STUDIES AND TEXTS

IN FOLKLORE, MAGIC,
MEDIAEVAL ROMANCE, HEBREW APOCRYPHA
AND SAMARITAN ARCHÆOLOGY

WITH 14 PLATES AND 5 ILLUSTRATIONS

STUDIES AND TEXTS

IN FOLKLORE, MAGIC,
MEDIAEVAL ROMANCE, HEBREW APOCRYPHA
AND SAMARITAN ARCHÆOLOGY

WITH 14 PLATES AND 5 ILLUSTRATIONS

COLLECTED AND REPRINTED
BY
MOSES GASTER, PH. D.

PROLEGOMENON BY
THEODOR GASTER

IN THREE VOLUMES
VOLUME ONE

"... and the feast of ingathering, at
the end of the year when thou
gatherest in thy labours out of the
field."   Exod. XXIII, 16.

KTAV PUBLISHING HOUSE, Inc.

NEW YORK

1971

FIRST PUBLISHED 1928

NEW MATTER
© COPYRIGHT 1971
KTAV PUBLISHING HOUSE, INC.

SBN 87068-056-0

LIBRARY OF CONGRESS CATALOG CARD NUMBER: 68-54864
MANUFACTURED IN THE UNITED STATES OF AMERICA

TABLE OF CONTENTS

Vol. I

Page

Vol. II

Vol. III

HEBREW SECTION

TABLE OF CONTENTS
ALPHABETICAL

LIST OF PERIODICALS

LIST OF ILLUSTRATIONS

MOSES GASTER
(1856-1939)

I

Until a few decades ago, a scholar in the area of the humanities was a very different being from what he usually is today. Today, he is primarily a specialist in a restricted department of learning, and whatever other interests he may profess tend to be regarded as extracurricular diversions or mere amiable "hobbies." In those older days, however, the development of new fields of inquiry had not yet demanded major concentration on initial spadework, nor had the precincts of the Muses yet been invaded by the trampling feet of the exact sciences. Scholars were far more of the nature of broad, encyclopaedic *humanists*. To be sure, they had their chosen areas of research, but their main interest was to set these within the context and framework of human culture as a whole, and to illustrate and illuminate any one particular subject in the light of their wide general reading. To adapt Browning's well-known phrase, their concern was with humanity's rather than *hoti's* business, and their work was informed more by subjective genius than by objective science.

It is against this background that the work and achievement of Moses Gaster is best assessed. A man of prodigious erudition and phenomenal breadth of vision, he took virtually all polite learning for his province, writing with equal familiarity and skill on such diverse subjects as Rumanian and Jewish literature, the Apocrypha and Pseudepigrapha, comparative folklore, medieval romance, and the writings and traditions of the

Samaritans. His distinctive contribution to learning and letters lies, however, not so much in the propounding of particular theories about particular texts (many of which were in fact wrong) as in a unique gift for correlating and cross-fertilizing areas of study previously kept apart. He was forever opening windows and revealing new and exciting vistas. Few men have done so much to put so many old things in so many new perspectives. It was Gaster, for instance, who first lifted the vast repertoire of medieval Jewish legend out of the narrower channel of rabbinic literature into the broad mainstream of world folktale as a whole. He was likewise the first to appreciate the importance of Samaritan traditions for the recovery of ancient Palestinian lore bypassed or discarded by so-called normative Judaism and to recognize their links with material preserved in the Apocrypha and Pseudepigrapha and in the writings of Philo and Josephus.

Yet, even this was not the full measure of his achievements. Gaster had, in addition, an uncanny flair for ferreting out important but forgotten ancient texts and for sensing the significance of what others had neglected. It was he, almost single-handed, who retrieved and assembled the whole vast body of Rumanian popular literature, who first collected and examined *in their entirety* the extant writings of the Samaritans, and it is to him that we owe also the recovery of the fascinating Hebrew *Chronicles of Jeraḥmeel*—a medieval legendary history of the world—and of a lost portion of the Hebrew text of Ecclesiasticus.

Nor was his contribution confined to his own books and monographs. Throughout his long life Gaster was the constant mentor and stimulator of countless other scholars—both seasoned colleagues and rank beginners. He was supremely generous both of his time and of the resources of his famous library. Works in which acknowledgment of his help is made run literally into the hundreds and cover the widest diversity of fields.

To be sure, such versatility had its price, and its weaknesses as well as its strength indeed appear in Gaster's work. Depth is sometimes sacrificed to breadth; there is a tendency to prefer broad sweeps to exacting minutiae, to base conclusions on a priori hunches and assumptions without adequate critical control, and even to confuse assertion with proof. Gaster was not a good editor of texts and, despite his rare linguistic attainments, was—except in Rumanian—an indifferent philologist. Moreover—as his critics were not slow to point out—he bedevilled much of his work by an obstinate proclivity towards predating by centuries (in one case by a millenium!) almost every text that he discovered, in the romantic belief that mere antiquity automatically enhances intrinsic value.

It is easy to be snide about such weaknesses. The fact is, however, that Gaster's mistakes are such as can be readily corrected, whereas his merits are virtually unique. Men of this Erasmian stamp have to be viewed in their own light, not in ours, and the only just gauge of their achievement is to consider not where they fell short of their latter-day successors, but where they outstripped them. In range of knowledge, combinative imagination, and intuitive empathy with the climates and patterns of ancient thought and with what actually moves and informs the "common folk" Gaster surely ranks among the giants of his time.

II

If it is true, as Milton said, that every good book is the precious life-blood of a master spirit, of few is this more true than of the present volumes. Moses Gaster's scholarly work was but one expression, or outlet, of his total personality. The same traits (even quirks) that inform it were manifested also in all the other aspects of his life. Accordingly, in order to appreciate his overall contribution—to see that work in the round and not merely as a series of disparate disquisitions—it is necessary to know something of the man himself.

The dominant characteristic of Gaster's temperament and outlook was a deep-seated and irrepressible *romanticism*. This came out in a passionate, even exaggerated, attachment to the past and in a somewhat rose-tinted view of the peculiar genius and creativity of "the common people." It was the mainspring, in particular, of his lifelong devotion to folklore and of his *penchant* for exotic peoples, like the Samaritans and the gypsies. Its roots are to be found, I think, in the time and place of his birth and in the intellectual and spiritual climate of his formative years.

Moses Gaster was born at Bucharest in 1856. During his adolescence, Rumania at last achieved recognition as an independent sovereign state through the union of several areas previously held under foreign domination. This political development was followed in short order by an intensive drive on the part of the new nation's intellectuals, writers and poets to give it a distinctive identity by retrieving and resuscitating the lost monuments of its popular genius and by "regularizing" its language. It was the same sort of activity as had been pursued, under somewhat similar conditions, by Jacob Grimm in Germany, by Tomasseo and Comparetti in Italy, and by Rangabé in Greece, and as has found expression also, in more recent times, in the work of Douglas Hyde, Lady Augusta Gregory and W. B. Yeats in Ireland. Such activity was informed, however, by something else besides patriotic fervor. It came hard on the heels of the Romantic Revival and was permeated through and through by the teachings of such men as Herder and Von Arnim, with their insistence on the glories of the past and on the distinctive genius of the common people in each country.

This was the spirit which Gaster inbibed in his early years, and which infused him for the rest of his life. No sooner had he graduated from the University of Bucharest, than he threw himself avidly into the new movement. A close associate of such intellectual leaders as Hasdeu, Creangă, Eminescu, Tiktin and Şaineanu—the charmed circle often met in his father's home—his first excursions into scholarship were in the domain of Rumanian language and popular lore. Before he was thirty years old, he had succeeded in recovering for his countrymen practically the whole of their traditional folk-literature, and his classic History of it (followed later by his equally classic Chrestomathy) soon established him as the Jacob Grimm of his native land.

The trend of interest and the romantic proclivities which had been engendered in the climate of Rumania were presently to be deepened from another quarter. In 1879, after receiving his doctorate at Leipzig, Gaster proceeded to the famous rabbinical seminary at Breslau. He was a favorite student of Heinrich Graetz and his classmates included such future paragons of Jewish learning as Wilhelm Bacher and David Simonsen. The seminary was the recognized center of the rising science of Judaeology (*Wissenschaft des Judentums*), the object of which was to place the study of Jewish history and literature on a solid scientific basis and thus, by means of critical scholarship, to achieve a renaissance of the Jewish cultural heritage. In broad perspective, this might be regarded as the Jewish wing of that same movement which had been sweeping so many European countries; and it was dominated spiritually by the same romantic trend and the same sentimental attraction to antiquity.

As he himself told me on several occasions, my father did not go to Breslau with a view to qualifying for a rabbinical career, but simply because he was attracted by the new movement and wanted to equip himself to be part of it. And that very soon he was. His contribution, however, lay not so much in the editing of texts or in the specialized study of particular periods of Jewish history—the main preoccupations of his colleagues—as in an effort to correlate monuments of the Jewish heritage with the general cultural life of the ages. His *Beiträge zur vergleichenden Sagen-und Märchenkunde* (Contributions to the Comparative Study of Tales and Legends), which first appeared in the seminary's *Monatsschrift* (and a second instalment of which followed after an interval of no less than *fifty* years!) was a pioneer attempt to trace the analogues of various Jewish legends in world folktale, and paved the way for all subsequent comparative study of such material. (Eventually, in 1924, this stupendous undertaking reached its culmination in the monumental *Exempla of the Rabbis,* which remains a classic of modern folklore.)

It was the same romantic attraction to the antique and unexplored that led Gaster to the third of his major scholarly interests. In 1906 he went on a journey to Palestine. Already in Rumania (before he was exiled, in 1885, for his championship of Jewish rights) he had played a prominent role in the movement to establish in that country the Jewish colonies of Rosh Pinnah and Zichron Jacob. Now he was himself to tread the sacred soil. During his visit he came into contact with the ancient and exotic community of the Samaritans clustered around Mount Gerizim, and the intensive study of its traditions became thenceforth one of the consuming passions of his life. The Samaritan priests conserve in manuscript a fairly large corpus of their ancient and more modern writings. Except, however, for their famous Targum (translation) of the Pentateuch, sundry portions of their liturgy, the work of their fourth-century theologian Marqah, an Arabic chronicle by a certain Abu'l Fath, and another falsely entitled *The Book of Joshua,* none of these had been explored, even though their titles had indeed been recorded. Gaster set about to obtain copies of them all. He entered into the most cordial relations with their priests (of whom two eventually visited him in London, and one of whom had to stay in bed while my mother sewed up his robe!), and he even invented a special typewriter (which I have inherited) in order to communicate with them in their own script. Through regular correspondence, carefully framed questionnaires, and a benevolent remembrance of them at each seasonal festival, he eventually assembled a library of Samaritan manuscripts (now in the British Museum and the John Rylands Library at Manchester, England, but originally ensconced in his wine-cellar!) which surpassed that of any public or private library in the world. For the rest of his life Gaster proceeded to transliterate and translate these texts, aided in the former task by those of his sons—especially my brother Mannie (to whom scholarship owes an incalculable debt)—whom he could press into service. He also hit on the fruitful idea of having the priests translate all of the Arabic texts into Samaritan, thus building up an invaluable repertoire of the language as currently spoken; and, when they came to London, he made recordings of their speech (on the old-fashioned cylinder records which now sound like nothing on earth!). His own English translations, it must be confessed, were sometimes hurried and inaccurate, but the latter was due largely to the fact that for over thirty years Gaster was virtually blind and had to rely on having the texts read to him by assistants who were not always as literate as might have been wished and who therefore often garbled words and jumbled clauses.

Unfortunately, here too—as in so much of his work—he was bedevilled by a priori obsessions. He convinced himself that Samaritan traditions represent, by and large, genuine relics of ancient Israelitic lore and, not being a trained Islamist, tended to underplay the manifest evidences of Muslim influence and acculturation. The result is that many of his broad conclusions about the sect now stand in need of revision, although, of course, the possibility must be allowed (as he persistently contended) that some at least of the Muslim parallels may indeed reflect far older material, itself picked up from the Samaritans. Be this as it may, it is Gaster's abiding merit that he, more than anyone else, succeeded in making the documents known and that he was the first to subject them in their entirety to investigation. The more intensive studies which have come in recent years from the school of John Bowman in Leeds and Melbourne are based almost wholly on manuscripts which Gaster collected and on the transliterations which he made or which were made for him. Even in this later generation his name and memory are still held in reverence and affection by the priests at Nablus, as I had occasion to see at a memorable banquet with them in 1968 (when it was even suggested that my lovely daughter marry into the priestly family, to cement the union between Israel and Judah!)

III

It is interesting to see how the romantic strain which infused Gaster's scholarly work found parallel expression, as I have said, in other facets of his life.

A prime example is his attitude to Zionism, in the early stages of which he was a major figure. Zionism was to him far more a Jewish cultural renaissance than a purely political

movement. To the end of his life he was especially proud
of the role he had played in sponsoring (or, as he claimed,
introducing) the cultural plank into the Zionist platform, and
there is extant an interesting letter of his to Martin Buber
stressing the resuscitation of the Jewish heritage—a return to
Zion, and not merely to Jerusalem—as the cardinal *raison
d'être* of the movement. It is significant in this respect that
during the preliminary maneuvers towards the issuance of the
Balfour Declaration, in 1917, Gaster's approach to such
British statesmen as Herbert Samuel and Mark Sykes was—
as they themselves admitted—to fire their enthusiasm for the
glories of the Jewish inheritance rather than to outline a
political program. Indeed, it was precisely because that romantic approach needed eventually to be supplemented by
concrete proposals that Gaster came to be superseded—to his
lasting chagrin—by more pragmatic politicians.

Take, again, his attitude towards Judaism as a whole.
Gaster was staunchly traditional in matters of observance, yet
withal no obscurantist. But he saw Judaism far more romantically than ideologically—as an identification with a religious
history than as the profession of a personal philosophy. He had
no bent for theology, and was impatient of metaphysical argument. Like most men of the Breslau school, he objected to the
use of the term "orthodox," with its implication of canonical
dogma; the loyal Jew, he insisted, was required rather to be
ortho*prax,* "ortho" meaning in this context conformity to traditional practices. Characteristic of this stance was his attitude
towards Reform Judaism. He never really bothered to examine
or understand its theological premises; his objection to it was
that the broad masses of those who espoused it thereby broke
with historical continuity and failed to conserve an ancient
heirloom. It was the attrition of time-hallowed modes rather
than the novelty of fresh concepts that disturbed and incensed
him. He recognized, of course, that Judaism had indeed passed
through a process of evolution and also that it was a sea fed
by many rivers, but he somehow balked at the logical inference that tradition itself was dynamic, not static, and he
seemed in practice always to envisage it in terms of where our

ancestors went from *there,* rather than where *we* go from *here.* His sermons, as Haham (Chief Rabbi) of the Sephardic community of London were, by common consent, masterpieces of oratory and exhortation, but they were magnificent rather than constructive. For all his prowess in the pulpit—unlike his great namesake's, his were no stammering lips—Gaster, it must be confessed, contributed little, if anything, to the development and advancement of Jewish *religious* thought. Others, perhaps, will dispute this judgment, but I can say only for my own part that while I learned much from him about the history and literature of the Jews, I never learned from him what Judaism as a system of religion was all about. Whenever I tried to press him on this score, he became either vague or thunderous, and I was told not to excite him. Looking back, however, in what I hope is a more mature perspective, I now realize that his irritation and impatience was simply that of a romantic lover asked to explain his passion.

A Judaism of Gaster's (and Breslau's) type is a Judaism of romantic attachment rather than of spiritual posture; and it owes more to formal education in the glories of a heritage than to the inner light. It is not surprising, therefore, that my father was always more concerned, in his rabbinic ministrations, with the cure of minds than the cure of souls. He sought to instruct more than to edify, and he was vexed more by the ignorant than by the unspiritual. The rabbi, he held— in accordance with Jewish tradition—should be primarily a scholar-teacher rather than a pastor, and one of his lasting causes of indignation was the degeneration of the rabbinate in England (largely under the authoritarian influence of Chief Rabbi Nathan Marcus Adler) to the level of "ministers" and "parsons." He tried hard to remedy this situation by turning the rabbinical school at Ramsgate which had been founded by Moses Montefiore into a first-rate scientific institution on the lines of Breslau. He endeavored to import trained scholars to serve on its faculty and to build up an outstanding library by the purchase of the famous Halberstamm and Zunz collections, and it remained one of the great disappointments of his life that after a few years this activity came to an end as the result of internecine intrigue.

What fired my father in these pursuits and in this attitude towards his rabbinical office was, I think, once again, his innate romanticism. Jewish education and scholarship were to him ways in which Jewish glories could be evoked, and it was attachment to such glories that were to him the real measure of the Jew. This was, in a word, Jacob Grimm in Jewish dress.

Sometimes these romantic trends came out on a less exalted level. It was characteristic, for instance, that he chose the name Mizpah for his house in London, in evocation of the place which Jacob had so designated when he met with Laban, in witness to the hope that "the Lord may watch between me and thee when we are absent from one another" (Genesis 31:49). It was no less significant that when he wrote the bicentennial history of his congregation he concluded the volume with a portrait of himself (in full ecclesiastical robes) ringed by the same frame as had originally enclosed that of his illustrious predecessor, David Nieto (1654-1728). It was likewise a romanticism for which I am lastingly grateful that led him to name me for his friend, Theodor Herzl.

IV

But not everything was romanticism. Gaster's lively sympathy with the past was inspired not only by poetic fantasy but also by a very sound and sober historical sense. This comes out especially in his attitude towards the Higher Criticism of the Bible. He welcomed freely the critical investigation of the Scriptures, and was an extremely active member (indeed a long-term Vice President) of the Society for Biblical Archaeology, to whose *Proceedings* he contributed some of his most arresting monographs. But his historical sense demurred at the basic assumptions of the prevailing school of purely literary analysis. His studies in other fields, and the wider vision which they had given him, showed him that these views were often fallaciously narrow (or narrowly fallacious). He insisted, for instance, that the historical books of the Old Testament had been orally transmitted (even from written texts), so that the date of original composition could not be determined by linguistic evidence drawn from the extant recension. He maintained also that archaeology, and not literary criticism, must be the decisive factor in reconstructing the history of Israel and the evolution of its religious thought, and that prevalent views of Hebrew accidence and syntax would have to be modified when more texts of the Biblical period came to light. It is true that his preference for the broad view over the minute detail led him at times to an arbitrary and cavalier dismissal of the results achieved by careful literary research; as a contemporary scholar has put it, he did not always "sweat it out." Nevertheless, in these broad insights—then considered eccentric and idiosyncratic, if not actually reactionary—he has proved in the event to have been not wrong, but simply in advance of his time, for they are today, in increasing degree, the basis of that marked revolution of attitude and approach which is the leading characteristic of contemporary Old Testament studies.

V

Gaster's innate temperament took toll not only scholastically but also psychologically. Usually ahead of his contemporaries, he was, alike in his work and in his life, always restless and frustrated, and this no amount of public acclaim and renown could altogether allay. He was *difficile* in committees and team-work, because he had almost invariably seen the wider ramifications and implications of an issue before his colleagues had got to them; and even when they did so, they plodded, where he raced. A constant impatience tended at times to beget intolerance and to foster a conviction of infallibility. I never heard my father admit that he was wrong, and I remember the consternation which beset us children when once, at a breakfast chat, Jacob de Haas thundered at him that indeed he might be. His Zionist colleagues found him obstinate and intractable. The fact is, however, that he usually turned out to be more far-sighted than they. He saw, before they did, the snares and pitfalls in the compromise wording of the Balfour Declaration and rightly, though unpopularly, predicted that it would come, in the end, to form the basis for whittling away Zionist claims and aspirations.

Three things especially contributed, I think, to this sense of frustration and isolation. The first was the virtual blindness from which he suffered for nearly forty years. Not only did this seriously impede his scholarly work (he had to rely entirely on having everything read to him and to depend on his memory), but it also prevented him from gauging the reactions of people when he spoke with them. Up to the end of his life I doubt whether he ever envisaged his younger sons and daughters but as the small children that they were when he last saw them clearly.

Secondly, except for brief periods in his early years, Gaster never occupied an academic position. To be sure, he enjoyed a wide circle of scholarly friends and acquaintances, and a full meed of acclaim and renown (even of flattery and adulation), but he was denied that constant sharpening of mind on mind, that persistent challenge from one's equals, and that invaluable tempering and chastening of dogmatism and idiosyncracy which comes from daily converse with colleagues at a great university.

Thirdly, his appointment as Haham (Chief Rabbi) of the venerable Sephardic community of London invested him with a kind of pontifical authority which tended to spill over into his scholarship. The community in question has always been distinguished more for its history than for anything else, and though his august association with it indeed fed his romanticism, in other respects it starved him. Instead of being a prince among peers, he was turned into a king among inferiors, a giant among pygmies, and that is a situation which scarcely breeds self-criticism, humility, and a sense of fulfillment.

Gaster was, all in all, a man of strange paradoxes. He rhapsodized about the antique, but one wonders whether it was not often the patina rather than the substance that allured him. He was obsessed with a passion for folklore, but he had no knowledge whatsoever of the things which really characterized the life of the people among whom he lived for the better part of his life—things like cricket and public schools and bank holidays and pubs and music-halls. He was full of dreams of a Jewish cultural renaissance, but he had no interest in modern Hebrew literature, and never even read Bialik. No one could tell a fairy tale as could he, but it was the virtuosity of a master narrator rather than the passion of a creative artist. He was imaginative and visionary, but he read very little poetry . . . and he admired Longfellow. Alike in his speeches and in his writing dexterity predominated over nicety, and flourish over balance. (The renderings of the Psalms which are incorporated in his revised translation of the Sephardic prayer book are, for instance, full of Victorian elegance but insensitive to the music of language or the magic of simple words.) He was defiant of crass bureaucracies and ill-educated "establishments," but he was impressed by what the Victorians called "high station." He was romantically infected by his congregation's past (though why, it is hard to say), but contemptuous of their present. He was one of the prime promoters of the early Jewish settlements in Palestine, and he could fire multitudes by his enthusiastic advocacy of the Zionist cause, but a sense of purely personal umbrage—or even a conviction that his own rejected policies were better—was sufficient to hold him aloof, a sulking Achilles, when the movement began to come to fruition. He was adorable to children, but could be tyrannical to his own. He was generous and lavish, but he could also be selfish and egotistical. He resented criticism and could even be savagely censorious of anyone who he thought might challenge him or cramp his style. The two major influences of his upbringing seemed, indeed, to coalesce in a paradoxical amalgam: He was at once the impulsive, exuberant, generous Rumanian and the authoritarian product of the German university.

VI

It is a difficult and delicate thing for a son—particularly when he treads the same paths—to sit down after a quarter of a century and calmly assess his own father's scholarly work and worth. What others may read simply as so many learned treatises, to be judged solely by the value of the new material which they furnish or the tenability of the conclusions which they advance, are to him at the same time pieces out of the mosaic of a man's life. He remembers, in many cases, the thrills, excitements and disappointments which went into the writing of them. Behind the bare lines of print he can see the flashing and ticking of the author's mind, and recognize the "fancies which broke through language and escaped." A cold critical judgment is therefore likely to be warmed by a certain glow of sentiment and affection. I shall make no apology for this. Indeed, it is only because I believe that scholarship is a subjective, not an objective thing, and that a man's total scholarly contribution ought to be viewed against the background of his personality, rather than in an academic vacuum, that I have accepted the responsibility (and risk) of writing this sketch.

My father's scholarly work was, as I have said, a natural expression of his peculiar temperament, and the significant thing about that temperament was that its strength always outweighed its weaknesses. Much of the work was careless in detail, slipshod in minutiae and sometimes even egregiously erratic in such points as the citation of references and the spelling of proper names. But there was scarcely a single book or monograph which did not move its subject into important but unexplored fields, which did not bring to bear vast stores of knowledge which everyone else had neglected or of which, as lying outside their specialties, they were in fact totally ignorant.

It is in Gaster's books that the excellencies and shortcomings of his approach are most clearly exemplified.

Take, for instance, his well-known edition of the Samaritan work, *The Asāṭir of Moses.*[1] Gaster's claim is that this title means "Secrets [Heb. *s-t-r*] of Moses" and that, since the work incorporates traditions which can be traced in some instances to Pseudepigraphic and other intertestamental literature, it dates back to the second, or even third century B.C.E. Both assumptions are radically wrong. Asāṭir (written with a *teth*, not with a *taw!*) is a common Arabic word, occurring already in the Koran, for "ancient tales and traditions," and the work is indeed known usually as *Al-Asāṭir* (with the Arabic definite article); while linguistic examination shows that it contains several Arabisms (sometimes even puns, and therefore original) which stamp it, as Z. Ben Ḥaim has proved, as a compilation of the eleventh century C.E.![2] Nevertheless, the edition has positive and abiding value for, although the titling and dating are manifestly incorrect, Gaster *did* see the relation of the traditions which it embodies to the earlier Pseudepigraphic material and to the sources of Josephus, and thus opened up the possibility of using Samaritan materials in wider context.

Take, again, his view that the Hebrew and Aramaic versions of such Apocryphal and Pseudepigraphic works as the Additions to Daniel and the Testament of Naphtali which are embodied in the medieval compilation which he published as *The Chronicles of Jerahmeel* really represent the lost originals of those works.[3] This view has commanded little general assent, but Gaster's publication is still valuable for the light it throws on the transmission of Apocryphal and Pseudepigraphic material in later Jewish and gentile literature.

The same preference for romantic theories over exact deductions likewise mars the basic thesis of his celebrated *Exempla of the Rabbis,* perhaps the most important and enduring of his works. Gaster claimed that the collection of some three hundred apologues and tales which he published under this title mainly from a late manuscript in his possession represented an ancient compendium from which the masters of the Talmud drew and that it originated in Palestine. A linguistic analysis of the texts reveals, however, that the process was clearly the other way about: Gaster's manuscript is simply a collection from Talmudic sources and from standard earlier repertoires, and that it did not stem from Palestine is shown by the fact that in those stories which have parallels in the Talmud, the dialect is Babylonian rather than Palestinian Aramaic. Moreover, the use of the tannaitic formula תנו רבנן to refer to Amoraim proves incontrovertibly that it is of late date. Yet, here again, the untenability of Gaster's particular theory becomes, in the long run, a minor consideration when set against the abiding merits of the volume. For no one has ever collected so assiduously and so exhaustively the parallels to these rabbinic stories in world literature, thereby placing them in the context of folktale as a whole. In doing this, Gaster has reared an imperishable monument, and his egregious error about תנו רבנן becomes virtually picayune.[4]

Of a somewhat different order is the famous controversy over the Samaritan-Hebrew Book of Joshua.[5] In 1906 Gaster acquired from the Samaritans several copies of a Hebrew work (in Samaritan script) which purported to be an independent recension of the Biblical book, like that which the Samaritans possess of the Pentateuch. This book, since it was not deemed by them to be canonical, had been interpolated with several additional chapters, some of which run parallel with a well-known Samaritan-Arabic Book of Joshua (really an extended chronicle) published by Juynboll.[6]

Gaster accepted the Samaritan claim and regarded the discovery of the book as one of the major scholastic triumphs of his career. In support of his claim he pointed out especially that the compiler of the Samaritan-Arabic work had declared expressly that he had relied in part on a *Hebrew* original. Other scholars, however, immediately retorted that, in the first place, the book was not a new discovery, but had been previously published (albeit in a shorter version) by the well-known Palestinologist A. M. Luncz;[7] and, secondly, that it was manifestly a translation from the Samaritan-Arabic work, full of ostensible Arabisms. Moreover, they declared, the Samaritans had confessed (an assertion repeated by them to the present writer) that the whole thing was a fabrication by a nineteenth-century writer named Murjan which they had unconscionably palmed off on Gaster's credulity.[8] This retort has been accepted by most modern scholars, and Gaster's claim has therefore been almost unanimously discredited. But the matter needs a closer look. Gaster never denied that the Samaritan-Hebrew Joshua had been interpolated from the Arabic and other sources. His contention related only to the Biblical chapters.

He showed that certain crucial phrases in the Masoretic text
(e.g. reference to "all the land of the Hittites" 1:4, absent
from the Septuagint Version), which modern exegetes had
long held suspect, were in fact missing or different in the
Samaritan text, and that the account of the distribution of
tribal territories seemed (as in Ezekiel) to presuppose an
Israelite rather than a Judean orientation. The textual variations, he contended, could not be blandly explained away,
as his critics supposed, by the assumption that a modern
Samaritan had faked a recension on the basis of Walton's
Polyglott, for none would have been equal to the task. Moreover, he argued, the statement that Murjan had written the
book had been misunderstood, because the Samaritan term for
"write" (כתב) refers only to the actual penning of a copy,
whereas for composition they employ quite a different word
(יתב).

It would be premature, therefore, to call the issue closed.
Further study is necessary, and the possibility cannot yet be
excluded that Gaster had indeed hit upon something important—even though his presentation was distorted—in recognizing behind the late Samaritan work the relic of what is
indeed an independent ancient recension of the Biblical book.

A final example of Gaster's combination of perception and
fantasy is his famous lecture (omitted from the present
volumes) on the origins of the Round Table in the Arthurian
romances.[9] Gaster contended that the whole story of Arthur's
knights had stemmed from the enumeration of King David's
thirty-seven "mighty men" (הגבורים) in II Samuel 23:8ff.,
the first of whom, Tachkemoni, is said indeed, according to
the Masoretic text, to "have sat in the seat" (ישב בשבת), in
which Gaster saw the origin of the Siege Perilous. (That
the latter phrase is, in fact, a textual corruption, is immaterial,
for the writers of the Arthurian romance would have used the
Vulgate, where it indeed appears in this form.) Gaster never
denied that the particular knights may then have been identified with Celtic or other heroes; he was speaking only of the
concept of the Round Table—the king and his circle of
paladins. There was nothing whatsoever to support this con-

jecture, but there is no saying outrightly that it is wrong. It thus affords an excellent illustration of the kind of original insight which makes Gaster's work at once interesting and unique. If it was not science, it was at least genius.

VII

Both the strength and the weaknesses of Gaster's approach appear likewise in the present volumes of his collected papers. The selection was made by himself and covers his scholarly activity over a period of fifty years. The volumes were originally published by Messrs. Maggs of London in 1925-28, but the remaining stock perished in the air raids of the Second World War. Since many of the periodicals in which these papers appeared are now extremely rare and hard of access, the present reissue will be especially useful.

Naturally, the progress of research has, in several cases, augmented Gaster's material or modified his conclusions. The following notes on some of the pieces, though by no means exhaustive, may therefore prove helpful.

VOLUME I:

Pp. 1ff. *Hebrew Versions of the Tobit Legend.* On these versions see now F. Zimmerman, *The Book of Tobit* (New York 1958). Gaster's Text I seems to be a late Hebrew retranslation dependent largely on the Latin version. The neologisms and echoes of the Prayer Book are more abundant than Gaster noted, e.g. iii. 16, גומל לחייבים טובות ; ib. 22, והצדקה תעביר רוע הגזירה ; iv. 10 והא לך אות ; v. 7 גבולי for גבולות .—Of particular interest is the identification of the demon who slew Sarah's previous bridegroom, as Resheph (vi. 4), for this has an ancient prototype in the Ugaritic *Legend of Keret,* where it is said of that monarch's sons: *yitsp Ršp.*

Pp. 69ff. *The Testament of Naphtali.* Fragments of a work closely related to the Testament of Naphtali have now been found at Qumran. Gaster's Hebrew version is clearly a late *rechaufée,* as is obvious from such expressions as ולא יעלה

בְּמִי שאמר והיה העולם) (vol. iii, p. 25); ולא יוריד כי לא משנה הוא
(p. 29); טפה באושה (p. 30).—The expression אז הפריד גוים
והנחיל והגדיל (p. 29) is a play on Deut. 32:8-9, and this
vindicates the variant והגביל in the Paris manuscript.

Pp. 184ff. *Hebrew Sirach.* The question of the origin and
authenticity of the Genizah Hebrew text is now put into a
new light by the discovery of portions of the Hebrew Sirach
at Masada; cf. Y. Yadin, *The Ben Sira Scroll from Masada*
(Jerusalem 1965).

P. 460. *Samaritan Amulets.* The amulet from Cod. Gaster
Or. 899 is a version of the Arabic *zaïrgeh*, the working of
which is described by E. W. Lane in his classic *Manners and
Customs of the Modern Egyptians,* chap. xi.

VOLUME II:

Pp. 660ff. *Jewish Coins and Messianic Traditions.* For
rabbinical legends concerning the reappearance in Messianic
times of the pot of manna, ordained to be preserved "throughout your generations" (Exod. 16:33), see L. Ginzberg,
Legends of the Jews, vi. 86.—The cup has been interpreted
also as the golden *'omer*-vessel in which an offering of barley
was measured for the temple on the second day of Passover;
cf. H. Hamburger, *IDB* s.v. Money.—See also: P. Romanoff,
Jewish Symbols on Ancient Jewish Coins (Philadelphia
1947); E. R. Goodenough, *Jewish Symbols in the Greco-
Roman Period,* vol. iv (New York 1954).

Pp. 711ff. *The Sepher Assufoth.* R. Isaac Raphael Finzi
(1728-1813), who once owned the MS., was the rabbi of
Padua, Italy, and vice-president of the Paris Sanhedrin in
1806. Mordecai Samuel Ghirondi (1799-1852), who later
acquired it, was appointed assistant rabbi of Padua in 1819,
and subsequently became Chief Rabbi. S. D. Luzzatto was
head of the rabbinical seminary in that city.

Pp. 731ff. *The Inscription from Rheneia.* The LXX reading of Deut. 32:43 to which Gaster finds allusion in this text,
is found substantially in a fragment of the Hebrew text

discovered at Qumran; see P. Skehan, in *Bulletin of the American Schools of Archaeology*, No. 136 (Dec. 1954), 12-15.

Pp. 814ff. *An Old Hebrew Romance of Alexander*. On the relation of the Bodleian Hebrew to other versions, see now Israel I. Kazis, *The Book of the Gests of Alexander of Macedon* (Cambridge, Mass. 1962).

P. 905. *The Legend of the Grail*. The connection of Corbenic with Hebrew *qorban*, "offering," mentioned in the Grand St. Grail, may be no more than folk etymology. R. S. Loomis, *The Development of the Arthurian Romance* (New York, Harper Torchbooks, 1963), 63, relates it to *cor benoit*, "blessed body" itself a distortion of the *corn* or 'horn' of Bran in the Welsh version.

Pp. 942ff. *Hebrew Version of the Arthurian Legend*. The text has been published and studied in detail by C. Leviant, *King Artus* (New York, 1969).

Pp. 1005ff. *Two Thousand Years of a Charm Against the Child-stealing Witch*. Earlier forms of this charm are found in the literature of the Ancient Near East. EGYPTIAN: A. Erman, in *Abh. Preuss. Akad. Wiss.*, Phil-hist. Kl., 1901, i. 12ff. BABYLONIAN: D. Myrhman, "Labartu [= Lamashtu]— Texte," in *Zeitschrift für Assyriologie*, 16 (1901), 141-200; C. Frank, *Babylonische Beschwörungsreliefs* (1908); F. Thureau-Dangin, in *Rev. Ass.* 18 (1921), 161-98; H. Klengel, "Neue Lamashtu-Texte," in *MIOr* 7 (1960), 334-55. HITTITE: cf. T. H. Gaster, in *Studi e Materiale di Storia delle Religione* 23 (1951-52), 134-37. CANAANITE (from Arslan Tash, 9th cent. B.C.E.): T. H. Gaster, in *Orientalia* 11 (1942), 41-79.—On the late Jewish version, see T. H. Gaster, *The Holy and the Profane* (New York 1955), 41-79.— The aliases of Lilith in the Jewish version can be traced to Greek sources. Thus *Ayylô Okô Pdô* are simply the child-stealing harpies *Aellô* (stormwind) and *Okypetê* (swift-flying) mentioned by Hesiod (*Theogony* 267). *Strîna* is an error for *Strîga* = *strix, strega; Abnuktia* is *epinuktios* "nocturnal"; *Kko Eidem* is a corruption of *Kakoeides*, "ugly" and *Klê Bduzâ* is *Kleptousa*, "female thief," i.e. kidnapper.—The

charm recurs in Edgar's song in Shakespeare's *King Lear*
(III, iv).

Pp. 1070ff. *The Motif of the Grateful Dead.* See now: S.
Liljeblad, *Die Tobiasgeschichte und andere Märchen mit
toten Helfern* (Lund 1927); G. H. Gerould, The *Grateful
Dead* (London 1908); Bolte-Polivka, *Ammerkungen zu
Grimm Kinder- und Hansmärchen* (Leipzig 1913-30), iii.
490ff.

On *the motif of the vanished shadow as an omen of im-
pending death,* see T. H. Gaster, *Myth, Legend and Custom
in the Old Testament* (New York 1969), § 302, where further
literature is cited. The superstition seems to underlie the LXX
text of Job 15:29.—See also J. Negelein, in *Archiv für
Religionswissenschaft* 5 (1902), 1-37.

P. 1122. *Rumanian Legends of the Virgin Mary.* "No new-
born was baptized," etc. The ensuing verses reproduce a
cliché in myths of the Disappearing and Returning God (or
Goddess). Cp. the Homeric *Hymn to Demeter,* 302-13 and
the earlier Hittite *Legend of Telipinu* (KUB xviii. 10, i.
16-18) and the Ugaritic *Poem of Baal* (IAB, iii-iv. 25-26).
See T. H. Gaster, *Thespis*[2] (New York 1961), 455ff.—I
myself drew my father's attention to the Hittite parallel,
which he discussed in the *Journal of the Royal Asiatic Society*
1930, 628-33, though he there relied on A. H. Sayce's antiquated and inaccurate rendering.

P. 1168. *Rumänische Beiträge zur Russischen Götterlehre.*
The deity Lelo (Lelie) may be a mere concoction from the
lelo-wail in dirges. For analogies elsewhere, cf T. H. Gaster,
Thespis[2], 32; G. Hoffmann, in *Zeitschrift für Assyriologie* 2
(1890), 229.—A similar Lelo appears in Basque folklore.

VIII

Here the pen balks. For all this assessment of Moses Gaster's scholarly strength and weakness and for all this attempt
to trace the sources of his distinctive outlook and temperament, something is missing. The portrait dissolves at this
point into a series of vignettes which may perhaps better

illustrate the diversity of his interests and the uniqueness of his personality. One thinks, for instance, of the two dominant characteristics of his home—its endless array of books, overflowing into every room, and its equally endless stream of visitors, men and women of all vocations and types and from all parts of the world, who poured into it daily. In my own dreams, I still relive fabulous explorations in that fabulous library. I remember, one day in my teens, extricating several leaves of a fourteenth-century manuscript of Euripides from the binding of an old Turkish prayer book, and the thrill of suddenly discovering in a forgotten closet a set of dog-eared notebooks containing the popular poems still current among the Jews of Corfu. I remember blithely carting to school a rare Italian edition of Aeschylus which my teacher subsequently informed me, with an awed raising of eyebrows, had all the value of a manuscript. I recall sitting in the musty basement "schoolroom" poring over first-hand reports of the Dreyfus trial in the bound volumes of *The Jewish World*—otherwise regularly used by the household cat for the delivery of her kittens. I remember trying to master the argot of Parisian gypsies from a tattered paperback which, so to speak, rubbed shoulders on the shelf with an equally intriguing and outspoken *Index Eroticus* in which a former owner had helpfully pencilled the English equivalents. I remember a set of ill-printed monographs on Jewish subjects published in India by the indefatigable Herbert Loewe while on service there during the First World War. I remember the prospectus of an institute in Paris run by two brothers named Leon under the title of the Tower of Babel which professed to teach anyone any language and any subject under the sun by correspondence. I remember digging out of a cupboard in the dining room a roll of leather inscribed with a portion of Deuteronomy in characters very like those of the Dead Sea Scrolls. (My father thought it might be part of the notorious Shapira frauds, but my recollection is that the script was very different and that the column was a narrow, vertical one, and not written longitudinally, as were those fabrications.) I remember midnight browsing in ancient leechdoms and hours spent in devouring the countless volumes of folktales. And I remember vividly (and still with indignation) the times when my father found it necessary to lock the door of the library against my depredations.

I remember the unending procession of scholars—the memorable luncheon with Bolte, Pettazzoni, Haggerty Krappe and others at the first Folklore Congress. I remember the regular visits of G. R. S. Mead, the Gnostic scholar, and how, towards the end of his life, he lumbered into psychic research and even inveigled my father into attending a couple of séances. I remember the more formidable visits of my father's Anglo-Jewish confrères, Adolph Büchler (a holy terror), Arthur Marmorstein and Hermann Gollancz. I remember Eleanor Rhode discoursing enchantingly of gardens, and Jessie Weston trying to find Ancient Near Eastern prototypes of the Grail Legend. I remember the clear blue eyes of Sir James Frazer and shouting into Lady Frazer's tremendous ear-trumpet. I remember the venerable William Hechler, the friend of Herzl, with his long roll on which, in a glory of varied inks, he had carefully calculated from the concluding chapters of the Book of Daniel the course of the world's history and the imminent annihilation of us all. I remember the encyclopaedic Robert Eisler trying to convince us all over dinner that the Biblical Dedan was none other than the Classical Tithonus—until the proof was literally interrupted by the pudding. I remember the redoubtable Isidore Scheftelowitz, who once shared my bedroom, rudely awakening me at five o'clock in the morning to enquire whether I had found any traces of a dual in the ancient Luwian language. I remember the weekly study session in which my father expounded the intricacies of the Zohar. (Cecil Roth, who attended these sessions with his brother Leon, once told me that it made no difference if the reader happened accidentally to turn two pages together!). I remember the atrocious table manners of Bialik and his wonderful description of England's Reform Jews as "withered souls" (*nephashoth yebeshoth*). I remember the succession of Rumanian students, who were always my father's special protégés and who seemed always to be part of the family.

And then come other pictures. I see my father rising majestically (never diffidently) at meetings of the Folklore Society to demonstrate, with all the wealth of his omnivorous reading, that the central character in a particular tale was a flea and not a bug. I see him emerging from taxis laden with the precious cargoes of books which he had been unable to resist at Hodgson's auctions and which he insisted on laying out on the dining-room table and carefully handling one by one while everyone waited for supper. I see him coming home from meetings of the Anglo-Jewish Association and similar august bodies in a blaze of indignation at the parish-pump politics of more plebeian minds. So-and-so, he would tell us, had merely said "Ah, ah, ah"; another, "Ugh, ugh, ugh," and a third "Oh, oh, oh"—all conveyed with appropriate histrionic gestures and grimaces. I see him spinning tops at Hanukkah and presiding over the kindling of the lamps (one for each of his twelve children, and extras for the grandchildren). I see him conducting the family *seder* (rarely less than forty participants and a dozen family squabbles!), or sitting in our beautiful *sukkah,* which the *ushpîzîn*—the traditional spirits of Israel's patriarchs and worthies—must surely have found their favorite hospice.

A major element in our home was my mother, the daughter of Michael Friedländer, principal of Jews' College, London and best known for his translation of Maimondes' *Guide for the Perplexed* and for his masterly volume, *The Jewish Religion.* It was my mother who especially shared my father's enthusiasms and thrills, who patiently endured the rages and furies, who suffered the less attractive of the endless visitors and who gently mediated between a somewhat authoritarian father and a bunch of not always respectful children. During the years of my father's near-blindness, it was my mother who served principally as his eyes and did a major part of the daily reading to him. Any presentation of his collected work must pay tribute to her selfless contribution, and it is fitting that the memory of her be associated also with these volumes.

The wings of the Shechinah rustle. It is impossible to convey the richness and utter uniqueness of that life which, in a few years, no one will any more remember. But it is all part of the spirit which moves in these volumes, and these are images which the reader ought to hold before him if a man's work is to be more than printed words.

*   *   *   *

Fate dealt hardly with Moses Gaster. Much of his famous Samaritan collection was ruined by a burst watermain during the blitz on London in 1944. "Mizpah" has been replaced by an ugly block of flats. The great horse-chestnut tree which fronted it has been felled, just as the last tree in the grove planted by the Caesars came crashing down when the last of them died. To the modern *sabra* the name Gaster is virtually unknown; you can look hard in modern Israel for any street, square or settlement which commemorates one who fought so valiantly in the cause of Zion. Perhaps this is simply what Housman called "the inevitable encroachment of oblivion." But perhaps, on the other hand, it is the measure of what Gaster was in life—one whose vision always outdistanced his attainment, whose reach always exceeded his grasp.

THEODOR H. GASTER

NOTES

[1]*The Asāṭir: the Samaritan Book of the "Secrets of Moses"* (London 1927).

[2]Z. Ben Ḥaim, "The Book of Asatir," in *Tarbiz* 14 (1943), 104-125; 15 (1946), 71-87.

[3]*The Chronicles of Jerahmeel* (London 1899).

[4]See William G. Braude's Prolegomenon to the re-issue of this work by the present publishers (New York 1968).

[5]"Das Buch Josua in hebräisch-samaritanischen Rezension," in *Zeitschrift der Deutschen Morgenländischen Gesellschaft* 62 (1908), 209-279, 494-549; "The Samaritan Book of Joshua and the Septuagint," in *Proceedings of the Society of Biblical Archaeology* 1909: 115-127, 149-153. Cf. also Gaster's paper, "The Samaritan-Hebrew Source of the Arabic Book of Joshua," in *Journal of the Royal Asiatic Society* 1930: 567-599, though the document there published seems far less ancient than he supposes.

[6]T. G. J. Juynboll, *Chronicon Samaritanum, arabice conscriptum, cui titulus est Liber Josuae* (Leyden 1848). English translation: O. T. Crane, *The Samaritan Chronicle or the Book of Joshua* (New York 1890).

[7]*Yerushalaim Yearbook* 7 (1902), 138-155.

[8]Cf. D. Yellin. "A Book of Joshua or a Sepher ha-Yamîm," in *Yerushalaim Yearbook* 7 (1902), 103 ff. (Hebrew); A. S. Yahuda, "Ueber die Unechtlichkeit des samaritanischen Josuabuches," in *Sitzungsberichte der Königlich Preussischen Akademie der Wissenschaften* 39 (1908), 887-914; S. Fraenkel, in *Theologische Literaturzeitung,* 15 August, 1908. —— On the other side, see now A. D. Crown, "The Date and Authenticity of the Samaritan Hebrew Book of Joshua as seen in its Territorial Allotments," in *Palestine Exploration Quarterly* 1967: 79-100 (especially, 95 ff.)

[9]*Jewish Sources of, and Parallels to the Early English Metrical Romances of King Arthur and Merlin.* A lecture at the Anglo-Jewish Historical Exhibition, 23 July, 1887. The lecture was published *in extenso* in the London *Jewish Chronicle* and subsequently reprinted separately. —— For a contrary view, see now R. S. Loomis, *The Development of Arthurian Romance* (London 1963).

TO MY CHILDREN
AT WHOSE REQUEST
I HAVE GATHERED IN
THESE LEAVES

PREFACE

I am reprinting in these volumes a number of studies and texts which have appeared during the last fifty years in various journals here and abroad. I have limited myself chiefly to texts which I had published for the first time, together with their translations, introductions and annotations, for whatever the value of essays and studies may be, that of texts remains the same. They are not affected by differences concerning origin, date and interpretation. On the contrary, they retain a permanent value, and form the basis for further investigation. Nor am I aware that any one of these texts has since been published elsewhere.

These studies and texts cover a somewhat wide field. They touch upon many subjects. A large number belong to the literature of the Apocrypha, others deal with the liturgy and Midrash; some belong to ancient fiction and mediaeval romance, and not a few are studies in folklore in the widest sense. A special section has been set aside for Samaritan texts, and notably Samaritan amulets. Biblical archaeology is the subject of some of the larger articles, and a few Rumanian texts with their translations have also been included. I have omitted however nearly all those Rumanian texts published by me without any translation. I have also been forced to omit others which have become inaccessible even to me. These articles written in many languages have all been reproduced in facsimile, reappearing here in the same form as they first appeared in the various journals. In spite of the incongruous appearance, the student, I think, will be grateful that I have retained them in their original form and with their pagination, references to them having been made by scholars; it will therefore be easy to trace them here. To the older pagination of each separate article, however, a continuous one has been added. The first two parts contain translations and studies in European languages, whilst those in Hebrew characters have been grouped together in a third volume. A full index is in preparation, but its publication has been deferred in order not to interfere with the issue of these volumes, the appearance of which has been delayed for a much longer time than I had anticipated (they have been in print already since 1925). A double table of contents will meanwhile facilitate the finding of the articles. One table shows the contents in consecutive order with the sources, and the other gives the articles in alphabetical order. I have to thank the various societies for permission to reprint these articles, chiefly the Royal Asiatic Society, with which is now incorporated the Society for Biblical Archaeology, and then the Folklore Society of Great Britain and Ireland. I also wish to express my special thanks to Mrs. B. Schindler, who is now engaged in the preparation of the aforementioned index, and also to Dr. Schindler for his ever-ready friendly help in passing this book through the Press. Like milestones on the way of a long and stormy life, these studies tell me that I am approaching the final goal. I am glad to be able to count them over again, now when I am in my seventieth year, and I render thanks to Him Who has granted me zeal and strength to toil and labour in His vineyard.

M. GASTER

London, *Mizpah*, 193 Maida Vale, W. 9.

September 11th, 1928.

TWO UNKNOWN HEBREW VERSIONS OF THE TOBIT LEGEND.

[Published for the First Time.]

BY DR. M. GASTER.

Reprinted from the " Proceedings of the Society of Biblical Archæology."

I.—INTRODUCTION.

Of all the Apocrypha of the Old Testament the legend of Tobit alone may be said to have come down to us in the greatest variety of texts and translations. There are no less than three more or less different Greek texts, which are not slight alterations of one and the same original, but differ often in essential points. Then there are two distinct classes of Latin translations: one the Vetus Latin, represented by a variety of texts, and agreeing in some points with the so-called Greek Sinaiticus (C), and the translation of Jerome, *i.e.*, the *Vulgate*. We have then at least two Syriac translations, both however imperfect, each of these representing a somewhat different text.

Up to a very short time ago only two Hebrew texts of Tobit were known. Both had appeared for the first time in Constantinople (I possess both editions) (*a*) in 1516, and (*b*) in 1519. The first is better known as Hebræus Munsteri (H.M.), and the second as Hebræus Fagii (H.F.), after the names of these two scholars who edited them in 1542. In 1878 Dr. Neubauer published* the till then unknown Aramaic text (Ar.), and furnished thus an important

---

* The Book of Tobit, Oxford, 1878.

1

addition to the literary tradition of the Tobit legend. In the light of Dr. Neubauer's discovery the question of the relation in which the different texts stand to one another became a little more simplified, but the material thus available was not yet sufficient to clear up, for instance, the true origin of Jerome's text. The result of the investigation, conducted by many scholars, and summarised here, has not been able to establish definitely which of the various Greek texts can claim absolute priority. Noeldeke, and following him Schuerer, adopted the view propounded by Fritzsche and others. They consider the text of our LXX (A) as the most ancient and best. The other two texts (B) and (C) are, according to them, secondary developments and modifications of that oldest text. From the same text (A) originate, so we are told, (a) the first fragment of the Syriac; (b) the Æthiopic translation; and (c) the Hebrew text (HF); this latter is not exactly a translation, but rather an adaptation. From the secondary Greek text, or a mixed text (B, C), arises to a certain extent (a) an old Aramaic text differing from that of Dr. Neubauer, which would also be more an adaptation with many characteristic changes and differences; (b) Vetus Lat.; and (c) the second fragment of the Syriac. That supposed more complete Aramaic text now lost (a), is then the reputed source of the Aramaic text discovered by Dr. Neubauer (Ar.), and also of the Hebrew version of 1516 (H.M.). To the same lost Aramaic source the translation of Jerome is also traced. The net outcome of this scheme formulated by Noeldeke is that we have on the one hand the Greek text A of the LXX forming a distinct group; and, on the other hand, a number of texts which seem to go back to one partly represented by Greek B, C, to which latter group all the Semitic versions as well as the Latin, both the Vetus and Jerome, except Syr. I, belong. Others again look to B, C as the primary source, and A as the secondary development and enlargement; so Reusch and others.

The connection between the Latin and Aramaic-Hebrew texts, and the reasons for such marked differences between them, has not yet found an adequate explanation. Nor, to my mind, has the priority claimed for the Greek text A or for any Greek text, been established on firm ground. It is very surprising that most of the versions should favour a text (A) which, according to modern scholars, would be far from being the authentic and the oldest one, and that the authors of these numerous versions should select, as

if it were, for their model, the secondary version B, C.   Still more
surprising is it that the old Latin, and especially Jerome, should so
completely neglect that old Greek version (A) and prefer instead, a
totally different text.   Nor have we any reason to doubt Jerome's
deliberate statement that he took his Tobit from an Aramaic
original ; Dr. Neubauer's discovery goes a long way to prove it,
although Jerome's Aramaic version must have been very different
from that of Dr. Neubauer.

In order to unravel the somewhat entangled skein of the
numerous versions, it is advisable to start from the text of Jerome,
about the date of which there cannot be any doubt.   Illgen, who
has written a very elaborate and minute study on the book of
Tobit,* has shown that Jerome has laid the older Latin version
under considerable contribution.   According to Jerome's own statement, the text he had before him was written in Aramaic, and a Jew
who knew both languages translated it to him into Hebrew, from
which language he made his Latin translation.   Not a word, however, is mentioned by him of the Old Latin, and it is not a little surprising to find in his version a number of incidents and details wanting
in all the others.   These additions and differences, which I will
enumerate afterwards, have been lightly set down as due to his
invention (Fritzsche).   I am not aware of any such liberty having
been taken by Jerome with any other canonical or apocryphal book
translated by him.   And although he may not have had a high
respect for the Book of Tobit, it is nevertheless singular that he
should have indulged in such a fanciful enlargement of a text,
which he knew to be held in esteem by the Church, and that he
should try to palm off his fiction as truth on the devout people who
wrote to him for the book.   This, as well as his silence about the
Old Latin, and the choice deliberately made by him in the selection
of this version in preference to that of the LXX, call for an explanation.   This can only be found, if we assume that he had
followed faithfully a text which contained those peculiar incidents
and variations.   That text must have had the reputation of being
the genuine version, and for that very reason had also been followed
in the main by the Old Latin translation.   I do not wish to say
that the Vetus Latin was translated directly from the very same
text which served Jerome as a source.   Vetus Latin follows in the

* *Die Geschichte Tobits.* Jena, 1800.

main Greek texts, which may have been, and probably were, a Greek version of the B C type, in its turn a translation from the Aramaic, and which served thus as an intermediary source for the Old Latin. Being in the main identical with his own text, Jerome could have recourse to the Old Latin for touching up his version, which he owns to have completed in one single day. There was thus no need for him to acknowledge more than one source, namely Aramaic, as the O. Lat. was of secondary importance, and merely used by him for the purpose of rectifying the translation where it agreed with his. He took from the Old Latin, if he has taken anything at all, only materials for verbal alterations, but none of the *realia*. They agree both, because both are based upon almost one and the same text. Jerome also differs from the Vetus Latin in not a few instances, showing himself independent of it.

Having cleared the road thus far, we proceed now to the study of his original, which according to his explicit statement was Aramaic. The text published by Dr. Neubauer differs, however, in most of the peculiar incidents characteristic of the version of Jerome, and must therefore be considered merely as a faint reflex, or as a later modification of the ancient and more elaborate version. This shorter version had been incorporated into a collection of homiletical interpretations of the Pentateuch, and has suffered in consequence. This is probably the reason for the abridgement. As we shall see later on, this text has a history of its own, and by means of undoubted evidence it can be proved that it had suffered curtailment and other changes, in consequence of that connection with the Liturgy. The Hebrew text H.M. is considered to be a translation from an older and more complete Aramaic text, but it differs also in many, if not in most of the essential points, from the version of Jerome.

Before proceeding further I will point out the most important differences between Jerome and the Greek text of the LXX (A). Gr. reads *Tobit* whilst Jer. reads *Tobias*. According to Gr. Tobit was *purveyor* to the king (I, 13); Jer. *he has leave to go whithersoever he would* (I, 14). Gr. (I, 19) Tobit *flees alone;* Jer. (I, 23) *he flees with his wife and child.* Gr. (II, 10) *sparrows* blind him; Jer. *swallow.* Gr. (III, 10) Sara wishes to *strangle herself;* Jer. *she fasts three days.* Gr. (IX, 2) the angel Raphael starts for Rages with *only one slave;* Jer. with *four.* Gr. (XI, 14–19) Sara comes to Nineveh *the same day as Tobias;* Jer. (XI, 14–19) after *seven days.*

The dog plays a very inferior part in Jerome, and it is not unlikely that it is a later interpolation (XI, 9). The three nights of continence are also peculiar to Jerome, not a trace of it in the Greek. Many passages that are in the Greek are missing in Jerome. Thus there is not a trace in Jerome of Tobit being maintained by Achiacharos during his blindness (II, 10), nor of the doctors attempting to cure him; and, on the other hand, not a trace can be found in the Greek of the parallel to Job (Jer. II, 12–15). The various prayers inserted in the texts are different. The wife of Reuel is called by Jerome *Hanna*, against all the other texts where she is called *Edna*. One could easily increase the number of variations, which point conclusively to a text different in many essential features from that of the LXX. Only here and there does the other text, B C, offer parallels to Jerome. The Aramaic text agrees with Jerome only in a few instances, such as the number of servants taken by the angel, the position occupied by Tobi at the court of Shalmanassar, whilst on the other hand it differs from Jerome's text in almost every other incident. The dog is not mentioned at all, and Aqiqar appears only in the commencement of the tale. Nothing better can be said of the more complete text H.M. In it there are a few other additions which are missing in the Aramaic; H.M. contains some of the same moral reflections as Jerome, and leans more towards the Greek B C than towards the Aramaic (Ar.). Another version which belongs to this cycle is the fragmentary Syriac from VII, 11, on. But this is still more remote from Jerome and from the other Aramaic text, as well as from the Greek versions in the form in which we have them. I will mention only one or two points which Syr. II has, contrary to all the rest. In XI, 13, the friends bring presents after the wedding. Tobias prays (VII, 8) for children. The angel does not say, as in the Greek (XII, 12), that he had brought the prayers before God, nor that he presents the prayers of the saints (XII, 15). On the other hand Syr. II calls the father Tobi; his friend Aqiqar; the wife of Reuel Edna, the man to whom Tobit had lent the money, is called Gabæl (Jer. Gabel)

Enough has now been said to show the great divergence that exists in not unimportant portions and incidents between the various texts belonging to this one group. Not any of these texts can, therefore, be considered as the probable direct source for the others. Neither the Aramaic, nor, so far, the Hebrew Munsteri, nor the Greek B C, nor the Syriac, though they have many points in common. And as for the Itala, and, in a higher degree, for Jerome, the resemblance between them and the others is of the slenderest nature.

What we are in search of is to find a single text, be it in Aramaic or in Hebrew, which should offer the same characteristics as the version of Jerome, without being a translation from the latter ; having also its own points of divergence, so that the original character of that text should be established beyond doubt or cavil. At the same time it must have points in common with one or the other Greek text.

I think, now, that I have discovered such an ideal text, which comes up to all the requirements of the case. It is a Hebrew text copied, latest in the 13th century, from an older MS. which, if my conjecture is correct, belonged to the 11th century. In its turn, it may be, and in every probability was a copy of the original text. The MS. in the British Museum Add. 11639 is one of the finest specimens of mediæval calligraphy ; it is of the choicest penmanship imaginable, and is placed among the Select on account of its artistic merits, being full of admirable illuminations and drawings. It was written by a certain Benjamin, the scribe, on very thin and perfect vellum. The larger part of the MS. is taken up by the Pentateuch, round the margin of which portions of the Hagiographa are written. Then follow prayers, poetical and liturgical compositions, laws, regulations, rules, calendar, and many other similar compositions and texts. Round some of the liturgical poems, this history of Tobit is written by the same hand and with the same care. The calendar on folio 563*b* begins with the moon-cycle 266, which corresponds to the year 5036, *i.e.*, 1276, probably the date of the writing. On folio 568*b*, however, the date 828 or 858 (= 4858) is given, which is probably the date of the original, and corresponds to the year 1068 or 1098.

The legend is written with special care ; in a few places corrections are added *over* the text, and in one instance (III, 20), not having been able to read an obliterated or erased word, the scribe indicated the lacuna by dots, and did not try to correct the text. In a few instances he did not distinguish correctly the letters of the original ; he writes, *e.g.*, the name of the place where Tobit and the angel went, *Dage*, instead of *Rage*. The mistake points to the form of letters in which that original, from which he copied, was written. In the Spanish and the old *Palestinian* cursive writing it is almost impossible to distinguish between Ꭰ and R. I must point out, however, what cannot be a mere coincidence, that in an ancient Hebrew version of the 12th century of the longer recension of Judith discovered by me, the town (I, 5) is called *Dage*, instead of *Ragau;* absolutely identical with the Tobit text.

The text is divided in verses. At the end of Chapter VI stands the word *Half*, exactly as it is customary with sacred texts. As our text is apparently not complete at the end, this division could not be the work of the copyist, but he must have found it already in his original. I point out all these minute details, as it is necessary to convince ourselves of the fact, that we have in our MS. a *copy* of a more ancient text, and not a production of the 13th century. The contents of this new version which, for brevity's sake, I will call H.L. (Hebrew London), had so thoroughly surprised me, that I had to convince myself by the examination of all the details, and by a careful comparison with the known versions, and more especially with Jerome's, that we have here a really genuine, independent and thus very important version ; and not merely a translation or slight adaptation of one of the known versions. For to state it briefly, we have here, if not the very original of Jerome's text, at least a version which comes nearer to that ancient version than any other, and may be the old original. All the peculiar incidents which distinguish that text occur also in this Hebrew version. The similarity is so great, that at the first glance, one appears to be the direct translation of the other. On more minute examination we find, however, a number of variants, great and important enough to secure the independence of the Hebrew from the Latin, but not so easily *vice versâ*. The Hebrew text is in some parts more enlarged, and in others shorter than Jerome. It is characteristic that both the dog and every mention of Aqiqar as well as of Nadan or Laban is missing in H.L. The latter part of the XIIIth and of the XIVth chapter are also wanting. The prayers are mostly different, and greatly resemble the prayers of the Hebrew liturgy. The language is modelled after that of the Bible, the phraseology of which is closely imitated, and is, in skill and expression, vastly superior to that of H.M. and H F., both of which betray the influence of the rabbinical terminology. The author of H.L. had the Bible at his fingers' ends. At the same time, there occur at least two direct parallels to formulas of the liturgy (VIII, 5, 6 ; XIII, 11), and numerous other reminiscences. But as these were known already in the time of the Talmud and probably in that of the Mishna, they are of comparatively great antiquity. A few might be interpolations made by the first copyist. The language seems in some passages rather forced and somewhat artificial.

And yet by a close examination we convince ourselves that it is to a great extent the language of the prayers formulated at the time of the Second Temple, and what is more important, that this peculiar form of biblical and postbiblical language is shared by the recently discovered fragments of Ecclesiasticus and also of other Hebrew apocryphal texts such as the Testament of Naftali and the History of Judith in the version to which I have referred above. This language resembles more that of the last writers in the Bible, such as Ezra and Nehemia, as well as Daniel, in spite of the frequent use of other more archaic forms borrowed from older texts. There are also a few peculiarities, which I point out at the end of this publication, that show the transition from the language of the Bible to the so-called New-Hebrew. We may therefore safely see in this text the *oldest reflex* of the very *original* from which all the rest has flown. That it should have been translated at a very early period into the vernacular (Aramaic) is not at all surprising, and being excluded from the Canon, the Hebrew original soon disappeared. For this reason Jerome speaks only of the Aramaic, which must henceforth be considered as one of the versions and not as the original.

One can also not easily set aside the argument of Prof. Graetz (*Monatschrift*, 1879 p. 145 ff.), according to which the " Aramaic " of Jerome may mean the Hebrew language of the postbiblical time in distinction of that of the Bible. Jerome had no name for this development of Hebrew, and as some Aramaic words had been admitted into this language, not having a better to designate it, he called it pure and simple Aramaic. Graetz has pointed out many mistakes in the Greek and Latin translations, which can only be explained as misunderstandings of a purely Hebrew text. True, against this view stand the explicit words of Jerome, that the original of Tobit had to be translated to him into Hebrew. The language of this newly discovered text is, however, so much akin to bibilical Hebrew, that if we believe this to have been the source of Jerome, it is somewhat difficult to explain the necessity for another translator. Jerome could have easily mastered the text without any further assistance from a Jew. But he may have had the Aramaic version of this text.

If H.L. should be a translation from another language, and in this case Aramaic is the nearest to be thought of, then the translator has disguised his dependence upon another text so skilfully that it cannot be detected. The deep-going differences from the Greek versions exclude these from our purview, and the frequent discrepancies between this text and Jerome's, make it equally impossible to look upon the latter as a possible source from which the Hebrew might have been translated. There are so many obscure passages in the Latin and Greek versions which are now satisfactorily explained through this text, that they warrant the assumption that we have in our text, thus far, not a translation, but the oldest and best Semitic form of that original, from which Jerome made his translation, and to which B.C. refer, though indirectly. Quite peculiar to this text is the fact, that the author introduces the three friends of Job, who come and speak to Tobit, in the same manner in which they spoke to Job. The author must have thought these two to have been contemporaries, both living in the time of the first Assyrian conquest of Palestine. He alone avoids the confusion between the various forms of tithes, so conspicuous in all the other versions. He alone gives a correct reason for the sleeping of Tobit outside the house and being blinded by it. There is no trace of the agnate-marriage of which so much has been made by Rosenmann* and others. The men die in the first night only because they are not those who were appointed by God to be wedded to Sarah. We find here the explanation of the mysterious passage in Jerome (vi, 20= Hebrew vi, 15), "In the second night thou shalt be admitted in the society of the holy patriarchs." The Hebrew has, "on the first night, remember the name of the holy patriarchs," which is in strict accordance with the Hebrew formulas of prayers, in which mention in the first instance is made of the names of the patriarchs, and their intercession is invoked on behalf of the one who prays to obtain grace from God. The prayers uttered by Tobit and Sarah are the outcome of that very injunction. Both appeal to the history of the patriarchs, and add : as God had heard their prayers, so may He listen to the prayers of these two youths. An ancient analogy is to be found in the liturgy of the fast day as prescribed in the Mishna (Taanith, ch. ii). There are besides other numerous analogies to the forms of the ancient Hebrew liturgy in this version

* Studien zum Buche Tobit : Berlin, 1894.

of Tobit, which if they are due to the author, and are not later interpolations and amplifications, might assist to fix the date of this composition.   As far as I have been able to ascertain, all these allusions and parallels are found also in the Talmud, and in those prayers which form the basis of the Hebrew service, and are not later than the last century before the common era.   The author knows, however. also the conclusion of the Amidah (the " Acathiston " of the Greek Church), to be Ps. xix, v. 15 (viii, 12), which may be much older than it has hitherto been assumed.   The formula of betrothal (iii, 5–7) is more archaic than that of the actual liturgy, and on the other hand there is a poem connected with it (V. 8) which is an alphabtetical acrostic, and has been retained in a fragmentary form in the German liturgy.   As it resembles similar hymns in the Hechaloth of R. Ishmael, it may also be very old. These indications do not allow us to see in our text a modern compilation or a translation made in comparatively recent times.   It reflects much more the time when the liturgy had not yet been fixed, and much latitude was given to the individual.   The form of these hymns and praises remind one of those in the book of Judith, the Song of the Three Children, and the so called Psalms of Solomon, all belonging to the first century before the common era.

Minor differences between this text and Jerome's, as this alone can truly be compared with it, I need not mention here. They are apparent to every one who reads the translation with the variations from Jerome which I have added thereunto.

The MS., as I remarked above, is very calligraphically written and with some care.   The original must however not have been very correct, as in many instances there are evident lacunæ and other mistakes, with which I should not like to charge the copyist, as he seems to have done his work with care and circumspection, noting what he believed to be a mistake, and omitting to write those letters which he probably could not decipher.

In publishing this text I have reproduced it exactly as it stands in the MS., and in footnotes I have, in the first instance, indicated the biblical passages which the writer or translator had used in his work ; I have also referred to the passages in the Talmud which present analogies to the liturgical portions, and I have inserted in brackets in the text itself all the corrections and emendations.

Looking now upon our newly-recovered Hebrew text in the light which I have tried to throw upon it, we may confidently assert that

we have here undoubtedly the oldest Semitic text extant—older
than Jerome and Vetus Latin, and coming nearest to the lost
Hebrew original, if it does not faithfully represent it.   I am not prepared to state dogmatically the relation in which this text stands to
the Greek, be it the B-C or be it the A version.   It is evident from
the comparison that B-C comes nearer to our text, but there are so
many points of difference even between B-C and H.L. that it is
exceedingly difficult to say with any certainty whether B-C depends
on H.L. or is independent of it.   There are also a few points of
contact between H.L. and A, although more scarce.

In apportioning the right place to H.L. in the history of the
texts, we are guided by the same considerations which must
have guided Jerome when he made his translation.   He preferred
the text, which was almost identical with H.L., to the Greek.   He
must have believed, if he had not known it for a fact, that that was
the original, while the Greek, in whatever recension, was an
adaptation and a revision of that Semitic text.   If that be the case,
and I am inclined to believe it, then H.L. will be the oldest and
best text, and of the Greek, B-C will represent the older version, as
Reusch and others thought, and not A, as has been asserted by
Fritzsche, Noeldeke, Schuerer, and others.

I publish together with the Hebrew text an English translation
and a few notes.   In order to facilitate research I have divided it into
chapters, following the division of the Greek version, and have
numbered the verses according to the division I found in the MS.   I
have also added the numbers of the verses according to A and to
Jerome's division.   As H.L. stands in the closest connection with
Jerome's text, I print in square brackets [] those portions wherein
H.L. differs from Jerome's text, and add in footnotes the variations
and the verses from Jerome missing in our text.   The numbers of
verses as added in round brackets are those of Jerome's version.

I pass now to the study of the other text, no less interesting than
the last, but from another point of view.   Whilst H.L. furnished us
a link upwards, this here furnishes a link downwards in the history
of the transmission of the text in the later literature.   Dr. Neubauer
published together with the Aramaic text a peculiar legend from
the Midraš Tanhuma, the first half of which contains a parallel
to the incident of Sara and her seven husbands who died, whilst
Tobit withstood successfully the attack of the demon, whose place
is taken in this legend by the angel of death.   The second half

belongs to a different cycle of legends of which the oldest and most complete version is found in my MS. No. 82, fol. 100a, No. 130 (cf. Jellinek, *Beth-hamidrasch* V, 152–154 and I, p. 83–84). That legend was added to the Tanḥuma by the editor of the Mantua edition, who indicates as his source the same work as that given for the Aramaic version of Dr. Neubauer, viz., the Midrash Rabba of R. Moses had Darshan (the Preacher). The connection between these two versions is however very slender. There are many intermediary links missing, which should explain the gradual shrinking of the elaborate tale to a small legend. Joseph Zabara, who lived about the year 1200, and who wrote his "Book of Delight" in Barcelona or Narbonne, introduces among other tales a peculiar version of the Tobit-legend (translated into English along with the other tales by Mr. I. Abrahams, in *The Jewish Quarterly Review*, VI, 1894, pp. 522–524). This version, reprinted by Hugin in מעשים טובים Bagdad, 1890, fol. 6a–8b, is almost a perversion of the legend. The only point of interest is that only three persons are mentioned in connection with Sara instead of seven, and in this number the Tanhuma agrees with Zabara. Not from this source however did the legend come into the Midrash, but, as we have seen, from the Midrash of Moses the preacher. I have discovered now the exact counterpart in Hebrew to the Aramaic text of Dr. Neubauer, and what is more, have found it also in a collection of homiletic interpretations of the Pentateuch. The MS. is private property, and I was allowed many years ago to take a complete copy of this Midrash. It was then already half deteriorated by age and dampness and portions of the leaves were crumbling away at the slightest touch. I have reason to believe that we may consider the original MS. as lost since. Happily I have a complete copy of the whole work. The original was written in a Spanish hand, and belonged in all probability to the 15th century, if not earlier. The character of this Midrash is very much like that published by Buber in 1894 under the title "Agadischer Commentar zum Pentateuch." My MS. (I may now call it my MS., the other being as good as lost) seems to represent an older and more complete text, as it also contains homilies to the Haphtaroth and to the various festivals, which are not to be found in that edited by Buber. In the contents there are also marked differences, but still both texts belong to one and the same group, having many points in common. In this MS. (Codex Or. Gaster 28), we find a homily for the second day of Pentecost, the first part of which is a literal translation of the Aramaic text, but very much shortened towards the end. The greatest stress is laid on the giving of tithes, and the history of Tobit is adduced as an example of the grace of God bestowed on the man who fulfils faithfully the duty of paying his tithes. The lesson for the second day of Pentecost commences with the verse, Deut. xiv, 22, " Thou shalt surely tithe all the increase of thy seed, that which cometh forth of the field year by year." The same words stand at the head of the Aramaic text and of the Hebrew. Here the introduction is more spun out than in the Aramaic text, which is merely an abridged copy of the original. Through this official connection with the liturgy one understands the reason why in the Aramaic and in this Hebrew version, which I will call H.G. (Hebrew Gaster), and in Ar. mention is made (II, 1) of the feast of Pentecost. Jerome and H.L. have merely a *feast of the Lord*. It may just as well be, that because this feast is mentioned in the legend the legend itself was brought in connection with the lesson of that day.

Now H.G. follows Aramaic as closely as possible, though leaving out the greater part of the legend ; all the minor incidents and almost all the prayers are missing, so that the whole book is reduced to a comparatively short tale. But whatever there is left, is a literal translation which sometimes forces the character of the Hebrew. Thus it proves also the fact that Aramaic texts were translated into Hebrew at a later period, and that the legend of Tobit enjoyed a great reputation, and was preserved mainly through its connection with the liturgy. H.L. is also included in a volume containing all those books and poems which are usually associated with the prayer-book and synagogue service. Through this connection one understands the reason for its continual dwindling in size. It served as an illustration of the teaching of the Law, and was treated as such.

By comparing H.G. with the Aramaic, we shall find that among other things omitted in both is that peculiar legend of the intended sacrifice of the two sons of Sennacherib, mentioned in H.M., chapter I. But the very same legend occurs in my MS. (28) in the homily preceding that of the Tobit legend. We have thus an indication of the probable source of this version (H.M.). It was in every probability taken from this or a very similar collection of homilies.

The minute comparison of the Aramaic (Neub.) with H.G. (for which that is the direct original), besides being interesting as illustrating the way how the abridgement was effected, is also of value for critical purposes. One point is especially important. When Tobi deposits the money with Gabael he received from him, according to the Greek, *a handwriting* (v, 3) or a *note of hand*, so also Itala and Jer. H.L. has, *a token* (iv, 10), Ar. and H.M. have instead *a bag*, which to say the least, is very incongruous. In H.G. we have *a ring* as a token, which seems to be superior to all the rest. With a slight alteration one could amend the word אמתחת, *bag*, of H.M., into חתמה, which means a *seal*. This would imply that the Aramaic is a translation from the corrupted Hebrew text and not *vice versâ*. But one example alone would not suffice to determine definitely the position in which those texts stand to one another. Without pursuing, therefore, this question any further, I limit myself merely to pointing it out. Many other similar contributions to the criticism of the text are to be found in this Hebrew version, for which reason I publish this also, and add an English translation to it. I have divided it into chapters according to the Aramaic and Greek, but without the division of verses, as these chapters are very small, and it is quite unnecessary to subdivide them any further.

In order to be as complete as possible, I will mention in conclusion another text of the Tobit legend, which although printed, has, so far as I have been able to ascertain, escaped the notice of every bibliographer, nor have I been able to find another copy in any library but my own. In 1851 there appeared in Lemberg a book called Osar Haqqodesh, which gives itself out to be a reprint of an older Amsterdam edition. I have not been able to trace it. Perhaps some one else will be more fortunate in that respect. Now this little book contains, in the first place, our Tobit legend in a very shortened form. The text is divided into twelve chapters, and agrees in the main, as far as the plot is concerned, with A., but not absolutely. Without being a literal translation, it is a more faithful reflex of A than H.F. A few incidents are worth noticing, such as the correct Hebrew name Ahmata for Egbatanis; the proper translation of the name of the river, as Hideqel instead of Tigris, though Rage is spelt Ragez, and Raguel instead of Reuel. In one point, this text agrees with H.L. alone, where all the other versions differ. When Sara prays in the anguish of her soul, she says in H.L., "I know that thou (oh God) hast appointed the right man to be my husband, and if it be Thy will, send him to me."

In Jerome we have a faint trace of it. Sara says (in III, 19),
"because, perhaps thou hast kept me for another man." In this
printed edition we find that she almost expects her relative to be
her husband but he would certainly shrink from marrying a woman
who would thereby cause his death, and she prays either to be
healed or rather to die. Nothing of this is to be found in the
Greek; there are also a few other incidents similarly independent
of the Greek. I must limit myself merely to point these out and
to draw the attention of scholars to the vast material in Hebrew
literature which has hitherto not been utilised for a thorough study
of the Apocrypha.

II.—TRANSLATION.

Tobit Legend I (H.L.).

I. **1** (1)* The words of Tobi, son of Tobiel, son of Hananel, the
son of Asael, the son of Gabatiel of the tribe of Nephtali in Galil,
on (the river) Pishon, behind the way of the going down of the sun
on the left side; and the name of the town was Safet. **2** (2) And
Tobi was made captive and exiled in the days of Shalmanasar, king
of Assur. (3) Even in his captivity he forsook not the way of
truth, and whatever he got he gave in equal parts to his brethren
the captives. (4) And he was the servant to the whole tribe of
Nephtali, and he did not pull away the shoulder from the work.
3 (5) And when Israel was dwelling in his land he went astray and
worshipped the golden calves, which Jeroboam, the son of Nebat,
had made; (6) but that man Tobi used to go and bring sacrifices
in the house of the Lord, and adored there the God of Israel.
4 (7) And all the first-fruits of his land and his tithes he brought
faithfully into the house of God even unto his temple in the third
year, the year of tithes; (8) and from his youth he kept the ways of
the Lord and his commandments. **5** (9) And when Tobi grew to
be a man, he took a wife from his tribe, by name Anna; and she
was with child and bare a son; and she called his name Tobiyah.
6 (10) And Tobi poured out his heart over him, and taught him the

* The numbers in round brackets are the verses according to Jerome and
LXX; and the passages in square brackets [] are missing in or differing from
Jerome's version.

ways of the Lord. And he walked in the ways of his father and abstained from all sin. **7** (11) And he and his wife and son came into the land of Assur, into Nineveh the great city, together with the whole tribe Nephtali. (12) And they all defiled themselves with the food of the Gentiles, but Tobi alone did not defile himself. **8** (13) And he served God with all his heart, and God gave him grace and favour before Shalmanassar, the king, (14) and he made him master over everything that he wished, and he gave him liberty to do whatever he wished in the whole kingdom. **9** (15) And he went into all the towns and fortresses to see the captivity, and to ask after and seek their welfare. **10** (16) And when he had come to Madai he had in his hand a large fortune, which the king had given to him, 1,000 talents of silver. (17) And he gathered a multitude of Jews from his tribe, and he entrusted the silver to Gabiel, and they saw it and were witnesses, and he gave him a token in remembrance of the money. **11** (18) After a long time Shalmanassar, the king of Assur, died, and his son Sennacherib reigned after him, and the children of Israel were evily treated. **12** (19) And Tobi distributed his goods and gave it to his kindred and comforted them. **13** And he gave to every one as he was able. (20) He clothed the naked and fed the hungry, and the dead that were slain he buried. **14** (21) And when Sennacherib had come back from the land of Judah with ignominy by reason of the slaughter that God had made about him because he had blasphemed and slandered, that Sennacherib having been humbled, slew many of the Israelites, and Tobi used to bury them. **15** (22) And it was told the king, and he commanded him to be slain, and all his substance to be plundered. **16** (23) And Tobi fled with his wife and son, and they (wandered about) naked and barefooted in the frost without any covering and without sustenance ; but wherever he went he found many friends. **17** (24) And it came to pass that after forty-five days the sons of Sennacherib, Essarhaddon and Sharezer, killed him, (25) and Tobi hearing of it, returned to his home, and all his substance was restored to him.

II. **1** (1) And it was after this there was a festival of the Lord, and Tobi prepared a great dinner in his house. **2** (2) And he said to his son Tobiyah : go and bring some of our tribe that fear God to feast with us. **3** (3) And Tobiyah went and returned and told his father that he had seen one of the children of Israel slain lying in the street. **4** And Tobi got up from his seat and left the dinner ; he ate

nothing (4) but went to the body, took it up and carried it privately
to his house, and when the sun went down he buried it,* (5) and ate
afterwards with mourning and fear.   5 (6) And he remembered the
word spoken through Amos the prophet, and I will turn your feasts
into mourning and your songs into lamentation.†   6 (8) And his
relations blamed him, saying : Thou knowest well that the king had
given out a command to slay thee because thou didst bury the dead,
and thou didst flee and savedst thyself by it, and yet thou still
holdest fast thine integrity.   7 (9) And he said : I fear the Lord of
Lords more than the king, who is, like me, formed also of clay.
8 And Tobi continued to go after the slain, and he used to bring
them secretly into his house and bury them at midnight.   9 (10) Now
it happened one day that Tobi was wearied with burying them, [and
he had not washed his hands nor cleansed them in water after the
burial of them.]   10 And he cast himself down on a bed by the wall
and slept, (11) and there was the nest of small birds (swallows or
sparrows), and their dung fell upon his eyes and his eyes were dim
so that he could not see.   (12) And God did this to him in order to
try him as he had done to Job.   11 (13) And whereas Tobi feared
God from his infancy, he did not for all this charge God with
foolishness, (14) and he clung to the God of Israel and trusted in his
mercy.   12 (15) And the friends of Job, Eliphaz the Temanite, and
Bildad the Shuhite, and Zophar the Naamathite came to him, and they
all mocked at him saying : (16) where is thy righteousness upon
which thou trustest, saying, I am just and I will bury the dead and
bestow mercy upon them ?   (17) And Tobi rebuked them and said :
(18) truly [I am clean and I am innocent, and my righteousness will
answer for me, and we must receive the evil as well as the good with
love and gladness of heart, for all the judgments of God are right].
14 For everyone whose faith is perfect will not change nor alter,‡ and
God gives him the life of the world to come.   15 (19) And his wife
was wise hearted to work in all manner of cunning workmanship, and
she worked for many and she fed her husband by the work of her
hands.   16 (20) Whereby it came to pass that every (l. one) day she
received a young kid for her wages and she brought it home.   [And
the kid went through the house bleating.]   17 (21) And Tobi heard

* J. reads : That after the sun was down he might bury him.
† J. 7 omitted here.
‡ J. 18 reads instead : For we are the children of saints and look for that life
which God will give to those that never change their faith from Him.

the voice of the kid and he said to her : take heed lest perhaps it be
stolen, restore it to its owners, for thus are we commanded by our
God, and it is not lawful for us to keep it over night in our house or
to take it to ourselves.   **18** (22) And she answered and said : if
thou art righteous as thou sayest, wherefore has all this trouble
come upon thee ?   Such was her custom to speak every day roughly
with him [until he was wearied of his life].

III. **1** (1) And when Tobi heard [all these rebukes] he sighed
and was sorely grieved, and he turned his face towards the wall, and
he prayed with tears : (2) And he said : thou art just, O Lord, and
thy judgments right and thy ways are mercy and loving kindness and
truth and judgment.   **2** (3) And now, O Lord, remember me [for
good and visit me with thy salvation], and do not remember the sins
[of my parents], and hear me quickly, and the offences of my
forefathers do not remember against me.   3 (4) For because we
have not observed thy commandments, therefore have we been made
to be a fable and a reproach among all the nations whither thou hast
brought us.   **4** (5) And now, O Lord, great are thy works,* (6) and
thou doest what is right in thy sight.   And thou, O perfect Rock, do
with me according to thy mercy, love, and truth, and take my soul ;
for it is better for me to die, than to live.   **5** (7) The same time it
came to pass that Sarah, the daughter of Reuel, brother of Tobi [was
praying to God], in Madai.   **6** [For] she had heard reproaches [and
contempts and she was despised in the eyes] of one of her father's
servants.   **7** (8) and she provoked her sore every day saying :
woe unto thee and to thy luck, for seven men were given unto thee,
and they died every one of them the very first night they went in to
thee, through thy witchcraft.†   **8** And how darest thou to lift up thine
eyes and to raise thy head to speak to me on either a great or a
small thing, as I am better than thou.   **9** But this was an untruth in
her mouth, as it was through no fault of hers, as Ashmedai the king
of the demons killed them on the first night, because she was not
appointed for them.   **10** (9) And every day she used to say to her :
lo, thou art unworthy of a husband or to have seed upon the earth,
and (10) now thou thinkest to kill me as thou hast killed them.
11 And it came to pass one day that she went up into the upper

---

* J. reads : "Great are thy judgments, because we have not done according
to thy precepts, and have not walked sincerely before thee."

† (8) different in J.   (8) Because she had been given to seven husbands, and a
devil named Asmodeus had killed them at their first going in unto her.

room and stayed there three days, night and day, she neither ate bread nor drank any water (11) and stood in prayers and supplication before God that he would avenge her [on that servant] who upbraided her. **12** [And she thought to have killed herself if she had not been afraid that she would bring down the gray hairs of her father in sorrow to the grave and that their enemies should not say in derision : " he had one single daughter and she has killed herself "]. **13** (12) And when the three days had come to an end she fell down and prayed to God, saying : **14** (13) Blessed art thou, O Lord God of Israel, who keepeth his covenant and mercy with them that observe his covenant and love his commandments. **15** Thou answerest in time of tribulation, thou deliverest, rescuest, and savest and bestowest benefits on the guilty. **16** (14) To thee I lift up my eyes, to thee, who dwellest in the heavens [for I know that I am dust and to dust I shall return]. **17** (15) To thee I pray now, and before thee I present my supplication with regard to those who reproached me undeservedly.* **18** (16) Thou knowest my heart, that I never coveted a husband, and I am standing pure befo e thee. **19** (17) I did not sit in the seat of the scornful, nor have I joined myself with them that play, nor did I walk with the wicked. (18) I would not have desired to take a husband, were it not for my reverence for thee† (19) nor was I appointed for them. **20** I know that thou hast kept (?) and appointed another man for me‡ (20) [and if it be thy will, send him to me], (21) for such is the law of the man who worshippeth thee in truth, that his end is hope. **21** And when tribulation and anxiety comes upon him thou deliverest him through thy mercy, (22) for thou art not delighted§ in the death of him that dieth, but that he return from his way and live, for piety averts the evil decree. **22** (23) Be thy name blessed for ever and ever. Amen ! (24) At that time her cry and that of Tobi were heard as they prayed together, and their cry went up before God. (25) And he sent his angel Raphael to heal them and to deliver them from their tribulation.

* J. reads : I beg, O Lord, that thou loose me from the bond of this reproach, or else take me away from the earth.

† J. reads : But a husband I consented to take, with thy fear, not with my lust.

‡ J. reads : And either I was unworthy of them, or they perhaps were not worthy of me : because perhaps thou hast kept me for another man.

§ J. continues :—in our being lost ; because after a storm thou makest a calm, and after tears and weaping thou pourest in joyfulness.

IV. **1** (1) *And Tobi was praying for his death, and he called his son Tobiyah, (2) and said: **2** My son, hear the instruction of thy father, and forsake not the teaching of thy mother, and bind their instruction upon thine heart.   **3** (3) When God shall take my soul, thou shalt take me and bury me after the burial of my fathers, and thou shalt honour thy mother all the days of thy life.   **4** (4) **And thou shalt be mindful of the tribulations which have come upon us** and upon her every day; (5) and when she will have fulfilled the days of her life, bury her with honour by me.   **5** (6) And thou shalt be mindful of thy Creator all the days of thy life, and take heed never to sin, and keep the commandments of thy God and his law. **6** (7) Thou shalt surely open thine hand to the poor [when thou seest the naked, do thou cover him.   **7** Deal thy bread to the hungry]† and hide not thine eyes from them, then God will bless thee in all the work of thy hands, (10) and he will open unto thee his good treasure, (11) for riches profit not in the day of wrath, but righteousness delivereth from death.   **8** (12–14) And fear God with all thy heart and all thy might ; do not join thyself with evil-doers and do not sit in the seat of the scoffers.   **9** (15) Render to every man according to his work, and give him his wages on the very day, and let not the wages of the hired servant tarry with thee. (16) Love thy neighbour as thyself, (17 and 19)‡ and seek the counsel of the pious. **10** (21) And now, my son, go and ask for the talents of silver which I have left in the hand of Gabiel, in the city of Dago (Rage). (22) And here is the token which I have given him in memory of the money. (23) Fear not, for God will be with thee wherever thou goest, if thou keepest his commandments.   **11** [Be not dismayed on account of the great tribulations which have befallen us, for I trust, through the fear of God, that we shall still have great salvation and deliverance, my son; fear not.]

  1 V. (1) Then Tobiyah answered his father and said : I will do all the things which thou hast commanded me, (2) but teach me

---

* J. reads :—Therefore when Tobias thought that his prayer was heard that he might die he called, etc.

† (8 and 9 of J. missing here.   (8) According to thy ability be merciful. (9) If thou have much, give abundantly : if thou have little, take care even so to bestow willingly a little.

‡ (J. 18 and 20) missing here.   (18) Lay out thy bread and thy wine upon the burial of a just man, and do not eat and drink thereof with the wicked. (20) Bless God at all times, and desire of him to direct thy ways, and that all thy counsels may abide in him.

and show me the way I should go, for I am only one, and how can
I go alone to bring the money? **2** (4) And he said: go outside
and seek thee out some faithful man that I should give him his hire
while I yet live [and he will go with thee to get the money].
3 (5) And Tobiyah went out that very day, and went [into the market-
places of the town to seek a faithful man. **4** And the angel Raphael
went out to meet him—he was sent by God to assist him]† (6) and
the lad knew not that he was an angel. **5** And the lad saluted him
and he asked him: who art thou, my lord? (7) And he said: I
am of the children of Judah. **6** And Tobiyah said: knowest thou
the way that leadeth to Naphtali? (8) And he answered and said:
I know all the boundaries of the lands and countries, **7** and I know
Gabael, our kinsman, who lives in the city of Dage (Rage), in Madai,
in the city of Nineveh, on the mount Abtanim (C. Egbatanis).
8 (9) And Tobiyah said: let not my lord be angry, I will only go
to my father and return. **9** (10) And Tobiyah went and told his
father,‡ and Tobi sent for the man. And (11) he came to Tobi and
saluted him. **10** And the angel said: gladness and joy mayest thou
obtain! **11** (12) And he said to him: What manner of joy can there
be to me who sit in darkness [like the dead] and cannot see any
more the light of the sun? **12** (13)§ And he said: let it not be
grievous in thy sight, for thy salvation is near at hand; thou wilt see
again and thy heart will rejoice, **13** (14) And Tobi said to him: I
have called thee to go with my son (to) Gabael, who dwelleth in Dage
(Rage) in the country of Madai, and when thou shalt return I will
pay thee thy hire.

14 (15) And the angel said: Here I am, ready to go with him.
(16) And Tobit said to him: Tell me what is thy name, and of what
family and what tribe art thou? **16** (17, 18) And the angel answered
and said: My name is Azaryah, son of the great (elder) Hananyah.||

* (J. 3) omitted here. (3) Then his father answered him and said: I have
a note of his hand with me, which thou shalt show him, he will presently pay it.

† J. reads: Then Tobias going forth found a beautiful young man, standing
girded, and as it were ready to walk.

‡ J. adds: Upon which, his father being in admiration, desired that he would
come in unto him.

§ Different in J. (13) And the young man said to him: Be of good
courage, thy cure from God is at hand.

|| (J. 17–18) Different. (17) And Raphael, the angel, answered: Dost thou
seek the family of him thou hirest or the hired servant himself to go with thy
son? (18) But lest I should make thee uneasy, I am Azarias the son of the great
Ananias.

I am descended from a noble family. **17** (19) And Tobi said : let it not be grievous in thy sight (do not be angry, I pray thee), and tell me of what family art thou ? And he answered : I am from the tribe . . . . .* (21) And Tobi said : may God be with you and send his angel before you. (22) And they prepared provisions for the journey, and they set out together. **18** (23–25)† And Anna his mother went with him until the outskirts of the town, weeping all the way she went. **19** [And she said to them : May God be with you and give you grace and mercy in the eyes of the inhabitants of the land. **20** And now let thy footsteps be apace to return quickly to us, before we die and go down in sorrow to the grave. **21** And when she returned home] she said to Tobi : what hast thou done that thou hast sent away from thee [thine only son whom thou lovest ? **22** If mischief befal him, then shall we bring down our grey hairs with sorrow to the grave. **23** For as long as our son was with us, he was to us] (as one who refreshes our soul and) a restorer of life and a nourisher of our old age. **24** (26) And he answered her : Fear not, my sister,‡ (27) for God has sent his angel with him, and he will make his way prosperous for him, and he shall restore him yet to us.§

VI. **1** (1) And Tobiyah went, and came to the River Hideqel (Tigris), and he stayed there. (2) And he went down to wash his feet, and behold a great fish suddenly leaped out, and would have swallowed (devoured) him, (3) and he was afraid, and cried out with a loud ˙voice, and said : My Lord,‖ save me from this great fish.¶ **2** (5) And the angel said to him : open it and take out its heart, gall, and liver, and lay them out safely, for they will serve thee as

---

* J. (20) Omitted here : and the angel said to him, I will lead thy son safe and bring him to thee again safe.

† J. (23–25) Different. (23) And when they were departed, his mother began to weep, and to say : Thou hast taken the staff of our age, and sent him away from us. (24) I wish the money for which thou hast sent him, had never been. (25) For our poverty was sufficient for us, that we might account it as riches that we saw our son.

‡ Jer. adds : our son will arrive thither safe and will return safe to us and thy eyes shall see him.

§ J. (28) omitted here, "at these words his mother ceased weeping and held her peace."

‖ Diff. in J : My Lord (Sir), he cometh upon me.

¶ J. (4) omitted here. (4) And the angel said to him, take him by the gill, and draw him to thee. And when he had done so, he drew him out upon the land, and he began to pant before his feet.

medicine.   **3** (6) And he took hold of the fish and divided it in the
midst, and they ate one half, and the other they made into provisions
for the journey, till they came to Dage (Rage) in the land of Madai.
4 (7) And the lad asked the angel, to what use is the heart and
the liver and the gall which we have put up safely?   **5** (8) And he
answered and said : take the heart to drive away evil spirits from
man or woman, if you burn it on fire.*   **6** (10) And the lad asked
him : where shall we lodge to-night?   (11) And he said : [in the city
of Rage].   **7** Behold [in this town] there is a good man whose name
is Reuel, of thy father's family, and he has neither son nor daughter
but one single daughter,† (12) and she inherits all the substance of
her father, (13) and when you come there, ask her father for her,
for he will not withhold her from thee.   **8** (14) And Tobiyah
answered and said : [hear me, and so may God hear thee !]   **9** [I
have heard, and my belly trembled.]   I heard [from many who
uttered slander] that she had been given in marriage to seven
husbands, and the first night on their going in to her, Ashmedai,
king of the evil spirits, came in the middle of the night and
killed them.   **10** (15) Therefore I hold back, and am afraid lest
(the same thing should happen to me) as to one of them.   I am
young, and an only son to my father and mother, and if the same
thing should happen to me, I should bring down their gray hairs
with blood to the grave.   **11** (16) And the angel said to him : be
not affrighted nor be thou dismayed, nor let thy heart faint, for
I will show thee how to drive him away from thee.   **12** (17) Know
that all these men who were killed were not suited (or fit) for
her that any seed should come from them, therefore has the
demon killed them.‡   **13** (18) But thou shalt do what I command
thee : be together with her in one chamber three days and three
nights, and do not approach her.§   **14** (19) And every night thou
shalt burn the liver on the fire [and fumigate the bed on which you
will lie], and the demon will fly away.   **15** (20) On the first night,

---

* J. (9) omitted here.   (9) And the gall is good for anointing the eyes in which
there is a white speck, and they shall be cured.

† (12 and 13) somewhat different in J.

‡ (17) Diff. in J. : For they who in such manner receive matrimony as to shut
out God from themselves and from their mind, and to give themselves to their
lust, as the horse and mule, which have no understanding, over them the devil hath
power.

§ J. adds : And give thyself to nothing else but to prayers with her.

remember the names of the holy patriarchs,* (21) on the second, pray to God that good men may come from you.† 16 (22) And on the third night, about the time of the cock-crowing, do thy will with the fear of the Lord, and he will bless thee.‡

VII. 1 (1) And they went into the house of Reuel, and he rejoiced very much, (2) and he kissed Tobiyah, and said to his wife Ednah: behold how like he is to the good man Tobi. 2 (3) And she [his wife] said: who are ye, and whence do you come? (4) And he said: from the land of Naphtali, of the captivity in Nineveh. 3 (5) And Reuel said to them: do you know my brother Tobi? [And the angel said:] we know him (6),§ and this young man is his son, and his name is Tobiyah. 4 (7) And Reuel went and fell upon his face and kissed him and wept upon his neck. 5 And he said: blessed be thou of the Lord, for thou art the son of a good man. (8) And they came, Ednah his wife (and his daughter), and they wept over him. (9) And they prepared a feast, and they killed a young goat and sat down to dinner. 6 (10) And Tobiyah said: Uncle! [I ask a great request of thee; I pray thee, my lord, deny me not.]‖ 7 Consent now to give me thy daughter for a wife [it is better that you should give her to me, than that you should give her to another man, as I am thy flesh and thy bone.] 8 (11) And Reuel was terrified, and he was afraid lest he should die as those men died through her, and he kept his mouth with a bridle. 9 (12) And the angel said: be not afraid, as fortune has come, and in the name of God, give her to him, for the others were not appointed unto her, and this one is appointed. 10 (13)¶ And Reuel answered: oh, would that it were as thou sayest!** [may

---

* J. (20): But the second night thou shalt be admitted into the society of the holy patriarchs.

† J. (21) On the third night thou shalt obtain a blessing, that sound children may be born of you.

‡ J. (22) And when the third night is past, thou shalt take the virgin with the fear of the Lord, moved rather for love of children than for lust, that in the seed of Abraham thou mayest obtain a blessing in children.

§ J. (6) reads: And when he was speaking many good things of him, the angel said to Raguel, Tobias, concerning whom thou inquirest, is this young man's father.

‖ J. adds, I will not eat nor drink this day unless thou, etc.

¶ J. (13) reads, I doubt not but God hath regarded my prayers and tears in his sight.

** J. (14) omitted :—And I believe he hath therefore made you come to me, that this maid might be married to one of her own kindred according to the law of Moses; and now doubt not, but I will give her to thee!

the Lord God of Israel make their house to be like the
house of Perez, and fulfil the wishes of their heart and their
desire for good] (15) and the God of our fathers Abraham, Isaac,
and Jacob be with them and command his blessing upon both of
you. **II** (16) And the elders of the town gathered themselves
together there, and they wrote the things down, (17) and they
blessed God, the bridegroom, and the bride, and they ate and made
merry.

I VIII. (1) And it came to pass after that, that they went both
into the inner chamber. **2** (2) And Tobiyah remembered the words
of the angel, and he took the liver and laid it upon burning coals,
and the smoke thereof ascended. (3) And the angel took the demon
and bound him and sent him into the desert which is before Egypt.
3 (4) And Tobiyah said to Sarah : arise, and let us pray to God
to-night, and the following night, and on the third night we shall be
in wedlock. (5) For we are children of saints, and we must not
walk in the statutes of the nations that are round about us. **4** (6) So
they both arose and prayed with reverence before God, [and they
poured out their heart in prayer (supplication) before God].
5 (7) *And Tobiyah said : blessed art thou, O Lord our God, king
of the universe, who has created gladness and joy, bridegroom and
bride. [**6** (8) Blessed art thou, O Lord, King of the universe, who
has created man after thy own image and likeness, and who hast
given him from the strength of thy power to know thee and to serve
thee.] **7** Thou hast given him a helpmeet for him, and thou hast
commanded them to be fruitful and to multiply their offspring in the
midst of the land.† **8** [Lord over all, creator of all, mighty over all,
who searches all, he is all powerful and exalted over all, all give
song unto him, he establishes law and commandment for all, he
is good to all, righteous and just to all, all powerful ; all give him
praise, he sustains all, he answers all, he delivers all the captives,
he is just and gracious to all, the Lord is nigh unto all, the
Lord is merciful and his mercies are over all ; all give hymn
unto him, his name supports all. **9** God of gods, and Lord
of lords ! merciful has thy name been called from eternity ;

* J. (7 and 8) reads : And Tobias said, Lord God of our fathers, may the
heavens and the earth, and the sea and the fountains, and the rivers, and all thy
creatures that are in them, bless thee. (8) Thou madest Adam of the slime of the
earth, and gavest him Eve for a helper.
† J. (7–10) correspond in our text to (**5–25**).

remember us according to thy loving kindness and mercy, for they have been ever of old. **10** And remember for me the pious acts of my father Tobi, who walked before thee in piety and truth ; save me and rebuke the Satan so that he should not touch us or hurt us. **11** Give me from this woman seed of men, that our offspring may know thy name and study thy law, and it shall be known among the nations that thou art the Lord and no other. **12** Then hear thou in heaven my prayer, as thou hast heard the prayer of our holy fathers, the saints, the prayer of Abraham in Ur Kasdim, and the prayer of Isaac on the Mount Moriah, and the prayer of Jacob in Bethel, and the prayers of all the just ; and put my tears into thy bottle. Let the words of my mouth, and the meditation of my heart be acceptable in thy sight, O Lord, my rock and my redeemer.* **13** And Sarah prayed and said : The Lord, the Lord is a god full of compassion, and gracious, slow to anger, and abundant in mercy and truth ; keeping mercy for the thousands of those who keep his laws and commandments. **14** O Lord, thou alone art one, and there is no second beside thee ; who is like unto thee, who can be likened unto thee, who can be compared with thee ? there is no other save thee, and there is none beside thee, and there is none to be equalled to thee. **15** Thou hast created everything, and there is no forgetfulness before thee ; therefore the hearts believe that thou art one, wondrous in all thy ways, hidden from every eye and no eye can see thee. Thou hast been before the world came into existence, and after its destruction thou wilt be, and thy years shall have no end. **16** Lo ! the host of heavens were made by thy word, and thy hand was not in their creation ; thou didst call them, and they all stood forth ; in thy hand is the power and might to destroy them, and to change them and to restore them to their original state. **17** In thy hand is life and good ; thou hast created this world to try man by the statutes and judgments which thou hast given to them. And the world to come thou hast created for thy pious men—those that love thee and keep thy covenant— and hell thou hast prepared of old for the abominable and for those who dealt treacherously with thee. **19** And thou art the Lord who hast chosen the seed of Jeśurun from among all the nations which

---

* J. (9) reads instead : And now, O Lord, thou knowest not for fleshly lust do I take my sister to wife, but only for the love of posterity, in which thy name may be blessed for ever and ever

are upon the face of the earth, and hast performed (wrought) signs and wonders in the face of all those who stood up against them. **20** And now, oh Lord, oh king, full of mercy, give ear to my prayer, and hold not thy peace at my tears, as thou hast listened to the prayer of our mother Sara ; when she prayed to thee because of her handmaid Hagar, and to the prayer of Rebecca when the children struggled together within her ; **21** and to the prayer of Rachel, the mother of children, who was the barren woman in the house at the time when her sister provoked her sore ; thou didst open her womb, and she bare children that are standing in thy courts to serve thee. **22** And the prayer of the prophetess Miriam, and the prayer of the wife of Elqanah, when her rival provoked her sore, in order to make her fret, thou appointedst a son from her to be a prophet, to stand before thee and to minister unto thee, so may my prayer ascend as a pleasure before thee, and may I be worthy of this man, and send us of thy blessings. **23** And rebuke the Satan that he should not touch my lord, and not stand at his right hand to be his adversary. **24** Therefore we praise thee, O Lord our God, for all thy miracles and numberless wonderful things, for heaven and the heaven of heavens cannot contain thee, still less is man able to investigate one of them. **25** Who can utter thy mighty acts, and show forth all thy praises ; thou art exalted as head above all. and extolled over all blessing.]*

26 (11) And it came to pass in the middle of the night, about the cockcrowing, that Reuel cried to his servants : " Arise and dig quickly a grave for Tobiyah, (12) for I know that mischief has befallen him as it happened to the other seven men who made marriage with us." **27** (13) And when they had finished digging the grave, Reuel returned to the house, and said to his wife : (14) Send the maid and let her see and ascertain whether the young man be dead or alive.† **28** (15) And the maid went, and behold, both were alive, lying in their bed and sleeping. (16) And she returned and brought the good tidings, and their heart rejoiced. **29** (17) And they blessed the Lord, and said : Blessed art thou, O Lord God of Israel, for thou hast done well unto us, and thou hast wrought wonders (18), and thou hast rebuked the Satan, so that he should not be able to

---

* Instead of vv. 13–25, J. reads : (10) Sarah also said, Have mercy on us, O Lord, have mercy on us, and let us grow old both together in health.

† J. adds, that I may bury him before it be day.

harm us nor our children for ever, (19) and all the nations shall know that thy name is called upon us.* (2c) And Reuel commanded them to fill up the pit from one end to another. **30** (21, 22) And he commanded, and they prepared a feast (slaughtered animals), and he called all his neighbours, and they ate and drank and made a great banquet.† **31** (23) And Reuel begged of Tobiyah to abide with him two weeks. **32** (24) And he gave him one half of his riches and substance, and treasures and his sheep, and his cattle and his oxen, and his household, and of whatever he possessed he would give (one half of) it to him in his lifetime, and after his death he would take it all.

IX. **1** (1, 2) And Tobiyah said to the angel: I beseech thee, my lord, let not thine anger burn against me, I have taken upon me to speak but this once, and do thou show more kindness in the latter end than at the beginning. **2** (3) And go for me to Gabael into the town (city) of . . . . and take these tokens into thy hands, and receive the silver from him, and invite him to come to the joy and to rejoice with us, (5?) as I cannot depart from here before the end of the two weeks, the days of the feast.‡ **3** (4) And thou knowest that my father will not rest nor be still until I return in peace. **4** (6) So the angel listened to him, and he took four of Reuel's servants and two camels with him, and came to Rage, and he gave the token to Gabael and took the silver from him. **5** (7) And he told what had happened to Tobiyah, the son of Tobi, and that he had asked him to come and rejoice with the invited on the day of his marriage, the day of the rejoicing of his heart. **6** [And Gabael arose and saddled his camel and went with him.] **7** (8) And when he had come into Reuel's house, he found him and Tobiyah with him, sitting at the table, and he fell upon his neck and kissed him and he wept. **8** (9) And he blessed him and said: The Lord bless thee and keep

---

* J. (18 and 19) reads: For thou hast shown thy mercy to us, and hast shut out from us the enemy that persecuted us. (19) And thou hast taken pity upon two only children. Make them, O Lord, bless thee more fully: and to offer up to thee a sacrifice of thy praise, and of their health, that all nations may know that thou alone art God in all the earth.

† J. (21 and 22) reads: And he spoke to his wife to make ready a feast and prepare all kinds of provisions that are necessary for such as go on a journey. (22) He caused also two fat kine and four wethers to be killed, and a banquet to be prepared for all his neighbours and all his friends.

‡ J. reads (5): And indeed thou seest how Raguel had adjured me, whose adjuring I cannot despise.

thee, for thou art the son of a good man, Godfearing and avoiding evil. **9** (10, 11) May thy house be as the house of Perez, who begat Hezron.* (12) And all the people answered : Amen ! and they ate and drank and made merry.

X. **1** (1-3) But Tobi was heavy and wretched, and it grieved him at his heart, and he said : my son, my son, why dost thou tarry, why are thy steps so long in coming ?† Such was his custom all the days. **2** (4) And Hanna wept and did not eat, for her sighs were many and her heart was faint.   **3** And she said to her husband : thou are verily guilty of this great tribulation which thou hast brought upon us, **4**‡ for thou hast sent away our son, the joy of our heart, the nourisher of our old age, under whose shadow we would live among the nations. **5** (6) And Tobi answered her : fear not, my sister, for [I trust in the lovingkindness of my God, that he will bring him back] in peace, as the man who went with him is very trusty [and he is an angel from the Lord of hosts]. **6** (7)§ Go outside, my sister, and see, perhaps it might be the will of God, through his mercy, that thou bring me tidings and rejoice my fainting heart.   Such was his custom all the time his son was abroad.‖   **7** (9) Tobiyah was thinking in his own heart, and he said to Reuel, his father-in-law : why dost thou make me tarry, and God has made my way prosperous, whilst the sleep has fled from my father and my mother, they do not rest nor are they still [until I return home in peace ?]¶   **8** [But Reuel said to his son-in-law : be content, I pray thee, and tarry with me ; fulfil these

---

* J. reads : (10) And may a blessing come upon thy wife and upon your parents ; (11) and may you see your children and your children's children unto the third and fourth generation, and may your seed be blessed by the God of Israel who reigneth for ever.

† X. J. (1-3) reads : But as Tobias made longer stay upon occasion of the marriage, Tobias his father was solicitous, saying, Why thinkest thou doth my son tarry, or why is he detained there ? (2) Is Gabelus dead, thinkest thou, and no man will pay him the money ? (3) And he began to be exceeding sad both he and Anna his wife with him : and they began both to weep together, because their son did not return to them on the day appointed.

‡ J. (5) (here missing) : We having all things together in thee alone, ought not to have let thee go from us.

§ J. (7) reads : But she could by no means be comforted, but daily running out looking round about, and went into all the ways by which there seemed any hope he might return, that she might if possible see him coming afar off.

‖ J. (8) (here missing) reads : But Raguel said to his son-in-law, stay here, and I will send a messenger to Tobias thy father, that thou art in health.

¶ J. (9) : And Tobias said to him, I know that my father and mother now count the days, and their spirit is grievously afflicted within them."

two weeks, and I will send thee away with mirth and with song.
9 But Tobi answered : no, my lord, listen to me, and send me away,
so that I go to my country, and my wife with me.] **10** (10) When
Reuel saw that he could not prevail upon him, he sent him away, and
his wife with him, with silver and gold, and precious things, and
cattle, and great household, and with great mirth. **11** (11)* And
Reuel blessed his daughter, and said : may the Lord God of Israel
give unto thee seed of men, and prosper thy way ! †

XI. **1** And they sent him away, and his wife [and all his relations and friends and acquaintances went with him one day's journey,
and they gave him gifts, everyone a ring of gold, a Qesitah and a
piece of silver ; (1) and they went on their way to the city of
Nineveh.] **2** (2) And when they came near the city, the angel of
the Lord said to Tobiyah : thou knowest that it is a long time since
we have separated ourselves from your father. **3** (3) Set thy steps
on thy walk and go quickly to thy father, and I will lead on softly
according to the pace of the flock. **4** (4) And Tobiyah said : the
word is good which thou hast spoken. And he hastened and saddled
his ass, and he arose and went.‡ **5** (7) And the angel charged
Tobiyah : as soon as thou shalt come into the house, forthwith give
thanks to God and bless him, and go to thy father and kiss him.
6 (8) And the gall of the fish which thou hast put up to keep, take
with thee and anoint the eyes of thy father, and he will see, and his
heart will rejoice. **7** Then Tobiyah went away from him and came
into the town ; (5)§ when he came near his mother perceived him
(6)‖ and she ran and told it to her husband.¶ **8** (10) And Tobi

* J. (11) : " saying, the holy angel of the Lord be with you in your journey,
and bring you through safe, and that you may find all things well about your
parents, and my eyes may see your children before I die."

† J. adds (12-13) : And the parents taking their daughter kissed her and let
her go. (13) Admonishing her to honour her father and mother-in-law, to love
her husband, to take care of the family, to govern the house, and to behave
herself irreprehensibly.

‡ J. reads (4) : And as their going pleased him, Raphael said to Tobias,
Take with thee of the gall of the fish, for it will be necessary. So Tobias took
some of that gall and departed.

§ J. (5) : But Anna sat beside the way daily, on the top of a hill, from whence
she might see afar off.

‖ J. (6) And while she watched his coming from that place, she saw him afar
off, and presently perceived it was her son coming.

¶ J. (9) omitted : Then the dog which had been with them in the way, ran
before, and coming as if he had brought the news, showed his joy by his fawning
and wagging his tail.

rejoiced exceedingly, and he arose from his bed and wanted to run to meet his son, and he dashed his foot against a stone [and he fell down, for his eyes were blind]. **9** And Tobiyah hastened (11) [and descended from the ass and lifted his father up from the ground] and kissed him, and they wept (12) and worshipped God ; they praised him and blessed him with a loud voice. **10** (13) And Tobiyah took the gall of the fish and annointed the eyes of his father with it (14, 15) and his eyes were opened ; and the white substance which covered the eyes fell off, and he rejoiced exceedingly.* **11** (16) When Hannah saw that her husband was seeing, she worshipped God. **12** (17) And she said : blessed be the Lord God of Israel, who has comforted us and has magnified his mercy.† **13** (18) And it came to pass after the completion of seven days that Sarah arrived with all the cattle and the young and the camels and beasts which her father Reuel had given her. **14** (19) And Tobiyah told his father all that had happened to him, and what the angel had done for him, and how God had prospered him.§

XII. **1** (1) And Tobi said to his son : in what manner shall we honour this man ? (2, 3) for all that thou hast, has come to thee through him. He has moreover killed the demon, and has done many wondrous things for thee ? **2** (4) And now, my son, call him, that he may take one half of the riches which thou hast brought. **3** (5) And he listened to his father, and called the angel. And he besought him and said : I pray thee, my Lord, man of God, behold the Lord has blessed me for thy sake : choose thee from all that I possess, and take one half thereof. (6) And he answered : I will not take anything ; **4** but do ye serve God with fear, and worship him and praise his holy name, for he renders to every man according to his work. **5** And blessed be now the Lord who has rendered thee thy reward, for thou hast acted towards the dead in piety and in truth. **6** And the strength of Israel will not lie or utter falsehood, for

---

* J. (14 and 15) : (14) And he stayed about half an hour ; and a white skin began to come out of his eyes, like the skin of an egg (15) and Tobias took hold of it and drew it from his eyes, and immediately he recovered his sight.

† J. (17) : And Tobias said, I bless thee, O Lord God of Israel, because thou hast chastised me, and thou hast saved me : and behold I see Tobias my son.

§ J. (20 and 21) omitted in our text. (20) And Achior and Nabath the kinsmen of Tobias came rejoicing for Tobias, and congratulating with him for all the good things that God had done for him. (21) And for seven days they feasted and rejoiced all with great joy.

he is truthful.   **7** (9) And righteousness (alms) delivers from death.*
8 (13) And God has tried thee and has brought upon thee tribulations,
and has purified thee as silver and has heard thy prayer.   **9** (15) And
he has sent me, the angel Raphael, one of the seven princes who
minister first in the presence of the King, the Lord of hosts.
10 (14) And he commanded me to heal thee and to save thee and to
conduct thy son and to bring him back ; for God had listened to thy
prayer and to thy reproach, and to the prayer and reproach of Sarah.
11 (16) And when they had heard his words, they were amazed one
at another, and they fell down upon their faces.   **12** (17) And he said
to them, fear not, † (18) for I came by the word of God, and by his
command have I done all these things [and not by any will of mine],
(19) and behold, at the sight of your eyes I appeared to eat and
drink,‡ and yet did I neither eat bread nor drink water.§   **13** (21,
22) So they arose and blessed God, and the angel had disappeared,
and they did not know it (see it), for they feared that they would die,
as their eyes had seen an angel of the Lord of hosts.

XIII. **1** (1) And they arose and blessed God the Lord their God.
And Tobi said : blessed art thou, O Lord, and great are thy works,
and thou shalt reign for ever and ever.   **2** (2) For [thine is the
kingdom], thou leadest down to Sheol and bringest up again, he
wounds and he heals, and there is none who could deliver out of
his hand. **3** (3)‖ O give thanks unto the Lord, for he is good : for his
mercy endureth for ever.   **4** Who can utter the mighty acts of the
Lord, or show forth all his praise ? unto thee praise shall be given.
5 Bless the Lord, O my soul, O Lord my God, thou art very great ;
thou art clothed with honour and majesty.   **6** Blessed be the
Lord God of Israel from everlasting even to everlasting.   And all

---

* J. (6–13) corresponding to end of **3** and **4–7** differs greatly ; J. (7–8) and
(10–12) are missing here. (7) For it is good to hide the secret of a king : but honourable to reveal and confess the works of God.   (8) Prayer is good with fasting and
alms, more than to lay up treasures of gold.   (10) But they that commit sin and
iniquity, are enemies to their own soul.   (11) I discover then the truth unto you
and I will not hide the secret from you.   (12) When thou didst pray with tears,
and didst bury the dead, and didst leave thy dinner, and hide the dead by day
in thy house, and bury them by night, I offered thy prayer to the Lord.

  † J. adds, Peace be to you.

  ‡ J. reads : but I use an invisible meat and drink, which cannot be seen by
men.

  § J. (20) omitted here : It is time therefore that I return to him that sent me :
but bless ye God, and publish all his wonderful works.

  ‖ (3) till end of chapter totally different from J.

the people say: Amen! **7** And it came to pass that before they had finished their repast Tobiyah was told: lo, thy wife has come with the cattle and the flock. And they arose and went to meet them with timbrels and dances, and they brought them into the house with mirth and songs. **8** And they fulfilled the days of the feast, and they blessed God with a loud voice: Oh that men would praise the Lord for his loving kindness, and for all the good deeds and the wondrous things which God has wrought for us. **9** And Tobi said: blessed art thou, oh Lord God of Israel, because thou hast not denied us thy love and thy truth, thou who art the keeper of the covenant, and of the love for those who love thee and keep thy covenant. **10** And Tobi said to his son and to his wife Sarah, O give thanks unto the Lord, call upon his name; make known his doing among the peoples, because he has dealt wondrously with us, and has changed our mourning into mirth, and our sorrow into dance and a day of feasting. And all the people answered: Amen! and Tobi said to his son Tobiyah: blessed be our Lord, of whose gifts we have eaten, and through whose goodness we live. And all the people answered: blessed be our Lord, of whose gifts we have eaten, and through whose goodness we live. **12** And all the people arose and blessed Tobi and his wife, and Tobiyah his son, and his daughter-in-law, and they said to Tobiyah: may thy house be like unto the house of Perez. And they answered: Amen! And they went, everyone of them, to their tents, joyful and glad of heart.

XIV. **1** (1) And Tobi lived after he had recovered his sight forty-nine years, and the days of his life were one hundred and seventy years. **2** (2) And he died and was gathered unto his people in a good old age in the city of Nineveh.* **3** (4) And the rest of his works were in the love of God, in gladness of heart and abundance in everything, and in the fear of God and clinging to him. **4** (5) And it was before his death, and he spake to his son, saying: come near to me, my son, and do not stand aside, for I will counsel thee before God, ere I (die). . . . .

BE STRONG.

---

* J. (3) omitted here: For he was six and fifty years old when he lost the sight of his eyes, and sixty when he recovered it again.

TOBIT LEGEND II (H.G).

Thou shalt surely tithe all the increase of thy seed, that which cometh forth of the field year by year. And thou shalt eat before the Lord thy God, in the place which he shall choose to cause his name to dwell there, the tithe of thy corn, of thy wine, and of thine oil, and the firstlings of thy herd and of thy flock; that thou mayest learn to fear the Lord thy God always. Our sages say: "Thou shalt surely tithe" (Asser te 'asser), which means. tithe in order that thou become rich, and tithe surely, in order that thou have no wants. This is an indication to those that travel on the high seas to give the tenth to those that are engaged in the study of the law. If thou tithest then it is thy corn, but if not, it is my corn, as it is said (Hosea ii, 11), "therefore will I take back my corn in its due time." If thou art worthy, it is thy wine, but if not, it is mine. Rabbi Levi said: (Prov. xxviii, 22) "He that hath an evil eye hasteth after riches, and knoweth not that want shall come upon him," this verse applies to the man who does not bring out his tithes in a proper manner. For R. Levi said: It happened once (a history is told) of a man who brought out his tithes in a proper manner (etc.), therefore Moses warned the Israelites to tithe surely.

1. The history is told of a man whose name was Tobi, of the tribe of Napthali, who all his days walked in the right path, and performed many good deeds for his brethren who were with him in the captivity in Nineveh: and he was left an orphan by his father, and he was brought up by Deborah his father's mother, and she led him in the right path. And when he became a man he took a wife of his own kindred and family, whose name was Hannah, and she bare him a son, and he called his name Tobiyah. And when he was in the captivity, in the city of Nineveh, all his brethren and kindred polluted themselves, and did eat the bread of the sons of the Gentiles. But he did not eat, for he feared God with all his heart. And therefore God gave him grace and favour in the eyes of Shalmanesser, the king, and he appointed him master over all that he had, to the day of his death. And at that time he committed to the hand of Gabael his kinsman ten talents of gold. And after the death of the king Shalmanesser, his son Sennacherib reigned in his stead. And in the days of Sennacherib Tobi did many

charitable deeds for the poor, and he fed the hungry and the orphans; and when he saw one of the Jews slain, cast out in the street, he buried him. Now when Sennacherib returned in haste from Judah, he went to Nineveh in fierce wrath against the ten tribes, and killed many of them, and their corpses were cast out in the streets, and none buried them. When Tobi saw that, his wrath was kindled, and he arose in the night and buried them; and thus he did many times. Once Sennacherib asked for the bodies of the slain, but found them not. And the men of Nineveh said to the king: Tobi buries them. And the king commanded that he be put to death. When Tobi heard it, he fled. And the king commanded that they should pillage his house, and he hid himself from him five and forty days, until Adramelech and Sharezer his sons killed Sennacherib with the sword, and Esarhaddon his son reigned in his stead. And the king appointed Aqiqar over all his affairs. And Aqiqar spake good words for Tobi, and he brought him back to Nineveh.

II. When the feast of Weeks came, his wife prepared a plentiful meal, and as he sat at the table, he said to his son Tobiyah: go, and bring to me some of our poor brethren, such as fear God, to eat with us. Then Tobiyah went and found a man slain, cast out in the street, and he told his father. What did his father do? he rose from the table and he went with him, and he took him from the street of the city, and brought him into a house until the going down of the sun, that he might be able to bury him. And he turned to his house and ate his bread in mourning. And he said: Woe that on us is fulfilled, "and I will turn your feasts and your songs into mourning." And he wept very sore. And when the sun went down he went and buried him. And he returned to his house, and he lay upon his bed, and his face was uncovered, and dust fell from the wall into his eyes. And in the morning he went to the physician to cure his eyes, but it did not avail him, until he became blind of both eyes, which lasted for four years. And Aqiqar his friend nourished him. After many days his wife did work for women, and they gave her a kid for her wages. And Tobi heard the kid bleating in the house, and he asked her: from whence hast thou this kid? hast thou stolen it perhaps? And his wife Hannah said: they have given it to me as the wages of the work of mine hands; I have not stolen it! But Tobi did not believe her, and they quarrelled concerning the kid. Hannah said to Tobi: Where are thy goodnesses and thy merits? hence thy worthlessness is manifest to all!

III. When Tobi heard this he was much grieved, and he wept and prayed to the Holy One, blessed be he, in the anguish of his soul, and he said: Lord of the universe! take my soul from me, for it is better for me to die than to live, so that I shall no more hear shame.   And the same day, Sarah, the daughter of Reuel, who lived in Agbatanis, in the land of Media, heard a great reproach because she had been given to seven men as wife, and not one of them came in unto her according to the way of all the earth.   And her maid said to her: it is thou who hast killed these men to whom thou hast been given in marriage, and not one of them has come in unto thee because thou hast hurt them.   And it came to pass, when Sarah heard the words o her maid she wept very much, and went up into the upper chamber to pray there in the anguish of her soul. And she said: Lord of the universe! thou knowest that I am pure, and I have not polluted myself with man.   I am the only daughter of my father, neither has he son to inherit his property, nor any kinsman; and behold, seven husbands are dead for my sake, and why should I live?   But if it please not thee to kill me, have pity on me that I hear no more reproach!   Our sages say that on that day the Holy One, blessed be he, accepted their prayers, and he commanded the angel Raphael to heal them both; to cure Tobi from the blindness of his eyes, and to give Sarah for wife to Tobiyah, the son of Tobi, and to take away from her Ashmedai, the king of the demons.

IV. At that time Tobi remembered the money which he had committed to the hand of Gabael.   And he called his son Tobiyah, and said to him, My son, fear the Lord thy God all thy days, and give alms all thy days, and do not walk with a thief or an adulterer, and set aside thy tithes as is proper, and the Holy One, blessed be He, will give thee great riches.   And now, my son, know that I have committed ten talents of silver to the hand of Gabael, and I know not the day of my death; go to him, and he will give thee the money.

V. And Tobiyah answered his father: All that thou hast commanded me I will do: but how can I take the money from the hand of Gabael, who knoweth me not, and I know not him?   His father said to him: Take this ring, which he has given me, and I have given him my ring.   And now, my son, seek thee a trusty man, who may go with thee, and I will give him his wages.   So Tobiyah went immediately to seek for a man who might go with him, and he found the angel Raphael standing by.   But he did not recognise him that he was an angel of the Lord. He asked him : From whence art thou? He answered him, From the Children of Israel. He said to him : Knowest thou how to go to Media ? And he said : Yes. Tobiyah said to him : Tarry a little for my sake, and I will tell my father. Tobiyah went and told his father. He said to him : Call him. And he said to him : My son Tobiyah desireth to go to Media ; art thou willing to go with him ? He said to him : Yes! And Tobi called his son immediately, and said to him : Prepare thyself, and go with this man, and may the Lord of heaven prosper your way and bring you back in peace.

VI. Both went then on their journey, and they came to the river Euphrates, and they passed the night there. And Tobiyah ran to the river to drink, and a fish came out and ate his bread, and he cried out. And Raphael said to Tobiyah : Lay hold of the fish, and do not let it go. Tobiyah went and laid hold of the fish and drew it out, and Raphael said to him : Open it in the middle and take its heart ; it is good to burn it before a man in whom the spirit of demons is, to make them flee from him ; and take also the gall, for it is good to anoint therewith the eyes in which there is blindness, and they shall be healed. So Tobiyah did as the angel commanded him, and they went to Media. And Raphael said to Tobiyah : My brother, thou comest to the house of Reuel, who is an old man, and has a daughter who is exceeding fair, whose name is Sarah, speak to him that he may give her to thee for a wife. Tobiyah said to him : I have heard that she has been given in marriage to seven men, and they died before they came in unto her. Raphael said : Fear not! when thou shalt be with her in the marriage chamber, take the heart of the fish and burn thereof under her garment, and the demon will smell it, and will run away.

VII. Raphael said to Reuel : Give thy daughter to Tobiyah for a wife. And he said : I am willing. And Reuel took his daughter Sarah and gave her to Tobiyah for a wife. And Reuel said to his wife : Prepare a bedchamber. Tobiyah and his wife Sarah went into it ; and Tobiyah remembered the words of Raphael, and he took the heart of the fish and put it on a censer and burnt it under the clothes of Sarah. And Ashmedai received the smell, and he fled instantly ; and both prayed to the Holy One, who had healed her. On the morrow, Tobiyah said to Raphael : Go to

Gabael, that he may give thee ten talents of gold. Raphael went immediately, and brought the money ; and Raphael said to Tobiyah : Thou knowest that thou hast left thy father and thy mother in great pain ; now let us go to prepare the house, and let thy wife come after us. So they both of them went. Raphael said to Tobiyah : When thou comest into the house of thy father, take the gall and put it in the eyes of thy father, and he will be cured. He did so. And Tobi said to his son : Tell me all that thou hast done. And he told him. And he said : Blessed be the Lord who hath sent his angel with my son, and hath prospered his way, and hath cured two poor people like ourselves. In after days God blessed Tobiyah also, because he fulfilled the command of his father, and gave tithes of everything that he possessed.

Hence we learn how great is the power of alms and tithes, and how, because Tobi gave alms and separated his tithes as is meet, the Holy One, blessed be he, rewarded him ! And because the Patriarchs of the world knew the power of alms and tithes they were careful in observing them. Therefore did Moses warn the Israelites, saying to them : Thou shalt surely tithe all the increase of thy seed.

THE UNKNOWN ARAMAIC ORIGINAL OF THEODO-TION'S ADDITIONS TO THE BOOK OF DANIEL.

By Dr. Gaster.

*Reprinted from the " Proceedings of the Society of Biblical Archæology,"
November, December, 1894, and February, 1895.*

I.—Introduction.

It is an universally admitted fact, which no one acquainted with the Greek translations of the Bible will venture to contradict, that the real work of Theodotion consisted in correcting and altering the old Greek translation known as the LXX, in accordance with the Hebrew text. Not much has been preserved of that improved edition of the LXX made by Theodotion, but the fragments alone would suffice to show his absolute dependence upon the Hebrew original.

Much more clearly is this fact evidenced by the whole book of Daniel, which has come down to us entirely in Theodotion's version. The translation of the LXX must have deviated very much from the original, so much so as to induce the Church from very ancient times to eliminate it from the official service, and to substitute for it that other translation of Theodotion. (The LXX text has, as is well known, come to light in the last century, and has been often reprinted.) The differences extend also to the apocryphal additions, which are missing in our canon, at any rate in the Hebrew canon of the Scriptures. These differences do not appear to be very great, but it is questionable whether Theodotion's text has not been altered after that of the LXX. Even in this form there are, however, marked differences which cannot be explained, unless we admit that Theodotion had a certain original before his eyes, exactly as was the case with the rest of the book. He corrected and amended the old translation, being guided by the language of that original. It would appear, otherwise, at least singular that he should have attempted a similar process of correction, if there was not such an original text to guide him. The presumption, *à priori*, is, therefore, that also for those portions which are now counted among the Apocrypha an original in a Semitic dialect must have existed, and that this was used by Theodotion when he undertook to amend the LXX version.

I do not think that one can lay great stress on the suggestion thrown out by Lengerke,* that these apocryphal additions have been interpolated at a later time from the LXX into Theodotion, as this would lead to a far more complicated question, viz., how to explain these differences in those two texts.

First, as to the "Song of the Three Children." Many a scholar has thought that he could detect traces of such an ancient Semitic original in peculiarities of the language. De Wette-Schrader† has collected all these peculiarities of the Greek which would point to such an original. They can best be explained by comparing them with words or forms that may have been misunderstood by the translator, or by his being influenced by the forms of that language, which may have been an Aramaic dialect akin to that of Daniel— and yet does De Wette doubt the existence of such an original. Schuerer, who devotes a whole chapter to the study of these additions to Daniel,‡ sums up his judgment in these words : "There is no reason to believe in a Hebrew original for any of these texts." It is doubtful whether he meant a purely Hebrew or an original written in any *Semitic* dialect, since, properly speaking, one could say that there is no Hebrew original for the greater part of the Book of Daniel, as it contains so many chapters written in Aramaic. Much more decided is De Wette in his opinion about the origin of the other additions, such as the history of Bel and that of the Dragon. He, as well as Fritzsche,§ say that there is not the slightest foundation for the idea that there was a Hebrew, or, as the latter adds, an Aramaic original for these. The differences between Theodotion and the LXX are. however, much more pronounced in these other portions than in the Song, and, as far as I have been able to see, no theory has hitherto been vouchsafed by any of these scholars that could give a satisfactory explanation of these discrepancies. If they are not to be explained by a difference of translation, how, and for what . reason should Theodotion have gone out of his way to alter the old-established version ; and why

* Das Buch Daniel ; Königsberg, 1835, p. 108.

† Lehrbuch d. histor.-Kritischen Einleitung, 8th ed. ; Berlin, 1869, p. 509.

‡ Geschichte des juedischen Volkes im Zeitalter Jesu, 2d ed., ii, pp. 716–720.

§ Kurzgefasstes Exegetisches Handbuch zu den Apokryphen ; Leipzig, 1851, p. 121, § 12.

should the Church feel it proper to accept this latter, if not for their conviction that this way is a more faithful rendering of the original ? Delitzcsh, in his study on Habakkuk,* has already drawn attention to a fragment of the Bel legend in an old Hebrew Midrash quoted by Raymundus Martini in the 13th century. The same has since been discovered by Dr. Neubauer in another fragment of the same Midrash Major, as that book is called. He has published this legend, together with the Aramaic version of the Book of Tobit.† The language of this text, however, is more like Syriac than Aramaic, and it differs in many important details from the old Greek versions. It can, therefore, not be considered as the probable original from which those translations have been made. They go, on the other hand, a long way to prove the existence of these legends in a Semitic dialect.

Another proof is furnished by the fact that all the additions to Daniel are found also in the Hebrew Josephus, better known as Josippon. We have there the throwing of Daniel into the den of the lions, and the prophet Habakkuk drawn by the lock of his hair from Palestine to feed him in that pit,‡ then the history of Bel,§ and that of the Dragon.‖ As will be seen afterwards, these portions were in the oldest known MS. of Josippon, and form part of that book ; they are not later additions or interpolations, but belong to the body of that work. As the question concerning Josippon is still an open one, and its relation to the Greek Josephus not yet sufficiently cleared up, I prefer not to take this parallel as a proof for the antiquity of these texts. They suffice to prove, however, the existence of Semitic parallels to the apocryphal additions to Daniel. It will become evident later on that the version contained in Josippon, which has some details which are wanting in the Greek versions both of the LXX and Theodotion, is not taken from these versions, but in every probability from the original Semitic source which served as basis to these Greek translations.

It is dangerous to dogmatise, and to try to settle definitely questions which later discoveries may easily upset. Such is the case with these additions to Daniel, which, as shown, are declared

* De Habacuci Prophetae vita, etc.; Leipzig, 1842. pp. 32, 33.
† The Book of Tobit ; Oxford, 1878, pp. 41, 42.
‡ Ed. Breithaupt, I, cap. x, xi, pp. 33–37.
§ Ibid., cap. xiii, pp. 40–42.
‖ Ibid., cap. xiv, pp. 42–45.

by all the recognized authorities to be of a purely Greek, probably
Alexandrinian, origin, though it be extremely difficult to reconcile
it with the fact that such texts were known in a Semitic language
from ancient times.

I think now to have recovered that very original, the existence
of which has hitherto been denied, on apparently insufficient
grounds.

In the Chronicle of Jerahmeel, who lived somewhat about the
10th century, if not earlier, I have found an Aramaic text which is
interesting from more than one point of view.   The compiler of the
Chronicle gives first a Hebrew translation of all those chapters in
Daniel that are in Aramaic.   Then follows a long rhymed introduction, after which the author says : " Now I am copying the missing
praises and songs which praised and sang the three young men,
which Theodosius found, and are not in the 24 (canonical) books.
And this is the text (chapter) which Theodosius the wise man, who
translated (the Bible) in the days of Commodus, the king of the
Romans, introduced (arranged) in his Corpus (Canon)*   It is not
found in the book of the Hebrews but in that of the Seventy
wise men, who translated the book of the Law together with Elazar
the high priest, who was killed in the days of Antiochus (his
bones may be ground to dust), who translated the whole Law in the
days of Ptolomæus, king of Egypt ; and the two men whose names
were Symmachus and Akilas, who translated in the days of king
Adrian, were translators (thereof) also.   And Akilas is Onkelos."

" And this is the text of that which is not written in the Corpus
(Canon) of the Hebrews and was found by Theodosius."

So far this remarkable introduction, which I have tried to render
in a more intelligible form.   The language is greatly involved and
the meaning is not perfectly clear.   But one point cannot be mistaken, viz., that the compiler wanted to convey the meaning that the
text which he incorporated into his Chronicle was the one found or
discovered by Theodosius.   In order to understand fully the whole
bearing of these few words, one must first settle the question as to
who this great man Theodosius was, of whom Jerahmeel speaks
with such a respect.   I say that this *Todos* or Theodosius, as I

---

* I draw special attention to the word סדר used here, as this seems to be the
exact equivalent of κάνον, and furnishes the best explanation of this term.   I am
preparing a special study on this term.

have translated this name, is no one else than *Theodotion*. It will at once be apparent why it is said that he *found* it. Bearing in mind the character of his work as a translator, that it consisted chiefly in adjusting the Greek text so as to reproduce the meaning of the Hebrew original more accurately, one can easily understand his anxiety to get hold also of the Hebrew or Aramaic originals of those portions which were not included in the Hebrew canon, but were to be found in the Greek of the LXX. Therefore it is said that he " found " this text, *i.e.*, he discovered the old original. A comparison between this Aramaic text and the Greek of Theodotion will soon convince us whether my conjecture is correct or not.

Before proceeding to this exegetical part, we have still to examine that introduction, which may yield some unexpected results. First again the name *Todos* and *Theodosius*. If this be identical with Theodotion, as I suggest, then this short notice will throw a flood of light on the history and biography of this otherwise very little known translator of the Bible. Hitherto all that was known is due to the short and not very clear notices of Irenæus, Hieronymus and Epiphanius, whose credibility has been doubted.* The only thing certain was that he must have lived before Irenæus (d. 202), *i.e.*, before the close of the second century. He may also have been a Jewish proselyte. Hieronymus makes him out to have been an Ebionite or *semi-christianus*. According to Epiphanius (Irenæus) he came from Ephesus, was originally a Marcionite, embraced afterwards Judaism, studied Hebrew, and made his translation in the time of the emperor Commodus. That is almost all that is known hitherto about this man. There is nothing improbable in the idea that Theodotion may have been a proselyte. Most if not all the Greek translations owe their origin to proselytes : such were Akilas and Symmachus. They felt more keenly the inadequacy of the existing translations, and strove after another which should render the Hebrew original in the most faithful manner, in order to have, if it were possible, the Hebrew original in a Greek garb. To the Jews the Greek was almost a matter of indifference ; not so to those to whom Greek was their natural language, and who had to acquire the knowledge of Hebrew afterwards in life by hard work. Only such a motive will explain the number of Greek translations. The same may have been the primary motive for Theodotion to

---

* *Vide* de Wette, *l.c.*, p. 101.

improve the older and not sufficiently literal translation of the LXX.*

From the comparative obscurity and uncertainty as to the date and personality of Theodotion in which we are left by the writers of the Church, he is lifted out by this attempted identification of Theodotion or Theodot (so in some MSS.) with Todos, the popular and shorter form of the same name.

Todos is a man well known in Talmudic literature. He is mentioned in both the Talmuds at least five or six times, and always as a rich man and in high position. He is a munificent supporter of the wise men, and assists them materially.† "He used to give to the people of Rome the passah-lamb prepared in a peculiar manner, in the same way almost as it used to be prepared in Jerusalem, so that it looked like the sacrificial lamb. The sages sent word to him saying : 'if thou wert not Todos, we would have excommunicated thee.'"‡

In all these passages it is R. Jose, (second half of the second century) who mentions this fact. In one place only the name of the rabbi who sent that threat is given as that of R. Simeon b. Shetah, of the time of Jannai the Makkabæan king ;§ but this name has crept in from the other incident mentioned a few lines higher on the same page, and is undoubtedly a mistake of the writer or printer. The parallel passage in the Jesusalem Talmud (Moed katan) proves it also to be a mistake. From this passage two things are evident : (1) that Todos wished to observe the commandment of the passah-lamb in the strictest possible manner, so strictly in fact that he almost brought down upon himself the censure and possibly the anathema of the authorities. If anything, this is the characteristic of the proselyte, who is more strict in the observance of the law than the man born in it. In his anxiety to do what he considered to be

---

* Theodotion, or, as he is called in the same MSS., *Theodot*, stands probably for the Hebrew *Jonathan*. It is rather a peculiar coincidence that the Aramaic translation of the Prophets is ascribed to a Jonathan, who is identified in the Talmud with Jonathan, son of Uziel, pupil of Hillel. In a similar manner we have the Aramaic translation of the Pentateuch ascribed to Onkelos, the counterpart of Akilas. I do not intend laying any stress on this peculiar coincidence, beyond pointing out the parallelism in the names of the Greek and Aramaic translators of the Bible. Nor do I wish it to be understood that I identify Jonathan the Targumist with Theodotion.

† Tr. Pesahim, fol. 53*b*, jer. Moed katan, III, § 1*f*, 81*d*.

‡ *L.c.*, v. Tr. Betzah, fol. 23*a*.

§ Tr. Berachoth, fol. 19*a*.

a divine commandment, he almost went beyond the Law; and (2) that the rabbis must have had a very strong reason to wink at his zeal, and deal leniently with his transgression. The reason thereof is not given in the Talmud; it is said only that he was a munificent supporter of the rabbis. This would not have weighed very much with them; we are therefore bound to look in another direction for this leniency. If Theodotion was a proselyte, this would explain admirably why he was allowed to go out scot free. He did not know that it was not permitted to offer the passah-lamb outside Jerusalem. It was an error of judgment committed from the purest of motives, hence his immunity. If besides we take into consideration that by the new translation of the Bible he may have rendered a signal service to the community, we easily understand why he has been treated with such regard.* He is not to be confounded with Theodoros the doctor who is a contemporary of R. Akiba;† this seems to have been a man from Alexandria. I make this remark because Levy in his Talmudic dictionary brings both under the same name Todos, and translates this latter as Theodoros, which is not correct.

There is one more reference to Todos in the old Hebrew literature which leads us straight to the question from which we started in our investigation, viz., the relation between this Todos and the additions to the canonical book of Daniel.

In the name of Todos we find in the late Midrash to the Psalms‡ a peculiar Aggadic interpretation of the martyrdom of the Three Children. "According to Todos the three children compared themselves with the frogs which, according to the word of Scripture, entered also the furnaces of the Egyptians at the bidding of God, (Exod. vii, 28), but they were not hurt, as God protected them : the more reason for them to hope, who had also the merits of their forefathers to assist them, and had moreover the duty to sanctify the Name of God, and to suffer martyrdom for His sake."

This line of argument harmonises very well with the character of Theodotion as we have tried to sketch it; he was a zealous and devout proselyte. That he should have just chosen the three children for the exponents of his views, corroborates the idea that

---

* *Cf.* also Jer. Betza, II, § 7, f. 61*c* ; Toseftah Betza, II, § 15, p. 204, ed. Zuckermandel.

† Tr. Berachoth, fol. 28*b*, and Toseftah Oholoth, IV, § 2, p. 600, ed. Zuckermandel.

‡ Ps. xxviii, *v.* 2, p. 229, ed. Buber.

he must have occupied himself more specially with these incidents recorded in the book of Daniel. There is in the whole of Hebrew literature, as far as I am aware of, no other reference to a biblical passage recorded in his name.

If we return now to the starting point of this inquiry, we shall find that Jerahmeel has preserved also the date when Theodotion lived. He places him under Commodus, and is thus in perfect agreement with the tradition of Epiphanius, who places him exactly under the same reign. Nor is this date contradicted by the quotations and references in the Talmudic literature. According to all these independent witnesses, Theodotion flourished during the second half of the second century after the common era.

The remaining portion of Jerahmeel's introduction is no less interesting. We have there so faint an echo of Aristeas' famous letter that it is scarcely recognisable. According to Jerahmeel, the Greek translation of the LXX dates from the first half of the second century before Christ, as he lets the High Priest Eleazar, who takes part in it, die in the days of Antiochus Epiphanes (*circa.* 170 B.C.). This may mean to signify the latest date when all the books of the Bible were translated, as Jes. Sirach (130 B.C.) alludes to thee existence of that translation, whether in whole or parts is not perfectly clear. The time of Antiochus may be the *terminus ad quem.*

As far as Akilas and Symmachus are concerned, the date assigned to them by Jerahmeel—the time of Hadrian—seems to be perfectly correct, although some would like to place Symmachus after Theodotion.

From the preliminary matter we pass now to the text itself. We first study the language in which it is written. It is a remarkable fact that it is more like unto the Aramaic of the Book of Daniel than to that of the Targumim. The only difficulty we have to contend with in this connection is that we have only one copy, no other MS. being known to exist; the writing of this MS. is also not perfectly clear throughout. But in spite of these drawbacks the character of the text stands out clear enough, and we find in it all the peculiarities of the Biblical Aramaic.* On the other hand, it is very remote from the Syriac form of the fragment of the legend of the Dragon mentioned above. The lexicon is somewhat richer, as new words are to be found which do not occur in the Biblical

* *Cf.* Driver, "Introduction to the Old Testament," 3rd ed., pp. 471-473.

texts, and these have the same archaic ring about them as the rest. Judging, therefore, only from the language, we would be justified in assigning a high antiquity to this Aramaic version of the Song of the Three Children, and of the legend of the Dragon, for both these have been preserved to us in the compilation of Jerahmeel.

If we proceed now to the comparison between the Aramaic text and the version of Theodotion, such as we can reconstruct it after the numberless interpolations, omissions and alterations it has been subjected to, we shall find an *absolute identity* extending to the most *minute details*. All those points brought out by Fritzsche in his exhaustive study of the Song of the Three Children—to commence with this—find their ample justification in our Aramaic text. All the changes introduced by Theodotion correspond with the Aramaic text; all those passages proved to be later interpolations are missing from the Aramaic; the inversion of order to be observed, especially in the actual song in the Greek of Theodotion, has its counterpar in our Aramaic, and many a hazarded suggestion advanced by one or the other commentator—who sought to find in an Aramaic original the source and reason of misunderstandings—will be corroborated by our text. The confusion in the order of things enumerated in verses 28–50, varying in various MSS. and translations, disappears completely when compared with the order in the Aramaic text. Here we have, first God, then the heavenly bodies, then follow all the phenomena of the air, such as rain, dew, snow, frost, clouds, and so on; then land, sea and birds; lastly man. The minute commentary, which follows later on, is intended to bring out all these points. From such a minute study it will become evident beyond doubt or cavil, that we have in this Aramaic text the long-sought for, often denied, and now proved Semitic original of Theodotion's translation. I publish it (in Part II) exactly after the original MS., adding my corrections in brackets, and I subjoin to it an English translation, the differences between this and the current one* are as much marked as they are when comparing the Aramaic text with the Greek texts of Theodotion and the LXX. In the commentary I will point out the more important passages which seem to be conclusive.

I pass now to the other portion containing the legend of the Dragon. As has already been remarked, this legend was found long

---

* Published by the Society for Promoting Christian Knowledge; London, 1881.

ago in an ancient Midrash, but this differs so much from the Greek versions that it could not be the probable original of these latter. Not so, however, is the case with Jerahmeel's text, which follows immediately upon the Song. This corresponds exactly to the true text of Theodotion, and this absolute identity helps us to restore that very text, which as appears now, has been a little curtailed and made to fit better with that of the LXX. Here and there a few words are omitted in the Greek, and in one verse a very important detail is not to be found in the latter, which however must have been in the original, as we find it also in the parallel in Josippon. Both these texts contain a more detailed description of the ingredients which Daniel put into the lump of food for the dragon. Pitch, fat and hair alone would not kill a dragon such as that worshipped by the Babylonians, accustomed as it must have been according to legend to devour whole animals. In both texts Daniel used these merely as blinds, as " he rolled them round iron hatchets and made one big lump of it, which he threw into the mouth of the dragon. When the dragon had swallowed it, the fat and pitch melted away in the stomach, and the sharp points of the iron hatchets caused the dragon to linger and die." It is not likely that this should be a later interpolation, as we find it in two independent texts, also in the Midrash Rabba on Genesis lxviii, f. 77 *c*, *d* (ed. Fcft) ad Genes. xxviii, 12. I cannot find a satisfactory reason for the omission, unless in the desire of reducing the divinity of that dragon to a still smaller scale. The LXX have felt the incongruity between the things used by Daniel in the making up of that lump, and have added therefore that " the weight of the pitch used was very great, no less than 30 manehs," the cause of death was thus this great quantity.

With the assistance of the Aramaic version we shall get rid also of the remarkable bowl with bread, which reminds one of the Buddhist monks with their begging bowl. In the Aramaic, the prophet puts his bread in his *sac*, which he carries probably on his back, as he perforce must keep in his hands the pottage sod by him for the reapers. One can easily increase the number of such instances where our text gives a proper meaning, and shows its incontestable superiority over all the other versions, the Greek included. The language is the same as that of the other piece, the same grammatical forms and the same general character, distinct from Syriac and not absolutely identical with the Targumim.

In order to obviate a possible objection, viz., that Jerahmeel may have got hold of another version of Josippon and have transferred these two texts from it into his Chronicle, especially as the copyist added here a note, included by me in brackets, to the effect that "from here on Jerahmeel copied from Todos and the Jewish Josippon," it is necessary to point out that these very texts are to be found also in his extracts from Josippon, totally different from the Aramaic text, and corresponding entirely with the printed editions of that book.   This alone suffices to prove the accuracy and faithfulness of Jerahmeel, who repeated the same texts twice, copying them from *two different* sources.   It gives further credibility to the authorship of these Aramaic portions in his Chronicle, a credibility which they fully deserve, as it is borne out by the comparison between them and the Greek translation of Theodotion.

III.—COMMENTARY.

I pass now to the detailed and minute comparison between the Aramaic text published here for the first time, and the two Greek translations, the LXX and Theodotion.   This comparison will show how far the contention is justified by facts that the Aramaic text is the very original of those translations, especially of Theodotion's, and is not a translation from any of the Greek texts, or any other text in existence. I have used O. F. Fritzsche's edition,* which so far seems to be the best available.

At the same time I will offer some emendations of the Aramaic text, and some observations on the state of its preservation.

A. *The Song.*

V. 1. Is almost identical with Theodotion, and just as short; differing from LXX. Instead of φλογος we have however אתון נורא יקידתא, "The furnace of burning fire," corresponding to the second half of the LXX, τῷ πυρὶ ὑποκαιομένης τῆς καμίνου. *Azarias* is the *only* one who prays, not *all* as in the LXX.

V. 2. בריך corresponds exactly to εὐλογητός; משבח settles the reading αἰνετόν, and refers to the name of God. The verb is in the third instead of the second person, in conformity with the old Hebrew forms of praise, ברוך ה' לעולם אמן אמן Ps. lxxxix, 53, and more especially Ezra vii, 27, with which the first half of v. 2 is identical.

V. 3. For the first ἀληθινὰ stands here קשוט, whilst for the second, which in some MSS. alternates with ἀλήθεια, we have the word מדימנין, identical with Syr. P. This is a proof for the original character of the Aramaic, where two distinct words are used instead of one and the same, as is the case in the Greek. We shall find later on similar examples of copiousness of language in Aramaic for various shades of identical notions, which are rendered however by one and the same Greek word. The two words יציב and מדימן are used together (Daniel ii, 45), and אמת ויציב is the form used in the morning prayer of the Jewish Liturgy, which dates from the times of the second Temple.

V. 4. Our text has the singular, דין דקשוט, "true judgment," corresponding to v. 7, ἐν ἀληθινῇ κρίσει, where the same words occur.

אייתיתת, twice so in the MS., must be altered into אייתיתא. the *scriptio plena*, which we find in most cases of 2 s. in our text. It corresponds to Theodotion ἐπήγαγες in both instances in this verse.

---

* Libri Apocryphi Veteris Testamenti Graece. Lipsiae, 1871.

σοῦ of the LXX is omitted by Theodotion and in our text. ὅτι ἐν ἀληθείᾳ καὶ κρίσει is not a very happy juxtaposition, it is contrary to the constant combination of ' *truth* ' with ' *judgment.* ' In our text we have the correct form *in true judgment,* or *judgment oj truth,* once before in the same verse, and in v. 7. *Cf.* also Nehem. ix, 33.

V. 5. ἐν πᾶσι of the LXX, neither Theodotion nor our text. ἀποστῆναι is as near a translation as can be found of וְאָעֲדִנָא, the Aphel-form of עֲדִי, to depart, to remove oneself from. It stands in the finite form, and is parallel with the two preceding verbs and the following וְשַׁטְנָא ; so also Syriac, ed. Lagarde.

V. 6. The Greek translator has read בְּכֹל as it is in the Syriac (ed. Lagarde) instead of מִכֹּל, hence the peculiar ἐν πᾶσι, which gives no satisfactory meaning. It ought to read ἐν πᾶσι ταῖς ἐντολαῖς, according to the Aramaic text. The whole text of the two verses (7 and 8) does not seem to have been well preserved in Greek. V. 7 looks like an unnecessary repetition of v. 4. In the Aramaic we have in v. 8 the justification for the true punishments, and the way how they have been carried out. The LXX reading of v. 7 seems to be the more accurate.

V. 8. ἐχθίστων ἀποστατῶν is omitted in the Aramaic text, which does not know of apostates, and which has, *wicked and bad kings,* מַלְכִין *pluralis,* instead of the singular of the Greek, which may have been interpolated into the Greek by a copyist who thought probably of Antiochus, "the wicked king." The difficulty felt of old about the " apostates " is thus solved, and the speculation about the wicked king falls to the ground. (*Cf.* Fritzsche, *l.c.,* p. 125.)

V. 9. The wording of the Aramaic favours Theodotion's Greek form ἐγενήθη against the senseless ἐγενήθημεν ; the construction is however somewhat different in both versions. The Aramaic text agrees with Daniel ix, 16 ; *cf.* Joel ii, 17 ; the Greek translator must have thought of Isaiah xxx, 5, as he has αἰσχύνη καὶ ὄνειδος as in Isaiah, instead of only αἰσχύνη as in the Aramaic text.

V. 10. The Aramaic text has, "thy *great and holy*" added to " name," which is missing in Theodotion and LXX. שְׂהִידְוָותָךְ corresponds to Hebrew עֵדְוֹתֶיךָ, "Thy law, covenant." תִּשְׁכַּח, wrongly translated διασκεδάσῃς. The idea of God *forgetting* the Covenant is taken from Deut. iv, 31.

V. 11. Abraham, "thy beloved," ἠγαπημένος, is not a very correct translation of רחימך, which ought to be rendered by, φίλος σοῦ, the usual title of Abraham. (*Cf.* Isaiah xli, 8.) The Semitic original for this translation has been suggested also by De Wette (*l.c.*, p. 509); Syriac has also רחימך.

V. 13. Instead of the word עזרנא, which does not exist in Aramaic, we ought to read זערנא, "we have been diminished," "we have become less," ἐσμικρύνθημεν.

ὅτι is impossible, it must be καὶ νῦν, ועד כאן, "and now."

ἐσμεν ταπεινοὶ is the inexact rendering of דמסכינין אנחנא, "miserable," "poor," and helps us to recognize the Semitic original.

V. 14. In the Aramaic is no trace of a *king*, as Fritzsche and others suggest. רב = ἄρχων, is the "leader" of the people; פחוותא וסגנין (copied from Daniel iii, 2, 3) are the "governors" and "deputies." In the Greek the last word is missing; the Syriac has, like our text, four offices, but in a different order: head and governor; prophet and leader.

"Incense" missing in Aramaic.

V. 15. Is based upon and modelled after Ps. li, 19. Fritzsche is perfectly right in omitting the interpunction before ὡς, which belongs to the preceding. The division of the verses is undoubtedly wrong in the Greek text, as is evidenced by the Aramaic. Here v. 16 commences with כדין, οὕτως.

V. 16. Is hopelessly corrupt in the Greek, as pointed out by Fritzsche; καὶ ἐκτελέσαι ὄπισθέν σοῦ is omitted by the Syriac. It may have been a marginal variant which has crept into the text. The Vulgata alone has preserved the old true reading, "ut placeat tibi," corresponding to לרעוא. Ethiopic has: "and let it (our sacrifice) be perfect with thee."

εσται, Theodotion for εστιν, LXX, is justified by the Itpael form יתכבלמון.

V. 17. בעין, "we pray," "we are desirous," has been evidently misunderstood by the translator as meaning 'quærere' (*cf.* Dan. ii, 13, 20), hence, "we follow thee" or, "seek after thee;" but in the Greek, the first καὶ is to be omitted, and the tense of the verb changed to the Infinitive. Ζητοῦμεν τὸ πρόσωπόν σοῦ is likewise not a correct translation of the Aramaic ונתבע מן קדמך, which means, "and we beseech thee." מן קדמך has been taken to have the meaning of Hebrew מפניך, and was translated accordingly. The verse does not finish here as now in the Greek, but is continued further, being connected with the following through דִי, "that thou puttest us not to shame," which gives an excellent reading.

In the same way is v. 18 to be connected with v. 19, καὶ being left out and ἐξελοῦ ὑμᾶς connected with σοῦ. Instead of בסגי, one could read also כסגי. κατὰ τὰ θαυμάσιά is identical with Jerem. xxi, 2, נפלאותיו, but whether it stood in the original is doubtful. In the Aramaic it is missing ; it may have dropped out.

V. 21. בלחודך, which means "alone," has been incorrectly translated Θεὸς μόνος, as if it stood אֵל חַד, and the whole sentence has got a dogmatic meaning alien to the Aramaic text. But no stress is laid on the *Oneness* of God, only on His *omnipotence*, just as in 1 Chron. xxix, 12, viz., that God is "the ruler over the whole world"; ἔνδοξος for שַׁלִּיט, rather freely.

V. 22 agrees more with Theodotion. οὐ διέλιπον has no counterpart in the Aramaic, unless it is added by Theodotion to make the statement more emphatic, or עבדין has been taken as a participle and constructed with נסיבו, as meaning, "and they commenced, or continued, to do." I am the more inclined to believe in such a misunderstanding, as the latter word is not translated at all. The ὑπηρέται are the שמשוהי, the word דמלכא seems to have followed it, instead of preceding it as in the Aramaic. Theodotion must have read כען נסיבו עבדין שמשוהי דמלכא, etc. גלילין occurs for a second time in the following Dragon legend, v. 6, where we have the verb וויגלול, to *roll*. I translate it therefore, "and they made *balls* of naphtha, pitch, and tow." Theodotion took it to be the plural of גילא or גלא, hence κληματίδα, (*cf.* Levy, Targum-Wörterbuch, I, p. 139, s.v. גילא).

V. 23. Commences then naturally with לאסגאה, "to increase." If we had here לאסקא, which means, "to light, to incense," and also "to ascend," then Theodotion must have mistaken the meaning and translated, "to ascend," "to stream out." In consequence thereof Theodotion omits נורא ושלהובירתא in v. 24, as an unnecessary repetition. The Aramaic text, however, is quite correct, as in v. 23 the intention of increasing the fire and flame is mentioned, and in v. 24 quite a new thing happened, those very flames "streamed out and burned them" (*i.e.*, servants of the king), "*and* all those Chaldæans that stood about the furnace." In the Greek יתהון is omitted, undoubtedly by mistake, the "servants" were probably understood to be included among "the Chaldæans."

V. 25. The Aramaic וְאִיצְטַנִין, which means, "and it *cooled down*," is rendered by the senseless, ἐξετίναξε "to smite out, to throw out" the fire from the oven. A misunderstanding of the original Semitic word, which becomes still more evident in the curious translation of v. 26, כְּרוּחָא דִי מְנַשְׁבָא טַלָּא, which means, *as a wind that blows (and causes) the dew (to descend).* This is very much alike to the formula inserted in the Eighteen blessings of the Morning prayer, dating from the time of the second Temple, where it alternates with the other formula, "Thou makest the wind to blow and causest the rain to descend." Both are based upon Ps. cxlvii, 18, "He causeth his wind to blow and waters flow." (*Cf.* Treatise Taanith, fol. 2A, first Mishna.) The Greek misunderstood מְנַשְׁבָא, and translated, διασυρίζον, whistling. May be that he knew only the other Aramaic form נתב as meaning to blow, and hence his misunderstanding of נשׁב.

This passage has also been pointed out by De Wette as proving a Semitic original; v. 27 will therefore have to be translated, "and he made in the midst of the furnace like unto a wind that blew down dew," etc. The Syriac has, "the angel *of dew* went down."

Theodotion, τὸ καθόλου = כֹּל. παρηνώχλησεν is rather inappropriate after ἐλύπησεν (*cf.* Daniel iii, 27), and is probably due to a misunderstanding of מִידְעַם, a word, by the way, that does not occur in biblical Aramaic.

V. 27. יְקִידְתָא is omitted in the Greek; the Syriac has אַתּוּנָא דְנוּרָא.

Vv. 28–65 of the Greek finish regularly with εἰς τοὺς αἰῶνας, or εἰς τὸν αἰῶνα, as if it stood in the original always לְעָלְמֵי עָלְמַיָּא, in sæcula sæculorum, or לְעָלְמִין. This is not appropriate, however, in all cases, and is due, in every probability, to a confusion of בְּעָלְמָא with דְעָלְמָא, the former meaning "*in the world*," or "*all over the world*," and "not for ever." In our Aramaic text we find indeed both forms used with the necessary discrimination between the two. God's Name is to be praised for ever; His *creatures* cannot very well praise Him for ever, as they themselves are transitory, but they can praise Him in this world and above everything. The former is therefore used more in vv. 27–34, the latter in all the subsequent verses, where the creatures are appealed to 'to raise

their voices in praise of God. Syriac has throughout לְעָלַם like
the Greek.

V. 28, absolutely identical with Theodotion, who has not πάντας,
as in v. 29, corresponding with the Aramaic כָּל ; also only in v. 29.
τὸ ὄνομα τῆς δόξης is an incorrect translation of the Aramaic שְׁמָךְ
ויקירא (רבא), " Thy great and glorious Name," רבא is omitted
by Theodotion.

V. 30. In Aramaic there is nothing for the Greek τῆς δόξης σου,
which proved a stumbling block from very ancient times (cf. Fritzsche,
l.c., p. 128).   May be that יקירא, from v. 29, or יקר, v. 31, was
added afterwards, in order to make the first half of the verse correspond with those two verses.   It is thus a later interpolation.

The Ithpaal forms of תשׁתבח and תתייקר explain the ἀπαξ-
λεγομ : ὑπερυμνητὸς καὶ ὑπερένδοξος, as the Greek translator felt
forced to translate those emphatic forms here and in v. 32.   For
יקר and its derivation, δοξα is always used.   I add here a list of the
translations of vv. 28–33, which will show the relation between the
original and the Greek.

משׁבח, v. 28, αἰνετὸς ; v. 29, ὑπεραινετὸς ; v. 32, ὑπερυμνητὸς ;
תשׁתבח, v. 30, ὑπερυμνητὸς ; v. 31, αἰνετὸς ; v. 33, ὑμνητόν.
(Theodotion read thus, משׁבח in vv. 28, 31 and 33, and תשׁתבח,
vv. 29, 30, 32.)

מרומם, vv. 28 and 29, and תתרומם, v. 31, are all translated
ὑπερυψούμενος ; תתייקר, v. 30, ὑπερένδοξος ; מהדר, v. 32, ὑπερυ-
μνούμενος, and תתהלל, v. 33, δεδοξασμένος.
The Aramaic is more varied in expressions and more original
in its forms, whilst the Greek is forced, and clearly an imitation of
the Aramaic.

Vv. 31 and 32. Theodotion now reversed (cf. Fritzsche, l.c.)
probably later alteration. V. 31. δόξης after θρονου in some codices
of Theodotion is justified by יקר. The expression is borrowed from
הדר מלכותו, Ps. cxlv, 12, " His glorious kingdom."

V. 32. דאשׁתקעתא, " who hast lowered the abyss," or "causest
the depths (abyss) to sink down," i.e., " established them down
below," is mistranslated, ἐπιβλέπων. Theodotion must have read
the word differently, probably some form derived from שׁקף:
" to look," דאשׁקפתא ? (cf. Deut. xxvi, 15 ; Ps. xiv, 2 ; Lament.
iii, 50, etc.) The whole Song is modelled evidently after Ps. cxlviii.

The same order is followed in both, only the subjects are more numerous in the Song.

V. 33. Like Theodotion, שמיא, "of the heavens," after στερεώμα, רקיע.

V. 35 of the Gre?k, which is only a repetition of v. 33, is missing in the Aramaic (*cf.* Ps. cxlv, 4).

V. 35 Aramaic = 36 Greek.

V. 36 Aramaic = 37 Greek. καὶ πάντα, which is out of place, is omitted in the Aramaic. καὶ has been omitted also by Theodotion (v. Fritzsche, *l.c.*), *cf.* Ps. cxlv, 4.

V. 37. חיליית, exactly the δυνάμεις of Theodotion = צבאיו, Ps. cxlv, 2.

V. 39 of the Greek is missing in the Aramaic. In Syriac B it is marked with an asterisk, as being a later interpolation (*cf.* Fritzsche, *l.c.*, p. 129).

V. 38 = Greek 40. שמייא, plural, whilst Greek τοῦ οὐρανοῦ.

V. 39. (Greek 41.) πᾶς, probably taken from the following verse, as it is here quite out of place. Omitted in the Aramaic.

V. 40. (Greek 42.) πνεύματα, an inexact translation of רוחיא, instead of the proper, ἄνεμοι. One proof more for the Semitic of being the original, and the Greek a translation (*cf.* De Wette, *l.c.*).

V. 41-44. (44 Greek.) The MSS. of Theodotion's version differ very much among themselves about the text and the order of these verses, which is far from being settled. Our Aramaic text is of extreme value for the reconstruction of the original text, and proves its absolute independence from the Greek.

Each verse in the Aramaic stands for two of the Greek. I divide them into *a* and *b*, the first and second half, for easier comparison, and I add also the numbers of LXX.

V. 41*a* = 43 Theodotion and 43 LXX, *fire and heat.* 41*b*, *cold and warm*, corresponds exactly with Theodotion 48, ψῦχος καὶ καῦμα, although he uses καῦμα also, v. 21, whilst the Aramaic has חמימא in the second instance. The LXX has, v. 44 (ed. Fritzsche, p. 76), ῥίγος καὶ ψῦχος, and the same idea of ice and cold and snow and frost is repeated at least four times (vv. 44-47) without any apparent reason, unless it is due to inaccurate translation. Vv. 45 and 47 of the LXX are omitted entirely by Theodotion, probably as unnecessary repetitions, and the position of the others is changed.

V. 42*a*. רעפיא must be read רעמיא, "*thunders and lightnings*" (literally, "arrows"); *cf.* the first half of Theodotion and

LXX, 50, ἀστραπαί. The "thunder" is left out. 42*b*. קברא must
be read קורא; the words קרח and קורא are taken from Ps. cxlvii,
17, where they occur together, *ice and cold*, Theodotion, v. 49,
πάχναι καὶ χιόνες. In the LXX we have the choice of vv. 46 or 47,
46 being a more accurate translation of קרח and קורא, πάγος καὶ
ψῦχος.

V. 43*a*. *Vapours and clouds* (Ps. cxlviii, 8), Theodotion 50, has
only νεφέλαι, whilst the LXX has, v. 45, δρόσοι καὶ νιφετοί, which
latter word could be a corruption from δ. κ. νεφέλαι. The alterations into νιφετοί may have suggested itself through v. 50, where
νεφέλαι is, however, not in its proper place, at least according
to the Aramaic text. 43*b*, *nights* and days, Theodotion, 46;
LXX, 48.

V. 44*a*. Light and darkness, Theodotion, 47; LXX, 49. 44*b*,
קובלא ועמיטתא, "blackness and gloom," or, as I would prefer to
translate, "dusk and dawn." These two are omitted in both Greek
translations.

The text has now a more systematic and harmonious appearance:
first heat and cold in the abstract, then thunder and lightning, then
ice, frost and snow, then vapours and clouds, then day and night.
All these are phenomena that happen in the air, the earth and its
elements follow naturally upon it.

V. 45*a* = Greek 51. Aramaic, the *lands*, plural; Theodotion,
γῆ. 45*b* (Greek 52), mountains and hills.

46*a* = Greek 53. 46*b* has only מבייעיא; these are "the fountains
of the deep" (*cf.* Genesis vii, 11), and must therefore be mentioned
before "the seas and rivers." The transposition in the Greek text
is therefore not likely to be due to Theodotion, who moreover
agrees with the Aramaic in omitting ὄμβρος (so the LXX), mentioned
already before, in v. 41. Similarly we must alter θάλασσα, v. 55,
Greek, into θάλασσαι = ימייא of the Aramaic.

Instead of נוניא, Theodotion must have read תנינייא, hence
κήτη instead of the simple *fish*.

V. 48*a*. (Greek 57.) τὰ πετεινὰ τοῦ οὐρανοῦ is as literal a translation of the Semitic ציפרי שמיא as can be wished. Theodotion
has παντα = Aramaic כל in 57 and 58, in the latter only before
θηρία, just as in the Aramaic.

חיותא means the wild, and בעירא the tame animals, and are
faithfully rendered by θηρία καὶ τὰ κτήνη; *cf.* Ps. cxlviii, 10, החיה
וכל בהמה, "beasts and all cattle."

V. 49. (Greek 59.) Theodotion, υἱοὶ τῶν ἀνθρώπων, without οἱ = Aramaic אנשא בני ; כל is omitted in the Greek.

V. 50. (Greek 61–62.)   The second half of this verse seems to have dropped out in the Aramaic, as each verse has as a rule *two* distinct parallel subjects; and here only priests are mentioned. Theodotion has δοῦλοί = עבדי, after ἱερεῖς, כהנייא, and κυρίου after each, just as in the Aramaic דיי.   We must therefore complete the Aramaic verse accordingly.

V. 51. (Greek) 63. רוחין ונשמי צדיקיא = πνεύματα καὶ ψυχαὶ δικαίων.   The wording leaves it undecided whether it is a question of the living or the dead (*cf.* Fritzsche, *l.c.*, p. 130).   The following half of the verse mentions however the living, ענוי לבב, ταπεινοὶ δὴ καρδία.   The קדישין, ὅσιοι, must necessarily also be taken as living.   (*Cf.* Daniel vii, 21, 22, 27), and we shall translate therefore : *the spirits and souls of the just.*   The juxtaposition of רוח and נשמה occurs in Job xxxiv, 14.   I cannot see here any idea of the trichotomy of man as suggested by Fritzsche.

V. 52. (Greek 65.) שאול is rendered ᾅδος.   Theodotion has ἔσωσεν before ἐκ χειρὸς θανάτου, as in the Aramaic פריק before מידא.

Theodotion εκ μεσου καμίνου = Aramaic מן אתון, "From the burning fire and flame He has saved us."   Of these words, דליק ושלהובין are missing in both Greek translations, omitted probably because they appeared an unnecessary repetition of the foregoing verse.   יציל is better rendered by ἐλυτρώσατο, LXX, than by ἐρρύσατο, with which Theodotion is credited; as שיזב is translated so in the same verse, and it is not likely that he should have repeated the same word when he had to translate another Aramaic word, ויציל.

53. (66.) הודין, Greek ἐξομολογεῖσθε corresponds exactly.

53*b* (67) differs completely from the Greek.   The whole verse is not addressed to anyone.   V. 52 concludes fitly with the three Children, all the others having been enumerated before.   There was no room for σεβόμενοι to be repeated, as they were included among the δοῦλοί, etc. (vv. 50 ff. Aramaic, 61 ff. Greek).   למרי עלמא, "The lord of the universe," must have been strangely misread by the LXX and Theodotion, as well as the following, הוא אלהין, "He is God."   They have τὸν Κύριον, τὸν Θεὸν τῶν θεῶν, "the Lord, the God of gods." This verse is evidently modelled after Ps. cxxxvi, vv. 2 and 3, the Targum of which runs thus :—. . . . שבחו לאלהי אלהיא . . . . שבחו למרי מריא. Theodotion or the LXX may have thought of these verses, and have changed the primitive form found in the Aramaic for the other more dogmatic, but alien to the text.

The result of this detailed comparison is, that the Aramaic is a more primitive and more correct text, agreeing in the main with Theodotion, but differing sufficiently from his text to show its independence from any of the existing forms of the Greek. It represents thus the oldest text of the Song, and helps us to reconstruct the primitive form of Theodotion's Greek translation as it must have been before it was altered and interpolated from the LXX.

By these means we shall be able to reconstruct also the original form of the version of the LXX, as this also must have suffered many alterations and interpolations from Theodotion and others. Those readings in Theodotion which differ from our text will have to be considered as originating from the LXX, and *vice versâ* those agreeing more closely with our Aramaic text than the corresponding portion in Theodotion, have crept into the LXX from Theodotion.

We shall thus obtain a clearer insight into the true character of the old LXX version before Theodotion, and understand better the reason for its elimination from the church service; for it will be found to differ very materially from the Aramaic text, with which Theodotion would then exactly correspond. For this very reason the former had been eliminated, and the latter substituted instead, though it has become rather mixed in the course of time. It must be borne in mind that the Song formed, from very ancient times, part of the Church Hymn book, and is often found added to the Psalter. Hence the profound alterations to which it was subjected, and the amalgamation of LXX and Theodotion.

We are much better off in the other legend, where such causes did not operate to alter the character of the two translations; and I pass on to the examination of—

Daniel and the Dragon.

V. 1. (LXX 23; Theodotion 23.) The Aramaic text has באתרא ההוא, "in that place," in common with LXX, ἐν τῷ αὐτῷ τόπῳ, and רב וסגיא, "great and mighty," with Theodotion μέγας.

תנין is rendered by both δράκων.

כל, missing in the Greek.

V. 2. (24.) Aramaic totally different. No trace in it of "brass,"
which was suggested in the Greek by the tale of the brazen idol Bel
(v. 7), nor of "eating and drinking." Instead of προσκυνησαν we
have צלי, "pray."

V. 3 is missing in LXX, but is v. 25 Theodotion, with which the
Aramaic text agrees in general, but has more than the Greek
למלכא, "to the king;" דאבהתיי, "of my fathers;" and
רב ודחילו, "mighty and awe-inspiring," which are all missing in
the latter. *Syriac* identical with Theodotion.

V. 4. (LXX 25; Theodotion 26.) איקטל, identical with
Theodotion, αποκτενῶ; and not LXX, ἀνελῶ. All the ancient
versions have then, "a sword and staff," μαχαίρας (Theodotion),
σιδήρου (LXX) καὶ ῥάβδου Syriac חוטרא. Only the Aramaic has
the proper word, חניתא, "lance," which must have been read
חוטרא from very ancient times. חרב וחנית is a standing phrase
in the Bible, *cf.* I Samuel xiii, 19, 22 ; xvii, 45, 47 ; xxi, 9.

V. 5. The Aramaic text is again more complete. The permission asked for by Daniel is granted in express terms, אנא יהיב לך =
Theodotion 26, δίδωμί σου, and not LXX, δέδοταί σε, and then follows
"leave to do unto it all that thou wishest," which LXX and Theodotion omit.

Vv. 6 and 7. (LXX 26; Theodotion 27.) I have already drawn
attention in the Introduction to the great difference between these
and the corresponding Greek verses. Among the ingredients we
have also וכיתן, "flax." μᾶζας, Theodotion, is proved by גליל,
"a round lump." The whole portion of the iron hatchets is missing
in the Greek texts, and thus no satisfactory reason for the death of
the dragon is given, at least by Theodotion. The LXX have the
large mass of 30 manehs for the lumps made by Daniel. Theodotion,
τὰ σεβάσματα ὑμῶν, is identical with Aramaic, which he must have
read הא כען דהויתין פלחון קרמוהי, omitting אלהכון, and
took it to be the plural. Totally different is the ironical question
of the LXX, οὐ ταῦτα σέβεσθε. Syriac differs from all.

V. 8. (27, Theodotion 28.) Almost identical with Theodotion,
ἠγανάκτησαν λίαν is an excellent translation of the idiomatic תקוף
להון, which is repeated in v. 10 (Theodotion 30), and has the

meaning "to be mightily (incensed) against . . ." *cf.* Targum to Psalm xviii, 8, רְתקִיף לֵיהּ, etc. Much clearer is the sentence in the Aramaic, "for we know now that thou art like unto one of the Jewish men." Theodotion, Ἰουδαῖος γέγονεν ὁ βασιλεύς; *cf.* Fritzsche (*l.c.* p. 152). Aramaic has, after ἱερεῖς, "of Bel and his temple," and, instead of κατέσφαξε, תברתא, "thou hast broken up."

V. 9. (Theodotion 29.) Aramaic much shorter, a continuation of the words spoken by the people in v. 8, and not a new statement, as in Theodotion. בביתך, *in* thine house, Theodotion has read וביתך, *and* thine house.

V. 10. (Theodotion 30.) Here Theodotion has rendered תקיף by ἐπείγουσιν σφόδρα (see above v. 8), and instead of דבעו למקטליה "they wanted to kill him," we find, ἀναγκασθείς, "constrained," which is rather a mild description of the danger threatening him. Some other Aramaic word must have stood in the original used by Theodotion, or, what is more probable, with the change of a few letters he may have read the words as ובאולצניה (מסר), "and in his being constrained, delivered," etc.

V. 11. (31.) ושויאו, "they placed," I should like to read instead ושדיאו, "they cast," as it corresponds exactly with Theodotion, ἔβαλον. Instead of αὐτόν we have in the Aramaic "Daniel."

Aramaic שבעה, seven, Theodotion and LXX ἕξ, six days.

V. 12. (Theodotion 32.) Aramaic has the addition of באתרא ההוא, 'in that place.' The real meaning of σώματα, which could mean also "slaves," is proved by the Aramaic פגרי אינשין to be "human corpses."

V. 13. (Theodotion 33.) The Aramaic בארעא דישראל is much more correct than Theodotion, Ἰουδαίᾳ, as the prophet Habakkuk lived in Israel and not in Judæa. ἤψησεν ἔψεμα is as litteral a translation of מבשל תבשילא, "sod a pottage" as could be wished for. Instead of σκαφην the Aramaic has שקידה, "his sack" or "knapsack." The Syriac has ערבא, a very scarce word, which is translated *dish*, and seems to be a *hapaxlegomenon*. I am inclined to amend the word into טורבא = Persian توبۀ = knapsack, which would make it absolutely identical with the Aramaic.

In the Aramaic we have also an addition of למיכל לחצדייא, "to feed the reapers."

14. (34.) Aramaic has also some small additions: והא, "and there was" (or "appeared"); in some codices ὁ is preceding ἄγγελος :

זיל is added to ואייתי in conformity with the spirit of the Aramaic, "go and bring." Instead of ἔχεις we have דבשילתא, "which thou hast cooked." After בבל the word קרתא, "town," is added here and in v. 15. והב ליה, "and gave it to him" (to Daniel), is also missing in the Greek.

V. 15. (35.) למלאכא not in the Greek.

V. 16. (36.) Here a peculiar confusion has crept into the Greek. Theodotion does not seem to have understood properly the word קדלא, which he translated κορυφή "the crown," whilst the true meaning of it is "neck." There is then no tautology with the following, "hair," or as the Aramaic has it, "lock of his head," צוציתא. Aramaic adds, "and he set him with the food that he had in his hands over the mouth of the lions' den which was in Babylon."

V. 17. (36, 37.) The Aramaic text helps us here also over one of the most perplexing passages of the Greek text, of which no one has hitherto been able to extract a proper sense. *Cf.* Fritzsche (*l.c.*, p. 153-4), who does not mend matters. The words כד תב רוחיה, must have been strangely misread, possibly as ברתחא רוחיה, "the vehemency," "fury," ῥοίζῳ, and has been united with the preceding verses, thus producing a totally unintelligible sentence. The Aramaic on the contrary is perfectly clear, and shows unmistakably that it must have been the original. The meaning is, "And when his breath came back to him." (or "he recovered his breath") which he had lost through the quickness of the flight, "Habakkuk called Daniel and said." After ὁ Θεὸς Aramaic adds, "thine," אלהך.

V. 18. (38.) Aramaic begins with ושבח וצלי, "and Daniel praised and prayed, and said," which is natural when beholding the unexpected divine help. Instead of καὶ we have די, "for." For the rest this verse is identical with Theodotion.

V. 19. (39.) Theodotion, παραχρῆμα LXX (38) τῇ αὐτῇ ἡμέρᾳ; Aramaic, בשעתא חדא, "in one hour." Theodotion read probably הדא, "*in that very* hour."

V. 20. (40.) Aramaic והוה, as in vv. 7, 8, 13, and 17. וקם ואזל, also a peculiar Aramaic construction similar to ושבח ואמר וקרא וצלי throughout the text. In the Aramaic there is no trace of πενθῆσαι. Did Theodotion read למיבכי instead of למידחזי?

V. 21. (41.) Aramaic מלכא, so in LXX, missing in Theodotion ; Aramaic רב וסגיא (*cf.* v. 20). Greek only, "great" (or loud). Aramaic has the third person, "is the god of," אלהיה Greek, εἶ, "art thou." Aramaic ויקירא, "and glorious" (*cf.* Song of Three Children, v. 29). Theodotion (and LXX) have instead καὶ οὐκ ἔστιν ἄλλος πλὴν σοῦ.

V. 22. (42.) Aramaic has ופקיד מלכא, "and the king gave orders." Theodotion omits these as well as the words מן גוב אריותא·

אכלו קורציה, idiomatic expression, which is paraphrased by αἰτίους τῆς ἀπολείας αὐτοῦ.

אמר מלכא, also missing in Theodotion and LXX.

בפריע, Theodotion, παραχρῆμα ἐνώπιον αὐτοῦ ; probably he read בפניו. Syriac has even more, "before him and before Daniel."

This minute comparison between the Aramaic text and Theodotion proves beyond doubt that the former is absolutely independent of the Greek. Not a single trace can be detected of any Greek influence, either in language or in construction. Both are pure Aramaic, agreeing in every point with the known characteristics of that language. No translation could be as perfect, and no text that we have can be looked upon as a probable or even possible original. But everything points to the contrary conclusion—that this Aramaic text represents the original from which Theodotion made his translation. Numerous instances of misreadings and misinterpretations have been adduced in the course of our examination, which prove conclusively the dependence of the Greek text upon this very Aramaic text. The close resemblance between the Aramaic and Theodotion in the Tale of the Dragon is beyond dispute. In this piece we recognise, more clearly than in that of the Song, how thoroughly Theodotion differed from the LXX, and we find in the Aramaic text the reason for the profound changes introduced by him into his translation. He tried to approximate it as closely as possible to this original from which the LXX had deviated so much. With the assistance of the Aramaic text, we are now in a position to remove many of the mistakes that have crept in, and to reconstruct the same text of Theodotion.

Not having found a place in the Liturgy, this tale has suffered less from interpolations, and we have therefore two distinct Greek texts, and not a mixed text as in the case of the "Song." In the

Tale of the Dragon we are therefore also in a better position to see how closely Theodotion follows the Aramaic text.

Judging the Song, then, in the light of this almost absolute identity of Theodotion with the Aramaic, we are forced to admit, as already indicated above, that the literary tradition of the two Greek texts is far from being correct, that the difference between Theodotion and LXX must have been more profound than is now the case, and that we shall have to recast the existing text of Theodotion and also that of the LXX, as both translations have exercised a mutually deteriorating influence upon each other, taking as basis for the reconstruction this Aramaic text, which, as I have tried to prove, is the original from which those translations have been made. The mistakes, which have their origin in wrong readings and misinterpretation, prove also conclusively that the original was Aramaic, and not Hebrew.

IV. TRANSLATION.

A. *The Song of the Three Children.*

V. 1. And the three went into the furnace of burning fire, praising and blessing the Lord. And Azariah stood up to pray, and he prayed thus ; and he opened his mouth and said : V. 2. " Blessed be he, the God of our fathers, and be his name praised and glorified for evermore. V. 3. For thou art true in all that thou hast done to us, for all thy works are true, and thy ways established, and all thy judgments faithful. V. 4. Yea, true judgment hast thou wrought in all (*the things*) that thou hast brought upon us, and upon Jerusalem the holy city of our fathers, for true judgments hast thou brought upon us, because of our sins. V. 5. We have sinned, and we have committed iniquity, and we have departed (withdrawn) from thee. V. 6. And we have turned aside (trespassed) from all the commandments which thou hast commanded us, as we have not been willing to keep and to observe them, that it might go well with us. V. 7. And because we have not done (observed) thy commandments and statutes, V. 8. thou hast wrought true judgment in that thou hast delivered us into the hands of lawless enemies, and into the hands of wicked and lawless kings in all the lands. V. 9. And now we cannot open our mouths, for thy servants who cling to thee have become a shame. V. 10. And we beseech thee not to deliver us up wholly, for the sake of thy great and holy name, neither to forget thy covenants. V. 11. And cause not thy mercy to depart from us, for the sake of Abraham thy beloved, and thy servant Isaac, and thy holy Israel. V. 12. To whom thou hadst spoken that (*thou wouldst*) multiply their children as the stars of heaven, and as the sand (*that lieth*) on the seashore. V. 13. And now we are become less than any other nation, as we are miserable (poor) this day in all the lands because of our sins. V. 14. And at this time we have neither a leader nor prophets, neither governors nor deputies, neither burnt-offerings nor sacrifices, nor oblations, as there is no place to bring all these before thee (*in order*) to find mercy. V. 15. But in a contrite heart and humble spirit let us be accepted like as burnt offerings and sacrifices of rams and bullocks, and like thousands of fat lambs. V. 16. Thus may our sacrifice to-day be acceptable in thy sight : for they shall not be confounded that put their trust in thee. V. 17. And now we desire with all our heart to fear thee. V. 18 and we pray unto thee, that thou puttest us not to shame, but that thou dealest with us after thy lovingkindness, and according to the multitude of thy mercy. V. 19. Deliver us and give glory to thy name, O Lord ; and let all them that do thy servants hurt be ashamed. V. 20. And let them be confounded in (in spite of) all their power, and in (in spite of) their strength let them be broken. V. 21. And they shall know that thou alone art ruler over all the lands. V. 22. And now the servants of the king and his attendants, that threw the three men into the furnace, took naphtha, pitch and tow, and made balls, V. 23. in order to increase the flame of the fire 49 cubits above the furnace. V. 24. And the fire and the flame streamed forth and burnt them and every one of the Chaldaeans that were standing by the side of the furnace. V. 25. And the angel of the Lord came down into the oven with Azariah and his fellows, and the fire of the oven cooled down. V. 26. And he made in the midst of the furnace like unto a wind that blew dew, and none of the fire touched them, nor were they hurt in any way. V. 27. Then those three with one mouth praised, and glorified and blessed God in the midst of the burning furnace, and said : V. 28. Blessed is the Lord God of our fathers, and to be praised and exalted for ever and ever. V. 29. And blessed be thy great and glorious and holy name, and praised and exalted over all the world. V. 30. Blessed art thou in thy holy temple, and to be praised and glorified over all the worlds. V. 31.

Blessed art thou upon the throne of thy glorious kingdom, and to be praised and exalted for ever and ever. V. 32. Blessed art thou, who hast lowered the abyss and sittest upon the cherubim and be praised and glorified in all the worlds. V. 33. Blessed art thou in the firmament of heavens, and be extolled and praised for ever. V. 34. O all ye works bless ye the Lord God, praise him and exalt him in the world. V. 35. All ye angels bless ye the Lord God, praise him and exalt him over the world. V. 36. O ye waters that be above the heavens bless ye the Lord, praise him and exalt him in the world. V. 37. All ye hosts of God, bless ye the Lord, praise him and exalt him in the world. V. 38. O ye stars of heaven bless ye the Lord, praise him and exalt him in the world. V. 39. O ye rain and dew bless ye the Lord, praise him and exalt him in the world. V. 40. All ye winds of God, bless ye the Lord, praise him and exalt him in the world. V. 41. O ye fire and heat, bless ye the Lord, O ye cold and warmth bless ye the Lord, praise him and exalt him in the world. V. 42. O ye thunders and lightnings bless ye the Lord, O ye ice and frost bless ye the Lord, praise him and exalt him in the world. V. 43. O ye vapours and clouds bless ye the Lord, O ye nights and days bless ye the Lord, praise him and exalt him in the world. V. 44. O ye light and darkness bless ye the Lord, O ye dusk and dawn bless ye the Lord, praise him and exalt him in the world. V. 45. O ye lands bless ye the Lord, O ye mountains and little hills bless ye the Lord, praise him and exalt him in the world. V. 46. O all ye things that grow in the earth bless ye the Lord, O ye deep fountains bless ye the Lord, praise him and exalt him in the world. V. 47. O ye seas and rivers bless ye the Lord, O ye fish and all that move in the waters bless ye the Lord, praise him and exalt him in the world. V. 48. O all ye fowls of the heavens bless ye the Lord, O all ye beasts and cattle bless ye the Lord, praise him and exalt him in the world. V. 49. O all ye children of men bless ye the Lord, O Israel bless ye the Lord, praise him and exalt him in the world. V. 50. O ye priests of God bless ye the Lord, *(O ye servants of God, bless ye the Lord)*, praise him and exalt him in the world. V. 51. O ye spirits and souls of the righteous bless ye the Lord, O ye holy and humble men of heart bless ye the Lord, praise him and exalt him in the world. V. 52. O ye Hananyah, Azariah, and Mishael bless ye the Lord, praise him and exalt him in the world, for he hath delivered us from Sheol and saved us from the hand of death; for he delivered us from the furnace of burning fire, and he hath saved us from burning fire and flames.   V. 53. Give thanks unto the Lord, for he is good, as his mercies (*endure*) for ever, and bless ye the Lord of the World, he is God, praise him and exalt him in the world.

B. *Daniel and the Dragon.*

V. 1. And in that place there was a great and mighty dragon, which all the Babylonians worshipped.   V. 2. And the king said unto Daniel, now thou canst not say that this here is no living god, therefore pray to him.   V. 3. And Daniel answered and said unto the king, I pray only to the Lord God of my fathers, for he is a living God, mighty and awe-inspiring.   V. 4. But if thou, O king, wilt give me leave, I will slay this dragon without lance or sword. V. 5. And the king said unto Daniel, I give thee now leave to do unto it all that thou wishest.   6. And Daniel went and took pitch and fat and flax and hair, and rolled them into one lump, and he made unto himself iron hatchets, and rolled all that round and round the hatchets, and he threw it into the dragon's mouth.   V. 7. And it came to pass when the dragon had swallowed it and it had gone down into his stomach, the fat and pitch melted away from the hatchets, and the dragon was injured by the (spurs) points of the hatchet, and died.   And Daniel said, lo, this is your god, whom you worshipped. V. 8. And when they of Babylon saw that the dragon was dead, they were all greatly incensed, and they gathered together and went up before the king, and they spake, saying, now we know that thou art like unto one of the Jewish men, for lo ! thou has destroyed Bel, and the dragon thou hast killed, and the priests of Bel thou hast broken up, together with his temple.   V. 9. And now, if thou deliverest not Daniel into our hands, we will kill thee even in thine house.   V. 10. Now when the king saw that they were all greatly incensed so that they wanted to kill him, he delivered Daniel unto them.   V. 11. And they cast Daniel into the lions' pit, and he was there seven days.   V. 12. For there was a pit in that place, in which there were seven lions, and they used to give them every day two carcasses, and two sheep ; and on that day they were not given to them, to the intent that they might devour Daniel.   V. 13. The prophet Habakkuk was then. in the land of Israel, and he sod a pottage to feed the reapers, and placed bread in his sack, and went to bring it to the reapers in the field.   V. 14. And lo, the angel of the Lord *(appeared)*, and spoke to Habakkuk the prophet, saying, go and carry now this pottage which thou hast made to the town of Babylon, and give it to Daniel, who is in the lions' pit. V. 15. And the prophet Habakkuk answered and said to the angel, my lord, I have never seen the town of Babylon, neither do I know the lions' pit. V. 16. And the angel of the Lord took him by the neck and bore him by the lock of his head, and he set him with the food that he had in his hands over the mouth of the lions' pit which was in Babylon. V. 17. And when he recovered his breath, Habakkuk called Daniel, and said, take now this food which thy God has sent thee. V. 18. And Daniel praised and prayed, and said, O Lord God, thou hast remembered me, neither hast thou forsaken all those that love thee. V. 19 And Daniel arose and did eat ; and the angel of the Lord carried Habakkuk back to his place in one hour. V. 20. And it came to pass on the seventh day that the king arose and went to the lions' pit to see Daniel, and he saw Daniel sitting in the den.   V. 21. And the king cried with a loud and mighty voice, and said, the Lord God of Daniel, He is great and glorious. V. 22. And the king ordered to draw Daniel out from the lions' pit, and those men who had calumniated Daniel, the king ordered to cast them in there.   And they cast them in the lions' pit, and the *(lions)* devoured them in a moment.

POSTSCRIPT.—I have since acquired a Hebrew Manuscript (now Cod. Hebr., 130 of my collection) written in a Spanish hand, of the end of the XVIth century. It is a collection of tales. One among these (No. 72 f. 162a–165a) is now the Hebrew translation of the Syriac text of Bel and the Dragon, published by Dr. Neubauer, from the Midrash Rabba de-Rabba. (The book of Tobit, Oxford, 1878, p. 39–43). This translation is as literal as possible, therefore of no small importance for the criticism of that text, especially as it contains a few remarkable variations. I select only one, as it corroborates the reading of our Aramaic text in one of the most interesting variants. V. 13 reads in this MS. : "Now Habakkuk was a prophet in Judah, and he had in his hands a pottage (seething) and in *his knapsack* bread, to bring to the reapers in the field :" וחבקוק היה נביא בארץ יהודה ובידו תבשיל "
agreeing thus exactly : ובאמתחתו לחם להביא לקוצרים בשדה,
with the Aramaic, in that Habakkuk carried the bread in a *sack*, and in nothing else, although the Hebrew-Syriac text has also the word עורבא for it.

THE HEBREW TEXT OF ONE OF THE TESTAMENTS OF THE TWELVE PATRIARCHS.

By Rev. Dr. M. Gaster.

*Reprinted from the " Proceedings of the Society of Biblical Archæology,"
December,* 1893, *and February,* 1894.

A careful study of the old apocryphal literature has proved beyond doubt that it was of purely Jewish origin, and was written in Hebrew, or in the Aramaic dialect spoken at that time in Palestine.

I speak of that literature which arose in the two centuries before and one century after Christ. Now preserved in translations, or entirely lost, that literature underwent in the course of time a considerable change. The less its authority was recognised, the more easier it was the prey of 'different sects, which shaped and changed and distorted it through omissions and interpolations, in order to suit the views of the then ruling or disputing sects.

This class of literature is popular literature. It is no man's land. Whoever chooses takes possession of it, and utilises it the best he likes. Yet the original cannot be entirely obliterated; it betrays itself by peculiarities of language, by references to other works, by contradictions where the hand of the interpolator was not skilful enough.

By the aid of these points, the fact has now been established beyond doubt that the Book of Enoch, the Book of Jubilees, and many other similar writings, were originally composed in Hebrew. The original seems to have disappeared, and only translations have come down to us, which are just as often mutilations of the original.

It would lead me far beyond the scope of the present investigation were I attempting to show that not one single Hebrew original has been lost. They have only undergone a certain transformation, carried on on a fixed plan. Not that there was any premeditation in the way how those texts were treated; circumstances, acting automatically, have had an uniform result. All those prophetic portions that bore upon actuality and foretold the fulfilment of certain events which were belied by the future, dropped out, and were soon lost. They discredited themselves, and the people discarded them. On the other hand, all that which was of a legendary, historical character, or of a poetical and visionary, were preserved. They still exist, and I trust to be able to finish, one day, my book, " On the Hebrew Fragments of the Apocryphal Literature."

One of those ancient books which shared the same fate with the Books of Enoch and Jubilees, is now that known under the title of, "The Testaments of the XII Patriarchs." From the first publication by Grabe down to Sinker, who published the Greek text with critical notes and introduction, many were the opinions concerning the date of the composition and the probable author.

Sinker summarises those opinions,* and I can do no better than reproduce them here in a more concise form.

" Grabe, the first who treated at length of the *Testaments*, thought that the writing in question was the work of a Jew shortly before the Christian era, and to account for the presence of passages which no Jew could possibly have written, he had recourse to the theory of Interpolation. This opinion, however, has found but little favour, and critics have generally agreed to the conclusions of Nitzsch, who definitely attributed the work to a Judæo-Christian writer, although admitting a grave objection to this hypothesis to exist in the language used with reference to St. Paul and the Gentile Christians."

" A new theory was first advanced with a view of obviating this objection by Ritschl (1850), who, for the reason above alluded to, maintained the author to have been a Christian of Pauline tendencies. In the following year this theory was attacked by Kayser, who upheld the old view, and got rid of the difficulty arising from the liberal views of the writer by supposing interpolations, more especially in the famous passage alluding to St. Paul."

" Shortly after appeared the essay of Vorstman, which advocated Ritschl's view, and attacked Kayser's arguments seriatim ; maintaining strongly the authenticity of the supposed interpolation, as affording one of the strongest arguments for the Pauline origin of the document. Strangely enough, within a month of the publication of Vorstman's essay, a second edition of Ritschl's work appeared,

---

* R. Sinker, " Testamenta XII Patriarcharum ; " Cambridge, 1869, p. 18 ff.

yielding a curious instance of the various effects of the same arguments on different minds ; for, influenced by Kayser's essay, Ritschl held now the Judæo-Christian origin of the book (in fact specifying so far as to maintain the author to have been a Nazarene), and thought that Kayser had succeeded in rendering probable his views as to the interpolation."

"Kayser maintains that the author of this writing was an Essene-Ebionite, and brings forward some reasons for his view."

Sinker's conclusion is, "that the idea of the book, its form, its Christology, its ethics, display unmistakably a Jewish hand. The evidence which has gone to prove the Judæo-Christian authorship of the *Testaments* points also, not indeed with certainty, but with a fair degree of likelihood, to the sect whom Jerome knew as the Nazarenes (the half orthodox Ebionites whom Irenæus distinguishes from those wholly heretical), rather than to those of whom he speaks under the title of Ebionites."*

Thus far about the origin of the writing. Concerning now the language, Dillman, otherwise so cautious in his remarks, when speaking of our writing, says : "Since the publication of Nitzsch's study, all are agreed that the Book is *not* a translation, but was originally written in Greek."†

Much more decided and outspoken is Mr. Sinker on the question of the language in which the book was originally written. "Not only is it of Judæo-Christian origin, but also, as to the question of the language, little need be said. The *Testaments*, in their present form, were no doubt written in the Hellenistic Greek in which we now possess them, presenting, as they do, *none of the peculiar marks which characterise a version*. Whether there were a Hebrew work on which the present was modelled, a supposition by no means improbable in itself, we cannot tell, nor is it a matter of much importance." And further on : "Everything points to the conclusion that the work in its present form is *no mere translation*, though thoroughly imbued with the Hebrew tone of thought, and no doubt written by one conversant with the Hebrew of his day."‡

We shall presently see how we stand about the language, and whether it is a matter of much importance or not.

* *L.c.*, p. 26–27.
† Herzog, Real Encyclopædie, s.v. Pseudo-epigraphen, XII², p. 362
‡ *L.c.*, p. 31.

Sinker, and all those who agree with his conclusions, must assume that the book, as we possess it now, is all of one piece, that there are no interpolations; in fact, that the text has not been touched up and remodelled.

This assumption, however, has been deeply shaken by Schnapp, who in his essay * takes again up the line of argument used first by Grabe, and then by Kayser. Taking especially the Testaments of *Levi* and *Judah*, Schnapp proves clearly that this book had the same fate as nearly all the writings of that period ; that besides an original text written by a Jew, there are many interpolations made by Christian compilers, many of which were introduced into the text very clumsily.

The Armenian version, examined since by Conybeare,† proves unmistakably that many a passage has been interpolated into the text which we possess. Only by eliminating some such passages which interrupt the text in an arbitrary manner, the true meaning can be found. Glaring contradictions can only be explained by the same theory.

We must, however, go a few steps beyond those reached by Schnapp and Conybeare. We must inquire into the sources of that writing, into the whole character and tendency of the Testaments, obscured through those strange elements introduced into them.

The book is not only imbued with the Hebrew tone of thought, but thoroughly conversant with Hebrew Aggadah, with the whole Hebrew legendary lore. Nay, more : The whole writing formed evidently originally a portion of the Book of Jubilees. The similarity in tone and contents has been pointed out by Dillman, and explained by the borrowing theory. It is, at least, singular, however, that the Book of Enoch should be quoted, and the other not even mentioned, though it stood in a more close relation to the latter than to the former.

My conviction is, that it formed originally part of the Book of Jubilees, and therefore it is not referred to as being one and the same. In the Book of Jubilees we have almost identical testaments of Abraham, Rebecca and Isaac. There was no necessity to invent one for Jacob, considering that his is given in the Bible.

---

* " Die Testamente der Zwölf Patriarchen ; " Halle, 1884.
† *Jewish Quarterly Review*, 1893, p. 375 ff.

Chapter ix of Levi's Testament refers distinctly to chapter xxxi of the Book of Jubilees.

The similarity is far greater still, if we go into minute details, one of which—the age of the Patriarchs—I shall mention later on.

Having once established the primitive unity of the XII Testaments with the Book of Jubilees, we are enabled to look for other parallels in Hebrew literature, especially in those writings which betray a certain closeness in their contents with that of the Book of Jubilees.

As first in rank and importance I mention the book called "Sepher ha-Yashar," or "Sepher Toledoth Adam," "The Book of the Generations of Adam."

In that work of mine, to which I have alluded above, I trace the Book of Jubilees step by step in that Book Yashar. If my theory be correct, then the XII Testaments ought also to be found in that Book. It suffices to say, then, that a great number of legendary instances of the XII Testaments find indeed their exact parallels in that very book of Yashar ; such as the names of the wives of the twelve sons, or the number of years each one of them lived, the dates in which they were born, and the order in which they died. (Book of Jubilees, ch. xxviii, S. ha-Yashar, f. 89*a*-90*b*, and 116*b*–117*a*, fol. 121*a*, ed. Pr., ch. lxi, *v.* 1 ff.). Nearly half of the Testament of Judah, the battle with the Emorites, finds its counterpart in the Yashar, ch. xxxvii to xxxix, with the same names of kings and places as in the Testaments of Judah. I intend devoting to this chapter a separate study, and compare all the Hebrew versions. This Testament rightly interpreted will, in my opinion, give us a clue to the date of the composition, and also to the probable author of these writings.

Coincidences of such a nature which extend to minute dates and names are not the result of chance. One must have borrowed from the other, or both have borrowed from one common source, viz., the Aggadic Midrash.

That such is really the case is shown by the fact that we find numerous parallels in the ancient Hebrew writings. Some of them are identical with those which I have pointed out to be common to the Testaments and to the Book of Yashar. We find, for instance, the ages of the Patriarchs given also in the Midrasch Tadshe,

---

* Ed. Jellinek, Beth-hamidrash, III, p. 171.

further in the commentary of Bahya (1291) to Exodus. This chronology is to be found also in the very much older Seder Olam Zutta, and can be traced very far back to the Hellenistic writer, Demetrius, quoted by Alexander Polyhistor.*

Bahya mentions also the wars of the children of Jacob with the Emorite kings ;† and a long list of parallels is given by Zunz and Jellinek.‡

A fragment of Levi's Apocalyptic vision, and his selection for the priesthood, has been preserved to us by R. Salomo Itzhaki (d. 1105) in his commentary to Gen. xxix, 34 ; I translate here the short passage : "There is an Aggadic Midrash in Deuteronomy major, that God sent the angel Gabriel and brought Levi up to Him, and He gave him a name, and the twenty-four gifts of the priesthood ; and because He accompanied him with gifts, therefore was he called Levi (companion)." Compare Testament Levi, ch. i–v and ch. viii. The selection of Levi for the priesthood is explained in the Book of Jubilees (ch. xxxii, v. 3),§ by a peculiar counting, in consequence of which Levi was the *Tenth*, whom he had promised to offer to the Lord. "And in those days Rachel became pregnant with her son Benjamin, and Jacob counted his sons from him on upwards, and the portion of the Lord fell upon Levi, and his father clothed him with the garments of the priesthood, and filled his hands." An absolutely identical calculation we find in the Palestinian Targum to Gen. xxxii, 25 ; in the chapters of R. Eliezer, ch. xxxvii, in the Midrash Tanhuma *ad loc.*,‖ and in fragments of the Jelamdenu published by Jellinek.¶

In the Testament of Reuben we find, ch. vi, the following meaningless sentence: "For to Levi the Lord gave the sovereignty, and to Judah and to me also with them, and to Dan and Joseph that we should be for rulers." A statement which is utterly irreconcilable with the clear words of the Bible, wherein Reuben is deprived of his sovereignty.

In connection with this passage stands another no less hopelessly

* J. Freudenthal, " Hellenistische Studien ;" Breslau, 1874, p. 51–53.
† Ed. Venice, 1544, *f.* 48 *a*.
‡ Zunz, " Gottesdienstliche Vortraege," p. 153, and Jellinek, Bet ha-Midrash, III, p. ix–x ; xiii–xiv.
§ *Cf.* Rönsch, "Das Buch d. Jubilaeen," p. 298, 300, etc.
‖ *Cf.* Zunz, "Literaturgeschichte d. Synagogalen Possie," p. 24.
¶ *L.c.*, vi, p. 80, *ad* Leviticus, xxvii, 32.

corrupt in the Testament of Levi (ch. viii) : "And they said to me, Levi, thy seed shall be divided into three branches, for a sign of the glory of the Lord who is to come, and he that hath been faithful shall be first; no portion shall be greater than his. The second shall be in the priesthood.* The third—a new name shall be called over him, because he shall arise as king from Judah."

These two passages become perfectly clear in the light of the Hebrew Midrash, (Palestinian Targum to Genesis xlix, 3, Genesis Rabba, ch. xcviii, and Midrash Aggadat Bereshit, ch. lxxxii): "Because Reuben had committed that sin (with Bilhah), the three crowns (which were to adorn him) were taken from him and given to his brothers. The crown of the firstborn was given to Joseph (as he got *two* portions) ; that of priesthood to Levi, and that of sovereignty to Judah."

With but slight alteration we can emend the text of the Testaments, and they will then give a good sense.

In like manner I could add numberless parallels from the Hebrew literature to the most essential portions of the XII Testaments. After these remarks and proofs there can be no doubt as to the sources of the XII Testaments, and as to their primitive unity with the Book of Jubilees.

It is no less easy to show that far from being written originally in Greek, the Testaments, as we possess them, are an *incorrect* and faulty translation from the Hebrew.

In order to prove this statement, I point out a few of such mistaken translations. The translator must have been only indifferently acquainted with Hebrew, in order to commit such blunders as the following : Simeon, ch. vi, "and save by Him *Adam ;*" καὶ σώζων ἐν αὐτῷ τον Αδαμ, which must have read in Hebrew כל האדם or ויושיע כל בני אדם, "and he will save all the children of *man*," or Levi, ch. iii : "the *ignorances* of the righteous," ταῖς ἀγνοίαις τῶν δικαιῶν, must have read in Hebrew, עוונות הצדקים, "the sins or the transgressions of the righteous." Levi, ch. viii : "for by *their mouth* shall the holy place be guarded," in the original stood undoubtedly על פיהם, the usual biblical expression for "according to the command," or "by order of." Levi, ch. ii : "And Korah was born in my thirty-first year, *towards the east.*" The last words have absolutely no sense. In Hebrew stood

---

* The Slavonic translation has here, "learning."

probably מְקֶדֶם or מִן קֶדֶם, which means *before*, or מִקֶדֶם, *first*, which the translator took for the more usual מִן קֶדֶם, towards or from the east. *Ibid:* "And *Jochebed* was born in my sixty-fourth year, in Egypt, for I was *renowned* then in the midst of my brethren."

This sentence can only be understood if we translate it back into Hebrew, for then the play upon the word כבוד, and the connection between being *renowned* and *Jochebed* become clear, whilst they are totally lost in the Greek.

Similar instances of mistranslations and of allusions which can only be understood properly if translated into Hebrew, can be easily multiplied. I omit them, as we have a much more decisive proof for the Hebrew original, viz., the discovery of an actual Hebrew text of the Testament of Naphtali.

In the light of this text, we shall be able to gauge much better the true tone and tendency of our writing. In the Hebrew text we have undoubtedly the original version of the Testament, free from any interpolation. It is in perfect concord with the character of those ancient pseudo-epigraphical writings.

We find now, what we expected, viz., that those Testaments are strictly circumscribed in their contents. Each Patriarch speaks from his own experience in life, and what there is missing in the biblical recital is supplemented from secondary legendary sources.

The most important event in the life of the greater number of the twelve Patriarchs is their selling of Joseph into slavery. Upon this very theme, and upon their relation to Joseph, expatiate indeed most of them in their Testaments, some extolling Joseph, some disparaging him; some praise his virtues, his consistency, others lay all the blame of the future on Joseph. Judah then speaks of his valour and his mighty deeds, told in the tale of his battles with the Emorites; Levi of his consecration to the Priesthood; Joseph of his own chastity; each one embellishing his narrative with legendary matter.

It is obvious that if this writing was to appeal to the people, and be considered by them as a genuine writing bequeathed from antiquity, it must be in accordance with Holy Writ, and with current oral tradition.

For this very reason one cannot admit the possibility that our Hebrew text might be a translation from the Greek. Even if we should not press the fact that there are blunders and mistranslations—one or two more, and very glaring, will be found in this **very** Testament of Naphtali—and the dependence of the Testament cn Hebrew legendary Midrash ; there remains still one very grave objection, which is insurmountable, viz. : that it would be a simple stultification to present the Jewish people with a book whose reputed author is one of the Patriarchs or Moses, and that book was to be in Greek ! Abraham or Moses writing in Greek ! Why, the thought alone would drive the Jews away from touching the book, still less to believe in its authenticity.

If it was to be accepted as genuine, it must have been written in the sacred tongue of the Bible, otherwise it would have been rejected *a limine.*

I am surprised that so simple an argument has not yet dawned upon any of the numerous students of the pseudoepigraphical literature. For, either the authors of these writings had a tendency, and were desirous, of influencing the masses, or the whole was a mere play of some idle spirits. The latter alternative is out of the question, and the first could never have been accomplished if the authors would have gone the very way which they had to avoid. A writing which pretends to be the work of cne of the Patriarchs, must have been composed in the language of that Patriarch, and not in one loathed, or at least disliked, by the descendants of those Patriarchs. Hebrew is therefore the original language of these Testaments, and the Testament which I have discovered is the real genuine original of the Greek.

The Testament of Naphtali, which I publish now here, is embodied in the great chronicle of Jerahmeel, a MS. of the XIIIth century, of which I have a complete copy. The original is in Oxford, MS. No.

In the same library there is another copy (B) of the XVIth century, greatly inferior to A as far as the accuracy of the text is concerned.

By far the best recension is presented by a MS. of the XIIth century, now in Paris (P), a copy of which I got on the 25th January, 1889. A fourth MS. is in Parma,* 563 De Rossi, but this has been inaccessible to me. In 1890 a Testament was printed in Jerusalem (J), by S. A. Wertheimer, which seems to be identical with P.

Of these various MS. I have prepared the present edition,

---

* *V.* Buber, Midrash Samuel : Krakau, 1893, p. 35, No. 27, and note 21.

taking as basis A, and giving the various readings in footnotes. I have introduced the better readings into the Testament, giving the original corrupted ones in the notes. The translation follows the corrected text.

In comparing this with the Greek version, we are struck by the great disparity between the two. In the Hebrew version, whole chapters of the Greek are missing, whilst in the Greek, the whole of the Hebrew is condensed into four and a half chapters, the contents transposed and mangled almost beyond recognition. The Greek counterpart of the Hebrew makes no sense and has no meaning at all; whilst the Hebrew is rounded off, and complete and perfectly clear.

It is evident that the Greek translator has illtreated his original, and has thus thoroughly changed the tendency of the Testament. One of the most curious mistakes of translation occurs also in this Testament (ch. vi): "And, behold, there came a ship sailing by, full of salted (things, fish?) ($\mu\epsilon\sigma\tau\grave{o}s$ $\tau\alpha\rho\acute{\iota}\chi\omega\nu$)." The translator read the Hebrew text badly: instead of בְּלֹא מַלָּח he read מְלֵא מֶלַח or מָלִיחַ, and translated the word $\tau\acute{\alpha}\rho\iota\chi os$ instead of *sailor*.

It turns out afterwards that the ship was filled with all the goods of the world. Another hand has added then in the Greek the correct translation, "without sailors and pilot."

No less curious and significant is another similar mistake, ch. ii: "the calamus for health," $\kappa\acute{\alpha}\lambda\alpha\mu o\nu$ $\pi\rho os$ $\acute{v}\gamma\epsilon\acute{\iota}\alpha\nu$. Sinker himself cannot make out what calamus means. It is a bad translation of the Hebrew קָנֶה, which means the *windpipe*. The translator mistook it for קָנֶה, reed. Hence the "calamus."

The Testament is modelled after the two dreams of Joseph, with characteristic modifications. Instead of giving Joseph preëminence, he is portrayed here as the chief cause of the ulterior schism and ruin. The future of Israel is foretold by the prophetic dreams of Naphtali. The riding of Joseph on the bull is undoubtedly based upon a legendary interpretation of Deuteronomy xxxiii, 1–7. According to a later legend, Joshua rode upon a bull at the conquest of Canaan.

The historical allusions are perfectly transparent. In Hebrew literature we find also parallels to the 70 angels presiding over the fate of the 70 nations.

Very interesting are then the parallels to the last chapter

(Hebrew, Greek, ch. iii) about the functions of the various organs in the body. I have mentioned above the curious mistranslation of the "windpipe. We find a similar description of the organs of the human body in the Talmud (Tractate Berachoth, f. 61a-b). The same passage occurs in the En Ya'akob Berachot, No. 134, but with a slight variation in the order of the organs, the number of which is twelve in these two passages. In a somewhat different order and diminished number we find the same passage in the famous Sepher Yetzira (ch. v, § 2, ed. Ritangelus), in the Othioth de R. Akiba, in two recensions ;* the last comes nearest to our text in the Testament. Last, not least, it occurs again in the Cuzari of R. Jehuda ha-Levi (ch. iv, § 25),† who quotes it from the Sepher Yetzira.

The number of organs mentioned in the "Othioth" is that of *seven*. This seems to be the original number. It stands undoubtedly in connection with the passage of the seven spirits of error enumerated in Testament Reuben, ch. ii and iii, which passage is based on it. We find there, for instance (ch. iii), "the spirit of fighting in the liver and the gall," which is explained by the peculiar characteristic of the angry liver and soothing gall in the Testament of Naphtali. Twice seven organs in the human body are enumerated in the Midrash Tadshe.‡ Again we find seven forms of sin and temptation in the Tana debe Eliahu Zutta, ch. xvi ; seven gradations of sin in the Tractate Derech Eretz Zutta, ch. vi, and seven things that cause affliction in the Talmudic Tractate Arachin, f. 17b.

Wherever we touch in the XII Testaments, we find that we are on Hebrew ground. It can therefore no longer be any doubt about the original language in which they were written, nor could any one say any more that, "to know whether there was a Hebrew work on which the present was modelled, is not a matter of much importance;" nor can one doubt the original unity of the Book of Jubilees with the XII Testaments.

* Ed. Jellinek, *l.c.*, III, p. 35, *sub. lit.* 3, and p. 42–43, *s. littera* 'ם.
† Ed. Buxtorff, p. 307 ff. ; ed. Hirschfeld, p. 273 ff., and p. xlii, No. 53.
‡ Ed. Jellinek, *l.c.*, p. 168–169.

This is the Will (Testament) of Naphtali, Son of Jacob.

When Naphtali grew old and came to an old age, and had completed his years of strength, and fulfilled the duty of the earth-born man, he began to command his children, and he said unto them : " My children, come and draw near and receive the command of your father." They answered and said : " Lo, we hearken to fulfil all that thou will command us." And he said unto them : " I do not command you concerning my silver, nor concerning my gold, nor all my substance that I leave unto you here under the sun, nor do I command you any difficult thing which you may not be able to accomplish, but I speak to you about a very easy matter, which you can easily fulfil."

His sons answered and said a second time, "Speak, O father, for we listen."

Then he said unto them : " I leave you no command save concerning the fear of God : Him ye shall serve, to Him ye shall cling."

They said unto him : " What need hath He of our service ? "

And he answered : " It is not that God hath need of any creature, but that all the creatures need him. He hath also not created the world for naught, but that His creatures should fear Him, and that none should do to his neighbour what he doth not like for himself.'

They said then : " Our father ! hast thou, forsooth, seen us departing from thy ways, or from the ways of our fathers, either to the right or to the left ? "

And he answered : " God and I are witnesses that it is even as ye say ; but I dread only the future to come, that ye may not err after the gods of strange nations ; that ye should not go in the ways of the peoples of the lands, and that you should not join the children of Joseph, only the children of Levi and the children of Judah shall you join."

They said to him : " What dost thou see that thou commandest us concerning it ? "

He answered : " Because I see that in the future the children of Joseph will depart from the Lord, the God of their fathers, and induce the children of Israel to sin, and will cause them to be banished from the good land into another that is not ours, as we have been exiled through him to the bondage of Egypt. I will also tell you the vision I have seen. When I was pasturing the

flock I saw my twelve brothers feeding with me in the field;
and lo, our father came and said to us: 'My children, go (run)
and lay hold here before me everyone on anything that he can get.'
And we answered and said: 'What shall we take possession of, as
we do not see anything else but the sun, the moon, and the stars?'
And he said: 'Take hold of them.' When Levi heard it, he took
a staff (rod) in his hands, and jumped upon the sun and rode on it.
When Judah saw it, he did in like wise; he also took a rod and jumped
upon the moon and rode on it. So also every one of the nine tribes
rode upon his star and his planet in the heavens; Joseph alone
remained upon the earth.

"Jacob, our father, said to him: 'My son! why hast thou not
done as thy brothers?' He answered: 'What is for the woman-
born in heaven, as in the end he must needs stand upon the earth?'"

"Whilst Joseph was speaking, behold there stood near by him
a mighty bull with wings like the wings of a stork, and his horns
were like unto the horns of the Reëm. And Jacob said to him:
'Get up, my son Joseph, and ride upon him.'

"And Joseph got up and mounted upon the bull. And Jacob left
us. For about four hours Joseph gloried in the bull, now he walked
and ran, anon he flew up with him, till he came near to Judah, and
with the staff he had in his hands he began to beat his brother Judah.

"Judah said to him: 'My brother, why dost thou beat me?'

"He answered: 'Because thou holdest in thy hands twelve rods,
and I have only one; give them unto me, and then there will be
peace.'

"But Judah refused to give them to him, and Joseph beat him
till he had taken from him ten against his will, and had left only two
with him. Joseph then said to his ten brothers: 'Wherefore run ye
after Judah and Levi? Depart from them at once.' When the
brothers of Joseph heard his words, they departed from Judah and
Levi like one man, and followed Joseph, and there remained with
Judah only Benjamin and Levi. When Levi beheld this, he
descended from the sun full of anger (sadness).

"And Joseph said unto Benjamin: 'Benjamin, my brother! Art
thou not my brother? Come thou also with me.' But Benjamin
refused to go with Joseph.

"When the day drew to an end, there arose a mighty storm, which
separated Joseph from his brothers, so that no two were left
together.

"When I beheld this vision, I related it unto my father Jacob, and he said unto me : 'My son, it is only a dream, which will not come to pass (will neither ascend nor descend), for it hath not been repeated.

"There did not pass, however, a long time after that, before I saw another vision. We were standing all together with our father Jacob, at the shore of the Great Sea. And, behold, there was a ship sailing in the middle of the sea without a sailor and a man (pilot).

Our father said to us : 'Do ye see, what I am seeing ?' We answered 'We see it.'

"He then said to us : 'Look what I am doing and do the same.' He took off his clothes, threw himself into the sea, and we all followed him. The first were Levi and Judah and they jumped in (to the ship), and Jacob with them. In that ship there was all the goodness of the world. Jacob said : 'Look at the mast and see what is written on it ; for there is no ship on which the name of the master should not be written on the mast.'

"Levi and Judah looked up, and they saw there was written : 'This ship belongs to the son of Berachel (the one whom God had blessed) ! and all the good therein.' When Jacob heard that, he rejoiced very much, bowed down and thanked God, and said : 'Not enough that Thou hast blessed me on earth, Thou hast blessed me on the sea too !' He then said : 'My children, be men, and what ever each one of you will seize, that shall be his share.'

"Thereupon Levi ascended the big mast and sat upon it ; the second after him to ascend the other mast was Judah, and he sat upon it. My other brothers then took each his oar, and Jacob our father grasped the two rudders to steer the ship by them. Joseph alone was left, and Jacob said unto him : 'My son Joseph, take thou also thine oar.' But Joseph refused. When my father saw that Joseph refused to take his oar, he said unto him : 'Come here, my son, and grasp one of the rudders which I hold in my hands. and steer the ship, whilst thy brothers row with the oars until you reach land. And he taught each one of us, and he said to us : 'Thus ye shall steer the ship, and ye will not be afraid of the waves of the sea, nor of the blast of the wind, when it shall rise against you.'

"When he had made an end of speaking, he disappeared from us. Joseph grasped both the rudders, one with the right hand and one with the left, and my other brothers were rowing, and the ship sailed on and floated over the waters. Levi and Judah sat upon the mast to look out for the way (course) the ship was to take. As long as Joseph and Judah were of one mind, so that when Judah showed to Joseph which was the right way, Joseph accordingly directed thither the ship, the ship sailed on peaceably without hindrance.

"After a awhile, however, a quarrel arose between Joseph and Judah, and Joseph did not steer any longer the ship according to the words of his father, and to the teaching of Judah ; and the ship went wrong, and the waves of the sea dashed it on a rock, so that the ship foundered.

"Levi and Judah then descended from the mast to save their lives, and every one of the brothers went to the shore to save themselves. Behold, there came our father, Jacob, and found us scattered (distressed), one here and the other there. He said to us : 'What is the matter with you, my sons? Have you not steered the ship as it ought to be steered, and as I had taught you?'

"We answered : 'By the life of thy servants, we did not depart from anything that thou hast commanded us, but Joseph transgressed the word (sinned in the affair), for he did not keep the ship right according to thy command, and as he was told (taught) by Judah and Levi, for he was jealous of them.'

"And he (Jacob) said unto us: 'Show me the place (of the ship).' And he saw, and only the tops of the masts were visible. But lo, the ship floated on the surface of the water. My father whistled, and we gathered round him. He again threw himself into the sea as before, and he healed (repaired) it, and he entered the ship ; and he reproved Joseph and said : 'My son, thou shalt no more deceive and be jealous of thy brothers, for they were nearly lost through thee.'

"When I had told this vision to my father he clapped his hands and he sighed, and his eyes shed tears. I waited for awhile, but he did not answer. So I took the hand of my father to embrace it, and to kiss it, and I said to him : 'Oh servant of the Lord ! Why do thine eyes shed tears?' He answered, 'My son ! the repetition of thy vision hath made my heart sink within me, and my body is shaken with tremor by reason of my son Joseph, for I loved him above you all ; and for the wickedness of my son Joseph you will be sent into captivity, and you will be scattered among the nations. For thy first and second visions are both but one. I therefore command you not to unite (combine) with the sons of Joseph, but only with Levi and Judah.

" I further tell you that my lot will be in the best of the middle
of the land, and ye shall eat and be satisfied with the choice of its
products. But I warn you not to kick in your fatness and not to
rebel and not to oppose the will of God, who satisfies you with the
best of His earth ; and not to forget the Lord your God, the God
of your fathers ; who was chosen by our father Abraham when the
nations of the earth were divided in the time of Phaleg.

" At that time, the Lord, blessed be He, came down from His
high heavens, and brought down with Him seventy ministering
angels, Michael the first among them. He commanded them to
teach the seventy descendants of Noah seventy languages.

" The angels descended immediately and fulfilled the command
of their Creator.

" The holy language, the Hebrew, remained only in the house of
Sem and Eber, and in the house of our father Abraham, who is one
of their descendants.

" On that day the angel Michael took a message from the Lord,
and said to the seventy nations, to each nation separately : ' You
know the rebellion you undertook and the treacherous confederacy
into which you entered against the Lord of heaven and earth, now
choose to-day whom you will worship and who shall be your Protector
in heaven.'

" Nimrod the wicked answered : ' I do not know any one greater
than that (these) who taught me and my nation the languages of
Kush!' In like manner answered also Put, and Mizraim, and Tubal,
and Javan, and Meseh, and Tiras ; and every nation chose its own
angel, and none of them mentioned the name of the Lord, blessed
be He.

" But when Michael said unto our father Abraham : ' Abram,
whom dost thou choose and whom wilt thou worship ? ' Abram
answered : ' I choose and I will worship only Him who said, and
the world was created, Who has created me in the womb of my
mother, body within body, Who has given unto me spirit and soul,
Him I choose and to Him will I cling, I and my seed after me, all
the days of the world.'

" Then He divided the nations and apportioned to every nation its
lot and share ; and from that time all the nations separated themselves from the Lord, blessed be He; only Abraham and his house
remained with his Creator to worship Him ; and after him Isaac and
Jacob and myself.

" I therefore conjure you not to err and not to worship any other God than that one chosen by your fathers.

" For ye shall know, there is no other God like unto Him, and no other who can do like His works in heaven and on earth, and there is none to do such wondrous and mighty deeds like unto Him.

" A portion only of His power you can see in the creation of man, how many remarkable wonders are there not in him. He created him perfect from head to foot ; to listen with the ears, to see with the eyes, to understand with his brains, to smell with his nose, to bring forth the voice with his windpipe, to eat and drink with his gullet, to speak with his tongue, to pronounce with his mouth, to do work with his hands, to think with his heart, to laugh with his spleen, to be angry with his liver, to digest with his belly (stomach), to walk with his feet, to breathe with his lungs, to be counselled by his kidneys, and none of his members changes its function, but every-one remains at its own.

" It is therefore proper for man to bear in mind all these things, Who hath created him and Who it is that hath wrought him out of a drop in the womb of the woman, and who it is that bringeth him out into the light of the world, and who hath given him the sight of eyes and the walking of the feet, and who standeth him upright and hath given him intelligence for doing good deeds, and hath breathed into him a living soul and the Spirit of purity. Blessed is the man who does not defile the divine spirit which hath been put and breathed into him, and blessed is he who returns it as pure as it was on the day when it was entrusted to (him by his) Creator."

These, the words of Naphtali, the son of Israel, which he (commended) to his sons ; they are sweeter than honey to the palate.

B

AN UNKNOWN HEBREW VERSION OF THE HISTORY OF JUDITH.

By M. GASTER.

Reprinted from the "*Proceedings of the Society of Biblical Archæology*," *March*, 1894.

In the Hebrew literature we find two forms of the Judith legend —one long and elaborate, the other short, concise. The former is almost akin to the Greek version, though not absolutely identical, and has been published hitherto two or three times. The short recension, however, has been known till now only in one single text : in the collection of tales attributed to R. Nissim of Kairuan (N. Africa, eleventh century).

It is not my intention to enter here into a detailed disquisition of this subject. Schürer has summed up the results of modern and ancient investigations, and to his book and bibliography I refer.*

The consensus of opinion is, that the Judith legend originated in the time of the Makkabæans, and that it was originally composed in a Semitic idiom, Hebrew or Aramaic. No one has, however, been able to establish this conclusion with any certainty, or to explain who the mysterious Holophernes was, or to fix the exact place (Bethulia) where the tragedy took place.

Many a minor incident in the Greek text is far from being clear, such as xii, 7 : "thus she abode in the camp three days, and went out in the night into the valley of Bethulia, and washed herself in a fountain of water by the camp." There is no reason assigned for this peculiar ablution, nor does it stand in any connection with the other religious ordinances, which we are told that she observed so punctiliously.

These very ordinances, such as her refusal to eat of Holophernes' food, have been used by modern critics for the purpose of determining the date of the composition of this book.

* *E. Shürer*, "Geschichte des jüdischen Volkes im Zeitalter Jesu Christi, II (1866), p. 599-603.

However difficult it may be to determine the relation between the two recensions, little doubt, I think, is left as to the true character of the larger recension.

This writing belongs clearly to that class of literary productions which Schürer classifies under the title of *parænetic* tales, *i.e.*, writings composed for the purpose of edifying and encouraging the reader ; they were written with a tendency.

It is therefore not very probable that this was the original form of the tale or history of Judith, unless we assume the whole to be a pure fiction, evolved out of the brains of the writer, without any foundation whatsoever on fact.

But whoever is acquainted with the old apocryphal and pseudo-epigraphical literature must reject a purely fictitious origin of "Judith." *A Judith* must have existed, and must have been—at least in the conscience and memory of the people—the author of some daring act, perpetrated by her in times of dire and cruel persecution.

This figure was then taken up by the writer of the romance, if I may call by this name the longer recension, and the simple ancient tale was carefully worked up ; prayers, sermons, addresses were freely added, until the whole assumed the form in which we find it in that recension.

That the original tale must have suffered under this poetical treatment need not be specially pointed out.   Hence the difficulty of determining the historical element in that romantic tale.

Those very elements which characterise the longer recension are missing however, in the shorter text.   In this we find nothing of a Holofernes, nor is Bethulia mentioned, nor anything about the food ; and as to the bathing in the fountain, it is only here we have a perfectly clear explanation, in conformity with the Law.

The only text of this recension which had been known hitherto, was printed for the first time in Constantinople, 1519, then Venice, 1544, and reprinted by Jellinek.   It is incomplete.   But even in this mutilated text neither Holophernes nor Bethulia are mentioned ; not one of the prayers and supplications ; also nothing of Achior.

I have now had the rare fortune of discovering another copy of this same recension, which is both much older and much more complete, and as will be seen anon of utmost importance.

Through the kindness of a friend I have come into the possession of a considerable number of very valuable ancient Hebrew manuscripts, all hailing from Persia, or rather, from Babylon. Among these MSS., of which I will give a more detailed description on another occasion, there is one of the highest interest (now No. 82 of my collection of Hebrew MSS.). It is a collection of close upon 300 Talmudic tales. A volume of 198 leaves octavo, paper, written in a very ancient character. It is the most complete and probably the oldest collection of this kind, as I consider the MS. to belong to the Xth or commencement of the XIth century. The language, especially of those portions that are written in Aramaic, is much purer, more archaic, and more akin to the Mandaic than that of the corresponding tales to be found in our editions of the Talmud. From this, or a similar collection, R. Nissim has drawn the tales which he incorporated into his book. We find in this MS. also some of those tales which are only alluded to in the Talmud, and which are found in a complete form in the Aruch, or Rashi, or in Nissim's collection, such as the history of the " weasel and the pit." The MS. must have been written somewhere in Babylon. The pages are covered with old Persian glosses, which a later possessor of the XIIIth or XIVth century has added in order to explain the text.

In this collection we find then also the tale of Judith's heroic deed. In comparing this text with the one hitherto known, which forms part of the collection of R. Nissim, one can see at a glance that the latter has borrowed it from our MS. collection, omitting exactly those incidents which are of the highest importance for our investigation. He omitted the *heading* and the name of the king slain by Judith. These two, fortunately preserved in my MS., throw an unexpected light upon the history and origin of the Judith legend, and what is more, furnish us with an historical date, which may assist us to fix definitely the period when it happened.

The heading runs so : " The eighteenth day of Adar, the day in which Seleukos came up." This heading is of the utmost importance. It is worded absolutely in the same way as all the dates *in the Megillath Taanith*. It is an established fact that this Megillah constituted the calendar of the festival days of the Makkabæan period. The days in which a victory was reported, was fixed as a day of rejoicing. The 18th of Adar is missing in the Megillath Taanith, which has come down to us in a fragmentary state. This date is now supplied by our text, which, as that wording unmistakably demonstrates, must have belonged originally to the old

Megillath Taanith. Considering that these festival days were abrogated before the middle of the third century, there is no wonder that portions of it have disappeared. It is a fortunate coincidence that we have recovered at the same time the day on which the Jewish feast was kept and a portion of the Megillath Taanith. This settles the Makkabæan origin of *Judith*. Instead of the unknown Holophernes we get then a historical name *Seleukos*, which makes the fact related in the tale at any rate less improbable. Judith is also not a widow, but a maiden; and it is questionable whether *Betulah*, בתולה (virgin), has not suggested to the romancer the otherwise unknown *Bethulia*, against which the also unknown Holophernes wages an unsuccessful war, which costs him his life.

In our text the town which Seleukos besieges is Jerusalem, and the reason which Judith gives for her coming is much more plausible, than the very curious and unsatisfactory one in the long recension.

In our text, which is as simple a narrative as can be conceived, we find also a satisfactory explanation of the bath : it is the ablution of purification prescribed by Leviticus xv, 19–28, and xv, 13.

I may mention further that the Synagogue has always brought the history of Judith in connection with the Makkabæan period. One of the variations of our recensions, published by Jellinek,* is actually embodied in a liturgical piece which was recited on the feast of Dedication, established by Judah Makkabee. Judith is mentioned in connection with this festival also by Abudarham (fourteenth century) in ed. Venice, f. 135 *a*. The longer recension is also found in connection with the history of the Makkabæans, in Hemdath-hayamin,† reprinted by Jellinek.‡ Of this longer recension there is—as I may mention by the way—another copy in the MS. Chronicle of Jerahmeel, from which I have published the Testament of Naphtali; and to the kindness of Dr. Neubauer I owe the information that Cod. 2240, 5 (Oxford) contains also the long recension.

The profound difference between the short and the long recension, precludes the possibility that the former may be an abbreviation from the latter; the changes are much too radical. In fact, every essential incident is so much altered in the latter that it can by no means be the result of mere abbreviation. If it were an

---

* Bet-hamidrasch, I, p. 132–136.
† Constantinople, ואתבנן, II, f. 62*b*–65*c*.
‡ Bet-hamidrasch, II, p. 12–22.

abridged text, names and situations would have been retained, and only the rhetorical portions omitted, which however is not the case. Almost everything is different in the two recensions.

We must therefore perforce admit that we have two distinct recensions, of which one may be, and probably is, the unvarnished simple popular tale, the recital of a memorable incident which had happened in the time of the Makkabæan struggles, in which a maiden Judith played an important *rôle*, and the other a romantical panegyric based upon that fact, and told in the form of a paraenetic tale, intended to convey comfort and edification to the reader.

In questions of this kind one cannot be cautious enough, and I have limited myself to state the facts, and to draw only such conclusions from them as are warranted by the words of the text, which follows here in the original and in translation.

THE HISTORY OF JUDITH.

" A tale. Our teachers taught : on the eighteenth day of Adar [*i.e.*, one is not allowed to fast]; it is the day on which Seleukos went up. As we are told, at the time when he besieged Jerusalem, the Israelites were fasting and had put sacks on. There was a very beautiful woman named Judith, daughter of Ahitob. On every day she used to pray to God in ashes and sackcloth. God inspired her with the thought that a miracle would happen through her. So she went to the porters of the gate and said to them : 'Open the gates for me, may be that a miracle will happen through me.' They said to her, ' Hast thou, perchance, turned to the other side ?' She answered, ' God forbid.' So they opened the gates to her, and she went to the camp of Seleukos, she and her handmaid with her. She said to them (*i.e.*, the soldiers of Seleukos), 'I have a secret errand unto the king. They went and told the king, and said to him, ' A beautiful maiden has come from Jerusalem, and she says that she has a secret errand unto the king.' He said, ' Let her come in.' She went before the king, and fell down upon her face before him.' He said to her, ' What is that thou wishest ?' She answered and said, ' My lord king, I belong to a great family in Jerusalem, my brothers and my father's house were kings and high priests. I have now heard them speak concerning thee, that the time has arrived when this town is to fall in thine hands, therefore I have come first to find favour in thine eyes.'

"When the king beheld her beautiful countenance and heard her words, she found favour in his eyes ; and he rejoiced at the tidings she had told him. Then he commanded his servants to prepare a great feast. Whilst they were preparing it, he ordered all the princes to leave, as he wished to have the company of the damsel. He asked her to sin. She answered and said, 'My lord king, for this very thing I have come hither with all my heart, but now it is impossible, as I am in my impurity; to-night is the time of my purification ; I therefore desire the king to herald throughout the camp, that no one should stay the woman and her handmaid, when she goes out in the night to the fountain of water. When I return I will give myself over to the king, that he do what is pleasing in his sight.'

"The wicked man did accordingly. In the night he invited all the princes, his generals and his servants, and they ate and rejoiced at that great feast and got drunk. When they saw that the king was nodding his head, they said, 'let us depart, for he wishes to have the company of the Hebrew maiden.' So all went forth and left the king alone with the maiden and with her handmaid. She then took the falchion and cut off his head. She took the head and went out. When they left the soldiers noticed them, and they said to one another, 'no one is to touch them, such is the command of the king.' So they passed (the camp) and reached Jerusalem in the middle of the night. They called upon the porters and said, 'open the gates for us, for the miracle has already come to pass.' The porters replied, 'is it not sufficient for thee to have defiled thyself, that thou wisheth to deliver the blood of Israel (to their enemies)?' So she did swear to them ; but they would not believe her until she showed them the head of that wicked king; only then they believed her and opened the gates unto her. That day they kept as a day of feasting ; on the morrow the Israelites went forth against that army and slew them until they had destroyed them completely. The residue left their horses and their money and ran away. And the Israelites came and spoiled everything.

THE APOCALYPSE OF ABRAHAM.

From the Roumanian Text, Discovered and Translated

BY DR. M. GASTER.

Reprinted from the " Transactions of the Society of Biblical Archæology."
VOL. IX, PART 1, 1887.

At the moment when the power of prophecy ceased, its place was taken by the mysterious metaphysical and emblematical *vision*, in which the future was likewise prognosticated, but in an allegorical and fantastical form.

There grew up the *apocalyptical* literature, especially in the period of time which elapsed between the Book of Daniel and the Apocalypse of St. John, and in the following two or three centuries.

Almost at as remote a period as it first arose, the *apocalyptic*, or rather the *apocryphal* literature, was seized upon by all who were desirous of exercising an influence on the masses. In the first instance, the heretical sects of Christianity utilized it. The populace, as a rule, understands nothing of the subtle and higher questions of dogmatism, and it is most easily approached by those who speak its accustomed language, by those who enter into its views, who use its word-pictures and metaphors. What could serve better to popularise creeds which branched off from the straight road of orthodoxy, than to present them in the guise of a religious story, of a biblical allegory, of an apocalyptic vision? Special books of religious and prophetical tendency were therefore ascribed to all the patriarchs from Adam onwards. Each sect had a special predilection for a different personage, and various books were written, or in some cases ancient ones were altered to suit the requirements of the sects, and thus these works increased in number.

Contest with the ruling Church began at the same early period. *Indices* of these heretical books were drawn up, in which their destruction was urged as a sacred duty.

Strange to say, *almost all* the forbidden *Apocryphas* have nevertheless been preserved to us. To the explorer in the territory of folk-lore opportunities frequently present themselves of recognizing the ancient apocryphal stories amongst the popular literature of the middle ages. *All*, however, have not been preserved from destruction. Amongst others there has been missing until now an apocryphal story concerning the *death of Abraham*. It is referred to by *Epiphanius* (adv. hæresos, 39, 5), and also by *Athanasius* (Synopsis). Nikephorus (Stichometria, No. 6) also speaks of an apocryphon of about 300 verses, with reference to Abraham.[1]

This apocryphal story, of which until now nothing certain has been known, has been preserved in the old Slavonian and in the old *Roumanian* language. In the former, as far as I know, it is only in two MSS. (of which one is a fragment), and in Roumanian it is in *four MSS.*, of which one is the translation of the Slavonic fragment. The complete text, discovered by myself, in three MSS., which are all in my possession, I propose to give now in a literal translation.

Before I proceed, I should wish to say a few words concerning this text, the more ancient of the two fragments, and especially regarding the connection of *this* text with that of the Slavonic one of the sixteenth century.

The first incomplete text, which, as I have before stated,[2] entirely agrees with that of the contemporaneous Slavonic, is only distinguished from the more complete text by greater brevity, and some features which are wanting in the latter.

The complete Slavonic text[3] is distinguished from our present one only by some unimportant features, and therefore points to a common and more ancient source. That the source of the Slavonic text (and hence of the Roumanian)

[1] E. Schürer, "Geschichte des jüd. Volkes im Zeitalter Christi," II, p. 688, Leipzig, 1886.

[2] Published by *Prof. B. P. Håsdeu*, Cuvente den bătrâni. II, Bucuresti, 1880, pp. 189–194.

[3] *Tihonravov*, Pamjatniki otrechennoj russkoj literatury. I, St. Petersburg, 1863, pp. 79–90.

is Greek, is beyond all doubt. The fathers of the Church, already quoted, expressly say so. But besides this we have historical and linguistic proofs, which necessarily point to a Greek origin.

Of the linguistic proofs I will only adduce one here. The name of the place—as we will see—where the angel first meets Abraham is called *Dria the Black*, which was taken from the falsely rendered $Aρυα$ $τῆς$ $Μαμβρη$, the translation of the Hebrew *Elone Mamre*. *Drüa* was considered as a proper name, and *Mamre*, changed into *Mavri*, was rendered by the Slavic translator as *black*. Thus arose this otherwise inexplicable name.

Of the historical proofs, the most incontestible lies in the fact that all theological literature, in the widest sense of the word, reached the Slavic through the medium of the Greek, and that even a Greek MS. of it seems to be preserved in 'the library of Vienna.[1]

The stories, however, came originally from the poetical East, with its fantastic imagery, and amidst the influences of similar pictures of olden times. The fathers of the Church, who have preserved for us the name of this apocrypha, have also recorded the name of the sect in whose midst it first arose, namely, the sect of the *Sethians*, who beheld in Seth the son of Adam the true Christ and Redeemer from hereditary sin.

It would carry me too far afield were I to be more explicit as to this, and especially were I to dilate on the heretical agitation in Asia Minor, and to follow out in these texts traces which have been almost obliterated by time. In reference to this I wish to point out the " *threefold Judgement* " mentioned here, of which the orthodox church knows nothing.

At every step we meet parallels to the various incidents of this legendary story, both in the corresponding Jewish literature, and in the *apocalyptic* which has developed out of it.

---

[1] *Cf. Fabricius*, Codex pseudepigraphicus Vet. Test. I, pp. 417–418, and, *M. Gaster*, Literatura populară română, Bucureşti, 1883, pp. 311-317.

I will reserve to myself for some future work the investigation of these parallels. For the present it will suffice if I merely refer to the principal sources, or rather the most striking parallels.

As an example present to the mind of the authors of this legend, I would cite the Apocalypse of the Apostle Paul,[2] especially the Oriental version, which has also been published in English from a Syriac original. In this legend the Apostle, who has been carried up to heaven, beholds a very similar spectacle of the Judgment after death.

The second part of the legend of Abraham, that relating to his death, shows a decided leaning towards the widely spread legends (of Jewish literature) relating to the death of Moses.

That some features have been altered, whilst others have been superadded, will excite no surprise in those who are even but partially acquainted with this very luxuriant literature.

In conclusion, I would here set at rest an objection which is contained in the question, as to whether this text is actually the ancient and hitherto undiscovered apocalypse?

The road usually taken by such apocrypha precludes any possible doubt. Brought from the East, they were in an early period translated from the Greek into the Slavonic, and thence they became also by translation part of Roumanian literature. Similarly to these manuscript stories, the "Lists" of heretical books were translated into the Slavonic, and here we find our text incontestibly figuring amongst the forbidden books.

Origen, in quoting this text, appears to labour under a slight misconception. The Angel of Good and the Angel of Evil do not dispute with regard to the salvation of Abraham *himself*, but in Abraham's presence the angels dispute concerning that of another soul. This is meant by the story related in the text, when the soul was placed in the mid-way until it was released by the prayer of Abraham.

Out of the three MSS. in my possession I have reconstructed the critical Roumanian text, which is published here

---

[2] Ed. *Tischendorf*, Apocalypses Apocryphæ, p. 34, *seq.*

for the first time. As a basis I took the MS. of *c.* 1750,
which although fragmentary at the beginning and end,
nevertheless represents the best version. In (   ) I included the corrections I considered necessary, and in [   ]
the additions taken either from MS. *b* (1818), or MS. *c*
(1777), or from both. The transcription is strictly pho-
netical, following the ordinary manner used in publishing
Roumanian texts. It is as follows: letters have the Italian
value, ţ = tz ; ş = sh; â, ă, î = ę (Lépsius); ĭ = y. Every
Cyrillian letter, in which the texts are originally written, is
reproduced by a Latin letter; and I went so far as to
preserve even the dialectical forms, for the MSS. bear a
Moldavian character. The translation is of the reconstructed
text, which has been divided by me in chapters.

The Life and Death of our Father Abraham the Just, written according to the Apocalypse in nice words. Introduction.

1. Our father Abraham lived more than 175 years. In his lifetime he was vigorous, very gentle, compassionate and just towards all, and very hospitable. He dwelt not far from the place called *Dria the Black,* at the cross-road by which all strangers had to pass. He received the wayfarers and entertained them. Rich and poor, kings and princes, boyards and voyevods, all neighbours, the weak and the sick, all were treated with the greatest kindness, for Abraham was good and just, and loving all men, till he attained to extreme old age, and the time and the hour drew nigh when he was to taste the cup of death.

2. Then the Lord called the archangel *Mihail,* and said unto him: Go down, *Mihail,* to my friend Abraham, and remind him of death, for I have promised him to increase his

---

Vieaţa şi moartea părintelui nostru cel drept Avraam, scrisă după Apocalipsi cu cuvinte frumoase foarte. Cuvânt înnainte.

1. Trăit-au părintele nostru Avraam, întru vieaţa luĭ piste tot 175 de anĭ; şi într' aceşti anĭ cu mare putere şi cu multă blândeţe, şi cu milostiviri şi cu dreptate asupra tuturor; şi era foarte ĭubitoriŭ de oaspeţi. Şi lăcuinţa luĭ era lângă *Diea* (*c.* Driea) cea neagră, întru răpaosul ce veniea drumurile, de să petrecea streinii; şi priimiea călătorii, şi-i ospăta, bogaţiĭ, bolnaviĭ, împăraţiĭ, domniĭ, boeriĭ, voevoziĭ, veciniĭ, slabiĭ, pre toţi îi cinstiea, că era bun, drept şi pre toţi âĭ ĭubiea, până ajunse la bătrâneţe şi venea vremea şi cĭasul să guste din paharul morţiĭ.

2. Atĭncea Domnul Dumnezeu chĭemă pre Arhanghelul Mihail, şi-i zise: pogoară-te, Mihaile! la prieatenul mieu Avraam, şi-i pomeneşte de moartea luĭ; că m'am făgăduit săĭ-

7

property and to multiply his descendants like the stars of
heaven and like the sand of the sea. And I have blessed
him. Therefore he is now richer and more just than all
in his goodness and hospitality which he displays until
his end.

3. And the archangel *Mihail*, who sat before the Lord,
went out of His presence and descended to Abraham in *Dria
the Black*. And he found our father Abraham near the village
with his servants and also other young men. And the
archangel approached him. Abraham seeing him, thought he
was a soldier, being so modest and fair in his appearance.

4. Then the aged Abraham arose in order to meet the
archangel. And the archangel said, "Rejoice, venerable
father, the chosen one of the Lord, righteous soul, friend of
the Ruler of heaven." And Abraham said to the angel,
"Rejoice, oh chief of the hosts (Arhistratig)! · Thou, who art
greater than any of the children of men, be welcome on my
return home. Kindly relate me, oh young man, whence
thou comest, and whence it is that thou art so beautiful?"

înmulțesc averea luĭ și sămănța luĭ ca steleie ceriuluĭ și ca
nisipul măriĭ, și l'am blagoslovit; pentru că (l.c. aceea) iaste
maĭ avut și maĭ drept decât toți întru toată bunătatea luĭ,
iubitoriu de oaspeți până în sfârșit iaste.

3. Iară Arhanghelul Mihail eșă de la fața luĭ Dumnezeu, și
merse și să pogorâ cătră Avraam la Diea cea neagră. Și află
pre părintele Avraam aproape de satu cu oameniĭ luĭ și cu alțĭ
voinicĭ adunațĭ; și merse Arhanghelul cătră dânsul. Iară
Avraam deaca-l văzu, iĭ păru că iaste ostaș, că era curat și
cuvios cu frumusețe.

4. Decĭ să sculă bătrânul Avraam de-l întimpină pre Arhanghelul. Iară Arhanghelul zise: bucură-te, cinstite părinte, alesul luĭ Dumnezău, drepte suflete, prietinul luĭ
Dumnezău aĭ susuluĭ. Adică și Avraam zăsă cătră înger:
bucură-te, stratilate! maĭ multu decăt toți fiĭ oameniloi:
bine aĭ vinit la a nostră plecare. Cu a ta voi, spune-mi-o de
unde aĭ venit, tănărule? Spune-mi (de unde) a ta frumsăță?

5. And the Arhistratig replied, "Oh, just man! I come
from the Great City, and I am sent by the Great Ruler, to
say to His chosen friend, that he should be prepared, because
the Ruler calls him." And Abraham replied, "Well! Let us
go back to the village." And the Arhistratig said, "Let
us go!"

6. And they went to the nearest village, and sat down to
rest. And Abraham said to his servants, "Go to the field,
where the horses are, and fetch two that are fit for riding,
and get them ready, so that I may mount one, and the
stranger the other one." But the Arhistratig said to
Abraham, "Let them not bring the horses, because I do not
ride on a beast with four legs. Oh, thou righteous soul, let
us go on foot to thy pure abode." And Abraham replied,
"Let it be so." And they walked from that village to his
house.

7. On the way there grew a lofty and mighty cypress.
And the tree exclaimed, by the will of God, with a loud
voice of man: "Holy one! Holy one! Holy one! The

---

5. Iar Arhistratigul zăsă: eu, drepte omule, de la cetatè
cè mare viu, şi sănt trimes de la împăratul cel mare, ca si
zăcu prietinului celui maĭ ales, ca să să gătească, că înpăratul
îl cheamă cătră el!—Şi zăsă Avraam: aleĭ dar, domnul mieu!
să mergimu pănă la sat!—Iară Arhistratigul zăsă: să mergim
dar!

6. Şi marsără în sat strein, şi şăzură de odihni(ră). Şi
zăsă Avraam ficĭorilor luĭ: păsaţĭ în oborul cailor şi aduceţ
doi cai blănzi, învăţaţi, şi îĭ gătiţ, să încalec eu pre unul şi
streinul pre altul. Iar Arhistratig(ul) zăsă cătră Avraam: Să
nu aducă cai, că eu mă ferescu ca să nu şăz pre vită cu patru
picĭoare; ce blem, drepte suflete, pedestri la casa ta cè cinstită.
Şi zăsă (Avraam): adevărat să fie! Şi veniră de la aceĭ sat
pănă la casa luĭ.

7. Şi pre cale unde vinè era un chiparos înnalt şi des;
din voe luĭ Dumnezău striga copacĭul cu glas mare de om,
şi zăsă: Sfinte! Sfinte! Sfinte! Domnul Dumnezău te

Lord God calls thee!" And Abraham held his peace, and replied not, for he thought the Arhistratig had not heard the voice of the tree.

8. Then they approached the courtyard, and sat down. Isaac, the son of Abraham, saw the face of the angel, and said to his mother Sarah, "Look at the man who is sitting with my father, he does not appear to me to be born from a human being." And Isaac ran to the angel, and bowed down before him. And the angel blessed him, and said, "May God give thee what he has given to thy father and thy mother!"

9. And Abraham said to Isaac, "Take the basin and pour in some water, so that we may wash the feet of this stranger, who comes from afar to us, and who is weary." And Isaac ran to the well and poured water into the basin and brought it. And Abraham went to wash the feet of the angel, and Abraham sighed and wept on account of this stranger. And Isaac seeing his father weep, wept also, and his tears ran down. And the angel seeing them both weeping, wept with

---

chĭamă! Iară Avraam tăcu şi nu vru să zăcă nimică, că-i păru că nu aude Arhistratigul glasul copacĭuluĭ.

8. Decĭ dacă să apropieră de curte şăzură; şi văzu Isac fiiul luĭ Avraam faţa îngeruluĭ şi zăsă cătră Sara maica-sa; ia cautâ de vezi, ce om este acesta ce şăde cu tatăl mieu! că nu este cunoscut (l. născut) de om de pre pământ. Şi alergă Isac spre înger, de-i să închină luĭ. Şi-l blagoslovi îngerul şi zăsă : să-ţi dăruĭască Dumnezău ce au dăruit tătăne-tău şi maicĭi tale!

9. Zăsă Avraam luĭ Isac : Ia lighĭanul şi toarnă apă într'ănsul, să spălăm picĭoarile acestuĭ streinu, că (de) departe vine la noĭ şi este ostenit. Şi alergă Isac la puţ şi turnă apă în lighĭan şi adusă. Şi marsă Avraam de-i spălă picĭoarile îngeruluĭ, şi suspină Avraam şi lăcrămă pentru acestu streinu. Şi văsu (l. văzu) Isac pre tatăl său plăngând, şi plănsă şi el şi lăcrămă. Şi văzu îngerul pre amândoĭ că plăngu, şi

them, and his tears fell down into the basin. And these tears turned into precious stones. And when Abraham beheld this miracle, he took away the jewels and hid the secret in his heart.

10. And Abraham said to his beloved son, "Go into the room and get ready two beds, one for me and the other for the stranger, because he is a wayfarer; and prepare everything well and carefully, and put candles in the candlesticks, and prepare the table, and light the incense-burner, and bring sweet smelling herbs of the paradise and put them on the floor, so that they may scent the place, and light seven candles, and we will sit down and rejoice with the stranger, who is greater than any human being on the earth, and mightier than kings." And Isaac prepared everything carefully, according to the directions of his father. And Abraham went with the angel in the room, where the beds were ready, and they both sat down, one on one bed and one on the other, and between them stood the table with food.

---

plănsă și el și lăcrămă; și-i picară lacrămăle în lighian și să făcură pietri scumpe fără-de-preț. Deci văzănd Avraam minune ca aciasta pre pămănt priimi [*b.c.* pietrile] întru furiș de ascunsă taina întru inima lui.

10. Iar Avraam zăsă cătră fiul său cel iubit: pas fiiul mieu în cămară, de rădică doă paturi și așterni; întru unul să mă culcu eu, iară în cela-l-ant streinul, că este călătoriu; și grijasti foarte bine și frumos, și pune lumănări în sfeșnice și masa cè bună, și tămaiază cu tămăe de cè cinstită, și iarbă de cè mirositoare din raiu să aduci, să pui în casi să mirosască; și aprinde șapte candeli, să șădem și să ne vesălim cu acest strein astăz; că acesta este [mai] proslăvit decăt toță oamenii de pre pămănt, și decăt înpăratul! Și găti Isac foarte bine după graiul tătăne-său. Și luâ Avraam pre înger și marse unde era paturile așternute, și șezură amăndoi, unul pre un pat și altul pre alt pat și între ei era masă plină de bucate.

11. And the Arhistratig arose and went out to take the air, and he ascended to heaven, and came before the Lord, and said to the Lord God, "Lord! Lord! know that Abraham is very powerful, so that I cannot mention to him of death, for I have never seen a man like unto him on the earth, just, compassionate, and avoiding all evil."

12. And the Lord spake to the Arhistratig, "Go to my friend Abraham, and eat of all that which will be put on the table; and I will send My Spirit unto his son Isaac, and I will show him the approach of his father's death, so that he may see all in a dream."

13. And the Arhistratig said, "The incorporeal beings of heaven do not eat, neither do they drink, and he has spread for me a table with all the good things of the earth; and now, O Lord, what shall I do? How can I become different, as we shall be all at one table?"

---

11. Şi să sculă Arhistratigul de işi afară pentru primblare, şi să sui în ceriu şi stătu înnaintè lui Dumnezău, şi zăsi cătră Domnul Dumnezău: Doamne! Doamne! Să ştiĭ că mare putere are Avraam, că eu de moarte nu-ĭ pociu pomeni, că bărbat ca acesta eu n'am maĭ văzut pre pămănt; drept milostiv, şi ferindu-să de tot răul; ce să ştiĭ că eu de moarte nu-ĭ pociu pomeni!

12. Zăsă Dumnezău Arhistratigului: pas la prietinul mĭeu Avraam, şi ce va pune pre masă să mănănci şi tu cu el; că eu voĭu trimete duhul mĭeu spre fiĭul mĭeu Isac, şi voĭu arăta aducere-aminte de moarte în inima luĭ ca să vază în vis toate.

13. Şi zăsă Arhistratigul: toate ale ceriuluĭ ce sănt fără de trup, nici mănăncă, nici beu, şi mie mi-au pus masă bună şi cu de ale pămăntuluĭ bucate, şi acum ce voĭu să fac? mă voĭu schimba? că şidem tot la o masă!

14. And the Lord answered him, "Go to My friend Abraham, and do not trouble thyself, for I will send spirits, who shall cause the food to disappear from thy hands and from thy mouth; all that is on the table shall disappear. And rejoice thou with him. But thou shalt interpret Isaac's dreams unto him, so that Abraham may know the hour of his death. For he has numberless properties and lands and houses, because I have blessed him, and I have increased his possessions like the sands of the sea and like the stars in heaven."

15. Thereon the Artistratig descended to Abraham's table, and they sat down. And Isaac had provided the supper. And Abraham said his prayer, as it was his custom. And after the meal they arose, said a prayer, and sat down each one on his bed.

16. And Isaac said to his father, "I should like to sleep here also, because I love with all my heart to listen to the words of this stranger." But Abraham replied to his son,

---

14. Iară Domnulu zăsă cătră el: pas la prietenul mĭeu Avraam, ĭară de acele nu griji, ce şăzĭ şi cu el; că eu voĭu trimete duhurĭ măngăitoare (*b.c.* măncătoare) şi le vor topi din măinile tale de lăngă gura ta, de toate căte vor fi pe masi şi te vezăleşti (l. vesăleşti) cu el întru toate; numaĭ visăle să i le dizlegĭ, ca să ştie Avraam cĭasul morţiĭ luĭ; că are avere multă fără de samă şi moşiĭ şi casi cu ispravă; că el (*b.* eu) l'am blagoslovit pre el şi averè luĭ [ca să să înmulţească) ca năsipul mărĭĭ şi ca stelile cerĭuluĭ.

15. Atunce s'au pogorăt Arhistratigul la masa luĭ Avraam şi au şăzut [*b.* la masă]. Şi marsă Isac de griji de cină. Şi făcu Avraam [*b.* molitvă] după cum le era obiceĭul. Şi după cină să sculară [*b.* şi ĭarăşi făcură rugăcĭune, şi şezură] cineşi în patul său.

16. Şi zăsă Isac cătră tatăl său: şi eu să mă culcu cu voi, că mi-i drag să ascult cuvĭntele omuluĭ strein cu tot sufletul mĭeu! Iară Avraam zăsă cătră fiĭul său: ba, fătul mĭeu!

" No, my son! go thou to thy bed and rest, so that we may not inconvenience this stranger." Then Isaac received his father's blessing, and went to his bed to rest.

17. And the Lord showed Isaac in a dream the approaching death of his father. And after the third hour of the night Isaac awoke from his sleep, and arose from his bed, and ran quickly to his father, where he slept with the Arhistratig, and called aloud, "My father Abraham, open the door quickly, so that I may enter and cling to thy neck, and kiss thee before they take thee away from me."

18. And Abraham got up and opened the door. And Isaac entered, and he embraced his father, and wept aloud; and Abraham wept also; and the Arhistratig seeing this, wept with them. And Abraham said to Isaac, " My dear child, tell me truly what has appeared to thee, so that thou camest so frightened to me ? "

---

ce pas la patul tău de te odihnești, ca să nu cădem greu acestuĭ strein. Atunce Isac priimi blagovenie tătăni-său și s'au dus la patul luĭ di s'au odihnit.

17. Și au aruncat (I. arătat) Dumnezău spre Isac aducere-aminte de moarte tătăne-său într'un vis. Și după al triile cĭas să deșteptă Isacu din somnu, și să sculă din pat și mărsă tare la tatăl său unde dormie cu Arhistratigul, și strigă tare: tătă Avraame! deschide-mĭ curănd ușa să întru, ca să mă spănzuru de grumazăĭ tăĭ și să te sărut pănă nu te eu de la mine!

18. Și să sculă [Avraam] de-i deschisă ușa și întră Isac, și să apucă de grumazăĭ tătăne-său și începu a plânge tare cu glas; și plânge și Avraam; și văzu și Arhistratigul Mihail și plănsă și el cu eĭ. Deci zăsă Avraam luĭ Isacu: fiiul mĭeu cel drag! Spune-mĭ cu adevărat, ce ți s'au părut și aĭ venit la noĭ așa înspăĭmăntat?

19. And Isaac wept, and said to his father, 'I beheld the sun and the moon, with luminous and far-stretching rays, resting on my head, and seeing this I was glad; when suddenly the heaven opened and a luminous man descended from heaven. And he was brilliant. And he removed the sun from my head and ascended to heaven. And shortly afterwards, while I was still sad, I saw the luminous man again descending from heaven, and he removed the moon from my head. And I wept, and I said to him, " do not take from me my pride, but have pity on me and listen to me, for thou hast taken the sun from me. Do not also take away the moon!' And he replied, 'Let them go, because the Lord of heaven wishes that I should bring them to him.' And they left their rays upon me."

20. And the Arhistratig said to them, " Listen to me, oh Abraham the just! Thou art the sun, seen by thy son Isaac his father; and the luminous man, descending from heaven, will take away thy soul. And know, oh just Abraham! that

---

19. Şi începu a plănge Isac şi a spune tătăne-său : Eu am văzut soarile di-asupra mea şi lumina (l. luna) cu razăle reşchirate şi luminate; iară eu unde le videm mă vesălem. Şi văzuïu ceriul că să deşchisă şi un bărbat prè-luminat să pogorăe din ceriu şi era strălucit; şi-mï luă soarele din cap şi să sui în ceriu. Şi după puţină vremi—încă eram jălnic—şi iară văzuïu pre acel bărbat luminat pogorăndu-să din ceriu şi-m luâ luna din cap; şi am plănsu mult şi m'am rugat : să nu-m ei şi slava mea dela mine, ce mă milueşti şi ascultă, de mi-aï luat soarile, nu-m lua şi luna. Iară el mi-au zăs : " Lasă tu să margă, că va împăratul de sus să-i ducă pre dănşiï acolo." Şi razăle [b. lor le lăsară] pre miní.

20. Iară Arhistratigul zăsă cătră ei : ascultă, drepte Avraami! soarile care au văzut fiïul tău, eşti [tu] tatăl luï ; iară bărbatul luminat ce s'au pogorăt din ceriu, aciala va să-ţi iai sufletul. Şi să ştiï părinte, cinstite Avraami, în

thou wilt soon leave this world to go to the Lord." And
Abraham replied, "Oh wonderful! I fear thou art the man
who will take away my soul!" And the Arhistratig said to
Abraham, "I am the angel *Mihail*, the greatest of the angels
standing before the Lord; and I announce to thee the news
of thy death. And thou wilt come to Him, according to thy
covenant." And Abraham replied, "Now I understand that
thou art he who will receive my soul—but I will not yield
to thee!"

21. After these words of Abraham, the Arhistratig disappeared; for he went up to heaven and stood before the
Lord, and related to him all that he had seen and heard in
the house of Abraham, and how Abraham had said, "I will
not yield to thee."

22. And the Lord replied to his Arhistratig, "Go to my
friend Abraham, and say to him as follows: I am the Lord
his God, who brought him out 'and led him to the Promised
Land; and I have blessed him, so that his descendants shall
become as numerous as the sands of the sea, and as the
stars in the heaven. And say to him, How hast thou dared

---

vreme acĭasta veĭ să părăsăștĭ lumè [acĭasta] și spre Domnul
veĭ mergi. Zăsă Avraam: O minune mare! că (l. eu) mă
tem că tu eștĭ cela ce veĭ să-m eĭ sufletul de la mine. Zăsă
Arhistratigul cătră Avraam: eu sănt Mihail îngerul, maĭ
marile îngerilor ce stau înnaintè Domnuluĭ și spuĭu adevărat
vestè morțiĭ, și să mergi spre el cum te-i făgăduit luĭ. Și
zăsă Avraăm: acum mă pricep că tu eștĭ cela ce-mĭ vrei
să-m priĭmeștĭ sufletul. Că nu-țĭ voĭu muri (l. c. prestăni!).

21. Iară Arhistratigul după cuvăntul luĭ Avraam numaĭ
de cât nu să maĭ văzu, că să sui în cerĭu și stătu înnaintè
Domnuluĭ, și-i spusă toate [ce] văzusă și auzăsă în casa luĭ
Avraam: că miĭe mi-au zăs că nu-m va prestăni!

22. Zăsă Domnul cătră Arhistratigul său: pas la prietinul
mĭeu Avraam și-i spune așa: că eu săntu Domnul Dumnezăul
luĭ, cĭala ce l'am scos de l'am dus în pămăntul cel poroncit
și l'am blagoslovit pre el să să îmmulțască sămănța luĭ ca
stelile cerĭuluĭ și ca năsăpul mărĭĭ! Și-i ză: căce aĭ înfruntat

to oppose my Arhistratig Mihail, by saying that thou wouldst
not follow him? "Does he not know that from the time of
Adam and Eve all have died? That neither the kings, nor the
forefathers have escaped death? because no one is immortal;
but all have died and have gone down into hell. But to him
I did not send either death, or sickness, or the scythe of
death, which should mow him down; but I sent to him my
Arhistratig, with a request, so that he might know my
decision and put his house and lands in order. But why did
he oppose my Arhistratig Mihail, saying that he would not
follow? Does he not know, that I will send the angel of
death, whose presence he could not endure?"

23. After receiving the command of the Lord, the Arhistratig descended to Abraham, fell at his feet, and repeated to
him all that he had heard from the Lord. And Abraham the
just said amidst many tears, "I entreat thee, Arhistratig of
the heavenly powers, because thou had honoured me, a
sinner, grant me one request. For the Lord God has always

---

pre Arhistratigul mĭeu Mihail [*b.* şi aĭ zis, că nu veĭ pristă-
nĭ]? Dar [nu] ştie, că dela Adam şi dela Eva toţi au murit
şi nimine din împăraţi sau din părinţi n'au fugit de moarte,
şi nu este nimene fără de moarte; ce toţi au murit şi toţi în
iad s'au schimbat (1. scoborăt)! Iară la el n'am trimes moarte
sau boală, nicĭ n'am trimes coasa morţiĭ să-l întimpine, ce cu
rugăcĭune al mieu Arhistratig l'am trimes, ca să să pricĭapă
cum iaste a luĭ stare, să-şi facă casăĭ bunătate şi moşiilor
tocmală. Dar căcĭ au înfruntat pre Arhistratigul mĭeu de
au zăs, că nu-i va prestăni? Dar nu ştie că voĭu trimete pre
moarti de nu o va putè răbda?

23. Adică priimi Arhistratigul poronca Susuluĭ şi s'au
pogorăt la Avraam, şi marsă de-i căzu la picĭoare şi-i spusă
toate ci-au auzăt de la Domnul. Atuncĭ îĭ zăsă dreptul
Avraam cu multe lacrămĭ: rogu-te Arhistratije al puterilor
celor de sus; însă de vreme ce pre mine m'aĭ învrednicit,
pre mine păcătosul, rogu-te să'mĭ posluşeşti de un cuvănt;
că la Domnul Dumnezău ce am cerut întru tot lucru mi-au

given me the things for which I have prayed, and has always fulfilled my wishes. And I know that I shall not escape death, but I shall certainly die. Know, therefore, that I expect that thou wilt fulfil this my request: I should like to see now, whilst still in the flesh, all the peoples and their deeds; then I will yield myself entirely."

24. And the Arhistratig ascended once more to heaven, and placed himself before the Lord, and told him all about Abraham. And the Lord replied to the Arhistratig, "Place Abraham the just in the chariot of the cherubim, and carry him to heaven." And the Arhistratig descended and took the just Abraham into the clouds and surrounded him with sixty angels.

25. And Abraham walked on the clouds, and he beheld another chariot behind him, and also some who walked (?). And in another part he saw people who were suffering, and much wrong-doing. And he said, "Oh Lord! command that the earth may open and swallow them." And in another

---

dat, şi toată pofta mĭ-au înplinit; şi eu ştĭu că fără de moarte nu voĭu să fĭu ce tot voĭu să morĭu; ce să ştiĭ ce voĭu să-ţĭ poruncescu, mă ascultă Doamne: oare întru aceste vremi de acum cu trupul va să mă vază (l. b. putea voĭu să văz) norodul şi faptele meale (l. lor)? Decĭ atunce mă voĭu pune (l. supune) întru averè (mea).

24. Şi ĭară să suĭ Arhistratigul în cerĭu şi stătu înnainte Domnuluĭ, şi-i spusă atunce (l. aceste toate b.) de Avraam. Iară Dumnezău zăsă Arhistratiguluĭ: prĭimeşti pre dreptul Avraam în carul Heruvimilor şi-l înnalţă în cerĭu pre el. Şi să pogoră Arhistratigul; şi luară pre dreptul Avraam întru noorĭ cu 60 de îngerĭ.

25. Şi mergè Avraam pre di-asupra noriloru, şi văzu şi alt caru într'altă parte umbländ pre di-asupra, şi pedestri; şi văzu într'altă partè şăzänd alţii (oameni) muncindu-să. Şi au văzut multă fără de-cale făcăndu-să, şi zăsă: Doamne, Doamne! poronceşti să să disfacă pămăntul şi să între acie!

direction he saw people plundering and stealing, and despoiling the stranger. And he exclaimed, " Oh Lord! command that fire shall come down from heaven and destroy them.' And fire came from heaven and consumed them.

26. And instantly there a voice came from heaven to the angels, and a thunder-clap reached the Arhistratig and he heard the words : " Turn round the chariot and depart with Abraham so that he may not see the people any more ; for if he sees them living in sin he will destroy them all to the very last," because Abraham could not endure those who did evil. And the Lord continued: "I have created the world, and I do not wish that any human being shall be destroyed, for I do not desire the death of the wicked, but that he should repent and live. Lead the just Abraham to the first gate of heaven, so that he may see the last judgment, and that he also may repent even more than the sinners."

27. And the Arhistratig turned round Abraham's chariot, and brought him to the first gate of heaven. And Abraham

---

Şi văzu şi într'altă parte bărbaţi jăfuind şi furănd din casă şi răpind pre streini, şi zăsă : Doamne, Doamne ! poronceşti să vie foc din ceriu ca să arză pre acie ! Şi numai decăt [b. veni foc din ceriu, şi-i arse pre toţi.

26. Şi făcăndu-se acĭasta, numaĭ decăt] veni glas [din ceriu] cătră Arhistratigul său, de-i zăsă : întoarce carul de du pre Avraam, ca să nu maĭ vază norodul tot, că-i va vidè pre toţi în păcate chinuindu-să şi-i va pĭerdi pre toţi pănă în sfărşit. Adică Avraam prè ceĭ ce-i vidè greşind nu-i suferè. Şi zăsă Dumnezău: Eu am făcut lumè şi nu voĭu nicĭ unul dintr'ănşiĭ să nu pĭară; şi nu voĭu moartè păcătosuluĭ, ce ca să să întoarcă şi să fie viu. Ce scoate pre dreptul Avraam pre uşa ceriuluĭ cè dintăĭ, ca să vază judecata cè de apoĭ, ca să să căĭască maĭ mult decăt păcătoşiĭ.

27. Intors-au Arhistratigul carul cu Avraam, de l'au dus la poarta cè dintăĭ a ceriuluĭ; şi văzu Avraam doâ căĭ: una

beheld two paths, one narrow and difficult to pursue, and the
other wide and extended. And on the narrow path he saw
a man sitting on a golden chair, and his face was terrible
like unto God. And he saw many souls pursued by angels
on the broad way, and but few souls conducted by the
angels on the narrow path. And the marvellous man, when
he saw all the wounded and sick souls on the wide way,
tore out the hair of his head and of his beard, and he cast
himself from his golden chair unto the ground and wept.
But when he saw many souls in the narrow path, he rose and
sat on his golden chair in joy.

28. And Abraham asked the Arhistratig: "Lord! who is
this marvellous man in such splendour? Sometimes he weeps,
and sometimes he rejoices." The Arhistratig answered:
"This is Adam, who was the first man created to adorn the
world, for all are descended from him. And when he sees
many souls traversing the narrow path he rejoices, because
that is the entrance to heaven, by which the just go to

---

strămtă şi cu anevoi a umbla pre dânsa şi alta lată şi întinsă.
Şi despre cale ce strămtă văzu un bărbat şăzănd pre un
scaun poliit şi faţa lui înfricoşată. [b. Şi văzu multe suflete
rănite (l. goniťe) de îngeri despre calea cea largă, şi văzu alte
suflete mai puţine aducându-le îngerii pre calea cea strimtă]
fără grigi. Dar acel ciudat bărbat [b. când] vide multe suflete
rănite şi betegi pre cale ce largă, iară el să apucă de păr şi de
barbă cu măinile de să zmulge şi să trănťie pre pământ din
giulgiul (l. jeţul b.) cel poliit plăngănd; şi cănd vide suflete
multe venind pre cale ce strimtă, să scula şi şăde în jălţul cu
multă vesălie şi bucurie.

28. Şi întrebă Avraam pre Arhistratigul: Doamne! cine
este acestu bărbat pre ciudat, întru atăta slăvire? Că uni-ori
plănge, iară alte ori să vesăleşti? Zăsă Arhistratigul: acista
este Adam, cel întăi zădit întru slava lumii; că toţi din el s'au
născut; ce cănd vede multe suflete întrănd pre cale ce strămtă,
atunce să bucură si să vesăleşti, că aceia este uşa ceriului

paradise. And when he sees many souls going on the wide
way he weeps and tears his hair, because that is the path of
the sinners, by which they go to hell. In seven thousand
years only one soul will be saved."

29. And while they were speaking, two angels brought
innumerable souls, and struck them with a whip of fire; and
one‚poor soul was supported by their hands and led on the
narrow way.

30. And he beheld again at the doorway a golden chair,
shining like fire; and on it there sat a man in the form of the
Son of God. And in front of him stood a table of precious
stones and pearls; and upon the table there lay a Bible, that
is a big book of twelve yards in length, and eight yards in
width. And there were two angels holding paper, ink, and
pens. And at the head of the table there sat a luminous
angel‑holding a scale in his hand; and at his left hand stood
an angel of fire, who held in his`hand a paper, and on it were
inscribed the temptations and sins. And that man who sat

[în] care întră drepţiĭ şi întră în raĭu. Şi cănd vede multe
suflete întrănd şi mergănd pre calè cè largă, el plănge şi să
smulge de păr; că aceea este calè păcătoşilor, care mergi în
ĭad. În cele şapte miĭ de anĭ numaĭ un suflet să va spăsi!

29. Şi grăind eĭ, ĭată doĭ îngerĭ aducè bătănd suflete
multe fără de samă cu biciul [*b*. de foc], şi pre un suflet, cu
milă îl ţinè între măĭnile lor, şi'l îndrepta spre calè cè
strămtă.

30. Şi au stătut de au văzut în mijlocul uşiĭ era un înger
(l. jeţ) înfricoşat de strălucie ca focul, şi şidè un bărbat în
chipul fiĭuluĭ luĭ Dumnezău, şi sta înnaintè luĭ [o] masă de
pietre scumpe şi de mărgăritarĭurĭ, şi pre masă o blibie, adică
o carte groasă de doĭsprezăci coţi de lungă, de optu coţi de
lată; şi sta doáĭ îngerĭ şi ţinè hărtie şi cerneală şi condeĭu.
Şi în capul mesăĭ şidè un înger prè-luminat şi avè în măna luĭ
cumpănă; şi di-a-stănga luĭ stan (l. sta un înger) de foc fără
milă, şi în măna luĭ ţinè o hărtie de carte, şi într'ănsa era
ispitele păcatelor. Şi un bărbat şidè de (l. *c* Şi bărbatul cel

there condemned or liberated the souls. And of the two angels who stood to the right and left, the one on the right wrote the virtues, and the one on the left hand wrote down the sins; and the one at the head of the table weighed the souls; and the angel of fire examined the souls.

31. And Abraham asked the Arhistratig: "What is it that I see?" And the angel replied, "That, which thou seest, oh just Abraham, is the judgment in the other world." And he saw the soul of a man brought before the judge by an angel. And the angel said to the judge, "Open the book and see the record of his sins and of his virtues .... and erase them, for he is neither to be condemned nor to be saved; therefore place him in the middle."

32. And Abraham said, "My lord! who are these judges, and these luminous angels?" And the Arhistratig replied, "Listen, oh just Abraham! He who sits in the chair and judges, is *Abel*, the son of Adam. He judges the righteous and the sinners. For the Lord hath said, that He will not

---

ce şedea în jeţ) giudeca şi lăsa sufletele; şi cei doi îngeri ce era unul di a stănga şi altulu de dreapta, [cel de a dreapta] scriè bunătăţile, iar cel di a stănga scriè păcatile; iară cel ce şidè în capul mesăi cumpăniè sufletile; [iară] îngerul cel de foc ispitiè sufletile.

31. Şi întrebă Avraam pre Arhistratigul: [*b*. ce sânt acestea ce văzuiu]? Iară îngerul zăsă: aceste ce vezi drepte Avraami, aciasta iaste giudecata lumii cè de apoi. [*b*. Şi văzu] adică un înger [ce] ţinè un suflet de om în măna lui, şi-l adusă înnaintè giudecătoriului. Şi zăsă giudecătoriul: deşchide cartè, de-i află păcatele şi dreptele, de-i le rade, că nu-i nici de păcat nici de mântuire, ce-l pune în mijloc!

32. Şi zăsă Avraam: Domnul mieu, Arhistratiji! cine este acest giudecători? şi aceşti îngeri ce luminează? Şi zăsă Arhistratigul: Auzi, drepte Avraami! acesta ce şăde în iălţul de judecă este Avel, fiiul lui Adam, carile judecă dreptii şi păcatoşii. Că au zăs Domnul că el nu va judeca

judge mankind, but that they shall judge each other. And to him (Abel) he has given the power to judge men, till the last judgment. Then the Son of God will judge perfectly and finally and for ever; and no other will be able to judge. Because men are descended from Adam, they must be first judged by a son of Adam; but at the second resurrection they will all be judged by the twelve Apostles; but at the third resurrection, our Lord and Saviour will judge them. For at the third time, at that terrible judgment, all will be ended. As it is written, 'By three witnesses shall the judgment be fulfilled.' And of the two angels the angel on the left records the evil deeds, and the angel on the right records the good actions; and he shines like the sun."

33. And Abraham asked his Arhistratig Mihail, "My lord! what is to be done with the soul which the angel brought in his hand, and which was placed in the middle?" The angel answered, "The judge has found that his good and his bad deeds shall be erased, and he is neither condemned nor saved, until the Lord, the Judge, shall come."

---

pre oameni, ce oameni să judece; şi au dat luĭ putere ca să judece pănă la vremè de apoi. Decĭ atunce va judeca fiĭul luĭ Dumnezău, Hs., desăvărşit şi de isprăvit şi de vecĭ; decĭ (l. căcĭ) nu va putè judeca nimine. Că toţĭ oameniĭ din Adam s'au născut, pentru aceea fiĭul luĭ Adam judecă întăĭ; iară la adouă învieri să va judeca de doisprăzăcĭ apostolĭ, tot norodul; iară a trie oară va judeca stăpănul Hs. şi măntuitoriul nostru Dumnezău. Decĭ tocma atunce a trie oară la acè înfricoşată judecată să va sfărşi, cum închipueşti: de triĭ marturi să astupă judecata. Iară ceĭ doĭ îngeri: cel di-a stănga scrie păcatele [iar cel de-a dreapta scrie] dreptăţile şi luminează ca soarele.

33. Şi iară zăsă Avraam cătră Arhistratigul său Mihail: Domnul mĭeu! sufletul cel ce l'au adus [b. îngerul] în măna luĭ, cum să judecă, de-l pus(ără) în mijloc? Zăsă îngerul, că aşa au aflat giudecătoriul păcatele luĭ şi dreptatè luĭ, să le şteargă, că nu l'au dat nicĭ la muncă nicĭ la drepţĭ, pănă va veni judecătoriul Dumnezău.

34. And Abraham asked, " What is wanting to this soul that it should be saved ? " The angel answered, " If he had performed one more good deed, he would had been saved." And Abraham said, " We will say a prayer for this soul, perhaps God will save it ! " And the Arhistratig said, " Amen ! so shall it be ! " And they both prayed, and God listened to them and saved this soul. And Abraham said, " I pray thee, Arhistratig, tell me where is the soul ? " And the angel answered, " It hath been saved, in answer to the prayer of thy holiness ! "

35. And Abraham said, " Oh, Arhistratig, let us entreat God for the sins of those whom I cursed before ! " And the Arhistratig listened to him, and they prayed for a long time, until there came a voice from heaven, saying, " Abraham ! I have heard thy prayer for those whom it appeared to thee that I destroyed. But I have saved them, and have preserved them alive. At the last judgment I will separate them. For, even if I destroy some on earth, I do not deliver any one entirely to death ; I wish that they may repent and live."

---

34. Zăsă ĭară Avraam : dară ce-i maĭ trebueşti sufletuluĭ acestue, să să mântuĭască ? Zăsă îngerul : numaĭ o dreptate de ar maĭ face să-i prisosască maĭ mult decăt păcatele, să va mântui. Zăsă Avraam : ian să facem o molitfă sufletuluĭ acestuĕ, sa videm, mântui-l-va Dumnezău ? Şi zăsă Arhis-tratiguł : amin ! aşa să fie ! Şi făcură molitfa ; şi ascultă Dumnezău, şi-l mântui pre suflet(ul) acĭala. Şi zăsă Avraam : rogu-mă, Arhistratiji, unde-i sufletul acĭala ? Îngerul zăsă : s'au mântuit pentru a sfinţieĭ tale molitvă.

35. Şi zăsă Avraam : rogu-mă Arhistratiji, ian să ne rugăm luĭ Dumnezău pentru greşalile celora ce i-am blăs-tămat ! Şi ascultă Arhistratigul, şi făcură rugăciunĭ înnaintĕ luĭ Dumnăzău mult cĭas, pănă veni glas din cerĭu, zăcănd : Avraamĭ ! auzătu-s'au rugăciunĕ ta, că ţ'au părut că i-am pĭerdut pre acie, ce i-am scos [şi] la vĭaţă i-am pus. Că la gĭudecata cĕ de apoĭ le voĭu alegi. Că eu căţi i-am pĭerdut pre pămănt viĭ, ce întru toate (l. c. moarte) nu-i voĭu lăsa [voesc să să întoarcă şi să fie viĭ].

36. And the Lord said to the Arhistratíg, "My servant! Turn the chariot, and take him back to his dwelling, for the end of his life is approaching, and he must put his house in order." And the Arhistratig turned the chariot of clouds and brought him back to his house. And Abraham went and sat on his bed.

37. And Sarah, the wife of Abraham, came and knelt ·at the angel's feet, and kissed them, and wept and thanked him, saying, "I thank thee, that thou hast brought back my lord, for it seemed to me, that he had withdrawn himself from our midst." And Isaac came and embraced his father; the servants also came and surrounded Abraham, thanking and blessing God.

38. And the Arhistratig said to Abraham, " Set thy house in order, and settle all with thy servants which concerns them; for thy last day draws near, when thy soul will depart from thy body; because the Lord has ordered it so, and He is just." And Abraham replied to the Arhistratig, "I will not obey thee!"

---

36. Zăsă Domnul Arhistratigului : slujitoriule! întoarce carul de-l du [la casa luĭ], că să apropie sfârșitul vieții luĭ, ce să 'și tocmască toate ale luĭ. Și întoarsă Arhistratigul carul cu noori și l'au dus la casă luĭ; și au mersu [Avraam] de au șăzut în patul luĭ.

37. Și vini Sara, muerea luĭ, și căzu la picĭoarele îngeruluĭ, de i le sărută, și plăngè și mulțămè zăcănd : mulțimescu-ți că încă me-i adus pre domnul mĭeu, că mi-au părut că s'au mutat de la noĭ. Și Isac veni de apucă de grumazi pre tatăl său; așijdire și roabile sta înpregĭurul luĭ Avraam de-i (l. de) mulțimiè și slăvè pre Dumnezău.

38. Și zăsă Arhistratigul cătră Avraam : fă-ți tocmală fecĭorilor și fetilor tale de cele ce le trebuescu, că s'au apropiet vremè zălii cei de apoĭ, aceea ce va să să disparți sufletul de trup. Că așa au zăs stăpânul; drept este! Și zăsă Avraam cătră Arhistratigul : că nu voĭu prestăni !

8*

39. When the Arhistratig heard these words, he ascended at once to heaven, stood before the Lord, and said, "Lord! Sustainer of all! I fulfilled Thy will, and Thy friend Abraham has seen all the earth and the heaven, and whilst still living he beheld the Judgment from the chariot of clouds, and yet he says that he will not obey me. I would willingly give him time, because he has done so much good on the earth that no man is like unto him; he is like an immortal king, and he is worthy of immortality. Oh Lord! what dost Thou command?"

40. And the Lord said, "Call Death hither!" And the Arhistratig Mihail went to Death, and said, "Go, for the Immortal King calls thee." When Death heard this, he trembled and ground his teeth, and went to the Mighty Lord, and stood before Him with much fear and trembling.

41. And the Lord said unto Death, "Go and disguise thy fearful face and thy countenance, and clothe thyself with gentleness and beauty and splendour; and go to My friend

---

39. Iară dacă auzi Arhistratigul, îndată să suĭ în ceriu și stătu înnaintè Domnuluĭ și zăsă: Doamne a-tot-țietoriule! voè ta toată am plinit, și prietinul tău Avraam ceriul și pămăntul au văzut, judecata în noor cu carul vĭu au văzut-o și ĭară zăsă, că nu mi-a prestăni. Eu îĭ dau vremi, că multe bunătăți au făcut pre pămăntu, căt nu este luĭ om asămine pre pămănt; ce-i ca un făr-de-moarte înpărat. Ce vei să fac?

40. Atunce au zăs Domnul: chemați prè moarte încoace! Și marsă Arhistratigul Mihail, și zăsă cătră moarte: pas, că te chĭamă înpăratul cel fără de moarte! Iară moartè auzi și să cutremură, și scărșini cu dințiĭ și marsă înnaintè înpăratuluĭ celuĭ prè puternic și stătu înnaintè luĭ cu multă frică și cutremuru.

41. Și zăsă Domnul: pas moarte de-ți ascunde frica (l. fața) ta cè groznică și cu răcoriala, și cu (l. *b. c.* și-ți ea) blăndețele și frumusățile și slava toată, și pas la prietinul mĭeu

Abraham and receive his soul and bring it to Me; and thou shalt not frighten him, but take it away in all tenderness." When Death heard this, he went away from the presence of the Lord, and changed his fearful countenance, and became gentle and luminous, and of great beauty.

42. And Abraham sat under a sweet smelling tree, resting his hand on his knees, awaiting hopefully the return of the Arhistratig Mihail. And he noticed the approach of a worthy and fine-looking man, and it appeared to him that it was the Arhistratig. And the angel beheld him, and bowed to him, and said, "Rejoice, venerable Abraham, just soul, friend of the Lord, like unto the angels!" And Abraham replied, "Rejoice, shining light, luminous man! From whence has this resplendent man come?"

43. And Death answered, "I tell thee the truth. I am the poison of death!" And Abraham said, "Art thou the cup which poisonest? And art thou he who takest away the life of man and the beauty of woman? Art thou the poison

---

Avraam, şi priimeşti sufletul luĭ, şi-l adă încoace la mine; şi să nu-l spariĭ pre el, ce cu măngăere să-l priimeşti. Aceste auzănd moartè, s'au dus de la faţa Domnuluĭ şi s'au schimbat faţa cè groznică şi s'au făcut cuvioasă şi luminoasă şi cu multă frumsăţă. Şi s'au pogorăt la Avraam.

42. Iară Avraam şidè supt un copacĭu [b. şi acel] pom [b. era] mirosătórĭu, şi'şĭ pusă măinile pre genunchi şi aştepta nedejdè Arhistratiguluĭ Mihail. Şi vini miros de om cătră el cu multă rugăcĭune şi ghizdăvie, că-i părè că este Arhistratigul. Şi-l văzu pre el, şi să închină şi zăsă: bucură-te, cinstite Avraami! drepte suflete, prietin ales a luĭ Dumne-zău şi într'un chip cu îngeriĭ! Şi zăsă Avraam: bucură-te frumsăţa soareluĭ! luminoase bărbat! De unde aĭ (l. a) venit la noĭ acestu bărbat proslăvit?

43. Zăsă moartè cătră Avraam: să ţi spuĭu cu adevărat. Eu sănt toapsecul morţiĭ! Zăsă Avraam: tu eşti [b. c. potirĭul ce otrăveşti, şi eĭ] viaţa oamenilor şi frumsăţa ghizdavilor? Tu eşti otrava morţiĭ? Iară zăsă moartè: eu

of death?" And Death replied, "I am the poisoned cup of death; and I speak unto thee the truth, for thus has the Lord commanded me."

44. And Abraham said, "Why hast thou come hither?" Death replied, "I have come for thy righteous soul." And Abraham said, "I understand! But, I do not wish to die!" And Death was silent, for he would not give any further answer.

45. And Abraham arose and went in and seated himself on his bed. And Death seated himself also on the bed, at the feet of Abraham. And Abraham said, "Depart from me, for I would rest." And Death replied, "I shall not depart from thee until I have taken thy soul." And Abraham said, "Fulfil my wish: show me the bitterness of thy poison when thou takest the souls of mankind." And Death replied, "Thou could'st not in any case bear to see my fearful countenance." And Abraham said, "I will see it; in the Name of the Lord, for He is with me."

46. Then Death cast off all his beauty, and he assumed a fierce and murderous and all-consuming expression, like unto

---

sănt cu adevărat [b. păhariul cu otrava morții]; că așa mi-au poroncit Dumnezău.

44. Zăsă Avraam: cum, în ce chip aĭ venit aicè? Iară moartè zăsă: pentru dreptul sufletul tău am venit. Zăsă Avraam: înțăleg ce zăcĭ; ce nu-ți voĭu muri! Iară moartè tăcu și n'au maĭ vrut să maĭ răspunză nimică.

45. Iară Avraam să sculă [și]marsă de să sui în patul luĭ. Și să sui și moartè cu el îm pat, și șăzu despre picĭoarele luĭ Avraam. Și zăsă Avraam: du-te de la mine, că voĭu să mă odihnesc. Zăsă moarte: nu mă voĭu dizlipi de tine până nu ți voĭu priimi sufletul. Iar Avraam zăsă: rogu-mă să mă ascult de ce te voĭu întreba: arată-mĭ amarul otrăvilor tale când eĭ sufletile oamenilor! Și zăsă moartè: că nu veĭ putè răbda nicĭ într'un chip groaza mè. Iar Avraam zăsă: putè-voĭu răbda, cu numile luĭ Dumnezău, că cu mine este!

46. Atunce moartè ș'au lepădat frumsăța sa și să făcu cu podoabă tălhărĭască, groznică și cu fața sorbitoare și cu de

the wild beasts; and (he assumed) a dragon's head with seven faces, and his countenance was as seventeen fiery faces; and he became like unto a fierce and dreadful lion and like a poisonous snake, and he had a mane like a lion, and he was like a thunderbolt, and like the waves of the sea, and like the stream of a rapid torrent, and like a very wild dragon with three wings. And from the fear of Death, seven thousand boys and girls died, and even Abraham the just was in danger of his life.

47. All this Abraham saw, and he said to Death, "I pray thee, poisonous Death, hide thy fearful countenance, and appear in thy former beauty." And Death resumed his former beauty. And Abraham said, "What hast thou done to kill so many souls? Hast thou been sent to kill them also?" And Death replied, "No, my lord! I was sent only on thy account."

48. Abraham said, "Indeed? How could'st thou kill them when the Lord did not command thee to do it?"

---

toate necurăție și ca de toate jiganiile sălbatece: cu capul ca de leu (l. c. zmeu) în șapte chipuri și fața în șaptesprezăce feță de foc; și ca de leu viclean și grozav, și [ca] aspide iuți și ca de leu la coadă (l. c. coamă) și ca o armă de foc cu tunet, și ca un val de mare și ca o vale de apă ce vine răpide și ca un zmău cu trii aripi ci este foarte sălbatec. Deci atunci au murit de groaza morții feți și fete 7 mii; si dreptul Avraam au venitu în cumpăna morții.

47. Aciasta au văzut dreptul Avraam și au zăs cătră moarte: rogu-mă moarte otrăvitoare! ascunde-ți toată groaza ta, și-ți ivești frumsățile tale. Și 'și au luat[moarte] frumsățile cele dintăi. Și au zăs Avraam cătră moarte: ce ai făcut de ai omorâtu atâte suflete? au doară ti-au trimes să-i omori pre aceștie? Zăsă iar moartè: bà, domnul mieu! ce pentru tine m'au trimes aice.

48. Și au zăs Avraam: adevărat! cum i-ai ucis pre acești de i-ai omorât și nu ț'au zăs Domnul! Și zăsă moarte ·

And Death answered, "Believe me, my lord, it is a wonder thou did'st not die with them. But I swear to thee in very truth, that I have in this hour the power of killing thee, and thy strength will not avail thee. Therefore put in order all that thou wishest to arrange."

49. And Abraham said, "I acknowledge now that the weakness of death is upon me, and my soul grows faint. But, I pray thee, oh poisonous Death to tell me, why hast thou killed so many boys and girls? Let us now both entreat the Lord to restore these boys and girls to life, and perchance He may listen to us." And Death said, "Amen! so may it be." And Abraham arose and threw himself on the ground on his face, and Death also cast himself on the ground; and they both prayed to God for a long time. And God sent the spirit of life unto the dead, and they were restored to life again.

50. And Abraham returned thanks unto God, and went to his bed. Death also went to the bed. And Abraham said to Death, "Depart from me; I would rest, for soon thou wilt take away my soul." And Death replied, "I will not leave

---

să mă crezĭ doamne, că mare minune este că nu te-i răpit şi tu cu eĭ. Şi eu îţi zăc cu gĭurămănt cu adevărat, că dreapta morţiĭ cu mine este într'acel cĭas, şi nu-ţĭ va folosă averè acĭasta; ce-ţĭ tocmeşti ce aĭ a tocmi.

49. Iară dreptul Avraam zăsă: cunosc acuma că aĭ (l. c am) venit în ameţala morţiĭ pănă am leşăn sufletuluĭ mĭeu; ce mă rog, toapsecul morţiĭ, cum făcuşĭ de omorăş atăţa feţĭ şi fete? ce vină să ne rugăm amăndoĭ luĭ Dumnezău, doară ne va asculta de vor învĭè aceştĭ feţĭ şi fete? Şi zăsă moartè: amin să fie! Şi să sculă Avraam şi căzu cu faţa la pămănt; şi căzu şi moartè cu faţă la pămănt, şi să rugă mult spre Dumnezău. Şi trimĭsă Dumnezău duhul vieţiĭ spre cĭi morţĭ şi au înviet.

50. Atunce dreptul Avraam au datu slavă luĭ Dumnezău. Şi s'au suit Avraam ĭarăşi în pat de au şăzut; şi au şăzut şi moartè cu el. Şi zăsă Avraam cătră moarte: du-te de la mine, că voĭu să mă odihnesc, si curănd vra să-mĭ eĭ sufletul

thee, until I shall have taken thy soul." And the patriarch Abraham became cross with him, and spoke angry words, and said unto Death, "Who has sent thee to me? Dost thou really believe that I will die?" And Abraham repeated again, "I will not follow thee."

51. And Death said, "Listen to me, oh, just Abraham! In seven epochs I shall destroy the whole world, and I shall cause all human beings and kings to go down into the earth, and to descend into hell; the kings, princes, rich and poor, old and young. Therefore I have shown thee the seven heads of a lion and the fiery faces, so that thou mayest arrange thy property and leave everything in order."

52. And Abraham said, "Depart from me, for I will see, if having the favour of God, I must still die, as thou doest demand of me!" And Death said, "I tell thee the truth, by God, there are seventy-two kinds of death, and I mow whomsoever I like; put therefore away thy doubts, oh just Abraham, and obey me, according to the will of the Universal Judge!" And Abraham said, "Depart from me for a while,

---

de la mine. Zăsă moarte: că nu mă voĭu dĭspărţi de tine până nu-ţ voĭu lua sufletul. Şi părintele Avraam l'au înfruntat cu mănie şi cu cuvinte posomorăte, şi zăsă cătră moarte: O cine tĭ-au trimes la mine? au doară zăcĭ, că voĭu muri? Şi ĭarăşi zăsă Avraam: că nu-ţĭ voĭu prestăni!

51. Şi zăsă moarte: ascultă drepte Avraami! în şapte veacurĭ voĭu să potopăsc toată lume, şi pre toţĭ oamenĭĭ, şi pre toţĭ înpăraţĭĭ, şi pre toţĭ în pămănt voĭu să i puĭu şi să i pogor, înparaţĭĭ, domnĭ, bogaţĭ şi săracĭ, bătrănĭĭ şi tinerĭĭ. Pentru acĭasta ţi-am arătat şapte capete de zmău şi obrazi de foc. Pentru [aceea] să-ţĭ tocmeşti averè ta să o laş cu ispravă, ca să-ţi tocmeşti casa şi bucatile.

52. Şi zăsă Avraam: du-te de la mine şi mă lasă: cu darul luĭ Dumnezău vom vidè oare a morţĭĭ sănt? [c. Zise (moartè) luĭ: amin zicu-ţi, cu adevărul luĭ Dumnezeu şapte-zăcĭ şi doao morţĭ sănt, toate căte voĭu vrea săcer] iată că-ţĭ zăcu drepte Avraamè, lasă-ţĭ toate cugitile tale şi vin-o de prestăneşti, precum este voè judecătorĭuluĭ tuturor. Zăsă Avraam: pas

so that I may rest for a time on my bed; for I have lost all
strength since mine eyes have beheld thee; all parts of my
body are weak, my head is heavy as lead, and my spirit is
trembling within me, so that I can no longer see thy face."

53. And Isaac came and cried bitterly; and all the
servants gathered him and cried bitterly. And Abraham
arose and set free all his servants and his maids. And he
called his beloved son Isaac, and kissed him tenderly, and
blessed him with the father's blessing. And he blessed his
wife Sarah, and he took leave of her and of all.

54. And the hour of his death approached; and Death
said to Abraham, "Come and kiss my right hand, so that
thou mayest revive for a while." And Abraham was deceived,
and kissed the hand of Death. But Death, when he gave
him his hand, gave him also the cup with the poison of death.
And at the same moment the Arhistratig Mihail. and numberless angels came and received in their holy hands the pure
and holy soul, and brought into the holy hands of the Lord's.

---

de la mine puținel, doară aș odihni ceva în patul mĭeu, că am
săcat decând ti-am văzut cu ochiĭ meĭ; vărtutè mi-au săcat
în (l. din) toate părțile trupuluĭ mĭeu, capul mi s'au îngreuet
ca plumbul și duhul mĭeu să bată în pieptul (mĭeu), căcĭ nu
pocĭu să-țĭ văz fața ta.

53. Și vini Isac, fiĭul luĭ Avraam, văĭtându-să cu amar, și
toțĭ au venit și roabile înpregĭur luĭ plăngând cu amar. Și
să sculă de-și ertă robiĭ (b și roabele) să fie slobozie. Și chiemă
pre fiĭul său Isaac cel drag de-l sărută dulce și-l blagoslovi cu
blagoslovenie părintească. Și pre Sara soțiea luĭ așijderea o
blagoslovi și o ertă, și de la toțĭ îșĭ luă ertăcĭune.

54. Și să apropiè cĭasul de moarte. Și zise moartea luĭ
Avraam: vin-o de-mĭ sărută mâna cea dreaptă, și-țĭ va maĭ
veni suflet și vieață! Și să înșălă Avraam de merse de-i
sărută mâna morțiĭ. Iară moartea cănd întinse mâna de-i
sărută Avraam, întinse și păharul cu otrava morțiĭ. Și numaĭ
decât stătu Arhanghelul Mihail cu mulțime de îngerĭ, și
apucară cinstitul și prea sfântul suflet în mâĭnile lor cele
sfinte și-l duseră în sfintele mâĭnĭ ale. luĭ Dumnezeu.

55. But the body was enveloped in clean and pure linen, and they sprinkled him with heavenly perfumes, and buried him with many heavenly songs. And all wept and lamented greatly. Isaac his beloved son, and Sarah, the mother of Isaac, and his servants, and his maids, and all his neighbours lamented for him, because they had lost their good and blessed father Abraham.

56. And they buried him in "Dria the black," with many hymns and with great honour. And they heard the voice of the Lord saying from heaven, "Take My friend Abraham and lead him into the paradise of joy, the abode of all the righteous; and to the eternal life, which is everlasting and without end."

*   *   *   *   *

There follows here a short "moralizatio," which has no bearing on the text itself, and which I therefore omit.

---

55. Iar trupul l'au învălit cu cĭarşafurĭ frumoase şi curate l au gătit; şi cu multe miroseniĭ dumnezeeştĭ l'au tămăeat, şi cu multe cântărĭ dumnezeeştĭ l'au îngropat [c. în Driea cea neagră], toţĭ plângându-l cu multi jale, Isaac fiĭul său cel ĭubit, şi Sara muma luĭ Isaac, şi toţĭ robiĭ şi roabele, şi toţĭ veciniĭ foarte cu jale l'au plâns, căcĭ să lipsise de bunul şi blagoslovitul părinte Avraam.

56. Şi cu multe glasurĭ de cântărĭ Dumnezeeştĭ şi cu mare cinste l'au îngropat la Diea cea neagră. Şi auziră glas din cer zicând Domnul Dumnezeu: luaţĭ prietenul mĭeu Avraam, de-l duceţĭ în raĭul desfătăriĭ, unde sânt toţĭ drepţiĭ, în vieaţa de vecĭ, cĭa netrecută şi fără sfârşit.

*   *   *   *   *

Decĭ şi noĭ ĭubiţilor mĭeĭ dragĭ şi pravoslavnicilor creştinĭ! veciniĭ, părinţiĭ noştri să cinstim, călătoriĭ streinĭ să-i priimim în casele noastre şi să-i ospătăm cu toată dragoste, bolnaviĭ să-i căutăm, pre ceĭ goĭ să-i înbrăcăm, celor flămânzĭ să le dăm de mâncare, pre setoşĭ să-i adăpăm, şi să urmăm întru toate faptele cele bune; ca să ne învrednicească Domnul Dumnezeu să dobândim şi noĭ vĭeaţa veaculuĭ ce va să fie, şi să slăvim pre tatăl şi pre fiĭul şi pre stântul duh Dumnezeu. Că a luĭ ĭaste înpărăţiea şi puterea în veciĭ vecilor. Amin.

Art XV.—*Hebrew Visions of Hell and Paradise.* By M. Gaster, Ph.D.

The recent recovery of the Revelation of St. Peter has again attracted attention to this branch of apocalyptic literature. Speculation has been rife as to the sources of that Revelation.

I intend publishing now, for the first time in English garb, the oldest extant Revelations which must have served as source to that of Peter, then to that of Paul, Ezra, Abraham, Isaiah, Virgin Mary, St. Macarius, and the host of others down to Dante and St. Patrick.

It is not here the place to enter into a more minute disquisition of the history of these visions. We find parallels in the old Ægyptian literature, in the Assyrian we have the well-known "Descensus ad inferos" of Izdubar (Nimrud). The Buddhist literature knows the Suhṛllekha, the letter of Nāgārjuna to King Udayana. In the Avesta literature we have the Nameh of Arda-viraf; in the Mahommedan we have the vision of Mahommed. All these Christian Revelations and of the others, at any rate the last two, are based directly upon those Hebrew visions, a fact which has hitherto not been noticed.

I reserve for a book, which I am writing, the fuller discussion of these points, and the study of the internal connection between these apocalyptic visions.

It would be bold to speculate on the relative age of each of the visions which I publish here. They all go back to the pre-Christian age, as is shown by the existence of those Christian visions almost verbally identical with the Hebrew. On the other hand one cannot doubt that they underwent some changes in the course of the ages. The substance remained intact, but many passages were interpolated or omitted. The different texts complement thus each other to assist us to arrive at a probable common source. The tendency of all these popular writings is to grow in the course of time, to attract and to assimilate various elements. We can see this process very clearly in the Revelation of Moses, which has been hitherto almost unknown. It has nothing in common with those known under that title. We have two recensions of it. A shorter one, and a longer which is more amplified and contains interpolations taken from the Zohar and the Talmud. Whether the biblical passages belonged originally to these visions is still a matter of doubt. They may have been tacked on to the narrative as a kind of scriptural proof, or they may stand as the beginning of a series of details and pictures which have been evolved out of them, by a rather fantastical exegesis, but by no means uncommon in the Oriental literature.

To each text I have added a full bibliography, and parallels from most of the extant apocryphal revelations. I have striven to be as literal as possible. The attempt to obliterate the Oriental touch by a polished translation, robs the text of its originality and local colour, which ought to be preserved.

I. The Revelation of Moses. (A.)

Heaven, Hell, and Paradise.

(*Gedulath Mosheh*, Amsterdam, 1854, v. Jellinek, Beth-hammidrash, II. pp. x., xiv. ff., and xix–xx.)

1. [As the apple tree among the trees of the wood, so is my beloved among the sons (Song of Songs, ii. 3). (This applies to Moses, upon whom be peace.)]
2. In that hour when God said unto him: "Go and bring out the children of Israel from Egypt, for I have heard their groaning, and I remembered the covenant, and the oath I swore to Abraham my

servant." Moses said: "O Lord of the Universe, who am I that I should go unto Pharaoh, and that I should bring forth the children of Israel out of Egypt?" (Ex. iii. 11). God said: "Thou hast humbled thyself in saying 'Who am I that I should go to Pharaoh?' but I will honour thee [as it is said: 'He that is of lowly spirit shall obtain honour' (Prov. xxix. 23)], and I will give the whole of Egypt into thy hands, and I will bring thee up even near to my throne of glory; and I will shew thee the angels of the Heaven." Thereupon God commanded Metatron, the angel of his presence (of the face), and said unto him: "Go and bring Moses with harps, and pipes, and drums, and dances, with joy, and songs, and praises."

3. And Metatron answered and said: "O Lord of the Universe, Moses is not able to come up and see the angels, for there are angels who are of fire and he is only of flesh and blood."

4. God said: "Go and change his flesh (body) into fire." And Metatron went to Moses.

5. When Moses beheld Metatron he trembled with fear, and said to him: "Who art thou?"

6. And he answered: "I am Enoch the son of Jared, thy father's father. The Almighty hath sent me to bring thee up to his throne of glory."[1]

7. Moses said: "I am only flesh and blood, and cannot look upon the angels." And Metatron changed Moses' tongue into a tongue of fire, and his eyes he made like the wheels of the heavenly chariot, and his power like unto that of the angels, and his tongue like a flame, and brought him up to heaven. 15,000 angels were on the right hand, and 15,000 on the left, Metatron and Moses in the middle. In this way was Moses carried up to heaven.[2]

[1] Ascensio Isaiae, ed. Dillmann, Leipzig, 1877. ix. 9 ; Apoc. Virg. Mary.
[2] Testament of Abraham, ch. 9 and 10, Rec. *A.* ed. M. R. James, Cambridge, 1892.

8. The first heaven to which Moses ascended corresponds
   to the first day of the week; there he saw the
   waters standing in lines.   This heaven was full of
   windows, and at each window stood an angel.   And
   Moses asked Metatron : " What are these windows ? "
   and Metatron answered : " These windows are—the
   window of prayer, the window of request, the window
   of supplication, the window of crying (tears), the
   window of joy, the window of satiation, the window
   of famine, the window of poverty, the window of
   riches, the window of war, the window of peace,
   the window of pregnancy, the window of birth, the
   window of the treasures of rain, the window of dew,
   the window of sin, the window of repentance, the
   window of smallness, the window of greatness, the
   window of death, the window of life, the window of
   disease among men, the window of disease among
   animals, the window of healing, the window of
   sickness, the window of health."   And Moses saw
   great things past finding out, "yea marvellous things
   without number " (Job ix. 10).[1]

9. Moses ascended then the second heaven, which corresponds to the second day of the week.   There he saw
   an angel whose name is X.[2]   His length is 300
   parasangs and 50 myriads of angels stand before
   him; they are of fire and water, and their faces are
   directed towards the *Shekina* above; and all sing
   hymns, saying : " Great is the Lord and highly to
   be praised " (cxlv. 3).

10. And Moses asked Metatron and said : " Who are
    those ? "   He answered : " These are the angels who
    are placed over the clouds, the wind, and the rain;
    they go and fulfil the will of their Creator and
    return to their places and praise the Almighty."

---

[1] Enoch, ch. 60, v. 12 ff. translated by Charles, p. 156 ff., B. of Jubilees,
ch. 1, v. Roensch, d. Buch d. Jubilaeen, p. 259; cf. *Sefer Raziel*, Amsterdam,
1701, f. 34[b] ff.

[2] In this recension the names of the angels are omitted.   They are to be
found, however, in the shorter.

And Moses asked: "Why have they their faces turned towards the Shekina?" And Metatron answered: "From that day when God created them until to-day they have not been moved from their position." [1]

11. Moses went up to the third heaven, which corresponds to the third day of the week. There he saw an angel whose name is X. His length is a journey of 500 years. He has 70,000 heads, in each head 70,000 mouths, in each mouth 70,000 tongues, and in each tongue 70,000 dictions; before him stand 70,000 myriads of angels, all of white fire; they all praise and sing to God [and say: "Thine, O Lord, is the greatness and power," etc. (1 Chr. xxix. 11)].

12. Moses asked Metatron: "Who are these? and what is their name?" And he answered: "Their name is *Erelim*; they are placed over the grass (herbs), and over the trees, and over the fruits, and over the corn; and they all go and fulfil the will of their Creator and return to their places."

13. Moses went up to the fourth heaven. There he saw the temple built; the columns of red fire, the sides of green fire, the thresholds of white fire, the hooks and the planks of blazing fire; the portals of carbuncle and the halls of sparkling gems. And he saw angels going therein praising (and saying) [as King David, upon whom may peace rest, said: "Bless the Lord, ye angels of His, ye mighty in strength, that fulfil his word" (Ps. ciii. 20)]. [2]

14. Moses asked Metatron and said: "Who are these angels?" And Metatron answered: "These are the angels, who are placed over the earth, and over the sun, and over the moon, and over the stars, and over the planets, and over the spheres, and ever sing they hymns unto Him." And he saw two big stars, each

[1] Enoch, *l.c.*; Jubilees, *l.c.*
[2] Testament Levi, ch. 5.

of them as big as the whole earth; the name of
one was *Nogah*, and the name of the other *Maadim*,
one standing above the sun, and the other above
the moon. Moses asked Metatron: "Why do these
stand above those others?" And he said: "The
one stands above the sun in summer in order to
cool the world from the heat of the sun, and that is
the star *Nogah*; whilst the other stands near the
moon in order to warm the world from the cold
of the moon (and this is the star *Maadim*)." [1]

15. Moses went to the fifth heaven and he saw there troops
of angels half of fire and half of snow, and the snow is
above the fire without extinguishing it, for God makes
peace between them [as it is said: "He maketh peace
in his high places," Job xxv. 2], and all praise the
Almighty.

16. And Moses asked Metatron: "What are these doing?"
He said: "Since the day when God created them
are they so." Moses asked: "What is their name?"
and he answered: "These are the *Erelim* who are
called *Ishim* [as it is said: 'Unto you, O Ishim
(men), I call,' Prov. viii. 4, *i.e.*: I call you
Ishim !]."

17. Moses went up to the sixth heaven, there he saw an
angel whose length was 500 years' journey; his name
was X., and he was wholly of *hail* (ice), and by him
stood thousands and myriads of angels, without number,
and all sung praises to the One who said and the
world was created [as it is said: the heaven proclaim
the glory of God (Ps. xix. 2)]. [2]

18. Moses asked Metatron: "Who are these?" and he
answered: "These are the *Irin Kadishin*, (the holy
watchers," Daniel iv. 10–14).

19. Moses went up to the seventh heaven, and he saw an
angel wholly of fire; and two angels, whose names
were X. These were fastened with two chains of red

---

[1] Cf. Pirke de R. Eliezer, ch. 6.
[2] Ch. 8–17, cf. Othioth de R. Akiba (Jellinek, Bet-hamm. III. 20–21).

and dark fire ; and each of them had the length of 500 parasangs.

20. Moses asked Metatron : " Who are these ? " And he answered : " These are wrath and anger, and God created them during the six days of creation, that they should fulfil his will." [1]

21. Moses replied : " I am afraid of these angels, and I cannot look on them." Thereupon Metatron embraced Moses, placed him in his bosom and said : " O Moses, beloved of God, be not frightened nor dread thou aught." And Moses was immediately calmed.

22. After this Moses saw another angel, whose countenance was totally different from those of the other angels, for he was ugly and his height of 540 years' journey, and he was girded forty times around his waist. From the sole of the foot unto the head he was full of fiery eyes, and whosoever looked at him, fell down in dread.

23. And Moses asked Metatron : " Who is this ? " He answered : " This is the angel of death, who takes the souls of men." [2] And he asked him : " Where is he now going ? " And Metatron answered : " He goes to take the soul of Job the pious."

24. And Moses said before God : " May it be thy will, O Lord, my God and God of my fathers, that thou shouldst not deliver me into the hands of this angel ! "

25. Then saw he angels standing before God ; each of them having six wings. With twain wings they covered their faces, so that they might not look upon the *Shekina*. With the other twain wings they cover their feet, for they have the feet of a calf, and with the other twain wings they fly and praise God. The length of each wing is 500 years' journey, and the width from one end of the world

[1] Cf. Rev. of Paul, ch. 11 (*Tischendorf*, Apoc. Apocryphae, Leipzig, 1866, pp. 34–69).
[2] Cf. Test. of Abraham, ch. 17.

to the other. And Moses asked: "Who are these?" and Metatron answered: "These are the holy Creatures." [1]

26. [Our sages tell[2] that at the time when Nebuchadnezzar the impious said: "I will ascend above the heights of the clouds; I will be like the Most High" (Isaiah xv. 14), the Holy Spirit came forth and said: "O impious man! How many are the days of the years of thy life? Threescore and ten, or even by reason of strength, fourscore years (Ps. xc. 10), and the distance from earth to heaven alone is 500 years, the thickness of the heaven again 500 years, and from the heaven Rakia to the heaven Shehakim 500 years, and its thickness 500 years, and from Shehakim to Zebul again 500 years, and its thickness 500 years, and from Zebul to Meon 500 years, and its thickness 500 years, and from Meon to Araboth 500 years, and its thickness 500 years, and the feet of the holy Creatures are equal to the whole; and their ankles are equal to the whole; and the wings of the creatures are like the whole, and their necks are like the whole, and their heads like the whole, and their horns like unto the whole, and upon them is the throne of glory which is equal to the whole. [It is like the terrible ice, Ezek. i. 22.] And there sits the King of Kings, the Holy, blessed be He exalted and high, and thou sayest: "I will ascend above the heights of the clouds, I will be like the Most High! Woe unto thee, O impious man and woe unto thy soul, for thou shalt be brought down to the uttermost parts of the pit (cf. Isaiah xiv. 15) to the seven regions of hell to be punished for ever and ever."]

[1] Cf. P. d. R. Eliezer, ch. 4.
[2] *Talmud B.*, Tractate Pesachim, f. 94a-b; *Yalkut*, II. f. 44c, § 286; cf. Tract. Hagiga, f. 12b.

27. And after that Moses saw an angel in the heaven called
Araboth, *i.e.* the seventh heaven, and this angel was
teaching the souls which were created by God at the
time of the Creation and have been placed in paradise.
The name of the angel was X. He teaches them in
seventy languages in the college on high, and they
answer : " Thus is the law of Moses given by
tradition from Mount Sinai [as it is said Dina was
set and the books were opened (Daniel vii. 10), and
Dina is none other than this angel, who is the
guardian angel of the Law and of wisdom." He
has also another name, they call him Jefefiyah, for
the name of the guardian angel of the Law is Iofiel].[1]

28. [(From the Zohar) R. Simeon, son of Johai, said : " At
that time when Moses went up to heaven an angel
sat before him and taught him 370 mysteries of the
Law, Moses then said to God, ' I will not depart from
here unless Thou wilt give me good gifts.' " God
answered : " Moses, my servant, faithful in my house,
I will give thee my Law wherein are good gifts,
as it is written : ' For I gave thee a good gift '
(Prov. iv. 2). Therein are also the commandments,
positive and negative, and not only this (I grant
thee) but also that the Law shall be recorded in thy
name, as it is written : ' Remember ye the Law of
Moses, my servant ' (Malachi iii. 22)." Whence do
we know that Moses did actually ascend seven
heavens ? We learn it from the verse, " And Moses
ascended to God." (It is further written, " God went
up amidst the sounds of trumpets ") (Ps. xlvii. 6).
Moses is therefore called Elohim like unto his Master,
for it is said :[1] " See I have made thee as Elohim
unto Pharaoh," therefore it is written : " Like an
apple-tree in the wood is my beloved among the
sons." This is Moses, master of the Prophets and
servant of God; he is like an apple in odour and taste.]

[1] About *seven heavens* v. Ascensio Isaiae and Test. Levi, ch. 3.

29. At that time a *Bath-Kol* came forth from underneath the throne of glory and said : " Moses, my servant! Art thou afraid of them ? " [It is written : " A wise man scaleth the city of the mighty and bringeth down the strength of the confidence thereof " (Prov. xxi. 22). Strength means the Law as it is said : " God will give strength to his people " (Ps. xxix. 11).]

30. God said then to Moses : " Moses, my servant! Thou camest up here and hast been worthy of the privilege of seeing all with thy (earthly) power ; and I have made thee ascend seven heavens, and have shown thee my treasures and I have given thee my law. Now thou shalt be worthy of seeing the two parks I have created in this world, one for the righteous and one for the sinners, viz. Paradise and Hell."

31. At that hour God sent Gabriel and said unto him : " Go with my beloved servant Moses and show him Hell ! "

32. And Moses said to him : " I cannot enter Hell, that blazing fire." He said to him : " Moses, there is a fire which burns more than all the seven Hells, and yet when thou wilt tread it with thy feet, it shall not burn thee."

33. At an hour when Moses entered Hell, the fire of Hell withdrew for 500 parasangs. The master of Hell said to him : " Who art thou ? " He answered : " I am the son of Amram." The Lord of Hell answered : " Not here is thy place." And Moses said : " I came to see the powerful works of God, blessed be He." And God said to the Lord of Hell : " Go and show him how men are in Hell."[1]

---

[1] I draw attention here to two more apocalyptic visions which do not seem to have been noticed hitherto. (1) The apocalypse of the Virgin *Mary* (v. *Tischendorf*, Apoc. Apocryphae, p. xxvii.; *Gaster*, Literatura populara română, Bucharest, 1883, p. 362–366; B. P. *Hasdeu*, Cuvente d. Bătrănĭ, II. Bucharest, 1879, p. 301–367) extant in Slavonic texts of the twelfth century. Greek, Roumanian, etc. ; Æthiopic and Syriac ? In this text the tortures of Hell are very fully described. (2) *Questions of St. Macarius*, of which I possess 6, *Roumanian* MSS. ; A *Syriac* Fragment of the twelfth century I found in the British Museum, Add. 17,262 (*Wright*, II. p. 867–8, No. 837), and a *Greek* text of the fifteenth century I discovered in Cod. Baroccianus (Bodleian), No. 147. f. 294ᵇ *sqq.*

34. Immediately he went with Moses, like a pupil before his master, and entered Hell together with him.

35. Moses saw there men tortured by the angels of destruction. Some of the sinners were hanged by their eyelids, some by their ears, some by their hands, and others by their tongues, and they cried bitterly. And he saw women hanging by their hair and by their breasts and in such like ways, all were hanging by chains of fire.[1]

36. And Moses asked the Lord of Hell, and said "Why are these hanged by their eyes and by their tongues and are so fearfully tortured and so sorely punished?" And the master of Hell answered: "Because they looked with an evil eye at fair women, and at married women, and at the money of their friends and neighbours, and gave false witness against their neighbours."[2]

37. Also saw he in Hell men hanging by their sexual organs and their hands were tied, and he asked: "Why do these hang?" The Lord answered: "Because they committed adultery, and stole, and killed, and murdered."[3]

38. He saw other men hanging by their ears and their tongues, and he asked: "Why are these .hanging by their ears and tongues?" And he answered: "Because they neglected the study of the law, and talked slander and vain words and empty words.[4] The women are hanging by their hair and breasts, because they used to uncover their breasts and their hair before the young men and desired them, and came thus to sin."[5]

39. Hell cried then with a bitter and loud voice, and said to the Master of Hell: "Give me the sinners, that

---

[1] Cf. V. 7. 15-19. Peter, ch. 9 (H. 24); *Robinson* and *James*, The Gospel according to Peter, etc., London, 1892, p. 37 *sqq.*; cf. A. *Harnack* (II.) Bruchstücke d. Evgl. u. der Apocalypse d. Petrus, Leipzig, 1893, p. 16 *sqq.*

[2] Cf. V. 15, 17. Peter, ch. 7 (H. 22); Paul, ch. 37, 38.

[3] Cf. Peter, ch. 9, 10 (H. 24-25); Paul, 32; Virg. Mary.

[4] V. 16.

[5] V. 17; Peter, ch. 9 (H. 22); cf. Paul, ch. 40.

I may destroy them." For Hell is always hungry and never satisfied, and crieth always for the sinners to devour them, but hath no power over the righteous.[1]

40. Moses went further and saw two sinners hanged by their feet with their heads downwards, and they cried by reason of the torture of Hell, and their bodies were covered with black worms, each worm 500 parasangs long. And these sinners cry and lament, saying: "Woe unto us, for the terrible punishment of Hell; would we could die." But they cannot die [as it is said: "They long for death but it cometh not" (Job iii. 21)].[2]

41. Moses asked the master of Hell: "What acts have these committed?" And he answered: "These are those who swore falsely, and profaned the Sabbath, and despised the learned, and persecuted the orphans; and gave bad names to their neighbours, and bare false witness. Therefore hath God delivered them to these worms to take vengeance on these sinners." And Moses asked: "What is the name of this place?" And he answered: "Aluka [as it is said; Aluka hath two daughters" (Prov. xxx. 15)].[3]

42. Moses went then to another place. There the sinners were lying on their faces; and he saw two thousand scorpions swarming over them and stinging them and torturing them, and the sinners cried bitterly. Each scorpion has 70,000 mouths, and each mouth 70,000 stings, and each sting has 70,000 vesicles filled with poison and venom, and with these are the sinners imbued and thus are they tortured; and their eyes are sunk in their sockets for fear and dread, and their cry: "Woe unto us, for our sins, and for the day of judgment."[4]

---

[1] Cf. Ev. Nicodemi, Greek form, ch. 20 ff.: "O all devouring and insatiable Hades."

[2] Peter, ch. 9, 13 (H. 24, 28).

[3] Cf. V. 16; Paul, ch. 39.

[4] V. 24; VII. 4; Peter, ch. 13 (H. 28).

43. And Moses asked: "What have these committed?" And he answered: "These have wasted the money of others; they have taken bribery, and elevated themselves above others; they have put their neighbours publicly to shame; they have delivered up their brother Israelite to the gentile;[1] they denied the oral Law and maintained that God did not create the world. Therefore God has handed them over to the scorpions to be avenged on them."[2]

44. He saw there another place where the sinners stood up to their knees; the name of that place is *Tit hayaven* ("miry clay," Ps. xl. 3). Angels of destruction tie them up with chains of iron and lash them with fiery whips, and they take fiery stones and break with them the teeth of the sinners, from morning until evening, and during the night they prolong their teeth again to the length of a parasang in order to break them anew next morning; [as it is said: "Thou hast broken the teeth of the wicked" (Ps. iii. 8)]. And the sinners cry: "Woe unto us, woe unto us!" but nobody takes pity on them.[3]

45. Moses asked the master of Hell: "What have these committed?" He answered: "They ate all kinds of forbidden fruit and gave them to Israelites to eat; they were usurers, and apostates and blasphemers; they wrote the ineffable name of God for Gentiles;[4] they had false weights; they stole money, and ate on the fast day of Kippur [for whosoever eats blood, or reptiles, or worms, and does not keep away from them is punished by being cut off], these are for ever punished in Hell, and therefore God hath delivered them to the angels of destruction to chastise them.[5]

---

[1] Peter, ch. 12 (H. 27).
[2] Paul, ch. 42; cf. Virg. Mary.
[3] Cf. Talmud, Tr. Berachoth, f. 54b.
[4] Probably on amulets.
[5] Cf. Paul, 36; Macarius, 40.

46. [He saw there further how they punish the wicked
with fire and snow; and torture them terribly.]
The Lord of Hell said then to Moses: "Come and
see how the wicked are punished in Hell with fire."
Moses answered: "I dread to go." But the Lord of
Hell answered: "Go and dread naught," [as it is
said: "Yea, though I walk through the valley of the
shadow of death I will fear no evil" (Ps. xxiii. 4)].

47. And Moses stood up to go, and he saw the *Shekina*
moving before him, so that he should not be in
dread of the angels of destruction. Each of these is
full of eyes, and hath fiery chains in his hands, and
his length is 500 years' journey.

48. Moses went and saw how the wicked were punished
by fire, being half in fire and half in snow, with
worms crawling up and down their bodies and a
fiery collar round their necks, and having no rest,[1]
except on Sabbath days and Festival days.[2] All
(the other) days they are tortured in Hell. Of
these speaks the verse: "And they shall go forth
and look upon the carcases of the men that have
transgressed against me, for their worm shall not
die, neither shall their fire be quenched" (Isaiah
cxvi. 28).

49. And Moses asked the angel of Hell : "What have
these committed?" And the angel answered: "This
is the punishment for those who have committed
adultery, sodomy, idolatry, and murder, and who have
cursed their parents. Therefore hath God delivered
them to the angels of destruction to be avenged on
them."[3] And Moses asked: "What is the name of
this place?" And he answered: "The name of it
is *Abadon*."

50. Thereupon Moses went up (to heaven) and said :
"May it be Thy will, O Lord, my God, and God

---

[1] V. *Bahya*, comment. to Pentateuch, Venice, 1544, f. 181ᵇ.
[2] Paul, ch. 44; cf. Pesikta rabbati, ed. Friedman, ch. 23, f. 112ᵃ.
[3] Peter, ch. 9 (H. 24); cf. Macarius, 22, 27, 39, V. Mary.

of my fathers, that Thou mayest save me and Thy
people Israel from those places which I have seen
in Hell."

51. God said •to Moses : "Moses, my servant ? I have
created two parks : Paradise and Hell. Whosoever
committeth evil deeds goeth down to Hell, and
whosoever doth good deeds cometh into Paradise "
[as it is said : "I the Lord search the heart, I
try the reins, even to give every man according
to his ways, according to the fruit of his doings"
(Jer. xvii. 10)].

52. Then Moses lifted up his eyes and beheld the angel
Gabriel ; and he fell down and bowed himself
before him. And the angel said : " Hast thou seen
Hell ?" He answered : " Yea." And the angel said :
" Come then, I will show thee Paradise, by the will
of God." So Moses went with him to Paradise.

53. When they came there, the angels said : " Thy time
is not yet arrived to leave the world." Moses
answered : "I came to see the mighty deeds of
God, and the reward of the pious in Paradise, what
is their condition there."

54. The angels began then to praise Moses and they said :
" Hail, O Moses, servant of the Lord ; Hail, O Moses,
born of woman, who hast been found worthy to
ascend seven heavens, hail the nation to whom such
belongs." [שככה such in arithmetical calculation is
equal to משה.]

55. When Moses went into Paradise he saw an angel
sitting under the tree of life. Moses asked the
angel Gabriel : " Who is this angel ?" He answered :
" This is the Lord (guardian) of Paradise and his
name is X."

56. This angel then asked Moses : " Who art thou ?"
He answered : "I am the son of Amram." He said
to him : " Why didst thou come hither ?" And
Moses answered : " To see the reward of the pious
in Paradise have I come hither."

57. The angel took Moses by the hand, and they went both together. Moses looked up and saw seventy thrones fixed, one next to another; all made of precious stones, of emerald, sapphire and diamond and precious pearls, and the foot of each was of gold and fine gold. Around each throne stood seventy angels. Amongst the thrones was one greater than the others, and twenty of the ministering angels kept ward thereover.

58. Moses enquired of the angel and said: "Whose is that throne?" He answered: "It is the throne of Abraham the Patriarch."

59. Thereupon Moses went immediately up to Abraham. Abraham asked him: "Who art thou?" He answered: "I am the son of Amram." And Abraham asked: "Is perchance already thy time come to leave the world?" Moses answered: "My time is not yet come, but with the permission of God I came to see the reward of the pious."[1] Abraham then said: "Praise ye the Lord, for He is good; for His mercy endureth for ever" (Ps. cvi. 1).

60. Then went Moses to the throne of Isaac, and he spake with him in a similar manner, and Moses answered in like wise.

61. Then asked Moses, the guardian angel of Paradise: "What is the length and width of Paradise?" The angel answered: "There is none who could measure it; no angel or Seraph can ever know the length and width of Paradise, for it is unlimited and boundless and immeasurable. The angels guard only the thrones and these are unlike to one another, for some of them are of silver, others of gold, others of bdellium, others of ruby, topaz, and carbuncle, others of emerald, sapphire and diamond, others of precious stones and pearls, others of rubies and carbuncles."

62. Moses asked the angel: "For whom is the throne of pearls?" He answered: "It is for the scholars

---

[1] Cf. Ascensio Isaiae, viii. 27, 28.

who study the Law day and night for the sake of
heaven." "And those of precious stones?" "For
the pious men." "And those of rubies?" "For
the just." "And those of gold?" "For the men
who repent;" "but the greatest throne is for thy
forefather Abraham, the other thrones are for Isaac
and Jacob, and for the prophets and righteous, and
the holy and wise pious men, each after his worth
and position and the good works he hath performed
in the world."

63. Moses then said to the angel: "For whom is that
throne of copper?" He answered: "For the wicked
man, whose son is pious; because through the merits
of his son he obtains a portion of heavenly bliss;
as thou seest in the case of Terah, who had worshipped all the idols in the world, but who through
the merits of his son Abraham obtained that throne
of copper [as it is said: "Thou shalt go to thy
fathers in peace" (Gen. xv. 15), thus announcing
to him (Abraham) that God would give (his father
also) a place in Paradise]."

64. Afterwards Moses looked and beheld a spring of living
water welling forth from underneath the tree of life
and dividing itself into four streams, [and it comes
from under the throne of glory] and they encompass
the Paradise from one end to the other. And under
each throne there flow four rivers, one of honey, the
second of milk, the third of wine, and the fourth of
pure balsam.[1] These all pass beneath the feet of the
just, who are seated upon thrones.

65. [It is said in the Zohar. King Messias said to R.
Simeon, son of Johai: "Worthy art thou of thy
portion in heaven, for thy teaching is divided (spread)
through 670 heavens, each heaven is divided into 670
lights, each light is divided in 670 arguments, each
argument is divided in (among) 670 worlds, each
world is divided in 670 streams of pure balsam.]

[1] Paul, ch. 23.

66. And all these streams flow round Paradise and beneath all the thrones. All these were created by God for the just, and whoso becometh equal to them in merit, sees and enjoys, as they enjoy, the splendour of the Shekina.

67. When Moses saw all these godly and pleasant things he felt great joy, and exclaimed: "Oh! how great is Thy goodness which Thou hast laid up for them that fear Thee, which Thou hast wrought for them that put their trust in Thee, before the sons of men" (Ps. xxxi. 19).

68. And Moses retired from there and went away. At that same moment a voice from Heaven (Bath-Kol) was heard saying : "Moses, servant of the Lord, faithful in His house; even as thou hast seen the reward which is preserved for the just in the future world, so also in the days to come shalt thou see the rebuilding of the Temple and the advent of the Messiah, and behold the beauty of the Lord, and meditate in His Temple" (Ps. xxvii. 4). (May it now be Thy will, O Lord, my God and the God of my fathers, that I and the whole nation of Israel may be deemed worthy of sharing in good and the great consolation, and the days of the Messiah, and the rebuilding of the Temple, and the everlasting life. Amen.)

II. THE REVELATION OF MOSES. (B.)

Heaven.

[*Ziyuni*, fol. 93 *c-d*, cf. *Yalkut Reubeni*, fol. 100*d*–101*a*; *Jellinek*, Beth-hammidrash, I. 58–64; *Pesikta Rabbati*, ed. Friedmann, sec. 20, fol. 96*a*–98*b*; *MS. Oxford*, No. 1466, 14 (Cat. Neubauer)].

1. Moses, our teacher, upon whom may rest peace, said to Israel: "Hear, O Israel, you the whole nation! I went up on high, and I saw all the Heavenly rulers. I saw

the angel *Kemuel*, the Janitor, who is placed over 12,000
angels of destruction, and who stands at the gates of heaven.

2. I saw further the angel *Hadarniel*, who is higher by 60
myriads of parasangs than Kemuel, and with every diction
that comes out of his mouth go forth 12,000 flashes of
lightning.

3. I saw further *Sandalfon*, the prince, greater than
Hadarniel by 500 years' journey.   Of him said Ezekiel:
" One wheel upon the earth besides the living Creatures,
for each of the four faces thereof " (Ezek. i. 15).

4. [This is the Sandalfon who weaves crowns for his master.
When this crown appears before the heavenly hosts, they
all shake and tremble and the holy Creatures are struck
dumb, and the holy Seraphim roar like lions, and they
say : " Holy, holy, holy is the Lord of Hosts, the whole
earth is full of his glory " (Is. vi. 2).   And when the
crown approaches the throne the wheels of the throne of
glory move, and the thresholds of brilliancy quake, and
all the heavens are seized with terror.   And when
the crown passes on to the throne of glory to its right
place all the heavenly hosts open their mouths, turn
to the Seraphim and say : " Blessed be the glory of the
Lord from his place."   They say :   " From his place "
(Ezek. iii. 12), because they do not know His actual place.
When the crown comes near to God's head He accepts it
graciously from His servants.   And the heavenly Creatures
and the Seraphim, and the wheels of the throne of glory,
and the heavenly hosts, and the Hashmalim and Cherubim
praise the Creator, acknowledge him as their king, and
exclaim unanimously : " The Lord reigneth, the Lord
reigned, the Lord will reign for evermore."] [1]

5. I saw further the fiery river *Rigyon*, which comes
out before God, from under the throne of glory, and is
formed from the perspiration of the holy Creatures who
support the throne of glory ; and out of dread of God's
majesty perspire fire.[2]   This river is meant by the saying

---

[1] Talmud B., Hagigah, f. 13b ; *Longfellow*, Sandalfon.
[2] Cf. Pirke de R. Eliezer, ch. 4.

" a fiery stream issued and came forth before him ;
thousand thousands ministered unto him, and ten thousand
times ten thousand stood before him ; the judgment was
set and the books were opened " (Dan. vii. 10).   For the
Almighty sits and judges the ministering angels, and after
the judgment they bathe in that river of fire and are
renewed.   Afterwards the river flows on and carries with
it fiery coals, and falls on the heads of the sinners in
Hell, as it is said : " Behold the tempest of the Lord, even
His fury is gone forth, yea, a whirling tempest ; it shall
burst on the head of the wicked " (Jer. xxiii. 19).[1]

6. I saw further the angel *Galitzur*, surnamed also *Raziel*,
who stands behind the curtain and listens to all that is
decreed in heaven and proclaims it.   This proclamation is
then handed over to the prophet Elijah and he proclaims
it to the world from the Mount Horeb.

7. The wings of *Galitzur* are spread and keep off the
breath of the holy Creatures, for otherwise all the ministering angels would be burned by the breath of the holy
Creatures.

8. I saw further *Michael*, the great prince, standing at
the right side of the throne, and *Gabriel* at the left ; and
Iefefiyah, the guardian of the law, standing before it ; and
Metatron, the angel of the presence, standing at the door
of the palace of God.   And he sits and judges all the
heavenly hosts before his master.   And God pronounces
judgment and he executes it.

9. I saw then a troop of the terrible angels who surround
the throne of glory, they were more powerful and mightier
than all the other angels.   All these whom I saw wished
to scorch me with the breath of their mouths, but out of
dread of the presence of the Almighty, the king of kings,
they had no power to injure me, for they all were full of
fear and agony and dread before Him.

---

[1] V. 23 ; cf. Peter, 8 (H. 23) ; Paul, 32 ; V. Mary.

III. The Revelation of R. Joshua ben Levi. (A.)

Paradise, Hell.

(*Orhot Hayim* II. Cod. 52, Montefiore College, f. 281ᵇ–282ᵇ; *Cod.* 28, Jews' College, London, f. 145ᵇ–147ᵃ; *Jellinek*, Beth-hammidrash, II. 48–51; with *Agadath Bereshit*, Warsaw, 1867, fol. 51*a–b*; *Kolbo*, §120; *Zunz*, Gottesdienstl. Vortraege, p. 141, No. *e*.)

1. R. Joshua, son of Levi, was a pious man. When the time approached that he should leave this world, the Lord said to the angel of death, "Go and fulfil whatever his wish may be." He went to him and said unto him: "The time is nigh when thou shalt leave this world, but now tell me what thou wishest, that I may fulfil it."[1]

2. As soon as R. Joshua heard this, he said: "I pray thee, show me my place in Paradise." He answered and said: "Come and I will show thee it." R. Joshua answered and said, "Give me thy sword, so that thou shouldst not frighten me." And he gave him his sword. So they went together till they reached the wall of Paradise. There being outside the wall, the angel of death lifted R. Joshua from the ground and placed him upon the crest of the wall, and said unto him: "Behold thy place in Paradise."

3. At that moment R. Joshua jumped down from the wall and fell into Paradise. The angel of death caught him by his mantle and said to him, "Get thee out thence." But R. Joshua swore by the name of God that he would not do so. The angel of death had no power to enter therein. The ministering angels seeing this, said to the Almighty: "Lord of the Universe, behold what R. Joshua hath done! By force hath he taken possession of his portion in Paradise." God answered: "Go and see if he has ever broken his oath, then shall this oath of his be likewise void and null." They searched and could not find any such case. So they came and said: "He hath never broken his oaths in his

---

[1] Cf. Test. Abraham, ch. 9.

lifetime." And God answered: "If it be so, let him remain there."

4. When the angel of death saw this, he said to R. Joshua: "Give me now my sword back." But R. Joshua did not fulfil his request till a voice came forth and said: "Give him the knife, for it is of necessity for His creatures."

5. R. Joshua then said to him: "Swear unto me that thou wilt not show it any more to the creatures at the moment when thou takest their souls." [For up to that time the angel of death used to kill men openly, as one slaughters animals, and he showed it even to the suckling in the bosom of their mother.] At that hour he swore unto him, and R. Joshua returned the knife to him.

6. After that began the prophet Elijah to proclaim and to cry out aloud to the just: "Clear the way for the son of Levi."

7. [He went and saw R. Joshua sitting in the compartment of the just, and he asked him: "Art thou the son of Levi?" And he answered: "Yes." He asked again: "Hast thou seen a rainbow in thy lifetime?" Again R. Joshua answered: "Yes." And he replied: "Then if this is so, thou art not the son of Levi."—In fact it had not been the case. Now R. Joshua had not seen a rainbow, but he did not wish to boast of it and to ascribe it to his own merits. He had asked him about the rainbow, for it is the sign of the covenant between God and the world; and when the rainbow appears then God (remembers) and pitieth his creatures; but when there liveth a just man, there is no longer any necessity for a rainbow, as through his merits the world is saved. As it is said: "And the just is the foundation of the world" (Prov. x. 25). Therefore did he ask him about the rainbow.]

8. The angel of death went to R. Gamaliel and told him: "So and so hath R. Joshua done unto me." R. G. answered and said: "He served thee right. But now please go and tell him I request him to search through heaven and hell their mysteries and to write them down and send it to me [also if there are idolators in hell]."

9. The angel went, and R. Joshua answered: "I will do so."

10. Thereupon R. Joshua went and searched through Paradise and he found therein *seven* compartments,[1] each of twelve myriads of miles in width, and twelve myriads of miles in length; the measure of their width being the same as that of their length.

11. The first compartment corresponds to the first door of Paradise. Here dwell the proselytes who had embraced Judaism of their own free will, not from compulsion. The walls are of glass and the wainscoting of cedar. As I tried to measure it the inhabitants rose to prevent me from doing it. Obadiah the just, who presides over them, rebuked them and said: "What are your merits that this man should dwell here with you?" (for they wished to retain him there). Thereupon they allowed him to measure it.

12. The second compartment corresponds to the facing of the door of Paradise. It is built of silver and the wainscoting thereof of cedar. Here dwell those who repent, and Manasseh, son of Ezekiah, presides over them.

13. The third compartment, facing the third door, is built of silver and gold. Here dwell Abraham, Isaac and Jacob, and all the Israelites who came out of Egypt, and the whole generation who had lived in the desert, and all the kings (princes), with the exception of Absalom. There is also David, and Solomon, and Kilab, son of David, still alive, and all the kings of the house of Judah, with the exception of Manasseh, who presides over those who repent. Over these here preside Moses and Aaron. Here are the precious vessels of silver and gold, and jewels, and canopies, and beds, and thrones, and lamps of gold, and precious stones and pearls. And I asked: "For whom are all these prepared?" And David answered and said: "They are for those who still dwell in the world whence thou comest." And I asked:

[1] Cf. Midrash *Kônen* in *Arze Lebanon*, Venice, 1601, f. 3a–b; Yalkut Reubeni, Amsterdam, 1700, f. 13d–14a.

" Is here perhaps one also from the Gentiles, at least
from my brother Esau ? " And he answered and said :
" No ; because the Almighty gives the reward of every
good deed they do in their lifetime in that world, but
after death they go down to Hell ; whilst the sinners in
Israel get their punishment in their lifetime in that
world, but after death they obtain the merit of their
good deed here." As it is said : " And he payeth." [1]

14. The fourth compartment, facing the fourth door of
Paradise, is beautifully built, like to the first compartment,
but its wainscoting is of olive-wood. Here dwell the perfect, and faithful, and just men. Why is the wainscoting
of olive-wood ? Because their life has been bitter to them
as olives.

15. The fifth compartment is of silver, and gold, and
refined gold, and of crystal, and bdellium ; and through its
midst flows the river Gihon. The walls are of silver and
gold, and a perfume breathes through it more exquisite than
the perfume of Lebanon. And beds of silver and gold are
there prepared, covered with violet and purple covers, woven
by Eve, and mixed with scarlet and made of hair of goats,
woven by angels. Here dwell the Messiah and Elijah in
a palanquin of the wood of Lebanon ; the pillars thereof
of silver, the bottom thereof of gold, the seat of it of
purple. Herein lieth the Messiah, the son of David, who
is the love of the daughters of Jerusalem, the midst thereof
is love. The prophet Elijah takes the head of the Messiah
and places it in his bosom and says to him : " Be quiet
and wait, for the end draweth nigh." On every Monday
and Thursday and Saturday and Holiday the Patriarchs
come to him and the fathers of the Tribes and Moses and
Aaron and David and Solomon and every king of Israel
and of the house of Judah, and they weep with him and
comfort him, and say unto him : " Be quiet and wait and
rely upon thy Creator, for the end draweth nigh." Also
Korah and his company and Dathan and Abiram and

[1] Cf. Othioth de R. Akiba (Jellinek *l.c.* p. 23).

Absalom come to him on every Wednesday, and ask him:
"When will the end of our misery come? When wilt
thou reveal thyself?"

16. He answereth them and says: "Go to your fathers
and ask them." And when they hear of their fathers they
feel ashamed and do not ask any further.

17. When I came to the Messiah he asked me: "What is
Israel doing in the world from which thou comest?" And
I answered and said: "Every day they await Thee." He
immediately raised His voice and wept.

18. In the sixth compartment dwell those who died
through performing a pious act.

19. In the seventh compartment dwell those who died
from illnesses caused through the sins of Israel.

20 R. Joshua, son of Levi, tells further: "I asked
the Messiah to allow me to look into Hell, but he did
not allow me, as the righteous should never behold Hell."
So I sent to the angel called *Komm* that he might describe
Hell for me. But it was impossible, for at that moment
R. Ismael, the high priest, and R Simeon, son of Gamaliel,
and ten just men were killed, and the news reached us, so
I could not go with the angel. I went afterwards with
the angel *Kipod* and the light went with me up to the
gates of Hell, and the Messiah came with me, and they
were open. The sinners who were there saw the light
of the Messiah, and rejoiced, and said to one another:
"This will bring us out from here."[1]

21. I saw compartments of ten miles length and of five
width, full of pits of fire, and these consume the sinners,
and after their destruction they are again made whole
and fall again into the fire. In that compartment are
ten nations from the Gentiles, and Absalom presides over
them. These nations say one to another: "Our sin is
that we have not accepted the Law · but what is your
sin?" And the other answers: "That is also our sin,
we are like you." They say then to Absalom: "Why

---

[1] Ev. Nicodem.

art thou punished, seeing that thou as well as thy parents hast accepted the Law?" And he answers them and says: "Because I did not hearken to the commandments of my father." Angels stand close by and with their staves drive them back into the fire and burn them. Then they hurry to Absalom to beat him also, and to burn him; but a voice calls out to them: "Do not beat him and do not burn him, for he is from the seed of Israel, who said 'We will do and hearken,' and he is the son of my servant David." So they leave him upon his seat and honour him with the honour of a king. They bring out afterwards the sinners from the fire just as if they had not been burnt and the fire had never touched them; and they burn them again. This they repeat seven times, three times at day and four times at night. Absalom alone is saved because he is the son of David.

22. After having seen this I returned to Paradise, wrote description of Hell and sent it to R. Gamaliel and the ten elders of the Jews, and I told them all what I had seen in Paradise and Hell.

IV. THE REVELATION OF R. JOSHUA BEN LEVI. (B.)

Paradise.

(*Jellinek*, Beth-hammidrash II. p. 52–53; *Yalkut* I. §20,
f. 7[a]; *Elia ha-Cohen*: Shebet Mussar, Constantinople,
720, ch. 25, f. 80–81[a].)

1. R. Joshua, son of Levi, tells: "Paradise has two gates of carbuncle, and sixty myriads of ministering angels keep watch over them. Each of these angels shine with the lustre of the heavens. When the just man approaches them they divest him of the clothes in which he had been buried and clothe him with eight clothes, woven out of clouds of glory, and place upon his head two crowns, one of precious stones and pearls and the other of gold,[1]

---

[1] Cf. Ascensio Isaiae, viii. 14, ix. 9, 24.

and they place eight myrtles in his hand and praise him
and say to him : " Go and eat thy bread with joy." And
they lead him to a place full of rivers (waters) surrounded
by roses and myrtles. Each one has a canopy according
to his merits, as it is said : " For over all the glory shall
be spread a canopy " (Is. iv. 5).

2. And through it flow four rivers, one of oil, the other
of balsam, the third of wine, and the fourth of honey.
Every canopy is overgrown by a vine of gold, and thirty
pearls hang down from it, each of them shining like the
morning star. In every canopy there is a table of precious
stones and pearls, and sixty angels stand at the head of
every just man, saying unto him : " Go and eat with joy
of the honey, for thou hast worked assiduously in the
Law," of which it is said : " And it is sweeter than
honey," and drink of the wine preserved from the six
days of Creation, for thou hast worked in the Law which
is compared with the wine," as it is said : " I would cause
thee to drink of spiced wine " (Song viii. 2). The least
fair of them is beautiful as Joseph and Johanan and the
grains of the pomegranate upon which fall the rays of the
sun. There is no night, as it is said : " And the light of
the righteous is as the shining light " (Prov. iv. 18).

3. And they undergo three transformations passing
through three wards. In the first ward the just is
changed into a child, and he enters the compartment of
children and tastes the joys of childhood. In the second
ward he is changed into a youth, there he enjoys the
delights of youth. In the third ward he is changed into
an old man, he enters the compartment of the old and
enjoys the pleasures of mature age.[1]

4. In Paradise there are eighty myriads of trees in every
corner; the meanest among them choicer than a garden
of spices. In every corner there are sixty myriads of angels
singing with sweet voices, and the tree of life stands in
the middle and over-shadoweth the whole Paradise; and

---

[1] Paul, ch. 22, 23, 45 ; Peter, ch. 5 (H. 19–20).

it has 500 tastes, each different from the others, and the perfumes thereof vary likewise.[1] Over it hang seven clouds of glory, and the winds blow from all the four corners and waft its many odours from one end of the world to the other. Underneath sit the scholars and explain the Law. These have each two canopies, one of stars and the other of sun and moon, and clouds of glory separate one from the other.

5. Within this is the Eden containing 310 worlds, as it is said: "That I may cause those that love me to inherit Substance" (Prov. viii. 21) [the numerical value of the Hebrew word for *Substance* is equivalent to 310].[2]

6. Here are the seven compartments of the just. In the first are the martyrs, as, for instance, R. Akiba and his companions. In the second, those who were drowned. In the third, R. Johanan and his disciples. [In what consisted his great merit? He said: "If all the skies were skins and all men scribes and all the forests pens, these scribes would not be able to write down all that I have learned from my teachers, and still am I no more than a dog liking the sea."] The fourth group is of those who were covered by the cloud of glory. The fifth group is that of the penitents [for the place occupied by a penitent not even a perfectly just man can occupy]. The sixth group is that of children who have not yet tasted sin in their lives.[3] The seventh group is that of the poor, who, notwithstanding that, studied the Law and the Talmud, and had acquired moral life. Of these speaks the verse: "For all that put their trust in Thee rejoice, and they shout for ever for joy" (Ps. v. 11). And God Almighty sitteth in their midst, and expounds to them the Law, as it is said: "Mine eyes shall be upon the faithful of the land, that they may dwell with me" (Ps. xci. 6). And God hath not yet fully unveiled the glory which awaiteth them in the world to come, as it is said: "The eye hath not seen, O God, beside Thee, that which Thou workest for him that waiteth for Him" (Isaiah lxiv. 4). Amen.

---

[1] Peter, ch. 5 (H. 15–16).
[2] Cf. Yalkut Reubeni, f. 14ᵃ⁻ᵇ.
[3] Cf. Paul, ch. 26.

V.

Hell.

(*Orhot Hayim*, Vol. II. Cod. 52, Montefiore College,
Ramsgate, f. 279*a–b* (=§§ 1–18). *Elia de Vidas*:
Reshit Hochma, Constantinople, 1736, f. 40 *a–b* (=
§§ 1–9, 19–21); cf. ibid. f. 40*b*, 41*a*. *Jellinek*, Beth-
hammidrasch V. 50–51 (=§§ 10–18).)

1. R. Johanan began his homily with the verse "Passing
through the valley of weeping they make it a valley of
springs." This means to say that the sinner confesses,
just as the leprous confesses, and he says: "I have committed such and such a transgression in that place, on that
day, in the presence of so-and-so, in that society."

2. Hell has three gates: one at the sea, the other in
the wilderness, and the third in the inhabited part of the
world. That at the sea is alluded to in Jonah (ii. 3):
"Out of the belly of Sheol cried I, and thou heardest my
voice." That of the wilderness is alluded to (Numbers
xvi. 33). "So they and all that appertained to them,
went down alive unto Sheol." And that in the inhabited
portion of the world (Isaiah xxxi. 9) "Saith the Lord,
whose fire is in Zion and his furnace in Jerusalem."

3. Nine different kind of fires are in Hell, one devours
and absorbs, another absorbs and does not devour, while
another again neither devours nor absorbs. There is
further fire devouring fire. There are coals big as mountains and coals big as hills, and coals huge like unto the
Dead Sea and coals like huge stones.

4. There are rivers of pitch and sulphur flowing and
fuming and seething.

5. The punishment of the sinner is thus: The angels of
destruction throw him to the flame of hell; this opens
its mouth wide and swallows him [as it is said: "Therefore Sheol hath enlarged her desire and opened her

mouth without measure and their glory and their multitude and their pomp and he that rejoices among them descends into it " (Isaiah v. 14.)] This all happens to him who has not done one single pious act which would make the balance incline towards mercy ; whilst that man who possesses many virtues and good actions and learning and who has suffered much he is saved from hell [as it is said : " Yea though I walk through the valley of the shadow of death, I will fear no evil for thou art with me ; thy rod and thy staff shall comfort me " (Ps. xxiii. 4). " Thy rod " means the suffering and " thy staff " means the law[1]].

6. R. Johanan began: " The eyes of the wicked shall fail and refuge is perished from them and their hope shall be the giving up of the ghost " (Job ii. 20). That means : a body which is never destroyed and whose soul enters a fire which is never extinguished ; of these speaks the verse : " For their worm shall not die neither shall their fire be quenched " (Isaiah lxvi. 24).

7. R. Joshua, son of Levi, said : Once upon a time I was walking on my way when I met the prophet Elijah. He said to me : " Would you like to be brought to the gate of hell ? " I answered : " Yes ! " So he showed me men hanging by their hair ; and he said to him, these were they that let their hair grow to adorn themselves for sin. Others were hanging by their eyes ; these were they that followed their eyes to sin, and did not place God before their face. Others were hanging by their noses ; these were they that perfumed themselves to sin. Others were hanging by their tongues; these were they that had slandered. Others were hanging by their hands ; these were they that had stolen and robbed. Others were hanging by their sexual organs; these were they that had committed adultery. Others were hanging by their feet ; these were they that had run to sin. He showed me women hanging by their breasts ; these were they that uncovered their breasts before men,

---

[1] Cf. Test. Abraham, ch. 12–14.

to make them sin. He showed me further men that were fed on fiery coals; these were they that blasphemed. Others were forced to eat bitter gall; these were they that ate on fast-days. He showed me further men eating fine sand, they are forced to eat it and their teeth are broken; and the Almighty says to them: "O ye sinners! when you used to eat that which you stole and robbed it was sweet in your mouth now you are not able to eat even this." [As it is said: "Thou hast broken the teeth of the wicked" (Ps iii. 8).] And he showed me men wallowing in the mire and worms were set upon them; these are they of whom it is said: "For their worm shall not die, neither shall their fire be quenched; and they shall be an abhorring unto all flesh" (Is. lxvi. 24). He showed me further men who are thrown from fire to snow and from snow to fire; these were they that abused the poor who came to them for assistance; therefore are they thus punished [as it is said: "Thou hast caused men to ride over our heads; we went through fire and through water" (Ps. lxvi. 12)]. He showed me others who were driven from mountain to mountain, as a shepherd leads the flock from one mountain to another. [Of these speaks the verse: "They are appointed as a flock for Sheol. Death shall be their shepherd and the upright shall have the dominion over them in the morning, and their form shall be for Sheol to consume that there be no habitation for it" (Ps. xlix. 15).] [1]

8. R. Johanan said: "For every sin there is an angel appointed to obtain the expiation thereof; one comes first and obtains his expiation, then follows another and so on until all the sins are expiated, as with a debtor who has many creditors and they come before the king and claim their debts, and the king delivers him to them and says: "Take him and divide him between yourself." So also is the soul delivered in hell to cruel angels, and they divide it among themselves.

[1] I. 34-49.

9. Three descend to hell for ever and do not ascend any more—the man who commits adultery, who blames his neighbour in public, and who is guilty of perjury. Others say : "Those who honour themselves by slandering their neighbours, those who make intrigues between man and wife in order to create disputes among them."

10. Seven descend to Hell: the judge, the butcher, the scribe, the physician, the barber and the teacher of very young children. These, if they have fulfilled their mission conscientiously for the sake of heaven, ascend afterwards again. Three, however, descend never to ascend : the man who blames his neighbour in public, the man who slanders his neighbour, and the man who commits adultery.

11. Hell has seven names : Sheol, Abadon, Beer Shaon, Beer Shahat, Hatzar Maveth, Beer Tahtiyah, and Tit Hayaven.[1] The length of Sheol is a three years' journey, and so are its width and height. Similarly are the others also. Hell is thus a 2100 years' journey. If a man deserves punishment he is handed over to the angels of destruction. These seize him and lead him to the court of death, darkness and gloom, [as it is said : " Let their way be dark and slippery " (Ps. xxxv. 6)]. But this is not all, for they thrust him into Hell, [as it is said: "And the angel of the Lord pursuing them " (Ps. xxxv. 6)].

12. When a man dies and is carried along upon his bier ministering angels walk before him and people walk behind the bier following him. If they say : " Happy the man, for he was good and praiseworthy in his lifetime ; " the angels say unto him : " Write it down," and he writes it down.[2] And this is not all, but two angels watch over the man at the moment of his death, and they know whether he has stolen or robbed during his lifetime; for even the stones and the beams of his house witness against him ; [as it is said: " For the stones shall cry out of the wall and the beam out of the timber shall answer it " (Habak. ii. 11)].[3]

[1] VII. 2.
[2] Cf. Macarius, 10–11.
[3] Macarius, 12–16.

13. When a man dies he is brought before Abraham, Isaac, and Jacob. They say unto him: "My son! what hast thou done in that world from which thou comest?" When he answereth: "I have bought fields and vineyards, and I have tilled them all my life." They answer: "O fool, that thou hast been! Hast thou not learned the words of King David, who said: 'The earth is the Lord's and the fulness thereof' (Ps. xxiv. 1)." Angels then take him away and bring another man before them, and they ask him in likewise. If he answereth: "I gathered gold and silver," they retort: "Fool that thou art!" Hast thou not read in the books of the prophets: "The silver is mine and the gold is mine, saith the Lord of hosts" (Haggai ii. 8).

14. When scholars are brought before them, they say: "My son! What hast thou done in the world from which thou comest?" He answers: "I have devoted my life to the study of the law." And the patriarchs answer: "He entereth into peace; they rest in their beds, each one that walketh in his uprightness" (Is. lvii. 2). And the Almighty receives them with grace.

15. There are five kinds of punishment in Hell, and *Isaiah* saw them all. He entered the first compartment and saw thère two men carrying pails full of water on their shoulders, and they pour that water into a pit which, however, never fills. Isaiah said to God: "O thou who unveilest all that is hidden, unveil to me the secret of this!" And the Spirit of the Lord answered: "These are the men who coveted the property of their neighbours, and thus is their punishment."[1]

16. He entered the second compartment and he saw two men hanging by their tongues, and he said: "O thou, who unveilest the hidden, reveal to me the secret of this!" He answered: "These are the men who slandered, therefore they are thus punished!"[2]

17. He entered the third compartment and he saw there

---

[1] Cf. I. 36.
[2] I. 38, 41.

men hanging by the sexual organs. He said : " O thou who unveilest the hidden, reveal to me the secret of this ! " And He answered: " These are the men who neglected their own wives and committed adultery with the daughters of Israel ! " [1]

18. He entered the fourth compartment and saw there women hanging by their breasts, and he said : " O thou who unveilest the hidden, reveal to me the secret of these ! " And He answered: " These are the women who uncover their hair and rend their veil, and sit in the open market place to suckle their children in order to attract the gaze of men and to make them sin ; therefore they are punished thus ! " [2]

19. He entered the fifth compartment and found it full of smoke. There were all the princes, chiefs, and great men, and Pharaoh, the wicked, presides over them and watches at the gate of hell, and he saith unto them : " Why did you not learn from me when I was in Egypt ? " So he sits there still and watches at the gates of hell.

20. On the eve of the Sabbath the sinners are led to two mountains of snow, where they are left until the end of the Sabbath, when they are taken back from there and brought again to their former places. An angel comes and thrusts them back to their former place in hell.[3] Some of them take, however, snow and hide it in their secret parts to cool them during the six days of the week, but the Almighty says unto them: " Woe unto you who steal even in hell ! " [As it is said : " Draught and heat consume the snow waters, in Sheol they sin." That means to say: " They sin even in Sheol."]

21. Every twelvemonth the sinners are burned to ashes and the wind disperses them and carries those ashes under the feet of the just [as it is said : " And ye shall tread down the wicked, for they shall be ashes under the sole of your feet " (Malachi iii. 29)].

[1] I. 36.
[2] I. 38.
[3] I. 48.

22. Afterwards the soul is returned to them and they come out black as the blackness of a pot, and they acknowledge the justice of their punishment and say : " Thou hast rightly sentenced us and rightly judged us. With Thee is righteousness and with us shame, as it is with us to-day." [1]

23. The other nations, however, and the idolators are punished in the seven compartments of hell, in each compartment for a twelvemonth. And the river Dinor floweth from beneath the throne of glory and falleth over the heads of the sinners, and it floweth from one end of the world to the other.[2]

24. There are seven compartments in hell, and in each of them are 6000 rooms, in each room 6000 windows, in each window (recess) there are 6000 vessels filled with venom, all destined for slanderous writers and iniquitous judges. [It is to that, that Solomon alludes when he says: "And thou mourn at thy latter end when thy flesh and thy body are consumed" (Prov. v. 2).][3] None of these will be saved unless they acquire learning and pious deeds. But at the end the Almighty will have pity on *all* his creatures, as it is said: " For I will not contend for ever, neither will I be always wroth, for the spirit shall pass before Me and the souls which I have made " (Is. lvii. 16).

VI.

Hell.

(*Nachmanides*, Shaar ha-gemul, Ed. Warsaw, 1878, p. 10 (= §§ 2-7) ; cf. *Orhot Hayim*, II. f. 282ᵇ–283ᵃ ; *Midrash Kônen, l.c.* f. 4ᵃ).

1. R. Joshua, son of Levi, says: "When I measured the first compartment of Hell, I found it to be 100 miles long and 50 miles wide. Therein are pits with lions ; all fall into

---

[1] Paul, i. 8.
[2] Cf. II. 5. Test. of Isaac, *James* and *Barnes*, Test. of Abraham, p. 147.
[3] I. 42, VII. 4.

those pits and are devoured by the lions, and the bones
are thrown into burning fire.[1]   I entered the second compartment and found it of the same size as the first.[2]

2. In the second compartment, in the second division, there
are ten nations, and their punishment is like unto that
of the first compartment.   Doeg presides over them and
the angel who punishes them is *Lahatiel*; but Doeg is
freed from chastisement because he is a descendant from
those who said: "We will do and hearken" (Israel).

3. In the third compartment there are other ten nations,
their punishment is the same.   The angel who punishes
them is *Shaftiel*.   Korah who presides over them and his
companions are free from punishment, for they also said:
"We will do and hearken."

4. In the fourth compartment the punishment is the
same.   There are also ten nations and Jeroboam presides
over them.   The angel who punishes them is *Maktiel*
(Matniel).   Jeroboam, however, has immunity for he himself had studied the Law, and he cometh from those who
had said: "We will do and hearken."

5. In the fifth compartment the punishment is the same.
Ahab presides over them.   The angel who punishes them
is *Hutriel* (Oniel).   Ahab has immunity because he is one
of the children of Israel who said on Mount Sinai: "We
will do and hearken."

6. In the sixth compartment the punishment is the same.
Micha presides over them.   The angel who punishes them
is *Pusiel* (Hadriel).   Micha is free from chastisement for
he is from those who said on Mount Sinai: "We will do
and hearken."

7. In the seventh compartment the punishment is the
same.   Elisha ben Abuya presides over them.   The angel
who punishes them is *Dalkiel* (Rugziel).   Elisha, however,
has immunity for he is a descendant from those who said
on Mount Sinai: "We will do and hearken."   This is
the punishment of the tens of thousand who are in each

---

[1] Cf. Test. of Isaac; *James* and *Barnes*, Test of Abraham, p. 147.
[2] Here follows in the text of Orhot Hayim, III. 21.

compartment, and they do not see each other, for it is
dark, and this darkness is that deep darkness which existed
before the world was created.[1]

VII.

Hell.

(*Baraita de Massechet Gehinom* : in *Hesed le-Abraham* of Abr.
Azulai in : Yalkut-ha-roim, Warsaw, 1858, f. 85, sqq.
Cf. *Midrash Kônen*, *l.c.* f. 3[b]–4[a].   *Shebet Mussar*, ch.
26, f. 84[a].)

1. We read in the Baraita of the Creation : " Beneath the
earth is the (abyss) *Tehom* under Tehom is *Bohu*, under
Bohu is *Yam*, under Yam is *Mayim*, under Mayim is *Arka*,
and there is, Sheol, Abadon, Beer Shahat, Tit-hayaven,
Shaare Mavet, Shaare Tzalmavet, and Gehinom. Here are
the sinners and the angels of destruction presiding over
them. There is darkness thick as the wall of a city, and
there the heavy and bitter punishments of the sinners are
enacted, as it is said : ' The wicked shall be put to silence in
darkness ' (1 Sam. ii. 9)."

2. The uppermost compartment is *Sheol*. The height
thereof is 300 years' journey ; the width 300 years' journey ;
and its length 300 years' journey. The second compartment
is *Beer Shahat*, of the same height, width, and length.
The third is *Tit-Hayaven* of equal size. The fourth is
Shaare Mavet of the same size. The fifth *Abadon* of the
same size. The sixth *Shaare Tzalmavet* of the same size.
The seventh *Gehinom* of the same size. That makes altogether the length of hell 6300 years' journey."[2] We read
further : the fire of Gehinom is one-sixtieth of the fire
of Shaare Tzalmavet, and so of every consecutive compartment till the fire of Sheol, and in Sheol is half fire and

---

[1] Peter, ch. 6 (H. 21) ; Macarius, 19 ; Virg. Mary.
[2] V. 11.

half hail (ice), and the sinners therein when they come out from the fire are tortured by the hail (ice), and when they come out from the hail (ice) the fire burns them, and the angels who preside over them keep their souls within their bodies [as it is said, "for their worm shall not die, neither shall their fire be quenched" (Isaiah lxvi. 24)].

3. We read further, "God created seven hells, in each hell are seven compartments, in each compartment there are seven rivers of fire and seven of hail (ice), the width of each is 100 cubits, its depth 1000 cubits, and its length 300 cubits, and they flow one after the other, and all the sinners pass through them and are burned, but the 40,000 angels of destruction who preside over them revive them and raise them on their feet and announce to them their deeds which were evil, and their ways which were crooked," and they say to them, "Pass now through the rivers of fire and hail and snow, just as you passed over and transgressed the law and the commandments which were given unto you on Mount Sinai, for you feared not the fire of hell and the punishment of Abadon. Now render account of your deeds!"

4. There are besides in every compartment 7000 holes (crevices), in every hole there are 7000 scorpions. Every scorpion has 300 slits (cavities), in every slit 70,000 pouches of venom, from these flow six rivers of deadly poison. When a man touches it he immediately bursts, every limb is torn from him, his body is cleft asunder, and he falls dead upon his face. The angels of destruction collect his limbs and set them, and revive the man and place him upon his feet and take their revenge upon him anew.[1]

---

[1] I. 42, V. 24.

VIII.

Paradise.

(In *Massechet Atziluth*, ed. Warsaw, 1876, f. 54 *a-b*; Siddur *Amram*, Warsaw, 1865, I. f. 12ᵇ–13ᵃ).

R. Ismael tells: "Sagansagel addressed me and said to me: 'My beloved! sit in my bosom and I will tell thee what will happen to Israel.' So I sat in his bosom and he looked at me and wept; and tears flowed from his eyes and dropped on my face. And I said: 'Glorious heavenly light! Why dost thou weep?' And he answered: 'Come and I will show unto thee what is awaiting my holy people Israel.' He took me and brought me into the innermost place, to the treasure-house of treasures and he took down the books and showed me the decrees of many misfortunes written therein. I asked him: 'For whom are these destined?' And he answered: 'For Israel!' Again I asked: 'Will they be able to endure them?' And he answered: 'Come to-morrow and I will show thee more calamities still.' The next day he showed me still more calamities, for some it being decreed to die by the sword, for others to die of hunger, others again destined for slavery. And I said: 'O glorious heavenly light! have they indeed sinned so heavily?' He anwered: 'Every day new calamities are decreed, but when Israel gathers in his prayer-house and repeats: "May His exalted name be praised" we retain those calamities and do not let them come out from these rooms.' When I left him I heard a voice speaking in Aramaic and saying: 'The holy temple is destined to be ruined and the temple to be a burning light, and the kingly palace delivered over to the owls and the young to slavery, and the princes to death and the pure altar to be profaned, and the table for the shewbread will be carried off by enemies, and Jerusalem will be a desert, and the land of Israel a desolation.' When I heard these

words I was terrified and trembled and I fell down.
Then came the angel Hadarniel and breathed into me a
new soul and lifted me upon my feet and said to me:
'My beloved! what hath happened unto thee?' And
I answered: 'O glorious heavenly light! is there indeed
no salvation for Israel?' And he answered and said:
'Come and I will show thee the treasures of comfort and
help stored up for Israel.' He brought me up and I
saw groups of angels weaving raiments of salvation and
making crowns of life and fixing in them precious stones
and pearls, and anointing them with all kinds of spices
and delights.[1] I asked: 'For whom are these all destined?'
He answered: 'For David, king of Israel.' And I said:
'Show me the glory of David.' And he said: 'Wait
three hours until David will come hither in his glory.'
So he took me and placed me in his bosom, and he asked
me: 'What dost thou see?' I answered: 'I see seven
lightnings running into one another.' He said: 'Shut
thine eyes that thou mayest not be dazzled by the light
which precedes King David.' At that moment the wheels
and Ophanim and holy Creatures and the treasures of
rain and snow, and the clouds of glory and the planets
and the ministering angels moved and shook and said:
'The heavens declare the glory of God' (Ps. xix. 1). I
heard then a loud voice proceeding from Eden crying:
'The Lord reigneth for ever and ever,' and lo! David
was in front and all the kings of his house after him,
each one with his crown upon his head; but the crown
of David surpassed them all, its lustre shineth from one
end of the world unto the other. And David went up to
the heavenly Temple, where a throne of fire stood ready
for him, whose height is of 40 parasangs, its length and
its width double the same. When David took his seat
upon the throne prepared for him, facing that of his
Creator, all the kings of Judah ranged themselves before
him, and the kings of Israel stood behind him. Then he

[1] IV. 1.

began to utter hymns and praises, such as no human ear has heard.[1]   And when he said : ' The Lord will reign for ever and ever.'   Metraton and his company responded : ' Holy, holy, holy is the Lord of Hosts,' and the holy Creatured praised and said : ' Blessed be the glory of the Lord in its place.'   The heavens say : ' The Lord will reign for ever and ever.'   The earth says : ' The Lord hath reigned, does reign, and will reign for ever,' and all the kings respond and say : ' And the Lord will be king over the whole earth.' "

[1] Paul, ch. 29.

THE SCROLL OF THE HASMONÆANS

(MEGILLATH BENE HASHMUNAI).

BY

M. GASTER, Ph.D.

I.—INTRODUCTION.

It is a peculiar fact that scarcely a trace is to be found in the whole ancient Hebrew literature of the glorious times of the Makkabæans. With the exception of the books now included in the Old Testament Apocrypha, no accurate coherent description of these events is known to exist in Hebrew. Talmud and Midrash are alike silent about Antiochus Epiphanes and his generals, about the various forms of persecution, and the great battles fought at Emmaus and at Eleasa, and of the various treaties with the Spartans and the Romans. Nay, more, Juda himself is scarcely ever mentioned, and the name Makkabee, which is known to the ancient writers of the Church, is absolutely unknown.

This is the more surprising, as the commemoration of the dedication of the Temple had been instituted as a religious ceremony. From the year 164 onward, the twenty-fifth day of Kislev is kept throughout Judaism as the first day of the feast of dedication (Chanukah). The lights are kindled and special blessings are recited.[1]

But what is more curious still is, that the only name which is mentioned in connection with that feast is not Juda, nor any one of his brothers, but only and solely Matithya, son of Johanan, their father, and a certain Johanan, high-priest. There must, therefore, be a good reason for this paucity of records, and for the complete ignoring of Juda and his brethren in a piece that was to form part of the liturgy. The events of the past must either have become obscured, through causes which we have to find, or their record must have been purposely preserved in a form greatly at variance with that of the books of the Makkabæans.

[1] The formula and the various liturgical ceremonies are treated in the Massechet Soferim, c. xx. § 1-12, ed. J. Müller, Leipzig, 1878, v. p. 283 ff.

The point from which we have to start in this inquiry is the establishment of that Feast of Dedication. This was the turning-point in the whole tragedy, and had therefore become from the very outset the most important memorial of the recovered purity of the worship. Whatever changes may come, this one would remain. It was too firmly rooted in the hearts of the people, and was undoubtedly kept up by the priests. It was the zeal and valour of a priest which that feast commemorated.

Different, however, it was with the person or persons themselves who acted in that drama. They soon deteriorated; they fell from the lofty pinnacle. The Makkabæan princes, the descendants of Matithya, soon became unlike their great ancestor. They committed first the sin to assume the title of kings, and to sit on the throne which tradition and religious feeling kept for the descendants of David alone. The Hasmonæans were priests, and had, as such, no right upon the royal position. It was a presumption which men like the zealous Assidæans of the time could certainly not tolerate, and still less acquiesce in. It remained a blot on the fair memory of the Makkabæans, of which practically only one kept free—Matithya, the Hasmonæan. To this the Makkabæans added another sin, no less heinous in the eyes of the orthodox, strict observers of the law. In the strife of parties which arose soon afterwards, they sided with the Sadducæans, persecuted the Pharisæans, the orthodox upholders of the law and the descendants of the Assidæans, who were the first to join Matithya, and to fight the Greeks.

Considering that the Pharisæans represented the popular party, and that the legal prescriptions, liturgical forms and ceremonies are mostly institutions fixed by them, one part of the mystery is cleared up. The staunch upholders of the law would not canonise, if I may use that word, men like Alexander Jannai and others whose death they celebrated as a festival, or introduce the name and memory of the Makkabæans, as they called themselves, in the history or in the liturgy of the nation. That explains also to a certain extent why the allusions to the Makkabæans are so scarce in the Talmud and Midrash. This literature is that of the Pharisees, and the Makkabæans were their bitterest foes.

The deliverance was due to divine intervention, but the persons chosen proved afterwards unworthy of the mission intrusted to them.

The result of this feeling was, that instead of having an exact record of those remarkable times, all that we have is, with but one exception (I. Makkabees), a mixture of truth and fiction.

This mutual hatred of the strictly religious and learned party and the Makkabæans, which developed at a very early period of Makkabæan ascendency, precludes the possibility of so-called Hasmonæan Psalms. Even if psalms should have been composed at that time, for which not a single proof is forthcoming, the Sopherim and learned men, the Pharisees, would certainly not have included them in the sacred canon. If they did not preserve in the ancient contemporary literature any detailed record of the great achievements of Judas Makkabee and his brethren, how much less would they compose encomia in their praise, or include them in the sacred psalter!

But a time came when the Hasmonæans belonged to the past, and their glorification could only tell against Herod, hated by all alike. It is to that period that I ascribe now the only connected description of the rise of the Hasmonæans, of the dedication of the Temple which has survived in its primitive Semitic form. An old tradition, which has been preserved in the Halachoth Gedoloth of Simon Kiyara,[1] says: "The presbyters (elders) of the schools of Shammai and Hillel (first century B.C.) wrote the 'Scroll of the house of the Hasmonæans,' but until now it has not become (canonical) for all times, till there will be again a priest who would wear the אורים and תומים. They also wrote the 'Scroll of fast-days' in the hall of Hananya ben Hizkiyahu, when they came to visit him, but the succeeding generation (Beth-Din) declared it apocryphal." This last Scroll contained the list of the memorable days from the Makkabæan period. Those days were kept as festival days and called fast days, i.e., in which it was not allowed to fast. With the destruction of the Temple these ordinances became invalidated. The difficult passage from the work of Simeon, which I have translated differently from others, is of the utmost importance for the chronicle with which I deal here. It shows us first the circle where that chronicle was composed. It is exclusively that of the orthodox party. It further points to the probable date of that composition; and thirdly, we learn to know indirectly also the language in which that Scroll was written.

However important the question may be, it is not here the place to discuss in what language were written the apocryphal and pseudo-epigraphical books of the Old Testament. As to the Books of the Makkabæans themselves, the general consensus of opinion is in favour of ascribing a Semitic original to the first, and of considering the others as being written originally in Greek. I doubt this latter

[1] Ed. Venice, 1547, f. 141d.; ed. Hildesheimer, p. 615, Berlin, 1891.

statement very much, as far as the II. Makkabees is concerned.   I
said a *Semitic* original for the I. Makkabees without specifying the
dialect.   In all probability it was originally written *not* in Hebrew,
though Grimm inclines towards a Hebrew original, but in the vernacular, the Aramaic dialect, which at that time already took the place
of Hebrew in all popular writings.   Of Tobith[1] and Judith[2] there
can be no doubt that they were written in that dialect.   In the same
dialect was now written the " Scroll of fast days," and this is the
language in which the Scroll of the Hasmonæans in its oldest form
has come down to us.   A most decisive testimony for the Aramaic
as being the original we have in the words of the famous Gaon
Saadya, who states most explicitly in his Sefer hagalui[3] that
"the sons of Hashmunai, Juda, Simeon, Johanan, Jonathan, and
Eleazar, wrote all that happened to them in a book in the language
of the Chaldæans, identical with that of the Book of Daniel."   And
further on he quotes a passage from it which we find really in our
Scroll.[4]   We learn also from Saadya that this book was divided
into *verses*, as all the Biblical books are.

Coming from the same school and belonging to the same period,
it can be no wonder that both Scrolls were written in the same language.   A careful examination of the contents will also show that
in tendency and form the Scroll of the Hasmonæans is closer allied
to that of Fast days than to the Books of the Makkabæans and to
Josephus ; but what is more, it seems to have been the *only* source
of all the fragments of the Makkabæan history which we find in the
Talmud and Midrash, and also of the prayers for the Feast of Dedication.   These all agree in the essential portions of the narrative.

Throughout the Jewish literature Juda is almost entirely ignored,
and everything is traced back to Matithya and Johanan the high-
priest ; and exactly so is the narrative of the Scroll.   Not a word
is further mentioned in the Books of the Makkabæans of the
miraculous flask of oil that lasted for eight days,[5] whilst this alone
is recorded in the Scroll of the fast-days and in the Talmudical
passages to which I refer anon.   One more remarkable point of
difference between the Scroll and the Books of the Makkabæans is the
era, as the former counts from the year of the building of the Temple,
whilst the Books of the Makkabæans have all the Seleucidian era.

It is further to be noted that the name *Chanuka* does not appear

---

[1] *Vide* A. Neubauer, The Book of Tobit, Oxford, 1878, p. xiv.-xv.
[2] A quotation in Nahmanides to Deuteron. xxi. 14.
[3] Ed. Harkavy, St. Petersburg, 1891, p. 150.   [4] *Ibid.*, p. 180.
[5] *Cf.* I. iv. 50-59 ; II. x. 1-8.

at all in this chronicle, though the feast is known from very ancient times under that name, *i.e.*, *The feast of the dedication of the Temple.* This ignorance of the official name goes a long way to prove the antiquity of the chronicle. It must be anterior to the time when this name obtained, otherwise it would be utterly inexplicable why it should not have been mentioned at all.

The following are the places in Talmud, Midrash, and rabbinical literature in which reference is made to the Hasmonæans and to the feast of dedication :—

Megillath Taanith, chap. 9 (month of Kislev). Tract. *Sabbath*, f. 21*b*. Tr. *Megillah*, f. 2*a*; *Rosh hashana*, f. 18*b*. (quotes Meg. Taanith), cf. *ib*. f. 19*a*. *Seder Olam Rabba*, ch. 30. *Seder Olam Zutta*. *Genesis Rabba*, sec. 23. *Exodus Rabba*, sec. 15, f. 113*b*. *Midrash Psalms*, to Ps. ix. 8, ed. Buber, p. 85, No. 65. *Jalkut*, to Kings i. 7, and Psalm xxxvi. *Midrash* quoted by Nachmanides ad Numbers ch. 7. *Sheeltoth*, ch. 26 and ch. 72. *Halachoth Gedoloth*, ed. Hildesheimer, p. 83. *Semag* of Moses of Coucy, ed. Ven., 1547, f. 250*c*. V. *Rabinowitz*, Dikduke Soferim ad Sabbath, p. 39, note נ.

The apparent anomaly in the official forms of thanksgiving which forms part of the liturgy of the feast of dedication finds its only explanation in the narrative of the Scroll. Many a commentator has in vain tried to solve the enigma of the words with which it begins, viz., "In the days of the Hasmonæan Matithya, son of Johanan, the high-priest, and his sons" (as it stands still in the last authorised English edition of the Prayer Book, 1892).[1] This reading is, however, corrupt. The oldest, recorded in a MS. of Masechet Soferim, is: "In the days of Johanan the high-priest, and the Hasmonæan and his sons," which the modern editor of Masechet Soferim did not understand.[2] In the light of the Scroll, this form is perfectly correct and intelligible. Johanan the high-priest is the man who, according to the Scroll, kills Nikanor, and is a person totally different from Matithya, who is here designated as "the Hasmonæan." He being also the son of *a* Johanan, not *the* Johanan the high-priest, this coincidence led to the confusion which we find in the various texts and in the readings of some of the Prayer Books.

If anything, this is a decisive proof for the authority the Scroll must have enjoyed in the sixth or seventh century, and that it was the *only* source of information for the Talmudic period and for the time when the liturgy was fixed for the Feast of Dedication. The question may now be urged whether we could not assume

[1] Ed. Singer, p. 52.   [2] Ed. Müller, p. 287.

that the original language of the scroll was Hebrew, and that it had been translated at a later time into Aramaic, this being like the Targum to other Biblical books. Against this theory there is— (1.) the direct testimony of Saadya; (2.) the old tradition in the work of Simon Kiyara, and the natural inference from the fact that all the other Apocrypha were written in Aramaic; further, that all the quotations in later times are in Aramaic. I have to add to these proofs some more which I have culled from some of the names that occur in the Scroll which we find afterwards in some of the most ancient liturgical pieces.

There is first the name of the Hasmonæans. As already observed, that of Makkabæans, as title of the family, does not occur even once in the old Hebrew literature; only that of Hasmonæans is known. So also does our Scroll not know the former, and bears accordingly the title, "Scroll of the Hasmonæans" (it being the Scroll of the Synagogue). Without entering into the origin of the name (חשמונ), we find it spelt in the Book of Makkabees Ασσαμωναιοι, hence our pronunciation *Hasmonæan*. The Scroll spells the name *Hashmunai* with *u*, and so it occurs in some of the oldest MSS. I have consulted, both in the formula of the prayer which is recited at the feast of dedication and in the poem of Joseph b. Solomon of Carcassonne, Byzantine Mahzor (Cod. Montefiore, Ramsgate, fourteenth century), Roman Mahzor (Cod. Montefiore, fourteenth century), again in a very old unique print of the fifteenth century. All these have Hashm*u*nai. The name of the king, Antiochos, is spelt Anty*u*chas, and that of the town *Antochia* in the Scroll and in these MSS. and prints—a coincidence which it is impossible to admit to be the result of mere chance; but one must be dependent on the other.

The reason why this Scroll did not obtain from ancient times to be read in the synagogue like the Scroll of Esther is one proof more that it was originally written in Aramaic, and not in Hebrew. Many centuries elapsed before the Targum was considered of sufficient authority to be recited in synagogue without the Hebrew text. Not before the seventh or eighth century was the authority of the Targum so far established as to be treated as something like a sacred text. About that time also this Scroll must have been invested with a certain liturgical character, and considered to be of some authority.

Thence poets drew the materials for their poems which they composed for the service of the feast of dedication. The Scroll itself formed then also part of the liturgy, and it has been preserved as such in the ritual of the Jews of Yemen. In former centuries that Scroll must also have been read in the European communities, as various authorities, from the twelfth and thirteenth centuries, point to that custom; and we find it in a great number of MSS. together with the five Scrolls or with other Hagiographa.   But this Scroll was translated early into Hebrew, which translation follows closely the original, often imitating the idiomatic forms of the Aramaic.   From that time on probably it was treated with greater reverence, almost as a sacred writing.   It was also inserted in MSS. of the Bible.   In a great number of MSS., the list of which is given later on, this Scroll is joined either to the Pentateuch, or more often to the five Megilloth, and in not a few instances to other Hagiographa.   In a MS. of the British Museum of the fourteenth century this Scroll follows the Book of Ezra and precedes the Scroll of Esther. 'In Eastern, specially Yemenite, MSS. it is as a rule accompanied by a literal Arabic translation, each Aramaic verse being followed by its translation, treated thus exactly like the sacred texts.[1]   The Arabic translation does not form one consecutive narrative, as is the case with the history of Hanna and her seven sons.   This is added as a complete independent tale to the chapter of Jeremia which is read as Haphtara on the ninth day of Ab, the day of the destruction of the Temple; so in an ancient scroll on red leather from Yemen in my possession, and so in the Bodleian MS. and in that of the British Museum, Or. 1127.

That treatment shows the religious character with which the Scroll was endowed in later times, whilst in olden times, as mentioned above, it was considered as the only authentic chronicle of the Makkabæan events.   The facts which were related therein were the only facts known in Talmudic and post-Talmudic times, to the exclusion of the books of the Makkabæans and of Josephus also.   These were either unknown, which is the most likely, owing to the language in which they were circulated from a very early period, or were not considered of sufficient credibility.   The former of the two hypotheses is the most probable.

So the Scroll of the Hasmonæans, which had the sanction of the then highest authorities, the schools of Shammai and Hillel, i.e., the whole orthodox party, was adopted as the only true one, not merely as far as the historical events contained therein are concerned, but also, what is more remarkable, the very peculiar chronology of the Scroll was accepted as true.   This chronology is very difficult to reconcile with the real chronology, and yet we find the same

---

[1] This text has been published by Dr. H. Hirschfeld in his Arabic Chrestomathy, London, 1892, p. 1–6.

in the oldest chronological attempt of Rabbi Jose b. Halafta
(second century) and in the Talmud (Tractat Aboda Zara, f. 9^{a}).
Rabbi Jose [1] says : " The Persian rule since the rebuilding of the
Temple lasted 34 years, and that of the Greeks 180, that of the
Hasmonæans 103, and that of Herod 103." This is repeated in the
Talmud in the same words.   Needless to say that thirty-four years
of Persian rule is unhistorical, and that what is assigned here to the
Greek period is more by about twenty years than the date given in the
I. Book of Makkabees (iv. 52), *i.e.*, if we take as last date the day
of Dedication.   In whatever way we count, 180 years, or 175, as
another text [2] has it, is inaccurate ; and yet it is the very same date
that we find in the Scroll (v. 5), " In the twenty-third year of his
reign, which was the year 213 after the building of the Temple,
he determined to go to Jerusalem "—213 = 180 + 33.   In one recension of our Scroll we find further the following computation
(v. 74) : " Thus the sons of the Hashmunæans and their sons'
sons kept the kingdom ever since up to the destruction of the
Temple for 206 years."   Exactly the same number of years is
assigned to the Hasmonæans and Herodians in the Seder Olam and
in the Talmud.   This absolute identity of dates goes far to prove
the antiquity and authority of our Scroll.   These dates must undoubtedly have been taken from the Scroll as *the* chronicle of that
period.   It is difficult to decide whether the last verses, with the
date of the Hasmonæan kingdom, belonged originally to the text of
the Scroll or were afterwards added.   If we admit them to have
belonged to it, it would settle at once also the question of the *age*
of the Scroll ; but it seems that they have been added later on, as
the *oldest* MSS. available (C. and B.) do not have these concluding
verses.   They may have been added soon after the destruction of
the Temple, for it is to be noted that not a single word about the
Romans is to be found in the Scroll, not even an allusion.

We turn now to the sources of the Scroll.   After all which precedes here, it is obvious that none of the Books of the Makkabæans
served as direct source to this compilation.   Nor do I think is any
direct written source to be thought of, but the Scroll rests mostly
upon oral tradition.   In this scroll, the mere outline of the events
are given, and in the light in which they appeared in later times.

We can easily understand the reason why only Matithya, Nikanor,
and Bacchides have been singled out.   These three names stood out
prominently ; *Matithya*, because he gave the signal of revolt, and

---

[1] Seder Olam Rabba, ch. 30, ed. J. Meyer, Amsterdam, 1699, p. 91 and 1143.
[2] Seder Olam Sutta, ib.

he alone had not assumed any regal title or prerogative; *Nikanor*, because the victory over him, recorded I. Makk. vii. 43–49, and embellished II. Makk. xv. 28 ff., was celebrated afterwards by a special day of feasting (13th Adar); and *Bacchides*, because Juda fell in the battle against him at Berea, when his whole army was destroyed (I. Makk. ix.). On these three names the popular fancy fastened, and these three alone are the chief personages in the narrative of the Scroll.

The salient points of the persecution and the names of those persons who were the representatives of persecution and deliverance have thus been preserved, and are embodied in the narrative of the Hasmonæans, but in a peculiar form. The relation between the Scroll and the first Book of Makkabees may be said to be akin to that of Hagada and simple text. Legendary embellishment can be traced already in the second Book of Makkabees, and still more in the Syriac translation of it. It is the same spirit, though not exactly the same tendency, in the Scroll as in the second Book of Makkabees. In the contents the Scroll approaches also more the second Book of Makkabees than the first Book, and uses often the same expressions as the Syriac paraphrase. The compiler of the second Book mentions now Jason of Cyrene as the author of the work from which he drew the materials for his own compilation. It is still doubtful whether Jason's work was written in Greek, or possibly in Hebrew or Aramaic. Should this latter have been the case, we could then see in that work the remote source for our Scroll. It is safer, however, to consider oral tradition as the foundation of this narrative of the Scroll, which served also to embellish the narrative of the second Book and the Syriac translation or paraphrase. In the footnotes to the English translation of the Scroll I have indicated the parallel passages from the Books of the Makkabæans.

It would have carried me too far should I have attempted to add the Syriac parallels to the text. I will point out, however, two or three of the more important parallels, especially the almost identical forms of the proper names. First, the very significant change from *Bacchides* into בַּכְרִיוֹס, Bakrios or Bikrios or Bikris (so in the three passages in which that name occurs, I. Makk. vii. 8; ix. 26; II. Makk. viii. 30), to which corresponds בגרים (Bagras or Bagris) in our text. The name מקבי is spelt identically in both versions, מַתִּיתָא Syr. and מַתִּתְיָה in our text, not Ma*t*atya, as in Greek and Latin; besides many other similarities of language which one notes easily when reading both texts side by side.

In the Targum to the Song of Songs, dating probably from the seventh century, we find also (ch. 6, v. 7–9) a short tale about the wars of the Makkabæans, which has, however, a thoroughly legendary character. The king whom the Hasmonæans fight is Alexander, and Matithya is called high-priest. Not one of his sons is mentioned by name; the whole credit of the victory is given to Matithya. Therein lies the identity with the recension of the Scroll, whence also the minor detail of the elephants and the warriors clad in coats of mail must have been borrowed.

For a few details, however, the Scroll of Esther served as model, and a few verses are almost identical. It is, however, noteworthy that the expressions used in our Scroll are totally different from the Targum of the corresponding verses in the Scroll of Esther. The one is therefore independent of the other.

Our Scroll being thus written or sanctioned by men of authority who lived in the first century before the Christian era, is of undoubted great value for historical as well as for philological researches. We have here one of the oldest writings in Aramaic, possibly older than the Targumim, which has been preserved, on the whole, in the original form. The quotations from it in other Talmudical writings, and by Saadya Gaon, agree exactly with the text of the Scroll, especially with the Eastern recension. As we shall soon see, we have two recensions of it, an Eastern and a Western. The former is the best and most accurate. It helps us also, as I think, to settle now finally the correct spelling of the name Makkabee.[1] If any one, those persons who lived nearest to the times when Makkabi flourished ought to know what that name meant, and how it was to be written. The Greek texts write uniformly Ma*kk*abaioi with two *k*'s; the Syriac translation of the second Book of Makkabees, which, as already observed, comes nearer to our Scroll, has always ܩ, and in the Scroll we find in all the Eastern MSS. מקבי, with the epithet קטל תקיפין, killer of the powerful, i.e., hammer or hammerer; and so in the poem of Josef of Carcassone, and in the Commentary קמחא דאבישונה, in the Roman Mahazor.[2]

II.

I turn now to the consideration of the text itself.

The Scroll of the Hasmonæans has come down to us in two forms, Hebrew and Aramaic. Of these two, the Hebrew version is the younger, it being in most recensions a literal translation from the Aramaic original. This translation was known only in Europe, and must have been made here at a time when the knowledge of the

---

[1] *Cf.* S. T. Curtis, the name Macchabee, Leipzig, 1876.   [2] Ed. Bologna, 1541, f. 152ᵃ.

Aramaic declined and the reading of the Targum began to be dis-
continued.   There are two recensions of this version : one, A., the
simple translation of the Aramaic text,[1] and another, B., that is also
based upon the same text, but the subject is treated with some
liberty.[2] Besides, there is also another amplified recension, C., into
which have also entered elements of the Judith legend.[3]   As this
recension had been versified by Joseph b. Solomon of Carcassonne
(in his liturgical poem, אודך כי אנפת, in the Roman and Italo-Germ.
rite, *v*. Zunz, Litgesch. S. P., p. 123), who is older than Rashi, it
must have been known in Europe, and specially in France, already
in the eleventh century.   Another poet, named Moses, probably of
the same period, makes use of this recension in his poem, but with
the omission of Judith and Holofernes.[4]

We must therefore admit that the recensions A. and B. belong
to a somewhat later period, twelfth or thirteenth century.

The Aramaic text shows also differences in the various MSS.
Those from the East, I., are far more correct, and more free from
interpolations, mistakes, and omissions than those which were written
in the West.[5]   The copyists of the Western group of MSS., II., are
not free from blame.   Their copies abound in blunders, and are not
so trustworthy as those copied in the East.   Here they formed part
of the liturgy, and, moreover, were treated with veneration and
care.   Like the other Targum texts in Eastern, especially Yemen
MSS., they have the vowels added, the system used being the Babylonian or superlinear, whilst the Western or European texts have
no vowel signs, and are in consequence thereof much easier exposed
to changes and to mistakes.   Hitherto only the Western recension
has been published, and this, too, from different MSS.   Not one of
these is satisfactory from a strictly scientific point of view.   No other
texts have been collated, no variants marked, no mistakes pointed
out, and not even the relation that exists between those texts that
were published has been so far indicated.

I have therefore decided, for the new publication of this Scroll, to
start not from the corrupted MSS. of group II., but from the far
superior MSS. of group I.   Being part of the liturgy, this Scroll is
found, as a rule, in all the prayer books of the Jews of Yemen.
Besides, it has also found a place in copies of the Bible.   It is in
such a copy from the fourteenth century that we find the oldest

---

[1] All the editions and Mahazorim.   [2] Hemdath Hayamim and Jell., i.
[3] Jellinek, i. 132-136.
[4] זכור מעללי יה , in Roman and Byzantine rite.
[5] These formed the basis of the Hebrew translations, which have those defects in
common with the Aramaic recension.

extant text of the Scroll. Unfortunately almost one-third is missing, as two leaves of the MS. are lost.

The basis of my publication is a comparatively modern copy of the Prayer Book (eighteenth century) in my possession. Though a recent copy, it seems to be the most carefully executed of all I could compare. It is the only one in which the Daggesh is to be found at all. I do not wish to discuss here whether that Daggesh is everywhere correctly put where we find it in that MS. The others have no trace of it. With this I have compared another MS. of the Prayer Book of the fifteenth or sixteenth century, also in my possession (B.), and a text from the fourteenth century (C.), giving in the footnote all the variants, not only of words, but also of vocalisation.

It is an undoubted fact that the vocalisation of the Targum in all our printed editions is decidedly wrong, it being a transcript from the Babylonian to the Palestinian system (as they are called), which has been deteriorating from one edition to the other. Only the texts with the Babylonian punctuation have preserved to us the correct pronunciation of the Aramaic language in which the Targumim were composed. Minute attention must therefore be paid to vocalisation of the Yemen MSS., and every variant carefully noted, as we shall otherwise never come to fix satisfactorily the true pronunciation of that language. The MSS. vary also among themselves, and one can show that changes took place in the course of time even in the system of vocalisation itself. So, for instance, we find in Cod. C. a sign of רפה on כ and ג, in the form of a small curved stroke over the letter, which disappears completely in subsequent MSS. On the other hand, we do not find one single instance of (ּ) against later MSS., where we find this complex sign over קבל קדם, and לקבל.

These peculiarities must not be undervalued, nor the interchange between Holem (ֹ) and Kamez (ָ), as this may show how these vowels were actually pronounced at the time of the scribe of each MS. All these variants have therefore been carefully noted. I have further collated the text with two MSS. from group II. (D.), the text published by Jellinek from a MS. of 1559; and (E.) a MS. from the fifteenth or sixteenth century (Cod. 219, Montef. College); and further (F.), Cod. Brit. Mus. 2212, a Yemen MS. from the fifteenth century, the copy of which I owe to the kindness of Rev. G. Margoliouth. I have transcribed the vowel signs, and added to the text an English translation, and in the notes to it I have adduced the parallel passages from the Books of Makkabees.

I will now give here the literature of our subject—a list as com-

plete as possible of all the editions and MSS. known, both of the
Hebrew versions and Aramaic originals, as well as the bibliography
of the studies that have appeared hitherto about this Scroll.

HEBREW.

Editions.[1]—In Mahazorim : Italo-Germ. rite, Venice, 1568, folio, i. f.
56a, 56b. ס׳תפלת ישרים, Venice, 1750, 8vo, f. 105a, 107b ; ib. 1772, 8vo,
f. 105a, 107b ; *ib. 1666, 8vo. Sabionetta, 1557, 4to, f. 24–25. Sephardi סדר תפלות, Amsterdam, 1661, f. 197a–199a ; ib. 1716, 8vo, f.
184a–185a ; ib. 1728, 8vo, f. 196a–198a. *Salonica, *Wien, 1819, f. 202.
In the Prayer book עבודת ישראל, ed. Baer, Roedelheim, 1868, p. 441–445.

Independently printed : added to the Pentateuch, from the Sp. Prayer-
book ; reprinted by Bartolocci, Bibliotheca Magna Rabbinica, i. 383 ff., with
a Latin translation (Rome, 1675). *Neapel, 1491. Constantinople, 1505.
*Mantua, 1557 ; ib. 1725. Hamburger Altona, 1720. Berlin, 1766.
Farhi, עושה פלא, Livorno, 1870, I. f. 13a–14b.

Reprinted : Jellinek, בית המדרש, i. p. 142–146. With the Aramaic text,
Filipowski, London, 1851 (together with מבחר הפנינים, p. 73–100). Slutzki,
Warsaw, 1864.

B. חמדת הימים, ed. Constantinople, in the year ואתנם, ii. f. 61c ff.,
reprinted by Jellinek, *l.c.*, i. p. 137–141.

C. Jellinek, *l.c.*, i. p. 132–136 (from the Leipzig MS.), vi. p. 1–3 (Cod.
Munchen, No. 117, 4).

MANUSCRIPTS.—British Museum, Harley, 5713 (published by Filipowski),
Or. 1480, Hebrew and Aram. Yemen MS.

Oxford, Cod. 30 (Neubauer) ad. Pentat., 1480 ; Cod. 32 ad. Pentat.
and Haphtaroth of 1483 ; Cod. 94 ad. Hagiographa, 1305, Spanish hand ;
Cod. 174 ad. Onkelos ; Cod. 2229, 6, Collectanea from the sixteenth to
seventeenth centuries (?) ; Cod. 2305 m. id., Italian cursive characters.

Paris, Cod. 43 (Zotenberg) at the end of Pentat. and Megilloth ; 46,
also at end of Pentat., middle of fourteenth century, Spanish hand. This
MS. seems to be the original from which a copy was made for Wagenseil,
now Cod. Leipzig, No. 32. Cod. 716, 10, fourteenth century.

Parma, De Rossi, Cod. 850, Pentat. etc. from 1469. Hebrew and Aram.,
Cod. 414, Pentat. and Hagiogr. sec. xiii.

Hamburg, Cod. 19 (Steinschneider), Hagiogr. 1480, formerly Hinckel-
man (Wolf, i. 204, No. 336).

Rome, Cod. 26, Vatican, before 1438.

Leipzig, Cod. xxxii. 4 (Delitzsch), Wagenseil's copy, with the variæ lect.
of the ed. Bartolocci.

ARAMAIC.

Editions.—H. Filipowski, London, 1851, from Brit. Mus. Harley, 5686
ff. 18a, 19b. (ס׳התדיר, written 1466, Prayer book), with the Hebrew parallel

---

[1] A star marks those editions which I have not seen.

and with an English translation. The MS., however, is incorrect, and Filipowski has completed lacunæ, &c., from the Hebrew, retranslating them into Aramaic. This edition has been reprinted by *D. Slutzki*, Warsaw, 1863, who has added a short introduction.

J. Lewinsohn retranslated the Aramaic text into Hebrew (Hamagid, 1873, vol. xvii. f. 61 ff.).

A. Jellinek, Beth-hamidrash, vi. 4–8, from a Cod. of 1559.

J. Taprower, Mainz, 1874; the Cod. Leipzig, II. (v. Harkavy, p. 207, No. 5).

MANUSCRIPTS.—*A. Western: British Museum*, Harley, 5686 (ed. by Filipowski).

Ramsgate, Cod. Montefiore, 219,. f. 49*a*–50*b*, Italian cursive hand (sixteenth century ?).

Paris, Cod. 20, Pentat. from 1301 ; Cod. 47, id. circa 1350, Spanish hand.

Parma, De Rossi, Cod. 414, end of thirteenth or fourteenth century ; Cod. 989 of 1400 ; Cod. 951, fifteenth century ; Cod. 1026, from 1474 ; Cod. 535, from 1484.

Florenz, Cod. 52 (Biscioni, p. 143), thirteenth century.

Leipzig, Cod. II. (Delitzsch), Pentat., formerly Wagenseil ; Cod. xxxii. 3, a copy of it made by Wagenseil, who added a Latin translation to it.

B. Eastern recension, all MSS. from Yemen.—Brit. Mus. Or. 2377, Hagiogr., fourteenth century ; Or. 2212, id., fifteenth century. Prayer books, Or. 1479 from 1674 ; Or. 1480, seventeenth century ; Or. 2417 from 1650 ; Or. 2418 from eighteenth century, and Or. 2673 from 1663. In Or. 2227 the scroll is *not* included.

Oxford, 2333, 5, the five Megilloth and scroll ; 2498, Yem. Prayer book.

Berlin, Cod. 89 (Steinschneider f. 55*b*), sixteenth to seventeenth century, and Cod. 91, seventeenth century, both Prayer books. To these I add the *two* MSS. in my possession.

TRANSLATIONS.—Besides the Hebrew translation, which in its turn served as original for other translations, the Aramaic text has been translated into *Persian*, Paris Codex, No. 130, 4 (seventeenth or eighteenth century), written with Hebrew characters, and into *Arabic*. This translation accompanies the text in all the Eastern MSS. following each verse. So, at any rate, in all the MSS. I have been able to see.

The *Hebrew* text, as I have just remarked, has been translated into

1. *Latin*, by Bartolocci, *l.c.* (*v.* above), reprinted by Fabricius, Cod. Pseudepigr. Vet. Test., i. 1165 ff., and Scip. Gambato Archiv. V. Test., p. 511 ff. Wagenseil added his translation to Cod. Leipzig, xxii.

2. *German*, Anonymous translation, Venice, 1548 (from this B. Frenk made a Hebrew translation, Wien, 1822). *Jacob b. Abraham* made a translation in prose, Amsterdam, s. l. and a. (eighteenth century) ; a translation in verse appeared s. l. and a., probably in Prag. (eighteenth century).

3. *Spanish*, under the title נס חנוכה, s. l. and a. (nineteenth century), together with Judith.

LITERATURE.—*Zunz*, Gottesdienstliche Vortraege, p. 124, note *f.*

M. Steinschnieder, Catal. Bodl., col. 206, 207.

C. L. W. Grimm, Kurzgefasstes exegetisches Handbuch zu den Apokry·
phen. Das Buch d. Makkabäer, Leipzig, 1853, p. xxx. (who declares the
book valueless for the study of the book of the Makkabæans, and decides
hat it was not composed before the war of Hadrian).

A. Jellinek, Beth. hamidrash, i. p. xxii.–xxv. ; vi. p. vii.–ix.

A. Harkavy, Studien u. Mittheilungen aus der K. Bibliothek zur Petersburg, v. 1, 1891, p. 205–209.

C. Josephson, Die Sagen über die Kämpfe der Makkabäer gegen die
Syrer. Breslau, 1889.

This is, so far as I have been able to ascertain, the bibliography and
literature of the Hasmonæan scroll. Should I have omitted any MS., or
edition, or translation, I trust a critical reader will be able to fill up that lacuna.

TRANSLATION

(1) And it came to pass in the days of Antiochas, king of Yavan. He
was a mighty and powerful king, and potent in his realm, and all the
kings obeyed him. (2) He conquered many countries, and powerful kings
he bound in fetters ; he destroyed their castles, burned their palaces with
fire, and bound their inhabitants (valiant men) in fetters. (3) He built a
mighty town close to the shore of the sea, which should be for him the
residential house, and he called it *Antochia* after his own name.[1] (4)
Also Bagras (Bakchides), who was second in command, built another town
opposite and called it the town of Bagras after his own name. (5) In the
seventy-third year of his reign, which was the year two hundred and
thirteen after the building of the house of God, he determined to go up
to Jerusalem. (6) He spoke to his councillors and said : Do you not know
the nation of the Jews who live among us ? They do not worship our God,
nor do they observe our laws ; they neglect the ordinances of the king
in order to fulfil their laws.[2] (7) They also hope for the day of the
destruction of the kings and rulers, and say : when will our king reign
over us, when we shall rule over sea and land, and all the world will be
delivered into our hand ? It is not for the greatness of the kingdom to
leave these upon the face of the earth. (8) Now let us rise and march
against them, and let us abolish the covenant that has been made with
them to observe sabbath, new moon, and circumcision.[3] (9) And this word
was pleasing in the eyes of his councillors, and in the eyes of his army.
(10) In that hour the King Antiochas rose, and sent Nikanor his second,
with a great army and large multitude, and he came to the town of
Jerusalem.[4] (11) There he made a great slaughter, and placed an idol in

---

[1] Probably Charax-Spasina, at the mouth of the Karun, v. Pliny, vi. xxvii.

[2] *Cf.* Esther iii. 8.   [3] 1 Mak. i. 44–50 ; *cf.* 2 Mak. vi. 5–6.

[4] The general Nikanor ; *cf.* 1 Mak. vii. 26 ff ; 2 Mak. xv. 6 ff (not at all like to
this Nikanor of the text).

the sanctuary on that spot where God had said to his servants the prophets: 'There I will rest my Shekina for ever.' (12) In that time they slaughtered a swine and brought its blood to the hall of the sanctuary. (13) And when Johanan, the son of Matityah, had heard of this thing, he felt sorely grieved and he was filled with anger and wrath, and his countenance was changed, and he meditated in his heart what to do in consequence thereof. (14) Johanan made him a sword two spans long and one span in breadth, and he girded it under his raiment.[5] (15) And he went up to Jerusalem and stood in the gate of the town. And he called to the porters and guards, saying: 'I am Johanan son of Matityah, the high priest of the Jews; I have now come to appear before Nikanor.' (16) The porters and guards went up and said to Nikanor: The high-priest of the Jews is standing at the gate. And he said to them: Let him come in. (17) Then Johanan was brought before Nikanor. Nikanor answered and said: Thou art one of the rebels who revolt against the king, and do not desire the peace of his kingdom. (18) Johanan answered and said: I have now come before thee to do what thou wishest. (19) Nikanor [1] answered and said: If thou desire to fulfil my wishes, take a swine, sacrifice it to the idol, and take its blood into the hall of the sanctuary, and I will array thee in the royal apparel, and I will cause thee to ride on the king's horse, and shall be as one of the king's beloved.[2] (20) When he had heard that word, Johanan replied and said: My lord, I am afraid lest the children of Israel might hear that I have done so, and they would kill me with stones. Let therefore all [that stand] before thee go out, so that they should not make it known to the children of Israel. (21) Then Nikanor let every man go out, who stood before him. (22) At that time Johanan, son of Matityah, lifted his eyes to heaven, and offered his prayer to the Master of the Universe, and said: 'My God, and the God of my forefathers Abraham, Isaac, and Jacob. (23) (and he said) Do not deliver me into the hands of this uncircumcised, lest he would kill me and go and offer praises in the temple of Dagon, his false god, and he will say: My idol has delivered him into my hand.' (24) At that time he walked up to him three steps and thrust his sword into his heart, and cast his corpse into the hall of the sanctuary. (25) Johanan answered and spake to the God of heavens: My Lord, put no guilt on me, for that I have slain this uncircumcised in the sanctuary. So mayest thou deliver [into my hand] all the heathen that come to Jerusalem to cause the children of Israel to err. (26) Then, on that day, Johanan went out and he arrayed battle against the heathen, and he made a great slaughter among them; and those that escaped from the sword fled in boats to the king Antiochas. (27) The number of the slain, that were killed on that day was of seventy-two thousand and seven hundred, for they slew each other. (28) In his residence (place), he erected a minaret [pillar] and called it after his own name, *Makbe, killer of the powerful.* (29) And when Antiochas heard that Nikanor, his second, had been slain, he was sorely grieved; and

[5] *Cf.* Judges iii. 16. [1] *Cf.* 1 Mak. ii. 17–18. [2] *Cf.* Esther vi. 8.

he sent and called Bagras the wicked, the misleader of his nation. (30) And
Antiochas, the king, answered and said to Bagras : Knowest thou not, or
hast thou not heard, what the children of Israel have done unto me ?   They
have killed my army and have spoiled my troops and commanders.
(31) Will you now rely upon your substance or upon the houses that you
have ?   Let us get up and rise against them, and let us abolish the covenant
that has been made with them (to observe) Sabbath, new moon, and circumcision.   (32) And Bagras the wicked rose with all his army and came to
the town of Jerusalem.   (33) He made there a great slaughter, and
decreed a strong decree against Sabbath, new moon, and circumcision.
(34) Thus when the command of the king [3] was urgent against every one
who would circumcise his son,[4] they brought a man and his wife and hanged
(crucified) them against the child.   (35) And a woman who had given birth
to a son after the death of his father had him circumcised when he was eight
days old.   She went upon the wall of Jerusalem and her circumcised son in
her hand.   (36) She answered and said : To thee, Bagras the wicked, be it
said, the covenant of our forefathers will not cease from among us, nor from
our children's children.   And she threw her son down to the bottom of the
wall, and she fell after him, and both died.[1]   And many of the children of
Israel did likewise, and would not change the covenant of their forefathers.
(37) At that time the children of Israel said to each other : Let us go and
retire into a cave, lest we should violate the Sabbath.   And the Jews were
betrayed before Bagras.   (38) Then Bagras sent armed men, and they
went to the entrance of the cave and said : Children of Israel, come out to
us, eat of our bread and drink of our wine, and do what we do.   (39) The
children of Israel answered and spoke to each other : We remember what
we have been commanded on Mount Sinai : six days shalt thou do all
manner of work, but on the seventh day you must rest.   It is therefore
better for us to die than to violate the Sabbath.   (40) Therefore as
they did not accept them (their proposals), they brought green wood and
lit it at the entrance of the cave ; and there died about a thousand
men and women.[2]   (41) Thereupon the five sons of Matityah, Johanan
and his four brothers, went out and arrayed battle with the heathen.
(42) They made a great slaughter among them ; and those that remained
escaped to the sea-provinces, for they trusted in the God of heavens.
(43) Then Bagras the wicked mounted a vessel and escaped to King Antiochas, and with him those who had escaped the sword.   (44) Bagras an-

---

[3] Cf. Dan. iii. 22.   [4] V. 34–36.   Cf. 1 Mak. i. 61 ; 2 Mak. vi. 10.
[1] Cf. 2 Mak. vi. 10.   [2] V. 37–40 ; cf. 2 Mak. vi. 11–16.

From D. E. : "After that, Bagras the wicked decreed that no virgin should be
married unless she came first to the king.   The Hasmonæans had a daughter, and
they intended to bring her to Bagras the wicked.   When the girl saw what their
intention was, she cried bitterly and loudly, tore her garments, and said to her father
and to her brothers : My brothers, are you thinking to do that unto me and to deliver
me into the hands of that uncircumcised ; instead of acting as your forefathers have
acted, and be zealous as they were zealous on behalf of their sister Dinah ; and He
who created heaven and earth will assist you therein."

swered and said to King Antiochas: Thou, O king, hast proclaimed a decree to abolish from among the Jews Sabbath, new moon, and circumcision, and there is great rebellion in their midst; but even if all the nations, peoples, and tongues should go against them, they will not prevail against the five sons of Matityah, who are stronger than lions, quicker than eagles, and more daring than bears. (45) If now, O king, my advice be acceptable to thee, for if thou wouldst array battle against them with this thine army thou wilt be ashamed before all the kings. (46) Therefore, send letters to all the provinces of thy kingdom, and let come the captains of the armies and with them all the nations, and the elephants clad in coats of mail. (47) Then this word was acceptable in the eyes of King Antiochas, and he sent and called the captains of the armies; and they brought all the nations, and with them the elephants clad in mail. (48) For a second time rose Bagras the wicked, and came to Jerusalem. He made into it thirteen breaches, and he stopped the water of the city and burned her stones until they became like unto dust.[1] (49) He thought in his heart and said: This time they will have no power to resist me, for my army is numerous and my hands strong; but the Lord of heavens did not think so. (50) And when the five sons of Matityah heard it they went to Mizpah in Gilead, the place where they had had salvation in the days of Samuel the prophet.[2] (51) They ordained a fast day, and sat on ashes in order to obtain mercy from the Lord of heavens. (52) Then there fell into their hearts a good advice. Their names were: Juda the first born, Simeon the second, Johanan the third, Jonathan the fourth, Elazar the fifth.[3] (53) Their father blessed them before sending them to battle, and he said to them: Judah my son, I praise (compare?) thy actions, as those of Judah the son of Jacob who was likened unto a lion. (54) And thee, Simeon my son, I praise thy actions as that of Simeon the son of Jacob, who slew the inhabitants of Shechem, who had sinned against Dinah his sister. (55) And thee, Johanan my son, I praise thy actions as those of Abner, son of Ner, the commander of the hosts of Israel. (56) And thee, Jonathan my son, I praise thy actions as those of Jonathan the son of Saul, who slew the Philistines. (57) And thee, Elazar my son, I praise thy actions as those of Pinehas the son of Elazar, who was zealous before his god and saved the children of Israel. (58) Thereupon the five sons of Matityah arose and entered into battle against those heathen and made a great slaughter; and Judah was killed from among them.[4] (59) At that time, when they saw that Judah was slain, they turned back and went to their father, and he said to them: Why did you come back? (60) They answered and said: Our brother Judah has been killed, who was considered alone to be equal to all of us. (61) Matityah answered and said to them: I will go out with you and join battle against these heathen, lest the children of Israel be lost; and ye

---

[1] 1 Mak. i. 31; Josephus, Antiqu., xii. 4, 5. *Cf.* 1 Mak. vi. 62; x. 2.
[2] Ver. 50 ff; 1 Mak. iii. 46 ff.   [3] *Cf.* 1 Mak. ii. 2–5, different order.
[4] *Cf.* 1 Mak. ix. 18 ff. (totally different account.)

be comforted concerning your brother. (62) And Matityah went out that day with his sons and fought those heathen. (63) And the Lord of Heavens delivered into their hands all the mighty of those heathen and they made a great slaughter among them, all who drew the sword or held a bow, and the captains and governors, and none escaped. And those who remained fled to the sea provinces. And Elazar was occupied in killing the elephants, and he fell (in) under the belly (dung) of an elephant. (64) And they searched for him among the living and the dead and could not find him. Afterwards they found him sunk under the belly (in the dung) of an elephant. (65) And the children of Israel rejoiced that their enemies had been delivered into their hands; some of them they burned with fire, others they hung on trees. And Bagras the wicked, the misleader of his people, the children of Israel burned with fire. (66) When King Antiochas heard that Bagras his second was slain, and all the captains that were with him, he embarked into a vessel and fled to the sea provinces. And wherever he came, they revolted against him and called him: fugitive, fugitive. And he threw himself into the sea.[1] (67) Thereupon the children of Israel went up to the sanctuary, and built the gates and cleansed the sanctuary from the slain and from the pollution.[2] (68) And they sought after pure olive oil in order to light the lamps, and they did not find anything but one bottle, sealed with the seal of the High-Priest, from the times of the Prophet Samuel. (69) Therein was sufficient for the lighting of one day; but the Lord of heavens, who caused his name to dwell there, gave a blessing therein, and they lit with it (the lamps) for eight days.[3] (70) Therefore the Hashmunæans ordained and enjoined upon them and the children of Israel (71) to make it known to the children of Israel, that they should keep those eight days with mirth and gladness, similar to the days of festivals prescribed in the Law;[4] to light (the lamps) on them, so as to make it known to those that may come after them, that their God had wrought salvation to them from heaven. (72) On those days they are not to mourn, nor to wail, nor to ordain any fast; only the man who has previously made a vow must pay it.[5] (73) But the Hashmunæan and his sons and brothers did not decree that on them work or worship should cease. From that time on the Greek kingdom had no name any more there.[6] (74) The sons of Hashmunai kept the kingdom, they and their sons, and their sons' sons, from that time on until the second destruction of the House of God, for 206 years. (75) Therefore the children of Israel keep those days in all the Diaspora and call them days of mirth from the 25th day of the month of Kislev. (76) And for ever will not cease from the sanctuary priests and Levites; and all their sages ordained upon them and their children and their children's children for ever. Blessed be the Lord for ever. Amen and Amen.

---

[1] 1 Mak. iv. 36 ff. cf. 6, 7.   [2] Cf. 1 Mak. iv. 50.   [3] Cf. 1 Mak. iv. 59.
[4] v. 2 Mak. i. 9, which is now clearly explained by this passage.
[5] 70–72 v. Esther ix. 27 ff.
[6] This means probably that the Seleucidian era was thenceforth abolished.

A NEW FRAGMENT OF BEN SIRA.

THE first find consisted merely of the fragment which forms now the lower portion of the page. It numbered all told three lines on each side. These lines correspond with chap. xx. 6, 7, 13 of the Greek. The rest was missing. The gap, numbering apparently six verses, opened up a vista of conjectures on the mode of writing, on the size of the leaf and other palaeographical topics. I indulged in them largely, giving free scope to fancy, until I discovered the missing portion, and much of my former work had to be recast. Meanwhile also, papers appearing in the last number of the *J. Q. R.* and of the *Revue des Études Juives* taught that other fragments belonging to the same book had been found elsewhere, viz. in Cambridge and Paris. In writing this I am not indulging in a description of futile attempts of reconstruction, but place on record the fact that any new discovery might and often does entirely upset results based upon conjecture. It applies to the whole text of Ben Sira with equal force, and the final word can then only be spoken, when the remaining portions will have come to light. The *variae lectiones* in the two recensions or groups of MSS. have in a similar manner thrown a new light on the marginal glosses, have set at rest doubts and hypotheses, and have still more complicated the question of authenticity. The present fragment will also not diminish these difficulties.

Before entering upon the minute study of the text itself, it is necessary to consider it from the purely palaeographical point of view, to describe the characteristic features, and to draw some conclusions as to the

חכם יחריש עד עת
וכסיל לא ישמור עת יש
חכם לרבים מחכם ולנפשו
הוא גואל · יש חכם
לנפשו יחכם פרי ד...
על גויתו חכם לנפ...
ישבע תענוג וכל ה...
ואשרוהו · חכם...
...ד ושמ...
עולם חכם...
במעט דבר נפשו טובת
בסילום ישענך חכמה

probable date of this MS.   Hitherto no attempt has been made to describe the other fragments from the palaeographical side, and Mr. Adler has attempted to determine the date of his MS. only from the paper on which it is written.   Assuredly an insufficient guide for the fixing of the age of a MS. without any other corroborative evidence.

The size of this MS. is smaller than that of any other.   It is well known that the smaller the leaves are the older they are, and precede in point of time the larger paper leaves. The length of a leaf seems to grow with its more recent date, especially in the case of leaves used in the making up of a book, destined to be folded in layers of four or more leaves.   Fragments of a very old Haggadah for Pesaḥ, with rudimentary illuminations, are of a similar small size and written on almost the same kind of thick yellow paper. The writing is in accordance with this supposed old age. Large and not clearly determined form of letters is a characteristic of such early writings.   Noteworthy among the archaic form of Hebrew letters is the short form of the final "Nun," the peculiar "Shin," the long "Vav" at the end of the word ; the long stroke at the left foot of the "Tau" and "'Ain" are similar proofs of early date. Another is afforded by the evident care with which the copyist has written the text exactly in twelve lines to the page and on an average four words to the line.   They are uncials or square as in B and not cramped as in Codd. A and C (i. e. the fragment published by Mr. Israel Lévi in the *Revue des Études Juives*, vol. XL, 1900, p. 1 ff.), both written in a cursive hand.   A is considered by Mr. Adler (*J. Q. R.*, p. 467) not later than 832.   The new MS. follows on the whole the text as represented by Cod. B inasmuch as an attempt is made as far as possible to write no more than a hemistich to the line ; so that two lines would correspond with one verse, written in Cod. B in one line across the whole page, with a blank space in the middle.   The oldest Codices of the Bible are written in narrow columns, and later copies retain this division, especially in Psalms,

Proverbs, and Job, as long as possible. The running of
one verse into the other is a sign of later age.

In all the known Codices of Ben Sira the end of the
verses are marked by two dots (:). This new text differs ;
the end of the verse is marked by a single dot (•) and
a blank space of two or three letters. The time when
double dots were introduced has not yet been exactly
determined. In my study of the Samaritan Biblical Scroll
I have pointed out, that the oldest of these Scrolls contains
already the double dot. But that would not make it earlier
than the twelfth or the eleventh century. In the eighth
century, however, it was declared illegal to introduce them
into the Sacred Scroll of the Pentateuch. In order to be
forbidden the practice must have existed and crept in. It
may have been used first in profane literature. This would
place the MS. with the verse-mark of one single dot not later
than the eighth century. Old is also the practice of placing
the dot high up, on a line with the upper portion of the
letter, and not in the middle or at the bottom, as is done in
modern times. In spite of it, however, this text cannot by
any means be so old as the eighth century. The only
guide in Hebrew palaeography, still in its infancy, is the
comparison with dated MSS. of the Bible. The oldest,
assigned to the middle of the ninth century, has no marks
at the end of the verse. It appears in the Codex
Petropolitanus of 916 ; but the small free space which
separates in our MS. one verse from the other has entirely
disappeared. On the other hand we miss there one very
important characteristic, viz. the lengthened letters. It is
well known that Hebrew words are not divided when they
happen to be at the end of a line. In old Codices the
device resorted to by the scribe was to fill the blank space
with parts of letters or with the first two letters of the
word fully written in the following line. Not before the
eleventh century can any trace of the system be found,
according to which some of the letters were lengthened, so
as to fill up the line. Both MSS. A and C have a good

number of such lengthened letters, as the writing goes to
the very edge of the line. The copyist of B, with ample
space at his disposal, had no need to resort to the use of
these letters. The new text has also lengthened letters,
introduced by the copyist for the same reason, i. e. to fill
up his line, although he was not sparing in blank space at
the end of the verse. Finding in one instance that he had
not sufficient room left for another word on the same line
(fol. a, third line from the bottom) he lengthened the final
" Mem " in the word חכם. We do not meet with such
letters in any Biblical MS. earlier than the eleventh century,
and even if we should admit that such letters were first
used in profane literature, before they were introduced into
sacred texts (not the Scroll!) none of these MSS. of Ben Sira
could be earlier than the end of the tenth century or the
beginning of the eleventh; the oldest of them being this
one, as it is more archaic than the others, and is the only
one, except B, written in uncials or square type.

Turning now to the contents, it is at once apparent that
we have in this leaf a further portion of the book of which
two leaves have been found in Cambridge, and one in
Paris, belonging to what I would call the "Abstract"
or "Compendium of Ben Sira," apparently an epitome of
the larger work. The place of this fragment has evidently
been after the first leaf published by Mr. Schechter, as the
author of this compilation follows generally the order of
the chapters in Ben Sira, though this very fragment seems
to offer an exception, indicating that he did not scruple to
go farther afield to borrow some verses from a different
chapter. As far as can be guessed he attempts to group
together sentences and maxims on one and the same
subject, avoiding repetition and reiteration, and he arranges
them in the sequence in which they are found in the fuller
text. Our text contains, according to the misleading
numeration of the Greek version, the following verses:
ch. xvii. 31–33; xix. 1–2; xx. 5–7; xxxvii. 19, 22, 24, 26;
xx. 13, altogether thirteen verses, of which four are known

already, and in two recensions, whilst the rest appears for
the first time, belonging to the chapters still missing.

It is a fortunate coincidence that the verses of chap.
xxxvii are found here also. This is the third copy of
one and the same passage found in the fragment of the
British Museum and in that of Mr. Lévi. In these, however,
the text is fuller, for the verses counted in the Greek as 20,
23, and 25 are found in C (Codex Lévi), and verses 20 and
25 BM (British Museum), 23 being added as a marginal
gloss. Verse 21 is missing in all the three copies. They
are, however, not found in the Hebrew in the same order
as in the Greek. The order in the former is: C 19, 20,
22, 23, 25, 24, 26, 27 ; and BM 19, 20, 22, 25, 24, 26.
This confusion in the order of the verses is the more
interesting, as the parallel passage in the Syriac shows
a similar want of order. Verse 21 is missing in the
Syriac and so is 25. The corruption of this passage in
the Syriac is, however, more apparent than real. The
counting of the Syriac verses is not to be relied upon.
(Mr. Lévi took them to be identical with the Greek text,
and he has therefore compared verses which have nothing
whatsoever to do one with the other.) In the London
Polyglott the numbering does not agree with Lagarde's.
For our purpose we must needs ignore this artificial
counting and divide the text as it stands before us in
the best way possible. We must then no longer compare
19 or 22 with what is counted as such in Lagarde ; but
19 with 22 (corrected as will be shown later on), G 22
with Syr. 23 ; G 24 with Syr. 24 and G 26 with Syr.
26. It must not be forgotten that ver. 25 does not exist
in Syriac, as well as in this Hebrew fragment. The
parallelism between the "Abstract" and the Syriac is now
as perfect as can be wished. The confusion noticed in B
and C is due to the same causes which have disarranged
the order of the Syriac, viz. to the desire of completing the
text by the assistance of other versions or MSS. from
which other verses have been interpolated.

I have dealt with this point at some length, as it is an important one, and may help to determine the relation in which the "Abstract" stands to the fuller recension. The close agreement in the order and also in the form with the Syriac, such as we have it, precludes the possibility that the "Abstract" has been made from the fuller Hebrew recension, as represented by MSS. A, B, and C. It would be a miracle to find the author of the "Abstract" to have omitted exactly those verses that are missing in S, and miracles are excluded from purely literary work. It may be further asked whether these verses are in their proper place in the Greek and Syr. (xxxvii. 19 ff.). It is known to every one who has followed up the internal history of the text that transpositions have taken place. These verses are felt to be incongruous in ch. xxxvii. They stand in no connexion either with what precedes or with what follows ; whilst in the Hebrew the connexion seems perfect. We must bear in mind that the compiler follows the original in a strictly chronological order, except in this one case. In the Paris MS. we have abstracts from ch. vi. 18—vii. 25, in the first leaf of Cambridge iv. 23—v. 13. In this fragment xvii. 31—xx. 13, and in the second leaf in Cambridge xxv. 8—xxvi. 19. (I do not mention the verses omitted, but only the starting and the last verse.) In the original from which the "Abstract" has been made these verses may and have assuredly formed part of ch. xx, filling up the gap here between verses 7 and 13. Ryssel also points out that in ch. xx, ver. 13 joins practically ver. 8.

The old Hebrew original, as far as the wording itself is concerned, cannot have been different from the full recension as recovered. The agreement is so close that no other text could have served as basis for the compiler. The portions found in this MS. which are identical with corresponding portions of the full recension have established this fact beyond doubt. The relation in which this text stands to the other versions will be discussed in the Notes.

It will be found that in some instances the text agrees with the Syriac, in other more rare occasions it agrees with the Greek. In this small fragment, in fact, verses 6 and 13 of ch. xx are missing in the Syriac. But with the actual state of these versions before us, it is more than rash to draw final conclusions either from the presence or from the absence of words and verses in one version or in the other; more decisive is the coincidence in the forms in which words and sentences have been preserved. Not one of these versions has come down to us in its primitive form, nor even in any reliable form. The changes and manipulations to which each one of them has been subjected have been manifold and varied; each has been corrected and interpolated from the other; Greek has been changed over and over again in the course of time; the hand of an Alexandrian author, well acquainted with the LXX, a Christian, and later editors, have modified the translation of Ben Sira; and the activity of the "Hexapla" revisers of the Greek text of the Bible did not stay their hands at Ecclesiasticus. The original from which the Syriac translation has been made was either corrupt or imperfect, and the Syriac text itself has not fared much better. It has seen many changes; alterations by Jewish and Christian hands, noticeable in the Greek, have not left the latter uninfluenced.

I do not wish to enter now into the discussion as to the authenticity of the Hebrew text. I must reserve that for a special study, begun with the first publication of Messrs. Neubauer and Cowley's text, and which is being amplified and completed in consequence of subsequent discoveries. I have no doubt that the Hebrew text now recovered is not the original Hebrew of Ecclesiasticus.

I am now publishing the text, with an interlinear Syriac version in square brackets, so as to facilitate the comparison between the two texts. Missing words and parts have been completed mostly with the assistance of B and C.

xviii. 31 ‏אל תשמח אל שמץ ‏32 ‏שונא ·

[דסנאה: ‏32 ‏לא תחדא בסוגאא]

תענוג אשר פי שנים רישו ·

[דתפניקא . דלא חד תרין תהוא מסכין .]

‏33 ‏אל תהי זולל וסובא ומאומ(ה)

(מסכ זו) (ופקק)

[לא תהוא רוי וזליל כד מדם]

xix. 1 ‏פועל׳ זאת ‏אין בכים ·

[בכיסך לית: פעלא רויא]

(לא י)עשיר ובוזה מעוטים

[לא נעתר . . . .]

‏2 ‏יין ונשים ‏(ית)ערער:

[נארת מסכניתא: חמרא ואנתתא]

(יפ)חזו לב ונפש עזה

[מפחזין לבא . נפשא חציפא]

xx. 5 ‏יש ‏(ת)שחית בעליה ·

[תובד מרה . אית]

(מחרי)ש ונחשב . . .

[דכד שתיק מתחשב חכימא]

יש נמאס בריב . . .

[ואית דמסתנא בסוגאא דשועיתה]

‏6 ‏יש מחריש מאין מענה

[. . . . .]

הלל ‏ויש מחריש כי ראה עת

[. . . . .]

xx. 7 חכם מחריש עד עת

[ונברא חכימא נטר עדנא]

יש xxxvii. 19 · וכסיל לא ישמור עת

ועולא

[ית :וגברא מרחא לא נטר עדנא: אית]

חכם לרבים נחכם ולנפשו

[חכימא דבכל עדן חכים]

הוא גואל· 22 יש חכם

[ומן כל איקר כלא נפשה: ואית חכימא]

לנפשו יחכם פרי דע(תו)

[דלנפשה חכים ופארא דעבדוהי]

על גויתו· 24 חכם לנפש(ו)

[מן חזוא דאפוהי: ודחכים לנפשה]

ישבע תענוג וכל ר(ואיהו)

[נסבע תפניקא]

יאשרוהו· 26 חכם (עם?)

[ונשבחונה כלהון חזיוהי: חכימא דעמא]

(ינחל) כבוד ושמו (עומד)

[נארת איקרא ושמה קים]

חכם xx. 13 · (בחיי) עולם

[לחיא הלעלם:]

במעט דבר נפשו וטובת קמ

[.............]

כבוד   כסילים ישפוך חכמה

[.............]

TENTATIVE TRANSLATION.

xviii. 31. The enemy. 32. Take not pleasure in much cheer, the poverty (caused) thereby is double. 33. Be not a glutton and a drunkard, (when) there is nothing in the purse. xix. 1. One who acts thus shall not be rich, and he that contemneth small things will become destitute. 2. Wine and women defile the heart (mind), and a bold (impudent) soul destroys its master. xx. 5. There is one that keepeth silence, and is considered wise; there is one who is contemned by much (babbling). 6. There is one that keepeth silence, because there is no (or, he hath not an) answer; and some keepeth silence for he seeth the time. 7. A wise man keepeth silence until the time, and the fool will not regard (watch) time. xxxvii. 19. There is one that is wise to many but to himself he is defiled (useless). 22. There is one that is wise to himself, the fruit of his understanding is upon his body (countenance). 24. A wise man to himself shall be satisfied with pleasure (delight), and all that see him shall count him happy. 26. A wise man of the people shall inherit honour and his name standeth for ever. xx. 13. A wise man with a little uttereth his desire, and the goodness of the fool poureth away wisdom.

NOTES.

In these notes special attention is paid to the relation in which the Hebrew text stands to the Syriac, with which it is in close agreement, and by means of which the meaning of the Hebrew is made more clear than by the assistance of the Greek. The Syriac is published here in the form of an interlinear arrangement in order to bring out in many cases the absolute agreement. The Syriac text is disfigured by many glosses and interpolations; a double translation has sometimes been introduced from the margin into the text, and in a few instances the order of the verses and of the hemistichs has been displaced. I have merely rearranged here and

there a word or changed the order in which the verse is standing in
the Syriac. It will then be seen how close the relation is, in which
the two texts stand to one another.

xviii. 31. שונא Hebrew and Syriac: singular. Greek: plural.

ver. 32. I have translated שמץ in accordance with all the versions,
"much." The Hebrew word occurs only twice in Job (iv. 12 and
xxvi. 14), in both cases translated by the Targum: קצת "little."
The talmudic use of the word agrees on the whole with the idea
of "little." The author of the Hebrew text of Ben Sira following
his usual custom, selecting scarce words of the Bible and hapax
legomena, has hit upon this word, and has given it a different
meaning. He surely could not inveigh against a "little" rejoicing
and pleasure; it is the surfeit of enjoyment which he reproves,
which alone would bring poverty in its train. (32 b) The Syriac
חד תרין means "tandem aliquando," inadequately represented by the
Hebrew פי שנים which can only mean "double," and occurs only
twice in the Bible: 2 Kings ii. 9 and Zech. xiii. 8. G. is totally
different from the Hebrew and Syriac; it reads: "neither be tied
to the expense thereof." Ryssel tries to correct the Greek text, and
he translates: "so that thy requirements be not in the long run
double as great." If we detach the first words of the following verse
in the Greek and attach them to the preceding, we find there also
the allusion to "not getting poor," which in the Greek as it stands
is taken to be part of ver. 33. But it makes there no sense whatsoever.
For what can mean: "Be not made a beggar by banqueting upon
borrowing, when thou hast nothing in thy purse." If a man "has
nothing in the purse" he evidently *is* already a "beggar," and cannot
become after banqueting on borrowed money! The fact is that we
must read the Greek (as the Syriac), "lest through double expenses
thou necessarily wilt become a beggar." The Hebrew word רישו
occurs only twice in the Bible—Prov. xiii. 18 and xxviii. 19; translated
in each case in the Targum by מסכינותא.

ver. 33. In the Syriac I have eliminated the word מסכין as it is either
due to a dittography, a senseless repetition of the concluding word
of the last verse, or a correction made from the Greek. The former
seems to be the more correct view. The parallelism between the
Syriac and the Hebrew is now perfect. The Hebrew expression
זולל וסובא occurs twice in the Bible in this connexion—Deut. xxi. 20
and Prov. xxiii. 21; cf. also ver. 20. The reference to the passage in
Proverbs assists us in explaining the difference between the Syriac
and the Hebrew of our Text in the following verse (xix. 1). Instead
of זאת the pronoun, the Syriac has in the first hemistich the noun
from the preceding verse רויא and adds the second noun, represented

by the synonymous expression, רחם בשרא, following the example in
Prov. xxiii. 20, where the Hebrew has זוללי בשר, and the Peshitto adds
the word בשר also in ver. 21.

The Greek of xix. 1 a reads like a wrong translation from
the Syriac: "A labouring man that is given to drunkenness."
H. 1 b agrees better with G. "and he that contemneth small
things." I have completed the last word to read יתערער. The
noun occurs in Ps. cii. 18, where the Peshitto translates צלותא
דמסכינא. The verb occurs Jer. li. 58 עַרְעֵר תִּתְעַרְעָר, but it is translated by all: "uprooted, destroyed, utterly broken." In his usual
way the author of this Hebrew Ben Sira selects the hapax legomena
and scarce words. It can have here no other meaning than in
Psalm cii: "utterly impoverished." The Syriac has נארת מסכניתא
"to inherit *poverty*." G. has: "shall fall little by little."

ver. 2 a. H. agrees absolutely with S., nay the very same words
are used in both, as I felt justified in completing the verb יפחזו,
corresponding in meaning and form to the Syriac מפחזין. This verb
is used more than once by the Hebrew B-S., v. the Glossary to
Neubauer-Cowley's edition, s. v. פחז, where reference is made to this
verse, with the hope that it may have been used. This expectation
has now been fulfilled by the discovery of the Hebrew of·this verse.
G. totally different. לב is taken as "men of understanding," and the
verb rendered by me "defile" or "make wanton" is rendered by G.
"to fall away"; Ryssel adds "from God." He has also misunderstood
the Syriac of ver. 1 b, and still more the following part of this verse.
I omit here the second half of Syriac, i. e. 2 b, as it is not found in the
Hebrew, and what is numbered as Syriac 3 is taken by me to be the
true 2 b. A glance at the Greek and at the Commentaries of Edersheim
and Ryssel will convince every one that this passage is corrupted more
than in the Syriac, though this has also suffered by the intercalation
of 2 b, a mere repetition of 2 a. Ryssel considers ver. 3 S. as a late
interpolation. In the light of the Hebrew text we must reverse this
opinion and reject 2 b as a late interpolation. Ver. 3 S. corresponds
exactly to H. 2 b, word for word. The Hebrew עזה has been rendered
by me "bold, impudent" as in Prov. עזות impudence, roughness,
not "strong." In G. 3 b seems to offer an analogy to this part of the
verse. If we omit in G. 2 b and 3 a, and join 3 b to 2 a we shall have
corrected the text in a much more satisfactory manner than has been
done by Ryssel and others.

xx. 5. Agrees with both versions, S. and G. Ryssel's suggestion
that in the Hebrew stood נמצא, for which G. "found." The Hebrew
here, however, is נחשב "considered," exactly as the Syriac. 5 b בריב
must evidently be read ברוב. I have translated accordingly.

ver. 6. Missing in S., agrees in the main with G. עת here and in
the following verses is used in the same sense as in Eccles. iii. 1 ff.,
"propitious, proper time."   In S. and G. 7 a the word is rendered
"opportunity."

ver. 7 a. H. agrees more with G. than with S. which has נטר in both
halves of the verse.   Both versions have "גברא" or "man" in
connexion with "wise," but in all the following verses it is omitted
regularly.   So throughout in the Hebrew, which has only חכם.
7 b. S. and G. have an addition (due to a marginal gloss) "wicked"
S., and "babbler" G., beside the "fool" which alone is found in H.
Ryssel observes that the true antithesis between ver. 8 (or 7) is ver. 13.
The intermediary would thus appear to be in a wrong place altogether.
Instead then of verses 9-12 found in G. and S. we have in our text
the verses which are now in G. and S. in chapter xxxii. I have already
pointed out above the relation in which the Hebrew stands to the
other versions.   I mention that these new verses have been edited
twice, once by Mr. Margoliouth in the JEWISH QUARTERLY REVIEW,
and a second time by Mr. J. Lévi.   Our present text agrees in the
main more closely with B (the text of Mr. Margoliouth) than
with C (Lévi).   But as the comparison has not been made with the
exactly corresponding verses in S, I must, however briefly, go over
the same ground once more.

xxxvii. 19. H. has the peculiar Aramaic form נחכם, whilst in ver. 22
it is the Hebrew form יחכם.   The parallelism between H. and S.
becomes evident the moment we recognize in S. a displacement of
the second hemistichs in each of the two verses, now S. 20 and 22.
Written in parallel columns one over the other, they have changed
places; 22 b ought now to be what it probably was at the beginning
viz. 20 b, and the latter ought to take its proper place after 22 a.
לרבים is represented in S. by "at all times," "at many times," and
not "for many men."   H. agrees with S. "נחכם=חכים being "wise";
G. has instead "teacheth."

Our text has יגואל like B, against C נואל.   The first appears to be
the more correct form.   It is to be taken as identical with the same
word meaning "pollution, defilement, unworthiness," just as Nehem.
xiii. 29 and other passages in the Bible.   It thus corresponds much
better with the Greek "useless," "unprofitable," for נואל would
have been rendered "foolishly."   S. has "omnique honore privet
seipsum."   The Arabic translation, which rests upon the Syriac,
"suumque deiiciat honorem" (Walton's *Polyglott*).   Surely no more
perfect equivalent could be found for the Hebrew or vice versa in H.,
for it means in all instances "he becomes unworthy."

ver. 22. B and C have ויש like S. לנפשו in all these verses must be

taken as "himself," the personif. of the wise. ‎גויתו in the same
verse corresponds to S. "vultus aspectu," "the outward appearance,"
the "countenance"; "ab eiusdem vultu." Arab. (Walton) in contra-
distinction to "‎נפשו."   C has here also ‎נחכם, not so B.   "The fruit
of his understanding," H., agrees better with G. than with S.   I have
completed the word in accordance with the other MSS. into ‎דעתו.

  ver. 24. This verse is a logical sequence to ver. 22.   Those who
are able to recognize the wise from his aspect, are praising him.
H. agrees with S. and not with G., which is totally different from
H. 24 a, whilst H. corresponds to S. word for word.   The order of
words of 24 b is reversed in C, agreeing even in that detail with S.
In our text the order is somewhat different.   In B this part is
missing through imperfection of the MS.   The verb ‎יאשרוהו is in
plur. as conjectured by Mr. Lévi.   Ryssel misunderstands here also
the passage, and Lévi, not comparing the corresponding verses of S.,
comes to most curious conclusions.

  ver. 26. H. like S. combines "the wise man" with "the people,"
and agrees also in the remaining portion closely.   G. different.
"Honour" adopted by Ryssel is found here also, and in S. Cod. 248
reads ἔσται, exactly as our text has ‎עומד, and so S.   I have added the
word ‎בחיי in conformity with the other text (C), but the true reading
ought to be ‎לחיי.   S. has also a similar form ‎לחיא.

  xx. 13. No S. for this verse.   This verse as it stands does not agree
with any version.   I have tried to translate ‎דבר not as a noun, but as
a verb: identical with the sentence in Micah vii. 3: ‎והגדול דבר הות
‎נפשו "and the great man uttereth his mischievous desire," or "the
desire of his soul."   It would then mean here: "The wise man is
able to utter his desire in a few words, whilst the goodness of the
fool poureth away wisdom like water."

  Thus far this new fragment.   I draw no conclusions.
The close agreement between this text and S. needs no
further pointing out.   Nor is it necessary to urge again the
fact that text and writing exhibit a very archaic character.
The relation between this text and the fuller Ben Sira
still requires careful study.   The problem as it presents
itself to me is to determine in the first instance the claim
of priority of one over the other, that is, to ascertain
whether the smaller depends upon the larger book, or
whether the larger is a later amplification of an older,
smaller text.   After this question has been satisfactorily

disposed of, it will then be time to open the question of
the authenticity of this Hebrew text. It will be the duty
of those who defend the authenticity to explain the surprisingly close and almost literal agreement with the Syriac,
which goes so far as to obliterate the Hebrew character
of this book, notably in its Syntax.

Among the fragments from the Genizah I have found
a small portion of a leaf, in a very bad state of preservation.
The writing, which is almost faint, is of a mixed character,
uncial letters alternating with cursive. Fol. a has six
lines visible, of which five are tolerably legible, though
torn in the middle, and much mutilated at the left side.
The reverse is in a worse condition, and only stray words
can still be seen. As the text seems to stand in some
relation to Sira, one or two maxims finding parallels in
the latter, I am publishing them also, to preserve them from
utter destruction. They are rhymed maxims, and resemble
somewhat the collection published by Prof. Schechter,
J. Q. R., pp. 459–460.

שמע בני והתבונן והתחזק במוסר : [אח]וך שמע . . . [אש] . . .
ושים כבוד לב[ראי]ך . ואל תקוץ במוסר : הותר וגם נאסר . . . .
ותן תודה וגם [י]ר[אה] אש[ר] בהם תיוסר : ב . . . .
ולא תשב מקום רבים [וחבר] . . . כל שר : לא . . . . .
בני כי טוב יא[מר] לך עלה ה . . . לא תוסר . . . . . .

[ה]אלים [נ]אנשים   שמעה
ולא עין דמעות
לבושה   עת   תמים
יק . .

ולא רוא[ה]ה [ו]לא [ת]שכן

THE STORY OF THE DAUGHTER OF AMRAM: THE SAMARITAN PARALLEL TO THE APOCRYPHAL STORY OF SUSANNA.

Very little is known of Samaritan literature in general. One might say that the knowledge of it is limited to the Pentateuch and to the liturgical hymns. One or two small chronicles written in Samaritan Hebrew have also been printed but without any reference to other documents. Besides these the Arabic chronicle of Abul Fath has also been published by Vilmar, and the Arabic Version of the Samaritan Book of Joshua by Juynboll. Of their apocalyptical literature nothing has been hitherto known, nor has any apocryphal literature been suspected. It must be mentioned that their canon is a somewhat reduced one for it is limited to the five books of the Pentateuch. They do not recognise any other prophet besides Moses, and therefore the Book of Joshua is considered by them only as a profane book of history. The large chronicle starts in fact with the book of Joshua, and it was in that chronicle that I discovered the Samaritan version of the Hebrew Book of Joshua. Of the Apocryphal literature I have now discovered in the Samaritan an Apocalypse of Moses, which will soon be published by the Royal Asiatic Society. And curiously enough a close parallel to the history of Susanna has been found by me embedded in their Chronicle as if it were an historical incident. It is this which I intend publishing here. I have found it in the Book of Joshua which differs greatly from the text published by Juynboll (Leyden, 1848).

This belongs to a class of MSS. so common among the Samaritans and among oriental historians in general in which later matter is successively added, and thus a chronicle which originally dealt with a limited period is the starting point for a chronicle extending over a much longer space of time. Juynboll proved that the Arabic text published by him which rested ultimately on a Hebrew original was not due to one author, and that in fact no less than three or four had contributed to swell the contents of that book. Even then in that extended and inflated state it was considered to belong in the Arabic form not later than to the XII century.

It is not here the place to discuss the authorship and the date of the various sections which go to make up the Arabic Book of Joshua. I have obtained from the Samaritans four copies of it, of which my MS. no. 1146 is the Arabic, MS. no. 1167 is Arabic with a Hebrew translation made by them for me, MS. no. 887 another copy of the Hebrew version, and MS. no. 1140 a different Hebrew translation from the same Arabic original. Now these though different in language agree absolutely in their contents. All these rest on a very old Arabic original of the XV century in their possession. These MSS. differ considerably from Juynboll's Arabic text.

But the greatest difference consists in the fact that this Book of Joshua instead of being brought down to the time of Muhamet, stops at the history of Alexander, chapter 46 of Juynboll's edition. After the history of Alexander this recension contains then the history of the daughter of the High Priest Amram. The same story occurs also in the Chronicle of Abul Fath. As the latter states distinctly that he had made use of the Book of Joshua, which is the main source of the first part of his Chronicle, there is scarcely any doubt that he has incorporated this story of the daughter of Amram into his compilation from the Book of Joshua.

Though all these texts agree with one another down to minute details, yet in one point they differ considerably, and this point is the date. There is a profound discrepancy between one MS.

and the other. In all but one a different date is given and in one case cod. 1146 no date at all is given. The difference between those that contain the date is of about 200 years. In all the texts the name of the father is Amram. This seems to be the only fixed point, but as to the time when this Amram is supposed to have lived or to have been High Priest, we find in MSS. 887 and 1167 the date to be 4196 from the creation according to Samaritan computation (ca. 120 B. C.); again in cod. 1140 the date given is 1387 from the time of the rule of the Israelites, and this is said to be identical with the year 87 from the "birth of Jesus the son of Miriam".

In Abul Fath (my Codd. 890; 1144) we find Amram placed immediately after Tobiah, which according to the "Chain of Samaritan High Priests", as published by me (J. R. A. S., 1909) makes him to be Amram IV, the 77th High Priest, and who was High Priest in the year 4381 of the Creation. But Samaritan Chronology is a puzzle which no one has ever yet solved. This date would agree to a certain extent with MSS. 887 and 1167 and would place the history of the daughter of Amram, who is the Samaritan counterpart of Susanna between 80 and 90 A.D., whilst according to the other text this history must have happened in the year ca. 120 B.C. We might infer that this discrepancy of date is due to the attempt of identifying the Amram, the father, with one of the High Priests of the same name.

I am giving here the literal translation of the version from the Book of Joshua, and I have divided it into verses for easier reference.

CHAPTER TELLING ABOUT THE DAUGHTER OF THE RABBAN AMRAM, AND WHAT HAPPENED TO HER.

1. And this Amram who became High Priest in the year 4169 from the Creation of the World had a daughter of beautiful countenance and pleasant to behold. 2. She was the mistress of wisdom and knowledge, walking in the way of righteousness and all the manner of her deeds were good. 3. And that young

woman from her early infancy wished to study the Torah and to keep the Law, and to read in it. And she wrote one with her own hand. 4. And there was no one in her time who could be compared unto her. 5. And it çame to pass in those days there were two men from the children of Israel of the Samaritans who were hermits (Nazarites) unto God. 6. And they kept in their seclusion (as Nazarites) five and twenty years. 7. And each one of them at the time when he became a hermit was thirty five years old. 8. And they were among the people of their generation like unto prophets until they called them the support (pillars) of this world. 9. For from the time that they separated themselves for that hermit life to the end of five and twenty years they had never come to the town of Sichem. 10. They did not move from Mt. Gerizim all these days. 11. But they built unto themselves houses on the mountain just below the top of the mountain and they dwelt therein. 12. In that time the daughter of the Rabban Amram begged of her father to allow her to become a hermit (Nazarite) for one year. 13. And her father built her a house in the neighbourhood of the above mentioned hermits. 14. And the young woman went up there and became a Nazarite unto the Lord, blessed be He. And she spent her time in hymns, and praises and prayers unto God day and night. 15. At the end of three months on one night the hermits went up to the roof of their houses to read in the light of the moon. 16. And they called to the daughter of the Rabban that they might study with her (learn from her) for when they could not understand the words she was to explain them. 17. So she came out and went up to her roof and she took with her the Scroll of the Law written by her own hand. 18. And that young woman was like the light of the sun. And they looked at her, and saw that her face was more luminous than the light of the moon. And its light fell upon her, and their countenance was troubled through her sight. 19. Then they became wanton and forgot the Lord and their nazirate of a time of five and twenty years. 20. And the one revealed unto the other the secret of their thought as

to her beautiful looks, and they agreed that they would ask
her to show them the Scroll of the Law so as to look into it.
21. And when she would bring it to them they would lay their
hands on her, and get hold of her cunningly. 22. And it came
to pass when they asked her for the Scroll of the Law she
quickly came down from the roof. And they came down to
her and laid hands on her at the gate of her house. And they
revealed unto her the secret thing. 23. And the young woman
started reproving them with strong reproof, and reminded
them of all what the Lord commanded, but they did not hearken unto her. 24. And when she saw their violence she said
unto them, "Ye wish to do this evil deed". 25. And they said
"Yes we wish to do it and if it will not be with thy good will,
it will be against thy will". 26. And she said "I listen and I
will do, but leave me until I will get into my house, and I will
change my garments and anoint myself and put on other
garments better than these, and then you may do with me as
is pleasing in your sight". 27. And she revealed unto them that
it was her desire more than theirs to do this thing. 28. And it
came to pass when they saw it was her will to do this thing,
then their joy grew great, and they said unto her "Pass on
and change thy garments and anoint thyself and come unto
us." 29. And then she passed on to her house, and she locked
the door, and she set herself down behind it and she opened
the Scroll of the Law, and she dishevelled her head. 30. And
she lifted up her hands to heaven and she said "O Lord God,
thou who hast forbidden the committing of any evil deed, of all
abominations, of all wickedness. 31. And I am of the seed of
Pinehas, the man of zeal, and I have no redeemer who is to
redeem me of these two men, and no saviour who is to save
me from the evil deed of these two men, who desire to do the
evil deed before thee, O Lord God. 32. My hope is in thee,
and I have no one besides thee, O Lord God. 33. And for thy
help I hope that thou wilt save me from the hand of thy enemies
and thou wilt not grant them power over me and remove their
wickedness from me. 34. For I have no help beside thee, O Lord

God, and no one else to protect me but thou. [35.] And thou art my refuge and upon thee I rely." [36.] And the young woman fell upon her face and prayed and cried all through the length of the night. [37.] And when the two men saw that the young woman did not return to them, they went quickly to her house so as to hasten her coming out. But they did not find the way. [38.] Then they drew near to break the door and God blinded them so that they did not know the place of the door, as God has said in His Perfect Word "And they were smitten with blindness from small to great, and got wearied to find the door" (Gen. 19. 11). [39.] And they went round and searched for the door the whole night through until the morning and they could not find it. [40.] And when they saw that the dawn rose and they saw that they could not do anything against her, there fell upon them fear and fright and trembling seized upon them for they were kept in great awe and in high repute among the whole congregation. [41.] And they decided to blame her before she could blame them. [42.] So they rose up and went down and they came to the town early in the morning. [43.] And it came to pass that when they came down the whole congregation was just coming out of the synagogue (Kinsha) after the conclusion of the morning prayer. [44.] And when the community saw them, they were astonished about them, and the whole town was upset because of them, for five and twenty years had passed since they had come down to Sichem. [45.] So they went up to the synagogue (Kinsha) and the whole of the congregation gathered round them. [46.] And the High Priest Amram came down to make obeisance to them. [47.] And the elders of the congregation said unto them "What is the reason of your coming this day, and in the name of the Lord and of Moses you have granted us life, and you have hallowed us". [48.] And then they stood before the priest and they wept and said unto him "O our master, it is very hard for us, that we should tell you this thing for the message causes us pain of the heart, for it is still heavier for us than it might be for thee". [49.] And the Rabban said unto

them, "Haste and tell me quickly". ⁵⁰· And they answered
and said "Last night we went out on to the roof to serve our
Lord God, and sing hymns unto him according to our custom,
and we saw thy daughter and behold a stranger was lying
with her. ⁵¹· We investigated this matter, and we are now
come to testify a true witness before our God. And thou shalt
now do unto thy daughter as it is pleasing in thy sight."
⁵²· And it came to pass when the Rabban heard these words,
he threw himself upon the ground and he strewed upon his
head dust from the ground, and he lifted up his voice and
wept. ⁵³· And the congregation did likewise. And the men
and the women went out to the place Serin. ⁵⁴· And the Crier
(Habta) called by the order of the Rabban all the Samaritans,
that all the men and women should gather themselves together
in the place Serin, so that they should see the burning of the
daughter of the Rabban. ⁵⁵· As the Lord has commanded,
may He be exalted, "And the daughter of any priest, if she
profane herself by playing the harlot, she profaneth her father:
she shall be burned with fire" (Levit. 21. 9). ⁵⁶· And accordingly
the whole congregation went out and the Priest and the Crier
(Habta) went out alone by the way of the vineyards. ⁵⁷· For
it was not meet for the Rabban to go with the people for he
never ceased weeping. ⁵⁸· And whilst they were walking they
suddenly came to a place where angels having come down from
heaven had taken the form of little Samaritan children. ⁵⁹· And
they had arranged a kind of court of justice. One child taking
the place of the High Priest, and two were in the likeness of
the hermits, and the rest of the children sitting down waiting
to see this judgement. ⁶⁰· And he who took the place of the
High Priest commanded that each of the witnesses should be
put in a different place separately. ⁶¹· And each of them should
come to him singly so as to hear what he had to say testifying
against the daughter of the Rabban. And their testimony
differed. ⁶²· And the boy who was taking the place of the
Rabban said, ⁶³· "The Rabban has not acted so, otherwise he
would have been able to discover the truth from the lie, and

thus it would have been far from him to condemn the pure woman for a wicked deed." 64. And when the Rabban saw this action of the young lad he awoke from his sleep, and he said to the Habta, "I am going to do likewise, as these have done". 65. And when they drew near to the threshing floors of Serin, and all the Samaritans had gathered themselves together then the Rabban judged in the same manner as he had seen the children do. 66. And thus the testimony of the hermits became contradictory. 67. And then they were ashamed and they became confused. 68. Whilst all this happened the daughter of the Rabban was on the mountain. 69. And when she came down from the mountain, and saw whole congregation gathered there she did not know the cause of the gathering. 70. And the Rabban commanded and they brought his daughter. 71. And when she came, all the people came out to see her, her father asked her about everything that had happened to her. 72. And she told him the whole truth of the thing. 73. And all the men recognised the truth of her words and the purity of her actions and that the hermits had been telling falsehoods. 74. And they confessed what they had done, and they begged of the Rabban that he should save them. 75. But the people did unto them as the Lord, may He be exalted, commanded "And ye shall do unto him as he had intended to do to his brother" (Deut. 19. 19). 76. And the whole community stoned them with stones until they died. And they also burned them with fire. 77. And Amram took his daughter, and he came into the town and he was in great joy and happiness. 78. And the High Priest Amram died three days after that had happened. May the mercy of the Lord be upon him.

Thus far the version from the Book of Joshua. I have prefered to translate this because there can be no doubt as to its extreme antiquity. It cannot be denied that the agreement of Abul Fath with the Arabic version of the Book of Joshua is so close that one must have copied from the other. A brief abstract of it appears in the Latin Introduction of Vilmar, page LXIV. Considering now that Abul Fath has laid under contribution the last mentioned book, there can be very little doubt as to which of the two is the older version. There is one point of difference between the two, and this seems to prove also the Book of Joshua to be the older one. The lads who play at court and deliver judgement, and thus show the High Priest how he ought to have investigated the accusation brought against his daughter are described in the Book of Joshua as angels who assumed the form of boys. Abul Fath who per sistently removes in his Chronicle every miraculous incident has also here eliminated the angels and left the decision to real children.

The parallelism between the Samaritan and Jewish version is so close that it cannot rest upon mere accident. Both no doubt go back to one more ancient source, a popular legend or tale which had been appropriated, as it were, by each of the two sects and adjusted to meet their own requirements. The numerous variants of the apocryphal tale go already a long way to prove that there has not been any fixed text, and that in fact many variants must have been known already at a very early time. It is not here the place to enter upon a minute examination of the apocryphal tale in which Daniel plays the chief rôle, nor would it be profitable to compare the two texts minutely. It suffices for our purpose to establish in the first place that the Samaritan version must be very old. And if, as is now admitted, that the Book of Joshua was originally written in Hebrew, the final composition of the Chronicle of which the Book of Joshua forms the first part cannot be much later than the time of Vespasian and before Adrian, the very time when most of the apocryphal books were composed. The Book of Joshua itself finishes practically with the death of Alexander.

It may be stated, without fear of contradiction, that the old literature of the Samaritans had become fossilised, and that they retained with remarkable accuracy whatever has been saved from olden times, and they have added very little in the course of centuries.

If we now compare the two versions we shall find that they have many points in common, which, if carefully studied might throw light on some obscure points in the apocryphal tale hitherto not even recognised as such. In both tales the heroine is the daughter of an important man of the community. According to the Jewish one, in my Jerahmeel, ch. 65, page 203, the young woman is the daughter of Shealtiel, and the sister of Zerubbabel and the wife of King Jehoiachin. Here she is the daughter of the High Priest. Two Elders are the accusers holding high offices. In "Susanna" they are more or less identified with prophets and in the Samaritan they are saints or hermits and also respected as prophets. In both they allege the same story, and in both they are unhesitatingly believed and no real examination takes place. It is through the influence of a child that the truth comes to light. In both cases the accused woman prays to God almost in the same terms, but the Samaritan version has added some legendary element missing in the Jewish. The scene is placed on the top of Mt. Gerizim, so as to localise it, for the High Priest was not allowed to leave the Kinsha according to the Law, so therefore the incident must happen close to his residence. In the Samaritan the miracle is like that which happened in Sodom, the hermits become blind and are not able to find the gate. We have a much more elaborate description of the means how children are instrumental in bringing justice to light.

I do not think I am going very far wrong when I state that this latter incident is the more ancient and probably the original form, and the story had afterwards been transferred in the apocryphal tale to Daniel. It must strike every reader as rather incongruous that the exclamation of a young man (Sus., verse 45) (in the Syriac version he was twelve years old) should so much have affected the course of justice and influenced the leaders of the people to such an extent that they should stop every proceeding and start on a fresh investigation.

And then when he decides judgement we find Daniel appealing to *angels* as the executors of his judgement (ver. 55, 59) which is somewhat extraordinary even in an apocryphal tale. It is therefore very probable that in the apocryphal tale we have a modification of the original tale where children, either real, or angels who had taken the shape of children, played a decisive part in the unravelling of the mystery. They arranged a court of judgement, they examined the witnesses separately, and thus showed the leaders of the people the proper way how to proceed in order to find out the truth just as we have it in the Samaritan version. Hence the *young lad* in "Susanna" and his appeal to angels. Later on as Daniel's reputation for wisdom grew, the lad who played the rôle of presiding judge and who displayed such wisdom was identified with him and he was made to appeal to angels. In the Samaritan version no such identification was required, to enhance the merit of the virtuous daughter of Amram.

The confusion of the dates concerning Amram may be taken as a proof that the Samaritan is merely an adaptation of a floating legend, and as the name Amram was known to be that of the father of the girl he was identified with an Amram who was a High Priest. In the Arabic version of the Book of Joshua no date at all is given. In the other codd., as already mentioned before, various dates are given. But no Amram is known to have been High Priest in the year 4196 (ca. 120 B.C.) as found in MSS. no. 1147, and 887, whilst the Amram as found in cod. 1140 is identified as Amram IV, who was High Priest in the year ca. 90 A. D. With this date Abul Fath, in a shorter chronicle, agrees. The mock trial is not an isolated incident in Jewish legendary lore. There is a similar trial in the David and Solomon cycle, where Saul is unable to give a proper judgement, and almost condemns an innocent woman, but is taught to recognise the error of his way by a mock trial arranged by David as a child. Saul witnesses it and the truth comes to light. ("Parables of Solomon", Const., 1516.)

14

A similar tale furthermore occurs in the Arabian Nights in the story of Ali Hodja. Other parallels could easily be adduced from other Oriental sources. We are touching here the cycle referring to the Clever Child, who puts to shame the elders and people held in the repute of wisdom and knowledge. I will content myself with referring to the story of Pseudo Ben Sira in the Alphabetum Siracidicum and the Legends in the Apocryphal Gospel of Jesus' Infancy (Evangelium Infantiae.)

In the light of this investigation the Story of Susanna ranges itself as a folk-tale along with the stories of Tobit, Ahikar, Bel and the Dragon, as part of ancient Folklore.

———————

THE SIBYL AND THE DREAM OF ONE HUNDRED SUNS
AN OLD APOCRYPHON

By M. GASTER

IN addition to the more or less accredited ancient Sibylline oracles, others circulated, under the name of the one or the other of the Sibyls, which also claimed to be of equal authority. The name was a recommendation for a special kind of apocalyptic literature, and the example set of old of foretelling the future was thereby continued for many centuries. The character of this Sibylline Oracle was akin to some of the old Apocalypses, in which the future was revealed in a symbolical form, and the events to come foretold by allegories and signs, which were interpreted by the Sibyl as by one of the prophets of old. By connecting such apocalyptic revelations with some ancient name and ascribing to men or women of the past works composed at a much later time, these compositions entered into the domain of that apocryphal Christian literature which made use of old formulas for disseminating new teaching and thus prepared the mind of the people for untoward incidents. These oracles were soon drawn into the cycle of the Doomsday; the legends of Antichrist and of the Last Judgment were incorporated with the older oracle; and thus an oracle which originally may have been a mere forecast of purely political events became a religious manifesto, a prophetic pronouncement on the course of events, leading up to the final drama.

Such an apocryphal oracle was then ascribed to the Sibyl of Tibur. This was one of the best known among the nations of Europe and has been preserved in two ancient Latin versions, known as the Sibyl of Beda, one, however, dependent upon the other. According to the researches

14*

of Sackur, it had assumed its last form in the ninth
century, though its origin must be much older and is to
be sought in the East. The most prominent feature in
this oracle is a dream seen by one hundred noblemen on
one and the same night, in which they saw seven or
nine suns appearing on the horizon, each one distinguished
from the other by some peculiarity. The Sibyl is called
upon to explain the dream and what the seven or nine
suns portend. This symbolical multiplication of the sun
and its diverse aspects and manifestations, by which the
future was to be foretold, and which required an expert
interpreter, is of Oriental origin. Important events in
the life of men and nations have often been connected
with wonderful apparitions and signs in the skies. The
appearance of the star which led the Magi from the East
to the cave in Bethlehem is only one of numerous similar
examples in Oriental literature. The Rabbinical literature
knows of a brilliant star appearing at the birth of
Abraham ; and of four stars fighting, three of which
were swallowed up by one at the birth of Moses. In
both cases astrologers are called in to interpret their
significance—in the one case to Nimrod, in the other to
Pharaoh.

In the interpretation of those nine suns there was
a wide scope given to the imagination of the successive
interpreters and adaptors of the old oracle. For, after
a lapse of time the same nine suns were represented as
signifying some such series of events as the writer of
the time took a more personal interest in. In the West,
e.g., the history of the Frankish kingdom was read into
it, and, as will be seen later on, in the East at a later
period Muhammedan history had to do duty and become
the object of the prophecy. The authors of these oracles
were invariably Christians, and therefore the eschatological
element was joined with the history of the appearance and
spread of Christianity.

The vaticination of the Sibyl did not stop at a list of
succeeding kings, but the last of them was to lay
down his crown at the gates of Jerusalem and thereupon
was to follow the time of the Antichrist and the final
struggle, until the Day of Judgment would put an end
to the rule of evil, and then would be ushered in the
kingdom of heaven. It was this final portion which
assured to the Sibyl the popularity which her prophecy
enjoyed. Professor Bousset, in his exhaustive study on
the Antichrist (*Der Antichrist in d. Ueberlieferung d.
Judenthums*, etc., Göttingen, 1895), has devoted a special
chapter to the investigation of the relation in which the
Latin Sibyl of Beda stands to other compilations of
a similar nature. He compared it with that of Adso,
Pseudo-Methodius, the Syriac homily of Pseudo-Ephraem on
the Antichrist, and the genuine writings of Ephraem. The
date of this apocalyptic prophecy he thus moved upwards,
first to the time of the irruption of the Arabs into the
West of Asia and their spread far and wide, then higher
up to the epoch of Leo the Isaurian (eighth century), then
the period of Heraclius, the time of the invasion of the
Huns, the allied nations from Asia, and still higher up to
the time of the establishment of a Christian emperor on
the throne of Byzantium. We are thus led back as far
as the fourth century for the latter part of the prophecy.
Curiously enough, the first part, the vision of the hundred
suns, is missing in those ancient texts, even in Pseudo-
Methodius (*Orthodoxographa*, Basel, 1555, fols. 387 ff., an
edition unknown to Bousset and others), and must have
been lost at an early period, so soon as the legend had
reached the West of Europe. In the light of Arabic
versions of the legend it cannot be doubted that the
dream of the hundred suns was not only an integral part,
but the very starting-point. In it lay the justification for
ascribing the prophecy to the Sibyl and ensuring to it
a wide circulation. It is precisely this first part which

claims our attention. Thus far no old parallels nor any
link have been shown to exist between the oracle of the
Sibyl of Beda and such Oriental versions as are preserved
in Arabic and Ethiopian.

Dr. J. Schleifer[1] has now published for the first time
these Oriental texts of the Sibylline apocryphon in Arabic
and Ethiopian. One of them is a Karshuni text, of
course Arabic, but written in Syriac characters. The
editor confines himself primarily to a critical edition of
these various texts, none of them very old, and yet each
one interesting in its own way. The Karshuni text,
the Ethiopian, and then three Arabic texts, are printed
in five parallel columns, and so arranged that the
relation between these texts should be seen at a glance.
In the foot-notes various readings are carefully noted.
A minute description of the MSS. used is given, and
a German translation in three columns. In this translation Dr. Schleifer has combined the three Arabic versions
into one, and given the result of the critical emendation of
these texts. In the foot-notes to the translation reference
is made to the Latin Tiburtan Sibyl (Beda), and the book
concludes with an examination of the relation in which
these versions stand to one another. They all go back to
one ancient original, to which the Karshuni text is most
closely related, and almost of equal value as the Arabic,
though differing from the latter sufficiently not to be its
immediate source. The latest is the Ethiopian, which
rests on a text closely akin, though not identical with,
Arabic iii.

This edition of the Oriental versions is of great
importance for the history of the apocryphal tale, which
has exercised so great an influence upon popular imagination, and was at the same time a reflex of the popular

[1] *Die Erzaehlung der Sibylle.* Ein Apokryph nach den Karschunischen,
Arabischen, und Aethiopischen Handschriften zu London, Oxford, Paris,
und Rom veroeffentlicht von. (Denkschriften der Kais. Akad. d.
Wissensch. Wien, vol. liii.) 4to ; pp. 80. Wien, 1908.

naïve philosophy of history, which sees in the present the realization of events foretold in the past, and finds in it a source of comfort and hope for the future, lifting the people above the temporary trials and holding out a promise of reward and of peace everlasting. For it is all fore-ordained, and it is part and parcel of the divine economy which shapes human life and leads the world on irresistibly to a final day of judgment, when the actions of man will be weighed—the good rewarded, the evil punished, and the destroyed harmony of the world re-established.

These Oriental texts start with the dream, and the interpretation given by the Sibyl brings us down to the time of the rule of Al-Ma'mun and his successors (ninth century), possibly also to that of the Crusaders and Richard Cœur de Lion. The king immediately before the appearance of the Antichrist will be the " son of the Lion " from the land of the Franks. In some points there is a close resemblance between these versions and the oldest Latin text. The question naturally arises : Where is the connecting link between the Eastern tale and its Western parallels, and which is their ultimate source ? Dr. Schleifer might have turned his attention to this question, the importance of which for the history of this apocryphon cannot be gainsaid, but he scarcely touches it. The Arabic version rests probably on an older Syriac text, for that the book is of Oriental origin there cannot be any doubt. The whole setting and the detailed history of the Muhammedan Empire down to the tenth century and later, exclude the possibility of an Occidental origin. No old Arabic book has been translated from the Latin. But the Syriac itself could hardly be anything but a translation from a Greek text. That the Arabic may have been translated from the Greek is rather a remote probability, for if the book was originally written in Greek it has no doubt reached the Arabs through Syriac mediation. A Greek text would be the natural link between East and West. Unfortunately, hitherto no such Greek text has come to light ; at any rate, I am not aware of its existence. I have now discovered another version, which may safely be taken to represent the hitherto undiscovered Greek original. As far back as 1883, in my *History of the Rumanian Popular Literature* (pp. 338–9), I have discussed at some length an old Rumanian legend of " The Sivila and the dream which was seen of one hundred Senators in one night", the very same dream of nine suns and of the "Sivila" interpreting the dream to the emperor. This Rumanian version in its turn is only a literal translation of a much older Slavonic version, which again rests ultimately on a Greek original. All the Slavonic and Rumanian apocrypha go back to older Greek originals which were as a rule literally translated, and then only slightly altered in those details that affected their own nation. At times they ventured also — but very rarely — upon some small interpolations. A comparison between these texts and the oldest Latin form of the Tiburtan Sibyl shows the closest possible parallelism. No room for doubt is left that the one must be dependent on the other, and the internal evidence goes far to prove the dependence of the Latin on the Greek (= Slavonic) version. Moreover, the whole Slavo-Rumanian text is very short, and all the eschatological portions, as well as every reference to the Antichrist and the Last Judgment, are entirely missing. The introduction is also very brief, and differs entirely from all other versions. Every apocryphal story or legend must be an addition to the history of the Bible. In one way or another it must embellish the narration of Holy Writ. By these means the apocryphal story enters the holy cycle and forms henceforth part of the " Historiated Bible " Only in the Slavonic version this connexion with the

Bible is found—a proof of its great antiquity and its independence of the Western versions. It is an attempt to connect the Sibyl with David, whose offspring she is in a marvellous manner. She is here the oldest form, if not the origin, of the legend of Reine Pédauque, and possibly the ancestor of "Mother Goose". Professor Vesselofsky has studied this cycle exhaustively in his *Opyty po istorii razvitiya hristianskoi legendy* (ii, pp. 351–3). There he refers also to the legend current in the name of the Venerable Bede, and he shows that it agrees in the main with the Sibylline oracle in a Slavonic version, of which a copy had been placed at his disposal by Buslaev and Drinov. Since then an old Slavonic original and the Rumanian version, of which I wrote in my *Literatura populară romănă* (Bucharest, 1883, 337 pp.), have been published by L. Miletitch in the *Sborniků* of the Bulgarian Minister of Public Instruction (vol. ix, Sofia, 1893, pp. 177–80). According to Miletitch the Slavonic MS. (now in the Library of the State Archives in Bucharest) of the sixteenth century is merely a copy of an older MS. which belongs at latest to the fourteenth century. The Rumanian codex (in the Library of the Rumanian Academy) from which I published many years ago, also a portion of the legend of Adam and Eve (*Revista pentru Istorie și filologie*, ed. Tocilescu, Bucharest, i, pp. 78 ff.), belongs to the end of the sixteenth century. It is an almost literal translation of the Slavonic. In a few details it differs from the text published by Dr. Miletitch and supplements the latter. I have now translated these texts into English, following in the main the Slavonian version as the oldest, and adding in brackets the variants of the Rumanian. I am also reprinting here the Rumanian text, for it is preserved in an unique copy ; the edition of Dr. Miletitch is unfortunately faulty in many passages, and the text is practically inaccessible in the Bulgarian Sbornik. Moreover, it is written in the old Slavonic or Cyrillian alphabet. I have transliterated it and corrected the mistakes which have crept into the last-mentioned publication.

The comparison between these texts and the Latin versions of the Sibylline oracles mentioned before proves identity of origin and close resemblance in details. The description of the nine suns in the Slavonic and in Beda and their peculiar appearance agrees in many points. The divergence begins with the interpretation, which has undergone the greatest possible change. It had to be adapted to local exigencies if it was to be of any use, and if it was to be believed in as an old prophecy of coming events. In the Slavonian, unlike the Latin, the name of the great emperor is called explicitly Constantin, which might settle one of the difficulties of the Latin texts where the names of the kings and emperors are not fully given ; they are indicated only by the initial letter, and it was left to the imagination of the reader to supply the remainder, thus leaving an open field to fantastic interpretation and interested guesswork. In other respects the Slavonic also differs in the names of the various nations that were to make incursions into the western world and bring trouble upon the peoples. No doubt, as often happens with texts in which the names of ancient nations since extinct appear, more modern names are substituted by the later copyists for those of the older nations that had come and gone. Thus, the Tartars have no doubt taken the place of the ancient Huns, and the Saracens that of the Persians in the older versions. These names indicate the latest date for these Slavo-Rumanian versions, and lead us to the time of the invasion of the Mongols in the thirteenth century, known among the nations of Eastern Europe mostly under the name of " Tartars ".

Peculiar to these versions is the animosity against the

Greeks and the exaltation of the "Iberians" of Armenia, whom they describe as a God-fearing, pious, and modest nation, just the contrary to the rapacious, impious Greeks, who have changed their faith three times, and are in-hospitable and greedy. This no doubt reflects the feelings of the Bulgarians, who were in constant warfare with the Byzantine emperors. The author of the translation and adaptation from the Greek probably belonged to the sect of the Bogomils, whose chief literary activity centred in the translation and dissemination of the old apocryphal literature. This predilection for the "Iberians" is found also in other apocryphal and popular writings which were translated from the Greek by the same agencies, the members of that famous sect, and then adapted to their own peculiar teaching. This may also be the reason why some of the eschatological details found in all the other versions, and which therefore formed part of the old original, are missing in the Slavonic text, and why the Archangel Gabriel, who was the special favourite of the Bogomils, is introduced as the restorer of peace at the end of days. I cannot here follow up in greater detail the examination and comparison of these texts. Until a Greek text of this apocryphal tale comes to light the Slavo-Rumanian version forms the connecting link between East and West.

THE HISTORY OF THE SIBYL AND THE DREAM OF THE HUNDRED SENATORS OF ROME.

Translated from the Old Slavonic and from the Rumanian.

King David was a man of overpowering strength, and it oozed out of him. The servant one day wiped the phial with some grass, and threw it out, and a goose came and ate it. No sooner had it eaten it than it laid an egg, and the egg burst, and out of the egg came a girl. They told it in secret to David, who when he heard of it understood what had happened, and gave orders to hide the child; and they hid her away in the land Gorskia (Rum. Ugorsku), (and she grew up and studied), and she was wiser and more beautiful than the whole world, and through her wisdom (she obtained the rule over the whole land of Ugorsku), and she became the ruler of Rome (Rimŭ), and she considered (or, pondered over) the word of the prophets, for God had said unto David: " Of thy seed will I place upon thy throne;" and she considered also what the other prophecies foretold. And her name was Maria, but for her wisdom they gave her the name Sivila. And she hoped that from her Christ would be born, and she kept her virginity for fifty years, until one hundred of the great boyars saw a dream, and then Sivila understood that it would not come to pass as she had hoped.

And the boyars came together and said: " Let us go to the Queen and tell her the dream which we have seen." And they came to her and said: " May it please your Majesty. We the one hundred boyars have had one and the same dream." And Sivila said: " Tell me the dream, and I will endeavour to explain it." And the barons said: "We have seen nine suns rising." Sivila replied: "Tell me how these suns looked." And they said: " The first sun rose clear and gentle, and it was a pleasure for us to look at it. The second sun, its light was three times darkened and hidden. The third was black, with dark rays round about it. The fourth sun was like flaming dark smoke. The fifth sun was (white) and burning hot; it was difficult for us to look at it. The sixth sun was white as snow. The seventh sun had a blood-red glow, and in the midst thereof there were hands. The eighth sun had soft and clear rays. The ninth was the most terrible and awe-inspiring, and hotter than all."

The Sivila replied: " The nine suns signify nine generations (or, periods). The first sun is the generation of the Bulgarians, who are good and hospitable and true believers and worship in the Christian faith. The second sun signifies the nation of the Greeks, for they have three times changed their faith and mix with other nations ; they are fond of money, publicans (or, taking bribes), and they betray the kingdom of God. The third sun signifies the Franks ; they will conquer all the nations, and from among them will be born a man from two nations (two origins or families ?), whose name will be Constantin, and he will conquer many nations, and he will wage great wars on the earth, and signs will be shown to him in the heavens ; and he will lift up the Greeks, and he will raise an empire among the Greeks, and he will build among them a town, and he will call it New Jerusalem, a fortress for the Greeks and a resting-place for the Saints. And to his mother the crosses of Christ will be revealed, and they will perform many miracles in the world. The fourth sun signifies the Arkadians, who will conquer the Franks and will take Rome. And Rome will again be rebuilt (or, sacked ?), and that man will be drowned (die) in the water. The fifth sun signifies the Saracens, who will destroy Jerusalem and take Syria. The sixth sun signifies the Syrians, who held Jerusalem and lost their throne ; and their country will be devastated for three hundred years. The seventh sun signifies the Jews. A woman will arise in their midst and give birth to a child from heaven, and his name will be called Jesus, and the girl that will give birth to him will remain a pure virgin. His throne is the heaven, and the earth his footstool. The name of the woman is Maria. And all the princes and judges will gather together and will hand him over to be crucified, and he will be buried, and on the third day he will rise and ascend to heaven. And he will send twelve men who will spread our faith, and that faith will grow strong, and that faith will have dominion from the rising of the sun to its setting."

The Jewish priests and the princes exclaimed then: "Be silent, O our Queen, for we wish to ask thee one thing more. Is it possible that God should descend from heaven and beget a son from a woman and destroy our faith?" And the Sivila answered: "O my foolish people! do not wonder at great and marvellous things. Consider well in your minds on what do the heavens hang and on what is the earth established that it does not move? Our law is not a good one, and I up till now had hoped that the Christ would be born of me, and I have kept my virginity for fifty years, but now I know that he will not be born of me.

"The eighth sun signifies the Iberians, a righteous and hospitable people (loving the stranger); they keep the Church and fear God, and (observe His holy Word). There is no guile among them, and it is of them that God says: 'Blessed are the meek ones, (for they will obtain salvation).' The ninth sun signifies the Tartars, who shed blood upon the earth, and no one can withstand them; they will eat up the whole earth, and they will destroy from among men the name of the archangels (and for a time they will be so strong that no nation will be able to stand up against them, but in the end they will be destroyed from among men by the name of the archangel Gabriel). Our God be praised for ever and ever."

THE RUMANIAN TEXT
Cuvântu de pré intelépta Savila

Davidı prorocul lui dumnezâu avé pohtâ mare cât eşiea vrătutea lui adecă plodul lui şi puné un vas şi pica in vası. Iarâ intr'o zi un inaşı al lui ştérse plodul cu nişte buruiane, şi le aruncâ afarâ. Şi eşi o gânscâ şi mâncâ burueanele. Şi cum le mâncâ îndatâ oô un ou, şi crepâ ôul şi din ôu eşi o pruncâ parte mueréscâ, şi intru ascunsı spuserâ lui Davidı. (Cum) a auzătı de aćasta Davidı bine inṭelése precum se făcu. Acieaši zise de ascunserâ fata acéea intru pâmântul Ugorscului. Ši ea crescu ši învăṭâ carte ši fu inṭeléptâ mai vrătos decâtъ toṭi oamenii ce petrecea in toatâ lumea. Ši cu inṭelepciuné ei dobândi ṭara Ugorscului toatâ, ši înpârâṭi in Râmъ, ši socotea zisele prorocilor, cum zise dumnezâu lui Davidъ : "Din sâmânṭa ta voi pune spre scaunul tâu," ši a altor proroci zisele le socotea. Numele ei era Mariea, ši pentru inṭelepciuné ei ii ziserâ Sivila. Ši trâgé nâdéjde câ dintru dânsa se va naště Hristos, ši feri feċoriea sa în 50 de ani, pânâ cândъ vâzurâ o sutâ de boeari mari toṭi un visъ. Atuncea înṭelése Savila câ nu easte acéea ce nâdâjdueašte.

Ši să adunarâ toṭi boearii ši ziserâ : "Blâmaṭi la înpârâtésa sâ spunem visul ce am vâzutъ." Ši venirâ câtrâ însâ ši ziserâ : "Sâ erṭi înpârâṭiea ta, iatâ cum avurâm noi o sutâ de boeari ai tâi un vis." Sivila zise : "Spuneṭi visul ši eu il voi dizlega." Domnii ziserâ : "Vâzut-am noao sori râsârindъ." Iară Sivila zise : "Spuneṭi-mi cum era acei sori." Ei ziserâ : "Soarele dintâiu curat ši lin râsâriea ši noi foarte cu drag îl ašteptam ši-l socotea(m). 2. Al doilé soare de trei ori intunecâ ši se ascunse lumina. 3. Al treilé soare cu zâri négre pregiur dânsul. 4. Al patrule soare ca o parâ de fum négrâ. 5. Al cincile soare albъ ši fierbinte era noaô a-l socoti. 6. Al šasele soare luminâ avé ca zâpada. 7. Al šaptele soare cu zare rošie ši în mijlocъ mâni avé. 8. Al optule soare zârile lui era line ši curate. 9. Al noôle soare de toti era mai groaznicъ spâimaṭъ era ši fierbinte."

Sivila zise : "Noao sori sântъ noao roduri. Cel soare dintâi este rodul Bâlgarilor, buni ši ĭubitori la oaspeṭi ši credinċoši, ši cea dréptâ credinṭâ creštinéscâ lui Dúmnezâu au închinatъ. Al doile soare sântъ Grecii, câ ei de trei ori credinṭa sa au lepâdat-o ši cu toate limbile sâ amésteca, ĭubitori de argintъ ši luôtori de adâmanâ înpârâṭie lui Dumnezâu dédera. Al treile soare sântъ Frâncii, ce ei vor câlca toate limbile, eši-va dintru dânšii om de 2 roduri, și numele lui va fi Constantin, și acela va câlca toate limbile și va face râzboae mari pre pâmântь și i să vor arăta lui sémne pre ceri și va râdica Grecii, și va face înpârâție întru Greci, și va zidi întru dânșii cetate și să va chiema Ierusalimul nou, ograda Grecilor și râpaosul svânților, și mâni-sa i să vor arâta crucile lui Hristos ce iale vor face sémne multe pre pâmântь. Al patrule soare aceștea sântь Arcadei ce vor birui Frâncii și vor câlca Rimul și iarâ va fi Rimul, și acela om într'apâ va muri. Al cincile soare, aceștea sântь Sârâcineștii (-nenii ?), ce vor pustii Ierusalimul și vor câlca Siriea. Al șésele soare, aceștea sântь Sirieanii, ce ținurâ Ierusalimul, și pierdurâ scaunul sâu și pâmântul lor va fi pustii trei sute de ani. Al șaptele soare aceștea sântь Jidovьi. Eși-va o mueare dintru dânșii și va naște fiu din ceri și-i vor zice numele lui Isus, și fata cea ce va naște va fi tot feсoarâ curatâ ; scaunul lui ĭaste ceriul, ĭarâ pâmântul ĭaste așternutь piсoarelor lui. Numele feсoarei va fi Mariea, aduna-să-vor toți domnii și toți gĭudecătorii, și-l vor da spre râstignire, îngropa-l-vor pre dânsul și a treea zi va învie și să va sui în ceri : și va trimite 12 bărbăți și aceea légea noastrâ vor râsâpi, și a lor lége vor întâri, și acéea lége va înpârâți de la râsâritul soarelui pânâ la apus."

Atuncea ziserâ popii jidovești și toți boearii : " Năi, taci înpârâțiea ta, câ încâ una te vom întreba. Poate acéea a fi, să pogoarâ dumnezâu din ceri și să să nascâ din feсoarâ și să spargâ légé noastrâ ? " Atuncea Savila a zis : " O nebun rodul mieu cel mare și minunatь ! nu vă mirareți de aсasta, ci socotiți cu înțelepcĭuné voastrâ, ci socotiți pre ce stâ ceriul aninatь și pâmântul întâritь și neclâtiь ; iarâ légea voastrâ nu spre bine stâ, câ și eu pânâ acum m'am nâdâjduitь câ dintru mine să va naște Hristos și mie-am ferit feсorиea mea în 50 de ani, iarâ acmu cunoscь câ nu-s eu aсéea."

Al optule soare, aceștea sântь Iverii derepți și ĭubitori

la oaspeți, beséreca pâzâscu, de dumnezâu se tem și
cuvintele svinției sale ćarcâ, și petrec fârâ de râutate,
i února ca acestora le zice dumnezâu : " Ferice la ceea
cė se plécâ aceea vor dobândi spaseniea." Al noôle soare,
aceea săntь Tâtarii ce varsâ sânge pre pâmântь și nimea
înaintea lor nu vor sta, mânca-vor toate țârâle și pânâ
la o vréme atâta putére vor avé câtь înnainté lor din
limbi nimea nu să va puté protivi ; ĭarâ cândь va fi pre
urmâ cu numele lui arhangel Gavriil ĭar de(n) oameni
vor peri.—Slavâ pârintelui și fiĭului și duhului svântь,
acum și pururé, și întru vécii de vécii amin."

JOURNAL

OF

THE ROYAL ASIATIC SOCIETY.

Art. XXIV.—*"The Twelve Dreams of Sehachi."*
By M. Gaster.

Among the tales that make up the well-known Kalilah and
Dimnah cycle, or the Fables of Bidpai, there is one which
has a history of its own. In the Syriac version published
by Bickell, probably the oldest text available, it is called
the "Gate of Bilar" (German translation, p. 93 ff.). In
the Arabic recension, and in the Syriac which rests upon
it, it is called similarly, "The Story of the Wise Bilar."
A full account of this text, together with an English
rendering, has been given by I. G. N. Keith-Falconer
("Kalilah and Dimnah," Cambridge, 1885, p. xxxi ff., 219 ff.,
and notes p. 301 ff.). By referring the reader to these "notes"
I can dispense with any lengthy discourse on the history
of this chapter within the frame of the Panchatantra. In
one form or another it has travelled, together with the rest
of the book, from one country to another, always forming
an integral portion of it. The curious point about this
chapter is, that hitherto no Sanscrit text of it has as yet
come to light. The reason assigned for its disappearance
has been, that it is of a pronounced Buddhist character and
that a humiliating position is given to the Brahmins in this
tale. The Brahmins, not being able to modify it by some

slight eliminations, have suppressed it entirely. To Schiefner is due the merit of discovering a Tibetan counterpart of it, thus making the Indian origin and Buddhist character of the tale perfectly clear.

The discovery of this independent Tibetan version is of special value, for apart from the fact that it proves a Buddhist origin, it shows conclusively that this tale circulated also independently of the book. I have often contended in my folkloristic studies, that single tales have been detached from larger collections and have led a distinct and separate life of their own. Some enjoyed greater popularity and spread much farther than the others which remained in the collection and travelled only with it. They developed often in a strange way, being more directly subjected to the operation of popular imagination. They were adapted to suit local or temporal purposes, and were treated similar to the old apocryphal and pseudo-epigraphical writings. They were made to serve dogmatic purposes when this was the requirement of the hour, and had to submit to strange transformations. None, e.g., is more curious than the change which created a "Barlaam and Josaphat" legend. Christian elements were introduced and gave the Buddhist Jataka the character of one of the *Vitae Sanctorum*.

The same has happened to the chapter of the Panchata-tantra which I intend investigating in connection with the publication of the Rumanian version from an unique, though modern, manuscript. It will become evident that this tale must have been taken up at a very early period, by the same agency which transformed Buddha into Barlaam, and subjected to a similar transformation. For it is now a tale with a distinct eschatological tendency, whose purpose is to be a premonitory warning of the "End of Days." The individual element has disappeared. The dreams seen by the king are no longer portents of coming good or evil as far as he personally is concerned, but warnings to the world on the things that are to be expected on the approaching period of the Last Days before the final Judgment takes place. From the time of the Sibyllinian

Oracles onwards more than one vaticination describing coming events appear in the Byzantine literature. They are mostly of Oriental origin, and are ascribed either to the prophet Daniel or to Bishop Methodius of Patara, to Leon the Philosopher, and to others (v. Krummbacher, "Byzantinische Litteraturgeschichte," 2nd ed., p. 628 f.). These prophecies were introduced into other writings of a similar character, especially into descriptions of dreams. Nothing could serve the purpose of telling the future better than to connect them with dreams, which play so important a rôle in the Bible. The transition was therefore easy from a Buddhist series of dreams, and their personal interpretation, to a Christian similar series of dreams, but with a Christian eschatological interpretation. The framework was retained as the best vehicle for transmission; the miraculous and mysterious is always sure to appeal to the people, only the interpretation had to be changed to make this non-Christian book thoroughly orthodox.

Following the example of Barlaam, we must look out for a Syriac and Greek text of these dreams, but none has yet been discovered. It may be that the attention now directed to this legend will help to stimulate a new search and will bring eventually such texts to light. Hitherto the "Dreams" were known only in Russia. Professor A. N. Vesselofsky, than whom there is no more competent scholar in that direction, has devoted a special study to the "Twelve Dreams of Shahaisha," as they are called in Slavonic ("Slovo o dvênadtzati snahŭ Shahaishi," St. Petersburg, 1879). With his usual thoroughness he not only published a critical edition of a fifteenth-century text, but he goes into minute details concerning the history of this text, and the influence it has exercised upon Russian and mediaeval European literature. He finds traces of these dreams in the cycle of Solomonic legends, in the Quest of the Graal by Chrestien de Troyes, in other romances, and also in popular Russian tales. These dreams exist in Slavonic in at least two redactions, one a more modern and more enlarged in its eschatological element, found among the "Raskolniks,"

the general term used for heretical sects in Russia, and
another somewhat shorter and evidently older. In both we
find, however, already traces of the Prophecies of Methodius
of Patara, one of the old Slavonic apocryphal books, and
a remarkable similarity with the Tibetan version, inasmuch
as this also partakes of the eschatological character in the
interpretation of the dreams. In these Slavono - Russian
MSS., of which a fairly good number is known, the name
of the king is called, with slight variations, " Shahaisha,"
and the philosopher who interprets the dreams, " Mamer."
Professor Vesselofsky sees in the former the Persian
" Shahinsha," " the Emperor," and finds " Mamer " in
" Mor-olf," " Memer-olt " of the old German legend of
Solomon (pp. 21, 22); and he concludes that the tale, for
which no parallels are found in European literature, must
have come to Russia straight from Asia, the same way as
the tale of the Judge " Shemyakin," whose peculiar cases
and judgments sound like riddles. They form part of the
Shylock cycle, and have been treated by me in my
" Beitraege zur vergleichenden Sagen und Maerchenkunde,"
1883, p. 16 ff.

But a Slavonic text of the fifteenth century, though
not yet found among the Southern Slavs, is of greater
antiquity than anything yet which has been proved to be
due in Russian directly to Oriental sources. The stories
of Shemyakin are comparatively modern, whilst all the
texts of a somewhat religious character rest ultimately on
Byzantine originals. Whether these are forthcoming or
not is merely a matter of chance. The negative argument
that none are known to exist can at any time be upset by
the discovery of such a missing text. We have a case in
point in the story of Aḥikar and another in this very tale
of the Dreams; for the discovery of a Rumanian text
sets all doubts at rest. The old apocryphal Rumanian
literature is based almost exclusively on South and Old
Slavonic originals, which, as remarked, in their turn
point to Greek sources. I had suspected the existence of
a Rumanian version from a curt note of the late Canonicus

Cipariu (Gaster, " Liter. pop. romana," p. 58), but short of seeing the MS. in question the surmise, based only on the title, could not be changed into a positive fact. Since the death of the owner the MS. has disappeared; may be it is now the property of the Rumanian Academy of Science and hidden away in their cellars, which have become the catacombs of Rumanian literature. Fortunately I learned from the Rev. Canonicus Voileanu, of Sibiiu, in Transylvania, that he possessed a number of MSS. written in the last century by his forefather Voileanu, and with a liberality which it is a privilege to acknowledge here, placed them all at my disposal. Among these I discovered also the text of the twelve dreams, written in the year 1786. As all the MSS. written by Voileanu have proved to be copies of much older texts, I have no hesitancy to recognize in the present text a copy of a much older manuscript. In many places it is evidently corrupt. By comparing it with the old and with the more recent Slavonic, both published by Vesselofsky (loc. cit., pp. 4–13), the absolute similarity cannot be gainsaid. They are clearly derived from one old text common to all, which had its origin among the Slavonians of the South.

The Rumanian text is the shortest of the three, and in many instances more archaic even than the fifteenth-century Slavonic version. Noteworthy among the differences is the name of the king, who is called in Rumanian " Sehachi," without a trace of the other form " Shahaishah," due no doubt to later popular etymology. With the disappearance of this Persian form disappears also one of the most potent arguments of Professor Vesselofsky for the immediate Oriental origin of the Russian versions. I see further in the name " Mamer," the philosopher, a corruption from the Syriac form " Bilar," due by careless writing of the letters b and l in Syriac, or to the Byzantine transliteration $\mu\pi\iota\lambda\alpha\rho = Mpilar$. A glance at K. Falconer's table (p. 303) will show how profoundly the names have been changed in the various versions of the Panchatantra.

The following is a faithful translation from the unique

MS. of the Rumanian version, to which I have appended a carefully transliterated copy of the MS. written originally by Voileanu, with the old Slavonic letters in use in Rumania up to fifty years ago. The text has become a mystical treatise, and is called:

A teaching concerning the End of Days.

"In a place called Vaihon there ruled a king called Sehachi. He once dreamed in a night twelve dreams, and there was none who could interpret them to him, until at last they found a man, by name Mamer, who was a great scholar and a philosopher. So he went to the king and said: 'My lord Sehachi, these dreams do not portend any evil concerning thee, but God has shown thee what will happen at the end of days. Tell me, then, what hast thou seen in thy first dream.' And the king replied: 'I have seen a golden pillar reaching from earth to heaven.' And Mamer replied: 'When the last days approach much evil will there be in the world. In that time justice will disappear and good thoughts, and no one will utter goodly words, only vile, and the old will become dotards, and all will fall into grave sins and not repent. There will be many famines, and the autumn will last all through the winter, and the winter will be prolonged beyond the middle of the summer; men will sow at all seasons, and one seed-time will miss the other (i.e. none will be at the proper time); they will sow much and reap little. At that time children will not respect their parents, and they will marry near relations (within the forbidden degrees), they will not beware of sin, and harlots will have children, not knowing who their fathers are. At that time kings and princes will act violently towards the poor. Many will forsake their faith and embrace another. The sun will get darkened, and the moon will not shine, the days will be short, and many signs will be seen. Priests will not be distinguishable from laymen, they will tell lies, and truth and justice will perish. This dream is an example for all!'

" The philosopher said : ' How was the second dream which thou didst dream, O king?' And the king said : ' I saw a woman holding in her hand a towel that reached from heaven to earth.' And the philosopher said : ' When the last days will be near the people will forsake their true faith and will begin to hold another, and no one will think of worshipping God. They will refuse to have any intercourse with their poor relations, and they will pass their time with strangers.'

"And the philosopher said : ' How was the third dream which thou didst dream ? ' And the king replied : ' I saw three kettles boiling over a big fire, one filled with fat, the other with water, and the third with oil ; some of the fat was running into the oil and some of the oil into the fat, but none fell into the water, which boiled by itself alone.' The philosopher replied : ' At the end of days men will plant villages in places where such villages had never been thought of before, and at one end of the village a rich man will live and at the other another rich man, and all the poor will live in the middle. And the one rich man will invite the other to feast with him, but he will ignore all the poor, even if there be a brother among them. All will be hypocrites, they will neglect their own relations, they will hate their parents and brothers and love only the wife's family. Women will leave their husbands and will run away with other men. Old women will marry young men and old men will marry young girls, for then shame will have disappeared from among men, and there will not be found a single pure woman.'

"And the philosopher said : ' How was the fourth dream which thou didst dream ? ' And the king replied : ' I saw an old mare chewing some hay and the foal neighing within its belly.' The philosopher replied : ' When the end of days approaches mothers will act immodestly and join their daughters with strangers with whom they will closet them, and they will be shameless.'

"And the philosopher said : ' How was the fifth dream which thou didst see ? ' And the king said : ' I saw a bitch lying in a pond and the puppies were barking within her belly.' And the philosopher replied : ' During the last days fathers will teach their sons properly, but the sons will not listen, and will say, "You have grown old and have lost your senses, and you do not know what you are talking about"; and the parents will be put to shame, and will keep silent.'

"And the philosopher said : ' How was the sixth dream ? ' And the king replied : 'I saw a large number of priests standing in a mire up to their necks.'   The philosopher replied : ' At the time of the end of days the priests will teach the people God's word, but they themselves will not observe it, and will only be gathering riches to themselves, and by this they will bring their souls to the everlasting fire.'

"And the philosopher said : ' How was the seventh dream ? ' And the king replied : ' I saw a beautiful horse with two heads, with one in front and the other at the back ; with the first it fed upon the grass and with the second it drank water.'   And the philosopher replied : ' When the end of days comes near they will deliver wrong judgment, accepting bribery, and the bishops will appoint ignorant priests— a thing which ought not to happen—only because they will be paid for it.   There will be many priests, but few good among them ; they will have neither fear of God, nor shame of men, and will not think that they will go down to the torment of hell.'

"And the philosopher said : ' How was the eighth dream ? ' And the king replied : ' I saw a quantity of pearls strewn upon the face of the earth, and fire fell from heaven and burned everything.'   And the philosopher replied : ' At the end of days all will become traders, and the rich will make the poor out to be liars, and will take away by wrong means everything from the poor ; by so doing they will lose their souls.'

"And the philosopher said : ' How about the ninth dream ? ' And Sehaicha said : ' I saw a large number of people working together in one spot.' And Mamer replied : ' At the end of days men will bring their riches

and put into other people's keeping. They will receive
them with love, but when they will be asked to return
the riches they will deny it, and say : " We do not know
what you ask for, nor that you have left anything with us,"
even when the people will claim their property under oath.
For doing which they will lose their souls.'

" And the philosopher said : ' How about the tenth
dream which thou didst see ? ' And the king replied :
' I saw a large number of men and women standing together
upon the earth.' And the philosopher said : ' At the end
of days people will practise trickery, and will pride themselves on it ; by so doing they will lose their souls.'

" And the philosopher said : ' How about the eleventh
dream ? ' And the king replied : ' I saw men wearing
beautiful flowers on their heads.' And the philosopher
said : ' At the end of days men will be slanderers and
misers and libertines, and no word of truth will be found
among them ; brother will be cruel to brother, and if a poor
man says anything wise they will all laugh at him, but
if a rich man says however stupid a thing all will exclaim,
" Hark ! that great man is speaking," and all will say,
" The master speaks well." For this they will go to the
torment of hell.'

" And Mamer said : ' How about the twelfth dream which
thou didst see ? ' And he replied : ' I saw a multitude of
men with terrible eyes, and with wild (hard) hair, with
nails like eagle's claws, and with long legs.' And Mamer
said : ' At the end of days the rich will strangle the poor,
and the poor will say, " Happy those that have died before
us, for they have not fallen upon such evil days." '

" Mamer, the philosopher, made then his obeisance before
the king and said : ' I am the servant of you all, and I say
again to you, my lord, that there will be great trouble at
the end of days.' "

Thus far the Rumanian version. The interpretation, in
which the Rumanian agrees in the main with the Slavonic
version, does apparently not fit in with the dreams. The

incongruity between the image, as given by the dream, and
the interpretation, which ought to show some similarity,
can only be explained by the distance of time which
separates us from the original form.   In the course of
transmission the interpretation, no longer corresponding
with any actual need or not answering any longer any
immediate dogmatic purpose, may have been changed almost
beyond recognition.   An intimate connection between dream
and interpretation must have existed originally.   The Tibetan
version shows it clearly.   In the change from a Buddhist
to a Christian tale the eschatological character has been
profoundly modified, and we can now only here and there
find a trace of this connection.   May be the dreams have
also been somewhat curtailed, which would increase the
difficulty of recognizing the relation between symbol and
interpretation.   Older Greek and Oriental texts alone will
solve satisfactorily this problem.

Invăţătură la vrĕmĕ de apoi.

Fost-au întru o cetate ce să kema Vaihon un înpărat ce-l
kema Sehaci, şi au văzut într'o noapte 12 visuri, şi nu să
afla nime să le dezlĕge, dară aflară un om ce-i era numele :
Mamer, şi era cărturari mare şi filosof.   Dĕcă mĕrsă la
înpăratul, zisă : dm̃ne Sehaci ! visele tale nu ţi-s de rău,
ci dm̃nezău au arătat ţie ce va să fie la vrĕmĕ de apoi.
Ce-m spune visu dintăi cum l-aĭ văzut ?   Zisă înpăratul :
Văzui un stâlp de aur din pământ pănă la ceriu sta.   Zisă
Mamer : când va veni vrĕmĕ de apoi, mult rău va fi preste
toată lumĕ, şi într'acĕi vrĕme va peri dreptatĕ şi gândurile
cĕle bune, şi cuvinte dm̃nezăeşti nime nu va grăi, ce tot
drăceşti ; şi bătrânii vor fi în minte pruncăscă, şi toţi oameni
vor cădĕ în păcate grĕle şi nu să vor pocăi.   Şi vor fi adĕse
ori foameţi, şi va băga toamna în iarna, iară iarna va fi pănă
în miază-vară ; şi vor sămăna oameni de toate sămânţălĕ (!),
şi sămânţă pănă la sămânţă nu va ajunge ; multe vor sămăna
oameni dar puţin vor secera.   Intr'acĕa vrĕme fecŏri nu vor
cinsti pre părinţi săi, şi nĕm aproape să vor luoa, de păcate
nu vor gândi, şi curvele vor face prunci, şi nu vor şti cine

le easte tată. Intr'acêa vrême dm̃ni și boeari vor lucra fără-de-lêge cu mișei, și mulți oameni vor lăsa lêgê lor și alta vor apuca a ține. Atuncê soarele să va întuneça, și luna nu'și va da lumina sa, zilele să vor mici, și multe seamne să vor arăta. Iară popii nu să vor cunoaște din oameni cei proști, ce vor fi mincinoși. Dereptatê și adevărul va peri. Acesta-i un vis de pildă la toți.

Iară al doilê vis zisă filosoful, cum l-ai (văzut?) înpărate? Și zisă înpăratul: Văzuiu o mueare țiindu o mănăștergură din ceri până în pământ spânzurată. Și zisă filosoful: când va veni vrêmê de apoi lêgê dirêptă vor lăsa și alta vor apuca a ținê, și toți oameni la slujba lui Dm̃nezău nu vor gândi, și de nêmul său cel mișel să vor lepăda, și cu streini vor petrêce.

Și iară zisă filosoful: al treilê vis cum l-ai văzut? Și zisă înpăratul: Văzuiu 3 căldări ferbând într'o pară de foc, într'una era său, într'alta era apă, într'alta era unt, și sărê din său în unt și din unt în său, iară în apă nu cădê, ce ferbe de sine. Zisă filosoful: când va veni vrêmê de apoi oameni vor face sate pe unde n'au mai fost sate, și într'un cap de sat va fi un bogat, și în cela cap de sat va fi alt bogat, în mijloc vor fi săraci; deci bogatul va chema pre bogat de-l va ospăta, iară pre cei mișei nu vor vedê macar i-ar fi frate. Și toți oameni vor fi fățarnici, nu-și vor căuta de nêmul său, ce-și vor urâ părinți și frați, și-ș vor îndrăgi nêmul mueri-și. Mueri îș vor lăsa bărbați și vor fugi cu alți, și muerilê bâtrâne să vor mărita după cei tineri, și oameni bâtrâni vor lua fête, că atuncê nu va fi rușine în oameni; și nice o mueare nu va fi bună.

Iară zisă filosoful: al patrulê vis cum l-ai văzut? Zisă înpăratul: văzui o iapă bătrână unde rodê niște fân iară mânzul râncheza dintr'ânsa. Iară zisă filosoful: când va veni vrêmê de apoi își va votri muma la fată să o mărite, și o va închide cu altul în casă și să vor înpresura (!), și de nime nu să vor rușina.

Iară zisă filosoful: al cincilê vis cum l-ai văzut? Zisă înpăratul: văzuiu o câțê într'un lac zăcând iar cățăi lătra dintr'ânsa. Iară zisă filosoful: la vrêmê de apoi atunca va

învăţa părintele pre fečor bine; iară fečori nu-i vor asculta,
ce vor zice, înbătrânit-aţi şi mintê v-aţi perdut şi nu ştiţi
ce grăiţi, iară părinţii să vor ruşina şi vor tăcê.

Iară zisă filosoful: al 6 vis cum l-ai văzut. Zisă
înpăratul: văzuiu preoţi mulţi într'o tină până în grumazi.
Zisă filosoful: la vrêmê de apoi învăţa-vor preoţi pre
oameni în lêgê lui Dmnezău, iăra ei cu sine nu o vor
ţinê, ce vor aduna avuţii multe, şi cu acêea îşi vor băga
sufletelê în focul nestins.

Iară zisă filosoful: al 7 vis cum l-ai văzut? Zisă
împăratul: văzuiu un cal frumos unde avê 2 capete, unul
dinaintê, altul dinapoi, cu cel dinainte pâştê, iară cu cel
dinapoi be apă. Zisă filosoful: când va veni vrêmê de
apoi atunča va judeca cu strâmbul pentru plată, şi vlădici
vor pune popi săi şi fără de carte, care nu s-are cădê, numai
pentru plata; şi mulţi popi vor fi, iară puţini buni şi drepţi.
De Dmnezău nu le va fi frică, nici de oameni ruşine, şi
nu-şi vor aduce aminte că vor mêrge în munca iadului.

Iară zisă: al optulê vis cum l-ai văzut? Zisă înpăratul:
văzuiu preste toată lumê mult mărgăritariu vărsat pre
pământ, şi căzu foc din ceriu şi arsă tot. Şi zisă filosoful:
la vrêmê de apoi atuncê toţi oameni vor fi negoţători, şi cei
bogaţi vor face mincinoşi pre cei săraci, şi vor luoa cu
strâmbul de la cei mişăi, şi cu acêea îşi vor pêrde sufletul.

Iară zisă Mamer: al 9 vis cum l-ai văzut? Zisă Săhaicê:
văzuiu lucrători mulţi unde lucra într'un loc. Zisă Mamer:
când va veni vrêmê de apoi atunča vor duce oameni avuţie
la alţi să o ţie, şi când o vor da, o vor primi cu drag, iară
când va fi de alurê (leg. a o luoa) o vor tăgădui şi vor zice:
nu ştim (ce) ceri, şi ce mêi dat; şi cu jurământ va să o ea
înapoi. Şi pentru acêea îşi vor pêrde sufletele.

Iară zisă filosoful: al 10 vis cum l-ai văzut? Zisă
înpăratul: văzuiu mueri multe şi bărbaţi unde sta pre
pământ. Zisă filosoful: la vrêmê de apoi vor unbla oameni
tot în vicleşuguri şi trufindu-să, şi pentru acêea încă îş vor
perde sufletul.

Iară zisă Mamer: al 11 vis cum l-ai văzut? Zisă
înpăratul: văzuiu nişte oameni purtând flori în cap foarte

frumoasă. Zisă filosoful: la vrêmê de apoi, fi-vor oameni scunpi și clevetitori și cu(r)vari, și vorbă drêptă nu să (va) afla, și frate cătră frate nemilostiv va fi. Și de va grăi vre un mișăl cuvânt înțălept, toți îl vor râde; iară de va grăi vre un bogat v'un (cuvânt) și cam prost, toți vor zice: ascultați, ca grăește cel boeari; și toți vor zice: bine grăește dmnul. Și pentru acêea vor mêrge în munca iadului.

Zisă Mamer: al 12 vis cum l-ai văzut? Văzuiu mulți oameni cu ochi grozavi, și aspri la păr, și cu unghi de vultur, și cu picoare lungi. Iară zisă Mamer: când va fi vrêmê de apoi, bogați vor sugușa pre cei săraci, și vor zice săraci: ferice de cei ce muriră înaintê noastră de nu ajunsă (!) acêste zile rêle.

După acêea să închină Mamer filosoful înnaintê înpăratului și zisă: a tuturor sânt slugă acestora, ce spun mării tale, însă mult rău va fi atuncê în zilelê cêlê de apoi.

Art. XIII. — *Contributions to the History of Aḥiḳar and Nadan.* By M. Gaster.

The history of Aḥiḳar and his nephew Nadan forms part of Eastern popular literature. When publishing my history of Roumanian popular literature seventeen years ago (Bucureesti, 1883) I devoted a special chapter to the Roumanian versions of this history (pp. 104–114). I was the first to recognize the connection between the Roumanian and Slavonic versions and those contained in the Arabian Nights. I then drew attention to the intimate relation between this legend and that which has entered the Greek life of Æsop. Since that time scholars have paid much attention to this legend, especially as through Meissner's studies it is being considered as one of the lost Apocrypha mentioned already in the Book of Tobit.

The whole material has now been collected under the title "The Story of Aḥiḳar, from the Syriac, Arabic, Armenian, Ethiopic, Greek, and Slavonic versions, by F. C. Conybeare, J. Rendel Harris, and Agnes Smith Lewis. London, 1898." In the Introduction (pp. vii–lxxxviii) the attempt is made to reconstruct the old Hebrew form of Aḥiḳar, especially in Chapters V and VI. Before examining this hypothesis, and many of the points touched upon in that Introduction, I will first give a direct contribution to the text itself by translating the Roumanian version. I have selected for this purpose, out of a number of manuscripts mentioned by me in my History of Roumanian Literature ("Grundriss der Romanischen Philologie," ed. Groeber), ii, 3, p. 387, the version contained in my manuscript No. 90, written 1777.

THE ROUMANIAN VERSION.

The History of Arkirie, the very wise, who taught his nephew Nadan in matters of wisdom and learning, that he should have sense and philosophy and good knowledge.

In the days of King Sanagriptu there lived in the land of Rodu (Doru) a man named Arkirie. This very wise Arkirie adopted a nephew, the son of his sister, of the name of Anadan (for he had no children). He fed him with white bread and honey and good wine, and taught him philosophy. And he said to him:

1. "My son, I teach thee first: Enter into no business with the mighty, nor buy anything from them, nor buy stolen goods, lest thy own goods perish with them.

2. "My son Anadan, honour thy father and thy mother, so that they should not curse thee, and let thy goods remain blessed and thou eat and rejoice in them (cf. Akyr. 25).[1]

3. "My son Anadan, when thou servest a wicked master, do not tell him that he is wicked and that he should have mercy on thee, but do what he orders thee.

4. "My son, do not talk in the presence of thy master, for thou wilt err and he will hate thee.

5. "My son Anadan, go to church on each holiday, and on Sundays, for God will feed thee (cf. Akyr. 33).

6. "My son Anadan, wherever thou seest a man sad and in sorrow crying, go to him and comfort him, and remind him that he will also die (cf. Akyr. 41).

7. "My son, when thou reachest a high position, then bow before everyone, for with thy wisdom thou wilt reach a higher place still.

8. "Be not hasty in thine anger lest thou repent afterwards (cf. Akyr. 97).

9. "My son Anadan, whatever thou wishest to obtain from God, pray continually, for in time God will grant it to thee.

---

[1] The references in parentheses are to the Slavonic version in the above publication of Conybeare, etc.

10. "My son, keep thy hand from theft; do not murder, and do not speak evil (cf. Akyr. 119).

11. "My son Anadan, flee from unchastity, especially from married women, for thou wilt lose thy head (cf. Akyr. 119).

12. "My son, listen to the wise man, though he be poor, for that is the way in which God acts; one day he gives to one and the other day to the other.

13. "As long as thou livest, beware from digging a pit for others, for thou art sure to fall in it.

14. "A wise man listens (to words), but the fool, even when thou strikest him, will never learn anything (cf. Akyr. 49).

15. "My son Anadan, take no bribes, for bribes blind the soul and make thee lose it, and darken the eyes of man (cf. Akyr. 53).

16. "My son, better be served by a righteous slave than by a wicked brother (cf. Akyr. 61).

17. "It is better to lie on the gridiron than to live with a wicked wife, and do not confide thy advice and thy faith to anyone (cf. Akyr. 68).

18. "My son Anadan, when thou speakest to thy master let thy mouth be locked with three locks — one on the heart, and the other on the mind, and the third on the mouth—for when thou once hast spoken, the word cannot be caught back either on horse, or by wind hounds, or by the hawk.

19. "Again, my son Anadan, honour and support the good and the wise, though he be only wise in his way and not rich.

20. "My son Anadan, if thou hast a wicked neighbour do not neglect him, for God will have mercy upon thee, and he will not be able to harm thee.

21. "My son Anadan, be not a liar, for a lie first goes to the bottom as heavy as lead, and at last it floats like a leaf on the water (cf. Akyr. 74).

22. "My son, it is better to carry stones with the wise than to feast with a fool.

23. "My son, honour thy brothers and thy friends, lest he speaks nicely in thy presence, but behind thy back he will hurt thee and smite thee.

24. "My son, if anyone throws stones at thee, throw bread, for the bread will come back to thee and the stone will return to him who throws it.

25. "My son, it is better that a wise man beats thee than that the fool honours thee.

26. "My son, when thou sittest at other peoples' table do not sit high up, for other people and greater people will come and move thee to a lower place; but when thou sittest at a lower end, and when once they have called thee up, they will no more move thee down.

27. "Nor shalt thou invite anyone to a stranger's table.

28. "Do not sit too long; better sit a little and let them regret that thou dost not tarry longer.

29. "When thou art invited come properly dressed, otherwise better stay at home and let them regret thy absence, instead of going unprepared, for he wishes to honour thee, and thou puttest him to shame.

30. "My son, do not go out in the night without arms, for thou knowest not whom thou shalt meet.

31. "My son, when thou startest on a journey, carry thy own food with thee, and count not on that of thy companions, for thou wilt remain hungry (cf. Akyr. 78).

32. "My son, do not start alone on a journey, and on the way do not eat all thy food, relying upon thy companion, for when thy food comes to an end he will not give thee; (for fruit in a stranger's sack get easily bad and rancid).

33. "My son, if anyone give thee good advice listen to it, for it will be very useful to thee; it will be like fresh water from a pure fountain to a thirsty man.

34. "My son, do not go to other tables uninvited, and

35. "What thou dost not like for thyself do it not unto others.

36. "My son Anadan, take care of the top of the sack and not of the bottom, for the bottom is also the end."

When he had instructed him in all the philosophy and wisdom and knowledge, Arkirie took his nephew Anadan and brought him to the King Sanagriptu. Bringing him to Court, Arkirie said: "Honourable King, I will present my nephew Anadan that he serve your Majesty, for I have grown old, and am not able to serve any longer." And the King Sanagriptu, in reply, said: "I am very pleased to fulfil your wish, Arkirie." And Arkirie said unto the King: "May it be thy gracious will to appoint my nephew Great Logothet." And he was appointed to that post, and it went well with him, and he was greatly honoured at Court.

But Anadan harboured evil thoughts in his heart, and he thought how he could destroy his uncle Arkirie, so that he should get all his property. So he wrote a false letter without the knowledge of the King, and he wrote as follows: "I, Anadan, in the name of the illustrious king Sanagriptu, send greetings and good health to my beloved friend and father, the wise Arkirie. The moment when thou receivest this letter assemble the warriors from that part of the country and come as fast as thou canst, for the king is in great trouble." When Arkirie read this letter he at once gathered his hosts, and started to go with all his hosts to the King. When Anadan knew that his uncle had approached the place, he took the king by the hand and led him to a high tower and showed him the army. The king was greatly astounded, and said: "What can this mean?" Then Anadan said: "There is my uncle Arkirie, who has risen in rebellion against thee." And the king said: "What am I to do to save myself from this great danger?" And Anadan said: "When he will have come much nearer I will go out and meet him, and with good words I will persuade him to come with me, and I will bring him to thee." And the king said: "If thou bringest him, there will be no one greater than thee in this realm." And the king said, "Go."

And Anadan then went and said: "Greetings to Arkirie, to my father, welcome in health. The king is waiting for thee, for he is oppressed with dangers from many quarters."

And he kissed his hand and he repeated : " Greetings
from the king." Arkirie said : " Hail unto thee, my son
Anadan ; and how is the king ?—is it well with him ? "
Anadan replied : " He is in great troubles, and he wishes
thee to come to him as quickly as possible." And Arkirie
replied : " With pleasure." So he got up and went to
the king as a faithful servant, not knowing anything.
Anadan made obeisance to the king with his uncle, and
the king said : " Is it right that thou shalt come with hosts
against me ? My father and I have been kind to thee, and
there was no one more honoured in the kingdom, and now
thou desirest to kill me, but instead of that thy punishment
will overtake thee." Arkirie replied : " I know nothing of
it, my lord." The king replied : " Why hast thou acted
in that manner against me ? " And the king said to his
counsellors : " How shall we punish him according to his
deserts ? " Not one of them answered, but Anadan said :
" The punishment shall be that his head be struck off and
carried one hundred feet away from his body." And the
king said to the great executioner : "Go and cut his head off."
    And Arkirie said to the executioner : " Remember the
kindness which I have done unto thee, and I pray unto
thee speak to the king on my behalf, and tell him Arkirie
prays that he be led to his own house to suffer there the
punishment, so that his wife and his slaves may weep over
him and bury him." And the executioner went to the king
and repeated his words. And the king said : "Take him
to his house and put him to death." So they brought
him to his house. On the second day they sat down and
feasted together, and Arkirie said to the executioner :
" Remember — and it is right that man should remember
the good that has been shown to him—that I have shown
friendship unto thee, and now has the time come to return
kindness to me. Put me not to death. There is a man
in prison who is like myself ; strike off his head and bring
it to the king." The executioner complied willingly with
his request, and struck off the man's head and returned to
the king. Arkirie made an underground dwelling in his

house, and there he lived for nine years, no one knowing anything of it with the exception of his wife. Anadan asked now from the king the houses and property that belonged to Arkirie his uncle. The king gave them to him. He went to the house of his uncle, and he began to beat the servants and slaves, and he held great feasts and dances over the grave of his uncle. And many other such things. Arkirie heard all this and suffered.

In another country there lived a king by name Pharaon. When he heard that Arkirie, the philosopher, had been killed, he sent a messenger to Annagriptu (1. Sanagriptu), saying : " I bid thee know, that the moment thou seest this my letter, thou shalt send me some workmen, for I wish to build a castle which shall be neither in heaven nor upon earth, and these workmen shall come, neither walking on foot nor riding on horseback ; they shall be neither dressed nor naked. If thou wilt not do as I wish, then gather thy hosts for battle." When Sanagriptu saw this letter he was greatly disturbed and wondered how to do it, for he had no one to counsel him, and he said to his counsellors : " If Arkirie had been alive, I should have had some one to advise me, but you have caused me to kill him, and now I am sure to lose my country." And all the counsellors were greatly vexed and wondered what to do. Then the executioner said : " O illustrious king, if anyone would bring Arkirie back alive, what wouldst thou do to him ? " And the king replied : " There shall be no greater man than him in my whole kingdom." So he went and brought Arkirie from his underground cell. When they brought him out, his hair reached to the ground, and his nails were like scythes, and his eyes were closed, for the hair of his lashes and eyebrows covered them completely ; and they brought him to the king.

When the king perceived him he greatly rejoiced, and said : " O Arkirie, what am I to do, as the king Pharaon has sent a missive asking me to send master-workmen to build a castle which shall be neither in heaven nor upon earth, and those masters shall be neither dressed nor naked,

and they shall come neither on foot nor on horseback."
Arkirie replied : " Be comforted, O king, and rejoice, for
I will accomplish this thing, but give me ten days grace
until I shall have recovered the sight of my eyes." The
king granted his wish, and after the ten days Arkirie came
to the king and asked him to give him two eaglets. He
took these eaglets with him and entered a boat, taking the
master-workmen with him dressed in fisher-nets, and so
they came to the king Pharaon.

When they reached the place the king did not recognize
him, and he asked them, "How did you come ?" And
Arkirie replied : "Neither on foot nor on horseback, and
now, Pharaon, be ready for to-morrow." On the second day
Arkirie took a boy and put him in a high bedstead (a cage),
and he tied the two eaglets to that bedstead, and the two
eaglets began to fly aloft, for the boy kept in his hands an
iron spit with meat on the top of it. He showed it to them
as if he were willing to feed them, and the eaglets were very
hungry, as they had been kept for three days without food.
The boy then cried : "Bring lime and stones, for the
workmen are ready, and we wish to build the castle in the
heights—neither in heaven nor upon earth." And Arkirie
said unto the king : "Give orders to the people to carry
up lime and stones, as the workmen are waiting for
work." The king wondered at it, and he said : "In
truth we are at fault now, as we cannot carry up the lime
and stones."

The king then recognized that it was Arkirie, and he said
unto him : "I want you to make me a rope of sand."
Arkirie went and bored a hole through the wall of a room,
and in the morning when the sun rose the rays of the sun
penetrated the room through that hole, and Arkirie said
to the king : "Send and tie the foals up quickly with that
rope, so that I may twist another." And the king wondered
and said, "Thou art truly the philosopher Arkirie !" and
he said unto him, "I am it"; and he told him all that had
happened to him, and how his nephew had spoken evil
against him.

He returned then from that place, and came back and made obeisance to the king, and said: "I wish you to deliver up to me my nephew Anadan that I teach him my philosophy, for I have hitherto not taught him sufficiently well." And the king said, "Go and take him." And he got hold of him by the chest and brought him to his house.

And he made four iron staffs and four clubs of wood with nails sticking out of them, and he put Anadan down and began to beat him. And Anadan said: "Forgive me, my father, and let me be the meanest of swineherds, only let me live." But Arkirie said: "No, my son, thou hast acted towards me in the same manner as the wolf acted when he went to the teacher to be taught; for whilst the teacher said A B C D the wolf said: 'For the lambs' and 'for the sheep' and 'for the goats' and 'for the kids'; in the same manner hast thou acted towards me, my son."

And he began to beat him. And Anadan said: "Have mercy on me, and I will be a shepherd." And Arkirie said: "Thou hast acted towards me as the wolf who followed the sheep and met the shepherd, who said to him: 'Happy journey to thee, wolf.' The wolf replied: 'Thank thee.' And he asked him: 'Whither art thou going so fast?' And the wolf said: 'I follow the track of the sheep, for an old woman had told me that the dust of the sheep was wholesome for the eyes.' In the same manner hast thou acted against me."

And he began again to beat him, but Anadan said: "Have pity on me, and I will groom thy horses." But Arkirie said: "No, my son, thou hast acted towards me like a man who, leading an ass on the road, tied it with a loose rope. The ass broke the rope and ran away. On his way he met the wolf, and the wolf said unto him: 'Happy journey unto thee, ass!' And the ass replied: 'Unhappy it will be, for the man tied me up with a rotten rope, so that I broke it and ran away, and he did not tie me with a good rope.'" And Arkirie continued to beat him until he died.

Thus far the Roumanian version in this manuscript, which is distinguished by some peculiar features from all the other versions known. Whilst some of the riddles are omitted like that of the Peculiar Tree, we have here, on the contrary, more details concerning the master-workmen which had to be sent to Egypt. The source for this text is probably Slavonic, but here again the differences are very marked between this version and that published by Jagic and reprinted in the English translation in the above-mentioned book (pp. 1–23). The proverbs and maxims are less numerous than in the Slavonic, and a large number are missing altogether from the Slavonic. The Roumanian text thus reveals a much more primitive form of this legend in the Slavonic, or maybe in the Greek original, than has hitherto come to light. The incident connected with the flying of the boy in the cage or bedstead is here also much fuller than in the Slavonic text, and presents striking resemblance to the ancient Solomon legends with which this part of the history is undoubtedly connected. Nor should it be forgotten that this text is merely one out of a number of similar texts, of which I have given a short description in my book on Roumanian Popular Literature, and recently in my History of Roumanian Literature in Groeber's "Grundriss der Romanischen Philologie," ii, 3, p. 387. Although all these MSS., and the printed texts published by Anton Pann (1842) rest ultimately upon one Slavonic or Greek original, yet there is no absolute identity among them. Each text differs from the other, either through the omission of some minor incidents and similes at the end of the tale or in the maxims and sentences, of which one contains a larger, the other a smaller number, and some again have new maxims inserted which are missing in other versions. These changes are sometimes radical, and yet they have evidently taken place within the last two or three centuries, as none of these MSS. is older than the eighteenth century.

The fact that even in one literature, and within a comparatively short period, profound changes have been introduced into it, is of no mean importance for the history of this tale. Similar changes have undoubtedly occurred also in the other versions of Ahikar, and it is more than doubtful whether we have in the versions that have come down to us, all of a comparatively recent origin, the old and primitive form of the "Ahikar" legend. The process of continual change is not limited to one period or to one circle alone. This is the rule for all popular books, and any conclusions that are derived solely from one or more versions, or even from all combined, must fall short of the truth so long as this factor is being ignored. In this change only the frame, i.e. the history of the hero, remains as a rule the abiding factor. The incidents are either amplified or altered according to the fancy of the copyist, and according to his greater or smaller amount of knowledge. The most fluctuant element is the gnomical —the maxims and proverbs that float about, as it were, in the air, and are eagerly caught up by the scribes to popularize the tale with the listeners for whom it is intended. These bear the imprint of the immediate environments; for they must have the local colour if they are to be retained by the copyist or translator. The figurative element will live longest in the East, the pregnant antithese will be appreciated everywhere.

I do not intend discussing here the history of the European proverbs. It suffices to point out the profound change which has taken place in the Greek proverbs. The Byzantine and modern Greek differ from the old not merely in form, but in tendency, as Krumbacher has convincingly shown. They resemble much more the Oriental conceptions and are also of a figurative character. In fact, they are identical with the Ahikar type, which in its turn resembles the old Hebrew ' mashal,' the maxims of the Books of Proverbs, Ecclesiastes, and Sirach. The Oriental proverbs have in their transmission from the East to the West a history of their own. Mutual borrowing can be followed up here no less clearly than in the case of tales and apologues. This branch of comparative folklore has, however, as yet scarcely been touched upon in spite of the great work of Wander and others. How far the East, and in speaking of it in this connection I limit myself to the Christian and Muhummedan East—is indebted to the West, i.e. Greece, and *vice versâ*, can only be matter of conjecture. In each country scores of witty sayings will have crystallized at one time or another round one prominent figure renowned for sharpness of wit and keenness of spirit. Collections of such proverbs have then been transferred from the one to the other. The similarity in many an incident and in a good number of maxims between Solomon, Ahikar, Æsop, and Loqman, is due to these causes of identification and adaptation from one local hero to the other. In fact, the bulk of the final portion is taken over bodily from the old cycle of Solomonic legends and adapted to the Ahikar cycle. The same has happened to individual maxims and proverbs. The route they take is not easy to follow. One single example must suffice to show how such maxims have come from the West to the East, to be enriched and amplified there, and to begin a new journey through the length and breadth of Europe.

It will at the same time disclose the true origin of the Ethiopic collection, which the editors do not seem to realize.

Honein b. Isaac translated in the ninth century from various languages—Greek, Syriac, and Hebrew—into Arabic a large collection of such maxims. It has deeply influenced European and also Oriental paroemiology. In the eleventh century already it was translated into Hebrew, and about the same time or a century later into Spanish. It forms the basis of Mubashir's collection, which in its turn is the basis of the Spanish "Bocados de Oro," translated then into French and English, not to speak of other translations dependent on either of these compilations (v. Steinschneider, "Uebersetzungen," p. 348 ff.). Among the component parts of Honein's collection we find also the so-called "Will of Loqman" and a goodly number of parallels to Ahikar. Steinschneider maintains now that the Ethiopic text is borrowed from this compilation, and thus the theory of the

editors, who believed in an independent Ethiopic version
of Aḥiḳar, falls to the ground.

In this transmission from literature to literature the links
are often missing. Parallelism is not sufficient proof for
determining the possible priority of one text over another.
Nor is it by any means clear, because in some versions of
the Book of Tobit, Aheiaharos and Nadan, and only the
ingratitude of the latter, are mentioned, that it refers to the
story in the form in which it has been transmitted. In the
short reference to him in Tobit, not a single allusion is made
to the teaching and to the maxims of Aḥiḳar. I see in
the 'story' of Aḥiḳar the combination of two independent
sets of tales. The first part of the tale—the adoption of
Nadan and the treason of the latter—is one independent
tale, whilst the 'wisdom' of Aḥiḳar is another, and it has
been amalgamated with the former at a later period. The
first is known only in connection with Aḥiḳar and Nadan,
no other name having ever been substituted for either.

There is no parallel known to this tale in any other
quarter. Wherever this tale occurs it is always associated
with the same names—copyists' errors in one of the Greek
texts of Tobit notwithstanding. Not so, however, with the
second part, containing Aḥiḳar's journey to Egypt for the
purpose of solving some riddles set by the king to the master
of Aḥiḳar, and the successful accomplishment of his task.
The very same incidents occur in the life of Æsop, and
Loqman has been credited with identical exploits. But all
these are merely the late reflexes of older cycles of legends
clustering round the name of Solomon, the oldest embodiment
of Oriental wisdom. The Queen of Sheba puts such riddles
to him, according to ancient legends; they recur also in the
recital of the riddles put to the same king by Hiram of
Phoenicia. He is also flying through the air in the same
manner as the boy in the legend of Aḥiḳar. This legend
has afterwards been transferred to Alexander the Great.
All these ancient sages are also credited with great wisdom,
and the 'Will' or last ethical exhortation is the concluding
portion of the narrative in each case.

I see, therefore, in this part of the Aḥiḳar legend, which
is common to so many reputed wise men, an older and
at the same time an independent part of it.   The same
applies for many of the maxims and ethical principles
put into the mouth of Aḥiḳar.   Their source must be
sought in the collections connected with names, such as
Solomon, Æsop, etc.   Very much depended on the translator
or copyists of the 'story.'   They played often the *rôle* of
authors, altering, omitting, and introducing such maxims
as suited them best.   Many a popular proverb has thus
been introduced which was of a totally different origin.
The one would favour Biblical reminiscences, the other look
to the Qorân for inspiration, and a good many to other
collections of proverbs and maxims.

How numerous such collections, e.g. of Greek proverbs
and maxims, have been can be gathered from the very rich
bibliography recently published by G. Polites in connection
with his publication of the Neo-Greek proverbs.   Such
proverbs were easily taken over by another and incorporated
into his work, to be borrowed anew from the latter by a third
compiler, and so forth.   To give again a modern example.
Negrutzi published in 1852 a collection of Roumanian
proverbs, into which he had incorporated verbatim almost the
whole of the maxims of 'Arkirie' without even mentioning
him!   Pann, again, introduced other popular proverbs into
his second and subsequent editions of Arkirie!

I adduce these examples because we can verify the sources.
In the light of proven facts we are justified to assume
similar procedures for ancient times, and we thus learn to
guard against rash conclusions drawn from similarity between
maxims or between single similes and incidents.

It needs hardly pointing out that under such circumstances,
before formulating any opinion as to the age and origin of
the Aḥiḳar legend, the first thing to be done is to try and
establish the primitive form.   All the MSS. containing the
story of Aḥiḳar are of comparatively modern origin.   They
differ among themselves very much, and show undoubted
traces of early indebtedness to the Bible in its widest

sense, and to many extraneous collections of maxims and
apophthegms.   An attempt to reconstruct a problematic
Hebrew original is, to say the least, premature; and the
attempt to penetrate behind the modern form with the
intention of finding a book contemporary with the Psalter
or with the Gospel narrative, as made in the Introduction,
is not warranted by any of the facts hitherto adduced to
strengthen this hypothesis.

I must dwell at some length on this point and on the
relation which is presumed to exist between Ahikar and
Tobit.   Much is made in the Introduction, p. xlviii ff., of
the sentence that occurs in Tobit, iv, 10—"Alms doth deliver
from death"—and the editor labours to prove the possibility
that in an older form much of the almsgiving of Ahikar
may have been mentioned, but which is now missing.   The
difficulty is to be met, then, by the identification of
'righteousness' and 'alms,' both expressed by the Hebrew
word 'sedaqah.'   He takes pains to explain the advice of
Tobit by means of finding also in Ahikar "a suggestion
of a confusion between 'righteousness' and 'alms.'"   The
passage in Tobit is, however, merely borrowed verbatim from
Proverbs, x, 2, or xi, 4, in which we find the same words
repeated twice: "but righteousness delivereth from death."
In my edition of the Hebrew Tobit this very verse is found
agreeing verbatim with Prov. xi, 4, thus dispelling any
lingering doubt.   This quotation has since become a popular
Hebrew proverb, exactly with the same meaning as in Tobit
and in Ahikar, 'alms' taking the place of 'righteousness.'
This change in the meaning of the Biblical proverb is due
to the change of the meaning in the word 'sedaqah' which
has taken place in post-Biblical times.   The Rabbinic
literature abounds with reference to 'almsgiving,' and the
regular word for it is only 'sedaqah.'   With this derivate
meaning the word entered the Qorân.   Its appearance with
that meaning among the sayings of Tobit, and especially
among the maxims of Ahikar, proves with absolute certainty
its late origin.   The change had already taken place, and
the proverb had become popular with the *altered* meaning

attached to it. Even now the sentence is written on the poor-box among the Jews, and it is repeated on occasions of burial, when the people are appealed to to give 'alms,' for "alms deliver from death."[1] There is nothing in it, therefore, that should "refer to the experience of Ahikar," as is maintained in the Introduction, p. liv, and no doubt can be entertained that the borrowing is entirely on the side of Ahikar.

Turning now to the parallels to the Psalms as given on p. lvii, the following sentence from Ahikar is considered to be parallel to Psalm cxli, 4:—Ahikar: "O my son, be not neighbour to the fool, and eat not bread with him." Psalm: "Incline not my heart to any evil thing, to practise wicked works with men that work iniquity, and let me not eat of their dainties." Much nearer, at any rate, is the following quotation from Proverbs, xxiii, 6: "Eat thou not bread with him that hath an evil eye, neither desire thou his dainties." It is significant that the next translation of Ahikar agrees apparently better with the Greek version than with the extremely difficult Hebrew original. Much more interesting is the third example adduced by the editors. Ahikar: "For he who digs a pit for his brother shall fall into it; and he who sets traps shall be caught in them." This is said to be a parallel to Psalm cxli, 10: "Let the wicked fall into their own nets, whilst that I withal escape." It has 'escaped' the editors that we have in Ahikar merely the transcript of Psalm vii, 15: "He that makes a pit and digs it, falleth into the ditch which he has made."

These few examples show that, far from the Psalms "containing an actual memorial of Ahikar," the very reverse has taken place. The sentences in Ahikar proclaim their youth by the form in which biblical reminiscences are found among them. The question may now be asked whether the references to Aheiaharos in the Greek versions of Tobit belong to the original form of that text? The oldest Hebrew version extant (published by me) has no

---

[1] v. Tendlau, "Spruchwörter Deutsch-juedischer Vorzeit;" No. 858.

reference whatsoever to Aheiaharos or to Nadan; and the Text of Jerome, which stands in close relation to this old Hebrew, has only one solitary allusion to this name. This is probably due to the influence of the Old Latin utilized by Jerome, which in its turn represents that Greek tradition which is found also in the Peshitto. Ilgen already in his commentary to Tobit pointed out that the two passages in which Aheiaharos occurs are probably due to a late interpolation. They interrupt the flow of the tale, and must therefore be of a different origin, introduced, as I believe, into the tale of Tobit in order to strengthen the moral weight of the ethical teaching contained in the ' Will ' of Tobit.

All this tends to diminish the probability of a Hebrew original of the story of Aḥiḳar, readily assumed by the editors. Not a single trace of the first part of Aḥiḳar has thus far been found in the Hebrew literature. Numerous parallels to the second part exist, as remarked above, but they are independent of Aḥiḳar; though a far larger number of parallels to the maxims can be found in Hebrew than those few given by the editors.

Hebrew paroemiology offers a vast material, which has hitherto not yet been utilized. The comparisons should not be limited merely to such coincidences which find their reason and explanation in the fact that they derive from the Bible, which is a source common to both. There are other collections in which parallels to Aḥiḳar will be found. But which is the primitive source? An answer to this question must be reserved until a complete translation of some of the more important collections will have been published by me, especially of those that go under the name and authority of Judah the Prince, Elieser the Great, and " The Canopy of Elijah " ascribed to Elijah.

In most of these collections the sayings are arranged in numerical groups exactly in the manner in which they appear at the close of Aḥiḳar's teaching, which undoubtedly is an imitation of those old ' Wills.' Such groups are found also massed at the end of a book called "The Sayings of the Fathers," by Rabbi Nathan, an extremely old compilation, dating probably from the fifth century. We find thus the following saying in "Maaseh Torah," ascribed to R. Judah, *sub* No. 4 : "The sages say the following four sentences : 'The fool will then become wise when a black man rubbing with a sack will become white; the young will then be possessed of knowledge when the ass will walk up a ladder; the daughter-in-law will live peacefully with her mother-in-law when the kids will dwell peacefully among tigers; and when a white raven will be found then also a woman without blemish ' " (cf. Akyr., No. 82 ; Khik., No. 83 ; Aḥik., No. 62 ; Haiq., No. 59).

From the Will of Elieser the Great: "My son, do not talk idle talk in the school-house, do not scoff at everything, do not scoff at everybody " (cf. Khik., No. 57).

"My son, honour the poor and assist him secretly, feed him in thy house, and turn thine eye away when he eats and drinks, for he is hungry and would leave off eating " (cf. Akyr. 81).

"My son, do not reveal thy secret to thy wife, be faithful and true to all; do not reveal thy secret to thy friend when thou art contending with him no more than when thou art at peace with him " (cf. Akyr. 68. 75; Haiq. 53; Khik. 59. 74).

"My son, do not cook in thy neighbour's pot (euphemism for 'do not marry a widow') " (v. Khik. 40).

"Be patient in anger " (Akyr. 97).

"My son, do not be without children, teach them the Law " (cf. Aḥik. 28; Haiq. 28; Khik. 20. 35).

"My son, do not wander about alone, nor be alone a judge, or judge and witness in one " (cf. Aḥik. 27. 56; Akyr. 27; Haiq. 27; Khik. 19).

"My son, be not a neighbour to the wicked, and do not associate with the slanderer "; and "My son, do not sit in the company of the slanderers and of the evil-tongued " (cf. Haiq. 19; Khik. 90).

"My son, rejoice not when thy enemy falls, lest God sees it and it displeases Him " (cf. Aḥik. 17. 60; Khik. 11. 97; Haiq. 58).

"My son, beware of a woman that is not worthy of thee, for she is sure to ruin thee" (cf. Akyr. 15; Aḥiḳ. 19. 72; Khik. 13; Haiq. 8).

"My son, love the wise and run after them, know thy Maker, live in peace with everyone, and speak the truth" (cf. Aḥiḳ. 12. 31; Khik. 6. 89; Haiq. 14).

These few examples suffice to show that many more parallels could be found in Rabbinic literature, though this parallelism proves very little for the Hebrew origin of Aḥiḳar.

The oldest version of Midrash Megillah

published for the first time from a unique manuscript
of the Xth century

by

Rev. Dr. M. Gaster,

Chief Rabbi of the Spanish and Portuguese Congregations of England.

The history of the miraculous delivery in the times of Haman and Mordecai held a prominent place in the affection of the people, during all the years of dispersion and persecution. It was constantly almost contemporary history, and conveyed to the people the message of comfort and consolation, of which they stood so much in need in those periods of dire hatred and threatening danger. Hence the innumerable versions of Agadic interpretations and Midrashim to this special book, which have come down to us, and which surpass by far the number of Midrashim to any other book of the Bible, the Song of Songs not excepted.

In reprinting the extremely scarce edition of Constantinople 1519, Ch. M. Horowitz added to it not only a very valuable commentary, in which he referred to the sources and parallels to this version, but also an elaborate introduction dealing with the various then known Midrashim and Targumim to the book of Esther. Since then, the indefatigable Buber has published the other Midrashim which were known only to exist in manuscripts, and has enriched his edition with the usual literary apparatus, which distinguishes his editions so favourably.

Another addition is made now by me by the discovery of the text which I am publishing here for the first time, in the volume intended to mark the high esteem

and the great appreciation in which Dr. Kohut was held by
the world of letters, and to express the feeling of the great
loss which Jewish science has suffered by the untimely de-
mise of the author of the "Aruch completum". It is a small
mite which I contribute to the memory of the man who had
made the Midrash his own domain, and who would have delighted in this new find.

The text which appears here for the first time, is taken
from my Codex hebr. No. 83. It is a quarto volume, composed of various Midrashim, most of which, if not all, are totally unknown. The various portions which go to make up
this volume, were written by different hands at various times, but all in the East. The portion which contains our
Midrash, although placed at the end of the volume, owing
no doubt to the carelessness of an ignorant binder, is in
fact the oldest document, and judging by the peculiar form
of writing and by the archaic style of paper and type of
letters, it must be assigned to the ninth or tenth century.
Dr. Neubauer, than whom there is now no greater authority
in hebrew palaeography, agrees with me, in assigning so
high an antiquity to this Ms. It is thus the oldest Ms extant
of any Midrash, and deserves as such, great consideration.

The great antiquity of this version is demonstrated by
the text itself, especially when compared with the other
known versions. In fact its simplicity and the Talmudic
elements contained therein, enable us to study the growth
and development of these Midrashim, in countries outside
of Palestine.

We have here the archetype of the Midrash to Esther,
which in all the other texts has gradually been embellished
by borrowing from every available source, in homiletical
literature Haggadoth of various origins were successively
added to the old stock, and thus there exists an internal connection between these diverse texts, which, however, differ
from almost every one separately. The individuality of the
compiler, the literature at his disposal, the surroundings and
other circumstances which had more actuality for his hearers or readers, are reflected in each of these versions sufficiently clearly, to enable us to discover by its form, the date
and local origin of each text.

As has been already remarked, we have in this text probably the oldest form of the Midrash to Esther, following upon the close of the Talmud, and based, I am inclined to say, exclusively on it. Should this be the case, and I have no reason to doubt it, judging by nine tenth of its contents, we may incidentally also learn something about the literary tradition of the Talmud. As it will be seen, not a few very characteristic legends which are in our Midrash, will be looked for in vain in the Talmud. It is not impossible that the author of this compilation may have had access also to other sources, from which he took those legends, but as the bulk is evidently borrowed from the Talmud, it is much more likely that also the other portions were borrowed from the same source. These were afterwards excluded from our text of the Talmud for the same reasons for which many more were left out in later times: *viz.* the fear of giving umbrage to captious readers.

The home of this text, judging by the peculiarities which distinguish it, seems to be Babylon or Persia. Among other things we find that special stress is laid on Niddah (cf. C. I. v. 12; II. v. 9) A prominent place is assigned in this text to Daniel. Two legends are related which, as far as I have been able to ascertain, are not to be found elsewhere Thus in Cap. I. v. 12. where Vashti refuses to obey the command of Aḥasveroš out of hatred to Daniel' and again C. IV. v. 5, where he is identified with the "Sarisim" of the Prophet Isaiah (LVI, 4); a peculiar reason is given for that mutilation. (As remote. parallels, but by mo means similar, cf. Tr. Sanhedrin, fol. 93b; Pirke de R. Eliezer, end of chap. 52; and Yalkut Machiri *ad loc.*, p. 213.) None of these are found in the Talmud. Proselytes seem to be viewed favourably by the author of this version. The legend of "Bithyah" daughter of Pharoah (II, 5) and the handmaids of Esther whom she is said to have converted to Judaism are mentioned. The latter also has no other parallel in ancient literature! That Haman should have sold himself as a slave to Mordecai in the desert, where he was dying of hunger, is again one of the legends peculiar to this text. I have a faint recollection of having seen or read this legend somewhere, but have not been able to discover it again. Remarkable is further the interpretation of Ps. X, 16 and Ps. XXXIII, 10 (C. III, 9) which is placed in the mouth of Haman to mean prayers against the other nations. In the mediaeval revival of the ancient calumny, I have thus far not found it based upon these verses of the Psalms.

Twice direct reference is made to the Talmud in I, 12 and IV, 11, both under the form: "Megillath Gemara".

The subject is treated, as in all the Midrashim, by constantly heaping various interpretations on one and the same verse, each commencing with: ד"א. There is no special prooemion, nor other introduction, as is the case for instance in the Midrash Rabba.

This much concerning the text proper, which, as will be seen by the accompanying notes, was by no means unknown to later compilers. The copy which we have here is therefore undoubtedly not the original but a later transscription of an older original. As this copy belongs, in every probability, to the IXth, or latest, the Xth century, we may assume a much higher antiquity for the original. We shall not be far from wrong, if under these considerations we assume it to have been composed about the VIIth or VIIIth century, not very long after the close of the Babylonian Talmud.

The Ms. is written, as already remarked, in a very archaic hand. The character of the script is Syriac-rabbinic, big bold letters, written on oriental thick paper. 7×5 with 19 lines on each page, and on the average 7 words on each line. A second and somewhat later hand has added a number of marginal glosses in Persian. These, and the fact that I have obtained this manuscript from central Persia, the ancient Babylon, prove the local Persian origin of this manuscript. With the exception probably of my "Tittled Pentateuch", which so far is the oldest copy of the Pentateuch extant, (VIIIth or IXth century) this manuscript of the Midrash Megillah is the oldest specimen of Hebrew writing from that part of the world. I regret that I am not able to add a photographic facsimile of the original.

I reproduce the text exactly as it stands in the Ms. On more than one occasion vowelpoints have been added to

the text. It is difficult to determine whether these have
been added by the first writer or by a later hand. I am
more inclined to ascribe them to the second source. I
have not omitted to put them also in my copy. They are
peculiar and point to a pronunciation which was current in
Persia. I have ascertained this fact from comparison with
other Hebrew texts of Persian origin, which have a similar
form of vocalisation. The Persian glosses have also been
reproduced here. They are with one exception, merely verbal renderings and require no further translation into English. That however to VI, 1, being of an explanatory character, has been translated by me. I have further added
the indication of the chapters and verses of all the Biblical
references.

In footnotes, which I have striven to reduce to the
shortest form, without impairing their completeness, I have
given all the parallels available. I start with the Talmud
and refer then to the following versions of the Midrash to
Esther.

I. Buber: *viz.* his edition of 1) Abba Gorion; (ספרי
דאגדתא, Wilna 1886, p. 1—42.) mere reference to Buber
means this text. A 1 is the text published by Buber under
the title of מדרש פנים אחרים נוסח א' (*ibid.* p. 45—51). A 2 is
the other published by him as מדרש פנים אחרים נוסח ב' (*ib.*
p. 55—82). Leḳaḥ Tob, is the fourth text published by
Buber (*ibid.* p. 85—112) and refers to that edition. In each
case I quote the page, as the passages can there be found
under the same verse as in our text.

II. Horowitz: is the reprint of the very scarce edition
of Constantinople 1519 with notes and an introduction (אגדת
אגדות, I, Berlin 1881, p. 47—75). As these notes and those
of Buber cover the whole field of literary references, it would
have been superfluous to reproduce them in this place. I
have pointed out only those that throw some light on our
text. Further reference has been made to the Midrash Esther in the Rabba collection. Chapter and § mean the
chapters and smaller subdivisions introduced into the modern
editions of the Rabba.

As desiderata I have left those, not unfrequent passages, for which I have thus far, not been able to find

the source or the parallel, and I trust that others may suc-
ceed in filling up the lacuna I was forced to leave, and complete the literary history of the oldest Midrash to the Book
of Esther.

One point is still to be noted, and that is, the writing
or rather the spelling of the Ineffable name of God in this
text, which is equally characteristic and one proof more of
its antiquity. It is written ‫יי‬ instead of ‫יהוה‬.[1]) This is the
orthography retained by the Karaites, who, as is well
known, hail originally from that country. This spelling is no
less instructive for the history of the writing of the name
of God in various countries and at various times. I am engaged in a special study of this spelling, which I trust will
prove a valuable aid, for determining the epoch and place
of writing of Hebrew manuscripts. Suffice it to state, that
this writing is the very oldest that obtained in Babylon and
ancient Persia, although it may be of Palestinian origin.

Another no less interesting point is the absence of any
parallel with the second Targum to Esther, which, as well
known, is of comparatively late, and moreover, Palestinian
origin. It was probably inaccessible or unknown to the author of our text. This might be adduced as a further proof
of the Babylonian origin of this text.

---

[1]) [This spelling, as also the following forms : ‫ייֺ‬, ‫ייי‬, may be found
in all Yemen Mss. On a Babylonian cup, inscribed with magic formulae,
recently discovered, three Jods are used. See on this point and others in
the same connection, Kohut's *Mansûr al - Dhamârî's* ‫سراج العقول‬
(New York 1892), p. 15. n. 3; his ‫نور الظلم ومصبح الحكم‬ *Light of
Shade & Lamp of Wisdom* . . . . . by Nathanel Ibn Yeshâya [1327],
(New York 1894), p. 25; and especially Steinschneider's article: "Abbreviatur
des Tetragrammatons durch drei Jod", in *Monatsschrift*, Neue Folge, vol.
40, (1896) p. 130—4. G. A. K.]

Ein Targum der Amidah.

Dr. **M. Gaster**.

———

Der Text, den ich hier zum ersten Mal veröffentliche, ist
durchaus ein Unicum. Bisher kannte man nur Targumim
zu biblischen Texten. Dass aber auch Gebete mit einem
Targum versehen worden seien, ist bis jetzt von Niemandem
geahnt worden. Die Tragweite dieser Entdeckung lässt sich
kaum ermessen. Von aramäischen Gebeten haben sich bekanntlich nur sehr wenige erhalten. Mit Ausnahme des Kaddisch
und des Jekum Purkan im Aschkenasischen Siddur sind nur
Fragmente von solchen Gebeten auf uns gekommen, wie das
Gebet für Kranke oder für Wöchnerinnen und die zwei Verse
im Seder ha-Jom, welche eigentlich das Targum der Keduscha
bilden. Von den Reschut an Schebuoth und von der Haphtara an Pessach sehe ich hier ab, da das poetische Stücke sind,
die mit der Liturgie doch nur in losem Zusammenhange stehen.

Mit Ausnahme des Targum zur Keduscha, welches seine Geschichte hat, kennt man jedoch keinen einzigen Theil der wirklichen Liturgie, der anders als hebräisch abgefasst und anders als in hebräischer Sprache gebetet worden wäre.

Im Siddur von Jemen haben sich ausserdem auch noch andere Fasttagsgebete und Litaneien erhalten, die aramäisch abgefasst sind, und von den in unseren Siddurim sich höchstens noch schwache Spuren nachweisen lassen. Im Allgemeinen jedoch hat sich das Aramäische eine Stelle in der eigentlichen Liturgie nicht erobert. Der Charakter derselben, ebenso wie der Ursprung, geboten das Festhalten an der heiligen Sprache für die Formeln des Gebetes. Die wesentlichsten Bestandtheile desselben sind ja eben Stücke aus der heiligen Schrift, aus dem Pentateuch und den Psalmen. Die einleitenden Segenssprüche (Jozer, Ahaba u. s. w.) reichen auch in eine Zeit zurück, in der wir das Hebräische als eine noch lebende Sprache anerkennen müssen.

Wie frühe sich die Uebersetzung in die „lingua vulgare" als Nothwendigkeit herausgestellt hat, und wann das Textwort der hl. Schrift in diese übertragen worden ist, um das Volk besser damit bekannt zu machen, lässt sich, trotz aller Forschungen, mit Gewissheit kaum bestimmen. Dass das Targum sehr alten Ursprunges sei, lässt sich kaum bezweifeln; ebensowenig, dass es im Laufe der Jahrhunderte mannigfachen Umwandlungen, Ergänzungen und Auslassungen unterworfen worden sei. Es verhält sich damit genau so wie mit dem Midrasch, dessen jüngere Form keineswegs immer den jungen Ursprung beweist.

Noch viel dunkler ist die Frage der Verbreitung des Targum. Wie viel davon ist nach Babylonien gedrungen? Und wie viel hat sich in Palästina erhalten? Wie viel ist orientalischen, und wie viel occidentalischen Ursprunges? Ich verstehe hier unter Occident und Orient Pälästina im Gegensatz zu Syrien. Die Antwort, dass Onkelos wenigstens in Form und Sprache babylonischen Ursprungs, das jerusalemitanische Targum dagegen palästinensischen Ursprungs sei, ist durchaus nicht befriedigend. Trotz Berliners werthvoller Ausgabe des ersteren, sind wir doch noch sehr weit von einer wirklich kritischen Ausgabe entfernt. Die Vocalisation der europäischen Ausgaben des XV. und XVI. Jahrhunderts ist sogar in diesen schwankend. Man braucht nur die Lissaboner Ausgabe mit der Complutensischen zu vergleichen und diese mit der Ausgabe, die Berliner der seinigen zu Grunde gelegt hat, um sich auf Schritt und Tritt davon zu überzeugen. Noch

viel bedeutender ist der Unterschied zwischen diesen und den alten
Hss. aus Jemen, die dem superlinearen Vocalisations-System folgen.

Noch viel verwahrloster ist das andere palästinensische
Targum von dem sich leider nur einige wenige Hss. erhalten
haben, die bisher auch noch nicht einmal mit unseren ge-
druckten Texten verglichen worden sind.

Ich habe diese Fragen hier berührt, weil sie, meiner Anschauung nach, mit einer anderen im innigsten Zusammenhange
stehen, die bisher auch noch nicht einmal aufgeworfen worden ist.

Woher stammen die Targumim in den Hss. der Juden
aus Jemen? Dass diese Frage keine müssige sei, wird sofort
einleuchten, wenn ich dann weiter frage: Woher stammt das
System der superlinearen Vocalbezeichnung, welches allgemein
als babylonisch oder syrisch bezeichnet wird? Ist dieses
wirklich orientalischen, d. h. syrisch-babylonischen Ursprunges,
wie ich selbst eine Zeit lang geglaubt habe, oder haben uns einige
alte und nicht sehr deutliche massoretische Notizen irre geführt?

Da ich auf dieses Thema bei einer anderen Gelegenheit
ausführlicher zurückzukommen gedenke, will ich den Gegenstand hier nicht weiter ausführen.

Es wird sich darum handeln, erstens nachzuweisen, welcher
Aussprache die Vocalbezeichnung des superlinearen Systems
entspricht, und zweitens, ob die Juden in Jemen mit Babylon
oder mit Tiberias in innigerem Verkehr gestanden haben, und
von welchem Orte sie, mit grösserer Wahrscheinlichkeit, ihre
Litteratur und Traditon bekommen haben.

Ich füge sogleich hinzu, dass das Resultat meiner Untersuchungen mich dahin geführt hat, einen Zusammenhang mit den
Schulen Palästinas als den wahrscheinlicheren anzunehmen.

In Palästina ist die Existenz eines, die ganze Bibel um-
fassenden Targums von Zunz unwiderleglich nachgewiesen.
Was babylonisch ist, ist eigentlich nur eine Modification einer
Schöpfung, die auf dem Boden Palästinas entstanden ist.

Nun erscheint auch noch dieses Targum des wichtigsten
Theiles des Gebetes, der eigentlichen Tefilla, welches ur-
plötzlich auftaucht.

In Sprache und Gedankengang schliesst es sich eng an das
Targum Palästinas zu den Megilloth, besonders aber an das Tar-
gum zum Hohenliede und zu Koheleth an. Die grammatischen
Formen, der Gebrauch der Partikel בני ארום u. s. w. deuten auf
jenen localen Ursprung hin. Die Citate aus dem Targum der
Propheten sind Jonathan ähnlich aber nicht mit ihm identisch.

Die Hs., No. 61 meiner Sammlung Hebr. Hss., kleines Octav-

Format, stammt aus Jemen und ist durch vielen Gebrauch an den Rändern abgegriffen, wodurch das Lesen des Textes sehr erschwert ist.

Sie ist eine Sammelhandschrift aus dem XVII. oder dem Anfang des XVIII. Jahrhunderts und enthält zunächst kabbalistische Formeln zu Beschwörungen und Amuletten, dann die arabische Uebersetzung der פטירת אהרון in kurzer Fassung und der פטירת משה in längerer Fassung; ferner Sand-Orakel und andere arabische und hebräische astronomische und astrologische Orakel. Auch sonst sonderbare Notizen, von denen ich das Eine oder das Andere hier weiter mittheilen werde.

Der Verkäufer, ein Jude aus Jemen, der die Hs. nur des kabbalistischen Inhaltes wegen hochschätzte, war nicht wenig überrascht, als ich ihm das Targum (f. 63 b — 67 b der Hs.) zeigte. Er war ein Gelehrter aus Sanaʿa, er hatte aber nie von einem Targum der Amidah gehört, weder in Sanaʿa, noch in irgend einer anderen Stadt.

Dass wir es aber mit einem unzweideutig alten Texte zu thun haben, geht sowohl aus dem Inhalte, als auch aus der Art, wie sich derselbe erhalten hat, hervor.

Der Abschreiber hat nämlich sehr viele Fehler gemacht. Er hat einen Text copirt, den er nur zum Theil verstand, und hat bald Worte getrennt, die zusammen gehören, bald aus mehreren Wörtern ein Wort gemacht. Ich habe nicht wenig Mühe gehabt, ihn leserlich zu machen, ohne eine andere Aenderung als Wortabtheilung und Vereinigung vorzunehmen. Verbesserungen habe ich in Klammern vorgeschlagen, und das Original unverändert gelassen. Auch habe ich durch Interpunction das Verständniss des Textes zu erleichtern gesucht. Es ist stets misslich, einen Text nach einer einzigen und dazu halb verwischten Hs. herauszugeben. Manches Zweifelhafte musste stehen bleiben, ohne verbessert zu werden. Vielleicht gelingt es Anderen, das eine oder andere aufzuklären, was ich als fraglich bezeichnet habe.

Was nun den Inhalt selbst betrifft, so ist er in der Beziehung den Megilloth-Targumim darin vollkommen ähnlich, dass auch hier die ganze Haggadahmasse im Anfang der Uebersetzung angehäuft ist, während der Rest fast nur wörtliche Uebersetzungen enthält (vgl z. B. das Tagum Scheni zu Esther). Mit dem Targum des Hohenliedes stimmt unser Targum darin überein, dass es die כנסת ישראל häufig als redend einführt, und mit dem Targum zu Kohelet berührt es sich durch den speculativen Inhalt (vgl. z. B. das Targum zu אתה קדוש) und

durch Hervorhebung des Lohnes der Gerechten und der Strafe
der Frevler. Die Klage über den Zustand im Exile klingt
durch das ganze Targum hindurch. Historische Momente, die
uns einen Fingerzeig für das Alter desselben bieten würden,
sind darin nicht enthalten. Der Islam ist gar nicht darin erwähnt und vielleicht gar nicht gekannt, woraus man vielleicht
auf ein verhältnissmässig hohes Alter zu schliessen berechtigt
wäre. Stutzig macht mich bloss die oben erwähnte Stelle zu
אתה קדוש, wo die Terminologie, bei der Beschreibung der
Engel und der irdischen Geschöpfe an jüngeren Gedankengang
erinnert. Ob dieses im Laufe der Zeit später hineingetragen,
oder ob es alten Ursprunges und gnostischen Einflüssen zu
verdanken ist, will ich unentschieden lassen. Die Theilung
von תשכון und את צמח ist ein anderer Fingerzeig. Die Form
der Amidah, soweit sie sich aus der haggadischen Umkleidung
herausschälen lässt, stimmt weder mit der Sephardischen noch
mit der Aschkenasischen Version genau überein. Im Allgemeinen
steht sie der Version des Siddur aus Jemen am nächsten, ist
aber auch damit nicht identisch. Uebrigens weicht diese
Recension auch in verschiedenen Hss. von einander ab. Sie
lautet in zwei Hss. aus dem XV. und XVIII. Jahrhundert,
die sich in meinem Besitze befinden, No. 4 u. 6, anders als in
einer Hss. des Montefiore College in Ramsgate (No. 380) aus
dem XVIII. Jahrhundert. Das Targum kennt nur eine Bene-
diction für ברכנו sowohl für den Winter als für den Sommer
und schliesst mit עושה השלום wie im alten Midrasch.

Die haggadische Erklärung der ersten Benedictionen ist
jedenfalls eigenthümlich. Für die erste könnte man auf Talmud
Joma, f. 69 b verweisen, aber für die anderen habe ich eine
Parallele nicht gefunden. Hoffentlich gelingt es Anderen, dieses,
und was ich sonst versehen haben möchte, nachzuholen.

Auf einen Punkt muss ich indessen noch aufmerksam
machen, und zwar auf die eigenthümliche Orthographie, die
ich, wie selbstverständlich beibehalten habe. א und ה wechseln
häufig am Schluss. ו und י werden ebenso häufig ausgelassen
als dort gesetzt, wo wir sie am wenigsten vermissen, bezw. erwarten würden. Eigenthümlich ist die Bezeichnung des Rafeh
der Buchstaben נדכת durch einen Punkt über denselben;
manchmal durch einen Querstrich ersetzt, besonders über ד.
ב und פ werden durch keinerlei diakritisches Zeichen unter-
schieden. Zu den arabischen Uebersetzungen der פטירת אהרון
und משה 'פ stehen dieselben Punkte über denselben Buchstaben
und auch über צ, welches im Hebräischen kein diakritisches

Zeichen hat. Ich habe diese beibehalten, da sie von nicht
geringem Interesse für die Aussprache des Targum sind.

Unerledigt muss, bei dem heutigen Stande unseres Wissens,
die Frage bleiben, wann und wie dieses Targum gelesen wurde.
Ob es je liturgische Bedeutung hatte? Ob es vom Vorbeter oder
von einem Meturgeman oder, wie es heute bei der Haphtara
der Fall ist, von einem Kinde Satz für Satz nach dem Vorbeter
recitirt wurde, als dieser die Amidah laut wiederholte? Alles
das muss so lange unentschieden gelassen werden, bis ein
neuer Zufall uns die Lösung der Frage bringen wird. Es
bleibt jedenfalls bedeutsam, dass das Gebet zu einer bestimmten
Zeit wie der Text der Bibel behandelt und mit einem Targum
versehen worden ist.

Sattsam bekannt ist, dass die Kabbalah sich sehr zeitig
desselben bemächtigt hat und von Juda b. Jakar an stets neue
Deuteleien hinein interpretirt worden sind.

Im Targum ist noch keine Spur von dieser kabbalistischen
Hermeneutik zu entdecken.

Nachträgliches zum „Targum der Amidah."

Von
Dr. M. Gaster.

Aus derselben Handschrift, die das jüngst mitgetheilte Targum der Amidah enthält, trage ich hier noch einige interessante Notizen nach.

Fol. 1 b hat folgende Notiz:

כמה אותיות בתורה ם רבוא כמנין ישראל יש ם רבוא אותיות לתורה.

וכמה הויות · מנין ודלת ראשׁי כארגמן · וכמה אדני ואלהים · מנין קלד וסימן קומתו דמתה לתמר · וכמה זרקות ושלשלאות בתורה · מנין אחור · ובנביאים מנין וקדם · ובכתובים מנין צרתני · וכמה הויות בתלים · מנין אכתריאל · וכמה מסכתות ופרקים וחכמים במשנה · וסימן כלי שמנה אשר · מסכתות · מנין כלי · שמנה אותיות משנה · ופרקים מנין אשר · וחכמים מנין קלנ.

אלו ימים צוה בהן מרעה · והם כד בשנה · ניסן ג : Fol. 2b:

ח · אייר ו וח · סיון ג וז · תמוז ב וכ · אב ד וט · אלול א וג · תשרי ב וי · מרחשון א וח · כסלו ג וכא · טבות (!) יא ויח · שבט ה וח · אדר א וכ · ושמע לה ישכון לבטח.

Diese Tage, an welchen nichts angefangen werden darf, haben eine weitverbreitete Geschichte und kehren in fast allen Litteraturen wieder. cf. Gaster, Literatura populara romana, Bucuresti, 1889.

למה אין בפי השור שיער · לפי שרכב עליו יהושע Fol. 6b. במלחמה ונצח · נשקו בפיו זכה אין בו שיער.

Scheint aus dem Alphabetum Pseudo-Siracidicum her zu stammen. cf. M. Steinschneider, Berlin 1858, f. 25 a.

ואל הבקר רץ אברהם · הבקר אותיות הקבר ללמדך Fol. 95 a: העגל רץ ואברהם רץ אחריו עד שהגיע למערת המכפילה וראה אדם וחוה יושבים ונר דלוק ומיטותיהם מוצעות ולכך חמדה אברהם לאחוזת קבר.

Diese wenigen Notizen werden genügen, um den Charakter der Handschrift zu kennzeichnen.

LA SOURCE DE YALKOUT II

Depuis la renaissance des études agadiques, le Yalkout est devenu l'objet de recherches minutieuses. Ce vaste recueil a conservé beaucoup de Midraschim, soit intégralement, soit partiellement. Les citations qui s'y trouvent sont quelquefois les seuls vestiges qui ont survécu à la perte de certains ouvrages. En outre, ayant été rédigé il y a bien des siècles, le Yalkout offre des leçons intéressantes pour la critique des textes midraschiques. Ces leçons sont souvent plus correctes que celles mêmes des manuscrits, et on ne saurait imaginer une édition critique d'un Midrasch sans la comparaison attentive du texte avec les fragments du Yalkout. C'est une vérité qu'ont mise, d'ailleurs, en lumière les recherches de Zunz, comme les publications de M. Buber.

Aussi est-il surprenant que malgré l'importance de cet ouvrage, on n'ait jamais, à ma connaissance du moins, cherché à déterminer s'il est vraiment original et ne doit rien à un recueil antérieur du même genre ; on se borne à le considérer comme l'œuvre d'un certain Siméon, ou d'un auteur unique, sans se demander s'il n'existait pas avant lui des travaux analogues dont il s'est servi et s'il a puisé directement aux sources. De la solution de cette question dépend la valeur à attribuer aux leçons du Yalkout ; il est évident que si ce n'est qu'un ouvrage de seconde main, il perdra de son importance pour la reconstitution des textes.

C'est la question que je vais essayer de résoudre, et je crois pouvoir démontrer que le Yalkout, au moins dans la deuxième partie, sur les Prophètes et les Hagiographes, loin d'être une compilation originale, reproduit simplement un Yalkout antérieur, avec des modifications, des interversions dans les citations et des suppressions partielles.

Si l'on examine les *renvois* de la deuxième partie, on remarque qu'ils se rapportent toujours, sauf de rares exceptions, aux pas-

sages contenus seulement dans cette deuxième partie, et jamais à
ceux du Pentateuque. Si les deux parties, comme on l'admet com-
munément, étaient l'œuvre d'un même auteur, on ne s'expliquerait
pas pourquoi il se serait interdit, dans la deuxième, de renvoyer à
la première, aussi bien qu'il renvoie à des passages de la même
partie. Il faut donc en conclure que ces deux parties, indépendantes l'une de l'autre, sont dues à deux écrivains.

En outre, si on dresse la liste des ouvrages utilisés dans les
deux volumes, on constate que certains ne sont cités que dans l'un
d'eux. Par exemple, le Midrasch *Abkhir* ne se trouve qu'une fois
dans le second volume (§ 56), et pour un fragment de deux lignes
seulement, tandis que le premier en a conservé cinquante extraits.
Le Midrasch *Abba Gorion* n'est cité que dans la deuxième partie.
L'*Agadat Samuel* n'est utilisée que deux fois dans le premier volume (§ 146 et 269), et vingt-neuf fois dans le second, non seulement dans les chapitres relatifs aux livres de Samuel, mais encore
dans Isaïe, Jérémie, etc. On trouve des extraits de *Debarim
Rabba* dans l une et l'autre partie, mais *Debarim Zoulta*, cité
treize fois dans la première, ne figure pas dans la seconde. *Echa
Rabbati* n'est cité que deux fois dans la première, et plus de
quarante, dont huit fois dans Isaïe seulement, dans la seconde.
Voici la liste des ouvrages utilisés par Yalkout I et qui ne
sont *jamais* cités dans Yalkout II : 1° דברי הימים ; 2° דברי
; מלאכת המשכן 5° ; מ' ויסעו 4° ; מדרש אספה 3° ; הימים דמשה
6° מ' לב' מדות ; 7° מ'ט מדות 8° ; מ' פטירת משה 9° ; מעשה דר'
יהושע בן לוי, quoique cette source ne soit pas explicitement in-
diquée dans nos éditions ; 10° ספרי זוטא ; 11° פסיקתא רבתי. On
pourrait objecter que ces livres ayant été écrits sur le Pentateuque, il est naturel que, pour commenter les Prophètes et les
Hagiographes, le Yalkout les ait négligés. Mais il faudrait en dire
autant de *Bereschit Rabba*, de la *Mechilta*, du *Sifré*, qui ne sont
également que des commentaires du Pentateuque, et cependant se
retrouvent fréquemment dans Yalkout II.

Ce n'est donc point être téméraire que de supposer que l'auteur
de Yalkout I n'est pas celui de Yalkout II.

Mais en serrant la question de plus près, on observe que l'auteur
de Yalkout II ne possédait que les plus anciens Midraschim, que
sa bibliothèque n'était pas aussi riche que celle du compilateur de
Yalkout I, que celui-ci possédait des ouvrages relativement modernes, ou existant en deux rédactions. En outre, il y a différence
entre les deux auteurs, pour la manière de citer les sources ; le
premier, par exemple, ne se sert de l'expression vague מדרש
qu'une cinquantaine de fois, et le second plus de trois cent cin-

quante fois dans un volume beaucoup moins grand que Yalkout I;
dans les citations de *Bereschit Rabba*, celui-ci ne manque presque
jamais (excepté quatre fois seulement) d'indiquer le *chapitre*,
Yalkout II l'omet plus de cent cinquante fois. Les différences sont
encore d'une autre nature. Examinons, en effet, la manière dont un
même texte est reproduit dans l'un et l'autre volume. Il est bien évident que les deux reproductions ne pourront pas beaucoup varier
entre elles, mais n'offriront-elles aucune divergence ? Que l'on compare, par exemple, le texte de la *Pesikta* dans I, § 471, et dans II,
§ 257, (= פסקא דברי ירמיהו, éd. Buber, 115 *ab*), ou de *Bereschit
Rabba* dans I, § 3, et dans II, § 310 ; I § 5 et II, § 323, on remar-
quera des différences qui ne peuvent être imputées aux exigences
de la manière de citer, mais à la divergence des manuscrits qui
ont servi pour l'une et pour l'autre partie. Or, il est impossible
que l'auteur n'ait consulté qu'un de ses manuscrits pour la première partie, par exemple, et l'autre pour la seconde.

A tous ces arguments négatifs, en quelque sorte, j'ajouterai une
preuve positive en montrant la source à laquelle a puisé l'auteur
de Yalkout II. Si notre hypothèse est admise, on verra du même
coup la manière dont procède cet auteur et l'origine même du titre
dont il s'est servi.

Il existe, en effet, un autre Yalkout, mais qui, justement à cause
de l'identité du titre, avait presque entièrement disparu. Ce qui en
reste est suffisant pour qu'on y découvre la source du Yalkout
Schimeoni. Ce recueil est le *Yalkout ha-Makhiri*, ou Yalkout de
Makhir b. Abba Mari, b. Makhir, b. Todros, b. Makhir, fils de
R. Joseph b. Abba Mari. C'est l'auteur lui-même qui nous l'ap-
prend dans l'introduction au Yalkout sur Isaïe. (Voir plus loin,
pièce I.)

Cette introduction, où l'auteur expose les raisons pour lesquelles il a entrepris cette œuvre, où il donne la liste des ouvrages
dont il s'est servi, et recommande aux savants son recueil en
en vantant la valeur, ne pourrait avoir été écrite, si l'auteur con-
naissait déjà un travail du même genre et portant le même titre.
Ce titre, il l'explique comme s'il en était l'inventeur, comme une
nouveauté.

Le livre de Makhir était un Yalkout sur les derniers Prophètes
et presque tous les Hagiographes. L'ordre dans lequel cette introduction range les livres de la Bible aurait lieu d'étonner si nous
n'en connaissions la raison : l'auteur les cite en suivant l'ordre
dans lequel il a composé son ouvrage. Il avait commencé par les
Psaumes et n'avait abordé qu'ensuite les autres livres. C'est pour
ce motif que, dans Isaïe, il renvoie à son Yalkout sur les Psaumes.

Malheureusement, de ce grand travail il ne reste que les chapitres
relatifs à Isaïe, aux douze petits Prophètes et aux Psaumes, et
encore ne sont-ils pas complets. Les premiers, sur Isaïe, se trouvent en ms. à Leyde (Ms. Scaliger, 7). M. Steinschneider en donne
une description dans son Catalogue de cette bibliothèque (p. 347-
349), mais il n'a pas fait remarquer la lacune du milieu du livre,
lacune qui porte sur près de 20 chapitres. Le ms. sur les 12 petits
Prophètes est au British Museum (Harlen, 5704), incomplet au
commencement et à la fin. Ni Azoulaï ni Wolf ne font mention de
ces deux recueils, et il n'en existe que ces exemplaires. Pour les
Psaumes, il n'en est pas de même ; outre le n° 167 de la Bodléienne
(Neubauer, Catal., col. 28), que Azoulaï a vu, avec celui de Job, il
en existe un autre que possédait feu Straschoun [1] et qu'a utilisé
D. Lurya pour son commentaire sur le *Pirkè R. Eliézer*. D'après
M. Steinschneider, il y en aurait encore un autre exemplaire à
Amsterdam [2]. Du Yalkout sur Isaïe et les petits Prophètes,
M. Neubauer a déjà publié ici même des extraits, mais du Yal-
kout sur les Psaumes, il n'a été encore rien édité. Prochaine-
ment le public sera en possession de l'ouvrage de Makhiri, car
M. Spira prépare l'édition critique du Yalkout sur Isaïe, et l'au-
teur de ces lignes, celle du Yalkout sur les petits Prophètes.

Avec ces éléments, il nous sera possible de justifier notre assertion. Pour cela, nous reproduirons ici quelques morceaux de ce
nouveau Yalkout, en renvoyant aux passages parallèles du Yalkout
imprimé, qu'il nous suffira d'indiquer par le numéro du paragraphe.

Avant de procéder à cette confrontation, nous donnerons la liste
des ouvrages mis à profit par Makhir. On voit dans l'introduction
que l'auteur a ébauché ce travail, mais il ne l'a pas poussé dans le
détail. Voici, outre les deux Talmuds, la Tossefta, les petites Mas-
sechtot, comme les Abot de R. Nathan, Masséchet Soferim, les
Midraschim que nous avons relevés : Bereschit Rabba, Veêlé
Schemot Rabba, Vayikra Rabba, Bemidbar Sinay Rabba, Elé
Hadebarim Rabba, Sifra, Sifrè, Tanhouma. Yelamdènou, Pesikta,
ou Pesikta de Rab Cahna, M. Tehillim, M. Mischlè, M. Kohélet,
M. Ruth Rabbati, Echa Rabbati, Ahaswerosch, ou Midrasch
Ahas., ou Haggadat A., M. Schir Haschirim, enfin Haggadat
Schir Haschirim, qui semble s'être perdu. Makhir cite encore un
לשהלוע, qui est probablement un Midrasch sur les Haftarot :
דנחמתא 'ג et דפורענותא 'ז. Cet ouvrage était indépendant de la Pe-
sikta. Makhir met aussi à contribution le Pirkè R. Eliézer et le

---

[1] Buber, *Midrasch Tehillim*, introduction, p. 80, n° 52.
[2] De la sans doute la note de Benjacob, *Oçar Hasefarim*, n° 230 de la lettre *yod*.

Séder Olam. C'est, on le voit, la même liste que nous a fournie Yalkout II (à l'exception de la Pesitka Rabbati) ; la coïncidence n'est évidemment pas fortuite et on ne s'expliquerait pas que deux auteurs différents se fussent rencontrés dans la connaissance des mêmes Midraschim et dans l'ignorance de certains autres. C'est l'indice certain d'une parenté entre les deux recueils.

Comparons maintenant les deux Yalkout. Nous reproduisons plus loin, pièce II, des morceaux du Yalkout Makhiri sur les ch. x et xi d'Isaïe et sur les petits Prophètes. Ces passages sont choisis à dessein parce qu'ils sont caractéristiques pour la richesse des citations et la manière dont l'auteur traite ses sources.

Ces citations, comme on peut le voir, sont intéressantes, elles réunissent les principaux ouvrages dont s'est servi Makhir, et particulièrement des fragments de ce Midrasch sur les Cantiques qui semble avoir péri. Les leçons et variantes en sont très instructives pour la critique des textes originaux. En outre, on y lit des passages messianiques dans leur forme primitive, avant leur altération ou leur mutilation par la censure. Mais, ce qui est plus important, pour l'étude que nous poursuivons, nous y reconnaissons aisément les morceaux qui ont servi à constituer Yalkout II, plus complets et disposés autrement que dans celui-ci. Malgré ces différences, ce sont évidemment les mêmes, et il est peu vraisemblable que Yalkout II ait eu recours aux originaux pour contrôler ou modifier le Makhiri qu'il utilisait. Tout ce que nous reproduisons du Makhiri se retrouve dans les §§ 284 et 285 du Schimeoni. Il en est de même pour le chapitre sur Obadia. Là, l'auteur du Schimeoni a encore abrégé plus que dans Isaïe.

En comparant ainsi les deux compilations, on arrive à cette conclusion que les droits de priorité reviennent à Makhir, lequel, on le sait, appartenait à une famille du midi de la France. Du même coup, la place que doit tenir cette œuvre dans les recherches sur les bonnes leçons des textes originaux devient considérable : c'est à cette source, plutôt qu'au Yalkout Schimeoni II, qu'il faudra désormais puiser des renseignements sur les plus anciennes leçons.

Maintenant, Makhiri n'a-t-il pas lui-même suivi un auteur qui l'a précédé ? L'introduction que nous avons reproduite nous donne satisfaction sur ce point, elle nous raconte, en quelque sorte, l'histoire de son travail, et rien ne nous autorise à mettre en doute cette notice. Il se peut, néanmoins, que Makhiri ait été inspiré par les écrivains chrétiens qui composaient des *Catenæ* sur l'Ecriture sainte ; mais il avait assez de modèles dans la littérature midraschique, puisque la plupart des midraschim sont de véritables

catenæ, pour qu'on n'ait pas besoin de recourir à une telle supposition.

Avant de terminer cette étude, je parlerai encore d'un autre
Yalkout manuscrit qui a déjà donné beaucoup de tablature aux
savants juifs. Ce ms., d'abord en la possession de S. D. Luzzatto,
passa dans la bibliothèque de M. Halberstam ; il est entré, sous le
n° 92, à la bibliothèque du *Montefiore Collège*, à Ramsgate.
Luzzatto s'en est occupé dans le *Kerem Chemed*, VII, p. 215-
221 ; Rabbinowitz l'a mentionné dans son étude sur les éditions
du Talmud [1] et l'a comparé avec le recueil des Agadot du Talmud
(Constantinople, 1516), qui lui ressemble beaucoup, offrant les
mêmes variantes et les mêmes erreurs de copiste. Rabbinowitz
conclut de cette comparaison que le rédacteur de ce Yalkout ms.,
qui, d'après lui, aurait vécu entre 1300 et 1350, aurait utilisé, pour
son travail, ce recueil d'Agadot. Quoi qu'il en soit, ce Yalkout rattache aux versets de la Bible les passages talmudiques qui s'y
rapportent, en suivant l'ordre des versets. Chaque citation est
précédée de l'indication du traité dont est pris l'extrait, exactement comme dans le Yalkout Makhiri et dans le Schimeoni, éd.
Salonique. Mais ce qui est plus curieux, c'est que dans cette compilation se retrouvent tous les textes talmudiques cités par le
Schimeoni, et cela assez souvent dans le même ordre que dans
celui-ci. Prenons, par exemple, la paraschat *Noah*, par laquelle
s'ouvre le ms., qui est incomplet ; voici les textes que nous y
trouverons : 1° גמרא ע"ז ; 2° סנהדרין פרק חלק ; 3° סנהדרין ארבעה
מיתות °4 ; סנהדרין, חלק ; 5° ברכות פ' הרואה ; 6° סנהדרין פ' חלק ;
7° עירובין פרק כושין פסין ; 8° ר"ה פרק ראשון ; 9° סנהדרין, חלק ; 10°
פסחים פ"א ; 11° פרק חלק ; 12° [פרקי ר' אליעזר בן הורקנוס] ;
13° פרקי ר' אליעזר בן] ; 14° כלה פ' יהודה אומר ; 15° ס' פ' חלק ; ס' ;
[והורקנוס] ; 16° קדושין פ"א ; 17° קדשים מסכת זבחים פרק השוחט ;
18° חלק פ' ס' ; 19° ס' פ' יומא פרק אמר כהם ; 20° פ"א קידושין ; 21° תלמוד
חזקה פרק נדרים ירושלמי, ; 22° סוכה פ' החליל ; 23° אין פ' חגיגה
דורשין ; 24° קידושין סוף פרק עשרה יוחסין ; 25° יומא פ' בא לו כהן ' אדם
קמא ורבע' קידושין פ' עשרה יוחסין ; 26° קמא ; 27° מיתות ד' פ' סנהדרין ; 28° יבמות
הבא פ' ; 29° הרואה וברכות דורשין, אין חגיגה ; 30° שבועות
העדות שבועות פ' ; 31° בן סורר פ' סנהדרין ; 32° הדר פ' עירובין
הנכרי עם ; 33° הנודר נדרים ; 34° ומורה סורר בן פ' סנהדרין ;
הכפורים יום פ' יומא ; 36° הספינה את המוכר פ' בהרא ; 37° יומא
הכפורים יום פ' ; 38° הכפורים יום ; 39° מדליקין במה פ' שבת ;
שנשברה חבית פ' שבה ; 41° חלק פ' סנהדרין ; 42° מגלה פ"א ;

שבת פ׳ אלו קשרים 45° ; פסחים פ׳ ערבי פסחים 44° ; יומא פ״א 43°
ע״ז פ״א 48° ; יבמות פ׳ הבת 47° ; כנהדרין פ׳ חלק 46°.

La plus grande partie de ces passages figurent dans le Schimeoni.

Mais cette concordance est encore plus grande entre ce Yalkout
et Schimeoni II. Voici la liste des textes cités dans Josué et dans
les ch. x-xiv d'Isaïe :

Josué. 1° (lisez ברכות) ; בתרא פ׳ אין עומדין 2° ; בתרא פ׳ ראשון
= S, § 5 ; 3° מנחות = § 6, ראה הקב״ה ; 4° חטאת פ׳ זבחים, = § 8 ;
5° סוטה אלו נאמרין, = § 14 ; 6° *Ibid.*, = § 14 ; 7° העריל פ׳ יבמות, =
§ 14, ch. v ; 8° הרב פ׳ ראשון מגילה ; 9° (הזר lis. עירובין פ׳ ראשון, = § 15 ;
= § 15 ; 10° מגילה, = § 16 ; 11° חלק פ׳ סנהדרין, = § 16 ; 12° בתרא
§ 17 ; 13° נגמר הדין פ׳ סנהדרין (lis. התענית), = § 17 ; פ׳ יש נוחלין
14° נגמר פ׳ סנהדרין, quatre textes l'un après l'autre, = § 17-18 ;
15° חלק פ׳ סנהדרין, = § 18, ch. viii ; 16° (סוטה, = § 14) ; 17° פ׳ סוטה
יבמות פ׳ אלו, = § 14, cf. § 18 ; 18° ע״ז פ׳ אין מעמידין, = § 22 ; 19°
אשה 20° (חולין, = § 22, ch. xiii ; 21° יש בקרבנות פ׳ תמורה, = § 26 ;
22° *Ibid.*, = § 27 ; 23° גיטין פ״א, = § 27 ; 24° חטאת פ׳ זבחים, = § 28,
ch. xvi ; 25° סוטה פ׳ אלו נאמרין (lis. בבא בתרא, 118 *ab*), = § 29 ;
26° יש נוחלין בתרא, = § 29, ch. xix ; 27° הגזלות פ׳ מכות (lis. הגולין)
= § 30 ; 28° הגולין פ׳ עדות (lis. מכות), = § 35 ; 29° אליעזר פ׳ שבת,
= § 35 ; 30° סוטא פ״א, = § 35.

Isaïe, ch. i-ii et x-xix. Ici je renvoie aux pages et aux lignes
de l'édition du Makhir qui se trouve maintenant sous presse. A ce
propos, il est nécessaire de remarquer que les paragraphes du
Schimeoni sur Isaïe diffèrent dans les différentes éditions. Dans
l'édition princeps (Salonique et Livourne), Isaïe commence au
milieu du paragraphe 385 et va jusqu'à 513 inclusivement ; Jérémie commence au paragraphe 254. Dans l'édition de Venise,
Francfort, Cracovie et Lublin, Isaïe va de paragraphe 253 à 374
et Jérémie commence aussi au paragraphe 254. Je cite cette édition
qui est la plus commune. 1° האשה פ׳ פסחים, = § 254, Makh., p. 2, l.
21 ff. ; 2° הלוקין פ׳ מכות, = § 254, M. p. 6, l. 35 ff. ; 3° (ברכות), =
§ 254, M. p. 9, l. 15 ff. ; 4° חבית פ׳ שבת, = § 255, M. p. 10, l. 25-27 ;
5° אין עומדין פ׳ ברכות, = § 254, M. p. 10, l. 34 ff. ; 6° היד פ׳ נדה, =
§ 226 ; § 254, M. p. 11, l. 19 ff. ; 7° ר׳ עקיבא פ׳ שבת, = § 256, M. p. 13,
l. 7 ff. ; 8° טיצירים שנ׳ פ׳ יומא, cf. § 256, M. p. 13, l. 27 ff. ; 9° (סנהדרין)
חלק פ׳, = § 257, M. p. 15, l. 21 ff. ; 10° (סנהדרין). = M. p. 18, l. 21 ff. ;
11° חלק פ׳ (lis. שבת, 139 *a*), = § 258, M. p. 18, l. 18 ff. ; 12° ברכות פ״א
= § 258, M. p. 19, l. 14-16 ; 13° האשה פ׳ פסחים, cf. § 258, M. p. 21,
l. 4-8 ; 14° סוטה (48 *a*), = M. p. 25, l. 14 ; 15° היה קורא פ׳ ברכות,
= § 261.

Isaïe, ch. x, vers. 28 à ch. XIV : 1° פ״א סנהדרין, = § 284,
M. p. 81, l. 9–18; cf. l. 29 ff.; 2° (סוטה), = M. p. 81, l. 38-40; 3° סנהדרין
חלק 'פ. = § 284, M. p. 85, l. 28-30; 4° המבלה 'פ נדה, = § 285, M. p. 90,
l. 13-19 ; 5° פ״א ברכות, = § 285, M. p. 91, l. 22; 6° יוחסין 'פ קידושין,
= § 285, M. p. 93, l. 10-12; 7° שואל 'פ שבת, = § 285, M. p. 92, l. 36-38 ;
8° חולין (?), M. p. 94, l. 8-12; 9° שואל 'פ שבת, = § 286, M. 94, l. 38-40 ;
10° *Ibid.* = § 286, M. p. 95, l. 8-12 ; 11° *Ibid*, = § 286, M. p. 95,
l. 33-36; 12° דורשין אין 'פ חגיגה, = § 286, M. p. 97, l. 5 ff.; 13° שבת
השואל 'פ, = § 286, M. p. 97, l. 32-34.

Ce qui ressort de ces tableaux comparatifs, c'est qu'il existe un
rapport entre ces différentes collections. Il est impossible d'ad-
mettre qu'elles soient indépendantes l'une de l'autre, les mêmes
textes se trouvant dans les trois recueils, et surtout, à l'exception de deux ou trois morceaux, *toutes* les pièces du ms. se
lisant aussi dans le Schimeoni. Mais la concordance de ces deux
dernières collections est plus intime encore qu'on ne croirait à
la simple vue des titres des morceaux parallèles. En examinant
ces citations de plus près, on est frappé de cette circonstance très
curieuse que celles du ms. sont absolument identiques à celles du
Schimeoni. Mêmes variantes et mêmes leçons du texte du Talmud,
même ordre et mêmes coupes dans les citations. Tandis que le
Makhiri a de longs passages talmudiques, le Schimeoni, comme je
l'ai montré, se contente de rapporter la partie qui se rattache
directement au verset biblique. De même, le Yalkout ms. ne cite
que de courts extraits et non tout le passage, comme le Makhiri.
Il semble donc que Schimeoni et le Yalkout ms. dépendent l'un
de l'autre.

Le résultat ne manquera pas d'intérêt pour l'histoire du Yalkout. Pour établir la nature des rapports des textes, j'essaierai
de montrer maintenant les différences qui règnent entre eux.

Le ms. contient, en outre des passages talmudiques, des gloses
insérées dans le texte. Dans les éditions modernes du Yalkout
Schimeoni, il n y a pas de gloses de ce genre, très rarement seulement on en lit quelques-unes à la marge. Ces notes ne sont pas
toutes modernes, l'édition princeps en contient et même dans le
texte Il sera permis de supposer que l'auteur du Yalkout Schimeoni II a ajouté aux textes, qu'il empruntait à Makhir, des gloses
explicatives, lesquelles ont été grossies peu à peu par les copistes
et éditeurs. Tandis que dans le Makhiri il n'y a pas trace de ces
notes, elles abondent dans la compilation qui est plus récente. On
s'attendrait donc à en voir plus encore dans les collections plus
modernes. C'est, d'ailleurs, ce qu'on observe dans les différentes

éditions de l'*En Yacob* et de l'*En Yisrael*. Ces notes marginales, gloses explicatives du Schimeoni, sont, pour la plupart, empruntées à l'*Arouch* et peut-être aussi à Raschi. Quant à l'auteur de la compilation manuscrite, il est certain qu'il avait sous les yeux le commentaire de Raschi, dont il tirait ses gloses, qu'il intitule toujours פי׳, c'est-à-dire פירוש.

Il n'y a pas à penser que ce ms. ait été mis à profit par le Schimeoni II, car celui-ci est beaucoup plus étendu, il a moins de ces gloses et cite plus exactement les sources talmudiques. Cette compilation manuscrite a donc vu le jour après celle du Schimeoni II ; elle s'est servie de celui-ci pour les passages talmudiques, qu'elle a enrichis de gloses empruntées à l'Arouch et à Raschi. Mais ce n'était pas le Schimeoni tel qu'il a été imprimé, de là les apparentes suppressions ou additions de cette collection ; les sources y étaient probablement indiquées moins distinctement que dans nos éditions, de là le changement de place de ces indications, qui se trouvent avant ou après le morceau auquel elles devraient être jointes. Ce ms. doit donc être pris en considération pour la critique des textes talmudiques du Schimeoni, qui, parfois, diffèrent tant de la leçon de nos éditions. L'auteur du Schimeoni II a écourté les textes qu'il prenait dans le Makhiri, aussi ne répondent-ils pas exactement à l'original, et c'est sous cette nouvelle forme que ces passages ont passé dans la compilation manuscrite.

Ce que nous avons dit suffit à montrer que le Yalkout Schimeoni appelle une nouvelle série de recherches sur les sources et la composition de cette compilation. Nous croyons avoir, pour notre part, démontré que le Yalkout Schimeoni II s'est servi du Yalkout Makhiri et ainsi remis en lumière l'importance de cette œuvre éclipsée par le Schimeoni. Désormais, pour toute édition critique des Midraschim il faudra donc avoir recours au Makhiri, qui bientôt sera accessible à tous les lecteurs.

THE APOCRYPHA AND JEWISH CHAP-BOOKS.

I have purposely chosen this title for the present article in order to put it in its proper setting, for it is not to be an investigation into the larger problem of the Apocrypha and the Jewish literature in general. It is, in a way, to show the form which this literature has assumed and to draw from it certain conclusions as to the nature and status of the apocrypha in the Jewish literature. One cannot emphasise strongly enough the fact that, literally speaking, there are no apocrypha in the Jewish literature. I mean thereby books which stand, as it were, in direct opposition to the Canon, books which were considered not to share either in the supposed inspiration or to have the authority of those books included in the Hebrew Bible. The idea of the Canon and, in consequence, the idea of books not forming part of that canon, belongs exclusively to the Church and not to the Synagogue. It may, perhaps, be of importance to mention here at the same time that not all the Books included in the Hebrew Bible share among the Jews the same authority. The Hagiographa do not stand on a level with the Law, and even the Prophets are not considered as having a binding legal force. The Church has probably used a word to which a different meaning is attached in Hebrew in a manner not compatible with the Jewish tradition. As will be shown by me elsewhere the word which has been taken as equivalent to Apocrypha (Genizah) in the discussion in the Talmud refers to books which are in the Bible, such as Ezekiel and Ecclesiastes, whilst not a single one of the other books which are contained in the Apocrypha of the Church is even referred to in that connection. Furthermore, no distinction is made in the synagogue between the few books found in the Greek Bible called Apocrypha and the larger number of books not included in it which are now called Pseudepigrapha. There is no real distinction between them, and their treatment at the hands of the Jews has been precisely the same. They all belong to that vast literature, paraenetic, homiletic, legendary, poetical, fantastical, paroemiological which fall under one heading called Midrash or Midrash Agada. It is a further development and expansion either of Bible texts and incidents or of extra-Biblical incidents in the history of the Jews and includes also books of wisdom and meditation. They have been treated as books to be read for education and entertainment, and some of them have been introduced into the service of the synagogue. They formed often the Homily for the festivals and memorable days. I see in this practice of the synagogue the origin—which, as far sa I know, has not hitherto been explained—of the lives of saints being read as homilies in the Church in precisely the same manner. It resolves itself into a panegyric of the saint on the day on which his martyrdom is being commemorated, and the miracles as performed by him are recounted. The origin of this practice and the pattern after which they have been formed is to be found in the use which the Jewish synagogue had made of these old tales, legends of the men of the past, and visions of heavenly bliss and punishment below. With the Jews they belong to the profane literature of tales, and from olden times collections have been made of such tales resembling greatly the "Golden Legend" of Jacob a Voragine, and even assuming the form of the Gesta Romanorum in which, *e. g.* we find Barlaam and Josaphat and other similar spurious saints. A similar fate has overtaken Jewish collections of tales, the oldest of which probably dating back to the fifth or sixth century, was published by the present writer in 1896. Many collections have been made and they occur in various MSS. some of which go back to the eleventh and twelfth century, and others are of quite a recent date, having been copied also by Jews as far distant as Yemen and Persia. From the beginning of the sixteenth century such collections have been printed in many forms and in many lands, some larger, some smaller, down to our very days, when a collection of such tales appeared in Bagdad. But what is still more important, in connection with our problem, is that these tales have been translated into the vernacular in olden times in Greek, then into Arabic, and in later times in European countries in such languages as the Jewish-German dialect now spoken by millions of Jews in Russia and Galicia, or into that popular Spanish (Ladino) spoken by the Jews who trace their origin from Spain, who from the end of the fifteenth century have left Spain and settled in the countries of the East. Side by side with these collections also single tales, especially the longer ones, have been reprinted separately either in the original Hebrew or in the translation alone or both together, and thus they become popular chap-books, circulating from hand to hand along with other books of different origin of a legendary or poetical character; nay some have assumed the form of Mysteries or Mystery plays, and have been preserved as such in the modern Jewish Chap-books. Reference will be made to a few later on, especially those printed quite recently. It is necessary, therefore, in the first place briefly to allude to the connection of these apocryphal writings with the synagogue.

It is self-evident that in the Hebrew literature those apocryphal and pseudepigraphical writings are most faithfully preserved in which the legendary and edifying element is more pronounced. The mystical has also its share, especially when it is connected with the life of Moses. To begin with it is thus not surprising to find that the history of the Maccabees should have been preserved in an Aramaic short version as part of the service of the Jews of Yemen, and in Italy during the festival of the re-dedication of the Temple or the celebration of the victory of Judas Maccabaeus. It is known as the Scroll of the

Hasmoneans, or the scroll of Antiochus (the text with variations and English translation was published by the present writer in 1892 in the Proceedings of the Oriental Congress held in London). From the Liturgy it has got into the Chap-books—I mean thereby the popular pamphlet circulating from hand to hand and read for mere amusement, quite independent of any religious service. It is joined with the story of Judith and Holofernes, often modified and enlarged or shortened until it became a popular tale. This can be found in various MS. collections of Hebrew legends, some of them going back to the twelfth century and some even earlier. The story of Judith has been connected with the war of the Maccabees. These tales are not an essential portion of the service, but they form appropriate reading matter. The last edition of the Jewish-German Chap-book called "The Miracle of Hanuka" appeared in Warsaw in 1904, and a Spanish translation some years previously, s. l. e. a. probably in Salonica.

The story of Tobit has been connected with the feast of Pentecost when they used to bring tithes into the Temple and in the story itself the feast of Pentecost is mentioned. It has also become a very popular tale. It is found in very old Hebrew MSS. One of the oldest, which stands in close affinity to the Latin version of Jerome, was published by the present writer from a MS. Prayer Book in the British Museum in the P. B. A. 1897. Ever since 1516, when it appears in Constantinople in print for the first time, it has been reprinted over and over again and has become a popular tale. It has been translated into the Jewish-German. The last edition in Jewish-German of the Story of the pious Rabbi Tobia appeared in Vilna in 1907 as a real chap-book. But Pentecost was principally the "festival of the giving of the Law" and "the Ascension of Moses to Heaven to receive the Law". It was the most propitious time for dwelling on this Ascension, for the heavenly hierarchy, all the wonders of heaven and earth and under the earth were beheld and described by him. The Jewish "Apocalypse" of Moses in a primitive form has been preserved under the name of the "Greatness of Moses", and is a real homily in the style of similar homilies in the Church. Many details of the visions of Enoch and Isaiah as well as Abraham, and later on the visions of Peter and Paul find their closest parallels in this glorification of Moses. Of this there are not only old editions but very modern reprints in Hebrew and Jew.-Germ., of which the following may be mentioned, Lemberg 1862, Czernowitz 1863, Vilna s. a. (but later than 1863), and Lublin s. a. An English translation of these visions was published by the present writer in the Jrnl. R. A. S. 1893.

An Assumption of Moses has been connected with the Festival of the Reading of the Law, the last lesson being read on the last day of the Feast of Tabernacles, and an "assumption" exists in Hebrew published with a Latin translation by Gaulmin, and is also one of the popular books read by Jews. The last edition in Jew.-Germ. as a Chap-book appeared in Lublin 1908. On the feast of Pureem, the Feast of Lots, the biblical story of Esther and Mordecai is recited from the scroll. In the Aramaic paraphrase of that scroll which has preserved to us the old homily of the day we find some of the apocryphal additions to the Canon, like the Prayer of Esther, the Dream of Mordecai, and other legendary matter, which has thus become part of the Jewish popular literature. It has been translated into the vernacular, but more than that it has become dramatised, for on that day a Pureem play like the ancient mystery plays used to be performed. An old version has been printed by Schudt Jud. Merkwürdigkeiten, Frankfurt, 1715, Vol. III. p. 202, under the title of "The Play of Ahasuerus" or the "Fall of Haman". Of this there are a large number of popular versions, little chap-books, printed in Lemberg 1879, Vilna 1890, and even in New York s. a., whilst the story of Mordecai, fully elaborated, was printed in Vilna, 1897. An old Spanish Jewish version of such a play is found in my MS. No. 1690 of the early seventeenth century. It was probably the only occasion on which the Jews indulged in mystery plays, and along side of the Ahasuerus play there also came the

Joseph mystery play preserved both in Hebrew and Jewish-
German as a popular book. Schudt (*ibid.* p. 226) has published
an old text, and modern reprints appeared in Kieff 1876, Lemberg 1879, Vilna 1895, etc., full of legendary matter some of
which goes back to the story of the fight with the Sechemites
told in the Testament of the Twelve Patriarchs, and others
found in the Joseph and Asaneth Apocryphon which have
filtered down through the ages in various writings until
they have become again focussed and crystallised in these
Jewish mystery plays, and also in the prose chap-books which
appeared in Warsaw, 1869, and lastly in Vilna, 1896. During
the Pureem festival also, stories, apocryphal and otherwise,
connected with the court of Babylon or Persia were told.
Among them probably the dreams of Nebuchadnezzer (last
edition Vilna, 1907), and the stories of Daniel inclusive of that
of Bel and the Dragon. Many variants of these stories are
found scattered in the Hebrew literature, and they have become
real popular books, chap-books, through translations into
Jewish-German.

The Jossipon, or the story of Joseph ben Gorion — the
Hebrew version of Josephus —has been one of the main sources
for the dissemination and popularisation of these tales. This
book contains chiefly the Wars. An English translation appeared
as far back as 1671, if not earlier, and has greatly influenced
English dramatists. The first chapters had not been translated
into English, and in these first chapters we find the story of
the three youths and their dispute before the king and the
wisdom Zerubbabel displayed, as told in the first chapters of
the book of Esdras, and, also the additions to Daniel and Esther.
Now as far back as the middle of the sixteenth century this
book had been translated into Jewish-German, and it appeared
for the first time in print in 1546. Since then, though bulky
in volume, it has been reprinted over and over again. The
oldest editions are adorned with very quaint woodcuts taken
from the Latin and German translations of Josephus. There
is in this book also the story of Hannah, and the martyrdom of

her seven sons, told as in 3 Maccabees. This was the prototype of the martyrs of faith of Synagogue and Church. Of this story of Hannah and her seven children there exists also an Arabic version which forms part of the liturgy of the Ninth Day of Ab, the great fast day kept by the Jews in commemoration of the final destruction of the Temple. To this day the history of that tragedy is read in Jewish-German, in Ladino, in Arabic, and in Persian as testified by the numerous MSS. and chap-books containing a full description of it. It gives occasion also for the reading of Messianic Apocalypses. The visions ot 4th Ezra, *e. g.* find their reflex in the Hebrew story of Zerubbabel, and in the description of the Last Days, the Story of the Ten Tribes, their dispersion and regathering (the Book of Eldad), the signs before the advent of the Messiah, the appearance of the Messiah, his fight with the enemy kings, just like the stories ot the Anti-christ in all the apocalypses foreshadowing the future, as in Enoch, Esdras, Baruch, etc. The apocalypse of Baruch, which is the subject of a homily in the Greek Church under the heading of "Remnants of the Words of Baruch" is found in the story of Abimelech and Jeremiah, connected with the history of the destruction of Jerusalem. It appears in the Talmud and then in various collections of tales studied by me as far back as 1883. It is impossible to exhaust here the whole literature, but I should like to mention finally the Testament of Naphtali, for it is extremely interesting. It shows how quickly a text dicovered so recently as 1890, and published by Wertheimer in Jerusalem and independently by me in London from another very old MS., has become a chap-book. I have no less than two of these printed as real chap-books both in the Hebrew original and one accompanied by a Jewish-German translation, one appearing in Warsaw 1898, and the other *ibid* s. a. The love for these ancient tales was not dependent upon their claim to any special authority. They live by their own beauty, by the moral lessons which they inculcate, teaching as they do fortitude, morality, humility, and at the same time satisfying popular curiosity in eschatological problems.

It is a futile attempt, I venture to think, to draw from these apocryphal writings deductions of a dogmatic or legal character as has hitherto been done by modern students of the apocryphal and pseudepigraphic literature. They represent passing moods of popular fancy, and legendary explanations of Biblical incidents. They have been treated by the Jews as such, unhampered by considerations of their canonical or uncanonical character. There is no such thing as a Jewish censorship, and none of these books has ever been considered as heretical. They have maintained their popular character and they have been treated as poetical folklore, so much so that to this very day they are popular chap-books among the Jews. I have picked them up on bookstalls and from dealers in chap-books, and all the booklets quoted are in my possession.

THE SWORD OF MOSES.

I. *Introduction.*

MAGIC has exercised the deepest influence upon mankind
from remote antiquity unto our own days. It either formed
part of the religion of the country, as it was the case in
ancient Egypt and Babylon and as it is now in some forms
of Buddhism (Tibet), or lived an independent life side
by side with the recognized religion. In some instances
it was tolerated, or rendered less obnoxious, by a peculiar
subdivision into white or beneficial and black or evil magic,
or was downright persecuted. Wherever we go, however,
and especially if we turn to the popular beliefs that rule
the so-called civilized nations, we shall always and everywhere find a complete system of magical formulas and
incantations. The belief in the witch and wizard, and
their powerful filters and charms, holds still stronger sway
upon human imagination than appears at first sight.

It is remarkable that we do not possess a good work,
or exhaustive study, on the history and development of
Magic. It is true that we find allusions to it, and sometimes special chapters devoted to the charms and incantations and other superstitious customs prevailing
among various nations in books dealing with such
nations. But a comprehensive study of Magic is still
a pious (or impious) wish. One cannot gainsay that such
an undertaking would present extreme difficulties. The
material is far too vast, and is scattered over numberless
nations and numerous literatures. Besides, much of ancient

times has disappeared; in fact, there is a profound gap between antiquity and modern times which is not by any means bridged over by the literature of the Middle Ages. In these times magical art and practice were ruthlessly persecuted by the Church, and the Councils teem with denunciations against the work of the Evil One. Moreover, it was connected in a certain degree with the teachings and practices of the various heretical sects, and the pursuit was anything but harmless. Thus it comes about that an exhaustive study of the origin and development of Magic is still a wish for the future, and the full influence which it has exercised upon mankind cannot be investigated in such a manner as to have a scientific value until at least a portion of the ancient literature will again have come to light.

The syncretistic character of the Gnostic teachings shows itself also in the adoption of Magic, and in the spiritual interpretation with which they invested the forms and formulas of Magic. The adherents of the various teachings of the Gnostics, and especially those that lived in Egypt and Palestine, adopted all the ideas that were floating about and transferred them into their system of superior Gnosis.

If anything of the teachings of the Gnostics has survived, it is the thaumaturgical portion of it. This has always been popular with the masses, as it afforded them those means which they wanted to defend themselves against the attacks of unseen evil spirits, and to the more speculative minds it afforded a clue to the mystery of the universe. It gave them the means to subdue and to put to their service the unknown forces of nature. This lies at the root of the general acceptance of magic formulas and enchantments, and gives to this practice the popularity which it still retains.

Being the most formidable sects that assumed an anti-Christian character, although some are anterior to Christianity, the Gnostics were the first to be attacked by the Fathers of the Church. Most of the ancient writings of the Fathers are filled with polemics against heretics, of which these are the foremost. The result of this campaign, which lasted for centuries, has been the absolute destruction of all the writings of the Gnostics. Sparse and incoherent fragments only have come down to us, and we are now compelled to study their systems and superstitions, if we may call them so, from the writings of their antagonists, Irenæus and Hippolytus, Tertullian and Epiphanius. A single exception is the work known as "Pistis Sophia," the date of whose composition is variously assigned to the second or fourth century. It certainly seems to belong to a later stage in the development of the Gnosis, as it contains some of the later ideas. It has come down to us in a very bad state of preservation.

Within the last few years the soil of Egypt has rendered some more fragments of this kind of literature, and magic Papyri have now enriched our hitherto very scanty stock of genuine ancient literature. These belong to the second and third century, and, being exclusively of Egyptian origin, throw an unexpected light upon the form which Magic assumed under the influence of the new order of ideas. It is a fact that nothing is so stable and constant than this kind of mystical literature. The very nature of a mystic formula prevents it from ever being radically changed. As there is no other reason for its efficacy than the form in which it is pretended to have been fixed or revealed to the Select by the Divinity itself, any change of *that* form would immediately destroy its efficacy. Dread preserved the form intact, at least as long as the practitioner stood under the influence of those divinities whose power he invoked for protection, or as long as he believed in the power of those demons whose malignant influence he tried to avert by means of that form of enchantment. This explains the uniformity of a number of such charms in whatever language we find them and almost to whatever time they may belong; as long as they are the outcome of one and the same set of religious ideas, which is the determining factor. But with the change of religion the charms also undergo changes, not in the *form* but

in the *names* of the divinities invoked, and these bring
other changes with them.   To take a modern example, the
charm against the Evil Eye will contain the name of Christ
or of a Saint in a Christian charm, the name of Muhammed
in the Muhammedan, and that of an angel or a mysterious
name of God in the Jewish formula, though all the rest
would be identical.   The same process happened also in
ancient times, and the Papyri mentioned above assist us
in tracing the change which the new order of ideas had
introduced in the magical formulas of the Christian era.

If we trace the first impulse of these changes to the
Gnostics, we must at once associate it with the sects of
Essenes and Theraupeuts that swarmed in Egypt and
Palestine, and with the most important sect of Gnostics
which produced the greatest impression, *i.e.* that represented by Valentin.   His is the one against whom
most of the polemics of the Fathers of the Church were
directed.   He is the author of the most profound and
luxuriant, as well as the most influential and the best
known, of the Gnostic systems.   He was probably of
Egyptian-Jewish descent ; and he derived his material
from his own fertile imagination, from Oriental and Greek
speculations, and from Christian ideas.[1]   In his system
entered also the mystical combinations of letters and signs
known under the name of cabbalistic formulas, and he
moreover favoured the permutations and combinations of
letters to express divine names and attributes.   To him
we owe the theory of Æons and the Syzygies, or divine
creative pairs, of which the two first form together the
sacred " Tetraktys."   I believe this to be the Gnostic
counterpart of the sacred "Tetragrammaton," and not, as
has hitherto been assumed by others, the Tetraktys of the
Pythagoreans.   For one can see in his system, and more so
in the mystical part of it, the direct influence of the Jewish
mystical speculations of the time.   Valentin lived, moreover,
in Palestine, and nothing would suit him better than to

---

[1] P. Schaff, " Anti-Nicene Christianity," ii, Edinburgh, p. 472 ff.

manipulate that mystical, Ineffable Name of God, round which a whole system had been evolved in the service of the Temple. Angelology and mysterious names of God and His angels are, moreover, intimately connected with the above-mentioned sects.

The mysterious Ineffable Name of the divinity which is invoked seems to be the centre of most of the ancient and even modern Magic. By knowing that Name, which is assumed to be the name by means of which the world was created, the man or exorciser in Egypt pretended to constrain the god to obey his wishes and to give effect to his invocation if called by his true name; whilst in Chaldea the mysterious Name was considered a real and divine being, who had a personal existence, and therefore exclusive power over the other gods of a less elevated rank, over nature, and the world of spirits. In Egyptian magic, even if the exorcisers did not understand the language from which the Name was borrowed, they considered it necessary to retain it in its primitive form, as another word would not have the same virtue. The author of the treatise on the Egyptian mysteries attributed to Jamblichus maintains that the barbarous names taken from the dialects of Egypt and Assyria have a mysterious and ineffable virtue on account of the great antiquity of these languages. The use of such unintelligible words can be traced in Egypt to a very great antiquity.[1]

It is necessary to point out these things in order to understand the character of the new formulas which take now the place of the old. To the old and in time utterly unintelligible names, new names were either added or substituted, and the common source of many of these names is Jewish mystical speculation. The Ineffable Name of God and the fear of pronouncing it can be traced to a comparatively remote antiquity. We find in those ancient writings that have retained the traditions of the centuries before the common era, the idea of a form of the

---

[1] Lenormant, "Chaldæan Magic," p. 104 ff.

Ineffable Name composed of 22, 42, or 72 parts, or words,
or letters, of which that consisting of 72 was the most sacred.
It is still doubtful what those 22, 42, and 72 were —
either different *words* expressing the various attributes
of God, or *letters* in a mystical combination; but whatever these may have been they took the place of the
Ineffable mystical name and were credited with the
selfsame astounding powers. By means of these every
miracle could be done and everything could be achieved.
All the powers of nature, all the spirits and demons could
be subdued, and in fact there was no barrier to human
aspiration. The heavens were moreover peopled at a very
early age with numberless angels arranged in a hier-
archical order and each endowed with a special Name, the
knowledge of which was no less desirable for working
miracles. I need only allude to Dionysius Areopagita
to have mentioned a complete treatise of such a divine
economy recognized by the Church, but we can go much
higher up and find these divisions and subdivisions of the
celestial hosts recorded in books that belong to the second
era before Christ. In the Book of Enoch (ch. vi) we have
a long list of such names of angels, and in a book, the date
of which has been differently put, the names of angels are
still more numerous, to which there are added also various
names of God. The book in question pretends to be
a vision of the High Priest Ismael, and is a description
of the heavenly Halls. Modern scholars who knew nothing
of the Gnostic and other heretic literature put it as late as
the ninth century, simply and solely because they could
not find early traces of it in the old literature, and because
it seemed to appear first in those times. A comparison
of it with the Ascensio Iesaiae, and still more with a
chapter in the "Pistis Sophia," easily convinces us, however,
of the fact that absolutely similar treatises were known as
early as the first centuries after Christ, if they were not,
in fact, later remakings of still more ancient texts. The
Greek Papyri already alluded to have also this peculiarity
in common with these texts, that they abound in similar

lists of names of angels and demons borrowed from
Egyptian, Christian, and Jewish sources. Among these
we find also numerous forms of the *Name* of God consisting
also of a number of letters, 7, 27, and others,[1] and also
most curious combinations of letters.

The Jewish idea of a mystical Name of God rests thus
upon the interpretation of the Tetragrammaton, or the word
JHVH, that stands for God in the Hebrew text, which from
very ancient times the priests first and then the whole people
refrained from pronouncing in the way it was written.
A substitute was found for it, so as to avoid a possible
profanation of the sacred Name. But it is an object of
millenary speculation what that substitute really was. As
already remarked, it is represented by a changing number
of elements, letters or words. The original miraculous,
powerful Name, however, was the Tetragrammaton known
as the "Shem ha-meforash." This word has presented
great difficulties to the following generations. It can
be translated either as meaning *explicit*, the "explicit"
Name of God, whilst the others are merely substitutes,
or *separate*, the name which is used exclusively for
the designation of the Divinity. These two are the
best known and most widely accepted interpretations
of the "Shem ha-meforash." In the light, however, of
our study it will appear that another translation will
henceforth be found to be the only true one, at any rate
for ancient times. Later on the true meaning of this expression was lost, and one or the other of the first-mentioned
philological translations was adopted. So we find in the
Testament of Solomon, *e.g.*, "the angel *called* Aphoph, which
is *interpreted* as Rafael." [This expression proves that
it is based upon a Hebrew original, and that the word
"perush" was taken to mean "interpretation."] Considering that this name was believed to be the only *true*
Name of God, the all-powerful name which was never
pronounced, "Shem ha-meforash" can only mean the
Ineffable, as we find it also in the "Pistis Sophia," and all

---

[1] A. Dieterich, "Abraxas," p. 185 (Papyrus Leyden).

throughout the ancient tradition. It is an euphemism; instead of saying: it is the " Ineffable" unutterable name, they used the word which meant: it is the "explicit" name, just as they said for a "blind" man—he is "full of light"; other examples can be easily adduced. In this way an ancient mystery and a stumbling-block for the translator of such texts disappears.

As the Tetragrammaton, or "Shem ha-meforash," was the Ineffable Name, and could by no means ever be uttered, others were substituted and were used by the priest when blessing the people. These also were endowed with a special sanctity, and were revealed only to the initiated. These substitutes were considered to be no less effective for miracles, and the knowledge of these mysterious Names was no less desirable than that of the true Tetragrammaton, for they were believed to represent the exact pronunciation of the forbidden word, and thus to contain part, if not the whole, of the power with which the Tetragrammaton itself was invested. Rab, a scholar who had studied in Palestine towards the end of the second century, says of these substituted names, and more especially of that of forty-two elements (Tr. Kiddushin, fol. 71a): " That this Name is to be revealed only to a man who stands in the middle of his life, who is pious and modest, who never gives way to anger and to drink, who is not obstinate. Whoever knows that Name and preserves it in purity is beloved in heaven and beloved upon earth; is well considered by man and inherits both worlds."[1] What these forty-two may have been has thus far been the object of speculation. When comparing the ancient tradition with the new texts in the Papyri, and in the mystical texts of Hebrew literature, there can no longer be any doubt that the Name of forty-two, or more or less, elements could not have been originally anything else but *words* consisting of that *number of letters*, which were substituted in the public pronunciation for the Ineffable Name consisting of one *word* and only *four letters*—the Tetragrammaton! In time these

---

[1] *Cf.* Bacher, "Agada d. Babylonischen Amoraeer," pp. 17, 18.

substitutes were also forgotten, or not divulged, and thus arose a series of new substitutes and variations for the divine Name. There was also the fear of profaning the name of God when writing it down in the way it occurred in the Bible, and therefore they resorted to manifold devices on the one hand to avoid a possible profanation, and on the other to obtain sacred or mysterious substitutes for the Ineffable Name.

Another element that came within the purview of this activity of coining new names was the new and greatly developed angelology that flourished at that time in Palestine and Egypt. The angels had to be provided with appropriate and powerful names, and the authors resorted to the same devices, of which I mention the most prominent, and which are the cause of many of the barbarous forms and names that abound in the magical rites and formulas and in the so-called practical Cabbalah. The biblical names of Michael, Gabriel, and others with the termination -*el*=God, served as a model for some of the new angels, such as in the Book of Enoch and in other similar writings. The first part was, as a rule, taken from the characteristic attribute connected with the activity of that new angel: so *Raphael*=the healing angel, in the Book of Tobit; *Raziel* =the angel of the mysteries; and in the same manner a host of similar names. Then came into requisition the system of permutation of the letters of the divine name: one standing first was placed at the end, and so on. Much more extensively were the change in the order or the substitution of other letters resorted to. In the Alphabet of R. Akiba no less than five different systems of this kind of substitutions are enumerated; either the last letter of the alphabet stands for the first (A-t; b-š, א׳ת ב ש׳, etc.), or one letter stands for the one immediately preceding such, as *b* for *a*; or the eighth and fifteenth stand for the first, and so on (A-h-s; b-t'-a, אחם בטע), or first and twelfth are interchangeable (A-l; b-m, אל ב׳מ). One can easily see how differently the same name could be written and employed in the same amulet, and all these various forms representing only *one* and the same name. The Tetragrammaton appears, therefore, either as מצפץ, or כוזו, or בקרק, or שעפע, etc. The number of such permutations and substitutions is not limited, however, to these four systems enumerated; they are innumerable, and it is almost impossible to find the key for all met with in these mystical writings, and especially on the amulets.

Other means employed for the purpose of devising new variations and protections for the sacred name, belonging to the very oldest times, were the combination of *two* words into *one*, of which one is a sacred name and the other an attribute, but the letters of these two words are intermingled in such a manner that it is not always easy to decipher them. An example, which has hitherto not been understood, we have already in the Talmud. The High Priest Ismael is said to have seen Iah אכתריאל *Aktriel* in the Temple. This word, which stands for the mysterious name of God, is nothing else than the combination of the two words כתר *Ktr*=Crown and *Ariel*, from Isaiah xxix, 1. In the text, which I publish here, we have the name שקדחזי *Skdhzi*=שרי *Saddai* and חזק *Hzk*=mighty, powerful. Names were further formed by leaving out one or two letters from the Tetragrammaton or from other sacred names of the Bible, the primary reason always being to avoid the possibility of profanation, as the profane utterance of the divine name brought heavy penalty upon the culprit. In this manner is the obscure exclamation in the Temple to be understood, אני והו *Ani vhu*, instead of the usual "O Lord" (help us): in each of these two words *one* letter has been left out—the *d* in the first, A*d*ni, and the second *h* in the second word. On other occasions strange letters were inserted between those of the divine name, and thus we get the puzzling form (Tr. Synhedrin, 56*a*=vii, 5) which is mentioned when the blasphemer who had blasphemed God was brought before the judges. The judges ask the witnesses to repeat the blasphemy uttered by the accused, and they say, instead of mentioning the Divine Name, the words יכה יוסהאת יוסי, which may have obtained this form in our printed texts through popular etymology, meaning "Jose beat Jose!" But originally we have here clearly the Tetragrammaton יהוה, and a strange letter inserted after each letter of that word, viz. כ, י, ס, and א.

This process continues still unto our very days, but from the thirteenth or fourteenth century onwards a change has taken place in the system of the formation of these mysterious words, considered to be so efficacious in amulets. The initials of the words of a biblical verse are combined into a new word without any meaning, or the letters of a verse are so arranged as to form uniform words of three letters without meaning, the commencement of each of these words being the letters of the Hebrew words arranged consecutively. The most celebrated example is the use to which Exodus xiv, 19–21 has been put for many a century. But these are a mark of more recent origin, and not a trace is to be found throughout the whole ancient mystical literature, and also not in our text.

If we should apply these principles to the Greek Papyri, there is no doubt that a key might be found for the innumerable curious names which crowd these fragments of a literature that at one time must have been very rich. Traces of it we find also in the "Pistis Sophia," where special stress is laid upon that Ineffable Name, communicated only to the initiated. The knowledge which a man acquires through the "Nomen Ineffabile" is described at some length (pp. 131–153). In another place we read that Jesus spoke the Great Name over the disciples whilst preaching to them, and blew afterwards into their eyes, by which they were made to see a great light (p. 233). The mysterious names of God and of the Powers are enumerated on pp. 223 and 234-5, whilst the following passage explains the power of that Name:—"There is no greater mystery than this. It leads your soul to the light of lights, to the places of truth and goodness, to the region of the most holy, to

the place where there is neither man nor woman nor any
definite shape, but a constant and inexpressible light.
Nothing higher exists than these mysteries after which
ye seek. These are the mysteries of the seven voices, and
their forty-nine Powers, and their numbers, and no name
is superior to that Name in which all the other names
are contained, and all the Lights, and all the Powers. If
anyone knows that Name when he goes out of the material
body, neither smoke nor darkness, neither Archon, angel,
or archangel, would be able to hurt the soul which knows
that Name. And if it be spoken by anyone going out
from the world and said to the fire, it will be extinguished;
and to the darkness, and it will disappear; and if it be said
to the demons and to the satellites of the external darkness,
to its Archons, and to its lords and powers, they will all
perish, and their flame will burn them so that they exclaim:
'Thou art holy, Thou art holy, the Holy of all the Holy.'
And if that Name is said to the judges of the wicked, and
to their lords and all their powers, and to Barbelo and the
invisible God, and to the three Gods of triple power, as
soon as that Name is uttered in those regions they will fall
one upon the other, so that being destroyed they perish
and exclaim: 'Light of all the Lights, who art in the
infinite lights, have mercy upon us and purify us.'"[1] This is
almost identical with the saying of Rab, with the difference
that in the "Pistis Sophia" the Egyptian influence is not
yet wholly obliterated These examples suffice to show the
character of the central point in the new Magic adopted
by the Gnostics, viz, the mysterious Divine Name and
its substitutes derived from the mystical speculations of
Palestine, and also the general tendency of syncretism and
absorption of various forms and invocations in that form
of Magic which henceforth will have the deepest influence
upon the imagination and belief of the nations of the West.

From that period, then, up to the twelfth or thirteenth
century there is a gap which neither Psellus nor the
Testament of Solomon fill sufficiently. All those ancient

[1] "Pistis Sophia," ed. Schwartze, p. 236.

magical books, being declared the work of the evil spirit, were successfully hunted up and destroyed. The link which binds the literature of the second half of the Middle Ages with the past is missing, and we find ourselves often face to face with the problem whether a book that appears after that period is of recent origin, or is an ancient book more or less modified? Such a book is, for instance, the so-called Sefer Raziel, or the book delivered to Adam by the angel Raziel shortly after he had left Paradise. It is of a composite character, but there is no criterion for the age of the component parts. The result of this uncertainty is that it has been ascribed to R. Eleazar, of Worms, who lived about the middle of the thirteenth century. One cannot, however, say which portion is due to his own ingenuity and which may be due to ancient texts utilized by him. I am speaking more particularly of this book as it seems to be the primary source for many a magical or, as it is called now, a cabbalistical book of the Middle Ages. Trithemius, the author of " Faust's Hoellenzwang," Agrippa, and many more, are deeply indebted to this book for many of their invocations and conjurations, although they must have had besides similar books at their disposal, probably also the Clavicula Solomonis, the Great Grimoyre, etc.

I must still mention one more fragmentary relic of that literature, viz. the inscribed cups and bowls from ancient Babylon with Aramaic inscriptions. These belong partly to the Lecanomantia, and are another example of the constancy of these formulas; for centuries these remain almost unchanged, and even in their latest form have retained a good number of elements from the ancient prototype.

It so happened, then, that some inquisitive men living in Kairouan, in the north of Africa, should address a letter to the then head of the great school in Babylon, Haya Gaon (d. 1037), asking him for information on various topics connected with magic rites and the miraculous powers ascribed to the Ineffable Name. I give here the gist of some of their questions, which date therefore from the second half of the tenth or the commencement of the eleventh century. They ask first, what it is about that Ineffable Name and other similar mysterious Names of angels through the means of which people can make themselves invisible, or tie the hand of robbers, as they had heard from pious men from Palestine and Byzantium that if written upon leaves of reeds (Papyri!) or of olive trees and thrown in the face of robbers would produce that effect; and if written on a potsherd and thrown into the sea, calms it; or placed upon a corpse, quickens it to life; and, further, that it shortens the way so that man can travel immense distances in no time. They have also books with these terrible, awe-inspiring Names, and with the *seals* of those celestial powers of which they are terrified; as they know that the use of these mysterious Names, without due and careful preparation, brings with it calamity and premature death. To these and other questions the Gaon gives a sensible and philosophic reply, warning them, in the first instance, not to place too much credence on the statements of people who pretend to have seen, but to try and see with their own eyes. Then he goes on to tell them that such books with mystical names are also to be found in his college, and that one of his predecessors was known to have been addicted to these studies, and to the writing of amulets and the knowledge of incantations, but, he adds, "only a fool believes everything." As for the books with formulas, he goes on to say: "We have a number of them, such as the book called 'Sefer ha-Yashar,' and the book called '*The Sword of Moses*,' which commences with the words, 'Four angels are appointed to the Sword,' and there are in it exalted and miraculous things; there is, further, the book called 'The Great Mystery,' besides the minor treatises, which are innumerable. And many have laboured in vain to find out the truth of these things." In the course of his reply Haya touches also upon the Ineffable Name and the name of seventy-two (elements), which, according to him, was the result of the combination of three biblical verses (*cf.* above, p. 11, where reference is made to Exodus xiv, 19–21), but he neither knows which

they are nor how they were uttered; as to the other of
forty-two, he says that it consisted of forty-two *letters*,
the pronunciation of which was, however, doubtful, resting
merely upon tradition. This name commenced, according
to him, with the letters אבגיתץ *Abgiṭṣ*, and finished with
שקוצית *Ṣ̌kuṣit*. He mentions further the books—"The
Great and the Small Heavenly Halls" and "The Lord of
the Law," full of such terrifying names and *seals* which
have had that dreaded effect upon the uncalled, and from
the use of which those before them had shrunk, lest they
be punished for incautious use.[1]

These abstracts suffice to show that the mystical literature
had not come to an end with the third or fourth century,
but had continued to grow and to exercise its influence
throughout the whole intervening period. The reasons
why so little is mentioned in the contemporary literature
is, that each period has its own predilections, subjects
which absorb almost exclusively the general interest, and
are therefore prominently represented by the literature of the
time, whilst other things, though in existence, are relegated
to an obscure place. The best example we have is the
modern folklore literature, that has assumed such large
proportions, no one pretending that the subject did not exist
throughout the centuries, although neglected by scholars.
It must also not be forgotten that we have only *fragments*
of the literature that flourished in Palestine and among
the Jews in the Byzantine empire, to which countries this
mystical literature belongs. Christian literature leaves us
also in the dark for this period, for the reasons stated above;
only Syriac might assist us somehow to fill up that gap,
but as far as I am aware very little is to be expected from
that quarter, as in the whole magnificent collection of the
British Museum I have not found a single MS. of charms
or magical recipes, except one single, rather modern, Mandaic
text. Two very small, and also rather modern, Syriac MSS.
of charms are in the possession of the Rev. H. Gollancz.
Of those books now mentioned by Haya Gaon in his

---

[1] Ṭaam Zekenim, f. 54*b* ff.

reply—all of which, by the way, seem to have been irre-
trievably lost—I have had the good fortune to discover
one, viz. that called "*The Sword of Moses,*" of which he
gives us the first words. From the answer of Haya it is
evident that he considered this book to be old and to be
the most important, for he is not satisfied with merely
giving the title as he does with the other books, but he
makes an exception for this to indicate the commencement
and to add that it contained "exalted and wonderful
things." A glance at the contents of the newly-discovered
text will justify the judgment of Haya, for it is a complete
encyclopædia of mystical names, of eschatological teachings,
and of magical recipes.

Before stating the contents I must first give a short
description of this MS., now Cod. Hebr., Gaster, 178.
This text has come to me with a mass of other leaves
full of magical formulas, all in a very bad state of
preservation and apparently hopelessly mixed up. Happily
there were custodes at the ends of the leaves, and by
their means I was enabled, after a long toil and careful
handling of leaves falling to pieces on account of old age
and decayed through dampness, to recover a good portion
of the original MS. and the whole of this text, which
occupies twelve small quarto leaves. The number of lines
varies. The writing belongs to the thirteenth or fourteenth
century, and is in Syrian Rabbinical characters. It is
evidently a copy from a more ancient text, and the copyist
has not been very careful in the transcript he made. Many
a letter is written wrongly, having been mistaken for
another similar, such as ר (*D*) for ר (*R*) and ם (*M*) for
ם (*S*). In many a place there are evident lacunæ, and the
copyist has often not understood the text. The language
is a mixture of Hebrew and Aramaic, Hebrew prevailing
in the first part, which I call the Introductory or historical,
as it gives the explanation of the heavenly origin of this
text, and deals with all the preliminary incidents connected
with the mode of using the text in a proper and efficacious
manner. In the last, which I call the theurgical or magical

part, Aramaic prevails. All the diseases are mentioned in the language of the *vulgus*, and so also all the plants and herbs, and the other directions are also in the same language. To no language, if I may say so, belongs the middle part, which is the real text of the "Sword." This consists of a number of divine and mysterious Names, a good number of which are the outcome of all those modes of manipulations with the letters briefly indicated above. It would be a hopeless task to try and decipher these names, and to transliterate them into the original forms of which they are the transformations and mystical equivalents. In this section we can recognize besides the unchangeable character of some of the magic formulas. What I said before of the Egyptians, who would not change any sacred Name, however barbarous it may sound, for fear of destroying its efficacy, holds good also for another number of Names found here in a bewildering variety. Almost every religion must have contributed to the list that makes up the "Sword." Eclecticism would be a mild word for this process of general absorption, that has made the "Sword" thus far the most complete text of magical mysterious Names which has come down to us. A small encyclopædia of a similar character is the Greek Papyrus of the British Museum, No. cxxi, and the Leyden Papyrus (J. 395), with which our text shows great similarity, but these Papyri mark as it were the first stages of this process of growth by the assimilation of various elements and combination into one single complete *vade-mecum* for the magician or conjurer. In the "Sword" we have the full development of that process, which must have run its course at a very early period.

Nothing is more fallacious than to try etymologies of proper names. The omission or addition of one letter by a careless copyist suffices to lead us completely astray. It is, therefore, difficult to advance any interpretation of even a few of the names found in this text that have a familiar appearance. If we were sure of the reading, we might recognize among those in No. 6, Isis (Apraxia,

Veronica), Osiris, Abraxas, and others; but, as already remarked, such an identification might easily lead us astray, and the coincidences might only be the result of mere chance. No doubt can, however, be entertained as to the complex character of this text, and to the astounding form of many of the names which it contains. It is a systematically arranged collection; in the apparent disorder there is order; and the names are placed according to certain leading features which they have in common. Thus we have a long string of names that are composed with the word Sabaoth (Nos. 24–37); others that are the components of the divine -el (Nos. 102–34). More startling still is a list of supposed names of heavenly powers that are represented as *sons of* other powers. These are undoubtedly derived from many sources, the author welding smaller texts and lists into one comprehensive list. The third part contains the directions for the application of these various Names. These are also arranged according to a certain system. The diseases follow, at any rate in the first portion, the order of the members in the human body, commencing with the head and its parts, then descending to the lower members; after which follow recipes for ailments of a different nature, to be followed by the directions for performing miracles and other remarkable feats.

Each of these 136 items (numbered by me) corresponds with a certain portion of Part. II, the words or the mystical Names of those portions in Part II being the mysterious words that alone were the proper to have the expected magical result. In order to facilitate research, I have subdivided Part II into such corresponding portions to which I give the same number. There is thus an absolute parallelism between the two parts—one the text and the other its magical application. We see that the book has been very methodically arranged by one who intended to prepare as complete a magical book as possible. By this parallelism, and by the partial repetition of the mysterious words in Part III, we have the means to satisfy ourselves as to the accuracy of the copyist, who does not come out very satisfactorily from this test. It may be that the original from which he copied was already partly corrupt, and the fear which such books inspired prevented him from attempting to correct what are obvious mistakes in the spelling of those Names. It not seldom happens that the same Name is written in two or three different forms in one and the same recipe. I have also not attempted any correction, as we have no means to decide which of these *variæ lectiones* is the true and which the corrupt. Another reason why the copyist may be exonerated from at least some of these inconsistencies, is the fact that he gives in many places what are intended to be different readings. He starts his copy with the marginal note, unfortunately half gone, the paper being destroyed in that place, that " there are differences of opinion as to the readings of the text and of the Names," or, as I would interpret this mutilated glosse, " the marginal readings are *variæ lectiones*." For, in fact, there are a good number of marginal glosses throughout Parts I and II.

There also are some in Part III, but these are of a totally different character. They are purely philological, and furnish one powerful proof more both for the antiquity of the text with which we are dealing and for the country where the MS. has been copied. Most, if not all, these glosses are, namely, *Arabic* translations of the Aramaic words of the original. By the mistakes that have crept into these Arabic glosses, it is evident that they have not been added by the copyist, who surely would have known how to write his own translation, but who would make mistakes when copying another MS., especially if it were in any way badly written or had suffered in consequence of age. The translation further proves that the original was written at a time when Aramaic was the language of the people, and that at a certain time when the copy was made from which this MS. is a transcript the language of the original had begun to be forgotten and required a translation, which, by the way, is not always exact. The Aramaic of this text is, in fact, not easy to understand; there occur in it many words of plants and diseases which I have not found in any dictionary in existence, and many of the grammatical forms present peculiar dialectical variations, which point to Palestine as the original home of our text, and deserve a special study. Here again we have to lament the fact that we deal with an unique manuscript and have no means to test the accuracy of the text. But even as it is, this text will prove an extremely valuable contribution to Semitic philology, and would enrich even Löw's book on Aramaic names of plants, where I have in vain searched for the names and words occurring in our text. I have therefore added a translation, which, however, in some places, does not pretend to be more than an attempt to grapple with a very recalcitrant text.

The title of the book seems to be derived from the last words spoken by Moses before his death. He concludes his blessing of the Children of Israel with these words (Deuter. xxxiii, 29): "Who is like unto thee, a people saved by the Lord, the shield of thy help, and that is the Sword of thy excellency," or "thy excellent Sword." The figurative "Sword" spoken of here must have been taken at a later time to signify more than a figure of speech. Under the influence of the mystical interpretation of Scripture flourishing at a very early period, it was taken to denote a peculiar form of the divine Name, excellent and all-powerful, which served as a shield and protection. It therefore could be made to serve this purpose in magical incantations, which did not appeal to the assistance of demons but to the heavenly hosts obeying the command of the Master of that "Sword." There is no wonder, then, that it came to be connected with the name of Moses, the very man who spoke of it, and whose last words were of that "Sword." In the Greek Papyri, Moses is mentioned as one who keeps divine mysteries (Brit. Mus., Pap. xlvi, of the fourth century, lines 109 ff., ed. Kenyon, in Catalogue, 1893, p. 68, and note to it); and again, in another Papyrus, cxxi, of the third century (*ibid.* p. 104, l. 619 and note), a reference to one of the magical books ascribed to Moses, called "The Crown of Moses." But what is

more important still, the Leyden Papyrus calls itself the
eighth Book of Moses. It resembles very much our text,
which has thus preserved the old name by which many of
these magical books went. Dieterich, who published the
Leyden Papyrus (Abraxas, Leipzig, 1891), looks to Orphic
origins for that magical composition and lays too great
stress on the Cosmogony in it. In the light of our text
it will become evident that these go all back to one common
source, viz. to the mystical speculations of those sects,
which he himself enumerates (pp. 136 ff.) ; and the " Logos
ebraikos " quoted by him from the Paris Papyrus (*ibid.*
pp. 138–141) shows more clearly still the same sources for
all these compositions. The overwhelming importance
assigned in these texts to the " holy Name " consisting of
a number of *letters*, and the book calling itself " The Work
of Moses on the Holy Name," justify us in seeing in it
an exact parallel to the Hebrew text, recovered now by
me. There is much internal similarity between the Hebrew
" Sword " and the Greek Papyri. The order of subjects
is similar; all commence with an eschatological part, which
in the Greek is more in the nature of a Cosmogony, in
the Hebrew that of the description of the heavenly hierarchy. In both follows the " Name," and after that a list
of magical recipes which refer back to that Name. The
constant refrain of the Leyden Papyrus after each recipe is :
" Say the Name ! " Here the Name is still simple; in the
Hebrew text it is represented by the rich variety which I
have pointed out, but an intimate connection between these
various texts cannot be doubted.

There exists besides another small treatise (B), also unique,
that goes under the same name as " The Sword of Moses "
(Cod. Oxford, 1531, 6). It is a short fragment of
a different recension, and has only a remote resemblance
with the first text (A). It consists of a list of mystic
Names, different in their form from the other text,
and has only sixteen recipes, which do not correspond
with *portions* only of the first part, but, as in the
Leyden Papyrus, the *whole* of this was to be repeated

after each recipe. Immediately upon this short text follows an invocation of the heavenly Chiefs, attributed to Ismael, the High Priest, the reputed author of the "Heavenly Halls." This addition corresponds to a certain extent with the first part of the "Sword" (A). In none, but very few exceptions, of B is there any trace of Aramaic, and a totally different spirit pervades the whole text. It is in the first place doubtful whether we have here the whole of it or merely a fragment. In two places we find the letters נג (NG) and נד (ND), which taken as numerals mean 53 and 54. If they stand for such, then we have here only the last two or three portions of a long text, of which the preceding *52* are missing. Again, on the other hand, as it is regularly recommended to repeat the *whole* of the "Name" after each recipe, an operation that would be well-nigh impossible for the inordinate length of that text, those NG and ND may not stand as numbers of paragraphs. This text presents besides many more peculiar traits that make it rather remarkable. We find here thus far the only trace in Hebrew literature of the "Twins" or "Didymoi" which appear in the Gnostic hymns of the apocryphal Acts of the Apostle Thomas,[1] and are brought into connection with the system of Bardesanes. The heavenly Powers mentioned in the "Sword" (A) under the form of *sons* of other Powers, point also to the same system of Bardesanes, of whom Ephraem Syrus said : "He invented male and female beings, gods and their children." [2] He may have taken these ideas from older sources. However it may be, this coincidence is none the less remarkable. We find further angels with double names, the one of which I translated "Kunya," *i.e.* the proper name, and the other the *explicit*, i.e. *Ineffable* unutterable name, corresponding entirely with that of the Testament of Solomon, where we find "the angel called Apharoph interpreted Raphael" (τῷ καλουμένῳ Ἀφαρὼφ, ὅ ἑρμηνεύεται Ῥαφαὴλ.—Orient, 1844, col. 747).

[1] Ed. Bonnet, pp. 36–38. *Cf.* Lipsius, "Apokryphe Apostelgeschichten," i, pp. 313 and 318 ff.
[2] Lipsius, *l.c.*, p. 310.

In the Gnostic prayer from the Acts of the Apostle Thomas, the Sophia is spoken of as the one "who knows the mysteries of the Chosen," or, according to the Syriac version, "revealer of the mysteries of the Chosen among the Prophets." With this the passage in the Hebrew text (B) may be compared, where the same idea is enunciated; and one feels almost tempted to see in the inexplicable word קינן ("Kinn") the Greek "Koinôn," the companion or partaker of the mystery; although it seems rather strange to find the very word in the Hebrew text. But there are many words that have a peculiar appearance in this text, and they look like transliterations of Greek words in Hebrew characters, such as "Chartis Hieratikon," etc. I have added, therefore, this second text also, making thus the publication of the "Sword" as complete as possible.

As a second Appendix I have added two conjurations found in the MS. of the "Sword" (A), both in Aramaic, and extremely interesting also for their similarity with the inscriptions inside the bowls brought from Assyria and Babylon. A detailed study of some of these magic bowls and their inscriptions has been published by M. Schwab.[1]

I have reproduced all these texts as closely and accurately as possible, without attempting any corrections or emendations, except in the case of obvious mistakes, which are pointed out by me as corrections. The glosses are given as notes, and the few corrections of obvious mistakes. I have refrained from referring to inscriptions on Gnostic gems and amulets, where we find "Ephesia grammata" similar to those of Part II of the "Sword" (A) and to some of Appendix I, and to the magical formulas in the terra-cotta bowls, which present a striking similarity with some portions of "The Sword." One cannot exhaust a subject of this kind, and the utmost one can attempt to do is to place as ample a material as possible at the disposal of those who make the study of Magic and theurgy and of the so-called practical Cabbalah the object of special enquiry. I have limited myself to

---

[1] Proc. Bibl. Archaeology, 1890, pp. 292–342.

draw attention to the relation that exists between these,
the Greek Papyri, and the Hebrew texts which I publish
here for the first time, and to point out the important fact
that we have now at least one fixed date from which to start
in the enquiry of a subject in which dates and times have
thus far been very doubtful. It is, moreover, a contribution
to Semitic philology, and by the addition of a facsimile of
the first page a contribution to Semitic palæography.

The origin of the "Sword" is none the less somewhat
difficult to fix. From the letter of Haya Gaon it is evident
that it must have been at least a few centuries older than
his time (tenth century). But it must be much older still.
As the Leyden Papyrus belongs at the latest to the third
century, and those of the British Museum to the third or
fourth century, we are justified in assigning to the first
four centuries of the Christian era the origin of our Hebrew
text, which throws so vivid a light upon those remnants of
Greek Magic buried hitherto in the soil of Egypt. Herein
lies also one side of the importance of our text, that
it shows how the connection between antiquity and the
later ages was maintained. The Greek texts had become
inaccessible and practically lost to the world, whilst the
Hebrew text, written in a language which was considered
sacred, the knowledge of which was never allowed to be
extinguished, preserved the ancient magical texts, with
their curious mystical names and formulas, and carried
them across the centuries, keeping up the old tradition,
and affording us now a glimpse into a peculiar state of the
popular mind of those remarkable times. The careful study
of those Greek fragments side by side with the Hebrew will
assist very materially in the understanding also of those
often very obscure texts, and lift the study from the narrow
groove in which it has hitherto been kept by the classical
scholars who have devoted their attention recently to
them. It will also help us in laying bare the fountains
from which flowed the whole of the magical arts of the
Middle Ages.

II. TRANSLATION.

I. *The Sword of Moses.*

In the name of the mighty and holy God!

Four angels are appointed to the "Sword" given by the Lord, the Master of mysteries, and they are appointed to the Law, and they see with penetration the mysteries from above and below; and these are their names—SKD HUZI, MRGIOIAL, VHDRZIOLO, TOTRISI. And over these are five others, holy and mighty, who meditate on the mysteries of God in the world for seven hours every day, and they are appointed to thousands of thousands, and to myriads of thousands of Chariots, ready to do the will of their Creator, X,[1] the Lord of Lords and the honoured God; these are their names—X. And the Master of each Chariot upon which they are appointed wonders and says: "Is there any number of his armies?" And the least of these Chariots is lord and master over those (above) four. And over these are three chiefs of the hosts of the Lord, who make every day tremble and shake His eight halls, and they have the power over every creature. Under them stand a double number of Chariots, and the least of them is lord and master over all the above Chiefs (rulers); and these are their names—X. And the name of the Lord and king is X, who sits, and all the heavenly hosts kneel, and prostrate themselves before Him daily before leaving X, who is the Lord over all.   •

And when thou conjure him he will attach himself to thee, and cause the other five Chiefs and their Chariots, and the lords that stand under them, to attach themselves to thee just as they were ordered to attach themselves to Moses, son of Amram, and to attach to him all the lords that stand under them; and they will not tarry in their obeisance, and will not withhold from giving authority to

---

[1] X stands for the mysterious names, which have not been transliterated. N for the name of the person who conjures.

the man who utters the conjuration over this "Sword," its mysteries and hidden powers, its glory and might, and they will not refuse to do it, as it is the command of God X saying: "Ye shall not refuse to obey a mortal who conjures you, nor should you be different to him from what you were to Moses, son of Amram, when you were commanded to do so, for he is conjuring you with My Ineffable names, and you render honour to My name and not to him. If you should refuse I will burn you, for you have not honoured Me."

Each of these angels had communicated to him (Moses) a propitious thing for the proper time. These things (words) are all words of the living God and King of the Universe, and they said to him:—

"If thou wishest to use this 'Sword' and to transmit it to the following generations, (then know) that the man who decides to use it must first free himself three days previously from accidental pollution and from everything unclean, eat and drink once every evening, and must eat the bread from a pure man or wash his hands first in salt (?), and drink only water; and no one is to know that he intends using this 'Sword,' as therein are the mysteries of the Universe, and they are practised only in secret, and are not communicated but to the chaste and pure. On the first day when you retire from (the world) bathe once and no more, and pray three times daily, and after each prayer recite the following Blessing:—

"'Blessed art thou, O Lord our God, King of the Universe, who openest the gates of the East and cleavest the windows of the firmament of the Orient, and givest light to the whole world and its inhabitants, with the multitude of His mercies, with His mysteries and secrets, and teachest Thy people Israel Thy secrets and mysteries, and hast revealed unto them the "Sword" used by the world; and Thou sayest unto them: "If anyone is desirous of using this 'Sword,' by which every wish is fulfilled and every secret revealed, and every miracle, marvel, and prodigy are performed, then speak to Me in the following manner, read before Me this and that, and conjure in such and such a wise, and I will instantly be prevailed upon and be well disposed towards you, and I will give you authority over this Sword, by which to fulfil all that you desire, and the Chiefs will be prevailed upon by you, and my holy ones will be well disposed towards you and they will fulfil instantly your wishes, and will deliver to you my secrets and reveal to you my mysteries, and my words they will teach you and my wonders they will manifest to you, and they will listen and serve you as a pupil his master, and your eyes will be illuminated and your heart will see and behold all that is hidden, and your size will be increased." Unto Thee I call, X, Lord of the Universe. Thou art He who is called X, King of the Universe. Thou art called X, merciful king. Thou art called X, gracious king. Thou art called X, living king. Thou art called X, humble king. Thou art called X, righteous king. Thou art called X, lofty king. Thou art called X, perfect king. Thou art called X, upright king. Thou art called X, glorious king. Thou art called X, youthful king. Thou art called X, pleasant king. Thou art called X, and thou listenest to my prayer, for Thou hearkenest unto prayer; and attach unto me Thy servants the lords of the "Sword," for Thou art their king, and fulfil my desire, for everything is in Thy hands, as it is written: "Thou openest thine hand and satisfiest every living being with favour."

"'I conjure you, Azliel called X; I conjure you, Arel called X, Ta'aniel called X, Tafel called X, and the most glorious of these Yofiel Mittron called X, the glory from above. With the permission of my king (I conjure) Yadiel called X, Ra'asiel called X, Ḥaniel called X, Haniel called X, Asrael called X, Yisriel called X, A'shael called X, Amuhael called X, and Aṣrael called X, that you attach yourselves to me and surrender the "Sword" to me, so that I may use it according to my desire, and that I find shelter under the shadow of our Lord in heaven in the glorious Name, the mighty and awe-inspiring X, the twenty-four letters from the Crown; that you deliver unto me with this

" Sword " the secrets from above and below, the mysteries from above and below, and my wish be fulfilled and my words hearkened unto, and my prayer (supplication) received through the conjuration with the Ineffable name of God which is glorified in the world, through which all the heavenly hosts are tied and bound; and this is the Ineffable Name—X, blessed be he! (I conjure you) that you shall not refuse me nor hurt me, nor frighten and alarm me, in the tremendous Name of your king, the terror of whom rests upon you, and who is called X. Fulfil for me everything that I have been conjuring you for, and serve me, for I have conjured you not with the name of one who is great among you but with that of the Lord over all, whose name ties and binds and keeps and fastens all the heavenly hosts. And if you should refuse me, I will hand you over to the Lord God and to his Ineffable name, whose wrath and anger and fire are kindled, who honours his creatures with one letter of his name, and is called X; so that if you refuse he will destroy you, and you will not be found when searched after. And you preserve me from shortness of spirit and weakness of body in the name of X, the guardian of Israel. Blessed art Thou, who understandest the secrets and revealest the mysteries, and art king of the Universe.' "

A voice was heard in the heavens, the voice of the Lord of heavens, saying : " I want a light (swift) messenger (to go) to man, and if he fulfils my message my sons will become proud of the 'Sword' which I hand over to them, which is the head of all the mysteries of which also my seers have spoken, that thus will my word be, as it is said : ' Is not my word like as fire? saith the Lord' " (Jer. xxiii, 29). Thus spoke X, the lord of heaven and earth; and I, Assi Asisih and Apragsih, the light (swift) messenger, who am pleased with my messages and delighted with my sending, ascended before Him, and the Lord over all commanded me : " Go and make this known to men who are pious and good and pure and righteous and faithful, whose heart is not divided and in whose mouth is no duplicity, who do not lie with their tongues and do not deceive with their lips, who do not grasp with their hands and are not lustful with their eyes, who do not run after evil, keep aloof from every uncleanness, depart from every defilement, keep themselves holy from contamination, and do not approach woman." When the Lord over all commanded me thus, I, X, the swift messenger, went down to earth, and I said on my way: "Where is the man who possesses all these that I should go to him and place this with him?" And I asked myself, and thought in my heart that there is no man who would do all this that I wished; and I found none, and it was heavy unto me. And the Lord over all conjured me by His mighty right arm, and by the lustre of His glory and His glorious crown, with an oath of His mighty right arm, and He conjured me, and the Lord over all strengthened me and I did not fall. I thus stood up, I, X, to put NN in the possession of the desired covenant, in the name of X."

"This is the great and glorious Name which has been given as a tradition to man—X, holy, glorious, glorious, Selah. Recite it after thy prayers.—And these are the names of the angels that minister to the son of man— Mittron, Sgrdtsih, Mqttro, Sngotiqtel, etc., etc., etc. (28 names)." "In a similar manner shall you serve me NN; and receive my prayer and my orisons, and bring them to God X, blessed be He! for I adjure you in His name, and I extol you (to ascend), like unto the bird that flies from its nest, and remember my meritorious deeds before Him and (make Him) forgive now my sins on account of my words of supplication, and you may not refuse me in the name of X, blessed be He! Sabaoth, Sabaoth, Selah. His servants sanctify Him and praise Him with sweet melody, and say: "Holy, holy, holy is the Lord of holy name; the whole earth is full of His glory"; and do not refuse me, in the name of X, who lives for ever, and in the name of Ditimon, etc., X, and in the name X of the great One from whom nothing is hidden, who sees and is not seen, and in the name of Him who is the chief over the heavens and is called X. And the King of the

Universe utters (this name) also in a different manner, thus—X. You swift messenger, do not tarry and do not frighten me, but come and do all my wants in the name of X, the great One, who sees and is not seen, AHVH, whose Ineffable Name is revealed to the heavenly hosts; and I conjure you by this Ineffable Name, such as it was revealed to Moses by the mouth of the Lord over all, X, the Lord Sabaoth is His name. Blessed art thou, O God, lord of mighty acts, who knowest all the mysteries."

And which are the letters which X communicated to Moses? He said to him: "If thou wishest to get wise and to use the 'Sword,' call me, and conjure me, and strengthen me, and fortify me, and say : ' X, with the great, holy, wonderful, pure, precious, glorious, and awe-inspiring secret Name X, with these letters I conjure thee to surrender to me and make me wise and attach to me the angels which minister to the " Sword," in the name of the Revealer of mysteries. Amen.' "

Write with ink on leather and carry about with you during those three days of purification, and invoke before and after prayer the following Names communicated to Moses by Mrgiiel, X, by Trotrosi, X, etc. (the 13 Chiefs mentioned at the beginning, and a long string of other mysterious names which are said to have been communicated to Moses). "And they have not hidden from him any of these sacred Ineffable names or letters, and have not given him instead the Substitutes of any of these sacred letters, for thus were they ordered by the Lord of all mysteries to communicate to him this 'Sword,' with these Names which constitute the mysteries of this 'Sword'; and they said to him : 'Command the generations which will come after thee to say the following blessing prior to their prayer, lest they be swept away by the fire ': 'Blessed art Thou, X, who wast with Moses; be also with me, Thou, whose name is X. Send me X, who is the cover of the Cherubim, to help me. Blessed art Thou, Lord of the Sword.' "

Whoever is desirous of using this ' Sword ' must recite his

usual prayers, and at the passage "Thou hearkenest to prayer" say: "I conjure you four princes, X, servants of Hadirion, X, that you receive my invocation before I pray, and my supplication before I entreat, and fulfil all my wishes through this 'Sword,' as you have done to Moses, in the glorious and wonderful name of the Lord of wonders, which is interpreted thus—X." He must then call the five superior Chiefs and say: "I conjure you, X, that you accept my conjuration as soon as I conjure you, and you attach to me those four princes and all the hosts of Chariots over which you preside, to fulfil all my wishes through this 'Sword' by this beloved name X." He must then call the three angels that are superior to these, and say: "I conjure you, X, the beloved of X, who is Hadiririon, that you attach yourselves to me and attach to me X, who are standing under your rule, to fulfil all my wishes through this 'Sword' by this unique name X." And then he must lay hold of the highest Chief over all and say: "I conjure thee, X, strong and powerful Chief over all the heavenly hosts, that thou attachest thyself to me, thou and not thy messenger, and attach to me all the Chiefs that are with thee, to fulfil my wishes through this 'Sword,' by the name X, which has no substitute, for thou art beloved and he is beloved, and I am from the seed of Abraham called the beloved. Blessed art thou, King of the mysteries, Lord of the secrets, who hearkenest unto prayer."

And he is not to touch this "Sword" ere he has done all these things; afterwards he will be able to do whatever he likes, everything being written here following in its proper order.

II. *This is the " Sword."*

[It consists of a series of mysterious names of God or angels, to which the recipes in Part III refer. The first list commences with Tobat, Tsbr, etc. (1–5). These numbers are added by me to make the formulas run parallel with their magical applications in Part III, as already explained in the Introduction. I refer to them as they break up this part in convenient smaller portions, and are easily discernible. After these follow the words] : "With these your Names, and with the powers you possess, to which there is nowhere anything like (I conjure you) to show me and to search for me, and to bring me X to do all my bidding in the name of X," and, again, a list of names, that have no special characteristic in common. Nos. 20–24 are all names commencing with *JJ*; some of these finish with *JH*. 24–36 all these names have the word *Sabaoth* attached to them. To 41–47 *HVH* is added. From Nos. 51–93 all the names are composite; they appear as names of *sons*, the name of the father being added to each of these, close upon 160 names, *e.g.*: Ssgnis, son of Srngia ; Ssgn, son of 'Arggis ; Atumi, son of Batumi ; Ahsuti, son of Kkthus ; Agupi, son of Abkmi, etc. Every name from 102 on to the end of this part finishes with -*el*, after which follow varying syllables and words: some are only *JH* or *JV* (Nos. 102– 105), or a word commencing with '*A*- and finishing with -*JH* (Nos. 106–111). Nos. 112–121 are followed by AHVH, whilst 122–127=JHVHH, and Nos. 128–134= HVJH. They conclude with the following words : " Ye sacred angels, princes of the hosts of X, who stand upon the thrones prepared for them before Him to watch over and to minister to the 'Sword,' to fulfil by it all the wants by the name of the Master over all; you Chiefs of all the angels in the world, X, in the name of X the seal of heaven and earth, ministers of X the most high God ; through you I see X in the world ; you are lording over me in all the place of the Master over all: I pray of you to do everything that I am asking of you, as you have the power to do everything in heaven and upon earth in the name of X, as it is written in the Law, 'I am the Lord, this is My name ! ' "

III.

1. If at full moon (?) a man wishes to unite a woman with a man that they should be as one to one another,

to destroy winds (spirits), demons, and satans, and to stop a ship, and to free a man from prison, and for every other thing, write on a red bowl from Tobar, etc. (No. 1).— 2. To break mountains and hills, to pass dryshod through the water, to enter the fire, to appoint and to depose kings, to blind the eyes, to stop the mouth, and to speak to the dead, and to kill the living, to bring down and to send up and to conjure angels to hearken unto thee, and to see all the mysteries of the world, write Nos. 1 and 2 upon the saucer of a cup and put in it the root of genip-tree (*genipa*). —3. Against a spirit that moves in the body write on a plate No. 3.—4. Against a spirit that burns write No. 4. —5. Against a spirit in the whole body write No. 5. —6. Against a demon (*shidda*) write No. 6.—7. Against shingles write No. 7.—8. Against quinsy (erysipelas ?) say the words of No. 8 over oil of roses and put it over his face.— 9. For pains in the ear whisper in the painful ear No. 9.— 10. For aches in the eye say the words No. 10 over water three days running in the morning, and wash the eye with it.—11. For cataract say the words of No. 11 over oil of sesame, and anoint the eye with it during seven mornings. —12. For grit in the eye say over Ḳohl No. 12, and fill the eye with it for three mornings.—13. For blood that runs from the head whisper No. 13 over the head early in the morning for three days, when you wash your hands before getting out of bed.—14. For paralysis say seven times over a vessel full of water and seven times over sesame-oil the words No. 14, "that it should move away and leave NN, Amen, Amen, Selah"; and throw the pail of water over his head and anoint him with the oil, and do this for three days; then write an amulet with the words from, "I conjure you" till "Amen, Selah," and hang it round his neck. —15. For pains in one half of the head (neuralgia ?) and for bad singing in the ear, write No. 15 and hang it round the neck.—16. For the bad deafening (of the ear) write No. 16 and hang it round the neck.—17. For pains in the ear say into the left ear the words No. 17 backwards.— 18. For deafness say over hemp water, whilst mixing it

with oil of " Idi " (sesame ?), the words of No. 18, and put
it into his ear as soon as it has become a little dissolved (or
warm).—19. For scabs, ulcers, itches, mange, shingles, etc.,
that befall mankind, say over olive oil No. 19 and anoint
with the left hand.—20. For jaundice say the words No. 20
over water in which radish has been soaked, and let him
drink it.—21. For pains in the nose and for the spirit in
the nose say No. 21 over oil of " Idi " (sesame?) and put it
into his nostrils.—22. For pains in the stomach (*lit.*
heart) and in the bowels say No. 22 over water, and
drink it.—23. For hot fever say No. 23 over water in
which rose-laurels are soaked, and he is to bathe in it.—
24. For tumors, etc., say No. 24 once over them and
once over olive oil, and anoint them for three days, but
do not let any water come near them—25. For an evil
occurrence (?) say No. 25 over seven white cups of water,
filled from the river, and throw them over the head.—
26. For ulcer (diphtheria?) spit out before him, and say over
his mouth, and over a cup of strong drink, No. 26, and make
him drink, and watch what is coming out of his mouth.—
27. For a man bitten by a snake or by another (!) poisonous
insect, he must say over the place of the bite or over the painful
spot No. 27 and drink it; the same he is to do whenever hurt
by any creeping thing.—28. For a woman who has seen
blood before the time say No. 28 over an ostrich egg, then
burn it, and she be smoked with it.—29. For pains in the
mouth say No. 29 over risen flour, and put it upon his
mouth.—30. For quinsy (croup) and for pains in the
shoulder, say No. 30 over wine and drink.—31. For a
painful nerve write No. 31 on a scroll and speak these
words over olive oil, and rub some of it on the scroll and
smear it over the painful spot and hang the amulet round
his neck.—32. For stone say over a cup of wine No. 32,
and drink it.—33. For hemorrhoids take tow and put salt
on it and mix it with oil, saying over it No. 33, and sit on
it.—34. For a man who suffers from swelling and from
venereal disease (?), he is to say No. 34 over water in which
radishes are soaked, and drink.—35. For sprains, either

you take a plate and write upon it No. 35 and put it upon
the place, and all around it will be healed ; or you take a ball
of wool and dip it in oil of (sesame ?), and say those words
upon it and put it upon the sprain.—36. When injured or
hurt by iron, and for every blow that it should not fester,
say No. 36 over white naphtha and rub it over the place of
the blow.—37. For (cramps ?) and for pains of heart say over
spinach and oil No. 37, and drink it.—38. For the gall and
the bowels take the water in which raisins have been soaked,
saying over it No. 38, and drink it.—39. For the spoiled
liver take (a drink) a sixth measure of water-lentils and
say No. 39, and swallow it slowly (?).—40. For the milt
say No. 40 over wine-lees and drink it, and repeat it for
three days —41. For the spirit who rests on the womb, say
No. 41 on camphor oil and put it on it with a ball of wool.—
42. For a woman who has a miscarriage, say No. 42 on a cup
of wine, or strong drink, or water, and let her drink it for
seven days ; and even if she should see blood and she repeats
it over a cup of wine, the child will live.—43. For a man
who is bald, say No. 43 over nut-oil and anoint with it.—
44. To conjure a spirit write on a laurel-leaf: " I conjure
thee, prince whose name is Abraksas, in the name of (No. 44)
that thou comest to me and revealest to me all that I ask
of thee, and thou shalt not tarry." And the one bound by
thee will come down and reveal himself to thee.—45. To
remove a rich man from his riches, say No. 45 upon the
dust of an ant-hill and throw it into his face.—46. To heal
leprosy, take the patient to the side of the river and say to
him : " I conjure thee, leprosy, in the name of (No. 46)
to disappear and to vanish, and to pass away from NN.
Amen, Amen, Selah " ; and he is to go down and dip seven
times in the river, and when he comes out write an amulet
with the words ".I conjure—Selah," and hang it round his
neck.—47. For diarrhœa write No. 47 on a red copper plate
and hang it round his neck.—48. If thou wishest that the rain
should not fall upon thy garden, write out No. 48.—49. If
thou wishest to see the sun (!) take . . . from a male tree
and stand in front of the sun and say . . . which art called

on the . . called . . . and the ears of barley (?) the words
of No. 49;[1] and he will appear unto thee in the form of
a man dressed in white and he will answer thee upon
everything that thou askest him, and he will even bring
a woman after thee.—50. Whosoever wishes to enter a
furnace is to write No. 50 on a silver plate and hang
it upon his haunch.—51. If thou seest a king or a ruler
and thou wishest that he follow thee, take a basin of water
and put into it the root of genip-tree, and the root of
purslane, and the root of (*Artilochia*), and say No. 51, and
place it on fiery coals in a white earthen vessel and throw
upon them leaves of olive-tree, and whatever thou decreest
he will bring unto thee, even a woman thou canst command.
—52. If you wish to overawe them, take water from the
fountain and say upon it No. 52 and throw it into their faces.
—53. For loosening (any charm) say over water No. 53 and
throw it over him and write it as an amulet and hang it
round his neck, and also for freeing a man from prison.—
54. To catch fish, take a white potsherd, and putting into it
leaves of olive-tree say over them No. 54 at the side of the
river.—55. If thou wishest a woman to follow thee, take
thy blood and write her name upon a newly-laid egg and
say towards her No. 55.—56. If a man is to follow thee,
take a new potsherd and dip it in black myrrh (gall)
and pronounce over his name the words of No. 56, and
walk on without looking backwards.—57. For a tree that
does not produce fruits, write the words No. 57 upon
a new potsherd and bury it under the root of the fruitless
tree, and water all the trees and these also which do not
produce the fruit.—58. For illness (dog) in the fruit write
on a new potsherd No. 58 and bury it in the cistern
(watering-place), and say these words also over water, ashes,
and salt, and water the earth with it.—59. For a suckling
babe write on an onyx slab No. 59 and whisper it into its
ears three times, spitting out' after the whispering; then
repeat them over a cupful of water 70 times and give it
the child to drink.—60. For one bitten by a rabid dog,

[1] There is something probably missing here.

write No. 60 on the halter of an ass and let the ass go; then repeat these words over sesame oil and let him anoint himself with it and put on new clothes and hang that halter (?) round him.—61. For fever and small fever, write on the skin of the brains of a ram or a goat No. 61, and hang it round his neck.—62. If anyone lose his way he is to say No. 62 over the four corners of his belt (?).—63. If thou wishest to ask anything of thy neighbour, say No. 63 over oil of sesame or of . . . or of . . . —64. If thou wishest that a woman is to follow thee write thy name and her name with thy blood upon her door, and the same upon thy door, and repeat the words of No. 64.— 65. If thou wishest to know whether thy journey will be lucky, take a field lettuce with open leaves, and standing before the sun say the words of No. 65 and watch the lettuce: if the leaves close and shut, then do not go; but if they remain in their natural state, proceed, and thou wilt prosper.—66. If thou wishest to deliver a man from prison (?) say No. 66 once to him, and once to the sun, and once to the prison (?) house.—67. To conquer (collect?), take dust from thy house and say over it seven times in the road of the town the words of No. 67, and then take dust from the road and do likewise and throw it into thy house.—68. If you wish to kill a man, take mud from the two sides of the river and form it into the shape of a figure, and write upon it the name of the person, and take seven branches from seven strong palm-trees and make a bow from reed (?) with the string of horse-sinew, and place the image in a hollow, and stretch the bow and shoot with it, and at each branch (shot) say the words of No. 68; and may NN be destroyed . . .—69. To send plagues, take (parings?) from seven men and put them into a new potsherd, and go out to the cemetery and say there No. 69, and bury it in a place that is not trodden by horses, and afterwards take the dust from this potsherd and blow it into his face or upon the lintel of his house.—70. To send dreams to your neighbours, write No. 70 upon a plate of silver and place it in the mouth (?) of a cock and kill it when it has gone down its mouth, and take it out from the mouth and put it between its legs and bury it at the end of a wall, and put thy foot upon that spot and say thus: "In the name of X, a swift messenger is to go and torment NN in his dreams until he will fulfil my wish."—71. If a snake follows thee say No. 71, and it will dry up —72. To stop a boat in the sea, say No. 72 over a potsherd or on a rounded flintstone and throw it against it into the sea. —73. To loosen it (from the charm), say No. 73 over dust or a clod of earth and throw it into the water, and as this dissolves the boat gets free to go.—74. If thou wishest to prevent an oven or furnace or pot from becoming destroyed (unclean?), say No. 74 over dust and throw it over them.— 75. If thou wishest them to be hot, spit in front of them and say No. 75, and they will boil.—76. If thou wishest to pass dryshod through the sea, say upon the four corners of the head-dress (turban) No. 76, and take one corner in thy hand and the other is (?) to precede thee.—77. If thou wishest to curse anyone, say in the 'Eighteen bene-dictions' No. 77, in the name of X.—78. To speak with the dead, whisper No. 71 into his left ear and throw into their holes (?).—79. To kill a lion, bear, an adder, or any other hurtful animal, take the dust from under the right foot, say over it No. 79, and throw it into their faces.—80. To catch them, take the dust from under your left foot, saying No. 80, and throw it into their faces.— 81. To open a door, take the root of lotos reed and place it under the tongue and say No. 81 against the door.— 82. To kill an ox or another beast, say into its ear No. 82.—83. To inflame his heart, say No. 83 over a piece of raw meat, and give it to him to eat.—84. To make a fool of one, say No. 84 over an egg and place it in his hands.—85. To destroy the house of thy neighbour, say No. 85 over a new potsherd and throw it into his house. —86. To expose (?) your neighbour, say No. 86 over oil of . . . and smear it at the bottom of his jug (?).—87. To make your neighbour disliked, take blood from phlebotomy, say upon it No. 87, and throw it upon his lintel.—88. To make a woman have a miscarriage, say No. 88 over a cup of water and throw it over her lintel.—89. To make a man ill, say No. 89 over olive oil and let him anoint himself with it.—90. To know whether a sick person will die or live, say before him No. 90 : if he turns his face towards you he will live; if away, he will die.—91. To catch a lion by the ear, say No. 91 and make seven knots in the fringes of thy girdle and repeat these words with each knot, and you will catch him.—92. To make thy renown go throughout the world, write No. 92 as an amulet and bury it in thy house.—93. To shorten the way, say No. 93 over a single lotos reed.—94. To cure hemorrhoids, take kernels of dates . . . and burn them in fire and say No. 94, and mix it with oil of olives and place it as an amulet over it, and it will be good.—95. For every spirit write upon a bowl No. 95 and hang it round the neck.—96. For subtle poison, as cumin-seed and calamint, write No. 96 upon an egg and put it into wine, and repeat over it the same words and then drink it.— 97. For the thunder that comes from heaven, take a ring (round piece) of iron and lead, and hang it on the spot you wish (to protect), and say over it No. 97.—98. To go before king or lord, say No. 98 over a piece of lion's skin dipped in black hemp(?) and pure wine, and take it with thee.—99. For blight, if it happen, take a sinew and soak it in turnip-juice in the night from Wednesday to Thursday, and say No. 99 over it; on the morrow sprinkle that water over the field.—100. If the fruit gets worm-eaten, take a worm from the mud and put it into a tube and say No. 100 over it; then close the tube and bury it in that place.—101. To free a man from prison (? shame), say over the grounds of Kappa (?) and unripe dates No. 101, and give it to him to eat.—102. For a field that does not produce fruits, take eight cups from eight houses and fill them with water from eight rivers, and put salt into them from eight houses, and say over them No. 102 eight times, and pour out two cups at each corner, and break them on eight paths.—103. If one does not know what a man is ailing

from, soak mullein (*verbascum*) in water, and say over it
No. 103, and let him drink it when he is thirsty.—104. To
make war, take the dust from under the left foot, say over
it No. 104, and throw it into the (enemies') face, and there
will appear knights with weapons in their hands who will
fight for thee.—105. To throw thy fear upon mankind, write
No. 105 upon a leaden plate and bury it on the west side of
the Synagogue.—106. To have always light in the darkness,
write No. 106 upon a chart (paper) and carry it always with
thee.—107. To catch (blind) the eye, write No. 107 upon
a scroll and expose it in a wicker-basket to the stars, but
you must not speak when writing.—108. To send a sword
which should fight for thee, say No. 108 over a new knife
wholly of iron, and throw it into their face.—109. If thou
wishest that they kill one another, say No. 109 over a new
knife wholly of iron and bury it with your heel into the
earth, and keep the heel upon it in the earth, and they will
kill one another, until you take it out from the earth.—
110. To make them pause, take the dust from under the
right foot, and, saying the same words again backwards,
throw it into their face, and they will stop.—111. If an
enemy has got hold of thee and wishes to kill thee, bend
the little finger of the left hand and say No. 111, and
he will run away from thee like one who runs away
from his murderer.—112. To catch the eye (blind), say
No. 112 over the skin of a lion and carry it with thee,
and no one will be able to see thee.—113. If thou fallest
into a (?) and wishest to come out, say No. 113, and thou
wilt come out in peace.—114. If thou fallest into a deep
pit, say in thy fall No. 114, and nothing will hurt thee.—
115. When thou fallest into a deep river say No. 115, and
thou wilt come out in peace.—116. If any burden or weight
falls upon thee, say No. 116, and thou wilt be saved.—
117. If the king's servants lay hold on thee, bend
the little finger of the left hand and say No. 117
before king or judge, and he will kill these people who
have laid hands on thee.—118. If a host has surrounded thee, turn thy face towards the west and say

No. 118 before king or judge, and they will be like unto
stones and will not move.—119. If thou wishest to release
them, turn thy face towards the east and repeat these
words backwards.—120. If thou walkest in vales or on the
mountains and hast no water to drink, lift thine eyes to
Heaven and say No. 120, and a fountain of water will be
opened unto thee.—121. If thou hungerest, lift thine eyes
to Heaven and spread out thine arms and say No. 121, and
a spirit will stand before thee and bring thee bread and
meat.—122. If thou wishest to call the angel (prince) of
man, say over thy mantle (?) No. 122, and the angel bound
by thee will come to thee and will tell thee whatever
thou wishest (to know).—123. If thou wishest to let him
go (depart), say before him the same words backward, and
he will depart.—124. If thou wishest that any heavenly
prince is to come to thee and teach thee, say No. 124 and
conjure him in the third hour of the night from : " in the
name of the Lord over the holy ones (No. 136) to the end of
the 'Sword,'" and " Send him to me that he reveal unto me
and teach me all that is in his power," and he will then disappear (!).—125. To walk upon the water without wetting the
feet, take a leaden plate and write upon it No. 125 and place
it in thy girdle, and then you can walk.—126. To become
wise, remember for three months running, from the new
moon of Nissan onwards, the words of No. 126, and add
in the 'Eighteen benedictions' : " May the gates of wisdom
be opened to me so that I should meditate in them."—
127. To remember immediately all thou learnest, write
on a new-laid egg No. 127, then wash it off with
strong wine early in the morning and drink it, and do
not eat anything for three hours.—128. To make another
forget what he has learned, write No. 128 in his name on
laurel-leaves and bury them under his lintel.—129. To
send an evil spirit against thy neighbour, take a green
grasshopper and say over it No. 129, and bury it in an
earth-hill and jump over it.—130. To send a plague, take
the bone of a dead man and dust from under him in a pot
and tie it up in a woven rag with saliva, and say upon it

No. 130 in his name, and bury it in the cemetery.—131. To tie and to fasten thiefs and robbers, say No. 131, and whilst saying it put your little finger in the ear.—132. To release them, say No. 132, and take thy finger out of the ear.—133. To guard thy house from thieves, say No. 133 over a cup of water and pour it out round thy roof. Thus also to guard a house.—134. To guard a house from hosts (robbers), take earth from an ant-hill and strew it round the roof, repeating the words of No. 134.—135. To guard thyself from Mazikim, say: "In the name of 'Nos. 1–5' may I, NN, pass in peace and not in hurt." The same must be done to excommunicate them when you meet them.—136. For every other thing that has not been mentioned say, No. 136 to the end of the "Sword."

And upon every amulet that you write from this "Sword" write first: "In the name of the Lord of all the holy ones, may this 'Sword' be effectual to do my services, and may the lord of it approach to serve me, and may all these powers be delivered over to me so that I be able to use them, as they were delivered to Moses, the son of Amram, perfect from his God and no harm befalling him!" If he will not act accordingly the angels of wrath, ire, fury, and rage will come near him to minister to him, and they will lord over him, and strangle him, and plague him all over. And these are the names of their leaders: the leader of the angels of wrath is Mzpopiasaiel; the name of the leader of the angels of ire is Zkzoromtiel; the name of the leader of the angels of fury is Kso'ppghiel; the name of the leader of the angels of rage is N'mosnikttiel. And the angels that stand under them are numberless, and these all will have power over him, and will make his body like unto a dunghill.

May the Lord preserve you from every evil. Amen!

End of the "Sword," with the assistance of God feared in the council of the holy ones. End, end.

APPENDIX I.

In the name of the Lord.   The Sword of Moses.

I. [A long list of mystical names; then follows:] and the angel over the animals, whose name is Ittalainma; and the angel over the wild beasts, Mtniel; and the angel over the wild fowls and over the creeping things, Trgiaob; and the angel over the deep waters and over the mountains, Rampel; and the angel over the trees, Maktiel; and the angel over the sweet-smelling herbs, Arias; and the angel over the garden fruits (vegetables), Sofiel; and the angel over the rivers, Trsiel; and the angel over the winds, Mbriel; and over man, X.—. . . hours are proper for man to pray and to ask for mercy upon man, be it for good or evil; and it is said that every hour is proper for man to pray, but during the three first hours in the morning man is to pray and to mention the hundred sacred names and the mighty ones, whose sum amounts to three hundred and four.   Amen. Selah!

. . . . X give me healing . . . .

Which is the great light?   All the . . . . X, I conjure you, mother of the (whether?) male and mother of the (or?) female, you, the "Twins," I conjure you, the hard (strong) spirits, in the name of God, the mighty hero, the living one [Michael], in the name of God [Gabriel], . . Raphael (save) me from the Lions, the powerful ones (Archons?), and the Twins.   I conjure you, strong spirits, in the name of God, the mighty hero, IH, IHVH, IHVH, I, N, son of N . .

II. Verily, this is the ("Sword of Moses") with which he accomplished his miracles and mighty deeds, and destroyed all kind of witchcraft; it had been revealed to Moses in the bush, when the great and glorious Name was delivered to him.   Take care of it and it will take care of thee.   If thou approachest fire, it will not burn thee, and it will preserve thee from every evil in the world.—
1. If thou wishest to try it take a thick (green) branch and

utter this "Sword" over it five times at sunrise, and it will dry up.—2. To catch fish, take sand from the sea and the root of the date (tree) (or the kernel of the date), and repeat this "Sword" over them, and the fish will come to the spot where thou throwest the sand.—3. To walk on the waters of the sea take the wooden helve of an axe, bore a hole through it, pass a red thread through it, and tie it on to thy heel, then repeat the words of the "Sword," and then you may go in and out in peace.—4. To run quickly (?), write the "Sword" on "Chartis hieratikon," then put water into a new earthenware pot, and let them drink it and wash their faces, and they will be victorious!— 5. To break it (?), write the "Sword" on a plate of copper (*kyprinon*) and put it in . . and they will be broken.— 6. To subdue a woman, write with the blood of thy hand thy (?) name upon thy gate, and write thy name upon a scroll of leather of a hart with the blood of thy finger, and say this "Sword," and she will come to thee.— 7. To make thyself praised in the community, take in thy left hand porret-seed and utter over it the "Sword," and throw it between them,[1] and descend (?) until the sun sets, and he will carry thee wherever thou wishest, and fast for three days, and burn incense and the smoke of white flower, and repeat the "Sword" in the morning and the evening, and he will come instantly and speak to thee and do thy bidding.—8. To get information through a dream, take balm and write upon "Chartis hieratikon," and repeat the "Sword" in front of a light, and put out the light with a stick of olive-wood, and lie down.—9. If thou wishest to go to a great man, take rose-oil and repeat the "Sword" over the oil and anoint thy hands and face with it, and he will hearken unto thee.—10. To make strife in the community, take the left hand full of mustard, speak the "Sword" over it, and throw it amongst them, and they will kill one another.—11. To separate a man from his wife, take ass's meat in thy hand and say over it the "Sword," and no harm will befall thee (?).—12. To destroy

---

[1] There is something probably missing here.

thy enemy, take a leaden plate and some of his hair and
clothes, and say the "Sword" over them, and bury them in
a deserted house, and he will fall down.—13. To walk in the
street and not to be recognized by anyone, take wormwood,
perfumes, and soot, and smoke thyself with it, and take
the heart of a fox, and say the "Sword," and go out in
the street.—14. If you are on the sea and the storm rages,
stand up against the waves and say the "Sword" to them,
and they will go down; then write on a plate, or potsherd,
or a piece of wood, and hang it in front of the ship, and
it will not founder.—15. To break an enemy, write the
"Sword" upon a potsherd that has not yet been burned,
and plaster it over, and throw it into his house.—16. To
obtain anything thou likest, take into thy right hand
wormwood, and say over it the "Sword" facing the
sun, and everything will be fulfilled, and purify thyself
for seven days, and thou wilt prosper in everything. Do
kind deeds to thy friends, take heed not to take an oath,
and walk modestly, and thus thou wilt prosper.

Write X upon the palm of thy left hand, take then a
new lamp and fill it with olive-oil and naphtha, and put
on new clean clothes, and sleep in a clean house, and the
angel will come at once and wake thee, and reveal unto
thee everything that thou wishest.

III. R. Akiba asked R. Eliezer the great: "How can one
make the Angel of the Presence descend upon earth to reveal
to man the mysteries from above and beneath, and the
speculations of the foundations of heavenly and earthly
things, and the treasures of wisdom, cunning, and help?"
He said thereupon to me: "My son! I once made him
come down, and he nearly destroyed the whole world, for
he is a mighty prince and greater than any in the heavenly
cohort, and he ministers continually before the King of the
Universe, with purity and separation, and with fear and
dread of the glory of his Master, because the Shekinah
is always with him." And he said to him: "My master,
by the glory which thou hast bestowed upon me, I conjure
thee to instruct me how to attach him to me." (And he

replied) : "In that hour when I wish to attach him to me
and to employ him, I sit and fast on that very day ; but
prior to it one must keep oneself free for seven days from
any nocturnal impurity, and must bathe in the fountain
of water, and not speak at all during those seven days,
and at the end of this purification, on the day of the fast,
he must sit in the water up to his throat, and before he
utters the conjuration he must first say : 'I conjure you,
angels of dread, fear, and shaking, who are appointed to hurt
those who are not pure and clean and desire the services
of my heavenly servants—I conjure you in the name of X,
who is mighty over all, and rules over all, and everything is in His hands, that you do not hurt me, nor terrify
me, nor frighten me; verily, in the name of the powerful,
the head of . . . ' After this he may commence his conjuration, for now he has fortified himself and has sealed
himself with the name of God of 42 letters, before which
all who hear it tremble and are frightened, and the
heavenly hosts are terror-struck.   He must then again
conjure, and say : 'X, chief, who of all the destroying angels
is the most hurtful and burning, with this Name and in this
way I call thee AVZHIA, angel of the Presence, youthful
minister before the King of the Universe, who art a prince
and chief of the heavenly hosts ; I conjure thee and decree
upon thee that thou attachest thyself to me to fulfil my
wish and to accept the decree of my conjuration and to
accomplish my desires and fulfil my wishes, and do not
frighten me, nor terrify me, nor overawe me, and do not
make my frame shake and my feet vacillate, nor cause
my speech to be perverted ; but may I be fortified and
strengthened, and may the conjuration be effective and
the (sacred) Name uttered properly by my throat, and may
no vacillation take hold of me and no trembling of the feet
by thy ministering angels confuse me and overawe me, and
weaken my hands, and may I not be overcome by the
fire and flame of the storm and whirlwind which precedes
thee, O wonderful and exalted one, whose Ineffable name
of X, of whose wrath the earth trembles, and nothing can

withstand his anger, twice blessed. Again I conjure thee
by thy 14 (!) names by which thou didst reveal thyself to
thy prophets and seers, to place in their mouths sweet words
of prophecy and to utter pleasant words; and these are
the Ineffable names and their surnames (Kunya): Spirit
Piskonnit, kunya, X; Atimon, kunya, X; Piskon (?),
Hugron, kunya, X; Sanigron, kunya, X; Msi, kunya, X;
Mokon, kunya, X; Astm, kunya, X; Sktm, kunya, X;
Ihoaiel, kunya, X; Iofiel, kunya, X; Ssnialiah, kunya,
X; Kngieliah, kunya, X; Zabdiel, kunya, X. I conjure
thee with these fourteen names, by which all the secrets and
mysteries and signs are sealed and accomplished, and which
are the foundations of heaven and earth. Four of these are
engraved upon the heads of the Hayoth (Holy Creatures),
namely—X, the lord of powers; X, master of miracles;
X, master of purity; and X, master of the yoke. And four
are engraved upon the four sides of the Throne, namely—
X, three times holy; X, Adir, Adiri, Adiron, etc., the king
of kings. And four are engraved upon the four crowns of
the Ofanim (wheels) that stand against the Holy Creatures,
as it is said: "When those went, these went; and when
those stood, these stood" (Ezek. i, 21); and these they are
—X, who is the mightiest over all; X, who rules over all
the inhabitants of the heights (?), and in whose hands everything is. And two are engraved upon the crown of the
most exalted and high King, and these they are—X, before
whom every knee bends and every mouth utters praises;
X, besides him there is no God and helper. With these
names I conjure thee, and firmly decree upon thee to
descend quickly to me, N, son of N, thou and not thy
messenger. And when thou comest down do not turn my
mind, but reveal unto me all the secret mysteries from
above and beneath, and the hidden secrets from above
and beneath, and all the secrets of wisdom and the cunning
of helpfulness, just as a man speaks to his neighbour. For
I have conjured thee with these Names, that are great and
mighty and wonderful and awe-inspiring, and proved and
arranged in proper order, through which the glorious

throne has been established and the beautiful seat of the
Most High, which has been wonderfully wrought, long
before thou and the heavenly hosts had been created,
"While as yet He had not made the earth nor the fields,
and the inhabitants of the earth and the creatures therein"
(Prov. viii, 26).

"'I call thee further by (the power) of the five
selected Names, to which only one is superior, and this is
their form—X. I conjure thee by these five Names,
which correspond to the five names of God, whose letters
are written on burning fire, and they circle round the
throne of glory, one ascending and the other descending,
so that the angels of the Presence should not behold them,
and this is their equivalent and form and glory—X.
I conjure thee by these, as thou knowest their praise and
greatness, which no mouth can utter, and no ear can hear,
no, not even one of them. Thou hast been commanded
and ordered by the Most High: "as soon as thou
hearest anyone conjuring thee with these names, to do
honour to My Name, and to descend quickly and fulfil
the wish of the man who makes thee hear them;
but if thou tarriest I will push thee into the fiery
river Rigayon and place another in thy stead." Do it,
therefore, for His Name, and come quickly to me, N, son
of N, not in a terror, and not in fear, not with fiery
coals, not with hailstone, and not with the sleet and
treasures of snow, and not with the howling of the storm,
and not with the provinces of the whirlwind that usually
accompany thee, and do my bidding and fulfil my desire,
for everything is in thy hand; by the permission of thy
God, the master over all and thy lord, and with His Names
I conjure thee to attach thyself quickly to me; come and
fulfil my wish, and do not tarry.

"'I further call thee with the greatest of thy Names, the
pleasant and beloved one, which is the same as that of thy
Master, save one letter, with which He created and formed
everything, and which He placed as a seal upon all the
work of His hand; and this is its equivalent—X, and the

other in the language of purity (permutations of the letters Yod, He) is read so—X. I conjure thee with the right hand of sanctity and with His beloved Name, in whose honour everything has been created, and all are terror-struck by His mighty arm, and all the sons of the internal heavenly cohort (servants) tremble and shake of His fear, which is X, and its equivalent by means of JHVH is X. Blessed be the name of His glorious kingdom for ever and ever. And all praise and extol thy Name, for they love thee. I conjure thee, and decree upon thee firmly, not to disobey my words, and not to alter my decree and my decision with which I conjured thee, and decreed upon thee, and established in peace. In the Name X, blessed be the name of His glorious kingdom for ever and ever, depart in peace, and do not frighten me in the hour of thy departure; in the name X, Lord, most high and holy, in the name of the Lord of Hosts, the God of Israel's battalions; in the name of the holy living Creatures, and in the name of the Wheels of the Chariot, and in the name of the river of fire, Ih, Zii, Ziin, and all His ministers, and in the name of IH, Ziin, Sabaoth, Z, El Z, Shaddai Z, X revealed Himself on Mount Sinai in the glory of His majesty.

"'With these Names, terrible and mighty, which darken the sun, and obscure the moon, and turn the sea, and break the rocks, and extinguish the light, I conjure you, spirits, and . . and Shiddim, and Satanim, that you depart and disappear from N, son of N.'"

APPENDIX II.

I. *Against an enemy.*—I call thee, evil spirit, cruel spirit, merciless spirit. I call thee, bad spirit, who sittest in the cemetery and takes away healing from man. Go and place a knot in NN's head, in his eyes, in his mouth, in his tongue, in his throat, in his windpipe; put poisonous water in his belly. If you do not go and put water in his belly, I will send against you the evil angels Puziel, Guziel,

Psdiel, Prziel. I call thee and those six knots that you go
quickly to NN and put poisonous water in his belly and
kill NN whom I mean (or, because I wish it). Amen,
Amen. Selah.

II. *Against an enemy.*—Write upon a new-laid egg on
a Nazarene cemetery : " I conjure you, luminaries of heaven
and earth, as the heavens are separated from the earth, so
separate and divide NN from his wife NN, and separate
them from one another, as life is separated from death,
and sea from dry land, and water from fire, and mountain
from vale, and night from day, and light from darkness,
and the sun from the moon; thus separate NN from NN
his wife, and separate them from one another in the name
of the twelve hours of the day and the three watches (?)
of the night, and the seven days of the week, and the
thirty days of the month, and the seven years of Shemittah,
and the fifty years of Jubilee, on every day, in the name
of the evil angel Tmsmael, and in the name of the angel
Iabiel, and in the name of the angel Drsmiel, and in the
name of the angel Zahbuk, and in the name of the angel
Ataf, and in the name of the angel Zhsmael, and in the
name of the angel Zsniel, who preside over pains, sharp
pains, inflammation, and dropsy, and separate NN from his
wife NN, make them depart from one another, and that
they should not comfort one another, swiftly and quickly."

THE WISDOM OF THE CHALDEANS: AN OLD HEBREW ASTROLOGICAL TEXT.

By M. GASTER.

Reprinted from the "Proceedings of the Society of Biblical Archæology," December, 1900.

Among other papers and MSS. obtained some years ago from old Nisibis in Mesopotamia, came also a number of half obliterated and badly damaged leaves of a MS. which at close examination revealed itself to be a collection of magical formulas and recipes, written in many old Oriental hands. With the new discovery of ancient Texts in the Genizah, our notions of Hebrew palæography are undergoing a complete change. It is now much more difficult to fix the age of a MS. only from the handwriting. It has been found that a form hitherto considered to be of a comparatively modern origin may after all be centuries older than anticipated. Still I would consider the writing of the principal part of this MS., reconstructed after long and painstaking trouble, not to be later than the XIVth century. The lower part of many a page has become illegible in consequence of dampness and age. The date of the writing is however not identical with that of the composition of the MS. It suffices to remember that the oldest Hebrew magical book known and lost one thousand years ago has been rediscovered by me in this very MS. From it I published the famous "Sword of Moses," which I have shown to be of the second or third century, standing in close connection with the magic Papyri and with the old magical books ascribed to Moses in Hellenistic times.

The MS. consists now of sixty-two leaves, a number of which is in a bad state of preservation. Some pages are written in Arabic, though with Hebrew characters, and these, as well as that portion which appears to contain the oldest texts, is written by a bold and careful hand. Other portions are written in a much smaller type, and at times less carefully. In the middle of the XVIth century it was the property of a certain Raḥamim, son of R. Samuel Malki or Milki. He tells us (fol. 17*b*) that "leaving once Egypt for Damascus he had hidden this book away. On his return no one knew where it had gone to, until he found it in the hands of a young man, from whom he bought it back at the price of seventeen 'grush.' In order that the book should not be purloined for a second time, and his title to it be called into question, he signs his name." He repeats the same statement fol. 22*b*. His writing is totally different from any of the writings of the MS. itself. From these notes, and from the whole character of the contents, as well as from the Arabic portions, it is evident that this collection has its origin in the East.

Among the non-Hebrew words that occur in the charms we find however some that are evidently Spanish. They are called "La'az"; thus, the name of the charm known as that of "the Mirror," "*Mirai*," and the conjuration itself, which is in Spanish. In another place we find the word "purga," in the meaning of purging (fol. 61*a*), also mentioned as "La'az." On the other hand, at least one of the mystical names invoked on some occasions seems to be merely the transliteration of Greek words, "megas Totma Tot." If all the mystical names in this Thesaurus of charms, numbering close upon four hundred in all, would be examined, many more will prove to be of an exotic character, grown on the field of that syncretism of Gnostic speculation and Egypto-chaldean incantations. In one place we find "Abraxel"; in another "The Paraclet" is invoked. The compiler has collected his materials from various sources, of which some are mentioned. The fact that a few Spanish words occur, proves that these have been brought back to the East from Spain, where the knowledge of mystical literature had existed from very early times. The authorities quoted by the compiler are: R. Jehudah Ḥasid (*ca.* 1200), fol. 13*a*, 14*b*, 61*a*; "The great Rabbi Eliezer, of Qarmisha or Garmisa," *i.e.*, R. Eleazar, of Worms (XIIIth century), fol. 6*b*, and his "Commentary to Genesis," fol. 10*a*; R. Aharon (fol. 13*a*), probably the famous Aharon of Babylon, possessor of mystical knowledge and of the wonder-working Name of God in the ninth century, as told in the Chronicle of Aḥima'aṣ, written 1055 (*v.* Neubauer, Mediæval Chronicles, II, p. 112 ff.); "Nahmanides," fol. 13*b*, 23*b*, 48*b*; "R. Samuel ibn Tibbon, in the name of R. 'Ezra," f. 47*b*; "R. Samuel in the name of R. 'Azriel" (the last two the well-known initiators of Naḥmanides into the mysteries of the Qabbala), fol. 46*a*. Another R. Samuel, fol. 42*a*, 42*b*, 45*b*. "A treatise of Sa'adya Gaon," fol. 56*a*.

Besides these more or less historical personages there are others less well known or mythical persons. The Patriarchs mentioned are Moses, Elijah, and Elisha, further the cup of "'Ezra the priest," fol. 53*b*. The charm communicated to the author by *R.* "mark the Rabbi, ! "Joseph the Shidda, nephew of the demon Samhoris," fol. 43*b*. (He is quoted also in the Talmud as communicating such knowledge to a certain R. Joseph, Treatise Pesaḥem, 110*a*, Erubin 43*a*; "R. Jequtiel," fol. 46*a*; "Menachem, the son-in-law of R. Baruch fol. 35*b*; "R. Eli'ezer the Sephardi," who is called "הרב הגאון" fol. 23*a*; R. Meshullam Ṣarfati, fol. 45*b*; R. Isaac Ṣarfati, fol. 50*a*; probably the Blind, one of the first enunciators of the modern Qabbala in the south of France, XIIth century. A certain "R. Dan," otherwise unknown, fol. 60*b*; Samuel Ladib, fol. 60*b*; (perhaps Latif). The mythical "R. Joseph de la Reyna" (of whom the legend exists that he had succeeded to chain the demon Samael) fol. 10*b*. Last, but not least, Rab Reḥimai, fol. 18*a*, mentioned also in the Zohar. He is evidently identical with the scholar whose name is spelt Rḥumi, Reḥimai, Riḥumi, etc. (v. Neubaueer Chronicles, s.v. in the index), who lived 456 B C. The great persecution under the Persian dynasty began in his time, and he is the last author connected with the compilation of the Talmud. No writing of his has come down to us, but a short treatise is ascribed to him in our MS. on the mystical name of God. I dwell on this name because I see in it the key to the mysterious "R. Ḥamai" or "Ḥamai Gaon," to whom many mystical treatises are ascribed, but who is otherwise absolutely unknown. This name is probably due to a wrong reading of "Reḥimai," taking the first letter R, not as the initial letter of the name, but as the abbreviation of the title "Rabbi," which stands before almost every old name of a scholar. Who "R. Tabshulim the prophet" may be, quoted f. 40*b*, is more than I know at present.

Besides these authors, anonymous books are also mentioned, from which the compiler had drawn his materials. In the first place, he often quotes the "Shushan Sodoth." There is a book in existence with a similar title ascribed to Moses ben Jacob (ed. Korzec, 1784) full of mystical speculations and interpretations of the prayers and of liturgical ceremonies. It has, however, nothing in common with the contents of our MS. Not a single charm or incantation is found among those speculations. A book of charms with such a title must have existed, however, for not only is it quoted here, but abstracts from that very book are given in many a MS. in my possession, all similar in character to this MS. (cf. my codd., Nos. 186, 265, etc.). Another work mentioned is the "Midrash of Simon the Ṣaddiq" (fol. 4a); "Another old book" (fol. 19b); "Other books " (fol. 15b); "Speakers of truth" (fol. 20a); "Other Qabbalists"; and so on. In one instance, when copying a text incomplete at the beginning, the copyist remarks: "I have found it only from here onward," showing the care with which he copied his texts. One of the recipes has the note appended " tried in שׂופרייא (Sophia)," (fol. 50a). I am doubtful, however, as to the reading of the name. It must be a place somewhere in Asia Minor or Spain, and cannot be identical with "Sofia " of Bulgaria.

It is remarkable that we find the greater number of these very names of authors, and especially the less well-known, and the anonymous works such as the " Midrash of R. Simon the Saddiq, very often quoted in the commentary to the Book Yeṣira of Moses Bottarillo. He wrote that commentary in Spain in the year 1409. The writings and authors mentioned by Bottarillo (vide the whole list in Steinschneider, Cat. Bodl. sv., col. 1781–1784) have been declared by Zunz and others to have been invented by him only and solely because they did not find them mentioned elsewhere. Our MS. corroborates now the veracity of the quotations of Bottarillo ; but whilst the latter limits his references to mystical speculations and qabbalistic interpretations which he gives in their names, the present MS. contains in their names charms, incantations and other mystical portions of practical Qabbala. I do not discuss the question whether those writings are genuine, or whether they have been wrongly attributed to these men, but we can no longer doubt the fact that these—genuine or pseudo-epigraphical — writings existed latest, in the XIVth century in Spain, if not before that date. Among the "Tossafists " to the Pentateuch of the XIIIth and XIVth century printed in " Hadar Zeqenîm," ed. Livorno, 1840, we find also some of these very names. Considering now that many of these men are not by any means known as such brilliant scholars, that works not written by them should have been ascribed to them with the intention of enhancing their value, nay, some being only known by these quotations of Bottarillo, I see no reason to doubt their genuineness.

This MS. is written by at least two or three almost contemporary hands. The ink is mostly the same, only the character of the writing differs considerably between what I would call the first old hand, especially noticeable in fols. 18–26, and the second. The actual compilation begins with fol. 5, and has as title "Segulloth." The numbering of the charms begins from here. On the preceding pages are Arabic (fols. 1–3) and later Hebrew recipes (fol. 4a). The numbering refers only to the remedies or charms. As the text is written in places very closely, the man who added the numbers has in consequence often missed one or two in the middle of the text. The true number would be nearer 400 charms. All the speculative portions unsuited for practical purposes are not included in the counting. The MS. being a compilation from different sources, not seldom happens that the same charm is found twice and even three times. The copyist merely transcribed whatever he found without much critical discrimination. This fact strengthens further the belief in the truthfulness of the copyist.

Among these charms, recipes, incantations and mystical prayers, we find now in that very part of the MS. which is written by the old hand, a text of an astrological character ascribed to the Chaldeans. This text is very striking from more than one point of view. In itself, it is a complete compendium of the astrological character of the Powers that rule in the course of the week. Each day is described, and its ruler or rulers. The image of that regent is delineated ; the mode of drawing him is indicated, and instructions are given how to make use magically of the image thus drawn, and of the formulas which accompany these magic operations. We are told to what profit this knowledge can be turned, the good and evil that can be performed by means of these divine images; we even learn the nature of the mysterious sigils or seals of these regents.

The revelation of these mysteries is ascribed in the first place to "Raziel," the angel, and then to the "primitive Enoch." Enoch as revealer of heavenly mysteries, and as the scribe who writes a book on the heavenly economy and hierarchy, is known from the old apocryphal and psuedo-epigraphical literature. The Book of Enoch, in its double or triple form : Greek, Slavonic, and Hebrew fragments, is too well known that I should dilate here at any length on it. I refer specially to chapter xliii, ed. Charles, and still more to the Hebrew fragments of the astrological book of Enoch (v. Jellinek, Bethhamidrasch V, p. 173 ff.). Of greater value is the fact that Enoch is beholding and describing the mysteries of the heavens in the Zohar, where his book is quoted, and in one passage he is also brought into intimate connection with the angel Raziel (I. fol. 55*b*. *cf.* fol. 37*b*.). To him and through him the astronomical mysteries of the world·are said there to have been communicated to Adam, Noah, Abraham, etc. It is the same tradition as that of our text, but with this noteworthy difference, that the knowledge is not communicated here to Abraham, but to the Chaldeans, who had speculated on the heavenly bodies, on their movements, and on the rulers who guide them. The essentially Jewish feature in the other tradition is clearly missing here. Much more important is, that in this piece alone out of the hundreds gathered in this compilation, the name of God is never mentioned, and that not one single citation is made of a Biblical text, nor is a single verse of the Bible alluded to. As a rule the basis or the efficacious portion of a charm consists either in the permutation of the letters of such biblical verses, or in their unchanged application. Here not a single trace is to be found.

The text is described as "the wisdom of the Chaldeans." References to Chaldean astronomy are extremely rare in Hebrew writings. We find them referred to, however, in what is considered to be the oldest astronomical book; I allude to the so-called Barayta of R. Samuel. The date of its composition has not yet been definitely established. Internal indications would place the final redaction in the eighth century. It is probably older, at least in some of its astrological portions.

Chapter IX of the Barayta is devoted to the interpretation of the astrological importance of the seven planets. Each one is minutely described in its ruling over human or other natural occurrences. To begin with Sabbetaï, "Saturn," which is mentioned first, "he rules over poverty, misery, illness, sickness and destruction ; over internal ailments, and over sin." In this fragmentary text, which belongs to the same category as our MS., no allusion is found either to the personal appearance of the planets viewed as heavenly bodies, nor are the ruling Powers or angels mentioned by name who move and guide the planets, and are the direct cause of the influence which they are said to exercise over human destiny. The text is evidently mutilated, as shown in my study on the version discovered and published by me in the "Chronicles of Jeraḥmeel." In this work we find a corporeal description of the planets, together with that of the influence which they exercise. The list begins (*ibid.*, chap. iv, parag. 5, p. 12 ff) also with Saturn. "He is appointed over the poor and needy, over women, over faintness and sickness, diseases of the body, and death.   His appearance is like that of an old man with a sickle in his hand."   We have thus here the description of the physical aspect of the planet.

The knowledge of these planets and their influence is much older in Hebrew literature.   In the introduction (Jerahmeel, p. lxi) I referred to the book Yeṣira (chap. iv, § 5 ff.), where the creation of the seven planets is explained in harmony with the fundamental theory of the " Book of Creation," viz., with the creation through the " Logos "—the spoken word, and how this operation was carried out in detail by the effects produced by each of the separate letters of the Alphabet.   In the commentary to this book by Sabbatai Donolo, who lived in the year 913, in Italy, a detailed list of the manifold influences which are exercised by these seven planets is given.   The order of the planets begins also with *Sabbatai* in the Book Yeṣira.   It is said to have been created on the first day of the week.   The author must have commenced his week with the Sabbath, and his order of the creation appears to be directly contradicting the biblical order of creation.   The Barayta of Samuel and Jerahmeel agree in this essential element with the Book Yeṣira. Either one is dependent on the other or both have borrowed from an older source.   This latter hypothesis seems to be the more correct one.   The author of the commentary to the same chapter of the Book Yeṣira, which goes under the name of Abraham ben David, knows the same tradition of the astrological influence of the seven planets, and he gives the fullest description, tallying in the main with that of the Barayta, Jerahmeel and Donnolo.   But in none of these occur the ruling angels.

In the commentary of Jehuda ben Barzillai of Barcelona, who lived at the beginning of the XIIth century (ed. Halberstamm, p. 247), in connection with the selfsame chapter of the Book Yeṣira, occurs then a list of angels who rule over the seven planets.   This list is absolutely identical with that of the rulers of the planets according the Chaldean wisdom of our MS.   We read there :—" These are the planets, Sun, Venus, Mercury, Moon, Saturn, Jupiter, and Mars, these are the seven rulers, the foundation of the world, corresponding to the seven hours (here follow a few words which are unintelligible, probably the names of hours).   Over them are appointed seven rulers, seven angels, to whit, Raphael the angel of the Sun, 'Anael the angel of Venus, Michael the ᴀngel of Mercury, Gabriel of the Moon, Qaphṣiel of Saturn, Ṣadqiel of Jupiter, and Samael of Mars." With the difference of one name only the same list occurs in the Book Raziel (ed. Amsterdam, fol. 17a). Here it is connected with the description of the astrological influence which each of these planets has on human destiny. The latter portion is directly copied from the Barayta of Samuel, following the original almost word for word. There can now be little doubt that the first portion containing the names of the angels, must have belonged originally also to the Barayta, but had been omitted in the mutilated text, preserved in one single MS., which has also since disappeared. The very same list of the seven tutelary angels occurs in our MS. for a second time, fol. 10b, where their seals are given.

Nowhere do we find any parallels to the images of these rulers, to their serving angels, or to the use to which they are put in practical magical purposes. The pentacles in the so-called "Key of Solomon" resemble these drawings only remotely. In some ancient calendars pictures of the seven planets are found, but they are reminiscences of Greek and Roman mythology. Mercury is drawn with the Caduceus, Saturn as an old man with a sickle, and so forth. More like those of our text are the drawings and pictures in the "Hoellenzwang" of Faust, ed. Schaible.

We must ascend to a much older tradition in order to trace the possible origin of this text. It pretends to be the exposition of the wisdom of the Chaldeans, and save for the Hebrew names of the angels, there is nothing specific Jewish in this text. The old Gnosis claimed Chaldean origin for its magical part. The Ophites especially utilised the old Chaldean astronomical and astrological notions for taumaturgical purposes. They drew the images of the Archons who ruled the seven planets. (v. W. Anz, Zur Frage nach Ursprung des Gnostizismus, Lpzig., 1897, p. 9 ff., and A. Dieterich, Abraxas, p. 44 ff.) Amulets with such images, and gems with similar incisions are the visible result of that symbolism, adopted and adapted according to their views by other Gnostic systems, such as that of Valentin, Basilides with his Hebdomas, and even Bardesanes, whose treatise "On the influence of the planets on the temperaments of nations" has been discovered and published by Cureton. Not without significance is the total omission of any allusion to the signs of the Zodiac, with which the planets have been invariably associated in all other astrological calculations.

In this text none of the extravagant interpretations or mystical applications of the seven planets are mentioned in connection with human salvation or with the soul before and after death, in fact none of the eschatological teachings of the Gnostic schools. It is all quite simple ; prominence is given to the magical powers alone inherent in the character of the angels drawn on tablets or on parchment, and in the invocations accompanying the operation. In how far this is due to Chaldean teaching or tradition pure and simple I am not in a position to state. A certain change from those Chaldean originals must at any rate have taken place. New names of angels have been substituted, all purely Hebrew, for the strange gods if taken over in their primitive form. But this change is quite natural, and in harmony with the tendencies of that very age, and but for it, the text itself might never have existed or would never have been preserved at all. The names of the angels are very transparent and offer few difficulties to the philologist. They have not yet assumed that curious and weird appearance as found in the Sword of Moses, in the Hebrew Hechaloth, in the Book Raziel, and in later magical writings and Amulets. They resemble the ancient forms and names known in Hebrew liturgy and liturgical poetry. A list of these has been compiled by Zunz (*Synagogale Poesie des Mittelalters*, p. 476–479). They occur also in most of the older qabbalistic collections (*cf.* the list of angels prepared by Mr. M. Schwab, *Vocabulaire de l'Angélologie*, Paris, 1897), differing by their simplicity from the complex and abstruse forms met with in the other works excerpted by Mr. Schwab.

It is curious to note, and a proof for the syncretistic origin of this text, that in one case the angel is described in the form of a woman. The influence of the notion that the regent of the sixth day is Venus, has been so strong as to cause the author to accept female angels in the heavenly hierarchy. It is a very strong proof for the non-Jewish origin of this text, as the conception of a female angel is contrary to Jewish notions.

One extremely interesting point in connection with the archaic character of this text is the clue it gives to a metaphorical expression often used in qabbalistic writings, but seldom clearly expressed. It is often stated that God, or the name of God, or of any of the chief powers is included in, and identical with, that of his serving or ministering angels. Save for the few exceptions where the one is bodily intercalated into the other, this expression has remained anything but clear.   In our text the very same expression occurs.   To each one of the chief angels of the day a number of angels is added as serving.   If we now examine these names we shall find that the first letters of the serving angels are the very letters of the name of the chief ruler.   They form an anagram of his name, and it is truly said that his name was included in theirs and their names in his.

The ruling powers of the day are angels, they are strictly separated from the planets, and not identified with them at all.   The planets are mentioned only to indicate the propitious hour for the writing of the amulets.

The reference to Enoch, identified from ancient times with Hermes, would make this treatise belong to the interminable list of " Hermetic " writings.   I consider it to be a reflex of the old Chaldeo-gnostic school which flourished so long in Palestine, and to belong in its primitive form to the third century.   The author of the " Book of Creation," as shown in my study on the " Shiur Komah," and the author of the " Barayta " in its fuller recension, must have drawn their astrological information from a similar source of which our text formed a part.   In later times the magical portions may have been allowed to drop out, as not quite in harmony with the teaching of Judaism.   They have been relegated to the domain of mysticism, which has preserved and protected many a doubtful product of ancient times.

The language of the text is throughout pure Hebrew.   In a few instances I think I can detect Arabic influence such as סיבין for סבין.   The *Scriptio plena ;* the form קלף בתול—a new masculine formation altogether—the use of שבכם and other peculiarities go to prove the antiquity of the language.   I do not pretend, however, to have said the last word on this " Chaldean Wisdom."

Translation.

THE WISDOM OF THE CHALDEANS.

This is the book used by the Chaldeans (which they composed) through their meditations and speculations in divine wisdom, and through the overflow of the spirit of prophecy upon them, by their strong adherence to their wisdom and to their mediations in the divine wisdom and their speculations concerning the spheres (planets) and the spirits that rule those spheres and move them. For in each sphere there is an angel that moves it. They investigated the nature of those angels and they found that they all partake of one nature, but that each one of them changes its nature in accordance with the changes in the appearance of the beings of the world. They further investigated whether each angel was fulfilling his message in person, and they found that the angels had servants who fulfilled those messages (tasks). And as the wisdom of man is greater than that of any other living being, they further investigated every subject, and they discovered the ways in which they could be used (or : discovered the things over which the angels were appointed). And from the time they used them, they (the Chaldeans) rejoiced mightily and they continued to search and to enquire, and they performed many deeds, and they wrote those books, and they made many books, but their successors did not understand how to study them until " Raziel" came and revealed the mysteries, and after him came the primitive Henoch. From that time on this science spread all over the world ; some understood it, others did not understand it. I pored over many books, and this is what I have gleaned concerning the seven angels of the week, and concerning the hours and their figures, and their position, and their use, and the manner in which one could make them serve one's purposes, and wherefore they are called by such names. These names are evolved out of the names of the rulers, as thou shalt see anon.*

II. The names are written over the heads of each of the angels for the different days. On the first day rules Raphael. His figure is like that of a man sitting on a throne with hands and feet outstretched. On his right hand serves Raḥabiel, on his left Phaniel, over his head Ariel, under his feet Lahabiel. Their use (work) is to cure all manner of disease, to preserve man from all wicked Shiddim and from all evil spirits which cause illness to man. If thou wishest to heal a man from enchantment, or from an evil spirit, or from folly (" madness "), or from any of the things mentioned, then draw the picture of a man on virgin parchment with both hands outstretched, under the right hand draw the image of a little man, and write on his shoulder Ariel ; at his feet draw the image of another man, but draw it with red ink, for this is an angel appointed over fire, and write on

* This passage corrupt in the original.

his shoulder (or, variant, on his forehead) Lahabiel, and under them the following conjuration : I conjure thee, Raphael, thou and thy servants who are called by thy name, and whose name is included in their names, viz., Raḥabiel, Phaniel, Ariel, Lahabiel, in the name of Azbuga, that thou healest so and so from all illness and all hurt and all evil spirit. Amen, Amen, Amen, Sela, Sela, Sela. If thou wishest to protect thyself from all evil, from every hurt and from wild beasts, make a drawing of all these angels on virgin parchment and carry it by thee, and no evil will happen to thee. Similarly, if thou wishest to protect a young babe from an evil spirit and from the host of Maḥalath, write these angels on a tablet of gold in Assyrian writing (Ashuri) and carry it by thee, and thou needs not fear any evil either from (for) a big man or a small child. It is of very great help. On the back of the tablet write the word *Mana*, for this is his sign (Sigil). It must be written during the hour of the Sun, in daytime and not at night. This is proven and sure.

III. On the second day rules Gabriel. This angel is like a man with horns. On each horn there is an angel in the likeness of a man. He also has ministering angels, as has been described above for the angel Raphael. His position is like unto a man with out-stretched hands. On his right hand serves Ga'ariel, on his left Kerubiel (var., Berukiel), on the right horn Raḥabibiel, on the left horn Ahariel, and at his foot serves Lahabiel. He helps to strengthen those that are imprisoned, further to conquer whatever it be, that thou wishest to conquer, be it in war or strife or in any other cause. Thou must then draw on a silver tablet the image of this angel as described. He has two horns, and his hands must be stretched out. Under his right arm draw the image of a little man and write on his shoulder Ga'ariel, under his left arm draw the figure of a little man, and write on his shoulder Kerubiel, on the horn (of the right side ?)* Ioel (?) Raḥabibiel, and on the left horn draw the figure of a little man attached to the horn. Write on the forehead or on the shoulder Ioel. On the back of it draw the image of a little man and write on his forehead Ahabiel, at his feet draw the figure of a little man, this is the angel of fire, and write on his shoulder Lahabiel. Carry this by thee and no one will be able to hurt thee from small to great, and thou wilt win in every strife and

---

* In the original there is some confusion, Ioel being mentioned twice, and instead of "right side" we find the word "shoulder."

battle. If thou placest this tablet among thy wares thou wilt soon sell them, and if thou writest these names of angels on parchment and carriest them by thee, they will be very good (useful) to thee. They must be written with green (Crocus) ink. On the back of the tablet thou must write . . . . .* for this is his sign (Sigil) and it must be written in the sight of the Moon.

IV. On the third day rules Samael. He is in the likeness of a man with outstretched hands. He has angels that serve him, as the aforesaid two angels, but he has no horns, and their position is as follows: on his right hand serves Sahariel, on his left Mahariel, behind him Ahzaniel, and at his feet Lahabiel. Their work is to destroy, to annihilate, to kill and to perform all manner of evil If thou wishest to be able to cut with a knife or sword better than any other man, make thee an apple of hard iron and write on it: "In the name of Samael and his servants," and make out of it a knife or a sword, and then thou wilt be able to cut whatever thou wishest and much easier than any other man. If thou wishest to win in any battle into which thou art entering, take a tablet of silver or of copper or iron and draw on it the figure of . . . . . . ,† under his right arm draw the figure of a little man and write on his forehead Sahariel, under his left arm draw the figure of a little man and write on his forehead Mahariel, behind him draw the figure of a little man and write on his forehead Ahzaniel, and under his feet draw the figure of a little man and write on his forehead Lahabiel. And make the drawing of a sword (placed) in the hand of the figure called Samael, and on that sword write the names of the following angels: Ḥatkiel, Imiel, Lahabiel and Hashmeriel, and in the other hand a human head which he is intending to cut off (or, in the act of cutting off). On the back of the plate write "Dal Dam," for this is his Sigil. And it must be written in the hour (time) of Maadim (Mars). If thou wishest to destroy a house, a town, a road or a village, write "Samael and his servants," with menstrual blood on the day of Mars on the garment of a hanged man (?), place it in the mouth of a frog and bury it in the room in which no man will dwell, and it will finally be destroyed. Thou must however stop the mouth of the frog with a little wax and write on the wax, "Dal Dam," and thus shalt thou act in every place wherever thou wishest. If thou

* The Sigil is omitted in the MS.
† Omitted in the original, evidently Samael.

wishest to kill a man, write, "Samael and his servants" on the garment of that person with the blood of a snake and place it in the mouth of a puppy and close the mouth of that dog with red wax, on which thou hast written "Dal Dam," and bury it at the parting (or crossing) of ways. That man is sure to die within sixty days, unless he go away from that place before the end that time.

V. On the fourth day rules Michael. He is like unto a man holding a horn in his hand and his hands are stretched out. On his right hand serves Ma'asael, on his left serves Iaḥtemiel; on that horn stands an angel called Kokabiel, behind him serves A'albiel, and at his feet Lahabiel. The benefit conferred (obtained) by these angels is to grant knowledge and wisdom to man. If thou wishest to be served by these angels, take a piece of pure (good) silver or lead and draw on it the image of a man with outstretched hands. Draw under his right arm the image of a little man, and write on his shoulder Iaḥtemiel, over his head draw the figure of a horn, and on that horn the image of a man holding that horn, and write on his forehead or shoulder Kokabiel, and under his feet draw the image of a little man, with red ink, for he is the angel of fire, and write on his forehead, Lahabiel; and this plate is very useful for gaining knowledge and wisdom and understanding. If a woman has difficulties in childbirth, place this tablet on her chest and she will soon be delivered of the child. If a man is ill, place this tablet on him whilst he is asleep. If he sleeps on quietly and does not wake, it is a sign for life, but if he wakes up quickly, know that it is a sign of death. If thou wishest to know whether a man is enchanted (charmed) or not, write the name of Michael and his servants on an egg with saffron (yellow), and place it under the bed on which he sleeps. If on the morning thou breakest it it is boiled *and there is a drop of blood in it, then it is a sure sign that he is under a spell. If thou wishest to make a child learn more than any other, then wash this tablet on every first night (of the month or week?) with white wine, then take the tablet in the right hand and turning towards sunrise utter the following conjuration : "I conjure thee, Michael, thou and thy servants who are called by thy name and whose name is included in theirs, in the name Ṭamaqashia, that thou givest me a heart to know all that I have been taught, and that I

---

* The original is here somewhat doubtful. It may mean : boil it, break it, and find, etc.

continue to learn, to hear and to understand all that I shall be taught in future. Open my heart to study, and my eyes to see, and my hands to write. And my ears to listen." He must then drink of tne wine and eat warm (fresh) bread with honey, and he will become wiser than any other man. He must write on the back of the tablet this name *Abg*, which must be done in the hour (time) of Kokab (Mercury).

VI. On the fifth day rules Ṣadqiel. This angel is in the likeness of a man with two horns, on one of these horns there is the likeness of a man. And he also has serving angels as the aforementioned angels. Their position is as follows. The angel who is in the likeness of man has the hands outstretched; on the right hand serves Ṣuriel, on the left Dahabiel. He has two horns, and serves Ia'aṣiel*; behind him serves (Apar) Aparsiel, and at his feet Lahabiel. These angels grant grace and favour to all those who carry them. If thou wishest to use them, make a tablet of silver or lead, and draw on it the image of a little man, and write on his shoulder Ṣuriel; draw then under his left hand the image of a little man, and write on his shoulder Dahabiel; then make on his head two horns, on the right horn draw the image of a little man holding fast to it, and write on his shoulder Qedoshiel, similarly do on the left horn, and write on his forehead Ia'asiel. Behind him draw the image of a little man, and write on his forehead Aparsiel, and under his feet a little man, and write on his forehead Lahabiel, written with red ink. The use of this drawing will be that whoever carries it about him will find favour and grace in the eyes of man and prince, and he will obtain all that he wishes. If he happens to fall in with a host of prisoners (or who is taken a prisoner),† he will not be bound (made a slave), and everyone will render homage to him. On the back of the plate write *Ili*, for this is his Sigil. If thou placest this tablet in a place where there are few persons, they quickly will multiply and become numerous, for they will come from every part to live there. If thou wishest to test (?) it, put it among bees and they will multiply and become numerous. Whoever carries it about him, no man will be able to prevail against him. It must be written at the hour of Ṣedeq (Jupiter). If thou placest the tablet on the

---

* "On one serves Qedoshiel," as mentioned below, is omitted here in the original part; the omitted words seem to have been added later on, on the margin, but they are now almost illegible.

† Not quite clear in the original.

seat of the ruler (Hegemon) or carriest it about thee every day, thou wilt prosper in greatness, and if thou placest it on the seat of a workman, he will get very much work.

VII. On the sixth day rules 'Anael. He is appointed on all manner of love. This ruler is in the likeness of a woman. She has in one hand a mirror in which she beholds herself, and in the other a comb with which she is combing her head. She, like unto other angels, has serving angels ; she also holds her hands outstretched. On her right arm serves an angel whose name is 'Arbiel, on the left one called Niniel, over her head one whose name is Lahabiel, and at her feet one called Ahabiel. If thou wishest to use them, make a tablet of fine silver, draw upon it the likeness of a woman in the name of the woman thou likest, then write on her shoulder her name and the name of her mother, and the name of the one who loves (desires) her, and that of his mother, and draw her hands outstretched. Draw then under her right arm the figure of a nice young man, and write on his shoulder 'Arbiel, under her left arm draw the image of another young man and write on his forehead Niniel, behind her draw the image of a man with red ink and write on his shoulder Lahabiel. The use of this picture of the woman on the tablet is that it gains for thee the love of that man or woman whom thou desirest, with a strong and unbreakable love. Thou hast only to touch this tablet and they will run after thee, especially that woman whose name thou hast written on the tablet. And thou must utter the following conjuration :—" I conjure thee, 'Anael, thou and thy servants who are called by thy name, and whose name is included in theirs, viz :—'Arbiel, Niniel, Ahabiel and Lahabiel, in the name of *Uriel*, with the countenance flaming all round, inflame so-and-so with my love and with my strong affection, and may her (Mazal) destiny, be united with mine, in the same manner as Adam was united to Eve. May she not have any chance to eat or to drink, or to sleep, or to stand, or to sit, before she is in love with me . . . . (?)* and until she comes to me and fulfils all my wishes and desires." Then warm the tablet on the fire and thou wilt see marvellous things. If the person in question is a man, then say : "That he may fulfil my wish," viz., this or that thing. On the back of the tablet write *Sit,* for this is his Sigil, and write it in the hour of Nogah (Venus). It is also somewhat in the figure of Ṣedeq† (or:

* Here is an unintelligible word in the original.
† Doubtful in the original.

write it also sometimes in the hour of Ṣedeq). And they say that if the image is drawn with the "thunderstone" and placed on a closed door, the door is sure to open by itself.

VII. On the seventh day rules Qaphṣiel. This angel is of bad augury, for he is appointed only over evil. He is in the likeness of a man in mourning, and has two horns, and angel servants as the other angels aforementioned. On his right hand serves Qubiel, on his left Phaṣhiel, on the right horn Ṣafriel, on the left horn Iaḥsiel, behind him stands Aḥiel, and at his feet Lahabiel. If thou wishest to make use of them to lower a man from his high position, make a tablet of tin and draw on it the likeness of an old man with outstretched hands; under his right hand draw the image of a little man, and write on his forehead Qubiel; on the left, the image of a man crying, and write on his shoulder Phaṣhiel; on the right horn, the image of a man flying on two wings, and write on his shoulder, or between his sides, or on his forehead, Ṣafriel; and on the left horn draw another man with wings outstretched flying, and the wings of the one must be touching the wings of the other, and write on his forehead, or on his shoulder, or on his sides, Iaḥsiel, and behind him draw the figure of a man with open wings, flying, with his hands on his forehead, and write on his forehead Aḥsiel, and at his feet draw with red ink the figure of a man, and write on his shoulder Lahabiel. The use of this tablet is that if thou placest it on the seat of a mighty man, or a king, or a priest, he will fall from his position, and if thou puttest it in a place where many people are assembled, they will scatter and go away from that spot. If thou placest it in a spot where they are building a town, or a tower, it will be destroyed. If thou placest it in hives, the bees will flee from there. Write the name Qaphṣiel, and those of his angels, on pure parchment, and place it in a reed cane with seven knots, and utter the following conjuration whilst thou ridest upon that cane: "I conjure thee, Qaphṣiel, and thy host, in the name of the most holy (the three times holy), guide me (carry me) to that and that place without hurt or harm." They say that a man will ride in one day the distance of an hundred days' travelling. Write and draw the images as described above and the name of a man and of his mother, and place it in anything thou likest (in whatever it may be), and tie it unto the wings of a dove, or of a bird of the desert, and conjure: "I conjure thee, Qaphṣiel, and thy whole host, that thou drivest away so and so, that he be wandering about, to and fro, in the same manner as the Lord

drove Cain away, to be wandering to and fro, so shall so and so be ;
he shall find no rest to the sole of his feet." He is then to let the bird
fly.   That man will be wandering to and fro without rest and without ceasing.   If thou can'st not find a bird, take a pot (bowl) and
place into it all that thou would'st have bound round the wing of the
bird, stop the orifice (mouth) of the pot with pitch, so that water
should not get into it,* and throw it into the river.   As long as the
pot is swimming on the river, so long will that man be wandering
about, until it breaks or water gets into it, or it sinks.   It must be
written in the hour of Shabbetai (Saturn).   On the back of the
tablet, or the parchment, write *Ani*, for this is his Sigil.

* In the original somewhat corrupted.

(*End.*)

ART. VII.—*The Logos Ebraikos in the Magical Papyrus of Paris, and the Book of Enoch.* By M. GASTER.

THE scholars who have studied hitherto the Greek magical papyri, such as Parthey, Wessely, Dieterich, and others, have either concentrated their attention upon the Greek forms contained in these documents, or have tried to find a connecting link between these books, notably between the weird notions contained therein and Greek and Egyptian parallels. Greek mysteries have been adduced in order to explain some of the curious notions prevailing in these papyri. Egypt had to serve for explaining the origin of some of the mystical names or angels mentioned therein. From time to time allusion has been made to so-called Cabalistic parallels, without any clear proof being furnished as to the dependence of one upon the other. But one branch of literature has been entirely neglected, which ought to have attracted attention in the first place, namely, the apocryphal and pseudo-epigraphic literature, which is the only truly contemporary literature. Similarity in tendency, claim of great antiquity, and open or covert allusions to heavenly mysteries show close affinities of no mean order. The authors in one case would be the very persons to avail themselves of the information furnished by the other. The world in which the writers of the apocryphal literature move has not been very much different from that in which the writers and speculators in this mystical lore, preserved in the papyri, have lived. And one would have thought that the material offered by the apocryphal literature would have been the first to be utilized for the elucidation of some of the problems connected with these magical papyri. Whatever the result, it would have been of extreme value.

The proof negative or positive of the acquaintance with, or ignorance of, the apocalyptic and pseudo - epigraphic literature by the writers of these papyri and of these incantations would be of invaluable service from every point of view. It would show, in the first instance, the medium in which each of them lived, the sources of their inspirations. Any borrowing or close connection between these writings would throw a flood of light on their origin, and it would also, to a certain extent, settle the date of their composition. No one denies that the intimate blending and mixing of the materials found in Egypt and Palestine had been going on for centuries, but the ingredients which formed these mixtures have as yet not been sufficiently sifted and explained. The following is to be the first attempt towards that process of sifting and elucidation.

Among the various portions that make up the papyrus Paris, No. 3,009, there is one which is called specially the "Hebrew Logos." A. Dieterich has reprinted it in his "Abraxas" (Leipzig, 1891, pp. 138–141), correcting and amending the first edition by Wessely, and adding critical footnotes and references to the passages in the Bible upon which that Logos seems to rest. He uses this publication for the purpose of showing that an Orphic-Jewish community, to which he ascribes that Logos, had taken part in enriching the spiritual property of the Gnostic associations which were beginning then to be established. From his notes, and from the whole tenour of his book, it is evident that he believes this and similar compositions to be the result of direct borrowing from the Bible and of an artificial piecing together of scattered verses, in order to make up this 'conjuration.' Before proceeding further, I prefer to now give a translation of my own of this text, corrected and amended according to my views, as shown in the notes appended to the translation.

The Greek text of the papyri is, as a rule, full of barbarisms; it abounds in mistakes, due either to the copyists or to the compilers. In the case of our text some mistakes may be due to wrong translation, if, as I have reason to believe, the original were Hebrew. Some are also due to the difficulties which confront the decipherer of these relics of ancient times. Want of interpunction and of marks of division make the reader run one text into the following. The meaning of some sentences is thus obscured, and what is directed against the demon to be exorcised reads in the present text as if it were addressed to God, in whose name the conjurer is to speak and whose assistance he is to invoke. I have therefore read the text in the light of similar conjurations, and in spite of apparent contradiction to the Greek text.

An Hebrew Logos.[1]

"An approved recipe of Pibekeus against those possessed of a demon. Take unripe olives and mastyx-plant and lotos and boil it together with wild (orig. 'colourless') marjoram, saying[2] . . . . (5) 'Go out of N. N.' Take then a tin-plate and write upon it this formula of protection. Iaobraothioth, etc., and tie (wind) it upon (round) the person that is affrighted and stands in awe of any (all the) demons. (10) Place thyself before the possessed and conjure. 'I conjure (thee in the name) of the God of the Hebrews, IAOO, Iabaie,[3] etc., who appeared in the flame (15), who expands in the midst of the fields[4] and snow and mist. May his terrifying angel descend and drive this spirit away which is fluttering around this creature, whom God has created in His holy Paradise, for I pray to thee Holy God upon AMMON IPSENTANHO. I conjure thee with the power (or 'energy') of (20)[2] . . . . I conjure thee with him who has shown himself to Israel in a column of fire and smoke daily and has delivered the people from the work[5] of Pharaoh, and has inflicted upon (25) Pharaoh the 10 plagues for his disobedience. I conjure thee, whatever spirit or

---

[1] The numbers are the lines of the Greek text in Papyrus Paris.
[2] A string of mystical names.
[3] Greek Ιησου is impossible if the text is of the second century B.C.
[4] Is this a wrong translation of ברד, 'hail,' read as בר, or of מדבר?
[5] Again wrong translation of עֲבוֹדַת = עֲבֹדוּת, 'slavery' = 'work'?

demon thou mayest be, speak, for I conjure thee with the
seal which Solomon placed upon the mouth of Jeremia, and
he spake.   In like manner speak thou (30), whoever thou
mayest be, in heaven or from the air, upon the earth or from
under the earth or inside the earth, (demon) of the Jebusites,
Gergesites, and Feresites.   Speak, whoever thou mayest be.
For I conjure thee with the light-giving, all-powerful God,
who knows what is in the heart of every living, (35) who has
formed the human race out of dust, who brings forth from
the dark (his hosts) (v. Ies. xl, 25), and thickens the
clouds, and waters the earth and blesses her fruit; whom all
heavenly powers praise and the Archangels of the Angels.
I conjure thee with the great God Sabaoth, before whom the
river Jordan withdrew (40) and turned backwards, and the
Red Sea let Israel pass—standing still—where there was
no road.   I conjure thee with Him who has taught 140
languages and has spread them through his command.
I conjure thee with Him who has struck the proud giants
(45) with His lightning, whom the heaven of heavens and
the winged (lit. 'the wings of') cherubs praise.   I conjure
thee with Him who has made the sand to be as a wall of
mountains around the sea, and has bound it not to pass
beyond it—and the sea obeyed.   So obey also thou (50) all
manner of a demon, for I conjure thee with Him who moves
the four winds from the four corners,[1] who is seen in the
heavens, in the sea, and in the clouds, who is light-giving,
all-powerful.   I conjure thee with the holy name . . . .
(55) of the One who dwells in the pure Jerusalem, where
the inextinguishable fire is ever burning, before whom the
fiery Gehenna trembles, and the flames roar, and the iron
(melts), and (before whom) each mountain is terrified in its
foundation.   I conjure thee all manner of a demon with Him
who rules over the earth and shakes its foundations (60) and
has created everything out of nought.   I conjure thee!'

   "The man who utters this conjuration must not eat
swine's flesh, and every demon and spirit will obey him.

   [1] The Greek text has here instead: "holy Aeons," evidently a corruption from
" four corners."

The conjurer must blow from the lower extremities upwards (65) until he reaches the face, and the demon will be driven out.

"Keep clean and pure, for this conjuration (*logos*) is Hebrew (*ebraikos*), and is preserved by pure men."

This Logos, resting on biblical passages and full of biblical reminiscences, is undoubtedly Hebrew, and is translated from a Hebrew text, as suggested by the footnotes, in which I have corrected difficult passages by means of Hebrew. It belongs, according to Dieterich (p. 143), to the second century B.C. The allusion to the Giants reminds him of the fragments of Eupolemos, who identifies them with people who lived in ancient Babylon, and who had been destroyed by the Gods in consequence of their wickedness. From the final sentence, where the "pure men" are mentioned, he concludes that the author of this Logos must have been a member of the old sect of the Essenes or Therapeuts who lived in Egypt. According to Dieterich they drew their inspiration from the Orphic mysteries. But these cannot account for the purely Hebrew origin of this Logos. It is now an extremely curious coincidence, not noticed by D. or by anyone else hitherto, that an absolutely identical conjuration is found in the apocryphal book of Enoch.

We read there [1] (Book of Enoch, chapter lxix, v. 3)—"And these are the chiefs of their angels and the names of the chief ones over a hundred and over fifty and over ten. (4) The name of the first, Jequn, that is, the one who led astray all the children of the angels, and brought them down to the earth and led them astray through the daughters of men. (5) And the second is called Asbeel: he imparted to the children of the holy angels the evil counsel, and led them astray so that they defiled their bodies with the daughters of men. (6) And the third is called Gadreel: he it is who taught the children of men

---

[1] I am following entirely the translation of Charles, though in some passages a slight alteration is suggested.

all the blows of death, and he led astray Eve, and showed
to the sons of men the weapons of death and the coat of
mail, and the shield, and the sword for battle, and all the
weapons of death to the children of men. (7) And from
his hand they have proceeded over those who dwell on the
earth from that hour for evermore. (8) And the fourth
is called Penemue : he taught the children of men the
bitter and the sweet, and taught them all the secrets of
their wisdom. (9) And he instructed mankind in writing
with ink and paper, and thereby many sinned from
eternity to eternity and until this day. (10) For it was
not intended when man was created (lit. 'men are not
created to the end') that he should give confirmation to
his good faith with pen and ink in such wise. (11) For
man was created exactly like the angels to the intent that
he should continue righteous and pure, and death, which
destroys everything, could not have taken hold of him,
but through this their knowledge they are perishing, and
through this power (of knowledge) it (death) is consuming
me. (12) And the fifth is called Kasdeja: he has taught
the children of men all the wicked smitings of spirits and
demons, and the smitings of the embryo and the babe,
that it may pass away, and the smitings of the soul, the
bites of the serpent, and the smitings which befall at noon,
the son of the serpent named Tabe't. (13) And this is the
number of Kesbeel, who showed the head (or 'power') of the
Oath to the holy ones when he dwelt high above in glory,
and its (his) name is Beqa. (14) And this angel requested
Michael to show him the hidden Name, that they might
mention it in the Oath, so that those who revealed all that
was hidden to the children of men might quake before that
name and oath. (15) And this is the power of that Oath,
for it is powerful and strong, and he placed this Oath *Akae*
in the hand of Michael (or 'Akae placed,' etc.). (16) And
these are the secrets (mysterious effects) of this oath : the
heaven was made strong through the oath, and was
suspended before the world was created and for ever. (17)
And through it the earth was founded upon the water,

and from the secret recesses of the mountains come beautiful waters from the creation of the world unto eternity. (18) And through that oath the sea was created, and as (or 'at') its foundation He laid for it the sand against the time of (its) anger, and it dare not pass beyond it from the creation of the world unto eternity. (19) And through that oath are the depths made fast, and abide and stir not from their place from eternity to eternity. (20) And through that oath the sun and moon complete their course, and deviate not from the path prescribed to them from eternity to eternity. (21) And through that oath the stars complete their course, and he calls them by their names, and they answer him from eternity to eternity. (22) And in like manner the spirits of the water, and the winds, and of all the zephyrs, and the paths of all the bands of the spirits. (23) And in it (or 'through it')[1] are preserved the voices of the thunder and the light of the lightnings, and in it (through it)[1] are preserved the chambers of the hail and of the hoar-frost, and the chambers of the mist and the chambers of the rain and the dew. (24) And all these believe and give thanks before the Lord of Spirits and glorify (Him) with all power, and their food is nothing save thanksgiving : they thank and glorify and extol the name of the Lord of Spirits for ever and ever. (25) And this Oath is mighty over them, and through it they are preserved, and their paths are preserved, and their course is not destroyed."

The situation, as it presents itself here, is clearly, first, a description of the angels or satans who are believed to be the primary cause of illness and disease. In connection with this fact, and through the mentioning of it, the author or the copyist of that curious text is induced to add the Oath, that is, to add at the same time the means for averting the illness caused by these evil spirits. This part of the book of Enoch is considered to belong to, if possible, an

---

[1] Cf. Hebrew בה.

older period than the rest of the book. It is called
a Noachic fragment, belonging originally to an apocalypse
of Noah. Accordingly, being written by a man who lived
before the Flood, Noah or Enoch could not mention any
event that happened in Jewish history after the Flood. The
'oath' is probably the mysterious word by which the world
was created and is maintained. The name Akae is the
mystical seal or sigle which stands for the ineffable name of
God, the knowledge and possession of which give to man
the power of acting almost like one of the superior beings.[1]
The description of the effect of that great name follows
here closely the order of the Biblical creation of the world.
This description is so close a parallel to the corresponding
portion of the Greek Logos that it helps us to understand
the passage of the four winds, not quite clearly expressed,
and which I had translated in the same manner before
having discovered the passage in the book of Enoch. In
the Greek text we find, however, not only the same
passages as in Enoch, but many more incidents, added
from the later history of the Jews, especially portions
dealing with the miracles of the going out of Egypt.
Solomon is mentioned, and the ancient nations inhabiting
Palestine before the Jews occupied it are connected somehow
with the demons conjured away.

There can be no doubt as to which of the two oaths or
conjurations is the older, or which is borrowed from the
other. The primitive character seems to be fully retained
in the book of Enoch. The narrative flows there in
regular sequence, from the creation of the heavens to that
of the other bodies. Not so in the Greek text. Here
the order of things is quite irregular. First, the going
out of Egypt is mentioned, then the creation of man,
then the creation of the world, and lastly allusion is made
to the heavenly spheres, to Gehenna, and to the heavenly
Jerusalem—if this last passage be at all correctly preserved
in the Greek. It is evident that the author of this magical

---

[1] If read Aïa it resembles absolutely the transliteration of the Hebrew
Tetragramaton as preserved by Theodoret (Quaest. xv ad Exod. vi) ('Aïa = אהיה).

formula in the Greek papyrus has had access to the book
of Enoch, for he borrowed even the expressions. In taking
over the Oath from the book of Enoch, adapting and
probably also translating it, he undoubtedly changed the
names of the satans or angels mentioned in that book, and
substituted for them other names of a barbarous sound,
viz., those of the nations which belonged to a prehistoric
period and known as worshippers of idols or demons. It
is not impossible that the author of the book of Enoch, as
well as the author of the conjuration, might have had
access to a much older text, which each of them adapted
according to his own special requirements, as it looks almost
like an interpolation in "Enoch"; but the change of those
names of angels in the Greek text goes a long way to
prove the author of the magical formula having borrowed
it directly from "Enoch." He must have belonged to that
class of people for whom the book of Enoch was written,
and who looked upon it as an ancient source of information.
He was probably an Essene living in Palestine; for it is
unlikely that already in the middle of the second century
B.C. this portion of the book of Enoch, or any portion of
it, should have been translated into Greek and accessible
to people living outside of Palestine. But however it
may be, it is a remarkable coincidence, and opens up
a new view in the study of the magical papyri and their
immediate sources. The connection between them and
the Jewish pseudo-epigraphical, notably mystical, literature,
must have been much closer than has hitherto been
anticipated. The one throws light upon the other, and
they enlarge our conceptions of the literary and practical
activity of those sects, of which so many contradictory
statements have come down to us. It is clear that the
authors and readers of the pseudo-epigraphical books were
also the authors and users of the mystical and magical
writings. They thus translated their speculations into
thaumaturgical practices

A NOTE ON "A HEBREW AMULET."

By M. Gaster.

Reprinted from the "Proceedings of the Society of Biblical Archaeology,"
May, 1910.

In the *Proceedings* for March (pp. 125–126) Mr. E. J. PILCHER
has published the facsimile of the obverse of a metal amulet with
a Hebrew inscription, and has offered a tentative reading and
translation.

OBVERSE.   REVERSE.

In the following pages I give new readings, on which are based
the new translation and added Notes which follow.

The larger portion of the amulet consists of abbreviations,
which must be filled up, and of cabalistical allusions, which make
the deciphering of such an amulet a somewhat difficult operation.
Mr. PILCHER has taken these abbreviations, consisting mostly of a
combination of the initial letters, and grouped them together as so
many Hebrew words, which he endeavoured to translate. I have
dissolved the groups, supplied all the words that are missing, and
added in brackets all the letters belonging to the initials which alone
are recorded in the amulet. In the Notes I explain the origin of
these words, and the reason why they have been used in the amulet.

It will be seen that my rendering gives to the amulet a totally
different meaning to that given by Mr. PILCHER's translation.

I think I have elucidated all the obscure points, and that the readings which I have substituted for those given by Mr. PILCHER will be found justified by a new examination of the original.

A

OBVERSE

1 ב(שם) י(הוה) א(להי) י(שראל) נ(עשה) ו(נצליח)

2 א(נא) ב(כח) ג(דולת) א(להים) י(הוה) צ(באות) א(להי) י(שראל)

3 ב(שם) מ(לאכי) א(להי) י(שראל) מ(שביע) אני) ע(ליכון) כל

4 מיני לילין וללתי

5 ושידין ושידתין

6 בכח הישם הקדוש

7 ק(בל) ר(נת) ע(מך) ש(גבם) ט(הרם) נ(ורא) כ(לול) (עם)

8 מקורו יהוה (שלא)

B

REVERSE

1 תכנסו לישום

2 מקום אשר יהיה

3 בו נ(א) ג(בור) ד(ורשי) לא תגעו

4 בו כלל ולא יקרב ב(כח)

5 השם הקדוש י(מינך) ת(תיר) צ(רורה)

6 י(חודך) כ(בבת) ש(מרם) הוא כלול עם

7 מקורו אדני ועם

8 שם בו ש(ועתנו) ק(בל) ו(ישמע) צ(עקתנו) י(ודע) ת(עלומות)

9 יהוה י(שמור) צ(אתך) ו(בואך)   מ(עתה) ו(עד)
    ע(ולם) א(מן) ס(לה)

10 ... יהוהפגיאו ?

TRANSLATION

A

OBVERSE

1. In the name of the Lord God of Israel we shall do and prosper.

----

2. "I beseech thee by the power of the greatness" of God, the Lord of Hosts, the God of Israel.

3. In the name of the angels of the God (of Israel) I conjure you all

4. kinds of Lilin, male and female,

5. and Demons, male and female

6. by the power of the holy Name,

7. "Accept the prayer of thy people, exalt them, purify them, O
    Thou who art tremendous," combined with
8. its root YHVH, that they do not

B

REVERSE

1. enter to any
2. place where there be
3. in it "O mighty one, those who beseech thee," nor shall touch
4. it at all, nor hurt by the power of
5. the holy Name "thy right hand shall loosen the bondage."
6. "Thy single ones, like the apple of thine eye, guard them,"
    combined with
7. its root (source) ADNI, and with
8. the name of 26 (letters) (the tetragrammaton) "Accept our entreaty
    and hear our cry, Lord who knowest the hidden things."
9. "May the Lord preserve thy going out and thy coming in from
    now and evermore." Amen. Selah.

The last line is hopeless.

This amulet is evidently modern, and made by a man who
reduced a larger formula so as to fit the space of the tablet. He
retained, therefore, in a rudimentary form, only the principal elements
usually found in the amulets written on paper or parchment.

These are : a short invocation to the God, Lord of Hosts, the
God of Israel, then to the angels, the intermediaries and messengers.
Then follows the conjuration, reduced here to a few words, and instead
of a whole string of demons, only two kinds are mentioned. These
are to be rendered powerless by means of mysterious names ; and
the conjuration finishes with a Biblical verse. There is nothing in it
of the "habitation of God," nor any "crushing of Satan," nor any of
the curious details found in the amulet, through a natural misconception of its true character.

The Title-line is often found in old amulets, as read by me.

Line 2. Invocation for the purpose of frightening the evil demons
away by means of the name of God and of his angels. Then follows
l. 3, the conjuration. In ll. 2 and 7, the holy Name is found in
the so-called mystical prayer ascribed to Nehunya, the son of Kanah.
The initial letters of part of this prayer (*cf.* M. GASTER, *The Book
of Prayer according to the Rites of the Spanish and Portuguese Jews*,
Vol. I, p. 11. London : 1901) have been introduced here into this

amulet as representing the mystical all-powerful Name of God, and
they occur in A, ll. 2 and 7, and B, ll. 3, 5, 6, 8. They occur
in a large number of amulets from the thirteenth century onwards, in
a bewildering multitude of permutations and combinations. The
prayer itself, consisting of seven verses, is much older, and has
enjoyed a great reputation. It had been endowed with a deep
mystical significance, for it had been contended that the initial
letters were, in truth, representatives of the ineffable wonder-working
mysterious Name of God. By specific calculations and combinations,
cabalists have sought to establish that identification. We find it
here expressed in the term used, A, l. 8, and B, l. 7, by the word
מקורו, meaning "its source," or "its root," not מקום, "place," as
read by Mr. PILCHER. It means that in those letters, used here
for the amulet and borrowed from the prayer, was found involved
the mystical name YHVH. For the specific purpose of obtaining
protection against Lilith and Demons, the writer of the amulet is
careful to add כליל; *i.e.*, combined, enclosed, involved' in those
letters is "The all-powerful Name of God," which is to drive the
evil spirits away.

In the translation the quotations from the prayer are given in
"quotes," to mark them off. They have been selected somewhat
haphazard by the writer of the amulet. He has used verses I, II,
III and VII, omitting the intermediary three verses.

In lines 2–3, A, the dots between the letters may be mere stops,
or they may be standing for the letter Yod (י) as the writing is very
clumsy. I have given the alternative reading also in the translation,
placing the word corresponding with eventual י in brackets.

Line 8. The "root," or "source" of the preceding group of letters,
i.e., the corresponding divine name is here YHVH. In l. 7, B, the
corresponding divine name is ADNI, but then it is supplemented
by the name whose numerical value is 26, which is again the tetragrammaton YHVH.

At the end of A, l. 8, I filled up the lacuna by the indispensable
word, שלא, "that they may not." On this word the whole intent
and purpose of the amulet hinges.

B, l. 4. The last word, בכח, "by the *Power*," had to be
supplemented, being identical with A, ll. 4 and 6.

L. 9. The missing letters at the beginning of the line could only
be יהוה, as the rest is the last verse of Psalm cxxi, concluding with
the usual Amen. Selah.

A GNOSTIC FRAGMENT FROM THE ZOHAR: THE RESURRECTION OF THE DEAD.

M. GASTER, Ph.D.

THE title which I have given to this fragment requires some explanation. The word Gnosticism has assumed a very wide application; almost every sect which did not conform strictly to the tenets of the orthodox Church of the first centuries, which used mystical or allegorical terms and evolved an independent system of cosmology, eschatology and soteriology, was indiscriminately described as Gnostic. The persecution of the sects was so ruthless that save for a few texts preserved in Coptic translations, scarcely any remnant has remained of a literature which must have been very rich, and even these have been greatly manipulated and modified; our knowledge of Gnostics and Gnosticism rests, therefore, considerably on the quotations found in the Patristic literature. To what extent it has been distorted can only be guessed, but that it is not a fair representation of these old systems can be safely assumed.

Yet in spite of all the drawbacks and the fragmentary and often unreliable information, it is apparent that all these systems have certain points in common. Modern scholars have brought to bear upon the investigation of these ancient remnants sound judgment and unbiassed appreciation. It is not here the place to refer to the huge literature which has arisen since the time of Baur down to Bousset and Cumont. The latter have, each in their several ways, attempted to sum up the leading principles which these Gnostic systems, including Mithraism, have in common. But if our investigation should be more fruitful, the Manichæan as well as the Mandæan doctrines must be drawn within the circle of our research. This last-mentioned is of the utmost importance and I incline to the belief expressed by Lidzbarski, Reitzenstein and Scheftelowitz, that of all the various systems, and especially in their relation to the so-called Iranian and Babylonian sources, the Mandæan has preserved in a purer form the oldest system of Gnosticism. Moreover, as will be mentioned anon, it took its rise neither in Egypt nor in Babylon but on the soil of Palestine, and was intimately connected with the movement whose outstanding protagonist was John the Baptist. It is, therefore, absolutely necessary to enlarge the field covered by the name of Gnosticism. So far the fundamental principle was believed to be the existence of the Adam Kadmon, the Protoplastes, the progenitor of the human race; but to a far higher degree has the centre of the movement to be found in the history of the soul. Not only was its origin to be disclosed or discovered, but still more so what happened to it after its departure from the body.

It is sufficiently well known that this Gnostic movement arose at a time of great spiritual upheaval. Unrest and doubt had seized upon the world, and a yearning had grown stronger and stronger to escape the fear of death. It may have been a morbid sentiment, but it was a sign of the decay of an ancient

civilization, which offered no satisfaction and no
stability to the mind and heart of man. The people
were anxious to obtain a solution of the problem and
the means by which to escape the terrible consequences
of complete annihilation. At the same time a moral
principle underlay this movement, or rather a sense of
justice, seeing that so many suffered innocently whilst
others prospered in wickedness and sin. The people
had lost their moral balance and it was to be adjusted
by the doctrine of punishment and reward meted out
to the soul after death. They wanted some assurance
to that effect and, if possible, to attain a glimpse of that
bliss in this world. The Gnosis offered them the
solution, for it promised to obtain everlasting bliss
to the purified soul which had been caught by dark
matter, but from which the initiate would free themselves step by step, and thus reach that high degree of
perfection which consisted in the adequate 'knowledge'
of the highest divine power. This was not to be
obtained by the exercise of reason, but by meditation
on and contemplation of the Divine. Whether complete absorption in the Divine was to be obtained is
not quite clear; but this teaching was a kind of
revelation, an apocalypse, a mystery, in which the
Rescuing Power, the Sotēr, Saviour, became the central
figure. He was a Divine power who, for the sake of
saving the souls from the bondage of matter, had
assumed a corporeal body and had undergone the same
trials as every mortal, nay had even submitted to
death only to rise again and thus conquer death. He
would then take the other souls with him along
the same road of trial and death to conquer over
it. Mystical names, formulas and prayers were communicated to the initiate, which were the outward

embodiment of that Gnosis or intuitive knowledge; and by means of these formulas, which served as amulets, the soul in its ascent was freed from the molestations of the evil spirits which barred its way. The wicked, the impure, those to whom Matter clung very strongly, could, of course, not obtain that free passage, that flight to the heights; they were dragged down and remained in the power of Darkness.

I must limit myself to this brief outline and must decline to discuss, or even to touch upon, the dualistic principle so prominent afterwards in the Manichæan teaching and in the Iranian; nor can I speak of the various theories of the origin of the Sotēr, the Fall of the Light—if I may call it so—into the power of Darkness, the rôle ascribed to the Plērōma, Archontes, Yaldabaot and even Achamot, except to point out that the last word is the dialectic pronunciation for Hahamot, 'Wisdom,' not in the usual meaning of this term, but meaning that intuitive wisdom obtained by contemplation, by which the mysteries of the world stand revealed and whereby the true Gnosis is obtained: in fact, it may be taken as identical with the Greek word 'Gnōsis.' There remains, however, one problem which, as far as I am aware, no one has yet touched, *viz.* what becomes of the body from which the soul has departed? Has this question ever been raised among the Gnostics? Hitherto all the attention has been concentrated upon finding out the fate of the soul; but no one seems to have troubled himself to discover the fate of the body according to Gnostic teaching. If one of the fundamental principles is the fight of Light with Darkness, which, at the end of time, is to end in the complete victory of Light over Darkness, the question remains, what becomes of the dark matter, which was only the result of a rebellious action, a deliberate separation from the source of Light? In the beginning all was Light. I am not going back to the obscure Babylonian myths of the fight of the gods with Tiamat, the great serpent, the dark abyss, which also finishes with the victory of Light over Darkness. But there again no answer has been vouchsafed as to what would happen at the end of time. This eschatological problem must have been present in the minds of those who preached the dogma of Light and Darkness, of Soul and Body and, above all, of the final victory of Light over Darkness, of Soul over Matter. Was that body then left to itself, although it had been the vehicle for the soul? In fact, was there a question of the resurrection, of re-uniting the Spirit with the Body, and of granting both such reward as they deserved after they had both undergone a similar state of trial and ultimate purification and perfection as had that Divine Power whose example they followed? Nay, what had become of the body of that Sotēr, in which he clothed himself when descending into this world? Did he or could he abandon it to utter decay and leave it behind as of no consequence, or did it also slowly assume a more spiritual form when he took his ascent to heaven? What could be understood by ' annihilation' of matter unless re-uniting in one form or another with the Divine Origin?

I venture to think that this problem agitated the mind of at least some of the Gnostics and, if we turn to the somewhat incoherent teaching of the Mandæans, very little doubt can be left as to the accuracy of this assumption. At the end of days when Anoš is to be victorious, he evidently will revive Adam and Eve and the whole Creation, which had been destroyed by fire and water (end of Book of John). In some of the Liturgies an echo of this belief can be found. But, of course, as so much stress had been laid upon the incompatibility of Matter with Spirit, of the wickedness and sinfulness of Darkness against the glory of the Light, this problem was more and more obliterated. Still, it is impossible to think of a whole system without taking into consideration the possibility, nay the plausibility, that it must have also included a final solution of the fundamental problem involved in the fight between Light and Darkness, between Spirit and Matter, in which the body would also in time be slowly raised to that higher perfection which was the ultimate end of creation. This would be a proper logical solution. It is this principle which is elaborated in the fragment recovered by me from the Book Zohar. The whole phraseology fully agrees with that used in the Mandæan books; even the same expression recurs over and over again, as can easily be seen by anyone who compares it with the teaching of the King of Light or the descent of Hibil-Zīwā to the regions of Hell, published by Brandt from the Genzā, and the similar teachings in the Book of John and the Liturgies published by Lidzbarski. They all breathe the same spirit, even the ' blotting out from the Book of Life ' is mentioned.

Before proceeding further, a word must now be said about the Book Zohar. The current ideas about that book are to my mind absolutely erroneous. Those who have studied the book have, I am afraid, not even taken the trouble to read the full title-page. It is ascribed to a certain Rabbi Simeon ben Yochai, a sage who lived in Galilee, in the second century, and it was not difficult for anyone reading the book to point out

a large number of anachronisms. It was therefore
alleged that the book was a spurious writing fabricated
by a certain Moses de Leon in Spain at the end of the
XIIIth century. The whole Book, which constitutes
a huge volume, was treated as a unity and, although
many portions have separate titles, they were still
considered as forming part and parcel of the original
composition.

I have dealt with this question fully elsewhere
(Hastings' *Encyclopædia of Religion and Ethics*, vol.
xii., pp. 858 ff.), and it suffices here simply to mention
that the results of my enquiries have led me to the
conclusion that this Book is a compilation made at
a later date from very ancient independent documents.
The editors or publishers, in the middle of the XVIth
century, were intent upon preparing a mystical commentary to the Pentateuch in addition to a book
originally called the 'Midrash of Rabbi Simeon ben
Yochai'; they gathered their material from every side
and joined this material together, reserving however
the title of each independent treatise, thus creating
out of a mass of incoherent matter what they believed
to be a consistent commentary to the Five Books of
Moses. It is, therefore, an idle attempt on the part of
scholars to formulate a mystical system of the Zohar.
There are in that Book not one but many such
systems standing side by side, sometimes supplement-
ing one another and sometimes contradicting one
another. Every mystical school of thought is represented in one part or another of that book. We have
thus in one fragment the principle of permutations
and the substitution of the letters of the alphabet,
resting on the theory of the Logos; for if the world
had been created by the 'Word,' a word consists of

letters, and probably the most efficacious of these letters must be those used to designate the Name of God. It is by combination of such letters that the creative Word could be re-constituted; hence all this play of letters which fills an ample space, not only in the Zohar and in the so-called practical Kabbalah, but which is already found fully represented in the ancient Magical Papyri and in the phylacteries of the Samaritans (see my publication in *Pro. Soc. Biblical Archæology*).

Side by side with this theory is that of emanations, the descending world of spheres, through which the world became slowly materialized, until it was finally condensed in our Earth. Then there is the purely allegorical interpretation, where to all the incidents of the Bible a totally different meaning is assigned from that found in the text. This allegorical interpretation is very well known through the writings of Philo, who follows therein an older example of Aristobulus. The process however has gone much further: the Biblical names stand for ideas and the whole simple meaning of the text has been sublimated and entirely obliterated. An arbitrary philology takes the place of sound grammar, and free play is allowed to the imagination unchecked apparently by any system of logic or reason. Many more systems could easily be discovered in the various sections of the Zohar. One can see, therefore, how irrational any attempt would be to evolve a uniform system from this complex collection. A further examination reveals the fact that the various treatises hail in all probability from schools which had flourished in Palestine, and especially in Galilee—they are written mostly in the Aramaic vulgar dialect spoken in that province,—and

that they belong to different ages and different
schools of thought. Some of these are undoubtedly
very old and it is due to simple chance that they
have survived. Mystic speculation was rife among
the Jews from very early times, whether it be
described as mystical speculations on the Heavenly
Throne, mystical speculations on the Cosmogony, or
on the ineffable Name of God, and they were known
long before the time of John the Baptist. Again, not
only Jews but other sects living in Galilee engaged in
such mystic speculations. Samaria must have been
a very centre; the figure of Simon Magus is sufficiently
well known to prove that fact, and many utterances of
John the Baptist, of Jesus and the Apostles, can be
properly appreciated only if it be assumed that they
referred to ideas and tendencies common among the
people. Their allusions could easily be understood,
for they moved in an atmosphere replete with such
notions. The world was at that time seething with
mysteries and mysticism, and it would have been
a miracle if the Jews alone could have remained
immune. But this is not the fact. On the contrary,
it is becoming more and more evident that Jews took
an important part in influencing and moulding these
various systems. Eschatology had already assumed
a very definite character, and the common belief in
reward and punishment beyond this world was strong;
one need only refer to the numerous apocalyptic
writings which then saw the light—not least among
them to the Revelation of John—to realize how greatly
the world at that time was beset with these difficulties and anxious to find a solution of the riddle
of Life and Death. No wonder, therefore, that
esoteric teachings like these would slowly crystallize

among various schools, and that traditions transmitted orally in the beginning should then be written down for fear of being forgotten or lost. Such beliefs formed the ingredients of the Zohar, and parallels to Gnostic teachings abound on every page. In a double set of treatises there is found the very central idea of the ascent of the Soul through various Heavens the gates of which are guarded by angels, whose secret name the Soul has to utter to obtain free passage, and, *vice versa*, the descent to Hell, where the soul has to pass through a similar process of examination by the demons watching at the seven gates corresponding to the seven gates of Heaven. It is fully elaborated, but it goes back to more ancient treatises of a similar kind which link it up with the Book of Enoch and other apocalyptic journeys through Heaven and Hell found in the pseudepigraphic literature.

Among other beliefs current already at that time and shared by Jews and Samaritans alike, as well as by other sects, was that of the Day of Doom and Judgment, to be followed by a period of peace and happiness. The Sibyl is already full of these ideas, and to them was added afterwards, as a necessary corollary, the Resurrection of the Dead; for if there were to be Judgment, then all those who had sinned had to rise and appear to receive Judgment.

At a more primitive stage in the evolution of this belief the idea of Judgment was not so prominently connected with the Resurrection. It was kept rather vague, and it is precisely in this form that the fate of the soul after death and its future re-union with its former body are described in a curious, solitary fragment found in the Zohar. For the reasons here advanced, I have no doubt that this fragment had originally

formed part of a much larger treatise concerning
eschatological problems. Some of the allusions are
still obscure, but by comparing others with the existing
mystical literature, they can be explained much more
easily ; so, *e.g.*, the 'great laughter.' It appears in the
Magical Papyri and has baffled every interpreter.
What is probably meant is the creative Laughter, the
Voice which alone suffices to bring the world into
existence without speaking a word, a continuous
modulated sound without letters and at the same time
a source of rejoicing and happiness, a characteristic
feature of the New World.

The allusion to Jerusalem, though based on
Biblical texts, finds a curious parallel in the Mandæan
teaching, where Jerusalem also is the spot for the
future revelation of Anoš. The soul is described
throughout as filled with Light, fed with Light from the
Divine Throne, shining in great lustre, being received
by the pious in the Heavenly Paradise, and even more
full of Light than the angels. The soul attains the
highest form of perfection, inasmuch as it is taught to
perceive and understand, to 'know,' the glory of God.
This is also reserved for the body, which is to be
slowly transformed into a more perfect being through
the agency of the Prince of the Presence, Metatron,
and becomes more translucent, *i.e.* spiritualized ; it
must be able to give the soul the 'secret sign' of that
highest knowledge which it has also attained, before
the soul can be re-united with it. The angel with his
ink-horn marks a sign on each one of the bodies which
are called to life again, just as we find it in the other
Gnostic writings.

But, again, it is a remarkable fact that nothing is
said here of the Day of Judgment, which proves the

extreme antiquity of this fragment. It had been taken over from a special Gnostic school and adapted to the Biblical text in a very deft manner. All the figures and all the incidents were treated allegorically, and references taken from other parts of the Bible and incorporated in this writing were treated in a similar manner. One can, easily, therefore, eliminate, as I have done, all the Biblical passages; nay, it is necessary if we are to reconstruct the old original.

The text which here follows forms an allegorical mystical interpretation of the story of the death of Sarah and of her burial, and then of Abraham sending Eliezer to find a wife for his son among his family and to bring her back to Isaac. Each name which occurs is interpreted almost in the manner of Philo; it no longer represents the human: Abraham stands for the soul, Sarah for the body that is interred in the field of Ephron who is the dust; the Het[1] is the representative of the pious; Eliezer is the servant of the soul and, therefore, the servant of his master, i.e. Metatron; and similarly Isaac and Rebecca as well as Keturah are interpreted to mean the soul and body in various stages. Further quotations are adduced from the Song of Songs, equally mystically interpreted, but not corresponding to the interpretation found in the Targum; for the dove here represents the soul and not the House of Israel as in the Targum. This whole section is called, in the Zohar, the 'Midrash Hane'elam,' 'The Hidden or Veiled Midrash.' I am simply joining together the portions which seem to belong to one continuous text referring to death and resurrection, leaving out all the Biblical references which have been adjusted in such manner to the text as to form the

[1] Or Hittite (Gen. xxiii. 3).

apparent basis for this interpretation which has. been placed upon the original.

THE VEILED MIDRASH FROM THE ZOHAR, FOL. 122Bff.

"And Abraham came to mourn over Sarah and to weep over her." That is what we have been taught. The soul of man watches over the body for seven days and mourns over it, as is said above. Abraham means the soul, Sarah the body. When the soul is worthy of it, she rises up and goes to her place ; the body rests in peace, and the soul goes straight to the place which has been appointed for it in the Garden of Eden. But when the soul is not worthy and deserves to be punished, then the soul returns desolate and visits the body in the grave every day. And so the soul goes on for twelve months, flitting about in the world and hovering over the grave. . . . But the soul that is meritorious, first protects the body for a while and then rises up to her high place. She also addresses the bodies of the others, the righteous, those who have been oppressed and overwhelmed in the world for the sake of their fear of the Lord, and who are now dwelling in the dust. And why is it necessary that it should be so ? Because they are all written down according to their number, and this body is entered into the same account. And this soul says to them with reverence and homage : "A stranger and a sojourner am I among you. For this body now is to be one of you in your company." Before the pious man dies, a Bath-kol proclaims every day to those pious men who are in Paradise : "Prepare a place for So and So who is coming here." And, therefore, they say : "A prince of God art thou in our midst, among the choicest of the pious. Enter him into our list, and none shall refuse him place among us, for we all rejoice and we offer him greetings of peace." And the soul reaches them first and rejoices with them, and then it reaches the angel who is appointed over them ; for we have been taught that an angel is appointed over the graves and his name is Dumah, and he proclaims every day among the pious those who are coming to be associated with them. Then the soul meets him, so as to ensure for the body a rest of peace, comfort and satisfaction. His name is mentioned as Ephron, because he is the one who presides over those who dwell in the 'Aphar (Dust). And all the registers in which the pious are entered, are handed over to him as well as those of all the company of the pious who dwell in the Dust.

And in the future time he is bound to bring them up according to the record; for in the time to come, when the Lord will decide to quicken the dead, He will call the angel appointed over the dead, whose name is Dumah, and He will ask of him the number of all the dead pious men and the pious proselytes and those who have been martyrs for the sake of His holy Name. And he will bring them forth in the same number as he had received them. But also the souls of the wicked are handed over to the same angel Dumah to carry them down to Gehinom and to judge them. And from the moment they are handed over to him, they are not free until they have been carried into Gehinom.

And the soul afterwards approaches him with the request to enter her own body into the list of the bodies of the other pious men. And the angel anticipates the request and says that the body's destination is to rest in the Dust; but the soul approaches him and requests him to place him in the list of the pious. These have already been entered before in the written record; for it has been decreed that this record should be kept by Dumah of all those that enter into the House of Burial; and by the same record they are in future to be brought out again. He is appointed over all those who dwell in the Dust,—the field which has been placed in his care as a place of great peace and rest. Every pious man is exposed two hundred times to be put to shame, and he also inherits two hundred worlds, for the sake of the study of the Law; for these are considered as if they were martyrs for the sake of His holy Name. . . .

We read in the Pentateuch: "And Abraham was old," and in the Song of Songs: "One is my dove," etc. Both are identical with the soul. The soul is called Abraham, because the soul is associated with the body like a man with the wife, the body representing the woman, whilst the soul which ascends above is like a woman compared to a man, and each one occupies the position accordingly, the soul being superior to the human whilst she is inferior in comparison with the heavenly spirit.

Four times every year drops fall from Eden to the Garden;

and these drops become a great river which divides up into four parts; and from these, eight-and-forty drops fall which water the trees of Eden. Where is that Eden? Some say it is above the Arabot;[1] others hold it is in the Arabot and that therein are the treasures of good life and of blessing and peace; and there also are the souls of the pious. This is the Upper Eden which is hidden, and to this corresponds the 'Garden' which is upon the earth, and which draws abundance every day from the Upper Eden. Eight-and-forty prophets have arisen and each one has obtained his 'wisdom' (Sophia, Gnosis or Higher Knowledge) by absorbing one of these drops, and through this he reached to the highest station, through the Holy Spirit which he had thus absorbed. Adam had partaken of all these drops, and it is easy to imagine how great was his wisdom. It must again be noted that with each drop which comes from Eden there comes with it the spirit of wisdom; it is this which caused the prophet to reach that high position, for only those who drink of this water become 'wise.' The souls of the pious are in that Eden and, if those who obtain only a drop reach a high state of wisdom, how much more must this be the case with the souls that dwell in Eden itself and partake of all the pleasures of Eden? As soon as the soul reaches the heavenly Jerusalem, the angel Michael meets her and gives her the greetings of peace, and the ministering angels look upon her in wonder and ask: "Who is this that 'rises up from the Desert'? Who is this one that comes up to the Upper World from the body which is like vanity?" Then he answers and says: "This is my 'only dove,' the 'only one to her mother,' which is the Heavenly Throne from which the soul is born and from which it has been separated. And the other souls that are there, which are called the Daughters of Jerusalem, come to see her. And the souls come and praise her and give her the greetings of peace. The Patriarchs, the pious proselytes, all assemble together to praise her, and thus the soul rises up and reaches everlasting life, i.e. the days which have no end.

Later on the soul returns to the body. Since the soul in the beginning had entered into a body of low origin, it is also likely that when the time comes the soul will re-enter that same body;

---

[1] One of the heavenly spheres.

for that body will then also have reached a very high standard of perfection. And it will be precisely the very same soul which will enter the very same body. Both will then be perfect of that 'perfect knowledge' which they had hitherto not been able to reach when they had been living in this world together.

Metatron, the Prince of the Divine Presence, who is called the Youth, the Servant, is appointed over the soul. He is to provide her daily with that Light which has been set aside for her; and he is the one who in future will take from Dumah the record of those who are buried in the grave, and he will show it to the Lord. He has been appointed to prepare the 'yeast' to rebuild the bones that are under the ground, so as to form the skeleton and to raise the body in a perfect condition, though as yet without the soul. He sends each one to his place, and it is he who in future will also beautify the bodies in the burial places. He is also appointed over all the hosts of the Lord. All these hosts receive the soul and rejoice in her light; for the light of the soul in the other world is greater than the light of the Heavenly Throne itself, although she has been taken from it, but the light of each one is in accordance with her own merits. And when Metatron goes to fulfil the command of God, all the hosts accompany him with his chariot, and they are fed by its lustre. The soul speaks to him and says: "Grant me thy help." And at the same time the soul causes him to take an oath saying: "When thou goest on this mine errand, thou shalt not take another body for this my soul to enter, even a strange body, which is not befitting me; but thou shalt take my very body from which I have departed. That body which had been full of suffering and pain and had no pleasure because of its devotion to the fear of the Lord, that very body shalt thou get for me, to laugh (to rejoice) with the joy of the pious, the joy of the Lord; for then will be the time of laughter in the world."

Then an angel will come with his ink-horn in his girdle and he will make a sign on the forehead of each body; and then the Great Prince, the Metatron, will come and perfect each one so as to make him fit to receive his soul. And that other angel will come before this Prince will start out on his errand. Those who have given their lives to the study of the Law, will be those who will be raised first; and this is sure to happen on the Friday, the eve of the Sabbath, which will be the sixth millennium, at the end of the sixth thousand, when the six thousand years of the world's existence will have come to an end. And then the soul will seek her own body; for although a man may have been a scholar, he still stands in need of perfection; but by the higher knowledge which he will then receive, they will be able to recognize one another. And the soul will say to the body: "It is necessary that thou shouldst give me the secret of thy knowledge concerning Him (God)." And then the body will say: "Thou hast also been like unto me, even a servant, and the knowledge which thou didst possess, has not been exalted above my knowledge of the Lord; for thou must realize that thou hast also been created like unto me. I know that where thou hast reached I have not yet reached; but I know also that I have the advantage over thee that I know thou hast been created from the brightness which has been given to thee." If the body give this sign, then the soul will know that the body has been handed over to her in consequence of these words; and then the soul will know that that is the body which belongs to her. And that is the fulfilment of the oath which the soul had caused the angel to take. And this body is holy because he has martyred himself in order to know and to apprehend his Creator, and he now becomes an associate of the intellect, a body joined to the mind and the brother of the soul, and the burden of ' wisdom ' is upon him. Then the angel Metraton will run towards him and say: "Give me a token of thy knowledge of thy Creator, as far as thou hast apprehended it in the world from which thou art now coming forth." Then the angel will gather up all the scattered bones and number them one with the other. [Then that body will rise up in the Land of Israel and there the soul will enter into it.] Tunnels are made by the Lord under the ground, and the bones are rolling through them from every part until they reach the Land of Israel. And the angel Gabriel leads them on towards the Land of Israel. And when the body has been completed and carried to the Land of Israel, there he will find the soul waiting to meet him. And then there will be great rejoicing in the world. And the soul will wait forty years for the body, and the place of meeting will be the Temple, because the soul will then love the body and comfort herself with him; and that will be the time of laughter and joy in the world. Now this soul will dwell beside the fountain of everlasting life with the knowledge of Him who is living for ever, to know and to apprehend that which she has never been able to apprehend in this world.

In addition to this text, there is also a small fragment of a similar treatise, which seems to refer to one incident only. It evidently belongs to the portion when Metatron goes to call up the dead and it runs as follows:

ZOHAR, I. 121A TOSEFTA.

The text of the Matnita.[1] We gathered together, we heard a Voice, turning from on high and below; there spread through the world a Voice which was breaking the mountains and splitting the mighty rocks. Great storms were raised, our ears were opened and it said: "Those who are resting under the shadow awake! And those who sleep in their deep slumber in their graves (lit. holes) stand up in your status!" The King speaketh, the guardians of the gate, those who are the rulers of the mighty hosts, stand up upright alive. They do not all respond. They do not know that the Book is open, that the name is entered and that the (angel) Dumah stands and takes account of those who dwell in the Dust. They sit outside and he draws near to count those who are not subject to the Turning Wheel (those who are not subjected to the Gilgul), and those who fall and do not rise up, the guilty ones that are to be blotted out from the Book of Dumah, those of whom account will be asked and those who have to render account. Woe unto them! Woe unto their lives! Woe unto their souls! Concerning them it is written: "They shall be blotted out from the Book of Life " (Ps. 69_{29}).

(Read at a Meeting of the Quest Society, February 8, 1923.)

---

[1] Name for ' Section ' in the Oral Law.

SAMARITAN PHYLACTERIES AND AMULETS.

Reprinted from the " Proceedings of the Society of Biblical Archæology,"
March, 1915.

The documents which I propose to publish now for the first time will no doubt cause as much surprise to those who will learn of their existence as they caused me when first I heard of it from the Samaritans. It took me many years to win their confidence, and even then it was only one by one that they disclosed the fact that such documents existed among them. The reason for their reticence is not far to seek. The very nature of these documents explains it. There is nothing which people keep more secret than that which would appear to others superstitious practices or ludicrous beliefs. There is also the fear that by making such things known they would lose their efficacy. However, in the course of twelve to fifteen years, by constant communications I succeeded in gradually obtaining practically all the documents of this kind in the possession of the Samaritans. These documents are, as I believe, nothing less than such phylacteries as are mentioned in Matt. xxiii, 5, and later on I shall have to draw special attention to the description of these phylacteries therein given. They are *not* frontlets, as has hitherto been universally supposed, but real amulets, worn for prophylactic purposes, as the very name denotes. Charms used for protecting the wearer from every possible hurt. Such amulets were not used for prayers : they would be worn constantly and they were also looked upon as superstitious practices used not only by the Jews but by almost every other nation of antiquity. The LXX does not translate the word *Totafoth* (Ex. xiii, 16, and Deut. vi, 8 ; xi, 18) as " phylacteries," but as " frontlets," thereby already differentiating between the two. It is the Peshitta or Syriac translation which translates the " phylacteries " in Matt. xxiii, 5, by *tefillin*. But it will be shown that the Jews had also separate phylacteries of a mystical and magical character quite independent of the *tefillin*. This is a literature which has hitherto been almost ignored because such phylacteries were believed to be amulets of a recent origin. The beginnings of mystical and superstitious practices are very difficult to trace. They are by-paths of faith and are studiously ignored by the select. They belong to the people, and as such the aristocrats of the spirit take no notice of them. Still they continue from generation to generation until a time comes when more attention is paid to them, and much of the mystical lore of the past stands revealed in these hitherto neglected documents. Because these were popular practices they were looked upon as superstitious and heretical and therefore hunted down. This is the reason why so much of the older magical literature has perished, and with it also the old phylacteries.

The wearing of such amulets was strictly forbidden on the penalty of death. We know that the wearing of *tefillin* fell under the same decree.

In outward appearance they resembled the *tefillin*, and could be easily confounded with them. According to a legend, when found wearing such *tefillin*, Rabbi Ishmael hid them in his hand where they became transformed into doves. This shows that the outward shape of the *tefillin* must have somehow been the same as, or similar to, that of the phylacteries. The contents of the latter, however, differed considerably from that of the *tefillin*, if we are to judge by the real phylacteries which have now come to light. The former contain merely four paragraphs from the Pentateuch without any trace of mysticism; the latter are nothing else than purely mystical amulets. It will be seen that they range easily among the other mystical and prophylactic literature known to us from antiquity. It will also be seen that it agrees in the main with certain mystical traditions among the Jews. Nor do these Samaritan phylacteries stand alone, as if they had nothing in common with Samaritan beliefs and traditions, and might therefore be considered as if they had been borrowed from another people and introduced into Samaritan from outside, and consequently not a Samaritan original and indigenous product. It is of course very difficult to establish the original or indigenous character of any mystical text. Such practices were common to many nations, and very often the one borrowed from the other. But there are some leading principles by which we can determine the origin of some of the formulae used. If the Tetragrammaton appears in a magical Greek papyrus, then one is absolutely sure that it is of Jewish or Samaritan origin. If an Egyptian name occurs, the Egyptian origin cannot be gainsaid.

This is the case with the Samaritan phylacteries. It will be seen that they are in perfect harmony with practices and beliefs specifically Samaritan. In some portions they run parallel to Jewish mystical writings. In others, on the contrary, these phylacteries are supported by Samaritan inscriptions and by other monuments in the Samaritan literature. Their age is not easy to determine. There is nothing in them which would preclude the possibility that they might belong to the first century of the Christian era. Everything in them points to a very high antiquity. It must also be remembered that magical texts in particular, and mystical literature in general, show a marvellous tenacity in preserving the old forms. The slightest change destroys their value. Hence the rigid retention of every minute detail with as little alteration as possible. There might perhaps be slight variations, but the general character will remain unimpaired. The Samaritans have moreover fossilized the past, and kept it with as few alterations as political conditions and literary activity allowed them to do. The comparison with the magical papyri, with stray references in the Rabbinical literature notably in the Talmud, with numerous Jewish real phylacteries, which have also been preserved but not noticed hitherto in their true character, with allusions to the Jewish mystical literature, will corroborate the assumption of high antiquity claimed for these Samaritan phylacteries. Of their genuineness there cannot be the slightest doubt. The very originals are all in my possession, and from a paleographical point of view they cannot be later than the eleventh or twelfth century, if they are not earlier. The writing is like that in the dated Bible scrolls of 1130–49—if anything the phylacteries seem more archaic. One of them is dated 1342 and is stated to be a copy of a much older one (see below). Here then after a lapse of so many centuries a whole mystical Samaritan literature, of which no one had hitherto even dreamt, is coming to light. In passing I should like also to draw another moral from it.

Here we have documents, fifteen in number, some of them very old, ranging from the twelfth to the nineteenth century, worn constantly by the Samaritans, in fact worn almost to shreds, and yet their existence was unknown, and until produced by me would not have been credited. There is among them a copy made towards the end of the nineteenth century, and if that alone had survived it would have been considered a modern composition, and yet it goes back to an immediate prototype of the fourteenth century, which in its turn is unquestionably a copy of a much older

original. No one knows yet how much is still hidden in the secret
recesses of the Samaritans in Nablus. Yet, when I discovered the
Book of Joshua in a comparatively modern copy of a Samaritan
chronicle some rashly doubted its genuineness and pronounced
it to be a modern compilation, if not a forgery, simply and solely
because they did not happen to know of any older original.
No one has ever heard till now of these phylacteries, and yet here
they are. And although no older copy of the Book of Joshua
has as yet come to light, still I have not the slightest doubt that
such an older original exists, and in fact some declare that they
have seen it.

So far by way of introduction. It will now be my duty to prove
in detail the statement which I have advanced of the existence of a
mystical literature among the Samaritans ; of the character and composition of these phylacteries—for there are more than one ; of the
relation in which they stand to Samaritan literature and to the kindred
non-Samaritan literature. A real chapter in Biblical Archaeology.

RELAND in the seventeenth century, and others before him, and
scholars ever since down to MONTGOMERY in 1907, are unanimously
of opinion that there is no trace of mysticism among the Samaritans.
They are described as dry, matter of fact, men, sticking closely to
the letter of the Pentateuch, not indulging in any speculation, and
free from every form of superstition and mysticism. The sources
of information upon which these scholars based their opinion were
very scanty. The correspondence from the seventeenth century
onwards between Samaritan priests and various men in Europe ; a
few liturgical poems published by GESENIUS, and more profusely by
HEIDENHEIM, besides a few stray notices in the writings of the
Fathers of the Church ; such was practically the whole material
available. The attention of scholars, moreover, centred almost
exclusively on the Samaritan Pentateuch, and very few enquired
of other books and writings in the possession of the Samaritans. Only
recently has the great collection of liturgical hymns appeared which
we owe to the industry of Dr. COWLEY of Oxford, but even these
yield practically very little in the direction of settling the problem as
to whether there was any mysticism known among the Samaritans.
If we consider, however, the fact that Palestine had been for centuries
the very centre of such mystical speculations and magical practices,
that there flourished numerous sects, each one more or less addicted
to such speculations—I need only mention the Essenes and Thera-

peutes, Ophites and Gnostics, and the latter in numerous variations (*v.* IRENAEUS and EPIPHANIUS)—it would have been a sheer miracle if the Samaritans, who at one time were more numerous than the Jews and who lived in the very midst of these warring sects, could have escaped contamination, and in fact they did not. Not only did they have mystical speculations, but, as was quite natural, they ran in parallel lines to those practised by the Jews, among whom mysticism was rife from very early times.

The root and basis of this Jewish mysticism, nay of all mysticism, is the belief in "words of power." The difference between one school and another often consists only in the difference between these words which the magician uses for his purpose, to subdue the "powers of evil" and to protect himself and those for whom he is acting by the knowledge which he possesses of these mysterious "words of power." Such words are originally spoken words ; later on they become written words, which must be read or worn. It is unnecessary here to dwell at any length on the fact that the words of power used in Jewish mysticism were in the first instance the ineffable Name of God, then numerous permutations of that Name, which were believed to consist of forty-two or seventy-two elements, and then on various combinations of verses and letters from the Bible. The principle underlying these practices is clear. No word could equal in power the word which stood for the Name of God in the Bible. Through God's word (*memra logos*) the world was created. It was by the utterance of a word that things came into existence. Now a word consists of letters; the Bible or the Law, in a restricted sense, is not only God's spoken word but God's written word, and therefore consisted of letters which in their combination and permutation must produce the very creative power which was contained in God's creative word. This is in brief the very root and basis of the whole range of mystical practices as far back as can be traced in Jewish literature. Whoever thus possessed the *Shem Hameforash*, that is, the Name, which is ineffable and yet has been made accessible by some means or other, was able to perform all kinds of miracles. He could heal the sick, or cure the blind, and the least he could do was to avert harm by wild beasts or evil men, or hurtful spirits, or sorcerers and wizards, and it has always been the aim and ambition of magicians to obtain the knowledge of these wonder-working words and names. Not only was this the case with the Jews (*cf.* GASTER, *Sword of Moses*), but also with all the other nations of Syria and Egypt. The Assyrian literature abounds in magic texts, and the soil of Egypt has yielded a good many magical papyri. In the latter especially we find a complete counterpart to these Jewish speculations, and we also learn how great was the influence hitherto supposed to have been exercised by the Jews upon this kind of literature. They abound in Hebrew names of God, and also in references to Biblical verses and scripture passages. Hitherto the belief has been that only Jews knew the use of the ineffable Name and of other divine names for such purposes, and it was therefore assumed that the authors of the Greek magical papyri owed much of their material exclusively to the Jews. In the light of the Samaritan phylacteries I venture to think that this opinion will undergo very serious modification, as well as that of the belief in the absence of any mystical practices among the Samaritans. But we must keep steadily in mind that there could not be any essential difference between Jews and Samaritans. The same principle will obviously underlie Samaritan practices, and formulae will then be found in the latter similar to those known to us from among the Jews, if both go back, as I believe they do, to very old traditions common to both.

In all questions affecting occult practices and occult literature we rarely come across ancient texts; many causes have contributed to their disappearance as already remarked. Any direct contact between these two sects intimate enough to allow the one to borrow such teachings from the other must be excluded. The hatred between the two was too deep to allow it.

It must now be established, in the first place, that the Samaritans treated the Tetragrammaton with the same respect and awe as did the Jews; that they looked upon it as the all-powerful name of God, and that it could not even be pronounced as it was written, that it was a real ineffable name.

However scanty the evidence may be on other questions, for this there is ample evidence that they avoided pronouncing the Name as written. One of the oldest accusations against the Samaritans was that they worshipped the Ashima, the goddess mentioned in 2 Kings xvii, 30, among those of the Kutheans settled in Samaria. It has long since been proved that this was merely the manner in which they pronounced the Tetragrammaton, which, to this very day, the Samaritans read Shema, *i.e.*, " The Name." This practice is so universal that in alphabetical acrostics, in some of the oldest poems in their liturgy, the first word in the line, which ought to begin with a *Shin* is sometimes replaced by the Tetragrammaton. It would not be difficult to connect this awe of the Tetragrammaton with the statement in Acts viii, 10, that Simon Magus was "that power of God which is called Great," if it is to be taken that he had that power of God which was called the Great (Name). For it was by such means that he was afterwards credited with having been able to perform miracles, to fly in the air, to cure the blind and heal the sick, revive the dead, etc. It must not be forgotten that he was a Samaritan, and whatever interpretation may be placed upon Simon as being an impersonation of Paul, or that some other Simon had been confused with him by JUSTIN MARTYR, IRENAEUS, and others, the unanimous testimony of the Fathers of the Church makes them all Samaritans, and no doubt they were credited with using such a wonder-working mysterious name of God. I have purposely brought in the name of Simon, for I believe that his name appears in a list of sorcerers found in the larger Samaritan phylacteries. But of this later on. Among the heresiarchs of the Samaritans there is one Dusis of uncertain date, sometimes confused with Dostan, also of uncertain date, but both belonging to the first centuries of the common era. Of these it is said in Samaritan chronicles, and by outside testimonies, that the former had accused the Samaritans of having deliberately altered the name of God. It seems that either the one or the other, unless they both be identical, had substituted the word *Elohim* for the Tetragrammaton, no doubt out of reverence, and for the same reason which forbade even the translation of this name in the Greek texts of THEODOTION in his translation of the Bible. When we approach MARKAH (fourth century), his poems on Moses abound with allusions to the mystical and holy names of God. He sees, in fact, mysteries everywhere, and he states in his last poem that, before writing the Law, God had written first the letters of the alphabet. Towards the end of that poem, in which much mystical interpretation of the value of the letters of the Hebrew alphabet is to be found, he discusses the divine names Elohim, IHVH, and Ehyh. As far back as Samaritan liturgy can be traced, there is frequent reference to the "Holy Name and Great Name" of God, which the High Priest is said to have uttered when he pronounced the Priestly blessing. (The same tradition prevails among the Jews concerning the High Priest in the Temple at Jerusalem.) In not a few passages that name is distinctly referred to as the *Shem Hamitfaresh*, exactly the same title as is given to the ineffable name in the Jewish literature.

The identical form for the name is found in the Palestinian Targum, Levit. xxiv, 11.

The author of the *Kafi*, JUSEF EL-ASKERI, who wrote his book on the Traditional Law of the Samaritans in 1042, says (Cod. Gaster, Nos. 821, 878) that the prayers finish regularly with the recital of "the holy names" by the officiating Kohen. Among these are to be understood, in the first place, the Tetragrammaton and, the other name (Ex. iii, 14) Ehye, consisting also of four letters. This occurs almost as often as the other in Samaritan prayers and invocations, perhaps more often.

When we reach the time of ABISHA (the middle of the fourteenth century—died 1376), we find mystical speculation almost at its height. There is a tradition that he was fully acquainted with these mystical names of God, and that he was able to make use of them in the same manner as the Jewish High Priest Ishmael was said to have done in the first century. By means of it ABISHA was translated alive into the Presence of God and saw the glories of Paradise, and the future advent of the Taheb or Messiah. He himself describes his vision in one of his poems in the Samaritan Service for the Day of Atonement. Older writers or contemporaries, for it is not easy to define the period when some of these poems were composed by, *e.g.*, JOSEPH HA-RABBAN and others, show a similar acquaintance with mystical names of God. Moreover, the Samaritan liturgical poems are full of them. To the same period, then, belongs a peculiar astronomical poem (Cod. Gaster, No. 876) by a certain JACOB, otherwise unknown, of the fourteenth century, which seems to have been used for the very peculiar purpose of, being recited before going to sleep, with the object of obtaining an answer from above in the dream of the night. A certain number of divine names are inserted in it, and the same names are used in another prayer (Cod. Gaster, No. 1170), precisely for the same purpose. It would be easy to multiply examples from the Samaritan liturgy showing the awe and reverence in which the Tetragrammaton was held, but this name formed the centre and basis of these holy and mysterious names. In order to get, as it were, the full significance and value, this name had to be submitted to many changes and permutations. To each letter a special significance was attached, as also to the position in which it stood; and if, therefore, these letters were changed or combined with those of the other mysterious name, Ehyh, the mystic evidently expected greater results. It was not sufficient to change the order or to group them in many forms, often multiplying the same group of letters over and over again in these permutations, but they often repeated the same letter very many times, thus, especially the a (א), which was at the same time the first letter of אהיה and of the alphabet. It will be found repeated as often as ten or twelve times and more. This by no means exhausts the list of the "holy names" which, as already remarked, are to be found in the poems of ABISHA, and in other poems, prayers, and allusions in Samaritan writings. The next step was the substitution of other letters of the alphabet for those of the divine names. As God had written all the letters of the alphabet, as His word was the creative power, as His name was one of the manifestations in the form of letters, and as the Law was the written word of God, therefore each letter was of divine origin, and one could take the place of the other if the initiated only knew which was the correct substitute for the letter in the divine name. Now there existed from olden times an interpretation which saw in the *Shem Hameforash*, not the Tetragrammaton as written, but as represented by forty-two or seventy-two elements, or, as found in the poem of ABISHA (Cod. Gaster, No. 835, f. 27ᵇ), of one hundred and six, or even three hundred and three, elements or words. This point was left in doubt, and to this day it has remained a source of keen speculation as to what was understood by this appellation of forty-two, seventy-two, one hundred and six, and so on. The solution which seems to have found favour with the oldest mystical teaching, was that it consisted of twenty-two, or forty-two, or seventy-two letters of the alphabet. Thus, a wide field was opened for speculation, and yet one can now trace a certain unanimity. It will be shown later on that chapters xiv and xv of Exodus have been singled out by the teachers of this doctrine. In chapter xiv there are three verses, 19, 20, 21, each of which consists of exactly seventy-two letters; what was more natural than to see in these three verses the very mysterious name of seventy-two. The idea is so abstruse that one would scarcely believe it could have been invented by two people independent of one another, and yet we find it in Jewish writings as far back as the eighth or ninth century, and now among the Samaritans.

It was a curious incident in connection with this chapter which, many years ago, roused my curiosity and became the starting point of these investigations into the mystical literature of the Samaritans. It is well known that the Samaritans have invented a peculiar system of cryptography, the like of which has not yet been found among any other nation. It consists in picking out letters from the text in such a manner that they form a vertical column in the text, which now becomes divided into two large columns, and these letters in the middle form the name of the writer and the date of the writing. When reading my Codex of the Bible, No. 800, I was struck by the peculiar phenomenon that, in the midst of the text of Ex. xiv, there appeared a vertical column written in the same cryptographic manner, and containing the Samaritan sentence, יהוה נצוחי קרביה, "The Lord is mighty in battle," the Targum of Ex. xv, 3. To pick out these letters in the midst of the text and to combine them into a Samaritan sentence, pointed to a special reverence being paid to this portion of the text, which forms a new section (ḳiṣṣa) in the Samaritan version of the Pentateuch. The writer evidently had a notion that these verses contained some potent value of a prophylactic character. I then examined all the available Samaritan MSS. of the Bible, and I found precisely the same sentence, and in precisely the same place, in the oldest Samaritan Bibles found in England, viz., the Crawford I, now Cod. Rylands, of the twelfth or early thirteenth century, and the Brit. Mus. Cod. Or. 2683, f. 86ᵇ, 87ᵃ of probably a century later. These three codices are copies of much earlier ones, and proved that, in or before the twelfth century at least, some special significance had been attached to this chapter and to these verses. The letters of these verses were then combined in groups of threes, into the details of which I cannot enter now (see below), but this combination is also of an extremely complicated nature. Each group of three letters is believed to represent one of God's mysterious names. In addition to these letters, then, we have the substitution of letters by various manipulations like אתבש, i.e., the first and last, the second and the last letter but one of the alphabet; or אלבם, the first and the twelfth, the second and the thirteenth, with innumerable variations in the grouping of the letters for substitution. Thus numerous variations have been created for the name of God by permutations, substitutions, and combinations. The antiquity of these permutations and substitutions is testified, among others, by the astronomical poem (Cod. 876), of the fourteenth century, and the apocalypse of Moses, which certainly belongs to a much higher antiquity, and may go back to the second or third century.

Coming down to the end of the fifteenth century, we find ABRAHAM KABASI of Damascus, one of the foremost men of his time, composing a commentary on Deut. xxxii, 2 and 3 (Cod. Gaster, No. 880). Therein he devoted a chapter (pp. 1–45) to the passage "for I called upon the name of the Lord," and endeavours to explain the meaning and value of this name of God. Here we find a further development of these mystical operations and manipulations. The letters are treated as mathematical figures, and thus mathematical calculations are derived from the names of God and from the various permutations and substitutions to which that name has been subjected; nay the very name by which these manifold operations were known in the Jewish literature seems to have been known among the Samaritans. I refer to the word usually written and read Gematria, which has hitherto been taken to be an equivalent with Geometria, although there is not the slightest connection between geometry and mystical calculation. The original form of the word was probably Grammata, "writings," which the people as a rule did not understand, and substituted for it the better known "Geometry" by a kind of popular etymology. These are no doubt the well known Fphesia Grammata so often recurring in ancient Greek mystical literature. No one has hitherto been able to explain this name, and I venture, in the light of what is to follow, to suggest a new reading of the first word of the writing. It has nothing whatsoever to do with Ephesus, but instead of reading Ephesia we ought to read Aphasia Grammata, and this means the "ineffable writings," an almost literal translation of the Hebrew *Shem Hameforash* or Samaritan *Shem Hamitfaresh*, with the meaning which has been attached to it from very olden times by antithesis the "ineffable name" or the "ineffable writing," and thus a mysterious title which has remained a stumbling-block to students of magical literature to this very day has now, as I believe, been entirely removed. Thus far then we have been able to trace the existence of mystical speculations centring round the name of God through the whole of the Samaritan literature as far as it is known. If we turn now to the phylacteries, we shall find every one of these mysterious names, forms, symbols, changes, and permutations, fully represented. It is almost a complete manual of these mystical names, in a richness and fullness more complete than any treatise that has hitherto been known even among the Jews, and certainly not among the Samaritans. And what is more we find here the two names of God, the Ehyh and IHVH, intertwined in a manner quite unlike the Jewish practice. Moreover, single letters are here repeated over and over again, almost whole lines being composed

of either the letter ה, or more especially the letter א. The alphabet
is grouped in many ways, and the names of God have been arranged
in squares and in other symmetrical forms. The two divine names
contain the five vowels, the ineffable name alone contains only three.
If, then, we compare this part of the Samaritan phylactery with the
Greek papyri we shall find that all the five vowels are there, and
moreover we shall be struck by the similarity between the strings
of the same vowel recurring in the Greek and those found in the
Samaritan, and what is still more surprising is that, in the Samaritan,
we find these groups of mysterious names of God which are the
result of a very composite combination of the three verses in
Ex. xiv, 19–21, to which reference has been made before. This
cannot be the result of sheer coincidence, one must have borrowed
from the other, but as the Samaritan seems to be independent of the
Jewish, and the Jewish no doubt equally independent of the
Samaritan, both must go back to a much more ancient common source
from which both have derived these names. It is also peculiarly
interesting to find that this Samaritan phylactery calls itself *Akhtaba*,
which is the perfect Samaritan equivalent of Grammata. I do not
think there can be any doubt with whom the priority for this title
lies, as the Hebrew Samaritan word "writings" is much clearer than
the Greek Grammata, which conveys very little and has in fact been
afterwards corrupted when taken over by the Jews and Samaritans.

SAMARITAN PHYLACTERIES AND AMULETS.

Reprinted from the "Proceedings of the Society of Biblical Archæology,"
May, 1915.

These Samaritan phylacteries are thus the real Aphasia Grammata known by reputation and now seen in the body. This does not exhaust the entire contents of the Samaritan phylactery. There is still another very important element which has entered into its composition, and which is not only thoroughly Samaritan but by means of which the high antiquity of this phylactery will be proved, for it stands, on the one hand, in close connection with the Samaritan inscriptions hitherto discovered, and, on the other, is the counterpart of sections of the prayer book of the Samaritans known only among them.

The Samaritan inscriptions which have hitherto been discovered, and which seem to range from the fifth to the fourteenth century, are of a very peculiar character. They are to a large extent inscriptions on lintels and doorposts. The lintels and doorposts were used as the places which were most conspicuous upon which to write or to make signs and marks of a symbolical character, as is testified by the command in Ex. xii, 22, that the Israelites in Egypt should sprinkle the blood of the Pascal Lamb over the lintels and doorposts so that the angel of destruction beholding the blood should pass over the houses of the Israelites and leave them unhurt. A more definite injunction we find in Deut. vi, 9, when it says: "ye shall write them upon the doorposts of thy houses and upon thy gates." This command has been taken literally by the Jews and the Samaritans. The Jews, however, have modified it inasmuch as they do not write the inscription on the very doorposts and lintels but use small scraps of parchment upon which they write two sections from Deut. vi, 4–9; xi, 13–21, which also form part of the *tefillin*. These are fastened to the doorposts and have thence taken the name of *mezzuzah*. The Samaritans have interpreted this command differently. They have taken "the words" mentioned in verse 9 to mean "the words," *i.e.*, the "ten words" or the "ten commandments," and we find therefore on some of these Samaritan monuments either the whole or part of the ten commandments, and to this day a stone with such inscription is embedded in the wall of the Samaritan Kinsha of Nablus.   But these are not the only words which are found in the Samaritan inscriptions the prophylactic character of which stands out most prominently when carefully examined.   Other verses have been selected from the Bible besides the ten commandments, as will be seen presently.

Besides the twelve inscriptions published by SPOER and seven by MuŠIL, there are about five or six in MONTGOMERY.   In addition to these the Samaritans have furnished me with copies of fourteen other inscriptions.   If we examine these thirty to thirty-five inscriptions we find that only two or three have the words of Deut. vi, 4–9, written upon them.   There are amongst them seven which contain either the whole of the Decalogue or portions thereof, the second as a rule beginning with "Honour thy Father," with which a section begins in the Samaritan Pentateuch.   The majority of the inscriptions, however, contain sympathetic and symbolical sentences from the Pentateuch, words of protection or of blessing, such as Gen. xlix, 25; Ex. xi, 23; xii, 13, 23 (which is very often repeated); xiii, 11; xiv, 14; xv, 2, 3; xx, 2, 3, 7, 12–17; xxii, 11b; xxiii, 25; xxxii, 12; Numb. vi, 24, 25, 26; Deut. v, 12a, 14; vi, 4–7; xiv, 31; xxvii, 4, 9; xxviii, 6, 8, 10, 12; xxxi, 8; xxxiii, 39.   Some of these refer to the destroying angel who should pass over the house without causing any hurt or harm to the inmates, or to the priestly blessing, etc. The verse (Ex. xv, iii) found as a cryptogram in the old Samaritan Bibles (see above) appears as the old inscription of Amwas of the twelfth century.   The only apparent exception is the inscription (MONTGOMERY, p. 274, Pl. II) which contains the Ten Words of Creation, i.e., ten short sentences from the first chapter of Genesis in which the name of God appears in connection with each one of the acts of creation.   These are the fundamental powerful words, the real *Logos*, and it is obvious from a mystical point of view that these words should be used as a protection.   The oldest Jewish speculation turns also on these words, and it is expressly stipulated that no public interpretation by any *Meturgeman* (interpreter) should be given of this chapter.   No interpretation is given of the "Story of the Creation" and the "Story of the Chariot."   The Ten Words of Creation are referred to already in the Chapters of the Fathers (chapter v, 1), and the Samaritans also discuss and group these Ten Words of Creation in Codex Gaster No. 1170 and by Kabasi as well as in the Malif (Codex Gaster 1169), but even this inscription contains other additional verses from the Bible. These inscriptions are of importance as they bear upon the character and construction of the phylactery. They are in fact phylacteries carved in stone instead of being written on parchment or on the doorposts in accordance with the injunction of the Law (Deut. vi, 9). Among the Jews only the parchment scroll has been used to this very day. These *mezzuzot*, unlike the *tefillin*, have indeed become phylacteries. Already from olden times we know that in addition to the two sections, Deut. vi, 4–9, xi, 13–21, other passages have been added of a similar character to those found in the Samaritan inscriptions, as well as mystical names and signs (APTOWITZER, *R.E.J.*, Vol. 65, 1913, p. 54 ff.); even mystical characters have also been inserted as already testified by RASHI in the eleventh century (see GASTER, *Journal R.A.S.*, July, 1913, p. 620). These seem to be, curiously enough, somewhat embellished letters of the Samaritan alphabet which claims to be the old Hebrew one, and if sanctity is attached to the Hebrew letters no doubt it would be given pre-eminently to the old real Hebrew characters. Mr. F. LEGGE has drawn my attention to an amulet of the Sabbatarian Sect of Crypto-Jews in Salonica, published by Mr. M. DARION in the *Journal Asiatique*, Paris, 1910, pp. 331–341. It is written wholly in this mystical alphabet and contains, besides quotations from the Zohar,—not recognized by Mr. DARION—similar Biblical verses at the end. In Cod. Gaster No. 443, which contains a number of such mystical alphabets, the one which agrees most closely with that of the amulet is, curiously enough, ascribed to Abraham the Hebrew. Christian inscriptions, of a similar character, found in Syrian Palestine on doorposts and lintels, show that this practice had spread from Jews and Samaritans to the followers of the new Faith (see W. K. PRENTICE, "Magical Formulae of the Christian Period in Syria," in *Amer. Journal of Archaeology*, Vol. X (1906), p. 137–150). The graphic form of the Samaritan inscription is also of special significance. We find here only portions of the Biblical verses; very rarely is the whole verse given, not even in the case of the Decalogue; parts of the verses stand for the whole. Moreover, even these words are not wholly written out. In not a few instances one or two letters represent the whole word, they are words represented only by the initial letters. It may be that consideration of space has been the reason for this kind of abbreviation, which reduces a whole verse to simple initials, or allows one word or two to take the place of the whole verse. Now, in form as well as contents, this is thoroughly and almost exclusively a Samaritan practice. Among the Jews, who have also resorted to abbreviations, no trace has hitherto been found, in the older rabbinical literature, of Biblical verses being thus reduced or quoted. The verses are cited in full or the first part is quoted, but a single word is not taken out of the verse and used to represent the whole of it. In later times, however, this practice begins to creep in, chiefly in mystical literature, when the Jews also freely adopted the use of Biblical verses in magical charms. A large number of instances is quoted by BLAU (*Zauberwesen*, pp. 68–71, Nos. 8–11). They were also used in incantations. So by Rabbi JOHANAN, against fever-heat (*Sabb.* 67[a]). But it is rather the Psalter which has been used for such prophylactic purposes, notably Psalms lxvii and xci.

In fact there exists a book called *Shimmush Tehillim* which seems to have served as a guide for the use of the Psalter for mystical and therapeutic purposes. (The English translation in the *Jewish Encyclopaedia* is unfortunately incomplete as the mystical element has been entirely omitted.) Out of these verses of the Psalter, abbreviations have been made and letters have been combined in bewildering variations. Verses of one psalm were often mixed up with those of another, and not only were initial letters combined, but medial and final letters also. A whole nomenclature of such mystical combinations has arisen, each one being regarded as having mystical power. Lists of these mystical names can be found in SCHWAB (*Vocabulaire de l'Angelologie*, Paris, 1897), and Codex Gaster (*Shemot Hamaleachim*). In course of time the words were forgotten, and many attempts were made to restore those of which only the initials have been left. So, in the blessing of the Kohanim and the so-called prayer of Rabbi Neḥunya, and ben-Haḳanah, such attempts have remained mere guess-work, and to this day the real words remain unidentified. I refer to these Jewish developments because they will also help us to determine the antiquity of the Samaritan phylactery, for none of these later combinations can be found therein, neither medial nor final letters are used, and only substitutions to which reference has already been made occur in the Samaritan. It may almost be considered as a key to the Samaritan inscriptions. The very Ten Words of Creation stand as it were at the beginning. Then, following the same principle, the same verses as found in the inscription are also to be met with among those inscribed in the phylactery. We very often find here that one single word stands for the whole verse, and, possibly to economize space, the same principle of abbreviation is carried out in the phylactery, the initials alone standing for the whole word. There are, moreover, a large number of Biblical verses of a sympathetic and prophylactic character, not only the words of Creation, but instances from the Pentateuch in which some healing process is described, such as the incident of Abraham at the Court of Abimelech (Gen. xx, 17), Moses' prayer for Miriam (Numb. xii, 13), or Moses' prayer for the people that the fire be quenched (Numb. xi, 2). We find also verses which refer to the miraculous power of God in smiting the wizards at the Court of Pharaoh, and other similar instances of a symbolical and sympathetic character.

There are also passages of blessings, such as Jacob blessing Ephraim and Manasseh (Gen. xlviii, 16), or blessing Joseph (Gen. xlix, 25), the Priestly Blessing (Numb. vi, 24), and other similar instances.

Special attention, however, has been paid to chapters xiv and xv of Exodus. These were taken as typical; one for the discomfiture of Egypt and the other for the triumph of the Israelites.

It may be a coincidence, but it is none the less a peculiar fact, that these two chapters are read with special solemnity in the Synagogue of the Sephardic Jews with the same cantillation as that of chapters xix and xx (Ten Commandments). If anything, this use of the verses goes to, prove the independent Samaritan origin of the phylacteries under consideration, for it accords entirely with the fundamental principle which governs the composition of the Samaritan Prayer Book. A characteristic feature of the Samaritan Prayer Book is that portion called the *Ḳaṭef*, literally Anthology. It is very unfortunate that, with the single exception of HEIDENHEIM (*B.S.*, II, pp. 1–4) no such *Ḳaṭef* has been published. COWLEY has entirely omitted it, and has thus greatly reduced the value of his otherwise excellent publication for a clear insight into the system and character of the Samaritan worship. This *Ḳaṭef* consists of a collection of verses of similar contents in which the same name or the same word recurs. These portions of the verses are culled from the Pentateuch mostly in the order in which they occur in the text. Very seldom, if ever, is a whole verse given, only that part of it which contains the word in question, *e.g.*, Joseph or Moses. These verses are then collected and form the *Ḳaṭef* for the Sabbaths of the First Month and for Passover (Cod. 839, f. 3*b*, 5*b*, 66*a*; *cf*. Cod. 844, f. 35*a*). There is also a *Ḳaṭef* for the Day of Circumcision (Cod. 827, f. 86*a*), with the names of God exactly as in the phylactery as if the one had been copied from the other. All these agree entirely, as it were, with the form of the Ten Words of Creation and the other inscriptions. Moreover, every Samaritan prayer practically begins with the recital of the first chapter of the Bible containing the Ten Words of Creation. And here we find ourselves on very ancient ground, for in the Temple of Jerusalem, also, the daily lesson contained consecutive parts of the first chapter of Genesis corresponding each day with the day of Creation. Again, the Song of Moses is recited by the Samaritans with the same responses and intercalations, and exactly in the same manner as are found in the phylactery, where we find also, curiously enough, the Samaritan translation of verse 3 which appears intercalated in the oldest known copies of the Samaritan text of the Pentateuch (see above).

Among the other elements which are used in the phylacteries, and which occur mostly in the intercalations, are numerous attributes of God, such as "the holy," "the merciful," "the gracious," etc. All these, and in still greater abundance, form one of the oldest prayers in the Service of the Samaritans (ed. COWLEY, pp. 7, 8), and are found also in two hymns printed by HEIDENHEIM from the Berlin MS. of PETERMAN (*B.S.*, Nos. 101, 102, pp. 206, 207), of which one (101) is missing in COWLEY. The Rabbis protested against such an accumulation of divine attributes in the prayer (see especially Tr. Megillah 18*a*, Berakh 33*b*, *cf.* also Ser. Berakh f. 12*d*, Midrash to Psalms, Ps. xix, 2), for, as they state, they cannot be exhausted. I see in this prohibition a protest against the Samaritan practice which might have appealed to some worshippers, and had therefore to be proscribed. The oldest form of Christian hymns in the Liturgy agrees more closely with the Samaritan practice than with the Jewish. How far the Rabbis have been successful with their prohibition belongs to the history of the Jewish Liturgy. It proves, however, the high antiquity of such prayers. These are specifically Samaritan traditions and Samaritan practices, and these phylacteries, even if some elements might have been borrowed from elsewhere, like the mystical combinations of the three verses, Ex. xiv, 19–21, which, however, is not likely to be the case, are a thorough product of the Samaritan mysticism, and representative of those magical practices which must go back to extreme antiquity, as does almost everything Samaritan.

We also find here the verses met with in the inscriptions represented likewise by single words, and, to save space, reduced to the initial letter. Herein the Samaritan phylactery differs profoundly from the Jewish, inasmuch as in the latter, as already remarked, medial and final letters are also used in abbreviations, permutations, and combinations. These are obviously later developments, whilst the Samaritan, on the contrary, give only the initial letters as is attested by the inscriptions, and, I believe, also by the Greek papyri. For, just as we find in the Samaritan phylacteries words consisting of initials besides those which are the result of substitution of letters by permutations of the alphabet—and curious words are the result of these initials—so may many a peculiar word in the Greek papyri be nothing else than the result of such a combination of initials. In this manner some of the riddles of the magical papyri might be solved, if the same principle could be applied to them as is applied to the Samaritan and Jewish phylacteries.

There is one more element of the Samaritan phylactery to which attention must be drawn. It is also a very characteristic and very ancient practice, that of *Palindrome*. Certain verses of the Bible, especially Ex. xv, 15, 16, are written backwards, starting, as it were, with the last word of verse 16 and going backwards, the order of the words, not of the letters, being reversed. Similarly Ex. xiv, 19 ff. ; xvii, 13, are written in the form of *Palindrome*.

This practice is known also to the Jews, and is referred to in the Talmud as למפרע = backwards (*v.* BLAU, *Zauberwesen*, p. 85). The usual practice in phylacteries of repeating important words many times (from three to ten) is also observed here, with specific words such as, " For I am the Lord that healeth thee" (Ex. xv, 26), which are repeated many times over, just like the names of God, which are repeated sometimes ten times and more.

It is remarkable that, and this is again a sign of its extreme antiquity, the Samaritan phylactery does not contain, in addition to the verses and names and mystical combinations, any of the peculiar drawings and designs found in other phylacteries—the only exception will be mentioned later on. No such geometrical figures and other drawings, except the square, are to be found in it. All these, on the contrary, occur in the Jewish phylacteries, and are, no doubt, of a more recent origin.

But this by no means exhausts the whole contents of the phylactery. The very character of this phylactery, and the use to which it has been put, are clearly indicated in the text. It is to be worn, and the writer starts from the very beginning with an invocation of some propitiatory verses for himself and for him who is to wear "these writings," to terrify all the demons and evil spirits. He becomes "clothed" with God's holy names. They cover him entirely, and, thus far, he has "God's names within him," like Exodus xxiii, 21, "for my name is within him"; and thus, though he is not identified with God, he wraps himself round and round with these mystical names as with so many means of protection. In one passage, Codd. D and G, the one who wears the amulet is believed to recite it, and he says: "From me the prayer, and from thee the healing" (Salvation), exactly as all the charms and exorcisms of olden and modern times finish.

It remains still to be shown first that this document is the phylactery mentioned in Matthew xxiii, 5, which has hitherto been taken to be identical with the Jewish frontlets. It has been seen before that this document called itself *Akhtaba*, the equivalent of *Grammata*, but in one MS., Cod. B, we find, instead of this word, the word *fnktra*, or *flktra*—as the writing is indistinct— and we have here the exact transcript of the consonants of the Greek phylactera. It is well known that the phylacteries have been worn, and are being worn, openly, in order either to catch the evil eye or terrify the demons and evil spirits, and sometimes they are carried in the bosom. They are worn constantly not like the *tefillin* which are only put on during prayer.

There cannot be the slightest doubt that the Jews also had phylacteries in the proper sense of the word, like all the other nations. Not only have a large number been preserved to this very day, although they are not older than perhaps the ninth century, but the older Rabbinical literature abounds in references to the so-called *Kameoth*, and by this name they are called. So long as these *Kameoth* were considered to be of recent origin, no attention was paid to them, but in the light of the present investigation it becomes clear that they are much older than had hitherto been assumed. In all essentials they agree with the Samaritan phylactery, and they show a regular organic development. The description of these *Kameoth* in the Talmudic treatise (Sabbath 115[b]) "As containing the letters of the Name and other quotations from the Torah," fits exactly the Samaritan phylactery. It reads as if it were part of the latter—so closely allied are they to one another—and what applies to the latter applies also to the former, when referred to in Matthew.

The objection that might be raised that the Samaritan phylactery was not worn outwardly, is set aside by the simple fact that the fragment in the British Museum is enclosed in such an ornamental metal case as is used to this day by the Arabs among others, on the edge of which is engraved in Samaritan characters with other sentences, the well-known verse from Exodus xiv, "The Lord will fight for you," etc., so often found on Samaritan inscriptions and in the text of the phylactery itself. No doubt, at a certain time, it became dangerous for any Samaritan to exhibit his nationality outwardly, and hence, instead of wearing the phylactery in a leather satchel or in a metal case in the sight of all, he preferred wearing it under his garment. The later practice proves nothing for that of previous centuries. The passage in Matthew is clearly intended to ridicule certain exaggerated practices of the Scribes and Pharisees, and the *tefillin*, *i.e.*, the frontlets used at prayer, are here deliberately described as if they were phylacteries used for superstitious and magical practices. They are described as "being made broad," which cannot be the case with the *tefillin*. But these phylacteries can be so folded that they can be made as broad as the wearer likes, a fact which helps to explain the passage in Matthew ; and similarly, instead of speaking of the fringes or *Ṣiṣith*, "the border of the garment," is referred to, just as, for the same purpose, instead of doing what might be the fulfilment of the Law, these Scribes and Pharisees indulged in practices which were condemned by the Law, as was the wearing of phylacteries.

From the examination of the Samaritan phylacteries, it is clear that we, in fact, find here a document the origin of which may be contemporary with the first century, or even still older, but it cannot be very much later. No trace of any other influence can be found in it: not a single Greek word, except the name phylactery which occurs in one MS. only. There is now one passage found in Codd. C and D, in which a string of names is given of reputed wizards and sorcerers. These seem to be Latin, and it would be remarkable if these strange names had been preserved for so many centuries without being corrupted. Had such been the case it would prove the extreme accuracy with which the scribes had copied the old original writings, and would strengthen the belief that we have here indeed a careful transcript of them. Among these names there occur Domninus, Sabina, a certain Nuna, and the list closes with Simeon and Eleazar.   If this Simeon could be identified with Simon Magus, then no doubt as to the antiquity of these documents could any longer be entertained.

It is possible that Nuna may be another form for Luna, one of the names recorded for the famous Helena, very likely written Hlna— (הלנא) in Semitic letters, from which Lena or Luna could easily be derived, the H (ה) being taken as the article, as if the name was to be read Haluna—the Luna—in course of time the H was dropped and we got the form Lena, Luna, Nuna.

Any further investigation will have to start from these names of the sorcerers or wizards here mentioned, which, when identified, will still more help to fix the date of the composition of these phylacteries.

The Samaritan phylacteries, or *Shem Hamitfaresh*, have been preserved in many forms: A.   Square sheets of parchment the size of a goat skin.   B.   In the form of a scroll of varying length and width.   C.   In the form of a little booklet, of which one single leaf has been thus far preserved   D.   In small scraps of paper of various sizes.   E.   In the form of metal coins.   And also F.   In the form of inscriptions carved in stone.   Each of these will now be briefly described.

SAMARITAN PHYLACTERIES AND AMULETS.

Reprinted from the " Proceedings of the Society of Biblical Archæology,"
June, 1915.

A brief description of each of the various forms of the Samaritan phylactery may now be given.

There are in my possession sixteen such phylacteries. Fourteen are originals, and two are photographic facsimiles of originals— one is in the British Museum, the other belongs to Mr. D. S. Sassoon, who most liberally allowed me to take a copy of it. Of these texts eight[1] belong to the first group. They all follow more or less the same type, at any rate in the writing and the outward appearance of the text. They differ somewhat in the arrangement of the contents. A certain latitude has been left to the scribe to manipulate and arrange the contents as he thought most suitable for his purpose. It may be that some artistic consideration in the grouping of similar verses and in the arrangement of the intercalary verses has led him to deviate from the original. It is also not impossible that these variations represent all the forms faithfully reproduced by the scribes who would not venture on innovations lest they should weaken the power of the amulet. Be it as it may, however much they may differ in the internal arrangement and sequence of the verses, in their outward form they follow as a rule one single type. It will therefore be sufficient to describe one of them only, but at greater length.

These phylacteries (or Shem) with one exception (I) which is written on paper consist of one goat skin cut into a square measuring from top to bottom between 17 inches and 22 inches. It is difficult to determine how much it measured from right to left. There is only one that has been completely preserved and this measures 27 inches. All the others are incomplete.

---

[1] Codd. Nos. 1101 (A), 1102 (B), 1100 (C), 1103 (E), 1104 (F), 1177A (I), Brit. Mus. Add. 27456 (N), Sassoon (P).

The skin has been well prepared and turned into parchment, and the writing is as far as can be ascertained on the fleshy, not on the hairy, side.

Among the Jews the rule is that on parchment the writing must be on the side nearest the flesh and on leather on the hair side, when used for having the sacred texts written on them.

All the Samaritan copies of the Pentateuch, both in the form of scrolls or in book form, are written on such parchment prepared from the skin of goats. In addition to the preparation necessary to make them fit for writing on, these skins seem to have been split. The art of splitting skins was not unknown in olden times, and the splitting of skins on which sacred scrolls were to be written is often mentioned in Rabbinic literature. The skins which are *not* vellum are extremely thin and there was a clear reason for making them thin and elastic. They had to be folded over and over again to such an extent that from a skin covering 16 inches by 24 inches, the phylactery was reduced to a small parcel of about 3 inches by 2 inches, and even smaller. The skin was divided into two unequal halves. Each of these was folded inwardly at least three times, so as to form long narrow strips which met in the middle. These were folded one on top of the other, and then a new doubling began from the top and the bottom of the long strip. Folded three times each way, they were then pressed one upon the other, and put in satchels of metal or cloth, so as to be worn round the arm, or the neck, hanging by a string. This multiple folding would have been utterly impossible unless the skin was thin and yet strong enough to stand the strain. Hence the necessity for reducing the thickness of the skin by splitting it. This folding of the skin was in a way the cause of its destruction.

However strong it may be, no skin can, with impunity, stand such a strain for centuries, to which must be added the continual friction of the edges. The inevitable result has been that it has given way all along these edges, and now, with but one exception, there is *no complete* phylactery. Most of them are only halves, either of the first or the second part, mostly of the latter, for the second half formed the innermost layer in the folding and was less exposed to loss or destruction than the first. The only complete text is my MS. No. 1100, which I have called C, and even in this case the above statement needs some qualification. Though the full skin is there, the two halves have parted, and some of the contents have been damaged by this breaking along each of the folds. The next one

in completeness is Cod. No. 1176, which I have called H.   Here
a gap has been produced between the two parts by which a good
portion of the text has disappeared in addition to at least one or
two columns at the end.   Worse has been the fate of the other
codices, A, B, E, F, N, and P; each of which is not more than
half, if so much, of the skin.   E, H, and P contain the first part,
and A, B, F, and N, the second part.   They vary in the degree of
deterioration, and in the size of the preserved portion.   The worst is
probably Cod. N, mere tattered fragments.   P is fairly good, the upper
portion is missing, gaps are between the folds, and the end is
entirely gone.   The best preserved of all is unquestionably F, of
which therefore a facsimile is given.   A and B follow suit.   In
addition to these must be mentioned Cod. I, which is written on
paper—the only specimen of this kind of phylactery.   Owing to the
fragile nature of the paper it has suffered even more than those on
parchment with the exception of N.   Only the first two columns
have been preserved with a break in the middle where it has been
folded.   It follows in its measurement and arrangement as well as in
its writing the other phylacteries, and it seems to be a fairly old MS.,
possibly fourteenth or fifteenth century.   By means of these fragments
it is possible to reconstruct a full text and in any case to complete
the lacunae and gaps on C and H, if only one could be quite sure of
their absolute identity in the order and arrangement of the text.   It
will, however, not be necessary to have recourse to any reconstruction
as will be seen presently, for, in addition to C a complete text has
been preserved in Group II.

Now all these codices follow one general rule in the writing of
the contents.   The skin is divided into seven columns of equal width
(3 inches).   These are separated one from the other by a space of
¾ inch, which has not been left blank.

These seven columns are surrounded on all four sides by two lines
of writing of which one is a Palindrome of verses from Exod. xiv, 16 ff.,
and xvii, 8 ff.   This writing is then continued in single lines filling
up the blanks between the columns.   In order to insert these lines,
the scribe has turned the skin to the left, and starting from the bottom
he wrote parallel to the side line.   In the same manner are the
other lines written.   If the phylactery is turned again to the proper
angle these lines are written exactly like the Mongolian script, one
letter standing above the other.   In these lines round and between
the columns one may detect the oldest form of illumination, the

verses and the letters preceding floral and other architectural illustrations.   In the Massora which accompanies the Hebrew MSS. of
the Bible the same symmetrical arrangement of lines above and
below the text is observed.   Here one can follow up the later floral
and architectural development.   If reference is made to this marginal
illustration it is done also for the purpose of showing that we are
dealing with extremely archaic " motives " faithfully preserved in the
phylactery.   These marginal and intercolumnal lines are written
regularly in very large characters like majuscules or capital letters,
and are the same as those used in the book-form of the MSS. of the
Pentateuch only, in which the leaves have writing on both sides, and
not in the scroll where the writing is on one side only and is in the
form of minuscules or uncials.   Very many goat skins would have
been required for a Pentateuch written in capitals ; not only would
the scroll become too heavy and unwieldy, but, which is more
important, it would deviate from the type used in that ancient scroll,
ascribed by the Samarians to Abisha, who is said to have written it
in the XIIIth year after the settlement of the Israelites in Canaan.
This scroll, which I have seen in Nablus, as well as *all* the other
scrolls of the law, are written in very small characters.   They are of
the uncial type and differ from the larger only by their size, otherwise
the character is the same.   The Samaritans have also a cursive type
which they call half-letters (חצי אות, pronounced *esi ot*) used by
them for every book except the Law.   None of the phylacteries
mentioned hitherto show even a trace of such cursive writing.   The
overwhelmingly larger part of the text is written in minuscules—if I
may call them so.   But in each column there are intercalated a
certain number of lines which often interrupt the text, and they are
written with capital letters, but no capital is used as an initial letter
of a column or paragraph.   The whole line is written either in
capitals or in minuscules.   The words are divided from one another
by dots, as is the regular custom of Samaritan writing.   But when
letters have been combined to form some mystical name they are
not divided by any sign.   Sometimes a whole line consists of letters
which are not divided up into words.   Accents, as I call them, or
rather graphic signs, are sometimes found at the end of single words,
when these stand for a whole " verse," and have been singled out as
the most important for the purpose of the phylactery.   An additional
reason for the use of the small type is to be found in the size of the
text.   If all that is found now in a phylactery was to be written upon

one skin, the smaller the type the better for the purpose, especially
if regard was to have been had to the symmetrical form of the
writing. As mentioned before, the writing of the phylactery follows
the example of the Scroll of the Law and the Prayer Book.
Identical words are written as it were in columns. Care is taken that
the same word occurring in two or more consecutive lines should be
so written that the same words should be found standing one upon
the other, forming as it were a column. For that reason blanks were
left in various lines so that the required word should be in the
required place. This involves loss of space which the writer of the
phylactery could ill spare. Hence, minute writing and multiplication
of abbreviations. Taking as an average 80 lines to a column and
7 columns to a phylactery, there are then no less than about 560
lines in the phylactery. If we multiply these lines by at least 20, for
this is the minimum number of a full line, we have no less than
11,200 letters in the space of 16 inches by 24 inches, not reckoning
the thousands of dots between the words. The facsimile here
reproduced will show how successfully the Samaritan scribes coped
with this difficulty. Cod. A has 356 lines, B has 244 lines, E has
94 lines, F has 226 lines, I has 335 lines, N has 201 lines, and P has
346 lines, fragments of lines being counted as full lines. These
details are sufficient. They show thus far the extent of the material
available for any future comprehensive publication.

All these texts agree furthermore in one point—they are
anonymous. By this I mean that neither the name of the writer, nor
that of him for whose benefit the amulet has been written, is
mentioned. It can be worn by anyone who happens to possess it or
to whom it may have been lent for the purpose of averting evil or
healing the sickness from which he suffers.

This anonymity no doubt helped to save these amulets from
destruction. Generation after generation they passed on from one
possessor to another. Each one hoped to get protection against foes
and sickness, for the charm was not limited to any person specially
mentioned in the phylactery.

On the other hand this general use has also contributed to reduce
these amulets to their present fragmentary state, such as is referred to
above.

Before proceeding to the second group, let me say a word about
the ink. The Samaritans seem to have made use of two kinds
of ink, both of course were vegetable ink, as is that which is used by

the Jews to this day for writing sacred texts. The Samaritans have one ink which is very black and glossy, and the other a very pale ink. The latter is not the result of any fading. I have parts of Samaritan scrolls of the Pentateuch written both in the black and the pale, and the fragments of the Samaritan scroll in the British Museum are also written in that pale ink. The black and glossy ink written on a hard surface like parchment is liable to peel, leaving a faint trace behind which soon disappears. The pale ink seems to sink deeper into the parchment, and thus the writing is better preserved. Most of the phylacteries are written with the black ink, the process of manufacturing which is a secret which the Samaritans will not reveal.

The second group consists of scrolls. The text is not written on a square piece, but in one long column. It is obvious that if the whole contents of Group I were to be entered on a scroll, more than one strip of parchment would be necessary. Patching is not favoured by magic. The amulet must as far as possible be of one piece, otherwise the evil elements may find some imperfection in the document and destroy its efficacy. There must have been some cogent reason for the use of the scroll. It is in fact an open question which of the two forms is the older. All the ancient sacred texts are written in scrolls and a number of magical texts in Greek, and later in Arabic, are in the forms of scrolls. The space is not so limited as in a given skin to which nothing could be added, but here strip could be joined to strip and the scroll will be continually lengthened until everything was written upon it which the magician would wish to write. There are two ways of writing on a scroll, either in short parallel columns corresponding to the width of the strip, which I would call horizontal writing, and the other vertical writing, running parallel to the right-hand edge-line, forming one continuous column from the beginning to the end of the scroll.

The Jewish and Samaritan scrolls of the Law and the Jewish frontlets are written in short columns. So also the Egyptian "Book of the Dead" and many old Greek scrolls. These lent themselves afterwards to an easy division into leaves, and this probably explains best why the oldest codices of the Bible, and even secular writings, are written in three narrow columns, and then later on in two columns, instead of being written across the whole width of the page. I am not aware that any explanation has hitherto been offered for this peculiar palaeographic phenomenon. In the Samaritan phylacteries,

however, the writing is what I call vertical, not from right to left
but from top to bottom, the whole text forming one single column.
It starts from the top end of the strip and is continued uninterruptedly to the end. He who reads it must turn the scroll upward.
And precisely in the same manner are the Jewish magic phylacteries
and amulets, the Arabic, and an old Greek roll in my possession.
Of such rolls there are three in my possession, 1105 (D), 1106 (G),
1107 (G2) and a fourth would be 1177 (K L M) if the three strips
are parts of one roll, not fragments of two or three as I originally
believed when I got them at different times, and all in a very
dilapidated condition. Of these four rolls one is on parchment and
the rest are on paper. The dates vary from the fourteenth to the
nineteenth century. The lines are perpendicular to the length of
the document.

The contents of these phylacteries are more or less the same
as Group I. The principle underlying the text is the same, and one
may be a copy from the other. There are, however, some important
differences between these two groups, In the first place they differ
in size : whilst all the square documents have from 500 to 550 lines,
some of Group II vary from 260 in Cod. G, to 625 in Cod. D,
G2 has 280 lines. It must be observed that the width of the lines
is the same in both groups—3 inches. The writing does not differ
materially. It is throughout the same small uncial writing alternating with larger capitals. Only occasionally does the scribe of
G2—who died in 1908—lapse into the use of the cursive letters.
Of these MSS. Cod. D is the longest. It is almost a verbatim
transcript of the square amulet (C) on a paper scroll. It is not
unlikely that the want of parchment had driven the copyist to this
expedient. He transcribed the other document upon material easily
obtainable. The top left-hand corner has been torn away probably
by an attempt to force this roll into a metal case; otherwise, it is
very well preserved, and is in fact the only perfect copy that has
hitherto been found among the Samaritans. It is for this reason
that I have selected this MS. for publication though it cannot be
older than the seventeenth century, if it is not of a later date. As
this copy has been well preserved one can see a marginal line running
down the length and breadth and enclosing the text all round. It
represents the marginal and intercolumnar lines of the MSS. in
Group I, though the wording differs. To the same class belong
Cod. 1177 (K L M), if, as mentioned above, they are fragments of

one phylactery. It is also on paper. The writing is very small and neat. It is, however, worn to shreds, the edges have entirely disappeared, the writing is in many places obliterated and the whole MS. so thin and frail that it breaks up into fragments if it is not handled very carefully. The length of the existing pieces joined together would be 37 inches. There are 179 lines, and it belongs probably to the sixteenth century.

The other MSS., G and G2, represent a shorter recension. Only a few of the biblical quotations have been retained and even these are often in an enigmatic form, sometimes represented by one single word or by a string of letters. Even the alphabet and mystical squares have been reduced to the smallest expression. Of these G is the oldest. It is written on parchment, but it has suffered so much through constant wear and tear that (though it is now backed) the edges are entirely frayed. Smaller and larger lacunae have contributed to mutilate the text. Happily in the modern copy (G2) all the lacunae have been filled up and the missing portions completed, as well as some new material added at the end. G has 260 lines and is dated 773 Heg. = 1364, and G2 has 280 lines and was written *circa* 1905. A space of close upon 600 years shows no difference between these texts. In G and D in some parts there are a few Samaritan Massoretic signs. The same care has been bestowed on the writing of these phylacteries as on those previously mentioned. Though not cramped for space, still the same abbreviations are also found there, probably because the copyist wished to keep close to the original, and if possible to copy it line for line as is seen in G2 compared with G, and in the alphabets in D compared with C or F. In spite of these similarities there is a profound difference between these two groups. Whilst the first group is for general use, the phylacteries in scroll form are *all* of a personal character. They are written for the special use and benefit of a person distinctly named. This practice was in a way fatal to the phylactery. With the death of the man in whose name it was written its efficacy must have disappeared. It became valueless and disappeared also. Hence the small number of the scroll phylacteries.

In a parchment scroll means were found to preserve its efficacy, and the name of the first person could be erased and that of the new wearer substituted. This has in fact happened with Cod. G, which as we learn from the name now found inscribed on the erasure belonged to no less a person than the actual High Priest

Jacob, the son of Ahron. This name is repeated three times. G2 is a copy made on paper by Azi, the son of this High Priest. He copied the old one in the possession of his father who is still alive, and substituted his own name for it. (Azi has since died, some five years ago.) He could not take the other, for his father kept it for his own protection until he parted with it to me in 1907. In this we find moreover an Arabic colophon giving us the ancient history of the phylactery, that it was copied by Jacob, the son of Sadakah, the son of Jacob, of the sons of Marḥib, from an older original in the handwriting of Harun (Ahron), the Haftavi of Nablus from an older copy in the handwriting of Abu Almuḥasin, the son of the Sheikh Abu Jacob Aben Dartah aben Salamah, son of Joseph, son of Dartah. All these details are missing in Group I. D was written for Abraham, of the sons of Daneftah, and in K L M the name of Joseph, son of Shalmah, son of Ab (Zahutah?) is found twice. In none of these except G is the date given. It may have been in K L M, but that part is missing.

There is still another profound difference between the scroll and the square, namely in Group II, except D, some cabbalistic signs are inserted after the first few lines. These twisted signs could easily be mistaken for an attempt at a primitive ornamentation. They are found, however, in other mystical writings, Samaritan and Arabic (see below), and they cannot be mistaken by anyone acquainted with cabbalistic signs and sigla. They prove that these scrolls follow a somewhat different practice than was tolerated in the writing of the square phylacteries.

Group III consists of one single leaf of parchment, Cod. 899 (O), almost faded, and discovered by me by a mere chance. The Samaritan who possessed it drew it out inadvertently from his bosom with an old parchment copy of the Pentateuch which he offered for sale to me. I purchased both together to the evident annoyance of the owner who was very reluctant to part with it. Pressed as to its meaning he stated that it was an ancient *Shem Hamitfaresh* of which this was the only remnant. The other Samaritans whom I consulted later on corroborated this fact, and up till now—it is more than twelve years since I acquired it—no other fragment nor anything like it has been shown by the Samaritans. The reading offered great difficulties. It is here reproduced, now being enlarged more than double its original size. It is a small piece of thin parchment of 3 inches by $2\frac{1}{2}$ inches. Less than half this space is occupied with

microscopic uncial writing. Within 1 inch by 2 inches no less
than 25 lines are written, divided into groups of 10 lines each. In
each line there are 10 letters divided often by stops. Between these
groups of 10 lines there are letters which are used as numerals. The
fragment begins with the 6th line of No. 4 and breaks off at the end
of No 10. It is the smallest Samaritan MS. I have ever seen, either
in the Libraries of Europe or among the Samaritans in Nablus. It
reminds one forcibly of the minute MSS. of the Manichaeans of
which some specimens have recently come to light. This phylactery
was in the form of a booklet with leaves, and differs entirely
from the other phylacteries hitherto described. Also the arrangement of the matter in groups of numbered lines differentiates it from
the others. As to the contents it would be difficult to say in how far it
agreed with the rest, considering that there is not one single complete
word in all these lines which could serve as a clue. They consist
only of single dotted letters, which the Samaritans themselves could
not entirely decipher, and still less supply the full word represented
by the initials, which alone fill the lines of this curious document.
Had not the Samaritans been unanimous in calling it a "*Shem
Hamitfaresh*" I should have thought it to be a book of *Sortes*—
a fortune-book—a kind of oracle, the answers being arranged in
certain groups. The MS. is stained and many letters have entirely
disappeared. In spite of these difficulties I have succeeded in most
cases in deciphering the letters, and a facsimile is given here. As
far as I have been able to compare them with the contents of the
other phylacteries they do not correspond with similar groups of
initials. They are probably Biblical verses, but hitherto have baffled
the ingenuity and skill of the Samaritans themselves. It is lucky
that this solitary leaf should have escaped the complete destruction
which has overtaken the rest of the volume of which it formed part.
Judging by the writing and by the fact that it is written on
parchment this fragment cannot be later than the thirteenth or
fourteenth century.

Among the Samaritan MSS. in the British Museum there are
two (Cod. Harley 5481 and 5495?) of the sixteenth century which
contain in addition to prayers some calendar notes. These are
written in the geometrical figures so characteristic of amulets.
They are preceded and followed (Cod. 4581, f. 54, Cod. 5495,
fols. 6, 16, and 24) by a peculiar formula. They are arranged
symmetrically in groups of 9 or 10 lines to the page, and each line

contains 5 or 10 words. They are written above and below the
calendar notes, but they are so arranged in Cod. 5491 that those on
the top must be read downwards, and those from the bottom
upwards, towards the central portion. It is precisely the order of
the surrounding lines of the phylactery. The contents also show
a slight variation of lines very similar to those in the phylactery. It
is, curiously enough, the same part of the Jewish liturgy of propitiation
which belongs to the oldest layer. As it consists only of a few lines
the translation may be given at the end of the present study. Its
importance lies in the possibility of its affording a clue to the
preceding text. It is here, as it were, an amulet connected with some
astrological notions. There can be no doubt that we have here a
portion of the old phylactery greatly reduced and adapted to
practical use.

This leads on to other shorter formulae, some of which are even
accompanied by mystical diagrams. They are all found in my
Cod. 884 (S) written by a modern hand on some additional leaves which
precede much older Arabic magical and mystical texts. Some of the
formûlae are in Arabic, a good number however are in Samaritan.
They consist of from two to six lines. They are for the most part
nothing else than detached portions from the old phylactery, the
palindrome of the "Shema," or verses from Exod. xv, or the blessing
of the priests, and again mystical combinations of initial letters and
mystical names of angels. In some cases "seals" and other signs
are added and directions are given for the specific use of each of
those formulae.

Though the copy is modern it would be rash to suggest that
these short formulae are also of modern origin—merely small
portions taken out of the larger phylactery. On the contrary
they may belong to the oldest elements of the phylactery. For,
curiously enough, they agree with the old inscriptions on stone dating
from the fifth century downward. The texts are very often the same,
and the Biblical verses are treated in both sets of monuments in
precisely the same manner. Whoever knows the tenacity with
which magical formulae will maintain themselves through the ages,
will not easily refuse to see in the magical prescriptions and amulets
of the nineteenth century the direct descendants of the ancient
prophylactic inscriptions carved on the posterns and lintels of the
gates. The existence of the larger phylacteries helped in the
preservation of these shorter formulae, which are written on scraps

of paper, worn by the patient. The Priest (Kohen) or High Priest is as a rule the person from whom the people obtain these amulets. The MS. in question belonged indeed to the actual High Priest Jacob, from whom I obtained it. Finally, the smallest formula is then the inscriptions stamped on bronze or silver-gilt coins and medals which are worn by babies for protection against evil eye and other occurrences caused by evil spirits. Such a coin is reproduced by MONTGOMERY, *Samaritans*, Pl. 8 (p. 272). The words there are practically copies of the inscriptions.

All these manifold phylacteries form one cycle. They are all phylacteries in the strict sense of the word, and prove beyond doubt that the Samaritans form no exception; that, in spite of repeated assertions to the contrary by those to whom that literature has hitherto been inaccessible, they have an ancient mystical tradition, which in its essence and fundamental principles is undistinguishable from the Jewish cabbalistic tradition. Moreover, that by the help of it some hitherto inexplicable features in Greek magical texts find a satisfactory explanation; and, finally, that one of the oldest forms of the real phylacteries has been preserved by the Samaritans in their *Shem Hamitfaresh.*

SAMARITAN PHYLACTERIES AND AMULETS.

Reprinted from the " Proceedings of the Society of Biblical Archaeology,"
February, 1916.

I have selected for publication, in the first place, the text contained in Codex D, though it is a scroll. My reason for doing so is that this text is the most complete with the exception of the first five or six lines, the top corner being torn away. The rest is in a perfect state of preservation and is the longest text thus far known. Moreover the space not being limited as with a skin, the copyist was able, in very many instances, to supply full words where, in the other codices, only the initial letters were given, and has thus avoided many of the obscurities and difficulties which baffled the investigator. He has also been scrupulously careful in his work, for, in a few instances, one can see that he has gone over the copy again after completing it, correcting his mistakes and supplying missing words and letters.

A curious fact which may be noted here is that I have been unable to find a single erasure in any of the copies of the phylactery. Mistakes have been corrected by writing the letter over the line, and words omitted have also been supplied in the same manner. The Samaritans evidently treated these texts with the reverence they accorded to sacred texts of the Law. Among the Jews it is well known that if a mistake occurs in the writing of the various names of God, the mistake cannot be corrected by erasure, the whole column must be cut out. But intercalations between the lines are not forbidden. The same seems to hold good for Samaritan scrolls, and, as far as can be ascertained, for these phylacteries also. In one instance, to which reference will be made later, an erasure has been made in Codex C. But this did not affect the text. Only the name of the first owner was erased, and that of the new possessor substituted. But in the text itself no erasures have been made. The reason, no doubt, is that such erasures would be regarded as mutilations which would vitiate the prophylactic character of the document.

The scribe has, moreover, been careful to preserve the twofold character of the script. Certain words and lines are written in the larger type and others in the minuscule. The only difference noticeable between this text and the older one is the omission of some of the signs of interpunctuation and abbreviation which are still found, *e.g.*, in Codices G and C. On the other hand, the words have been divided by dots as in most of the MSS., although in Codex E (1103), which is unfortunately incomplete but seems to be the oldest in existence, the words are, but with rare exceptions, not separated at all. The lines consist of a series of letters which can be read only by those thoroughly familiar with the language. By its completeness Codex D can form the basis for all future investigations, and by its close similarity with Codex C, and with some of the other full texts, it will help in the elucidation of many difficult passages caused by the bad state of preservation and the large number of abbreviations and single letters used in these texts.

With the aid of Codex D one can study the inner history of the phylactery, for, no doubt, it must have grown in the course of time. Other elements have unquestionably been added so as to make it more powerful and more efficacious. It is of the essence of magic to be eclectic and syncretistic. It gathers its elements from many sources and increases the strength of its magical operations by the addition of elements, taken from elsewhere, to which similar thaumaturgical importance had been given. It is also a feature of amulets that new matter is added to its contents whilst none of it is eliminated. This feature has not been sufficiently studied, though, by means of it one could follow up, in the various amulets, the history of their origin and growth. It will be found that the oldest portion is always that which stands at the beginning, and the latest addition is that with which the amulet concludes. There are sufficient indications in the text to enable us to separate one section from the other. We can trace them in Greek magical papyri and in almost every magical phylactery or amulet. Each section, as it were, begins with a similar formula of invocation of the Great Power. Thus Codex D, not less than most of the other codices, has preserved this characteristic feature in the repetition of the opening formula: " For I call upon the name of the Lord," etc., which, no doubt, marks a new section. This is the opening formula of the Samaritan prayer. As there is some strong similarity in the grouping of verses, and graphical symmetry between the amulet and some codices of the Pentateuch, and, above all, certain sections of the Prayer Book, to which reference has been made on page 139, there can be no doubt, therefore, that this formula marks such a new beginning. With our present knowledge it would be impossible to establish the period to which each of these sections belongs. They may be coeval in their origin, or they may have existed independently, belonging to different strata of thought in belief and practice. They have been united at some period so as to form one amulet containing all the elements of which each of the others boasted separately. If we now examine more closely the contents of these various sections, as I call them, we shall find that there is a difference between the first and the other part, which becomes more and more marked as we reach the end. Broadly speaking, there are two main divisions : the first (from lines 1 to 296) the symbolical and sympathetic as well as imprecatory and invocative, consisting mostly of Biblical verses and allusions to Biblical incidents : the second (lines 297 to 598) is purely mystical.

Of these sections the first is undoubtedly the oldest and agrees in its main features with the Samaritan Liturgy. All the lapidary inscriptions, as well as all the other forms of Phylacteries, can be found here. No artificial use has as yet been made of the Biblical verses—which are mostly from Genesis and Exodus—or of the words and letters, and the names of God, they contain ; there is not even a *palindrome*. This section is found at the very beginning of every other full copy and, in a shortened form, in the smaller texts. The second section, starting from line 150, differs in some respects from the first. The quotations are no longer from Genesis and Exodus. They are more of an invocative and imprecatory character. Palindrome and other artificial combinations of Biblical words and letters occur. It is probably a somewhat later development, but follows in the main the leading principles of the first section. Few quotations of this section are found among the ancient inscriptions. It is, moreover, not an integral and immutable part of every Samaritan Phylactery. As far as can be judged from the fragmentary character of Codices E and P, only a few quotations of this section seem to have been used. Totally different in conception and execution is the text of the third section, or second part. Here we find ourselves in the midst of the so-called practical Cabbala : mystical and magical formulae consisting chiefly of permutations and combinations of the names of God, groupings of the alphabets in symmetrical and progressive lines, mystical squares and other combinations of letters. It would be difficult to determine the age of these cabbalistic forms and manipulations. They are, however, at least as old as those in the first and second sections. They are the common property of Jew,

Samaritan and Greek, and rest on the mystery of the Ineffable Name. Here we find these peculiar groups of letters, which are used in Hebrew as *matres lectiones*, and which appear as vowels in the Greek Papyri. In fact, every magical treatise, from ancient times down to the most recent amulets, can furnish ample and surprisingly close parallels to this section, which I call the Cabbalistic Part. It may have existed originally in a separate form, and independent of the other sections, to which it has been joined in order to increase the potency of the charm—the prophylactic value of the amulet—which thus became a complete "armour" against the attacks of sorcerers and wizards, of demons and wild beasts, of every form of sickness, fever, and hurt.

An abstract of this section is found in the other texts, often very much curtailed and only understood when compared with the fuller text. The copyists have also taken greater liberties in the manipulation of the elements in the second part.

I have reproduced the text exactly as found in the MS., line for line, keeping also to the comparative size of the type, and, as far as possible, to the graphical peculiarity, which, however, is not so pronounced here as in the square codices.

The lacunae have been completed from Codices C, E, and H (1176).

I am adding a literal translation, together with such explanatory notes as may be required to elucidate some of the difficulties of this text, as well as to show the parallelisms between the Samaritan and other—especially Jewish—magical literature. Not all the difficulties and obscurities have been elucidated in spite of many years of study spent upon it, but it is hoped that the little that has remained unsolved will attract the attention of students of this mystical literature, who, no doubt, will continue to work, and solve the few remaining problems.

In the following translation every fifth line is marked excepting where a new section of the text occurs, when an additional number shows the corresponding line in the original. Explanatory notes are given in small figures above the line. The square brackets denote matter supplied from other codices. This translation is as literal as possible, for the importance of an amulet depends on its wording. References have been given to all the Biblical passages, and where the Samaritan recension differs from the Jewish, attention has been drawn to the fact.

Cod. D. 1105.

TRANSLATION.

(**1**) For I call in the name of the L(ord) and [ascribe ye greatness unto our G(od), Dt. xxxii, 3]¹. In the name of the L. G. of Israel [do I begin, for in the name of the L.] I call (Dt. xxxii, 3). There is none like the G. of Jeshurun (Dt. xxxiii, 26), [arise O L. for him who has written] these writings, and for the name of him who wears [this writing. In the beginning] (**5**) created the L. (Gn. i, 1). And the L. will pass over [the door and will not suffer] the destroyer to come into your houses to smite you (Ex. xii, 23).² [And I will in the name of the L.] call and ascribe ye greatness unto our G. [He is the rock, His work is perfect.] For all his ways are judgment. A God of faithfulness [and without iniquity. Just] and right is he (Dt. xxxii, 3, 4).³ The L. is our G., the L. is [one (Dt. vi, 4).⁴ Blessed be] (line 5) (**10**) our G. for ever, and blessed be His name [for ever].⁵ The L. is great (*cf.* Dt. x, 17), the L. is mighty (Ex. xv, 3, according to Samaritan recension), the L. is fearful (Ex. xv, 11), the L. is my banner (Ex. xvii, 15). The L. is consuming fire (Dt. iv, 24).⁶ I the L. am thy G. (Ex. xx, 2). Thou shalt have no other gods before me (Ex. xx, 3).⁷

(**17**) In the beginning G. created the heaven and the earth (Gn. i, 1). And G. said, Let there be light: and there was light (Gn. i, 3). And G. said, There shall be an expanse between the waters (Gn. i, 6). (**20**) And G. said, Let the waters be gathered together (Gn. i, 9). And G. said, Let the earth bring forth grass (Gn. i, 11). And G. said, Let there be lights in the expanse of the heavens (Gn. i, 14). And G. said, Let the waters bring forth (Gn. i, 20). And G. said, Let the earth bring forth the living creatures (Gn. i, 24). (**25**) And G. said, Let us make man in our image and in our likeness (Gn. i, 26). And G. said, unto them, Be fruitful, and multiply (Gn. i, 28). And G. said, Behold I have given you every herb bearing seed (Gn. i, 29). And G. saw everything, and, behold, it was very good (Gn. i, 31). And G. finished (Gn. ii, 2). And G. blessed (Gn. ii, 3). And the L. G. formed (30) and breathed into his nostrils the breath of life (Gn. ii, 7), and Adam became a living person (Gn. ii, 7) [in the day] that the L. G. made (Gn. ii, 4). The L. G. [had not] caused it to rain (Gn. ii, 5), and the L. G. formed (Gn. ii, 7), the L. G. planted (Gn. ii, 8), and the L. G. made to grow (Gn. ii, 9), and the L. G. took (Gn. ii, 15). (35) And the L. G. commanded (Gn. ii, 16). And the L. G. said (Gn. ii, 18), the L. G. formed (Gn. ii, 19), the L. G. caused to fall (Gn. ii, 21). And the L. G. builded (Gn. ii, 22) the L. G. made (Gn. iii, 1), for G. said (Gn. iii, 3), for G. doth know (Gn. iii, 5), and ye shall be as gods (*ibid.*). The voice of the L. G. (Gn. iii, 8) (40) and the L. G. called (Gn. iii, 9), and the L. G. said (Gn. iii, 13, 14), and the L. G. made (Gen. iii, 21), and the L. G. said (Gn. iii, 22), and the L. G. sent him forth (Gn. iii, 23)[8] for ever. The L. will fight for you, and ye be silent (Ex. xiv, 14). G. will surely heal him who is (45) clothed[9] (לבושי) with it (= the amulet) Amen. Then they began to call on the name of the L. (Gn. iv, 26) on the day G. created Adam in the day that G. created man in the likeness of G. (Gn. v, 1) in the image of G. he made Adam (*cf.* Gn. i, 27). Do not fear, Abraham, I am thy shield (Gn. xv, 1). And He said unto him, I am the L. that brought thee out of Ur of the Chaldees, to give (50) thee this land to inherit it (Gn. xv, 7). I have lifted up my hand to the L. the high G., possessor of heaven and earth (Gn. xiv, 21). And the L. said unto Abraham (Gn. xii, 1). And the L. appeared unto Abraham (Gn. xvii, 1), and he called thereon the name of the L., the everlasting G. (Gn. xxi, 33). By Myself have I sworn, saith the L. (Gn. xx, 16), dwell in the land and I shall be with thee (55) and I will bless thee (Gn. xxvi, 2). We have truly seen that the L. was with thee (Gn. xxvi, 28). And behold the L. stood above it, and said, I am the L. the G. of Abraham thy father, and the G. of Isaac: the land whereon thou liest, to thee will I give it, and to thy seed; and, behold, I am with thee, and will keep thee whithersoever thou goest (Gn. xxviii, 13–15a), (60) for I will not forsake thee (Gn. xxviii, 15). He called it the L. G. of Israel (Gn. xxxiii, 20). Besides me G. shall not give Pharaoh an answer of peace (Gn. xli, 17, according to Sam. recension of the text). And he said unto the magicians (Gn. xli, 8 : so according to Sam. recension). And the magicians could not (*ibid.*) (65) and He said, I am the G. of thy fathers, the G. of Abraham, the G. of Isaac, the G. of Jacob (Ex. iii, 6 : so according to Sam. recension). This is My name for ever, this is My memorial unto all generations (Ex. iii, 15) : who hath made man's mouth ? Or who maketh a man dumb, or deaf, or seeing, or blind, is it not I, the L. ? (Ex. iv, 11). (70) And G. said unto Moses, I am that I am [A(hyh), a(sher), A(hyh)] (Ex. iii, 14).[10]

And I appeared unto Abraham, unto Isaac, unto Jacob as God Shaddai, but by My name IHVH (Ex. vi, 3). Therefore, say unto the children of Israel I am the L. and I will bring you out from under the burden of the (75) Egyptians and I will redeem you, and I will take you to Me for a people, and I will be unto you G. (Ex. vi, 6, 7). I am the L. the G. of Israel (no such verse in Mass. text) : the G. of the Hebrews has called upon us (Ex. iii, 18 ; v, 3). There is none like unto Me in the whole earth (Ex. ix, 14) to recount My name in the whole earth (Ex. ix, 16), that I the L. am in the midst of the earth (Ex. viii, 18, 22) : And the L. (80) went before them (Ex. xiii, 21). And the magicians said unto Pharaoh, This is the finger of G. (Ex. viii, 15, 19). And the magicians could not stand before Moses (Ex. ix, 11) (*v.* lines 64 ; 124 ; 363), and as the magicians could not stand before Moses, so may they not be able to stand before him who is clothed with Thy name O L. (the possessor of this writing).[11] Do not fear, the L. will fight for you (Ex. xiv, 14) the salvation of the L. (Ex. xiv, 13). Do not fear, the L. will fight for you the salvation of the L. The L. will help. The L. (85) is mighty in battle, the L. is His name (Ex. xv, 3 ; so Sam. recension). Thy right hand, O L., is glorious in power ; Thy right hand, O L., dasheth in pieces the enemy (Ex. xv, 6). Who is like unto Thee, O L. ? (not in Mass. text). Who is like unto Thee, O L., among the gods ? Who is like Thee, glorious in holiness (90) fearful in praises, doing wonders (Ex. xv, 11). Till Thy people pass over, O L., Till Thy people pass over which is Thy possession (Ex. xv, 16*b*). The L. will rule for ever and ever (Ex. xv, 18*b*), and sing ye to the L. And Moses led Israel onward from the Red Sea, and they went unto the wilderness of Shur; and they went three days in the wilderness and found no water. And when they came to Marah, (95) they could not drink of the waters of Marah, for they were bitter: therefore the name of it was called Marah. And the people murmured against Moses, saying, What shall we drink? And he cried unto the L. and the L. shewed him a tree, and he cast it into the waters and the waters were made sweet. There He made for them a statute and an ordinance, and there He proved them, and He said, If thou wilt (100) diligently hearken to the voice of the L. thy G., and wilt do that which is right in His eyes, and wilt give ear to His commandments, and keep all His statutes, I will put none of the diseases upon thee, which I have put upon the Egyptians, for I am the L. that healeth thee (Ex. xv, 22–26). L. G. heal him who is "clothed"[12] with it (105) of all sickness, Amen, Amen. (106) I will make all My goodness pass before thee, and will proclaim the name of the L. before thee; and I will be gracious to whom I will be gracious, and will shew mercy to whom I will shew mercy (Ex. xxxiii, 19). And the L. passed by before him and proclaimed the L., the L. a G. full of compassion and gracious, slow to anger, and plenteous (110) in mercy and truth; keeping mercy for thousands, forgiving iniquity and transgression and sin, and that will by no means clear the guilty; visiting the iniquity of the fathers upon the children, and upon the children's children, upon the third and upon the fourth generation. And Moses made haste, and bowed his head toward the earth and worshipped. And he said, If now I have found grace in Thy sight, O L., let the L., I pray Thee, go in the midst of us; for it is a (115) stiffnecked people; and pardon our iniquity and our sin, and take us for thine inheritance. And He said, Behold, I make a covenant: before all thy people I will do marvels, such as have not been wrought in all the earth, not in any nation (Ex. xxxiv, 6–10a).

(120) May the L. remove from thee all evil and hurtful thing from before him who is clothed[13] with Thy names, O L., through Thy righteousness. The L. by the L. (twice). The L. our G. Thy right hand, O L., will pursue the enemy (Ex. xv, 6; so in Sam.) and the L. The L. shall remove their words and their name.[14] And the magicians would not stand before Moses (Ex. ix, 11) and

may they not stand before him who is clothed (**125**) and who is clothed with Thy name, O L., consuming fire (Dt. iv, 24), and may it not be allowed by thy G. (or by Thee O G.) that thou shouldst be hurt by anything that is in the heaven or anything that is on the earth or anything that is in the waters under the earth. The L. is great. The L. is G. (**130**) May none of the magicians be able to stand neither with strong hand nor with strong face against him who wears this writing, Rebekah and Mrglitah and Baubs and Dmninah and Nunah, Gibi and Killah, Ahvh (her brother?) and Sbinah and Rbth and Simeon and Mrklah and Elazar and Mlksh and Nnah and Hisdorah. [C, line 114, has the following names after the words "holy writings": Rebekah, Mrglita, Baubs, Brkah, Frskah, Mlḳah, Nunah, Domnina, Gibah, Killah, Ahvah (probably the brother), Sbinah, Rbtah, Simeon, Mrklah, Elazar, Maksah, Nnah, Hisdorah, Teodorah.][15]

May none of the (**135**) magicians under the heavens be able to stand up against him who is clothed with this writing, neither by strong hand nor by strong might (El.), for he will be loosening the charm. The L. is His name and Ya is His name.

(**138**) Alphabet נ–א.[16] (**140**) Single letters, probably initials, and single words taken from Biblical verses each one representing a verse such as Zilpah, How can we justify ourselves? (Gn. xliv, 16).— Abraham, Isaac, Jacob, Joseph, and our master Moses the prophet and Aaron the priest, Elazar the trusted one, Itamar the honoured one, Pinehas the holy one, and Joshua the king. He made the laver of brass, the base thereof of (**145**) brass and the appearances (images) of the hosts which trouped at the door of the tent of meeting.[17] In the name of the L. G. of Israel. He made the laver of brass, the base thereof of brass and the appearances (images) of the hosts which trouped at the door of the tent of meeting (Ex. xxxviii, 8).

(**150**)[18] and I will turn unto you forever, saith the L. The L. is righteous, the L. is great. The L. is mighty, the L. is awe-inspiring. The L. is my banner (twice). The L. is His name, slow to anger and plenteous in mercy and truth (Ex. xxxiv, 6). (**155**) The L. He is our G. The L. He is our G., the L. is one. The L. the L. is great, the L. is awe-inspiring, the L. is mighty. The L. is king of the kings, for the L. is greater than all the gods (Ex. xviii, 11). Behold, unto the L. belongeth the heaven, (**160**) and the heaven of heavens, the earth and all that therein is (Dt. x, 14). For the L. your G. He is G. of gods, and L. of lords, the Great G., and the mighty and the terrible (Dt. x, 17).

(164) For ask now of the days that are past, since the day the G. created man upon the earth, (165) and from the one end of heaven unto the other (Dt. iv, 32). For the L. He is G. and there is none besides him.

. That the L. He is G. in heaven above and upon the earth beneath: there is none else (Dt. iv, 39). For the L. He is my strength, (170) as the days of the earth and thou wilt forgive. Our G. is in our midst, G. is great and mighty and awe-inspiring (v. lines 152, 153). And I will remember the covenant with Jacob, (175) and also My covenant with Isaac and also My covenant with Abraham will I remember (Lev. xxvi, 42). (177) May the L. bless thee and keep thee; may the L. cause His countenance to shine upon thee and be gracious unto thee: may the L. be favourable unto thee and give thee peace, Amen (Nb. vi, 24 ff.). (180) Rise up, O L., and let Thine enemies be scattered, and let them that hate Thee flee before Thee (Nb. x, 35), Amen (four times). For their shadow is removed from over them, and the L. is with us: fear them not (Nb. xiv, 9). And all the earth shall be filled with the glory of the L. (Nb. xiv, 21). Wherefore it is said in the book of the wars of the L. with Vaheb in (185) the storm (or, with Vaheb in Suphah) (Nb. xxi, 14), that He may take away the serpent from us, and Moses prayed for the people (Nb. xxi, 7), and for thee (?) (so in the MS.). The dread of thee and the fear of thee upon the peoples that are under the whole heaven, who shall hear the report of thee, and shall tremble, and be in anguish because of thee (Dt. ii, 25).

Thou shalt be blessed above all peoples: (190)[19] there shall not be male or female barren among you or among your cattle. And the L. will take away from thee all sickness; and He will put none of the evil diseases of Egypt, which thou knowest, upon thee, but will lay them upon all them that hate thee (Dt. vii, 14, 15). For the L. thy G. is in the midst of thee, a great G. and an awe-inspiring (Dt. vii, 21), the L. is great. (195) For if ye shall diligently keep all this commandment which I command you to do it; to love the L. your G., to walk in all His ways, and to cleave unto Him; then will the L. drive out all these nations from before you, and ye shall possess nations greater (**200**) and mightier than yourselves. Every place whereon the sole of your foot shall tread shall be yours; from the wilderness, and Lebanon, from the river, the river Euphrates, even unto the hinder sea shall be your border. There shall no man be able to stand before you: the L. your G. shall lay the fear of you and the dread of you upon all the land that ye shall tread upon, as He hath (**205**) spoken unto you (Dt. xi, 22–25). The L. the L. is great,[20] the L. is mighty, the L. is awe-inspiring, the L. the L. He is the ruler. The L. is our G., the L. the L. is one, He is single. (**210**) For the L. your G. is He that goeth with you, to fight for you against your enemies, to save you (Dt. xx, 4), Amen (five times). And the L. will take away from thee all sickness, and He will put none of the evil diseases of Egypt upon thee, (**215**) but will lay them upon all them that hate thee (*cf.* 189 ff.) (Dt. vii, 15). For the L. your G. is He that goeth with you to fight for you against your enemies to save you (Dt. xx, 4). Behold, I send My angel before thee, to keep thee by the way (Ex. xxiii, 20) (**220**) from the hands of the magicians and sorcerers. Wherefore now do ye transgress the commandment of the L., seeing it shall not prosper? (Nb. xiv, 41). There shall not be found with thee anyone that maketh his son or his daughter to pass through the fire, one that useth divination and that practiseth augury, an enchanter, a sorcerer, a charmer, a consulter with a familiar spirit, a wizard or a necromancer. (**225**) For whoso-ever doeth these things is an abomination unto the L. The L. thy G. doth drive them out from before thee (Dt. xviii, 10–12). And the way of the magicians will not prosper, for the L. thy G. is in thy midst, fear them not (Dt. vii, 21; *v.* line 193). The L. his G. is with him, and the shout of a king is among them. G. bringeth them forth out of Egypt; He hath as it were the strength of the wild ox. Surely there is no enchantment with Jacob, (**230**) neither is there any divination with Israel (Nb. xxiii, 21–23). Wherefore it is said in the book of the wars of the L. with Vaheb in Suphah (Nb. xxi, 14, *v.* lines 183, 184); for the L. thy G. is a merciful G., He will not fail thee, neither destroy thee, nor forget the covenant of thy fathers which He sware unto them (Dt. iv, 31); (**235**) that the L. may turn from the fierceness of His anger, and shew thee mercy, and have compassion upon thee (Dt. xiii, 18 (17), for the L. thy G. is a merciful G. He will not fail thee, neither destroy thee (Dt. iv, 31), that the L. may turn from the fierceness of His anger and shew thee mercy (Dt. xiii, 17). And He will multiply thee (Dt. xiii, 18 (17), and then the L. thy G. will turn thy captivity and have compassion upon thee (Dt. xxx, 3), and the L. thy G. will put all these curses upon thine enemies, (240) and on them that hate thee, which persecuted thee, and thou shalt return (Dt. xxx, 7). The L. shall cause thine enemies that rise up against thee to be smitten before thee (Dt. xxviii, 7). The L. shall establish thee for a holy people (Dt. xxviii, 9), for I will proclaim the name of the L. (Dt. xxxii, 3). For what great nation is there, that hath a god so nigh unto it as the L. our G. is whensoever we call upon Him (Dt. iv, 7). (245) The L. alone shall lead him, and there is no strange god with him (Dt. xxxii, 12). Behold, now, that I even I am He and there is no god with me (Dt. xxxii, 39). There is none like unto G., O Jeshurun, Who rideth upon the heaven for thy help, and in His excellency on the skies. The G. of old is the dwelling place, and under His arm is (250) the world : And He thrust out the enemy from before thee and said, Destroy (Dt. xxxiii, 26, 27 ; so Sam. reading). A people that is saved by the L., the shield of thy help, and that is the sword of thy excellency ! and thine enemies shall submit themselves unto thee : and thou shalt tread upon their high places (Dt. xxxiii, 29).

The L. is our G., the L. is one single (Dt. vi, 4). For[21] I will proclaim the name of the L. (Dt. xxxii, 2 ; v. line 241). And a wind of G. moved (255) upon the face of the waters (Gn. i, 2). And He breathed into his nostrils the breath of life (Gn. ii, 7). And G. made a wind to pass over the earth (Gn. viii, 1). And they were a grief to the spirit (Gn. xxvi, 35). And put a wind[22] betwixt (Gn. xxxii, 16 ; so Sam. interprets). A man in whom the spirit of G. is (Gn. xli, 38). And the spirit of Jacob revived (Gn. xlv, 27). For shortness of wind (Ex. vi, 9). And the spirit revived (Gn. xlv, 27). (260) And the east wind (Ex. x, 13). And the L. turned a west wind (Ex. x, 19). By an east wind (Ex. xiv, 21). And I will take of the spirit (Nb. xi, 17). And He took of the spirit (Nb. xi, 25). And the spirit of G. (Gn. i, 2). And they were a grief to the spirit

(Gn. xxvi, 35. And an east wind (Ex. x, 13; v. line 260). And the L. turned a (265) west wind (Ex. x, 19; v. line 260). And ye shall repeat[23] the spirit . . . . . And He took of the spirit (Nb. xi, 25) by the spirit. A man in whom the spirit of G. is (Gn. xli, 38. And the spirit rested upon them (Nb. xi, 26. And He filled him with the spirit of G. (Ex. xxxv, 31). When there passes over him a spirit of jealousy (Nb. v, 14). The G. of gods of the spirit of all flesh. (270) And the L. saw (Gn. i, 4). And the L. added [this verse is not found in the Mass. Bible; probably scribe's error]. May the L. heal the boil, and He healed; heal, heal her, O L., I beseech Thee (Nb. xii, 13). And he called the name of it the L. nissi (Ex. xvii, 15). O my master Moses (forbid them)[24] (Nb. xi, 28). My master Moses, speak to the leader of the hosts. Save us from the hands of our enemies. My master Moses, speak to the leader of the hosts. Save (275) us from the hands of our enemies. My master Moses, speak to the head of the wonder-working powers. Save us from the hands of our enemies. My master Moses, speak to the leader of the hosts. Save us from the hands of our enemies. My master Moses, say unto the head of all the great gods. Save us from the hands of our enemies. My master Moses, (280) say to the head of the high G. the possessor of the heaven and earth that He may save us from the hands of our enemies

(281) Palindrome.[25] The L. our G. giveth thee all the days (Deut. iv, 40b). (282) The L. is our G. The L. is one (Deut. vi, 4) single. (283) The great one, the mighty one, the awe-inspiring.

(284-296) Palindrome of Deut. iv, 35-40.—Unto thee it was shewed that thou mightest know that the L. He is G.; there is none else beside Him. Out of heaven He made thee to hear His voice, that He might instruct thee: and upon earth He made thee to see His great fire; and thou heardest His words out of the midst of the fire. And because He loved thy fathers, therefore He chose their seed after them, and brought thee out with His presence with His great power out of Egypt; to drive out nations from before thee greater and mightier than thou, to bring thee in, to give thee their land for an inheritance, as at this day. Know, therefore, this day, and lay it to thine heart, that the L. He is G. in heaven above and upon the earth beneath : there is none else. And thou shalt keep His statutes and His commandments, which I command thee this day, that it may go well with thee, and with thy children after thee, and that thou mayest prolong thy days upon the land, which the L. thy G. giveth thee. **(297)** In the name of the L. the merciful G. and in thy name, the L. the great G.

(299–312) Seventy-six groups of mystical names of G. formed by a combination of the letters of Ex. xiv, 19–21. The groups consist of three letters each, with the exception of the last five groups which consist of two letters, formed of—(*a*) the letters of verse 19 from the beginning to end; (*b*) the second letter in the group is taken from the letters of verse 20 backwards; (*c*) the third letter is taken from the letters of verse 21 going forwards.[26]

(313–338) Ex. xv, 1, continued by an imprecation against enemies, the alternate lines being the names of God with the attributes.

Then sang Moses :

(313) The great L.
(315) and the children of Israel,
(316) G. the awe-inspiring
(317) the song.
(318) The L. is my banner.
(319) This to the L.
(320) G. is my might.
(321) They said as follows :
(322) The L. is mighty,
(323) May the L. destroy,
(324) The L. is great,

(325) the nations,

(326) the L. is mighty,

(327) the sorcerers,

(328) The L. is my banner,

(329) and the wizards.

(330) The L. is awe-inspiring

(331) may cause them to perish before Thee

(332) The L. healeth.

(333) The L. their name,

(334) The L. is His name,

(335) from under the heavens.

(336) Amen (three times).[27]

    This man and woman and child male and female.

(337–342) Terror and dread falleth upon them. By the greatness of Thine arm they are as still as a stone. Till Thy people pass over, O L. Till the people pass over which Thou hast purchased (Ex. xv, 16, written first as in the text and then backwards as palindrome). (343) And Moses prayed unto G. and the fire was quenched (Nb. xi, 2). (345) And Moses prayed for the people (Nb. xxi, 7). The L. is our G. (twice), the L. is one. The L. save, the L. enlighten, the L. fight. The L. be gracious, the L. be merciful, the L. protect, the L. be kind, the L. (three times). And he made (350) the laver of brass and the base thereof of brass and the appearances (images) of the hosts which trouped at the door of the tent of meeting[28] (so Sam. Ex. xxxviii, 37, v. line 144). This writing is good for every man who is clothed with it Amen. (354) In the name of the great G., the L. is great, the L. is awful, the L. is the holy ruler, the G. of every god A. a. A. who sees every hidden thing, A. who sees and is not seen. May the L. remove everything evil. My L. O G. may He answer thee (probably or keep His eye over thee. Some mistake). (360) May He save me from everything evil and from every hurt. May the L. save and help. May the L. help, protect (flutter). May He rise up, may He befriend, may He be gracious, may He shield, may He be merciful. And the magicians could not stand before Moses (Ex. ix, 11, v. line 80), and so may they also not stand before those who are clothed with Thy name, O L., be it male or female. (365) May the L. G. be with thee. Rise, O L., in all places and at every time. There is no G. but one, no prophet like Moses, and no Law (Torah) like His Law (Torah) and no worship than that on Mt. Garizim His inheritance, and no other selection than His congregation and assembly. (369) The letters of the whole alphabet.

(370) IHVH (ten times) then follow the three words, Great, pray, end.[29]

May it not be exterminated (or, cut off), and pray thee may it not turn back (or, return), may every man who is clothed with this good phylactery[30] be freed from every demon and every spirit (creature) and every wicked (or guilty) one and from every harm and from every beast. Amen (three times). (375) Rise, O L. (v. lines 393 ff.). Return, O L., to him who is clothed with these writings. Save him from every evil thing and from every bad thing, Pishon, Gihon, Dkl, and Perat.[31] For I am the L. that healeth thee (Ex. xv, 26). Keep me, O G. of the holy Tabernacle. (380) Keep me, O G. of the sanctuary. Keep me, O G. of the Prophet. Keep me, O G. of Mt. Garizim. Keep me, O G. of the Kohanim (Priests). Keep me, O G. of the holy ones. Keep me on the way upon which I walk and do not pass over my prayer, for this reward me and save me from all evil. (385) The L., the Holy One, may He be praised. IHVH (ten times ; v. lines 408, 409), the great, mighty, awful, the G. of the spirits of all flesh, flesh. The G. of the praises (390) of songs and hymns (of exaltation). There is no G. but one and no prophet like Moses. Rise, O L. (v. lines 375 ff.). Turn, O L., to those who are *clothed* with *these* writings. Save them from every evil, and from every (395) hurtful thing and from every demon and from every wild beast, and from every Pishon, every Gihon, every (Hi)dkl, and every Perat (v. line 378), for I am the L. that healeth thee (Ex. xv, 26). For I am the L. Save us from the nations which are around us, (400) and enlarge us from this distress, and from all the strange gods ; may they all turn away (depart) from before the L., the holy L. who is in me (or in my midst). Keep me holy, G., and save me from every evil. May He bless these young men (Gn. xlviii, 16); the L. the L. the holy one, great G., L. G., may He be praised, exalted, blessed, sanctified, worshipped (405) for ever. There is no G. but one. IHVH (ten times, v. lines 387, 388). This is My name for ever and this is My memorial from (410) generation to generation (Ex. iii, 15). Whoever wears this writing, may the fear of You and the trembling before You be upon all the beasts of the land and all the birds of heaven. In Your hand have I given it (Gn. ix, 2; so Sam. version). And Jacob[32] said, the G. of my father Abraham, the G. of my father Isaac, O L. which saidst unto me, Return unto thy country, and to thy kindred, and (415) I will do thee good. I am not worthy of the least of all the mercies, and of all the truth which Thou hast done unto Thy servant: for with my staff I passed over this Jordan, and now I am become two companies. Deliver me, I pray Thee, from the hand of my brother, from the hand of Esau: for I fear him lest he come and smite me, the mother with the children. And Thou saidst, I will surely do thee good, and make thy seed as the sand of the sea, which cannot be numbered for multitude. And he lodged there that night (Gn. xxxii, 9–13). (420) The G. before whom my fathers Abraham and Isaac did walk, the G. which hath fed me all my life long unto this day, the angel which hath redeemed me from all evil, bless these lads, and let my name be called upon them and the name of my fathers Abraham and Isaac; and let them grow into a multitude in the midst of the earth (Gn. xlviii, 15, 16). (425) And he blessed them that day saying, In thee shall Israel bless, saying G. make thee as Ephraim and as Manasseh; and he set Ephraim before Manasseh (Gn. xlviii, 20). I have waited for Thy salvation, O L. (Gn. xlix, 19). By the G. of thy father who shall help thee, and by the Almighty who may bless thee with the blessings of heaven above (Gn. xlix, 25). Amen A(men).

A. a. A. who sees the hidden things. A. who seest and (430) art not seen, L. G. of heaven. And ye will lie down and none will frighten you, and I will rid evil beasts out of the land (Lev. xxvi,

6). O G. of heaven and earth and of all that is in them, the G. of the great heavens, G. of all the greatnesses, and G. of all the mighty deeds and wonders, the G. of all that exists (lit., stands up). (435) Arise, O L. Turn, O L. May all the strange gods depart from before the L., the holy G. is within me. He who rideth the heavens, my Master the holy G., save me from all evil. IHVH (five times). G. of gods, enlarge me from all stress and anguish, and remove from us the snake.

(440) And Moses prayed for the people (Nb. xxi, 7). The G. of all and mighty over all (lit., who can do everything), and who knows all, the G. of the heavens and of the heavens of heavens. IHVH (ten times),[33] IHVH Elohim, IHVH (three times), Elohim IHVH Elohim (445) IHVH Elohim, Adam,[34] Noah, Abraham, Isaac, Jacob, Joseph, Levi, Kehath, Amram, Moses, Aaron, Eleazar, Ithamar, Pinehas, Joshua, Kaleb, the Seventy Elders. Mystical letters ANGDKNH.[35] Master, be good unto me, Master by these Names corresponding to the 86 names mentioned before these.[36] (450) Arise, O L., and let Thine enemies be scattered and let them that hate Thee flee before Thee (Nb. x, 35). Amen (three times). Rise, O L., for every one who is clothed with this writing by Thy name, O G. Ahyh Elohim (twice), IHVH (ten times). Ahyh Elohim. Remember for me the holy spirit who is the name of the G. of the world, who is the guardian and protector against the hatred of all who stand up against me. The G. of all (455) who is all-powerful and in whose hand everything is. IHVH (ten times). Look down from the holy place from the heaven (Dt. xxvi, 15a).

(458) May the L. open unto thee His good treasure.

(459) The L. G. the L. the L. our G. the L.

(460) the heavens to give the rain

(461) the L. is one L. The L. is single, the L.[37]

(462) of thy land in its season (463) and to bless all the work of thine hand : and thou shalt lend unto many nations and thou shalt not borrow, and the L. shalt make thee the head and not the tail (Dt. xxviii, 12). Amen (three times). (465) A. a. A. IHVH our G. IHVH is one alone. And the L. thy G. will put all these curses upon thine enemies, and on them that hate thee, which persecuted thee. And thou shalt return and obey the voice of the L. thy G. (Dt. xxx, 7, 8). And the L. is He who goeth before thee and He will be with thee. (470) He will not fail thee nor forsake thee, fear not, and be not dismayed (this line 470 is repeated ten times ;[38] so in text, differing from Mass. Dt. xxxi, 6). (481) Amen (three times). And thy enemies shall submit themselves unto thee ; and thou shalt tread upon their high places (Dt. xxxiii, 29). Amen (three times).

The L. is holy. The L. is great, the L. is mighty, the L. is awe-inspiring. The L. He is the ruler, (485) the L. He is G. The L. He is the healer. The L. killeth. The L. bringeth to life, the L. is our G., the L. is one.

Thou art the L. our G., the honoured one, permanent A. a. A. Found in all places, Thou seest, but art not seen : Thou hast made the luminaries and stars that they may shine through Thy goodness upon the whole earth. Mayest Thou be praised for ever. (490) In the name of the L., the L., the L. Every day and night we bow down to Thee, O high G., and we bow down and we pray to Thee, and we exalt Thee for there is none like Thee, our G. and the G. of our fathers. Grant us help from Thee and send an angel by Thy goodness, and bless us in everything and keep us from our enemies and our adversaries by Thy goodness, the mighty (495) G. of spirits of all flesh. Master of masters, our G. do not forsake us.[39] Ahyh (twice ten times), high G., King, merciful, awful.

(499) Mayest thou remember this

(500) The L., the holy of the holy ones (the most holy)

(501) by the holiness of

(502) G. mighty of the mighty (the most mighty)

(503) this prayer

(504) G. the awful of the awful (the most awful)

(505) which I am praying

(506) the L. the great of the great (the greatest)

(507) Thou who art exalted above everything

(508) The L. the ruler of rulers.

(509) victorious in battle[40]

(510) A line of letters not divided up by dots into words, evidently initials.[41] (511) And he and whoever causes it. (512) The L. is victorious in battle (Sam. Ex. xv, 2). The L. is His name. (513) And he smote it (Gn. xxxii, 9); and we may not smite him (Gn. xxxvii, 21), etc.[42] (515) Thirty times AH with occasional intercalation of the letters דהוזחטי and preceded by one or two א.[43] And Joshua, the son of Nun, was filled with the spirit of wisdom, for

Moses had put his hand on him (Dt. xxxiv, 9). And Abraham

prayed (520) unto G., and G. healed (Gn. xx, 17). And he was

healed therefrom (so Sam. Ex. iv, 26), for I am the L. that healeth

thee (Ex. xv, 20), and he was healed. Heal. Let us be healed.

O L. heal (Nb. 12, 13). I have wounded and I heal (Dt. 32, 39),

For I am the L. that healeth thee [44] (Ex. xv, 26). (I pray thee)

Abiel the angel who rules over the fire, may the fire be on the enemy,

and may be saved from the fire of burning heat everyone who wears

this (525) writing.[45] A group of sixteen letters probably initials.

And Moses prayed to G., and the fire was quenched (Nb. xi, 12)

so may the burning fire be quenched of him who is clothed with it.

Abraham, son of Ab Sakua [46] the Danafite, Amen. And Moses

cried to G. saying, O L. heal her I pray thee (Nb. xii, 13). And

Abraham prayed to G., and G. healed (Gn. xx, 17). (531) And

Moses prayed unto the L. and the fire was quenched (Nb. xi, 2) (the

whole sentence repeated seven times).[47] And Moses prayed for the people (Nb. xxi, 7).

(539-560) The Hebrew alphabet arranged in twenty-two lines of twenty-three letters in each in such a manner that the top and bottom, as well as left hand line, should form a complete alphabet and the letters are so grouped that the letter א should form a diagonal line from the first to the last, dividing the square into two triangles, the base of which on top and bottom are formed by the whole alphabet whilst the lines between are filled up with letters which in this grouping do not form a complete alphabet as some of the letters are repeated.[48]

(561) In the name of God the G. of gods.

(563-568) Series of letters not separated by dots, probably initials of words which are often repeated in various combinations, and which fall into groups each beginning with ב.

(569-578) A square composed of the words, The L., great G., in ten lines of eleven letters each, so arranged that the top line and the two vertical lines contain exactly the same words. Moreover, the first and last letters of each line are identical, and each line, vertical and horizontal, contain the same letters. This square is also divided like the preceding alphabet into two triangles by the letter ל. Each letter is enclosed in a square. The square is flanked right and left by two lines written vertically. May be exalted this great name. May it be hallowed and uplifted. May it be beautified and honoured. May it be praised and declared mighty.[49]

(579) L., master of the world. This is My name for ever (Ex. iii, 15). The L. is righteous (Ex. ix, 27): (580) that they may believe that the L. has appeared unto thee (Ex. iv, 5). The L. is mighty in battle, the L. is His name (Ex. xv, 2), the people believed in the L. (Ex. xiv, 31; so Sam.). And ye shall know that I am the L. (Ex. vi, 7). And the children of Israel cried unto the L. (Ex. xiv, 10). And Moses said, Fear not, stand still and see the salvation of the L. (Ex. xiv, 13). Who is like unto Thee, O L., among the gods (Ex. xv, 11).

Till Thy people pass over, O L. (Ex. xv, 16), and Moses cried unto the L. (Ex. 17, 4). (586) Behold, I send an angel before thee, to keep thee on the way (Ex. xxiii, 20). And ye shall serve the L. your G. I will remove sickness from the midst of thee (Ex. xxiii, 25). And I will send My fear before thee (Ex. xxiii, 27). (590) And they shall know that I am the L. (Ex. xiv, 4). And ye shall know that I am the L. (Ex. vi, 7). And the L. passed before him (Ex. xxxiv, 6). And ye shall know that I am the L. (Ex. vi, 7). I, the L., am thy G. (Ex. xx, 2). In the name of the L. I will speak and prosper by the names by which I am victorious. (595) Their shadow has passed away from them, and the L. is with us: fear them not (Nb. xiv, 9). For the L. your G. is He that goeth with you to fight for you against your enemies and to save you[50] (Dt. xx, 4; seven times [51]) Amen (three times). Hear, O Israel, the L. is our G., the L. is one (Dt. vi, 4). (600) Do not destroy thy people and thy inheritance (Dt. ix, 26). Israel safe alone: the fountain of Jacob in a land of corn and wine (Dt. xxxiii, 28).

Mystical combinations of the first ten letters always preceded by א three times probably the initials of A. a. A., and finishing with the complete alphabet.[52] **(606–7)** Alphabet divided into two lines of eleven letters each. **(608)** Groups of letters in which the last two are repeated in the succeeding word : sk, isk, msk, mais, lmnos, ins, ashr, ishr.[53] **(609)** May they become dumb like the stone.[54] May their hearts be closed up concerning me. **(610)** Amen (three times). A. a. A. Victorious in battle : subdue the power of the enemies and adversaries by the mighty power of Thy name zealous G.

The L. is consuming fire (Dt. iv, 24). **(615)** A. a. A. who was, is, and will be permanently, the L. G. of heaven, and the G. of earth ; G. of the spirits, and G. of the Sabaoth. **(618)** Blessed art Thou, and blessed is Thy holy name for ever. There is no G. **(620)** but one. And may the peace of the L. be upon the prophet, the righteous, the perfect pure and faithful Moses, who was free from every blemish.[55] Amen !

Notes to the foregoing Translation.

[1] This line belongs to the frame which surrounds the text and starts with this verse. With this same verse almost every prayer in the Samaritan liturgy begins.

[2] This invocation (line 5) corresponds entirely to the Samaritan inscriptions on various stone lintels used as a prophylactic against evil spirits and other enemies. It forms also the blessing upon the writer and wearer of the amulet (v. Proceedings, 1915, p. 135 ff.).

[3] The Song of Moses (line 6 ff.) is held in special reverence by the Samaritans, and these verses are evidently invested with a special significance. This song is read by the Samaritans to a dying man, and is also recited by the Jews in their burial service; GASTER, Prayer Book, I, p. 197.

[4] Line 9. This is used by the Samaritans as a constant refrain in prayers and hymns. They omit the first words, "Hear, O Israel," which the Jews have retained in their liturgy.

[5] Line 10. A common Samaritan and Jewish doxology; cf. Psalms lxvi, 20; lxxxvi, 35; lxxii, 19; Neh. ix, 5; 2 Cor. xi, 31, etc.

[6] This collection of divine names occurs very frequently in the phylactery and forms an integral part of many prayers. The amulet relies practically on the cumulative effect to be produced by the reference to the numerous appellations of God. This seems to be the oldest form of prayer among the Samaritans, who never tire of invoking whole strings of such divine appellations. One hymn consists of nothing else but these names (cf. Cod. 847, f. 20b). In my Cod. 1170, f. 193, a list of 76 such divine names is given under the heading of the "mysterious name of 76," to which reference will be made later on. It is to be noted that among these 76, only four out of the 32 of the attributes of God are included, as found in Ex. xxxiv, 6. If closely examined some of the oldest forms of the Jewish liturgy, especially the Amidah and introductory prayers to the Shema, seem to be collections of divine appellations. The very name of the amulet is Shem Hamitfaresh, which the Samaritans explain to be the fully interpreted name of God. God is only known by His actions, these being recorded in the scriptures by His numerous acts, especially the Creation, and the various forms of help, assistance, and punishment. All these will be found here in the amulet grouped together, so as to give, as it were, a complete record of God's manifestations to man. These are the appellations: for God shows Himself powerful, merciful, and loving above all words; creating and averting danger, etc., and these altogether represent The Name. This tendency of cumulating names of God in prayers must, at a certain time, have become so pronounced that a great scholar had to rebuke a reader for attempting to multiply these divine attributes whilst reciting the prayer. It was considered as a mark of heresy. Probably the Samaritans indulged in it, and they were referred to under the name of Ninim, i.e., heretics (Mishna Berach v, 3). For a list of divine attributes combined with the word king instead of God, v. Pirke Hecholoth, ed. WERTHEIMER, ch. 18, 4 (cf. Beth. Hamedr., Vol. III, ed. JELLENEK, ch. 16), and for a similar long list of 64 names

(*ib.*, ch. 24, 4). In Beth. Hamedr. is a much shorter list (ch. 23, 3), and also in Pirke Hecholoth (ch. 25, 4 = Beth. Hamedr., 24) ; cf. also *ib.* (ch. 26, 4 = Beth Hamedr., 26, 3) a hymn of similar attributes addressed to God. For a still fuller list in alphabetical order of divine attributes of God, like Hecholoth, 18, 4, combined with the word king, numbering close upon 400, *v.* Clavicula Salomonis, or Mapheteah Shelomo, ed. H. GOLLANCZ, Oxford, 1914 f., 71a–72b.

⁷ The Ten Commandments (l. 16) occur very often on the most ancient Samaritan monuments. They interpret the passage, "these words," in Dt. vi, 6, as referring to the Ten Commandments, and verse 9 is carried out by them literally ; and coming after Dt. xxxii, 3, they complete the frame round this MS. The Samaritans, moreover, recite them daily in their service.

⁸ Lines 17–42 are an epitome, or as the Samaritans call it, a " katef" of God's Creation chiefly by speaking. The theory of the creative logos rests upon the first chapters of Genesis. These verses are also found on the Samaritan inscriptions in the same abbreviated form (*v.* Vol. XXXVII, p. 140 ff.), and were probably even then considered to be of a magical and mystical value. They formed part of the daily Samaritan prayer and were also a part of the daily prayer of the Jews in the Temple (*ibid.*). They form the basis of mystical speculations, and from olden times it was forbidden to indulge in such speculations or to attempt any public interpretation to the people in the assemblies of worship (*v.* Mishna Hagiga, II, 1). "A Book of Creation" (Sepher Yeṣirah, the most complete edition, Warsaw, 1884) is mentioned in the Talmud connected with the great Name. The knowledge of it gave to the initiated divine powers of creation. Another book of a similar title, ascribed to Abraham or to Akiba, has come down to us which contains the oldest treatise on the mystical value of the letters of the alphabet, the element of the logos of the creative word (*v.* Zunz, G. V², p. 165 ff. esp. 174). In the Midrash Tadshe, in which ancient traditions have been preserved, it is said (ch. X) that there are 70 names of God in the first three chapters of the Bible (more accurately Gn. i–iii, 14), and these chapters also contain 70 verses. This 70 is the round figure instead of the 72 or 76 to which reference will be made later on (note 25). So there are 70 nations, 70 names for Israel, 70 names for Jerusalem, and 70 names for the Torah, *v.* JELLINEK, *B.H.*, III, pp. 172 and XXXIV ; and ed. EPSTEIN in his Mikadmonioth, or *Beitrage z. jud. Alterthumskunde*, Vienna, 1887, p. XXV.

⁹ Line 44. This term is frequently used for its wearer throughout the amulet. It has no doubt a mystical meaning and refers to the divine garment with which, if a man is covered, he becomes raised to the status of an angel. It plays an important rôle in the apocryphal literature ; v. Slavonic Enoch (ed. MORFILL and CHARLES, Oxford, 1896, ch. 22, 8, p. 28), and the references to it. It appears also in the Odes of Solomon, xi, 10. In the Jewish literature a mystical book existed called the Sepher Hamalbush, fragments of which are now preserved in the Sepher Raziel (ff. 2b–7 ; *v.* also Zunz, G. V², p. 176). It is presumed to have been given to Adam by the Angel Raziel. A series of permutations and combinations of the alphabet, to which reference will be made at line 539, is given under the title of Malbush in the Sepher Yesirah, ed. Warsaw, 1884, pp. 53 and 54.

¹⁰ Whenever this name is repeated it will be given as A.a.A., according to the initial letters.

¹¹ *V.* note 9.

¹² *V.* note 9.

¹³ *V.* note 9.

[14] Line 123. This means the magical conjurations and actions of hostile magicians.

[15] Lines 131 ff. We have here evidently a list of reputed male and female sorcerers. If they could be identified, the date of the composition of this amulet could be more easily determined. There are Greek and Latin names among them like Margareta, Marcelah, Isidorah: others are Biblical names as Rebekah, Simeon, and Eleazar: and others are of unknown origin. They do not seem to have suffered much corruption at the hands of copyists. Unfortunately, very few names of sorcerers have come down to us. If we could see in Dmninah the Idaean Daktyle Damnamenus mentioned by EUSEBIUS, *Praep. Ev.*, X, 6, and by CLEMENS, *Strom.*, I, 75,—he occurs together with other names in the Ancient Greek cursing tablet ed. WUNSCH, *Antike Fluchtafeln*, No. 3, p. 9,—then this would show that we are dealing here with names known in the first centuries of the Christian era. If Simeon could be identified with either Simeon Magus or Simeon Peter, and Nunah with Lunah (Helena), the famous wife of Simeon Magus, this would still further corroborate the date assumed for the origin of the amulet. It was the practice in ancient conjurations to introduce a list of names of demons or of divinities, for it was believed that by mentioning the enemy by name one destroyed his power for evil. In the charm against Lilith, her power is broken by being forced to mention the forty-three names by which she goes. Some of these names in a Greek charm mentioned by PRADEL, *Griechische und suditalienische Gebete Beschoworungen und Rezepte des Mittelalters* (Giessen, 1907), p. 23, remind us of this list without being exactly like it. In other charms long lists of names of Saints have taken the place of demons, *v.* SYRKU, *Rukopisnye*, etc. (St. Petersburg, 1896), pp. 8 ff., 15 ff., as being more efficacious in averting the dreaded danger(*v.* Greek charms published by VASSILIEV, *Anecdota Graeca* (Moscow, 1893), I, p. 20, 7). ORIGEN says that to Biblical names a special mystical and supernatural importance has been attached for magical purposes, and so with the names of the Patriarchs (ORIGEN, *c. Cels.*, I, 24, V, 45; PAULY, *R. Encycl.*, Vol. IV, p. 1406). The same holds good also for the names of the rivers of Paradise (*v.* note 30). The names of the Patriarchs occur also in the present phylactery (lines 141, 445).

[16] Here starts a series of combinations and permutations of the letters of the alphabet, to which mystical importance has been attached as being the elements of the logos (*v.* note 8), the representatives and substitutions for the divine names.

[17] This seems to be the Samaritan interpretation of Ex. xxxviii, 8, according to the Samaritan Targum. Curiously enough, there existed in ancient times a Jewish mystical treatise with the same heading, "The Images of the Hosts," written in the Aramaic language on the unity of God. It is quoted by MOSES ABEN GABAI in his *Abodat hakodesh*, 14, 2, ch. 24. This verse is taken as being of a symbolical character. The Samaritans have evidently given to the word במראות the meaning of "images."

[18] With line 150 begins a new chapter starting, like line 10, with a list of the attributes of God, all expressive of His might, but here given much more fully and not as direct quotations from the scriptures. Then this is followed by verses from Dt., also explanatory of God's might and more of a prophylactic character, inclusive of the Priestly Blessing (line 177).

[19] Lines 182–253. From here the character of the amulet changes as far as the quotations are concerned. They are no longer verses or portions of verses, but whole passages taken from the Pentateuch. They contain complete incidents—

nay, small sections of the Bible—in which the promises of divine protection are repeated in full, as well as the divine blessing. The priestly blessing occurs already in some of the oldest inscriptions, and is a standing feature of magical amulets. These incidents from the ancient history are then taken in a sympathetic and prophylactic character. The wearer of the amulet invokes the same divine protection for himself as was promised by God to his forefathers, and implores divine assistance by means of these quotations against all manner of evil, be it from beasts, be it from enemies, or be it from evil spirits. Especially pronounced and often repeated is the imprecation against the machinations of wizards and sorcerers (v. lines 220–226). In Jewish and Christian, as well as Mahomedan, amulets similar practices prevail. The very Logos Hebraeikos in the Paris Magical Papyrus, to which reference has often been made, is nothing else but a whole chapter lifted out from the book of Enoch, as shown by me (*J.R.A.S.*, Jan., 1901, p. 209), and some of the oldest Christian prayers resemble very closely this kind of invocation (v. MICHEL, *Gebet und Bild in Frühchristlicher Zeit*, etc., Leipzig, 1902, p. 34 f., especially HEIM, *Incantamenta Magica*, Leipsig, 1892, pp. 520–25). The transition from this kind of magical invocation to prayer is often very difficult to trace.

Of the books of the Bible, however, the Psalms seem to have been those specially selected for similar purposes. There is a complete treatise, *Shimmush Tehillim*, to which reference has already been made, where the line of demarcation between prayer and magical invocation cannot be definitely fixed. Indications are given of the use to which each of these psalms is to be put for averting evil, or for healing, and so on. Sometimes the whole psalm is used, but occasionally also only verses, and even mystical names of God have been constructed out of single letters in these psalms, to which the same value has been ascribed as to the recital of the whole psalm. How persistent the use of the psalms has been for mystical purposes, see K. KAYSER, "Gebrauch d. Psalmen zu Zauberi," *Z.D.M.G.*, 1888, Vol. 42, pp. 456 ff. The suggestiveness of such incidents from Biblical history recurs afterwards in most of the ancient charms, in which either a god or a hero or an apostle or a saint is introduced whose experience is recited, and the cure which he effected or the safety with which he emerged from the trial is applied in the invocation to him who is using it. This is so constant an element that any collection of ancient charms contains abundant examples, as in the Papyri, as well as in other Greek and Latin collections (v. HEIM, *l. c.*, p. 495 f.). In the Samaritan Phylactery we meet the oldest and most primitive form, which shows us the various stages of development through which the later amulets and charms have gone. This is the reason why from olden times a confusion has arisen between the phylactery amulet and the *tefillin*, as in both whole sections of the Bible were found, and it was difficult to distinguish between the one and the other. The same happened also to the two smaller sections of the *tefillin*, i.e., Deut. vi, 4–9, and xi, 13–21, which were, and still are, used as inscriptions on the doorposts, the *mezzuzah*. To these even Jews ascribe a prophylactic value, and a number of such *mezzuzahs* have been found, some very ancient, on which, in addition to the two small sections from the Pentateuch, either whole psalms or verses of psalms have been added, and also magical characters have been inserted, so as to increase their prophylactic value (v. APTOWITZER, *Rev. Étud. Juives*, 1913, p. 54 ff.). The names of God are also found among them, inserted in squares or round each letter, and also substitutions of letters immediately following in lieu of those of the Tetragrammaton, the practice which has persisted to this very day. It belongs to the system of permutations foreshadowed by lines 540 ff. of this phylactery (*v.* note *ad. loc.*).

[20] The same attributes are here as in line 10, and similarly, in a slightly different form, lines 170–182, where the formula concludes with four times Amen. Here it is repeated five times. In the former it also contains the priestly blessing and may therefore be taken as the conclusion of a smaller section. The priestly blessing in the Samaritan Service is pronounced at the end, and Amen is always taken to mark the end of prayer or blessing, and is here used for the end of a section in the conjuration.

[21] Here the introductory formula marks a new section containing various groups of quotations, the first (line 254) is one in which the word ruaḥ, רוה ("wind or spirit") occurs. This belongs to the category of the Ḳaṭef, of which numerous examples are found in the amulet.

[22] Line 257. The Samaritan here reads the word ruaḥ instead of revaḥ as in the Massoretic, and is here translated accordingly.

[23] Line 266. Possibly copyist's error for "he took."

[24] Lines 273–81. This is the second group of invocations in which the intercession of Moses with a peculiar heavenly hierarchy is sought. It is quite unlike any hierarchy known in Jewish or Christian literature. This peculiar hierarchy consists here of the Hosts' wonder-working powers—of the Great gods, of the high God, of the Possessor of Heaven and Earth—a remarkable hierarchy, of which no parallel exists. The head of each category may perhaps be taken as identical with God, but there seems to be a gradation beginning with the Hosts and finishing with the Possessor of Heaven and Earth. There is no trace of gnosticism in it. But in the traditions about Simon Magus and his mystical claims, traces of this kind of speculation can be detected.

[25] Lines 281–296. Here we have three quotations from the Bible gradually increasing in size, and each one is written backwards. In the translation the original order of the text has been kept, but in the text the last word corresponds with the first word of the translation. In the use of the palindrome there are also various forms where the letters of the words are kept in their proper order, but the whole words are written backwards, so that the last word of the verse should be at the beginning of the quotation, or the letters in the words are also written backwards. Both practices seem to be very old. In the Talmud we find (Tr. Sandhedrin, folio 22a) many examples of this kind of metathesis, besides the writing backwards being referrred to by a special term. Abracadabra is the well-known specimen of this kind of palindrome, and no doubt many hitherto unexplained passages in the Greek magical charms and incantations will, on careful examination, be found to be nothing less than Biblical or other verses written backwards. Its use is universal in magical literature, and the object is to confuse the demon, who would not be able to read the wording in its proper sequence, and would, in consequence, get confused and terrified. The frame lines and the intercolumnar lines in the phylactery of the first group square sheet are all written on this principle, as a facsimile of Codex F will show. This is also an additional proof that the text before us is a real phylactery or an amulet, for only in such documents do we find palindromes.

[26] Lines 299–312. These verses have also been taken by the Jews (*v. Proceedings*, 1915, p. 100) in a similar manner, with the difference that they make of them 72 groups whilst the Samaritans make 76. Each of these groups is considered to be one of the mystical names of God. There is a whole literature of the attempts

which have been made to explain these names, either by words, or by verses more easily understood. Each of these groups of three letters, and also of two in the Samaritan 76, or the 72 of the Jews, was considered to be a special mystical Name of God, and as such, an attribute or a name. Various endeavours were then made to find the equivalent or a proper interpretation of these groups. One consisted in trying to find words whose initial letters corresponded to the letters of the group and to thus express a certain meaning ; or they were looked upon as equivalents for such words as strength, love, grace, etc. Among the Samaritans reference has been made to them by Abisha (my Cod. 872), and a list of such interpretative names is found in my Cod. 1170, f. 193 (*v.* note 6). The 76 words have been enumerated there ro doubt as the equivalents of the 76 mystical names evolved out of the combinations of the letters of the three verses. Among the Jews it suffices to refer to the literature mentioned by ZUNZ, *Literatur-geschichte der synagogalen Poesie*, Berlin, 1865, p. 146, and especially to BLAU, *Jud. Zauberwesen,* p. 127 ff., especially p. 137. In the Sefer Raziel, f. 24*b*–31*b*, there are at least three such different interpretations and substitutions (*v.* also note 33). So well known was the use of initials as standing for the whole word, that there exists even a technical term for it in Talmudic literature, *i.e.*, Notarikon, probably the shorthand writing of the notary. Even words of the Bible were treated as if they consisted of the initial letters of as many words as there were letters in the word. In a Biblical Commentary of the twelfth century ascribed to ELEAZAR of Worms numerous examples of it are found, as also in the commentary of Asheri known as Baal ha Ṭurim. A similar work is mentioned by AZULAI as Sefer Gematrioth. To this may be added the fact that a prayer consisting of 72 verses said to be representative of the 72 names of God is contained in the Jewish Liturgy and is recited by those who are mystically inclined. (*V.* note 48 ; also GASTER, *Literatura Populara Romana.* For Christian names and substitutions see the literature given there, p. 401 ff.). Not only among the Jews, but also among the Karaites this mystical number of 72 names of God, derived from precisely the same verses of Exodus as mentioned here, seems to be well known. AARON, son of Elijah of Nicometia, thirteenth century, refers to it expressly in his *Commentary to the Peutateuch Keter Torah.* ed. GOSLOV, Vol. II, folio 38 b. He explains there the manner in which the three verses have been used in order to form these groups. No mystical figure is so widespread as this figure of 72. It would be impossible to enumerate all the attempts which have been made to elucidate the origin or to chronicle the use of it. It must suffice to refer to REITZENSTEIN, who, in his *Poimander,* p. 300, believes it to be of Egyptian origin. He points out that the Kynokephalos had 72 members and the earth has 72 nations. The full literature of ancient and mediaeval writings has been collected, as far as possible, by J. BOLTE, *Zeitschrift d. Ver. f. Volkskunde,* Vol. XIII, pp. 444–450 ; and *ibid.,* MARZELE, 1913, pp. 69 ff. and 190.

[27] Lines 313–38. A similar refrain with the hóly names intercalated between short Biblical passages in the Samaritan service (my Cod. 829 f., 32 *a* and *b*). The Song of Moses is recited by the Samaritans, especially on festivals, with intercalations and repetitions. MARKAH, the oldest Samaritan poet (third or fourth century), writes his great hymn on this Song of Moses, forming the chief part of Book II, Cod. 1162 f., 45 *a* ff. (not in HEIDENHEIM). It is to be noted that this Song of Moses forms part of the weekly and festival services of the Jews. In ancient Greek Psalters the Song of Moses was added at the end of the Psalter, probably to be used in the services as one of the hymns sung in the Church. But this Song of

Moses seems also to have been used for magical purposes. From line 337 onwards it is written straight and as palindrome. It is a remarkable fact that, moreover, ch. 15, verse 16, written in the same manner straight and as palindrome and exactly as here in lines 337–342, forms part of the Jewish service of New Moon. It is also followed by Amen three times and Selah three times (GASTER, *Prayer Book*, Vol. 1, p. 146). This part of the service can be traced back to the treatise Soferim V, 2. In older versions to Ex. xv, 16, 17 also is added. So Abudarham, Rokeah, etc., Yalkut 188, Mekhilta (Ex. Bō), *v.* Sefer Ḥasidimd 230. Landshut Hegyon Leb. 391 ff. (the whole literature), Beer Abodat Israel 338 (Rodelheim 1868). REIFMANN suggests that these words were omitted by Maimonides because they were like charms, probably used originally at the eclipse of the moon. They are, however, remnants of mystical prayers connected with the New Moon which plays such an important rôle in the magical literature of charms and amulets. The magical character of that quotation from the Bible is shown by the prayer which follows. It is of precisely the same sympathetic and symbolical character as the Samaritan, for it says, "As we attempt to leap towards thee but cannot touch thee, so may those who attempt to injure us be unable to reach us"; exactly as we find it here in the formula often repeated "as the sorcerers could not stand up against Moses so may they not be able to stand up against him who wears these writings" (*cf.* l. 363 ff.) ; a complete parallel which could not have been noticed hitherto—as the Samaritan phylactery was unknown— and proves the extreme antiquity of each other. (On Palindrome *v.* BLAU, *ibid.*, p. 85.)

[28] See note 17.

[29] Probably single words standing for whole verses, like Great is our God. Heal I pray.

[30] Here we have the very name of this amulet, for it is nothing else than "phylactery" by simple metathesis of the two letters, for phikltra means philktra. It is more than a mere coincidence that the very same transposition of letters should occur in that identical word in the only quotation in the Talmud Treatise Sabb., f. 103, where all the commentators seem to have gone wrong. The word is written פנלאטורין, which is nothing else but פלנטורין, in which, according to the Aruch, groups of the first letter of the alphabet (א) are said to have been written, the document being an amulet. The two letters א are there explained to be the initials of the word Amen repeated twice (*v.* Aruch, *s.v.* א). The same word is used in the Logos Ebraikos of the Paris Papyrus to denote purely and simply an amulet. It agrees entirely with the character of the Samaritan phylactery, and proves beyond doubt that, as mentioned before (*Proceedings*, 1915, p. 96), phylactery is not a correct translation of *tefillin* (*v.* DEISSMANN, *Light from the Ancient East:* London, 1910, p. 256).

[31] Line 378. These four rivers of Paradise play an important rôle in mystical conjurations and amulets. They occur not only often in Jewish amulets, but they are also found in the Greek text published by PRADEL (*Griechische und suditalienische Gebete Beschoworungen und Rezepte des Mittelalters*, pp. 35, 60). They are found in the Greek questions ascribed to BARTHOLOMEW in Vassiliev, *Anecdota Graeca*, 20, 6, and probably lie at the root of the allusion in Rev. ix, 14, which would thus carry it back to the first centuries of the Christian Era. Ancient Biblical names of rivers or nations have been invested with a demoniacal character : so the seven nations mentioned in the Bible occur in the Logos Ebraikos practically as names of demons (*cf.* DEISSMANN, *l.c.*, p. 256).

[32] After concluding the imprecation against sorcerers, there begins a series of quotations from the Bible of blessing, which are now symbolically to be transferred to him who wears the amulet, and who, by the power of the divine Names, has frightened away all evil beings or harm.

[33] From here (line 443) begin the mystical combinations of the divine Names IHVH and AHYH. It would be impossible to attempt, even remotely, a complete list of parallels. This is a common feature in all ancient and

mediaeval magic. It lies at the base of the Gnosis and Cabbalah. The divine Name, especially IHVH, is the essentially potent factor : it is repeated very often, simply or in combination with other names, or is represented by substitutions of other letters. It is to be found in the whole of the vast literature of phylacteries, be they Greek, Hebrew, Samaritan or Latin. In Greek and Latin we find groups of vowels, which correspond to the letters of IHVH and AHYH, which are also vowel-signs in Hebrew. I limit myself here to some of the most important known parallels, where also the whole of the literature is given. My Samaritan Cod. 1170 contains (f. 299) a prayer for him who wishes to obtain a prophetic answer in his dreams. This prayer begins with a similar group of IHVH. KABASI's work on the Name has been mentioned on p. 105 ff. (*Proc.,* Vol. XXXVII) ; it abounds in Greek magical papyri, *v.* DIETERICH, *Abraxas passim ;* DEISSMANN, *Light from the Ancient East :* London, 1910, p. 270. On Aramaic magical bowls, *v.* MONTGOMERY, *Aramaic Incantation Texts from Nippur,* Philadelphia, 1913, p. 273, and the full literature thereon, p. 60. In Hebrew literature *v.* BLAU *Zauberwesen,* pp. 123 ff. ; an exhaustive study so far as the Rabbinical literature is concerned. For the later literature *v.* Sefer Raziel, *passim,* *Sword of Moses* (ed. GASTER), and GASTER, *Charms,* in *Hastings Encyclopaedia of Religion and Ethics,* p. 451, and especially the literature at the end (p. 455). One of the most important works on the divine Name by a leading mystic is the Ḥayē Haolam haba or Perush Shem Hameforash, "The Life of the World to come," or the explanation of the ineffable Name, by the famous Rabbi ABRAHAM BEN SAMUEL ABULAFIA (b. 1240) still inedited. My Cod. 1054 (of the fourteenth or fifteenth century) is a masterpiece of caligraphy. It contains upwards of 200 mystical circles formed out of the letters and substitutions of the divine Name. On f. 37*b*-38*a* is a similar group of IHVH, and on f. 39*a* is a similar group of permutations of AHYH. Also no less than ten different groupings of the 72 names of three letters each all derived from the same verses in Ex. xiv, 16 ff., the first part of which is identical with the group here, line 299 (*v.* also note 25). The divine Name is here repeated ten times in accordance with the ancient tradition that the world was created by " Ten words " for ten times "the Lord said " is found in Gn. i. In Jewish literature, *v.* Chapter of the Fathers, v. I (TAYLOR, *ad. loc.,* p. 87, 2nd ed.), and for the Samaritan, *v.* the Commentary to Genesis by Meshalmah the Danafite (Cod. GASTER, 1186, f. 1*b*). It is sufficient also to refer to the Ten Commandments for the mystical importance attached here to the number ten. The repetition of the divine Name occurs also in lines 451–3, 456–7. The use of the ten is progressive. AHYH is repeated twice ten times in lines 496–8, and AH with other letters is repeated three times ten in line 515 ff. (note 43). Similarly a group of three times א occurs ten times followed by the first ten letters of the alphabet (line 602). In the same way the Biblical verse in line 470 is repeated ten times (note 38).

[34] Line 445. *V.* note 15.

[35] Line 447. Mystical letters, Cod. F. has ANGRMN.

[36] Line 449. Evidently the reference is to the 76 groups in line 299 plus ten times IHVII. The second letter is, however, indistinct, and may be read 76, which of course would be the exact number of line 299 ff.

[37] Lines 458–61. For this system of intercalation *v.* note 27. The verse, Dt. xxviii, 12, is the same that already occurs in the ancient inscriptions.

[38] Line 470. Ten seems to be the symbolical figure, as the name of God was repeated ten times, *v.* line 144, *v.* also note 33.

[39] *Cf.* the introduction to the Incantation in the Logos Ebraikos, DEISSMANN, *l.c.*, and the other ancient opening formulas in the *Aramaic Incantation Bowls* (MONTGOMERY, *l.c.*). Line 491 ff. is also the concluding formula of the Samaritan Morning Prayer.

[40] Lines 499–509. Here again intercalated prayer, *v.* note 27.

[41] Line 510. The letters used are אהוחימסר and the line finishes with the three-fold א, probably A.a.A. and with ah and ah, the same vowels as are often found in Greek Papyri. So also lines 515-7.

[42] Lines 513 and 514 contain single words each one of which represents a whole verse or part of a verse of the Bible.

[43] Lines 515–518. These three lines consist of a group of thirty times (which is three times ten) Ah. No one to my knowledge has hitherto given a satisfactory explanation of these peculiar groups of vowels in the magical incantations, especially in the Greek Papyri. These have been the only documents available in which such groups notably of the vowel *a* abound. Some, like DIETERICH in his *Abraxas*, have tried to explain the use of the Greek vowels by attributing to them the mystical value, which, according to the Pythagorean teaching, is attached to the letters of the Alphabet. It does not help us, however, very much. For, why should only the vowels have been singled out? It is true they represent a peculiarly harmonious scale. One fact has been overlooked, and it is an important fact: these groups of vowels have been found only in incantations and magical formulas of a syncretistic character, in which Jewish or Samaritan influence can be traced. I see now in these groups of vowels nothing more than the graphic representation of a peculiar cantillation. The Charms have been first *chanted*,—hence the name Incantation,—before they were written down. And even then they were written down for the private use of the magician. He was to recite all these words and prayers, or rather chant them to a certain tune, and here we have in these vowel-groups the indication of how it was done. The practice of "chanting" an Incantation has persisted to this very day; but what raises my hypothesis to a reality is the fact that even now the Priests, *i.e.*, Cohanim the descendents of Aaron the High Priest, recite the Priestly Blessing among the Jews as well as among the Samaritans with precisely such a cantillation as is found in the Phylactery. They repeat over and over again the sound of "ah" at the end of each word, and more so at the end of each of the three verses which compose it. For at least two thousand years this practice in the synagogue and kinsha has continued almost daily. And if one realizes that this blessing is characterized as "putting the Name upon the people," it will be understood how natural it was for one who used the Name for conjuration or incantation to imitate this very form of cantillation, with prolonged and multiplied repetition of the "ah" sound. Graphically, it moreover represented one half of the divine Name *Ah*yah, and this would be an additional recommendation. A reason could also be found for this cantillation which is faintly indicated in a description of the Temple Service found in ancient Literature. On the Day of Atonement the High Priest pronounced clearly the Ineffable Name. In order, however, that the assembled multitude should not be able to catch the real pronunciation, the other priests chanted the remaining words in such a manner that the "Name" became, as it were, swallowed up in the sounds they made. This was the most solemn occasion for the recital of the Blessing. It set the example for all other times during the existence of the Temple, and has been handed down as a living tradition to our days.

I have been able to obtain from the Samaritans an impression on my phonograph of their recital of the Blessing, and it also contains the same cantillations, which is the best proof of its extreme antiquity. This seems to be the only possible explanation of the otherwise inexplicable groups of vowels in these Incantations, in the Papyri, and on the Aramaic Incantation Bowls. When the Hebrew characters were transliterated into Greek it is not impossible that, forgetting in later times that they were musical notes, they were interpreted and modified in the light of Pythagorean harmonies and other mystical manipulations of vowels and letters. The intercalated letters are intended to be the first ten letters of the alphabet as in line 602 ff.

[44] Lines 519–522. Here we have a Katef, with the leading word "healing," where verses have been gathered together in which this word occurs, to be used as a sympathetic means towards a cure.

[45] From line 522 is a very remarkable prayer inasmuch as it is the only one in which the name of an angel,—here the angel of fire (Abiel)—is mentioned in the phylactery. This is not the place to discuss Samaritan angelology, but it will be seen from my forthcoming publication of the Samaritan Apocryphal Book of Moses that the Samaritans knew and recognized the existence of angels from olden times, and that many of them have distinctive names. So also in my Cod. 884.

[46] Line 527. Here we have the name of the man for whom the amulet was written. By the insertion of the name of the owner or wearer the scroll is distinguished from the square parchment. It is difficult to identify this Abraham of the family of Ab Sakua who belonged to the section of the Danafites, as they are numerous. If this Abraham, who evidently had written this phylactery, as no other name of a scribe is mentioned, could be identified with the father of Murjan the author of various liturgical hymns who lived about 1720, then this Abraham lived in the second half of the seventeenth century, the date which I have ascribed to the scroll.

[47] Line 531. This is a repetition of the verse seven times as a prophylactic. Here we have the figure seven endowed with the same mystical importance as the figure ten in the preceding lines.

[48] Lines 539–60. In other copies of the phylactery the grouping is different. In some of them care is taken that each line should contain all the letters of the alphabet plus one. This forms the basis of innumerable possibilities of substitutions and permutations, for each letter in the succeeding line can be taken, and has been taken, as the representative of the letter in the line above for which it can afterwards be substituted. This practice is already mentioned in the Talmud (Sanhedr 22a). The Milesean formula is based on the same principle of substitution of the letters of the alphabet (v. PAULY, Real Encyclopadie (Stuttgart, 1864), Vol. IV, p. 1400). It has been fully developed in the Jewish mystical literature. It also forms the basis of steganography and all the ciphers used in secret scripts. Various tables have been drawn up similar to the Samaritan phylactery. A few may be mentioned here. In Hebrew literature the principle of the permutation of the letters of the alphabet as the secret of creation is found in the Book Yeṣirah, ch. 2, para. 4. BOTAREL in his Commentary to the above passage (ed. Warsaw, 1884, p. 81) elaborates a number of tables of permutations similar to the Samaritan, and the author of Or Hadash (ed. Warsaw, 1884), ibid., p. 83, supplies another set. Other sets of alphabets are found in KNORR, v. Rosenroth Cabbala Denudata, pp. 179–194 ; v. furthermore, AGRIPPA, in his mystical works, Vol. III, p. 25, ed. SCHEIBLE. The writing in the Samaritan

phylactery of the square so as to be the result of two triangles is not without mystical importance. It is the application of the principle of continual attenuation seen in the Abracadabra in which in every succeeding line the two end letters are dropped so that the last line consists of one letter, the apex of an inverted triangle, symbolical inasmuch that, as the writing diminishes so may the illness diminish until it reaches vanishing point. This seems to be the reason of the two triangles joined together here, yet still distinctly kept apart by one letter forming the diagonal, preserving thus the character of diminished writing of the alphabet, as it is reduced to a single letter, the apex of the triangle, with the same symbolical meaning.

[49] Lines 569–78. Here the same principle is applied to the great Name of God as it is called in the margin. It must be noted here that throughout the whole phylactery the letters have not been used as numerals. The whole of the mathematical cabbala, that is the use of letters according to their numerical value, is not hinted at in this phylactery. The grouping of the square lends itself to this kind of mathematical speculation, although it is not used here for any such purpose. This is the best proof of its high antiquity. In Rev. xiii, 18, traces of it can already be found : the mystical figure 666 representing a name ; and in the Epistle of Barnabas, chap. ix, the figure 318 is taken as the mystery of three letters there explained. This mathematical cabbala in its later growth overshadows all other mystical speculations. It is found among Jews, Christians, Mohammedans (v. LANE, *Modern Egyptians*, London, 1890, Chap. XI, p. 239), and the latest form of the Samaritan phylactery presents many examples. The Samaritans themselves are not ignorant of this use of letters. Already in the Kafi (beginning of eleventh century), traces of this use can be found in the interpretation of the Bible ; and occasionally in the apocryphon of Moses but more so in the work of KABASI. It is utilised for the purpose of obtaining from the text of the Bible indications of the date of the appearance of the Taheb, of the length of the Fanutah, even for the appearance of Jesus and Mohammed (v. MERX, *Taheb*, Giessen, 1909, p. 91 ; but more complete in my Cod. 879 f., 18a). The name given by Jews and Samaritans to this art of computation is Gamatria, which is not to be identified as hitherto with Geometria but with Gramatia. It is only in the light of these mystical tables that the true meaning of this often wrongly interpreted word has now been made clear. It can only have meant, originally, the use of letters in permutations and substitutions in accordance with the groupings in these tables (v. note 48).

[50] Lines 579–93. Another Katef with the leading word " Lord," in connection with the preceding permutations and combinations of the divine name.

[51] In the middle of line 597 the letter occurs standing by itself as meaning a numeral which, in connection with the word following, means seven times, i.e., that the whole passage is practically repeated seven times, and that may be an indication that the phylactery was not only worn but may have been recited as a powerful exorcism by the Samaritan magician ; otherwise there is no obvious reason for this note, unless the writer found the passage too long to copy out seven times in succession.

[52] Line 602. These Alephs cannot be Amen, for this word is always fully written out and stands *only* at the *end* of a sentence : never at the beginning. They may be the initials of Ahyh hasher Ahyh, or they are possibly a different mode of cantillation similar to, yet not identical with, the one in line 515 (v. note 43). This duplication and triplication of Aleph must have also been characteristic of

the ancient Jewish phylacteries mentioned by the author of the Aruch, *s.v.* אא (wrongly interpreted as meaning Amen).

[53] Line 608. It reminds one of the Ephesian Gramata with a similar end rhyme. They sound almost alike : Aski Pataxi (or Pataski), Lix (Aix), Tetras (Tetrex), Damnamenos : *cf.* also the peculiar formula against gout " huat, hanat, huat, ista, pista, sista, domiabo, danna, ustra" (PLINY, *H.N.*, 28, 2 ; CATO, *Rer. Rustic.*, n. 160).

[54] Line 609. Referring again to Ex. xv, 16, the same verse to which reference has been made (note 27), as one used in the Jewish ritual of the New Moon.

[55] Line 620. This is the usual formula for ending almost every Samaritan prayer, and every Samaritan writing.

SAMARITAN PHYLACTERIES AND AMULETS.

By M. Gaster.

Reprinted from the "Proceedings of the Society of Biblical Archæology," February, 1917.

Codex Gaster No. 1104 (F).

The facsimile of Codex F (shown on Plates I and II) contains the last third of a whole skin, and is the best preserved of all the known Samaritan phylacteries belonging to this group. Although the MS. is slightly reduced in size the text is easily read, and all the phylactery characteristics are clearly seen. There are the frame lines, the intercolumnar lines, the uncial and the minuscle writing. Furthermore, the symmetrical groups, the alphabets with the diagonal and the divided squares, and the contents, are practically identical with those of Codex D: line 3 F corresponding to 441 D.

In order to show how close is the resemblance between the two I give a table of comparison between the various lines, giving first the list of those in which both codices agree, so that, with the help of one the other can easily be deciphered. But there are also a few lines in which the copyist of Codex F has followed a slightly different original, and also, from want of space, he has sometimes reduced to initials, words found written out fully in D. On a few occasions lines are omitted in F which are found in D, and vice versa. I have given lists of these lines also.

It will be evident, from a comparison of these two texts, that although they are separated from one another by at least 400 years, there is really no great difference between them. Occasionally even the copyist of D starts the lines in the same way as F, so faithfully has he transcribed the old document; a proof of the influence of tradition on Samaritan manuscripts.

Codex F collated with Codex D.

The following lines in F agree with those in D :—

Codex F.	Codex D.
3–6	441–442
7–8	444
9–14	445–449

PLATE I.

S.B.A. Proceedings, Feb., 1917.

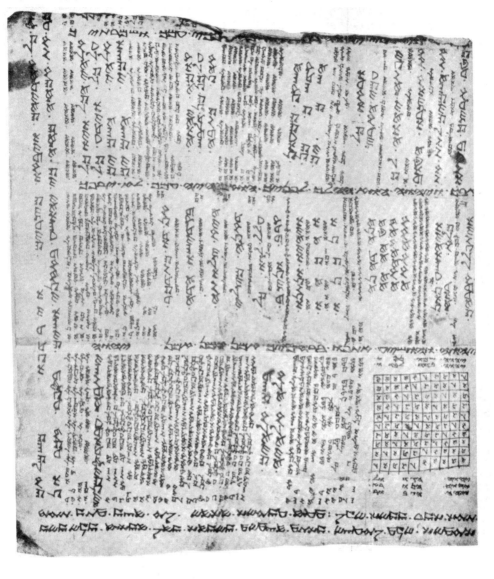

PLATE II

S.B.A. Proceedings, Feb., 1917.

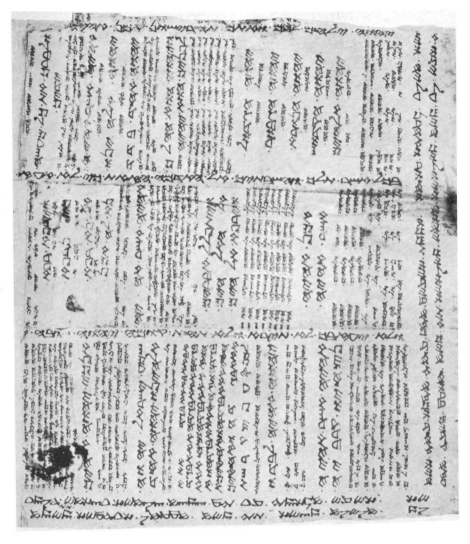

	Codex F.	*Codex D.*	
	15–24	450–454	
	26–31	456–457	
	45–50	463–465	
	54–58	467–469	
half of each line omitted }	60–64	470–479	
	65	480	(latter half)
	66, 68, 70, 74	484	
	82–86	486–490	
	87–95	491–498	
	96–100	499–503	
	101	506	
	102	505	
	103	504	
	104–106	507–509	
	107	510	(letters : but *not quite* the same)
	108–110	511–513	
	112	513	
	113–114	514	
	115–122	515–517	(letters : but *not all* the same)
	123–129	518–521	
	124–135	521–522	(parts agree)
	136	522	
	138–143	523–524	
	144	523	
	145–156	527–537	
	172–193	539–560	(different arrangement of squares)
	194–195	561–562	
	196–205	563–568	(letters : but *not all* agree)
	206–215	569–578	(different arrangement of squares)
	216–224	578–585	

[N.B.—In Codex F the last word or two of these lines have been omitted; but in some lines the last two or three letters, which can be traced to the end of words in Codex D, are inserted.]

Codex F.	Codex D.	
225–234	593–601	
235–241	602–605	(letters: but *not all* the same)
244–248	608–612	
256	619	

The following lines, which are in Codex D, are omitted in Codex F:—

[N.B.—Between ll. 9–14 לוי קחת עמרם.]

half l. 455
458–462
538
586–592
606–607
620–626

The following lines, which are in Codex F, are omitted in Codex D:—

1–2
25
32–44
51–52 (inclusive)
half 65
67, 69, 71, 72, 73
76
78, 79, 80, 81
111
137
157–172
242–243
249–255

PLATE III.

S.B.A. Proceedings, Feb., 1917.

The frame lines, starting from the bottom, and reading backwards, contain :—

A. (Outer frame line.) Exodus xiv, 21–23, beginning with the word את, and finishing with the word סום.

B. (Inner frame line.) Exodus xvii, 12–14, beginning with the word וישב, and finishing with the word זכר.

C. (Intercolumnar lines, from the right, reading from the bottom upwards.) Exodus xiv, 14. Genesis xxviii, 15, to the word אעזבך. Deuteronomy xxxi, 6, from the word כי to the word יעזבך, followed by these words :—

לא תירא ולא תחת קומה יהוה שובה יהוה והושיע אתנו ברחמך
אמן אמן אמן יהוה.

"Do not fear, and do not be dismayed. Arise, O Lord! Turn, O Lord! and save us by thy mercies, Amen. Amen. Amen. Lord."

CODEX GASTER No. 899 (O).

(PLATE III.)

The full description of this Codex has been given in these *Proceedings* (Vol. XXXVII, 1915, pp. 171, 172). I have since discovered parallels in other Codices which fully corroborate the statement of the Samaritans that this forms part of a phylactery. It is so in Codex 1103 (E), ll. 124 ff. and in Codex P, ll. 278 ff. The former, from a palaeographic point of view, may belong to the second or third century, but unfortunately it is in a very mutilated condition, and is only a fragment. Still, that part which contains the parallel passages is clearly legible, and has enabled me to give here as exact a transcript of Codex O as would not otherwise have been possible, the MS. being almost illegible. Very fragmentary also is Codex P, but it afforded some help of which I have availed myself in deciphering Codex O. The facsimile has been enlarged to double the size of the original, and even then the letters are so small, and the writing so much effaced, that but for the assistance I had from the Samaritans and from these two Codices the transcript would have remained very doubtful. In spite of this help some letters cannot be deciphered. Their places have been marked in the transcript by a small line. The last line in Group ז, however, cannot be deciphered at all. In the original, every letter is marked by a dot, and each group finishes with three letters which are the initials for קדש יהוה קדש. There are ten lines in each group and ten letters in each line. They are unquestionably initials of words, but up to the present time neither the Samaritans nor myself have been able to find the exact words of which they are the initials. Perhaps, now that this document has been made available, someone may, by a happy inspiration, hit upon the elucidation of this obscure text.

CODEX GASTER No. 899 (O).

ו

ה	ב	ו	מ	ה	י	י	נ	י	נ
י	כ	ק	ה	ו	ש	נ	ה	ו	ר
נ	ע	ל	ה	א	א	נ	ו	א	י
-	א	י	נ	ה	א	פ	נ	י	ו
נ	ל	-	•	י	ה	ה	ע	ה	ה
-	ל	כ	ו	נ	ל	י	י	ה	ד
ש	ה	ה	י	פ	ו	ד	ו	ה	ל
י	א	ו	י	ה	ו	י	ה	ה	י
א	מ	ק	ו	ו	ל	ה	נ	ה	-
ש	ו	א	ת	ת	ש	נ	ש	ת	מ

ז

ל	ו	א	כ	ר	-	-	-	י	-
-	נ	ד	ש	ל	י	ל	א	-	-
ל	ו	א	פ	ז	٠	ל	ה	ל	ל
ו	ז	ו	ח	א	-	ר	א	ה	מ
ע	ו	א	ו	כ	ת	ע	-	א	נ
כ	פ	ס	י	א	ה	ק	י	י	ל	ו
ו	ד	ק	ק	א	י	-	ו	נ	י
ת	א	ה	א	נ	-	-	א	י	ע
י	כ	נ	ה	ו	-	א	י	ו	ל
-	-	-	-	-	-	-	-	-	-

ח

ו ב י ה י ה ג ה א ה
ו י ו ו ל ו ו א ה ה ה
- א ו ו י ב ש ה נ נ ד
ד י ל ו ו י ד י - י א
א ל ה ה נ ה כ ה ו ו י
א - - נ - ה א ה א א ו
א ל ל נ - י - מ ס מ - ה
ר ו - כ ע ת ע ה י ת
ה כ ד ו - - ' - - - ה
ה ל א ו ת א נ ה נ נ ק"י

ט

ה י י א כ ש ע י י ל י
פ מ ה ח ל ' ר ו י ע
ל ל - כ ו ע א פ ג ל
ו נ נ ו מ ל - י א א
מ כ י ה ' - י ה א נ
ז ה ו ל כ - ו ה ה א
ז ה א י ל ל נ נ מ י
ר ס י י ש ' י ע א ר
- ב ה ל - ר - ה נ
- - - - - א ר א ל ק"י י" ק"

י

ו נ י - ד ה מ נ י ו
ד י - ה ר ק כ י ו ו
ו ה - י נ מ י ו כ א
ה - כ י מ ו א ל י י
ת ל י ל ח א ' כ ה ה
ר י ו א ז ה ה ה ר ל
ע ב א צ ש ו כ ה ד א
ו ר י נ י ת ק נ ו כ ו
ו כ ה י ש ב ע י ו מ
מ ק"י י" ק" ל ה ה ל א ו י
ת ו ב א צ

A SAMARITAN MS. OF THE SECOND OR THIRD CENTURY: A PALÆOGRAPHIC STUDY

ALL the elements are missing for even a moderate attempt at establishing definite rules for Samaritan Palæography. Of all the MSS. of the Pentateuch known in Europe only a few specimens have hitherto been published in facsimile, and, as far as I am aware, not one of them dated. The same holds good for all other Samaritan documents, prayer-books, letters, etc. There is therefore practically nothing to go upon, except personal experience, and the examination as far as possible of the materials available to as large an extent as circumstances allow. It is the course which I have endeavoured to pursue, but as will be seen the examination of MSS. hitherto known does not lead us further back than the eleventh or twelfth century. With all modesty I may claim to have seen most of the Samaritan MSS. in England and in Nablus. In the rest of Europe they are an almost negligible quantity : possibly the oldest dated fragment of a scroll of the Bible is in my possession. I have seen all the scrolls in the Kinsha in Nablus, inclusive of the famous one ascribed to Abisha, grandson of Eliezer, the son of Ahron the priest, and I have obtained copies of the Tarikh, or as they call it of the Teshkul (pronounced Tesh'ul), i.e. the date of most of them. I have taken a photo of the scroll of 1140, and done my best to get an insight into Samaritan palæography, intimately bound up as it is with the history of the Bible. If anywhere, it is among the Samaritans that the ancient traditions have been fossilized, and their scribes betray a most touching anxiety to imitate the originals as closely as possible.

Professional scribes will often retain the archaic characteristics of the script which they are copying. This is best seen in connexion with the scrolls of the Bible among the Jews, and what holds good for the Jews holds good also for the Samaritans. If not for some differences in the general character of the letters which mark off Oriental from Occidental forms, due to recognized traditions and not due to the vagaries or differences introduced by the scribes, it is often impossible to fix even an approximate date for such scrolls. It now often happens that a document discovered in the Genizah judged by outside appearance is considered to be of a more recent date, yet by the date which it bears it is found to be of far greater antiquity. We learn to our astonishment that the script which we considered modern is really very ancient, and that the scribes of a later date had retained intact the old form for centuries with the utmost fidelity. If we had to determine the date of these documents on the basis of palæography alone, we should have set them down as belonging to a period three to four hundred years later than they really are. If this is the case with Hebrew MSS., of which the libraries in Europe count about 10,000, not to speak of the equally great number of Genizah fragments in England alone, how much more fallacious must any estimate of the age of a Samaritan undated MS. be ! The Jews have established long ago—how long it is impossible to guess—standard codices of the scroll of the Law, for subsequent scribes to imitate word for word, line for line, column for column. To this very day such models are placed in the hands of the scribes. This probably is also the practice followed by the Samaritans, and I have had therefore four or five scrolls copied for me by the Samaritans in order to find out the principles followed and the originals which served as their model. Given the reticence of the Samaritans on many points affecting the scrolls in their possession, this was the only means of obtaining some reliable information as to the rules followed by them. A large number of Pentateuch copies in book form, some anterior to 1480, others of more recent origin, even a copy of the Triglott and the Targum, yielded important material towards an attempt to establish Samaritan palæography. I should like to add that the oldest fragment of the Bible scroll in Europe (belonging to the twelfth century) is in my possession. I also possess a large number of fragments of various ages and dates, of which each one contributed its quota to the elucidation of the problems connected with Samaritan palæography.

I reserve the detailed description for a special study on the palæography of the Samaritan Pentateuch. Yet in spite of the examination of so many ancient and modern Samaritan MSS. I must own that an attempt to fix the age of an undated MS. must still be more a matter of conjecture and hypothesis. There are to my knowledge no Samaritan MSS. available anterior to the twelfth century, except probably the famous Abisha scroll, the date of which will only then be determined when the study of the palæography of the Samaritan Pentateuch is established on a sound and definite basis. I have been informed by Mr. Warren of Michigan that a photographic copy has been taken of the whole of it by the American Society, and that the plates are now stored away in Jerusalem. One can only hope that they will survive the devastation of the War.

All this is mentioned here to show that I have spared no effort to reach some satisfactory result from the study of as full a material as could be gathered together under actual circumstances.

Nothing, or scarcely anything reliable, however, exists

older than the eleventh or twelfth century by means
of which the age of an older MS. could be fixed with
any hope of reliability, and none with certainty unless'
and until other dated texts are discovered. As far as
I am aware there is little hope for such a contingency.
No facsimile has been published of the Samaritan
fragments from the Genizah of Nablus, carried away
under false pretences by Firkovitch some seventy years
ago and now deposited 'in the library of St. Petersburg.
Among them there are a number of dated Ketuboth, a list
of which had been furnished by Harkavy to Nutt, and
published by the latter in his Samaritan Targum (p. 166).
Still, the oldest is dated only from the year 916 Heg.
(1510), the rest from the seventeenth to nineteenth
centuries. It is a pity that none of these had been reproduced in facsimile, and thus no help is forthcoming in
that direction, nor would it carry us higher up beyond
the beginning of the sixteenth century. But in addition
to the MSS. there is other material available, that
of the Samaritan inscriptions, of which a fairly good
number has recently been discovered, and most of which
have been reproduced in facsimile by Spoer Musel
Lidzbarski and by Montgomery. Paradoxical as it may
sound, these inscriptions are probably posterior to written
documents. They owe their preservation to the in-
destructive material—the stone or clay—on which they
have been engraved. But writing is undoubtedly older,
especially in Jewish and Samaritan literature, than any
of these inscriptions, which merely attempt to copy the
script which they followed as closely as the hard material
allowed. Unfortunately most of these monuments are
undated. The dates assigned to them rest mostly upon
mere conjecture and on the comparison of the writing
with other known inscriptions which are either dated or
whose age has been determined by the names and incidents
recorded thereon.

The dated monuments are helpful in showing the form which letters had assumed at a given period, and that a monument whereon the letters differ must be of a different age. If in addition to certain graphic details there is no other indication through the contents, it would be impossible to state which of the two monuments thus compared is the older or younger unless we follow the historical evolution of the script on the Semitic inscriptions through the ages. We are thus reduced to the comparative study of the alphabet and other details. The absence of old Samaritan inscriptions greatly adds to the hypothetical character of the results thus obtained. Still, though a wide margin may be given, I hope that this internal evidence and the comparison with old inscriptions may lead to results as much assured as has hitherto been the case with other ancient North Semitic or rather Palestinian epigraphic monuments.

The epigraphic material is thus the only available, but unfortunately it is very scanty. There are only very few old Samaritan inscriptions known, and they are of uncertain date. Some are ascribed to the fifth century, and others possibly to a little earlier period (third or fourth century). No convincing proof has been given for the dates, but there is nothing to contradict these views. No palæographical criterion has yet been established by which to determine the real age of these inscriptions. Montgomery in his Samaritans has reprinted a number of them. He has evidently not been guided by the assumed antiquity of each of them in the order in which he published them, for those numbered 1, 2, 3 are not the oldest. They are ascribed to a period anterior to the sixth century (the destruction of the Temple by Justinian before 531). Only No. 4, the inscription of Emmaus, of which more anon, may claim, in my opinion, to be the oldest hitherto recovered. For if we examine the writing on plates 1, 2, and 3 we shall find that the characters differ very considerably in their outlines, and in the manner in which the strokes of the letter have been drawn from the oldest available Hebrew, Phœnician, and Aramaic inscriptions, and approximate more closely some of the oldest Samaritan MS. fragments of the Pentateuch in book form.

The lines are quite horizontal, especially the lower lines of ב כ מ. The ד has no stroke or jot at the right or left of the foot and the top. The ה is very slanting, and the middle stroke passes through the back. The ו is broken in the middle; the vertical line of ק does not protrude above the top lines, and the vertical line of the י is not perpendicular, but rather slanting. On the whole the letters are not slanting. Characteristic is also the form of the י. Owing to the hardness of the stone the rounding of the letters, notably the top parts of בכפדר, is not complete. Very characteristic is the ל, whose lower stroke forms a sharp angle with the upper one, which slants from right to left. This letter has undergone a remarkable development. In the oldest Phœnician and Aramaic inscriptions the lower horizontal line is very small, but it has grown continually in the course of centuries to such an extent that it has become the most prominent part of the letter, and has reduced the upper line to a mere fraction of its original size. In these Samaritan inscriptions the lower line is already greatly developed, and the upper one has become completely slanting. All these features are especially noticeable in the Schechem inscription of the Ten Words on Creation reproduced by Lidzbarski on a larger scale and in smaller form by Montgomery (plate ii). As already remarked, it is extremely difficult to compare inscriptions cut with the chisel on hard stone with the writing by a reed pen in some soft material like papyrus and parchment. But the general outlines would no doubt be the same and in each case characteristic of the age of each of these monuments.

What I mean to say is this : that definite characteristic
features in the shape and outlines of letters would be
found in written as well as in cut letters, and that the
ornamentation, slanting or upright position, of the letter in
one set of monuments is sure to correspond with the same
size, form, shape of the letters in the other, independent of
the material upon which they have been produced. The
changes that supervene in the course of time will be seen
in either of them, though, as already remarked, it is much
more easy to retain archaic features in written documents
prepared by expert scribes, and notably in those cases in
which they copy ancient and sacred documents. They
would then be inclined to imitate also the outward form
of the letters whilst copying the contents. I have already
referred to this peculiarity in connexion with the writing
of sacred scrolls or anything invested with a sacred
character. Close imitation is almost part of the scribe's
duty, and yet in spite of this slavish imitation changes
are slowly introduced into the writing. But these will be
almost imperceptible at the beginning, and a long time
must elapse before a definite change can be recognized.
This, on the one hand, increases the difficulty of fixing the
date of any such document, and on the other hand helps
us approximately to fix the date, for if a decided difference
can be noted between one document and another, and
taking into consideration the slowness of the evolution
and the change, one is justified in assuming that a long
space of time must separate one from another. Centuries
must have elapsed in those cases. If we thus compare
the Emmaus inscription with the preceding three in
Montgomery this difference in type will at once be
noticeable. There are practically no lower horizontal
lines in the letters בכמ. There is only a short slanting
line in lieu of the vertical and horizontal, the lower stroke
of the ל is short in comparison to the upper line, and
there seems to be also a slight stroke on the left-hand

corner of ר which approximates this inscription very
closely to Phœnician forms, and to a certain extent to the
old Siloam and also slightly to the Moabite inscription,
though centuries must have elapsed between e.g. the
Siloam and the Samaritan inscriptions. There is now
another point—the interpunction. In the Aramaic inscriptions, which curiously enough have all come to light
during the last fifty years, we find the words separated
from one another by a dot. No such separation of words
takes place in any of the numerous Phœnician and Punic
inscriptions, nor is a dot found separating the words from
one another on the Hebrew coins. On the other hand, all
the Samaritan documents which have come to light—I refer
here especially to the written documents—have this dot of
separation between one word and the other. If we turn
now to the Samaritan Schechem inscriptions we find that
instead of one dot there occur two dots—the colon—which
separates the words from one another, and is not used as
syntactic interpunction, either separating sentences or
marking the end of greater divisions. I am not aware
that anyone has yet drawn attention to this problem of
word separation by one or two dots. In any case it is
a very remarkable fact that these dots and colons do not
occur on Phœnician inscriptions. In view of the fact
that the dot separating the words occurs already in the
Aramaic inscriptions at Zindgerle and on the Moabite Stone,
if the latter be genuine, would carry this marking up to
very high antiquity, and the same would be the case with
the Siloam inscription if it is carried back to the time of
Hezekiah, and thus the question arises : Why should the
Phœnician not have used the dots to separate one word
from another ?

There are evidently two different traditions here, and
the problem becomes complicated if we turn to the
Samaritan literature. Did the Samaritans use these dots
for separation of words from one another in very ancient

times, or are they of a later origin? In the absence of
decisive documents the question is an extremely difficult
one to answer. The epigraphical evidence would point in
the direction that the Samaritans did not use originally
a dot to mark the end of a word, but rather two dots—
a colon—appear in the Schechem and other inscriptions,
whilst no dot at all is found in the Emmaus inscription.
In the facsimile published by Montgomery there may be
a dot found in the second, but I doubt its existence, and
only one dot is found in No. 3, which, however, may have
a syntactical and not a diacritical value. In the absence
of other evidence it would be idle to inquire when the dot
had been introduced, and to what influences that dot is
due. All the MSS. available, even the oldest, have these
single dots. If now a document should be discovered
in which the words are not separated by any dots, either
single or double, unquestionably that alone would suffice
to mark it as an extremely ancient one, anterior in any
case to the inscriptions of the fifth or sixth century, and
much nearer in age to the Emmaus inscription, and if the
character of the letters would also agree in the main with
the first Emmaus inscription this would have to be accepted
as sufficient evidence for the document to be considered as
one of equal antiquity and if possible even older, unless
there would be direct internal evidence to show that such
an assumption is impossible.

Among the Samaritan documents in my possession there
is a large number of phylacteries or amulets. I have
recently published in the PSBA. for 1915–17 one of the
most complete of these amulets. I have endeavoured to
show that by their contents these amulets led us back
to the first centuries of the Common Era, if they are
not even older. For I see in these amulets the very
phylacteries mentioned in the New Testament. I have
gone into a minute description of the palæographical
peculiarities of these documents (ib. 1915, pp. 163 ff.), and

I have pointed out their very archaic character. Not
wishing to make them out too old, I see now that I have
erred on the wrong side in making them out to be much
younger than I am inclined now to think. The constant
occupation with them has sharpened the sight for many
minute points originally overlooked, and minute points
count for much in these delicate investigations, and their
importance has grown with the closer study of the
Samaritan inscriptions.

Among the phylacteries there is one (my Cod. 1103)
which has all the characteristics referred to above in the
epigraphic monuments, and marks it out as probably the
oldest Samaritan MS. which has thus far been recovered.
A careful examination of this document will convince us
of this fact. Not only do the letters bear close resemblance
to the first Emmaus inscription, but this is also as far as
I am aware the only Samaritan document in which the
words are not separated by dots, and the whole writing is
consecutive. It is remarkable that the words are not
separated from one another. All the letters are written
close to one another just as they are found in Phœnician
inscriptions, and not in the other phylacteries with the
words carefully separated by dots. If the whole were not
a collection of Biblical phrases these documents would
offer to the scholars the same difficulties of decipherment
and interpretation as those Phœnician and Punic inscriptions offer. It cannot be suggested in explanation of the
omission of the separating dot that because the phylactery
would be used for magical purpose the text would be
written consecutively, as may sometimes be the case for
magical formulæ, but as the text consisted of Biblical
sentences the writer would not have ventured to alter the
Biblical text and to make it as it were unintelligible by
the omission of dots if he had found them in the original.
No doubt, at his time, the Biblical text had not yet been
separated into words marked off by dots, and this would

carry it back to very high antiquity. It represents in
a faithful manner a much older original, the scribe not
venturing to take any liberties with the older original
which he transcribed and which he wanted to use as
a prophylactic against all kind of hurt and evil. This
is the more remarkable as the scribe knew the value of
the dot as a diacritical sign, for he used it as such and not
for the purpose of separating one word from another, but
to mark the pause between certain words which evidently
had to be pronounced emphatically, like the word *kadosh,*
" holy." It is used at the end of certain groups of mystical
letters, notably in the second column. He also knows the
value of the colon, but it is used only and solely for the
purpose of dividing certain lines into two equal halves,
each consisting of ten letters. Now there are in Samaritan
orthography also diacritical points corresponding more or
less to the Hebrew accents. They were described by me
and fully explained in my article in *Noldeke Festschrift*
under the title " Massoretisches im Samaritanischen ".

The older the Samaritan MSS. of the Bible are, the more
carefully do we find the accents and orthographic signs
inserted in the text, and probably because they have been
connected with the sacred text of the Bible use is made
of them also in most of the phylacteries, and the same
phenomenon can be observed in these as in all Bible MSS.,
for the older they are the more carefully are these accents
entered in the text. This MS., however (Cod. 1103), again
shows no trace of any of these diacritical points and
accents. Only occasionally there appears a vertical stroke
at the end of a whole paragraph more or less like
the Hebrew Silluk, but none of the other signs, dots, or
hooks, or any of the graphic signs found in all the other
Samaritan MSS. I take this to be another proof of
the high antiquity of this MS. If, as I suggest, those
Samaritan accents had been invented and introduced
about the fourth or fifth century, then their absence alone

would already prove that this MS. must be anterior to the
fourth or fifth century.

We turn now to the letters. We shall be struck by the
close affinity, not only with the Emmaus inscription, but
on the whole with the older Phœnician inscriptions. This
is a point of extreme importance inasmuch as it shows
that the Samaritans borrowed their alphabet from the
Phœnician and not from the Hebrew, or that all go
back to a common stock, yet in their development the
Samaritans kept close to the Phœnician, but the Hebrew
and Aramaic developed their alphabet on more independent
lines. It will be noted that there is scarcely any straight
horizontal line under בפמב —they are all on the slant—
but also that the מב have practically, in most cases, no
horizontal line at all. They finish the upper part with
a kind of tail slightly turned on the left exactly as we
find them in the Emmaus inscription, and as we find these
letters in the old Phœnician inscriptions. It agrees with
col. 3 in Montgomery's table, which is early Hebrew,
meaning thereby the Siloam inscription, and even more
closely with col. 4 (middle Phœnician) with the exception
of one or two letters. If we turn to the ל we find the
lower stroke very small and the upper line curved upwards
and not straight, slanting to the right. The ה is in most
cases standing upright, quite perpendicular, and the upper
line protrudes beyond the stroke on the right and not in
the middle as in the inscriptions of Nablus, and in all
subsequent monuments. The ר has also an upper stroke
and we find it revived afterwards by the scribe of the
eleventh or twelfth century, and on the foot of the דד
there are strokes to the left.

These archaic forms in the present text cannot be mere
graphic vagaries, for it is a long document consisting of
no less than 185 lines, and this is only half of the
original document; the other half has been torn off, and
who knows whether it is still in existence ? The

preservation of these documents is almost a miracle in itself, and with one single exception, my cod. No. 1100 (C), there is no one single whole phylactery known to exist anywhere. They are all only fragments of one-half or two-thirds of the original, all written with great care, and are copies of much older documents as mentioned before. They are the oldest representatives of the amulets current in Palestine, not only in the first century but unquestionably much earlier. The agreement between these phylacteries and the oldest Greek magical papyri is very close. What is still more pertinent to our purpose now is the fact discovered by me that all the Samaritan inscriptions hitherto discovered contain precisely the same text in the same order with the same abbreviations as found in the phylactery. They were in fact phylacteries in stone put there for the same purpose of protection. They contain the very same phrases and even the same abbreviations, and the very inscription of Emmaus is found here in line 13 of this phylactery (excluding the two top frame lines). This makes the graphic comparison even much more easy.

There is now another point. In all the other phylacteries we find two kinds of writing, small and big letters, and although the practice of writing small and big letters is very old, still this is the only document of its kind in which the whole writing is in one single alphabet. It is neither the real minuscule nor a real majuscule, but a bold full-sized type, the same for the text as for the surrounding marginal lines and the frame lines, as I call them, which in all other MSS. are written in very big type. In the other phylacteries there are in addition to the two frame lines also intercolumnal lines separating one from the other, and the text of the frame lines is continued in these intercolumnal lines. In this MS. there are no such intercolumnal lines.

There is one interesting feature to which attention may

be drawn now in this connexion. The Samaritans, like
the Jews, have two kinds of alphabet; the latter have one
called the square and the other called by a misnomer
Rashi type, for it seemed to have been used for the first
time in Europe for the writing of the commentary of
Rashi to Bible and Talmud, but recent discoveries have
shown that this second type of writing is much older than
Rashi (twelfth century). Documents of the seventh and
eighth centuries in the Genizah are already written with
this alphabet, and it is not at all unlikely, nay, very
probable, that we have in this cursive writing a direct
development of the older Aramaic script in the papyri.
Many of the letters agree much more closely with the
latter, and in fact it is suggested that the so-called square
character is nothing else than a further development of
the much more ancient Aramaic writing going through
the intermediary of the Palmyrene. Be it as it may, the
characteristic features of the cursive writing and of the
older Aramaic is that the letters are supported by a long
vertical stem, which, in the course of time, seems to have
been bent over to the left so as to form a kind of
rectangular basis of the body of the letter above it. Now
the Samaritans have also in addition the well-known
alphabet which can only be compared with the Hebrew
inasmuch as it has a definite character; it is by no means
square, a kind of script, which they call half letter
(*heṣi-ōth*). Hitherto, all the Bible MSS. known are
written with the full-letter alphabet and not in the half-
letter alphabet. I have discovered, further, among the
Samaritan fragments, old scrolls of the Bible written with
these half or cursive semi-uncial letters. This fact proves
that this alphabet must have been much older than one
would have been inclined to believe from the MSS.
in which it has been used, all thus far comparatively
modern (fourteenth century downwards). But this
writing must have been considered by the Samaritans

to be of equally sacred character as the uncial alphabet,
or otherwise it would never have been used for the
writing of sacred scrolls.   Samaritan palæography has
hitherto taken absolutely no notice of this alphabet, and
yet in the light of the discovery of the present document,
the Samaritan phylactery, one will be able to trace the
close connexion between the semi-uncial writing and the
oldest script used by the Samaritans themselves.   The
very letters כב, and especially כ (cup-like, on a slightly
bent stem), show the very same characteristics—the
absence of any horizontal line at the base of the letters
and the prevalence of plain strokes downwards in lieu of
these straight horizontal lines.   The same is the case with
the ל and פ.

A special feature of the semi-uncial is the letter ב, and
in modern copies the lower stroke has been prolonged to
such an extent that it sometimes runs under the whole
length of the word.   It is only by this peculiar feature
that it is distinguished from the ר.   The ו agrees also
with the form as found in the oldest Emmaus inscriptions,
where the script approximates also closely to similar
writing in the cursive alphabet.   We thus have a parallel
development among the Jews and Samaritans in the use of
their alphabet.   In both the more ancient forms seem to
have survived in that cursive writing, the study of which
hitherto had been almost entirely neglected.   The
Samaritan documents are thus a link again between
the past and the present.[1]

[1] The ע in this Samaritan alphabet is quite characteristic, with the
exception of the Emmaus inscription, where the ע resembles a circle ;
in all the other Samaritan documents and monuments the ע has the
form of a triangle.   Now it may be a mere coincidence, but in Christian
iconography we often find a triangle depicted either on the altar or
on the porch outside the church with a human eye inside and the rays of
light shining out from the three sides ; sometimes the Hebrew tetragrammaton is written either inside or over this triangle.   It is clear
that this picture is intended to represent the eye of God inside this
triangle, which probably stands as a symbol for the Trinity.   The

A brief description of the document may now be given.
It is written on parchment, consisting possibly originally
of four columns, only two of which have been preserved,
and even those in a somewhat dilapidated condition.
The text agrees in the main with the one published by
me, although it presents some very curious variations, to
which reference has been made in the other publication in
connexion with Cod. O [Cod. Gaster 899]. The writing is in
the main carefully done, but the alignment is occasionally
not so straight as in the other documents, especially in
the lower half.   The copyist does not follow any definite
rule in the number of letters in each line, varying from
17 to 23 letters, and when writing shorter lines he follows
the same tradition as found in the Samaritan Bible
codices, viz. he leaves a blank space in the middle of
a word and finishes the line with either one or two final
letters of that word.   From every point of view, therefore,
this MS. may be considered as belonging possibly to the
second or third century, and is probably the oldest
Hebrew Samaritan MS. in existence anterior to any
document in these languages that has come down to us.
But this would not exhaust the full importance of the
present· text, which goes far beyond its value for
palæography.   It must be remembered that most of the
contents of this document, which is a phylactery or
amulet, are taken literally from the Pentateuch.   We
have therefore here one of the oldest fragments of the

connexion, however, between the triangle and the eye is not so clear.
But if we look at the Samaritan writing we shall find this very letter
𐎠 is such a triangle, only with the apex downwards.   The name of
that letter is in Samaritan as well as Hebrew *'ayin*, which means "eye".
Now the connexion is obvious.   The triangle is the letter 𐎠, which means
"eye", that very eye which is painted within, and the word of the
Psalm thus applied to it, " Behold, the eye of the Lord is upon them
that fear him" (Ps. xxxiii, 18), and the commentary to it is thus
pictorially expressed.   On another occasion I may be able to show the
close connexion which exists between the Samaritan teaching and
practice and primitive Christianity, when the explanation of ancient
symbolism will not appear as a mere fortuitous coincidence.

Hebrew Bible either in the Samaritan or Jewish Hebrew recension. No older MS. is known to exist, and although the phylactery is only a fragment, still the quotations from the Bible are numerous enough to be most helpful in the direction of elucidating some of the problems connected with the Pentateuch. In the first place, of course, also from the archæological side, for if this is a true representation of the text in its oldest form with undivided words, we have here, as already mentioned before, a clear evidence of the existence of such a text. No dot or other mark separates the words from one another. Moreover, we have then a further proof that at the time when that ancient original was compiled of which this is only a copy, the original being probably many centuries older, the Samaritans were then already in possession of a text which in every detail down to the most minute agrees with the recension in their possession, notwithstanding some minute differences from the text published by me in PSBA. The rest agrees also with the Hebrew recension in many instances, even as far as the *scriptio plena* and the *scriptio defectiva*. I do not wish to draw conclusions for the antiquity of the Pentateuch. But if this document is as old as it seems to be, as this is only a copy of a much older document, then it is obvious that the Samaritans must have been in possession of their Pentateuch at a very early time. For in this document we find catchwords as shown by me which represent either whole sentences or even small sections, and presuppose the existence of a text divided up into small sections and also into sentences, sufficiently distinct to be able to be recognized by one single word—the catchword—being taken out of the contents. That ancient codex of the Bible must have already been written in conformity with definite rules still prevailing among the Samaritans, for we find them followed implicitly by the writer of this document. The reason why I consider this amulet to be a copy is obvious. The whole principle underlying this charm or phylactery must have already been fully elaborated, and a complete compilation must have been made of various elements before it assumed the actual shape in which we find it here. In this document we do not recognize a first attempt. On the contrary, it represents a definite final formulation, a kind of *ne varietur*, which the other documents followed at whatever time they were written; whether the copy was made in the twelfth century or the fourteenth century or the nineteenth century, they are all faithful copies of one or two originals rigidly transcribed. It agrees, moreover, in all its minutiæ with the actual recension of the Samaritan Pentateuch, especially the graphic details, and yet it is much more ancient by centuries than any scroll yet found among the Samaritans. How has it escaped destruction? The answer is obvious. Its very nature and character assured for it the greatest care, for with its preservation he who wore it preserved himself from every hurt and evil. His own safety was, as it were, bound up with the safety of the amulet. In spite of all the persecution under the Greek emperors when the whole literature of the Samaritans was destroyed, even then though the wearing of amulets was equally strongly forbidden, it was possible to conceal it, for to this very day however large the sheet of parchment be on which these amulets are written they are folded so many times until they occupy a very small space, so small that one could conceal it almost in the palm of one's hand. It was worn next to the skin, and every care was taken to hide it. Should the views here set forth be accepted—and I do not see how they could be controverted—then one might venture to look upon this document as a most valuable contribution to Hebrew and Samaritan palæography, and a new means for determining the date of similar documents should they be discovered.

I am reproducing here in facsimile the top part of the manuscript in question — about one-fourth of the whole — and I am subjoining the transliteration in Hebrew square characters of the first thirty-five lines, which are in a better state of preservation, to which I am adding a few explanatory notes. It follows the original line for line, and no attempt is made to divide the words, so as to give to the reader an exact impression of the original. The English translation will facilitate the reading of the original.

THE FIRST EMMAUS INSCRIPTION

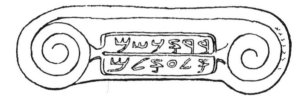

It reads ברוך שמו לעולם, "Blessed be his name for ever."

Cod. Gaster No. 1103 (E)

בשמ׳יהוה׳הגדול׳ 1
בשמיהוהאלהייישראלאשרי
כיבשמיהוהאקראאינכאליישרון
קומהיהוהעלדכאהנכתבועלשם
סבולזההמכתבבבראשיתבראאלהים 5
ופסחיהוהעלהפתחולאיתן
המשחיתלבואאלבתיכמלנגפ
כיבשמיהוהאקראוהבוגדל
לאלהינוהצורתמימפעלוכיכל
דרכיומשפטאלאמונהוהואינעול 10
צדיקוישרהואיהוהאלהינו
יהוהאחדברוכאלהינולעולם
וברוכשמולעולמיההגדול
יוההנוראיהוהנס׳

A Samaritan Phylactery of the Second or Third Century. Upper half. Codex Gaster 1103 (*E*)

15 יהוהאשאכלה:

. עשותוהאלהים : המטריהאלהים

ויצריהאלהים : ויטעיהאלהים

ויציהאלהים : ויק חיהאלהים

ויצויהאלהים : וייהאלהים

20 ויצריהאלהים : ויפליהאלהים:

ויבניהאלהים : עשהיהאלהים

כיאמראלהים : כיידעאלהים

והייתמכאלהים: קוליהאלהים

ויקריהאלהים : וייהאלהים

25 ויאמריהאלהים: ויעשיהאלהים

ויאמריהאלהים: וישיהאלהים

עדעולמיהוהילחמלכמואתמתחרי

שון

רפאירפאאלהים

לבושה...נאמן:

30 כיבשמיהוהאקראויאמראלהים

יהיאורויה[י]א[ו]רויצריהוה

אלהימאתהא[ד]מעפרמנהאדמה

ויברכאלהימאתנחואתבניו

ואברכמברכי[כ]ומקלליכאאראל

35 עליונקניש[מ]ימואארצאתהאל

Translation

[1] In the name of the Lord the great one. [2] In the name of the Lord God of Israel do I begin, [3] for in the name of the Lord I call (Deut. xxxii, 3). There is none like the God of Jeshurun (Deut. xxxiii, 26). [4] Arise, O Lord, for him who has written these writings, and for the name of [5] him who wears this writing. In the beginning created the Lord (Gen. i, 1). [6] And the Lord will pass over the door and will not suffer [7] the destroyer to come into your houses to smite you (Ex. xii, 23). [8] For in the name of the Lord will I call, and ascribe ye greatness unto [9] our God. He is the rock, His work is perfect. For all [10] His ways are judgment. A God

of faithfulness and without iniquity. [11] Just and right is He (Deut. xxxii, 3, 4). The Lord is our God, [12] the Lord is (Deut. vi, 4). Blessed be our God for ever, [13] and blessed be His name for ever. The Lord is great (cf. Deut. x, 17) [the Lord is mighty ?]. [14] The Lord is fearful (Ex. xv, 11), the Lord is my banner (Ex. xvii, 15). [15] The Lord is consuming fire (Deut. iv, 24). [16] The Lord God made (Gen. ii, 4). The Lord God caused it to rain (Gen. ii, 5), [17] and the Lord God formed (Gen. ii, 19). The Lord God planted (Gen. ii, 8), [18] and the Lord God made to grow (Gen. ii, 9), and the Lord God took (Gen. ii. 15). [19] And the Lord God commanded (Gen. ii, 16). And the Lord God said (Gen. ii, 18). [20] The Lord God formed (Gen. ii, 19), the Lord God caused to fall (Gen. ii, 21). [21] And the Lord God builded (Gen. ii, 22). The Lord God made (Gen. iii, 1), [22] for God said (Gen. iii, 3), for God doth know (Gen. iii, 5), [23] and ye shall be as gods (ibid.). The voice of the Lord God (Gen. iii, 8), [24] and the Lord God called (Gen. iii, 9), and the Lord God said (Gen. iii, 13, 14), [25] and the Lord God said (Gen. iii, 22), and the Lord God made (Gen. iii, 21), [26] and the Lord God said, and the Lord God sent him forth (Gen. iii, 23) for ever. [27] The Lord will fight for you and ye be silent (Ex. iv, 14). [28] God will surely heal him [29] who is clothed with it. Amen. Amen. [30] For I call in the name of the Lord (Deut. xxxii, 3). And God said [31] let there be light, and there was light (Gen. i, 3). And the Lord God formed [32] Adam from dust from the earth (Gen. ii, 7). [33] And God blessed Noah and his sons (Gen. ix, 1). [34] And I will bless them who bless thee, and those who curse thee I will curse (Gen. xii, 3). God [35] the most high one, possessor of heaven and earth (Gen. xiv, 19). Thou art . . .

Note to translation

In this text the Ten Words of Creation found in other phylacteries after line 15 have not yet been inserted. They form partly the contents of the Sichem inscription.

In ll. 16 ff. the Tetragrammeton is often represented in an abbreviated form by the first two letters ה י, and some other words are equally abbreviated.

THE CHAIN OF SAMARITAN HIGH PRIESTS.

INTRODUCTION

THE Samaritans possess three Chronicles, written in that mixed Hebrew idiom peculiar to them. In substance identical with one another, they differ in form. One is quite short, the second a little more expanded, and the third a further enlargement of the two previous ones. Of these Chronicles the second has been published by Dr. A. Neubauer, " Chronique Samaritaine " (*Journal Asiatique,* 1869 ; and separately, Paris, 1873), from a copy made by the present High Priest under the title *Tolidoth* (T.). The third, by E. N. Adler and M. Seligsohn, " Une nouvelle Chronique Samaritaine " (*Revue des Études Juives*; and separately, Paris, 1903), taken from a modern copy made by Ab-Sakhīvā in 1900 from an older MS. in the possession of the Samaritan priest Phineas. I quote it as " Chronicle " (Ch.). Both editions are accompanied by a French translation and a few stray notes. But the shortest of all, obtained together with copies of the other two Chronicles, and copied by the same High Priest, Jacob son of Aaron, has hitherto not yet been published. It goes by the name of *Tolidah* and of *Shilshelat.* As the former name has been given to the Chronicle edited by Dr. Neubauer, the name *Shilshelat* or *Chain,* i.e. of tradition, is given by me to this Chronicle published now for the first time.

The Samaritans have also some Chronicles written in
Arabic, the best known of which are the so - called
Arabic Book of Joshua and the Chronicle of Abul-Faṭḥ.
Others are still in manuscript. All these are in the
form of the ancient annals. It is purely annalistic
writing, not real history. The annalist merely writes
down contemporary history and brief entries, which his
successor continues where his predecessor has left off.
He retains what he finds in the older writing and
sometimes adds new facts, amplifying it. The result
is, that such a compilation contains at the same time
very old and very recent materials. The old is thus
carefully preserved in the last, and the time in which the
last copyist lives is not the date of the entire book. The
first part may be many centuries older than the last chapter
of such a Chronicle. It is necessary to dwell on this fact
in order to understand the true character of those three
Hebrew Chronicles. The text of the first and shortest
recurs without any change of wording in each of the
succeeding writings. To the brief note, however, a few
details are added to fill up gaps or to complete the story
briefly indicated in the first, but otherwise the old is found
intact in the new. The comparison between these three
texts is a study in ancient chronicle-writing, not without
interest and importance for the history of the Samaritan
literature.

Of greater moment still is the fact that the oldest
Chronicles of the Samaritans were originally written in
Hebrew, and that the Arabic compositions are translations
and amplifications of the materials found in the older
Hebrew writings. Abul-Fath mentions in the Introduction
to his Chronicle a large number of Hebrew Chronicles used
by him as sources for his own compilation in addition to
those written in Arabic. Of the Hebrew sources one is
called "Tolidah" and the other "Dibrei Hayamim", or
"Genealogy" and "Chronicle", the latter a more elaborate

composition, the other containing practically only the genealogy or chronology of the Samaritan High Priests. These are the very Chronicles Ch. and T. published hitherto.

But the Samaritans had a still more extensive historical literature. Not only do they constantly refer to their "Dibrei Hayamim", i.e. "The Chronicle" in Hebrew, but Abul-Fath himself, in addition to the two books just mentioned, refers explicitly (p. 139) to an elaborate Hebrew Chronicle, which contained not only a detailed description of the many deeds of Baba Rabba, but, according to him, also elaborate legends which had circulated about that great man, the greatest among the Samaritans. From Baba Rabba dates the Renaissance, or better, the consolidation of the Samaritan Commonwealth in the third or fourth century A.D. In his time lived their greatest poets and writers—Markah and his son Nana. Such an elaborate Chronicle of the fourth century had, evidently, been preserved in Hebrew among the Samaritans down to the period of Abul-Fath (fourteenth century). Who knows whether it will not sooner or later come to light as so many other writings of the Samaritans hitherto unknown, and how much of it may be found in those already known ?

However large the number of such Samaritan Chronicles and Annals may be, it is no proof of their reliability.

Through their annalistic character these Chronicles practically start from one and the same ancient source, which they follow with literal fidelity. Comparing e.g. the more elaborate Arabic Chronicles among themselves, it will be found that Abul-Fath copies out verbatim the work of his predecessor, and more recent compilers do likewise. Similarly, in "The Chronicle" the whole of the *Tolidah* can easily be found embedded in other material gathered from different sources, and one and all resting ultimately on the *Chain*. A mistake in one is, therefore, faithfully reproduced by the succeeding compiler, and confusion grows apace. This could, however, be detected by a critical examination of the more ancient texts. The real difficulty lies elsewhere—how to determine what a given date in a Samaritan Chronicle may mean; to which of our better-known dates does it correspond ?

Of all the problems connected with the Samaritans none is more difficult than that of their Calendar and of their system of chronology. In spite of the admirable work done by Scaliger and the attempts by De Sacy, we are still far off from a clear and comprehensive description of the Samaritan Calendar, and of the mathematical and astronomical principles upon which it is based. The Samaritans ascribe the invention of their Calendar, upon which the whole system of religious festivals depends, to Phineas, the son of the High Priest Eleazar, who had entered the land of Canaan together with Joshua, and who had taken the meridian of Sichem as the basis for his calculations.

For all that, very little is known to this day how they calculate the new moon, how they compute the year, and how they manage to synchronize the lunar and the solar year by the intercalation of a thirteenth month at stated and astronomically-fixed intervals. This has a distinct bearing on their chronology, and on the calculation of the corresponding year of any other era, be it the Greek (Seleucidan) or the Muhammedan or the Christian era. Nor are the Samaritans agreed upon one single era. I have found among them no less than four different systems of computation, even in the dates inserted into the sacred Scrolls of the Law. Some are dated according to the era of the Creation, others according to the entry of the Children of Israel into the land of Canaan under Joshua; again, others are dated according to the Muhammedan era, and in their Calendar (my Cod. 820) I found also the computation according to the era of Jezdegerd. In a MS.

of the British Museum (Or. 5034) we find, in addition, also the Greek era and the era of Diokletian. As this is the oldest-known dated MS. of Samaritan liturgy, it is of some interest to repeat here briefly the "Tarikh" or "Tishkal", as it is called by the Samaritans, and the corresponding dates. This "Tarikh", made out in the usual Samaritan form by singling out certain letters from the text, to which a numerical value is assigned, gives the date of the MS. according to the era of the Exodus and not that of the entry of the Israelites into the land of Canaan, as the year 2903. The corresponding date according to the "Kopts" is the year 1972 of "Diokletian, the last king of Egypt". According to the Persian era it was the year 1635 of "Yezdegerd, the last of the kings of Persia". According to the computation of the "Rum", i.e. Greeks, it was the year 1577 of "Alexander the son of Philis the horned" According to the Arabians it was the year 656 of "the Kingdom of the Ishmaelites". Lastly, another date is added, which has not yet been deciphered, but which I read " וק. וכ: ", i.e. 620 according to the Jewish (Samaritan?) computation ".[1] There is so much apparent discrepancy between these various dates and eras that they may well tax the ingenuity of scholars. The copyist would certainly not make mistakes in each and all of them. It is not here the place, nor now the time, to enter upon the solution of this problem. Suffice it to remark that if we add the intercalary months, which play a similar important rôle in the Samaritan Calendar as in the Jewish, and we subtract the thousand from the other eras, a certain approximation is obtained which justifies the belief that the corresponding dates are correct.

On flyleaves of liturgical MSS. and of ancient Samaritan Bible codices, also chronological data are found which

---

[1] Cf. a detailed description of this MS. by the Rev. G. Margoliouth, Zeitschr. Deutsch. Morgenländ. Gesellschaft, 1897, p. 499 ff.

contradict one another and increase confusion. In my
Cod. 806, an ancient copy of Numbers on vellum, I have
found on the paper flyleaves, added by a late hand, three
short chronologies differing in details from one another.
The author of those notes quotes four different traditions
and calculations of the dates from Adam to his time (1262
Hedg.=1845), and he refers specially to the חשבן קשטה
("Correct Calculation" or Calendar) for one set of figures
and to the " Tolidah " for another. As to the time when
the " Fanutah " will come to an end, i.e. the advent of the
" Taeb ", he also gives two different dates. According to
one, 3,896 years passed from Adam to "Ezrah the Scribe",
and 2,204 [1. 2,104] have still to elapse so as to complete the
6,000 years. Immediately after this calculation he says
that, according to the Master Pinehas, the " Fanutah " will
last 2,947 years from the time that the Ark was hidden.
He also has a list of the High Priests, which, however, is
incomplete.

Of these numerous eras only that of the Creation has
been used in the " Chronicle " The " Tolidah " has only
the dates of how long each High Priest was in office ;
occasionally reference is made to the Muhammedan era.
No consecutive date is given. From this scant information
it has hitherto been very difficult to fix the date when
any of these priests lived. But that is not all. The
student of Samaritan chronology is confronted with
another difficulty due to the tendency of the Samaritans to
modify the dates in order to harmonize them with certain
dogmatic views of theirs of the duration of the "Fanutah",
i.e., the disappearance of the Divine favour, and the time
of the advent of the expected " Taeb ", the Restorer, as
exemplified by the two calculations just mentioned. They
therefore divide the time into certain definite periods,
and alter accordingly the dates of events and of persons.
Vilmar [1] has already drawn attention to this peculiar

[1] Abul-Fath, ed. Vilmar (Gotha, 1865), pp. xlix ff.

tendency, which vitiates considerably the reliability of their chronology.

The importance of the " Chain of tradition " which I am publishing now for the first time from my MS. Cod. No. 862 (Cod. A) lies in the fact that it helps in settling some of these chronological difficulties. It has been copied or compiled by the actual High Priest, Jacob son of Aaron, who has written it in his usual admirable calligraphical hand. No more perfect penman among the Samaritans than this High Priest, whose copies are a model of neatness and clearness, and, on the whole, absolutely reliable for their accuracy. It is possible—nay, probable—that he merely copied a more ancient text and completed it down to his time, for I possess also a second copy of the same book, Cod. 877 (Cod. B), which, however, is written very carelessly. The unknown copyist has altered and changed the entries and corrected many a passage. It looks much more like a rough draft than a final copy, and differs also in some details from A. But both are identical in the essential feature which characterizes this " Chain "   Both contain not only the same brief account of these names of the patriarchs and priests, but they have the same system of synchronistic notation of the dates. No less than three eras are consecutively given. First that of the Creation, then the entry into Palestine, and thirdly the Muhammedan era, in parallel columns. Moreover, in the first column, starting from Adam, the date is given how old the person was when his first son was born, or how long he was in office as High Priest ; in the second a computation of the era of Creation which is continued to our very days. When the time arrives for the entry of the Children of Israel into the land of Canaan, a third column is added giving then the era of the entry. Finally, with the advent of Muhammed begins a fourth column with the last-named era. The " Chain " contains thus three different eras placed synchronistically side by side, and helping thereby to fix the chronology, at least for the time, from Muhammed on, and, if possible, to work it backwards towards the more remote beginnings.

A brief description of the MSS. used for this edition may now follow. Cod. A (No. 862), small octavo, 16 pp., neatly written by the High Priest, with carefully ruled lines in red, carries the chronology down to the year 1325 H. = 1907.

Cod. B (No. 877), rough quarto of five folios, leaves off at the year 1306 H. = 1888. Unfortunately a page in the middle is missing, covering the space of 1,380 years. The copyist follows in the main the original of A, but the notes in the margin and the dating on the tops of the pages are in Arabic, and not Hebrew as in A. B differs besides slightly from A, inasmuch as B counts the consecutive number of the persons enumerated, and divides them, at least in the beginning, into groups of sevens and tens. In lieu of writing out the dates in words as in A, B gives the figures in Arabic notation. Other discrepancies are of minor importance and are due to carelessness on the part of the copyist.

In order to make this edition as complete as possible, I have compared the dates of this " Chain " with those found in the other two Chronicles and with that of Abul-Fath, noting the differences in the footnotes. I cannot say that even after all this comparison we shall have. arrived at a complete harmony of the Samaritan tradition, but through the synchronistic table some stability may have been introduced into it.

The text published is taken from Cod. A. Mistakes, which even the High Priest did not avoid, are corrected in the text ; the reading of the MS. is given in the footnotes ; also the variants of B, the " Tolidah " (T.), "Chronicle" (Ch.), and Abul-Fath (A.F.). I have added the details from B not found in A, and enclosed them in square brackets. An English translation has also been added based on the critically emended and corrected text.

One word must be said now about the transliteration of the proper names. It is based on the Hebrew pronunciation of the Jews. The Samaritan pronunciation differs somewhat from that of the Jews, and they moreover pronounce all the gutturals, inclusive of the letter koph (*k*, ק), without any apparent distinction. Thus Noaḥ becomes *Na* ; Isaaḳ, *Yesa'* ; and so on.

The study of the Samaritan names would also yield interesting results. I cannot dilate on them here. Suffices it to draw attention to the fact that, like the Jews, so also the Samaritans evidently have avoided for centuries to give to their children the names of Biblical patriarchs, Noah, Abraham, Isaac, Moses, etc. In other respects there seems to be further close parallelism between the two sects in the names themselves which they have given to their children at certain times. For the Samaritans have also double names ; one which may be considered the equivalent of the " holy " or " sacred " name of always a purely Jewish or rather Biblical one, and another often borrowed from the Onomasticon of the other nations, Greek or Roman in ancient times, Arabic since the conquest of Palestine by the Arabs.

This multiplication of names has introduced an element of doubt and complexity into the scant literary history of the Samaritans. No list is known of equivalents of these two names ; the identity of some Samaritan authors is now often difficult to ascertain. The High Priests, however, seem to have shunned this practice. All the Samaritan Chronicles, including those written in Arabic and giving the names in Arabic transliteration, have only the purely Hebrew names of the priests without any equivalent in another language. Nor have I found in modern times the High Priest having any Arabic equivalent, but most of the other Samaritan priests, and even the sons of the

High Priest, have an Arabic name in addition to their Hebrew one. Thus Abisha is called Nadgi, Azi, and so forth.

The discovery and publication of all the records still kept by the Samaritans, but perishing fast under foreign, and not the best, influences working upon the dwindling community in Nablus, may still solve some of the problems in the history of the Samaritans, of their chronology, and of their Calendar.

TRANSLATION

THE CHAIN OF THE HIGH-PRIESTS.

THESE ARE THE GENERATIONS FROM ADAM ·TO THIS DAY

I. DATE OF BIRTH AND PRIESTHOOD.   II. THE ORDER OF THE PERFECT BOOK (THE LAW) (I.E. DATE OF CREATION)

	I.	II.	
[1]	130	130	Adam.
[2]	105	235	Seth.
[3]	90	325	Enosh.
[4]	70	390	Ḳainan.
[5]	65	460	Mahalalel.
[6]	62	522	Yered.
[7]	65	587	Enoch [7th].
[8]	67	654	Matushelah.
[9]	53	707	Lamech.
[10]	502	1209	Noah [10th].
[11]	100	1309	Shem. In the 18th year of his life was the flood upon the earth, as it is said: "And he begat Arpachshad two years after the flood" (Gen. xi, 11).[1]
[12]	135	1444	Arpachshad.
[13]	130	1574	Shelah.
[14]	135	1708	Eber [7th].
[15]	130	1838	Peleg.
[16]	132	1970	Reu.
[17]	130	2100	Serug.
[18]	79	2179	Nahor.
[19]	70	2249[2]	Terah.
[20]	100	2349	Abraham. Upon whom be peace. The 10th from Noah.
[21]	60	2409	Isaac. Upon whom be peace. The 7th from Eber.

[1] B and A.F. count No. 10 = 600 and No. 11 = 2. Ch. agrees with A.
[2] In A wrongly 2349.

	I.	II.		
[22]	87	2496	Jacob.	Upon whom be peace.
[23]	52	2547	Levi.	
[24]	71	2619	Kehat.	
[25]	52	2671	Amram.[1]	
[26]	83	2754	Aaron.[2] First of the Priests. [Moses.]	
	40	2794	Moses [3] the Prophet. Peace of the Lord upon him. He started as Prophet when 80 years old.	

III. The Entry of the Children of Israel into the Land of Canaan.

	I.	II.	III.	
[27]	50	2844	50	Eleazar (1).
[28]	60	2904	110	Pineḥas the First (2) [7th].
[29]	40	2944	150	Abisha the First (3).
[30]	50	2994	200	Shashai the First (4).
[31]	35	3029	235	Baḥki the First (5).
[32]	25	3053 [4]	260	'Uzzi. At the end of his priesthood did the Lord hide His Holy Tabernacle.[5]
[33]	39	3093	299	Shashai.
[34]	23	3116	322	Baḥki.
[35]	28	3144	350	Shebet [7th].
[36]	55	3169	375	Shalum.
[37]	20	3189	395	Ḥiskiah.
[38]	28	3217	423	Jonathan. In his time reigned David the son of Issa.
[39]	22	3239	445	Yair.[6]
[40]	25	3264	470	Dalyah [10th].
[41]	19	3224?	489	Yair. [7] In his 'days did Shelah build his Temple in Yebus.
[42]	28	3311	517	Jonathan [7th].

[1] A.F. 55.

[2] B combines Nos. 26 and following, and has I 123 ; II 2793.   A.F. om.

[3] A.F. 120.   [4] Tol. 3055 ; A.F. 3054.

[5] A.F. reckons from 'Uzzi to Muhammed 1993 years.

[6] Between Nos. 39 and 40 A.F. mentions four names—Zedekiah, 28 years ; Aḥiyah, 20 ; Maaḥar, 21 ; Yoṣadak, 25 ; but cf. Vilmar, *ad loc.*, p. 176, Arab. note to line 16.

[7] A.F. 29, but v. Vilmar, note 1.

I.	II.	III.	
[43]	26	3337	543	Ishmael.
[44]	28	3365	571	Ṭobiyah. This priest was killed by the Ishmaelites.
[45]	20	3385	591	Ṣaddoḳ.
[46]	28	3413	619	ʿAmram the First.
[47]	24	3437	643	Ḥilḳiah.
[48]	28	3475	681	ʿAmram the Second.
[49]	36	3511	717	ʿAḳob [7th].
[50]	39	3550	756	ʿAḳabyah. This priest was taken prisoner with the Children of Israel in the first Exile, which is the Exile of Boḥtnaṣar. [10th.]
[51]	45	3595[1]	501	Ḥilal (Hillel ?).
[52]	40	3635	841	Serayah. This priest returned with his people from the Exile.
[53]	50[2]	3685	891	Levi.
[54]	51[3]	3737	943	Netanel the First.
[55][4]	35	3772	978	ʿAzaryah. This king was taken prisoner by the King of the Chaldeans[5] in the 10th year of his priesthood.
[56]	40	3812	1018	Abdael. This priest returned from the Exile; and the number of his community was three hundred thousand, and he returned in the 35th year of his priesthood.
[57]	30	3842	1084	Ḥisḳiah.
[58]	24	3866	1072	Ḥananyah.
[59]	32[6]	3898	1104	ʿAmram the Third. The son of this priest saw in a dream the daughter of Derus (Darios ?) the king, and she married him, but when he came with his wife to this country the Samaritans rose up against him, and killed him and his wife and all that were with him.

---

[1] In the text 3591, a mistake of the copyist between ה and א.
[2] Ch. 30, yet II 3685 !   [3] Ch. and A.F. 52, yet II 3737.
[4] From here missing in B to No. 85.   [5] B: of the Greeks.   [6] Ch. I 24; II 3890.

	I.	II.	III.	
[60]	25 [1]	3924	1029	Hana. This is the man whom the King of Ashur hath taken and married to his daughter, and who was killed by the Samaritans.
[61]	21 [2]	3944	1150	Hiskiah.
[62]	42 [3]	3986	1192	Dalyah.
[63]	40	4026 [4]	1222	'Akob.
[64]	35	4061	1157	'Akabyah.
[65]	41	4102	1298	Levi.
[66]	44	4146	[5]	Eleazar the Second.
[67]	36	4182	1388	Manasseh.[6]
[68]	39	4221	1427	Yair the Third.
[69]	41	4262	1468	[Netanel.]
[70]	[32	4294	1500]	Yoyakim. In his days Jesus appeared in Bethleem.
[71]	27	4321 [7]	1527	Jonathan the Third. In his days the Jews killed Jesus in the cursed Shalem.
[72]	33	4354	1550	Elishama. In his days was Kisariyah captured by the King of Edom, Sianes (Vespasianus).
[73]	10	4364	1560	Shemayah.
[74]	8	4372	1568	Tobiah.[8]
[77]	9	4381	1277	'Amram the Fourth.
[78]	30	4411	1607	'Akabon the First.
[79]	40	4451	1647	Pinehas the Second.
[80]	25 [9]	4476	1682	Levi. In his days came King Adrianus, and

---

[1] Ch. I 33 ; II 3923. De Sacy reckons here I 24 (cf. ed. of Ch., p. 37). Evidently some confusion between Nos. 60 and 61.

[2] Ch. I 24 ; II 3944. A mistake, for the exact number ought then to be II 3947 !

[3] Ch. agrees, and has II 3986 ! III, wrongly in A 1182.

[4] A mistake : 4016.

[5] Lacuna in A.

[6] This priest (No. 67) is missing in A.F., who inserts, however, after Yair (No. 68) another High Priest, Netanel I, 41 years ; so also Ch. I 41, II 4262 ; and then both have Yoyakim, I 32, II 4294. I have accordingly adjusted the order.

[7] A, I 4221, mistake.

[8] A.F. inserts here two more names—[75] 'Amram, 11 years ; [76] 'Akob, 9 years.

[9] Ch. I 45, and yet II 4476.

I.	II.	III.	
			he showed great mercy and did favours to the Samaritans and destroyed the sanctuary of the Jews.
[81]	32	4507	1714 Eleazar the Third.
[82]	28	4536	1742 Baba. In his days there were great changes in the heavens.
[83]	41	4577	1783 Eleazar the Fourth. In his days was Platamas (Ptolemæus?), the grandfather of Yezdegerd.
[84]	23	4600	1806 'Akabon the Second. This was the uncle of Baba Rabbah.
[—]	32	4632	1838 Netanel the Third. This was the father of the king Baba Rabbah.
[85]	26[1]	4658	1864 'Akabon the Third. In his days was the bastard Dusis.
[86]	31	4689	1895[2] Netanel the Fourth. The handmaid loved his son Aba'onai, and for that he burned her with fire.
[87]	20	4709	1915[3] 'Akabon the Fourth.
[88]	25	4734	1940 Eleazar the father of Miriam.
[89]	24	4758	1964 'Akabon the Fifth, who built the Kinsha on the " Piece of Land ".
[90]	17[4]	4775	1981 Eleazar the Sixth [10th].
[91]	30	4805	2011 'Akabon the Sixth.
[92]	40[5]	4845	2051 Eleazar [7th].[6]
[93]	31	4876	2084 Netanel the Fifth. In his days was the king Zinon [the accursed].

[1] A.F. mentions Netanel as the son of Baba Rabbah, but does not reckon him as one of the High Priests: B, which starts here again with No. 85 for 'Akabon, must have also omitted Netanel, and counted the two names mentioned after No. 74 by A.F., and thus 'Akabon becomes the 85th in the list.

[2] B, II 1890.

[3] B, II 1910 ; A, 1815, mistake.

[4] A.F. I 27.

[5] A.F. 41 ; v. Vilmar *ad loc.*

[6] Dropped out by mistake in A, as the figures of No. 93 show.

	I.	II.	III.	
[94]	25	4901	2107	Eleazar the Eighth. At the end of his life came Muhammed [the Prophet of the Gentiles].[1]
[95]	20	4921	2127	Netanel the Sixth.

IV. The Era of the Muhammedans.

	I.	II.	III.	IV.	
[96]	18	4939	2145	38	Eleazar the Ninth. In his days were Amar (Omar) the son of Alḥatab and Otman the son of Ophan, king of the Gentiles.
[97]	30	4969	2175	68	'Aḳabon the Seventh, who was drowned in the waters of the well-known Jordan.
[98]	16	4985	2191	84	Eleazar the Tenth. In his days was Abdulmalik the son of Merwān.
[99]	20	5005	2211	104	'Aḳabon the Eighth [7th].[2]
[100]	22	5027	2233	126	Eleazar the Eleventh [10th].
[101]	21	5048[3]	2254	147	'Aḳabon the Ninth. In his days the valiant ones of the Gentiles went over to the Abbasides.
[102]	26	5074	2280	173	Eleazar the Twelfth. In his days was King Aaron Alrashid of the children of Abbas.
[103]	7	5081	2287	180	Simeon. In the 2nd year of his priesthood asked the King of Ashur, Karozai (Chosroes ?), from the Samaritans many men, and in the 4th year of his priesthood came 'Arḳala (Heraclius), the king of Rome, and conquered the Holy Land, and after twenty-two years came the Ishmaelites and conquered all the towns, and they carried into captivity the inhabitants of Ḳisariyah.

[1] Thus far Abul-Fath. [2] Placed by B here by mistake. [3] A by mistake 5088.

	I.	II.	III.	IV.	
[104]	31	5012	2318	211	Levi.
[105]	12	5124	2330	223	Pineḥas the Third.
[106]	2	5126	2332	225	Netanel the Seventh.
[107]	11	5137	2343	236	Baba.
[108]	9	5146	2352	245	Eleazar the Thirteenth.
[109]	20	5166	2372	265	Netanel the Eighth.
[110]	7	5173	2379	272	Eleazar the Fourteenth.
[111]	8	5181	2387	280	Pineḥas the Fourth.
[112][1]	55	5236	2442	335	[Netanel the Ninth.]
[113]	[16[2]	5252	2458	351]	Abdael the Second. In his days was built the town of Ramleh.
[114]	35	5287[3]	2493	386	Eleazar the Fifteenth.
[115]	20	5307[4]	2513	406	Abdael the Third. In his days was an Ethiopian king of Egypt. And after this priest I have found in the Tolidoth three priests mentioned, namely, Eleazar the son of Abdael, who was priest for 29 years, Abdael his son, who was priest for 17 years, and his brother Ahron 19 years. So that the sum-total of their priesthood would come to 69 years, but this cannot be explained in accordance with the record of the Chronicle, unless they were priests not in the chosen place (Sichem), but they were priests in Damascus, who acted as priests under the authority of the priest of the place (Sichem).
[116]	38	5345	2551	444	Eleazar the Sixteenth.
[117]	14	5359	2565	458	Ahron.

[1] B. I have inserted the second part of No. 112 from B dropped out in A, and in No. 113 I have added the figures from B, so as to harmonize the list.

[2] B, I 12.   [3] A, II 5278, mistake.   [4] A, II 5317, mistake.

I.	II.	III.	IV.	
[118] 12	5371	2577	470	Ṣadakah. Towards the end of his priesthood he appointed his son 'Amram.
[119] 39	5410	2616	509	'Amram the Fifth.
[120] [22	5432	2638	531][1]	Aaron. In his time lived Abul-Fath, who was well known through his good deeds, and the Kinsha of Sichem was built in his time.
[121] 28	5460	2666	559	'Amram the Sixth.
[122] 26	5486	2692	585	Aaron.
[123] 19	5505[2]	2711	604	Netanel the Tenth. At the end of his priesthood came the priest Itamar from Damascus and was later on appointed High Priest.
[124] 48	5553[3]	2759	652	Itamar. This is the priest who had come from Damascus in the year 102 (?).
[125] 15	5568[4]	2774	667	'Amram the Seventh. In the 6th year of his priesthood the country was conquered and many men were killed in Sichem. Of the Samaritans, many men, women, and children, and with them 'Uzzi, the son of the above-mentioned priest, were carried away captives to Damascus, and the Samaritans of Damascus ransomed them and sent them back to Sichem.
[126] 22	5590[5]	2796	689	'Uzzi. In his days the Muhammedans took away from the Samaritans the Kinsha of the " Piece of Land " (v. No. 89), and this was at the

[1] These figures had dropped out from A and are supplied from B.
[2] Ch. I 17 ; II 5503.   [3] Ch. I 48, and yet II 5551.
[4] Ch. I 15 ; II 5566.   [5] Ch. I 22 ; II 5588.

	I.	II.	III.	IV.	

time of the king Yerek̩, who was killed at the time of the priest Joseph.

[127] 19 5609[1] 2815 708   Joseph. This priest came from Damascus.

[128] 56 5665[2] 2871 764   Pineḥas, his son. He was the father of the Raban Abisha—the author of liturgical hymns—and of his brother Elisha.

[129] 25 5690 2896 789   Eleazar, his son, the Seventeenth. He was the brother of the above-mentioned Abisha.

[130] 56 5746 2952 845   Pineḥas the Sixth [the Nazarite]. In his days lived the elder Abdalah the son of Shalma. This Pineḥas was the son of Abisha, the author of the liturgical hymns.

[131] 34 5780 2986 879   Abisha.

[132] 36 5816 5022! 915   Eleazar the Eighteenth.

[133] 41 5857 3063 956   Pineḥas the Seventh. He was in the blessed spot (?), and he saw his place and that of his community in Paradise.

[134] 48 5905 3111 1004   Eleazar the Nineteenth [7th]. In his time they built a bath for purification for the Samaritans.

[135] 19 5924 3130 1023   Pineḥas the Eighth.

[136] 10 5934[3] 3140 1033   Shalmiyah. He disappeared from among the priests and went to a place that was called the River of Sand, and there he called and cried to his Master three times, " All-Merciful ! " and

[1] Ch. I 21 ; II 5609.
[2] Ch. I 52 ; II 5665 !
[3] Ch. I 11 ; II 5936.   All these figures in Ch. are obviously wrong.

I.	II.	III.	IV.	
				he was answered three times, "Lo, here I am." And this was heard by the people who were with him.
[137] 27	5961[1]	3167	1060	Ṣadaḳah.
[138] 45	6006	3212	1105	Isaac.
[139] 40	6046	3252	1145	Abraham.
[140] 20	6066	3272	1165	Levi.
[141] 36	6102	3308	1201	Ṭabyah. This priest went to the Samaritans in Gaza and stayed with them four years, and married from among them.
[142] 42[2]	6144	3350	1243	Shalmah. He was appointed priest when he was 15 years old, for when his father died he was only 3. During his childhood the functions of priest were performed by one of the Samaritans, Shelah son of Isaac.
[143] 33	6177	3383	1276[3]	'Amram, his son.
[144] 49	6226	3432	1325[4]	Jacob the son of Aaron, the son of Shalmah. A seventh from Aaron, unto this very day.

[1] Ch. I 26 ; II 5961.

[2] B inserts before Shalmah an interregnum of twelve years from II 6102 to II 6114 in which there was no priest from the house of Levi, and instead of I 42 he has there I 30.

[3] Ch. I 32 : II 6176.

[4] B, I 31 ; II 6207 ; III 3413 ; IV 1306. The date of the compilation.

The Biblical Lessons: A Chapter on Biblical Archæology

A custom which is not proved from the Torah is nothing else than the result of an erroneous conclusion.—Soferim xiv. 10.

As the title indicates this article is a study in Biblical archæology and palæography. It is not undertaken with a view of strengthening, or in any way affecting the established customs and rites. In fact, this study is one section out of a larger work dealing with the history of the Bible, and is undertaken from the modern comparative point of view. The investigation is to lead us on step by step, from fact to fact, eschewing as much as possible hypothesis or imaginary combinations, so that we may reach results which rest on verified facts. The materials accumulated in our ancient literature will be treated from an independent point of view, and new light may be thrown upon ancient problems from our examination of all available data. A study of this kind is beset with many difficulties, the greatest of which is the indefinite character of all beginnings, the difficulty of tracing tradition to its starting-point, and, above all, the scantiness of the materials and the uncertain character of the sources, which, in many cases, cannot be chronologically fixed. It is difficult to determine, especially in our Jewish literature, how much of that which is found often in a late book is of a much earlier origin, and how much of it represents events contemporary with the author. Nowhere is this difficulty greater than in dealing with Jewish literature from the Second Temple, and down to the close of the period of Midrashic activity. I include here pseudo-epigraphic as well as Agadic literature. And there is another point which increases the difficulties to be surmounted, viz. that everyday occurrences, customs and rites, with which the people are familiar, are very seldom committed to writing. The beginnings of Jewish literature are just as much shrouded in darkness as the beginnings of the Christian, though this latter is of a much younger date, and one might have expected to find more definite information. It will be seen, later on, that in a way we are still better equipped to explore our past than those who undertake to unravel the mystery of the beginnings of the Samaritan, Christian, Mohammedan and other religious faiths, which have all developed during the last two thousand years. One result which is outstanding from these investigations coincides with the result obtained in modern times in other fields of archæological investigations. The ancient traditions, so long misunderstood, ignored or rejected, are being fully vindicated by the latest discoveries and by the latest investigations. It is not here the place to discuss the bearing of the results achieved by the diggings in Babylon and Egypt, in Mycene and Cyprus, nor will I refer to the new chapter which has been opened by the discovery of the papyri of Elephantine, or by the Greek papyri, which throw a flood of light on Jewish antiquities, and tend to corroborate the truth of the ancient traditions almost down to the minutest detail. Now the problem which I wish to attack here is the rôle which the Bible has played in the liturgical service of the Jews, both in public and in private. Since when has the Bible been used for such educational purposes and in what manner has it been used ? The tremendous influence which this reading of the Bible has had need not be emphasised here. It is too self-evident. It lies at the very root of modern civilisation, and it has given to the divine worship a character not dreamt of by the followers of other faiths. Others have dwelt already eloquently on this unique feature of the Jewish worship, and have drawn conclusions so exalted for the uplifting of the world that it suffices to have mentioned them. I am dealing with the more mechanical side—if I may say so, the practical working of this great principle. As indicated above, the investigation falls into two parts, (*a*) the archæological, including the palæographical, and (*b*) the historical. How far back does the tradition lead us, and how far is this tradition corroborated and strengthened by the Law ? Since when was it considered a religious duty to inculcate the reading of the Bible in the Jewish worship ? Our ancient tradition is unanimous on this point. It says emphatically that Moses ordained that the Law should be read to the people on every Sabbath, festival and Holy Day throughout the year.

A second tradition supplements the former, and says, Ezra established the reading of the Law to take place also on Mondays and Thursdays. There are minor differences as to the rule concerning the reading of the Law on the Sabbath afternoon, and as to the number of verses to be read on the last occasion. These will be treated later on. Here we have, then, a definite statement which is based on the injunction, Deuteronomy XXXI. 10, tracing from it a practice known throughout the whole of Jewry. That records have come down to us that the reading of the Law accompanied the prayer need not be mentioned here ; it is understood. It formed part of it, and it has never been conceived independently of it in public worship. True, prayers are mentioned where no reading of the Law may have taken place, but never the reverse. In addition to this general tradition, we have a definite fact stated in the Law that the king was expected to read the Torah on certain occasions (Deut., *v.* below), and no less emphatic is ancient tradition that Ezra himself read the Law on one of those solemn occasions (Neh. VIII. 1–8 ; IX. 3). At an earlier date also we find the High Priest, Hilkiah (II Kings XXII. 8–13 ; XXIII. 1–3), reading the Law in the presence of the king and the people, not to speak of the still more decisive testimony in Joshua VIII. 34. To this practice, therefore, cannot be denied extreme antiquity, and the tradition which connects it with Moses and Ezra means that the practice is so ancient that it owes its origin almost to the time of Moses. It is necessary that we should go step by step, and establish the fact that this was not mere tradition, but tradition resting on real fact. We are told that the Haftarah was introduced at the time of the Hasmonean revolt, when Antiochus Epiphanes, in the middle of the second century, forbade the reading of the Law, and therefore the people substituted the reading from the prophets for the reading of the Law. Though this tradition is only mentioned by Abudarham, no one has ventured to dispute its value as far as the fact is concerned, that the Law was read before that time, and that at the time of the defilement of the Second Temple it was forcibly interrupted. Sirah, in his introduction to his well-known book, speaks of his grandfather as one of those who read the Law and the prophets. It cannot be doubted that it was not meant only for private purposes, but as we shall see, the High Priest and the other priests used to read a portion of the Law and the prophets in public. In the Mishna Yoma I, it is clearly stated in the preparation for the service of the Day of Atonement, that the sages of the time used to teach the High Priest to read certain portions of the Law, which he was then to read aloud to the people at the conclusion of the sacrifice. And, moreover, we are told (*ibid.*) that the sages used to read also some of the books of the Holy Writings, such as Job, Daniel, Chronicles, etc. If we come down to a little later period, we find that Philo, and at least on one or two occasions Josephus, speaks in no uncertain voice as to the reading of the Law on Sabbaths and festivals; nay, he also traces the introduction back to Moses (Josephus, *Contra Apionem*, II. 17, 175): "But Moses . . . demonstrated the law to

be the best, and the most necessary instruction of all
others . . . enjoining the people to assemble together
for the hearing of the law, and learn it exactly, and this
not once or twice or oftener, but every Sabbath."
And finally the information culled from the pages of the
New Testament (Luke IV. 16–20, etc.). Jesus and Paul
enter the Synagogue and read the Law and the prophets
to the assembled people. Talmudic and Midrashic
literature often repeats this tradition. At the time of
the Mishna no question was raised as to the regular
reading of the Law throughout the lands whither the
Jews had gone. It is so much of an established custom
that only incidental differences, exceptions in the reading
which occurred during the reading of the Law, are
mentioned to be discussed. The practice itself is so
firmly established that it requires no special mention;
it is taken for granted. I turn from the Jews to the
Samaritans. It is necessary to do so for reasons which
will be shown later on. With them the same practice of
the reading of the Law on every Sabbath prevails; and
this practice is never questioned, it is taken for granted
as with the Jews. Their literature, however, is so
scanty, and the information which has reached outsiders
so small, all their literary monuments are comparatively so young, that it is impossible to find in them
any reference to that institution of an early date. None
the less, sufficient proof can be found in the literature
for the Samaritan view, not only that they have been
continually reading the Law in their public service,
but that they trace this institution back to the earliest
time, nay, to Moses. Thus, in the earliest letters sent
by the Samaritans to Europe, or more properly to
Scaliger, towards the end of the sixteenth century from
Nablus and Egypt, the High Priest of the time—Eliezer
—writes distinctly that they read the Law on every
Sabbath and Holy Day, and he mentions even one of
the sections read on Pesach. Similarly in the letter
from Egypt the same fact is mentioned of the constant

reading of the Law on Sabbath and Holy Days (Letters published by de Sacy; in Eichhorn's *Repertorium*, Vol. XIII, 8, page 257 ff.). And in a Samaritan MS. on their customs and rites (my Cod. 872) the Samaritans distinctly state that the custom of reading the Law on every Sabbath, festival and Holy Day is a tradition handed down to them from Moses, Pinehas and the seventy Elders mentioned in the Bible. An older authority we find in Abul Fath, in his *Chronicle*, and even as far back as 1041 Josef Al Askari refers to it distinctly in his *Al-Kafi* (my Codd. 821, 878, 1159).

Close investigation extending over fifteen years ripened in me the conviction that the Samaritans have preserved for us in an almost fossilised state customs which go back to the time of the Second Temple. They represent a phase in Jewry of Jewish rites, of Jewish practices, of Jewish religious conceptions and views, which one may call pre-Talmudic, pre-Rabbinic, which concur in a remarkable degree with the traditions and customs prevailing also among the Jews outside of Jerusalem, and agree also with the most ancient traditions and customs of the Christian Church.

Justin Martyr (1st Apol. I. 67), who was a Samaritan, at least born in Samaria, and intimately acquainted with the Samaritans, refers distinctly to the custom of the public reading of the Law among the early Christians. I mention him here on the score of Samaritanism, not the Christian Church. The practice of the Christian Church, as far back as can be traced, fully corroborates the public reading of the Law. There was a regular reading of the Holy Scriptures during the public worship. At the beginning the lessons were taken only from the Old Testament. Later on also from the New. So Tertullian, Origen, and apostolic constitutions; the latter not only mention, but decree (II. 39 and 57) that the Old Testament should be read before the New; and later on more ample reference will be made to these, and to the practice of the Christian Church and the

order of the lessons in the Christian worship. This fact,
that the Samaritans also have the regular reading of the
Law on every Sabbath, festival and Holy Day, at once
sets at rest the suggestion, which has been made, that
the very reading of the Law had been introduced among
the Jews as a distinctive feature against the Samaritans.
Whether this may hold good for the reading of the Haftarah is a matter which cannot be discussed here, but
that the reading of the Law had been taken over in
common by the Jews and the Samaritans alike cannot
be doubted, both following a much older tradition sacred
to both.   And this at once forces the establishment of
the institution back to a much older date than even
those records which we have been able to quote.   The
distinction between Jews and Samaritans was brought
out in a much more decisive manner in the public
reading of the Ten Commandments, on every occasion
of worship in the Temple and in the synagogues.* For
just in that, the most important section of the Torah,
the Samaritan text differs most profoundly from the
Jewish, and the very ground of separation between
Jews and Samaritans centres in the additional verses
which the Samaritans have added to the Ten Commandments ; counting those verses as the Tenth Commandment in which the selection of Mount Gerizim seems to
be not only indicated but justified by the very words of
Scripture.   The public reading of the Ten Commandments alone would thus bring home much more
emphatically this difference which separates Jews from
Samaritans, than the reading of the Law, which both held
in common as the most sacred book, and in which, with
few exceptions, the other differences are of a minor
importance.   The abolition of the practice of reading
the Ten Commandments, owing to taunts of the
" Minim," was really due to the fact that the " Minim "
claimed authenticity for the rest of their text of the
Pentateuch.   Through the selection by the Jews of the

* A practice which obtains to this very day in the Samaritan worship.

Ten Commandments only, as points of difference, they would thereby tacitly admit, as it were, the correctness of the other portions. This seems to me to be the correct interpretation of this abolition. It will be seen presently that there is indeed a much more close agreement between the two texts than has hitherto been suspected, and a complete examination of the agreement will, I trust, be of no little importance for the elucidation of some of the most difficult problems in the archæology and palæography of the Bible. But before proceeding further, it was necessary to establish the fact that the practice of reading the Law was of very ancient date.

It behoves us now to endeavour to establish the manner in which the text was read. But here we are entering upon the palæographical investigation of the books of our Bible. How the whole of our Pentateuch had been written originally we do not exactly know, except for the very obvious statement in the Talmud that it was written in small scrolls, " megilot " as they are called. But no doubt the whole must have been subdivided into smaller sections, otherwise it would have been too unwieldy for any purpose, for teaching as much as for reading. Names are often the most trustworthy indications of ancient practices. The very fact that the Bible has not one title or one name for the whole of its contents brings out more clearly than anything else the fallacy of the idea of a Canon, established or sanctioned by the Synagogue. If the Synagogue had at any time established such a Canon, it would have coined a proper name for it. The absence of such a name is sufficient proof to doubt, nay; even to deny such a Canon of the Synagogue. It may be a startling proposition, but it will be discussed in another essay, forming another chapter of my studies in the history of the Bible. The Pentateuch goes by the general term Torah. The five great divisions have no proper names. Three of them are mentioned in the Mishna by a paraphrastic description, such as Torat Kohanim (=Leviticus), Homesh Ha-

pekudim (=Numbers) and Mishneh Torah (=Deutero-
nomy). These now take their names from the initial
words. The only ancient division is into five books,
each one called a Fifth (Homesh). In the Sam.
MSS. to this day, the books have no titles.

The colophons at the end of each book (corresponding
to the Massoretic colophons of the Hebrew Bibles) call
the books the First, the Second, the Third, the Fourth,
and the Fifth, without any specific names. The Greek
translation represents a later tradition, and affixes
a title to each of them. It calls Bereshith Genesis, Shemoth Exodus, and Debarim Deuteronomium. But we
know the books only by the initial words Bereshith,
Shemoth, etc. It will be seen that this practice has been
continued when these books were divided into smaller
sections. It is a matter of some importance; for if a book
or a section is known only by the initial word, it shows
a widely spread popular practice. The people must have
been sufficiently familiar with those books and these
sections to recognise them at once, as soon as the first
word was mentioned. And just as the five books were
called by the initial word, so we shall find this practice
applying to smaller sections, which are also known from
such initial words. There are exceptions when the titles
are given from the contents and not from the initial
word, and it will be interesting to see which of these
sections was called by its contents rather than by the
initial word. For it will be found that such sections
were not popularly so known. It was a mere scientific
title and not a popular one. How was the Bible divided?
I will limit myself, in the first place, and for our purpose,
almost exclusively to the division of the Pentateuch.
There are definite indications of the Massoretic texts,
which give us an undoubted clue to these ancient
divisions. The whole text was subdivided into small
paragraphs called by the general term Parasha. I want
to make it perfectly clear that this word was not
originally applied exclusively to the weekly lesson or

Perikope. This application dates from a somewhat later period, and almost entirely owes its origin to the liturgical use of the Bible. But one must not lose sight of the fact that the study of the Bible was the primary object and aim. The reading of the Bible was merely popularisation. But first and foremost the Bible was to be studied, and in order that it should be taught properly, it had to be divided into smaller sections. This ancient and to my mind oldest division of the text has been preserved with the utmost fidelity in the scrolls of the Law; and the Massora, that guardian of the ancient tradition of our Scriptures, has preserved these divisions to our very day, and has transferred them from the written to the printed text. Happily, no one has yet interfered too much with these divisions, so as to obliterate their graphical character. It may be taken as an axiom not open to doubt or discussion that the scroll, as found now in our synagogues, has preserved to us the text in the oldest form available, and the writing and arrangement date from a period which one would be justified in calling pre-Massoretic. The Massoretic rules and prescriptions have had the object of not allowing the text, as it stands, to be modified or altered in the slightest degree. " The Massorah is a fence round the Torah," as stated in the Chapters of the Fathers. The best proof for this is that neither the Massoretic rules nor indications are found in the scroll: neither the marking of the verses, nor vowel points, nor accents, are allowed in a scroll: no names, no titles, not even dates in any shape or form, are to be found therein. The severity and rigidity of the rules for the writing of the text has reached almost its extreme limit. Not many erasures, not many corrections are allowed, and, in fact, everything that could be done to preserve the text intact and to reproduce the original with the utmost fidelity and correctness has been done with great efficiency and with excellent results. We may boldly state that the scroll read to-day does not deviate in any shape or form from those scrolls which were torn up in the time of Antiochus and the Hasmoneans. The justification for such statements rests on the palæographic proofs which have been hitherto not sufficiently recognised, nay entirely ignored. Certain rules, no doubt, must have been laid down by the Soferim, following probably older examples, for the manner in which the text of the Pentateuch ought to be written down. It had to be written in columns; sufficient spacing between words, lines and columns had to be allowed; and the divisions between the five books had to be clearly marked in an unmistakable manner. In addition to these, other minor divisions have been introduced into the text which, as must be stated with all emphasis, were used for didactic purposes as the text-book of the moral and religious life of the people, the source of its information, and the spring of its inspiration. The study of the Law precedes the reading. The object of the reading, then, is to convey to the people as simply as possible the contents of the Law, so that it be known not only to the Sages and Pupils, but to the whole nation. It must therefore be added that the same tendency prevails here in the tradition surrounding the books as can be seen in other literature which follows lines of normal development. With us perhaps this tendency assumes a more definite form. The tendency is to preserve the older and to join on to it the results of later developments. We do not relinquish the past at the expense of the present, but utilise the present to strengthen the past. The fences round the Law double and treble in course of time, but not one of the old fences is given up. We add prayer to prayer in the development of our liturgy, but we do not substitute one for the other. And so this happened also with the system of preserving the Law, especially when it was transcribed from the scroll into book form. The scroll represents to us the text in the oldest form in the sacred service. But for didactic purposes the scroll is found to be difficult to handle, and so it was written in pages, and here the Massora then added notes, rules and injunctions destined to preserve the original text intact. None of these marks, information, rules, etc., have found their way into the ancient scroll. It is not here the place to discuss the history of the writing of the Bible, which would form an interesting chapter by itself. It is only with the one aspect of the writing I am dealing here : division introduced into the text and marked off graphically.

It will be noticed that there is not a single column, with the exception of the two songs in Exodus and Deuteronomy, which is not broken up into two or three smaller sections, divided off in olden times very clearly one from the other by a white line. At least one line has been left unwritten so as to mark off the division. The size of this section varies : sometimes it is of eight or ten lines, and other times two or three lines. Originally these also may have been separated from the other by a large white space between. Later on in some MSS. they were separated by a small space sufficiently clear, however, to show that there is a break in the text. According to the writing these spaces have been designated as Petuhot, meaning open, that is, leaving a full blank line, or Setumot, closed section, with a blank space within the line. Meiri, in 1306, going minutely into the graphical character of the scroll, and endeavouring to establish it, in its minute details, says then that no special information has come down from olden times as to the Petuhot and Setumot. No rules had been given authoritatively as to these sections, fixing which are to be open and which are to be closed. The Talmud knows these divisions, and goes so far as to say that no Petuhah should be written Setumah, and no Setumah should be written Petuhah. Such a mistake in the mere writing of a section, or failure in marking off graphically the divisions, suffices to annul the whole column. It must be cut out from the scroll and another column substituted for it. He goes on to say that neither in the Mishna nor in the Talmud, nor even among the writings of the Gaonim, is there found any direction for the Petuhot and the Setumot. But he follows old model codices like that used by Maimonides and another of Toledo to fix these divisions. Maimonides, before Meiri, has given in the thirteenth century laws on these open and closed sections, but he also relies on the same authority as Meiri. How old are these sections, and by what name were they known ?

The silence of the Talmudic and Rabbinical literature is easily explained. People do not put down in writing information which they assume to be known by everybody, but happily we are able to prove by means of comparative palæography that this division in the text is extremely old, the very first into which the text of the Bible had been broken up, and that it must go back to the earliest possible written copies of the Pentateuch. For curiously enough the Samaritans have also divided their scrolls of the Bible in exactly the same manner as the Jews ; they follow and preserve the very same, ancient tradition which lies at the base of the Jewish and Samaritan text. They also write the Torah in the form of a scroll, and like the Jews they have no marks in the scroll of any Massoretic character, although, as has been shown by me, they also have ancient Massoretic accents dating back probably to the fourth or fifth century. Yet they are not found in the most ancient scrolls which are known to me, and which go back to the twelfth century. But I may claim to have seen also that old scroll of the Law which they declare to have been written by Abisha, in the thirteenth year after the entry of Israel into the land of Canaan, and therefore, according to them, being more than three thousand years old. It is in a very dilapidated state, the ink has eaten through the parchment. The fact of its being written on parchment detracts very considerably from the claim. But that it is very old there can be no doubt. There also I have found the writing to be in columns, and the text divided into small sections, just like other scrolls of the twelfth century, partly in my possession and partly photographed by me. There are no signs otherwise of internal mark or division except the blank space between section and section. The verses are not divided off by colons, and the small sections agree with the large inasmuch as a complete blank line has been left between one and the other, even where the latter consists of only one or two lines. The five books are divided from one another by large spaces, just like in the Jewish scrolls. If we turn to the Samaritan Pentateuch in book form, we shall find that whilst they have preserved with absolute fidelity the small and large divisions of the text, they have inserted there the marks for dividing the verses. They have also introduced accents, and, moreover, special signs between larger divisions, to which we shall refer later on. It should be noted that to each book they have added, as we have done in our Bible in book form, Massoretic notes, giving us the minuter details of these sections. This form of outer agreement is as close as can be thought. It will be seen that the inner agreement in the selection of the portions and in the manner in which they have been divided is much more complete than has ever been dreamt of. It cannot be mere coincidence, as the agreement often goes to the minutest details. The Samaritans were certainly not the people to borrow from the Jews. On this point anyone who knows the Samaritans, their history, their life and their literature cannot come to any other conclusion. But this closeness in the outward agreement might still be challenged, and perhaps some would insist that the one, in this case the Samaritan, would depend on the other, the Jews, and that the Sam. Pent. would be a late copy of the Jewish scroll. On this point the study of the Sam. scroll must set such opinions at rest. That the Jews should have taken from the Samaritans, no one would ever think of suggesting. It is as unlikely in this case as I hold it to be in the other. This being the case, the only solution of the problem is that the Samaritans must have taken over their scroll like the Jews at the very earliest date from a common original, and the division therefore would be proved to belong to very great antiquity. Yet there is a third test which comes to our assistance, and proves that this division is the first and the very oldest, and precedes any other into which the Bible may have been subdivided for liturgical or homiletical purposes. The Greek translation, known as the Septuagint (LXX), that of the seventy, has in a remarkable manner also preserved the very same division of the text into minor sections. Unfortunately, no reference has been made to this paleography of the Greek text, even in the admirable introduction to the Septuagint by Swete. But the old MSS., the Sinaiticus, Vaticanus, and the Alexandrinus, have all preserved the divisions. Tischendorf unfortunately has omitted to mark the blank spaces between one section and another. Swete, on the contrary, has fortunately preserved them. In this latter edition the spaces look like the Hebrew Setumot.

The agreement is so close that it proves, if proof be still required, that we have in these divisions the first and oldest attempt of arranging the text into smaller portions. The Greek translators have certainly not invented these divisions, they merely followed the Hebrew original. It is well known how anxious they were to reproduce down to the minutest detail the Hebrew original, especially in the translation of the Pentateuch. They did not shrink even from the transliteration of the Hebrew words if they offered difficulties, and in every particular they followed their text with an almost absurd faithfulness. It is just because of this accuracy and fidelity that the Greek translation was held in such high, nay, sacred, repute among the Greek-speaking Jews of Alexandria.

Its literalness served even as a basis for arithmetical and mystical speculation. The divisions, therefore, are

the divisions of the ancient text. This is not a mere
hypothesis. A comparative table, which I have drawn
up, and of which I give here a few specimens, will show
such agreement, so as to remove any doubt, and to
bring out a result as convincing as it is surprising of the
antiquity and permanence of this division. It will show
how faithful the Massora has been in the preservation
of the text, and will satisfy us as to the reliability and
antiquity of the Samaritan tradition. I take the first
chapters of Genesis, and show how close this agreement is.

CHAPTER I

1st sec.	1–5	Mass. Pt.	Sam. idem.	Greek idem.
2nd ,,	6–8	Mass. Pt.	Sam. idem.	Greek idem.
3rd ,,	9–13	Mass. Pt.	Sam. idem.	Greek idem.
4th ,,	14–19	Mass. Pt.	Sam. idem.	Greek idem.
5th ,,	20–23	Mass. Pt.	Sam. idem.	Greek idem.
6th ,,	24–31	Mass. Pt.	Sam. idem.	Greek idem.

Here the Greek divides into two, and takes into the
2nd section, first part of II. 1.

CHAPTER II

7th sec. 1–3   Mass. Pt. Sam. idem. Greek idem.

In chapter II. Greek and Samaritan agree still more
closely because they subdivide chapters II. and III. into
more minute sections than the Massora and yet agree
very closely with one another. Thus :—

8th sec. 4–7   Heb. Pt. Sam. idem.   Greek idem
9th ,, 8–17   Sam. and Greek idem.
10th ,, 18–25   Sam. and Greek idem.

CHAPTER III

11th sec. 1–13   Sam. and Greek idem.
12th ,, 14–17   Heb. Pt. and Sam. idem.
13th ,, 18–22   Heb. Pt. Sam. and Greek idem.
14th ,, 22–24   Heb. Pt. Sam. and Greek idem.

Chapter IV (No Hebrew Division)

15th sec.	1–8	Sam. and Greek divide.
16th ,,	9–16	Sam. and Greek divide.
17th ,,	17–24	Sam. and Greek divide.

Chapter V

18th sec. 1–5   Heb. St. and Greek divide.

Sam. takes verses 1 and 2 with previous division.

19th sec.	6–8	Heb. St.	Sam. idem.	Greek idem.
20th ,,	9–11	Heb. St.	Sam. idem.	Greek idem.
21st ,,	12–14	Heb. St.	Sam. idem.	Greek idem.
22nd ,,	15–17	Heb. St.	Sam. idem.	Greek idem.
23rd ,,	18–20	Heb. St.	Sam. idem.	Greek idem.
24th ,,	21–24	Heb. St.	Sam. idem.	Greek idem.
25th ,,	25–27	Heb. St.	Sam. idem.	Greek idem.
26th ,,	28–31	Heb. St.	Sam. idem.	Greek idem.
27th ,,	32	Heb. St.	Sam. idem.	Greek idem.

This at the same time settles another vexed problem, the relation between the Samaritan and the Greek. It shows that whilst there is a close affinity, there is also some definite difference between the two, and on the other hand such a close agreement between the three texts—the Hebrew, Samaritan, and the Greek—that the dependence of Samaritan on Greek can no longer be maintained. There are many more details affecting this question, which, however, cannot be dealt with here any further.

On the other hand, if we compare the divisions of the last two chapters of the Pentateuch the same parallelism will be found between all three texts, not only in the problem of dividing up the texts, but also in following certain graphical peculiarities. The Song of Moses (Deut. xxxii.) is written in our scrolls in hemistichs, absolutely identical in the Jewish and Samaritan scrolls, and in the same form also in the Greek. It is otherwise

absolutely undivided, it forms one whole section, and
it has been preserved like that in the Samaritan, and
no doubt also in the Greek, where the writing of the text
in verses makes it difficult if not impossible to trace
any sectional division. The same obtains in the last
chapter in the Greek with two or three small exceptions,
where it is written in prose. But the agreement between
the Hebrew and Samaritan continues down to sections
of one or two verses only, equally separated in both.
The agreement rests upon a very old and unshaken
tradition. The principle which the scribes—Soferim—
followed in writing, so that the books of the Law could
easily be studied, is seen more clearly in the Samaritan
text than in the Hebrew. Here the ancient division has
been obliterated by later superposition of other divisions
and where the distinction between one section and
another has now almost been entirely forgotten. They
are marked in our printed editions only with a letter
P or S, having lost entirely their original meaning. The
Samaritans, on the contrary, preserve the clear division
of the books as it is found also in our scrolls, and they
go even further, they are exceedingly careful to finish
the column with such a division, never breaking it up.
Each column begins with a new division, a practice
which has not been followed by us—only a fragmentary
tradition has still been preserved by the Massoretic
indication of the initial letters of six columns, the letters
ביהשמו the first letters of the initial words of the
columns. Some writers persist in starting every column
with the letter ו (creating the tradition of ווי העמודים)
or, as some scribes do, with המלך in the scroll of
Esther. The result of the Samaritan practice, as
seen in their scrolls, is that the last lines of the
columns are often cramped, and the writing greatly
reduced, so as to squeeze the words into a narrow space.
In order to obviate such cramped writing no doubt
our sages have dispensed with that rule, which is still
followed by the Samaritans, and which can be seen in

their oldest scrolls. The division was no doubt introduced to mark the change of ideas : a new statement,
the beginning of a new incident, or the introduction of
a new name, were reasons for dividing that portion off
from the rest. We find now in the Jerusalemitan
Talmud the peculiar statement of Rabbi Joshua ben
Levi, who says : " I have constantly refrained from
reading in books of Agadah. Only once I looked into
such a book of Agadah, and I found therein that there
are 175 Parashiyot in the Torah of speaking, saying,
commanding, and those 175 correspond to the life of our
father Abraham. I found, moreover, that the Psalms
were divided into 147 corresponding with the years of
Jacob, and that there were 123 Halleluyahs corresponding with the years of Aaron." There are two or
three points of importance in this statement which
require to be studied. The author lived in the third
or fourth century, and he found in a book containing
legendary and homiletical interpretations of the Law
the statement that the Pentateuch was divided into 175
sections, and the reason given was in the regular homiletical style, because they corresponded with the years
of Abraham, and he says, what is of importance now
for our investigation, that they were, as it were,
characterised by the very words of "speaking,"
" saying " or " commanding," which means that
these sections started no doubt with, or were marked
by, the words which are so often found in the Pentateuch, " and God spake " or " and God commanded."
Here we have then a clear indication of the leading
principle in the division of the Law. Wherever in the
text was found a portion that was sufficiently large
and coherent enough to form a section they marked it
off as such, whenever it began with these words,
ויאמר (vayomer), וידבר (vayedabber) and so on, or when
the whole contents were filled up with one special
command, or one incident in the Bible in the life
of the Patriarchs which would lend itself to form a

complete section. The examples quoted above of the way in which the Hebrew, Samaritan and Greek divide the first and last chapters of the Pentateuch, explain very easily and clearly this system of division. Each one begins with vayomer, or, as in the last chapter of Deuteronomy, each section is given to another tribe, however small the size of it may be. In the second chapter of Genesis the Samaritan carried out this system of division more rigidly still, as he divided it up into still more minute sections. The Greek, who is the third in the order of development, carried this principle of division even to greater length. Not only in the Pentateuch, but he also divided all the other books of the Bible in a similar manner, and I have been able to trace it in some of the oldest texts in the New Testament, where the words " Jesus said " are often introduced at the beginning of these sections into which the books are so divided, whilst these words are missing in other copies not so divided. Here we find then a clear principle for the division of the text.

We gather from the words of R. Joshua ben Levi that these divisions were called Parasha, or Parashiyot (plural). The Samaritans have for this division the name Kissa from the root Kss, meaning to cut off, divide, practically like the Latin *divisio*, or section.

Another word used may have been Piska. This latter name may have changed its original meaning when a new use was found for it. It may therefore be that the oldest name for such division was Piska or Pissuk. It cannot have meant " verse," because the Bible was not yet divided into verses, and it is the exact word corresponding with the Samaritan Kissa, division or section. There are many indications that this was the original meaning of the word. It would explain what has hitherto remained somewhat of a riddle, and what had erroneously been taken as a proof for the very great antiquity of the Massoretic division of the text into verses, when we find in the Talmud, etc., that Aher the scholar, or Nero the Emperor, or Haman are said to have asked the boy coming home from school to recite his Pissuk, hitherto translated " verse." Considering that the reply is seldom limited to one verse, and that the pupils were not expected to study in school only one verse during the day, this interpretation cannot be correct; but if it is understood that the boy was to quote something out of the Piska, of the section which he had studied, the difficulty of the question is removed. The boy could easily recite two or three verses, as indeed happened. And again the Pissuk te'amim mentioned in the Talmud, which has been taken to mean the division according to accents, when such accents had not yet been invented, will now be fully explained in the light of the above investigation, for it means division of the text according to its contents, according to the Ta'am, and in complete agreement with the division known throughout the Talmudic tradition. And this corresponds entirely with the division of the Bible as described above, a division guided by the contents of the text.

This will be made much more apparent later on, when a more detailed description of the Pesikta will be given. The chapter of curses is called the Piska of Curses.

The name, however, for the division of the Bible which has obtained the widest currency, and has retained its character almost unchanged to our very day, is Parasha. Originally it does not refer at all to the weekly lesson, but to every section, especially when used for liturgical purposes, either in the Temple or outside. It is so designated in the Mishna as Parasha. There are no other older documents to show the use of the term Parasha, but there is proof from the manner in which the portions of the Bible are mentioned as Parashiyot in the Mishna. It is there taken for granted that a mere allusion is sufficient to mark the section to be read, and to know that not only is the reference to a section of the Bible, but, still more, which section of the Bible is referred to. Unless the use had been an already long-established one, and unless the divisions marked off were known as such, a mere citation of one word (the initial word) would not have sufficed to make the identification so complete as was evidently intended should be the case, even for the casual reader or listener. The section, for instance, dealing with the blessings of Bileam, is quoted as the Parasha Bileam (Num. xx. 21–25). The portion in Deuteronomy dealing with the duties of the king is known as the Portion of the King. But this calling of the section by the name of Parasha goes still further back. The meaning in which it was used is the same as mentioned before when dealing with the division in the Pentateuch, and it seems that the name Parasha is as old as the division of the Torah into five books. The initial word of the Parasha was taken as the title, and we find it thus in the section dealing with the service in the Temple on the Day of Atonement, when the High Priest was expected to read certain sections of the Law (Mishna Yoma VII. 1, and Sota VII. 7), for these sections are mentioned by the initial word such as Aharei Moth (Lev. XVI. 1) and Akh Beasor (*ibid.* 23, 27). He read also Numbers XXIX. 7, where Numbers is called the fifth of the Pekudim.

Still more fully is this the case in the lesson which the king was expected to read. As this chapter of the Mishna is of far-reaching importance for our investigation I will give the literal translation of the text, as found in Sota VII. 8 :—

" At the going out of the first day of the Feast of Tabernacles (at the end of the seventh year and the beginning of the eighth) they made him a seat in the court of the Temple, and he sat on it as it is said (Deut. XXXI. 10, 11). 'And Moses commanded them saying, At the end of every seven years, in the set time of the year of release in the Feast of Tabernacles, when all Israel is come to appear before the Lord their God in the place which he shall choose, thou shalt read this law before all Israel in their hearing.' Then the Hazan (overseer) of the Synagogue takes the scroll of the Law and gives it to the head of the Synagogue, and then the head of the Synagogue gives it to the Segan, and the Segan gives it to the High Priest, and the High Priest gives it to the King. The King, standing up, takes it, and, sitting down, he reads. The King Agrippa stood up and took it and read it standing, and the sages praised him. And when he came to the passage (Deut. XVII. 15), ' Thou mayest not put a foreigner over thee,' his eyes shed tears, and they said unto him, 'Fear not, Agrippa, thou art our brother, thou art our brother.' The King read from the beginning of Deuteronomy until Shemā (Deut. VI. 4), and then he read Deuteronomy XI. 13. Then chapter XIV. 22, Thou shalt surely tithe, and afterwards from XXVI. 12, When thou hast made an end of tithing. Then the Section of the King XVII. 14, and then the blessings and curses, Deuteronomy, chapters XXVII. and XXVIII., until he finished the whole Parasha. The benedictions which the High Priest spoke the King uttered also, with the exception that he substituted ' remembrance of festival ' instead of ' remission of sin.' " Thus far the Mishna. In this Mishna we have a description of an historical event which had happened in the Temple, and certainly not the first of its kind, on the contrary, perhaps the last, if this Agrippa who is mentioned here as king is the Agrippa of the time of the destruction. In the preceding Mishna we find a description of the service in the Temple as conducted by the High Priest himself. In these chapters of Mishna numerous Parashiyot are mentioned by name, and each of them derives its name only and solely from the initial word, with the single exception of the Parasha called that of the King. It is furthermore important to note that only the beginning is given, and nowhere an indication where each of these portions came to an end.

It is obvious that there was no doubt in the mind of the hearers and readers how far each of these portions went. Certainly not further than marked off by the ancient division. Everyone knew where it came to an end. This custom of mentioning the Parasha by the initial word has obtained also among the Samaritans. In one of their oldest poems, ascribed to Abisha (fourteenth or fifteenth century), sections of the Bible are also quoted by the initial word, and the Targum of the Samaritan Bible has the initial word of the section as it were as a title written over each section. So in some very old fragments from the Genizah in the Cambridge Library, and so in a copy of the Targum in my possession, and similarly in the Arabic translation of the Samaritan Pentateuch in MSS. of the thirteenth or fourteenth century. Everywhere the same custom prevails.

There can be no doubt as to the universal application of this name of Parasha to the section, and also as to the antiquity of the name applied to the section. It was sufficient to quote the first word in order to know exactly which Parasha was meant, and where a doubt existed, as in the case of the third portion read by the High Priest, then the name of the Book of the Pentateuch in which it occurred was added for elucidation. One might linger for some time over these Mishnayot, so important are they for the history of the service. I may have to refer to them once more when dealing with the reading of these sections in the Synagogue. For the time being it was necessary to point out that the name Parasha was given to portions of the Law, in smaller or larger sections, used for liturgical purposes. If we pass on to other references in the Mishna, we shall find that the portions allocated for special Sabbaths, like those preceding the Feast of Passover, are also mentioned under the name of Parasha, such as Parasha Shekalim, thus called because it deals with the Shekalim contribution by every Jew to the treasury of the Temple, or Parasha Zakhor, in which the remembrance of Amalek is mentioned, or the Parasha Hahodesh, the important Parasha which ushered in the very important first month of the year. It would be almost superfluous to multiply these examples in the Mishna and Talmud to prove the use of the word Parasha to denote thereby sections of the Bible, especially when connected with the service.

In the reading of the Maamadot of Genesis, ch. I., verses 1–5 are called a great Parasha, and 6–8 a small Parasha, and it is said that the great Parasha is read to two persons and the small Parasha to one person. The reading is as follows : The first person reads verses 1–3, and the second 3–5, and the third 6–8, each one three verses. The second day (Monday) verses 6–13 divided in the same manner, the third day (Tuesday) verses 9–18, the fourth day (Wednesday) 14–22, the fifth day (Thursday) 19–24, and the sixth day (Friday) verse 23 to chapter II. 2. Here we have then the small section called Parasha just like the larger section mentioned above. Occasionally other sections in the Prophets and Holy Writings are mentioned by the name Parasha, but quite exceptionally. No other word is used for the designation of these sections, no other title ever alluded to, no other was so deeply rooted as this word for denoting the Sections. In the oldest Halachic Midrashim, notably in the Sifra, belonging probably in its original form to the second century, this very division has still been re-tained, with the name of Parasha. Occasionally this Midrash has preserved also the name Dibbur or Dibra, which has been mentioned above. It would be perhaps hazardous as yet to discuss the name of Parashiyot in the old Halachic and Agadic Midrashim unless we have established the contention on unassailable ground that down to a very late period, perhaps down to the sixth or seventh century, no other name has been applied to these sections.

In what manner were these sections used for the

liturgy in the Temple and outside the Temple ? We
shall have to distinguish between the use made of
special sections of the Law or the Pentateuch for select
occasions like New Moon, specially appointed days in
the Bible for holy observances, when additional sacrifices had to be brought, and when other ritual ceremonies were prescribed to be performed in conjunction
with sacrifices such as heave-offering (the Ōmer), the
firstlings (Bikkurim), etc., and the other readings of
the Law in the Temple, like the reading by the
King on the Jubilee. In addition to these we shall
have to consider the consecutive reading of the Law
for didactic purposes and in the liturgy. Here we are
face to face with a difficult problem, not easy of solution.
What was the form of the worship of the Jews outside
the Temple ? They could not offer up sacrifices on those
specially appointed days and seasons. What kind of practice did they institute in order, as it were, to perform so
sacred a duty incumbent upon them ? That they had
synagogues cannot be doubted, places of assembly for
worship and prayer, and no doubt also for study.
That they gathered on festive occasions, especially
on Sabbaths, New Moon, and other great days, requires
no proof. The evidence given at the beginning of this
article satisfies us amply on that head. It does not
affect our question, what kind of service they had in
the Temple of Yeb, or rather Assuan, as disclosed by the
papyri. The references are too vague to allow us to
come to a definite conclusion. But a careful examination has satisfied me that no real sacrifices were sanctioned. Only incense offerings, and other bloodless
offerings, seem to be referred to in these precious fragments of the past. In the Temple of Onias in Alexandria, we are distinctly told that they read the Law
publicly ; no mention is made of any sacrifices. The
service of the Maamadot may help us however, if not
to solve, at any rate to approach the solution of these
problems, and if we study in addition the Samaritan

liturgy and some other indications in the history of our own liturgy, what may have been an hypothesis will be raised to a certainty. We have, moreover, the unanimous tradition of Jews and Samaritans on this point, namely, that in addition to the first chapter of Genesis other portions—Parashiyot—were selected in their entirety and read one after the other ; and that on such special occasions, like New Moon, New Year, Pesaḥ, etc., those small sections—Parashiyot—in which the observance of that special day was enjoined, or the actions to be performed on that day were described, these sections were read in lieu of the sacrifices in which they could not take part, the Temple being too far away. This happened whilst the Temple existed. And still more so, when they were no longer in a position to perform them after the destruction of the Temple. In the liturgy, notably in that of the special days, we find, in fact, incorporated in the part of the prayer such short sections or Parashiyot taken from the Bible which refer to the special character of the day.

The Samaritans on their part have not only retained the first chapter of Genesis, reading that also in small portions every day like the Maamadot did in olden times, but they call them almost by the same name as they are called in the Mishna, " The Chapters of Creation," *Kisse deberiah*, and then they read a whole series of short Parashiyot or Ḳissin, as they call them, inserting as we do precisely the same Parashiyot from the Pentateuch on the several special occasions, notably when they happen to be on the Sabbath. The reading of the Shemă is also the Samaritan practice. The first Mishna of Berakhot already speaks of the reading of the Shemă as an old-established custom, and calls it by the initial word Shemă, although it embraces three independent sections, and we find later on in the Talmud a question by R. Napha why the two sections of the Shemă are arranged in an order contrary to that in Deuteronomy. (It is unfortunate that all this part which gives us a clear insight into the liturgy of the Samaritans has been entirely omitted by Dr. A. Cowley in his edition of the Samaritan liturgy. Not a trace is left, and the references that are made sometimes in the text are therefore absolutely unintelligible.) I refrain from referring to the other parts of our liturgy, consisting of a mosaic of Biblical verses, selected with a view to the festival, or the special occasion when they are to be recited, such as verses referring to the Sabbath or New Moon, or on other occasions such as in the Selihot the Musaph Amidah of New Year, etc., collected together. On an elaborate scale this practice is found among the Samaritans and Karaites. This is mentioned here for the purpose only of showing that there was a further development in the introduction of Biblical verses in the liturgy after the time when the use of the smaller portions had become rigidly fixed. The part forming the prayer proper in which these had taken their place did not exhaust all the requirements of the service. The people were not satisfied with the shorter sections which merely informed them on occasions of the Biblical injunction referring to the importance and character of the day they were celebrating. The Bible could not remain to them a closed book, and probably the reading of the Law in its entirety preceded the Order of the service proper. The latter found its expression by the worship in the Temple, and by such devotional exercises as they were ready to institute in imitation of the Temple worship. But the study and reading of the Law stood by itself, and it was not confined to the centres of the learned. Tradition tells that the institution of the public reading of the Law goes back to the very beginnings of the foundation of the people as the People of God. Throughout the Bible we read, "Thou shalt meditate on it," and "Thou shalt read it"; and, "Delight in the Law." It is too well known to require any further proof that the study of the Law was considered a most meritorious act, and to read publicly in the Law was to make it possible for others to partake of that merit. As far back as our tradition goes, public reading and private study of the Law seem to be an integral part of the religious life of the people. I am dealing with these questions later on when following up the course which these practices have taken during the centuries, but no one denies the fact that the Law was read publicly to the people, as mentioned by Josephus, Philo, etc.

The question which we have now to face is: Upon what system was this reading of the Law carried out? Here again the same old tradition informs us that Ezra had appointed that the curses in Leviticus should be read before the Feast of Weeks and the curses in Deuteronomy before the New Year. This is a definite starting-point which shows unmistakably that the reading of the whole of the Pentateuch must have been completed in one year, otherwise it would have been impossible so to regulate the reading that these portions should fall in their consecutive order at those fixed periods. It is impossible to imagine that only select sections could have been meant, for there would have been then no reason to fix a definite period. The rule which is laid down that close upon four months must elapse between the last chapter of Leviticus and Deuteronomy XXVII. and XXVIII., gives us just the space required for the two books (Numbers and Deuteronomy I.–XXVII.), whilst the other seven months could be allotted to the first three books of the Pentateuch. The month of Tishri was given up to the reading of the select sections referring to the Festivals and Holy Days. The tradition in the Mishna knows, in fact, no other division of the Pentateuch; it assumes the annual cycle, and the discussion as in Megillah, 29 ff., turns on finding a way to adjust the reading of the weekly portions with the additional readings for special Sabbaths, such as the four special Sabbaths before Pesaḥ, or that Sabbath on which

Rosh Hodesh may happen to fall, meaning the Sabbath in Hanukah. The question was, how to arrange for the reading of Parashat Nesiim (the portion of the offerings of the princes) or those in which the Shekalim, Amalek, and others are to be mentioned in conjunction with, or in lieu of, the regular weekly portion. These and all the other references to the reading of the Law presuppose only an annual cycle.

How was the Bible then divided? Into weekly Portions. The old division into Parashiyot was not touched. There is no new larger portion which breaks up the smaller section or begins in the middle. It is always a Petuḥa (rarely a Setuma) which separates the preceding from the succeeding portion. The only change which has taken place, if change it be, was to give to the word Parasha a somewhat different and more restricted meaning, which becomes more and more identified with the weekly portion, to the detriment of the older application of the word, causing thereby some confusion. Anyone who finds, for instance, either in the Samaritan Letter or in the Rabbinical documents, the name of one of the divisions quoted as Parasha has no doubt as to what it really means. The difficulty arises when reading older documents, Mishna, etc., and to some extent the Sifra, to understand exactly what was meant by that term. The meaning of Parasha as weekly portion became soon an established fact. The Samaritans, who call their smaller portions Kissa, have chosen the same word Parasha, writing it like the Hebrew, but pronouncing it Barasha, to designate the weekly portion into which they divide the Bible. This investigation has not the aim of proving that the Torah was read publicly. The question which we are pursuing and endeavouring to settle is the manner in which the public reading, and to a certain extent the private study and reading, was carried out. Was there no other system except the annual? Is there no trace of any different system of reading found in the literature clearly and unmistakably enunciated as such ? And do we find in the Palæography of the Biblical text any indication or justification for such an assumption ? These are the main points and to these we shall adhere. It was necessary to establish, in the first place, the primary division into Parashiyot or Sections as the very basis for the division of the Law into Portions. I have then proceeded to trace the way in which these smaller Sections were used in the public worship in the Temple by the High Priest, and by the King on the one hand, and by the delegates as Maamadot in private worship. The latter has shown us how certain portions were read, in what may be termed a semi-public service. It was only carried on during week-days and by a select few. We have, moreover, seen that other Sections—Parashiyot—were embodied in the service outside the Temple, i.e. in the Synagogue, and on special occasions, notably on the Sabbath, New Moon, Festivals, etc. Furthermore, that in accordance with the whole Jewish tradition, the Law has been divided into as many portions (lessons or Perikopes) as there are weeks in the year. The number has been fixed at fifty-four. During the year there are at least a few Sabbaths on which Festivals occur, for which separate readings have been instituted. These larger portions have also been called Parasha, and have assumed the names of the initial smaller Parasha or section with which they begin. The name by which the latter was known was transferred to the weekly lesson. Originally, no doubt, the first and the last of the smaller Parashiyot were mentioned in order to cir-cumscribe and define exactly the extent of the weekly portion. But later on, the custom having become deeply rooted, it sufficed to mention only the name of the initial small Parasha.

Now the fact that these portions are quoted by the initial words is the best proof possible that they

had been already established for a long time, and
that the Bible had been subdivided for public readings in such manner, for the mere reference to the first
word was enough to characterise the portion meant.
The reference to Lekh Lekha, or Noah, was quite sufficient for the people to understand to what it referred.
The Samaritans, in fact, have retained the older form of
quotation.   Originally the portion was, e.g., from Lekh
Lekha to the portion Vayera, or Mikkes to Vayehi,
and the Samaritans to this very day so designate their
Portions, although in some instances for brevity's sake
they quote only the beginning (v. Letters to Scaliger
quoted above).   They also know only the annual cycle,
as observed by Jews and Karaites.   The Samaritans
have done exactly the same, though in not a few instances they differ considerably from the Jews in the
starting-point of their Parasha.   They sometimes begin
in the middle of one of our Parashiyot, but they follow
the same system and provide like the Jews also for
a larger number of Parashiyot for the intercalary year,
when four Sabbaths are added.   They do it in the same
manner as we do, by dividing three or four longer
Parashiyot into six or eight shorter ones, or vice versa,
combining two or three into one, agreeing even in this
detail in some instances with the practice of the Jews.
They combine, e.g., Matot and Mas'ei together with
Pinehas, and the Portion corresponding to Nissabim,
Vayelekh, as we do.   A close examination furthermore
shows that they never started from the middle of a
Kissa.   Like the Jews, they start invariably from the
beginning of those smaller Sections marked by us as
Pet or Set, as the case may be, and clearly distinguished
by them as a Pet by a blank line between. Dr. Cowley
has reprinted the list of Parashiyot as found by him
in one of the Petermann MSS. in Berlin.   But unfortunately he has not noticed that the list for Genesis
which he published, is the extended list for the Leap
Year, and thus creates some confusion in the under-

standing of the division (*J.Q.R.*, Vol. VII, 1894, p. 137 ff). He starts Exodus with number 14, while he leaves off Genesis with 18. The same list is also found in my Cod. 1135.

It being of importance I reprint here in the Appendix the whole calendar for one year like my Cod. 1150, with all the indications week by week of the Portions read, wherein also other calendaristic details of the highest interest are given. That the Samaritan division has not been done haphazard, but rests on very ancient tradition, is evident from the fact that on one or two occasions they start the " Barasha " with the very Portions which we have selected for our Festivals and Holy Days. I will refer to them anon, when examining the Sifra and Pesikta.

Before I proceed to describe the way in which the Portions are read, it is necessary to draw attention to the further parallelism between Jews and Samaritans, showing the extreme antiquity of the practice followed by both. Both begin the reading of the Law immediately after the Feast of Tabernacles. It must be remembered that the King read the Law at the Jubilee, also at the end of Tabernacles, and this, no doubt, remained a starting-point for the annual reading for the future. What is still more significant in the highest degree is the arrangement in which both Jews and Samaritans agree that the curses in Leviticus are read before the Feast of Weeks, and those in Deuteronomy before the New Year. A Leap Year makes no difference with this arrangement, for the Samaritans expand the fourteen Portions into which they divide Genesis into eighteen, in order to provide for their four intercalary Sabbaths. They begin the reading of the second book of the Law invariably on the first Sabbath of the eleventh month (Nisan is the first), and Leviticus with the first Sabbath of Nisan. From this rule they do not deviate. Remembering then that this arrangement of the reading of the curses and blessings is traced back

by tradition to Ezra, we have here an unexpected cor-
roboration by the reading of the Samaritans. No less
curious is, that on the last Sabbath of the eleventh
month (or the first of the twelfth) an additional
Portion is read, namely, Exodus xxx. 12, the well-
known additional Section to our Parasha Shekalim read
by us precisely at the same time. These are not
haphazard coincidences, for they run parallel in the
minute details of liturgical arrangement. Both point
thus to a far greater antiquity than has hitherto
been believed, for it cannot be stated often enough that
the Samaritans have borrowed just as little directly
from Rabbinical Judaism as the Jews have borrowed
from the Samaritans.

We shall now consider the way in which the weekly
lesson is read by the Jews, Samaritans, etc. How was
this weekly Portion read ? Did the people take any part
in the reading, and if so, in what manner ? It is impossible to assume, as some have done, that originally
the people read only one verse, and that three verses
formed the whole of the weekly Portion. The very
size of the ancient Parasha, which very seldom is less
than three verses and often consists of a larger number
of verses, precludes even the hypothetical assumption
of the possibility of such a short reading. It would
be almost ludicrous to imagine that men should be called
to read before the public one single verse, considering
that they were reading so many Parashiyot in their
prayers like those mentioned above, whilst the whole
of the reading of the Law should consist of one verse.
That three men should be called up on a solemn day
to exhibit the greatness and beauty of the Law by the
reading of one single verse each seems too preposterous
to be believed. There is not a shred of evidence for
such a system. The Mishna cited above makes it
perfectly clear that in the week-day semi-public reading
of the Maamadot, each of the persons was expected to
read at least three verses. Note that this was for a week-

day lesson. Why the minimum of three verses should
have been established is not mentioned anywhere.
But the reason is not far to seek. The priestly
blessing consists of three verses, and this no doubt was
taken as a model for the reading. The analogy of the
Samaritans does not sufficiently assist us in the history
of the reading of the Law, at any rate in one direction ;
although their practice is very suggestive in other directions. They do not read from the Scroll as far as I have
been able to ascertain. They have the Scrolls, it is true,
and they have used them in ancient times. In the later
centuries, however, they only take them out from the
Ark, show them to the people at the conclusion of the
prayer, and then settle down to read from their MS.
books. The cause may be that not being able to obtain
pure parchment from goat skins sacrificed ritually and
properly prepared owing to the loss of the ashes of
the Red Heifer, and being in a state of Levitical
impurity, they had no more "pure" parchment from
the fifteenth century on, as they assured me, and are
therefore, no doubt, afraid to wear out the few parchment
Scrolls by too constant use. They therefore use their
books, which are mostly written on paper. They have
a double system : one at the conclusion of the morning
service and one at the conclusion of the midday service.
In both the whole congregation takes part. The reading
in the morning is not, however, carried on in the " Kinsha " (their Synagogue), but in the " Bet-kahana " (the
house where the priests are dwelling), and there the
reading partakes of a character reminding one as emphatically as possible of the injunction mentioned in
the Talmud, that every man should read the Bible,
each verse twice in Hebrew and once in the Targum.
This system of reading the text twice and the Targum
once, I have seen done by the Yemenite Jews in Jerusalem on Shabuoth afternoon, when squatting on the floor
in their Synagogue they read the Book of Ruth in such
manner. The Samaritans similarly read alternately ;

the reader—always one of the priests—reads and the congregation joins in either by repeating the verse or reading the verses alternately during the morning service. They have now forgotten the Targum, which they used to read alternately with the Hebrew text, in the same manner, I understand, down to about 150 years ago, when the practice ceased, because the people had lost the knowledge of the ancient Samaritan tongue in which the Targum is composed, and therefore it had lost its meaning. They read the whole Parasha, verse by verse, in the morning. At the midday service we find they read the whole Parasha again, but then the priest starts and reads the first three or four verses of each Kiṣṣa corresponding to our small Section, and the people afterwards read the other half until they finish the whole of the weekly lesson. Calling up therefore does not exist. With us the former practice of reading the text with the Targum alternately, now also given up, had been the general rule, and has had an influence upon the study of the Law to a far greater extent than has hitherto been surmised. " It is incumbent upon every individual to read the whole of the weekly portion to himself, twice in the Hebrew text and once in the Targum " (Berakhot, 8a). This will be considered in connection with the private form of study. But we are still discussing the public reading, where the Meturgeman had his place, and where, no doubt, the reading was carried out exactly in the same manner as the Samaritans did and do. Faint indications of this are preserved by the way in which the Song of Moses was read alternately by precentor and people, and by the practice of the congregation chiming in at the end of the sections in the Sabbath Portion. This is merely a remnant of the older practice in which the congregation, no doubt, repeated the Hebrew text, verse by verse, and listened to the Meturgeman who explained it to them in the vernacular.

As regards the minor subdivision or the calling up of

people to the reading of the Law, we find that the
Levites in the Temple already are stated to have read
the Portion in precisely the same manner, dividing
the weekly Portion into seven smaller Sections as we
do. A Synagogue from which the Scroll of the Law is
taken is mentioned in the Mishna referred to before.
It is from that Synagogue that the Hazan took the
Scroll and gave it to the High Priest, and he to the
King. So there must have been a Synagogue within
the precincts of the Temple itself. This division into
seven is not an artificial one as it might appear from a
casual study of the passage in the Talmud, where a
gradual development seems to be indicated by the
enumeration of the various occasions in which the
number of people to be called up—that is who are to
take their share in the public reading—is successively
increased from three on week-days to four on New
Moon, etc., until seven on Sabbath. The seven portions,
no doubt, correspond with the seven days of the week,
and are unquestionably a very old practice. But this
is a minor point which I cannot pursue any further
here.

What part the Kohen, as such, may have taken in the
public reading of the Law is one of the problems which
await solution. It is intimately connected with the
question raised by me, as to the form of the Jewish
worship outside the Temple. In close relation to it
stands, of course, the position held by the Kohen in the
community.

The fact that the Samaritans still give to the Kohen
a pre-eminent position in all religious questions cannot
be overlooked. Of no less importance is the Christian
practice which gives to the priest functions absolutely
identical with those claimed by the Jewish Kohen. He
alone was and is allowed to deal with the Sacraments and
holy offices. In the Church he is primarily, or the only
person who leads and reads the prayer. He was presum-
ably also the leader and reader in the Synagogue, and

hence his claim to be the first to take part in the reading of the Law, just as the Samaritan priests do to this very day, in their service. If, as suggested above, the reading of three verses is an imitation of the threefold blessing of the priest, it is obvious that the Kohen should be expected to read also, in the first instance, the portion of the Law and afterwards to retain at least the first position in the reading. To return now to the system of reading, the practice of the Church shows that it knows only an annual cycle. The Church extended it over the Old and New Testaments, originally reading only the Old, until the New was considered to be of equal sanctity, that is, when the Heathen-Christian element prevailed over the Jewish-Christian. Then they slowly eliminated the reading of the Old, and substituted for it almost exclusively the reading of the New Testament, retaining, however, the system of an annual cycle. The general principle of the lessons of the Church is exactly the same as that of the Jewish lesson. On festive occasions special portions fitted for the occasion are read from the Old Testament and New Testament bearing on the importance of the day ; and throughout the special season of the year selections are made from the Bible for the same purpose of public reading. The comparison which I established before when dealing with the sectional division between the Hebrew, Samaritan, and Greek Bibles will help us to understand the practice of the Church. It follows here absolutely and entirely the example of the Synagogue and the Kinsha. The lessons from the Old Testament for the Christian Lectionaries, notably in the Triodion for the Quadragesima, are sections taken from the LXX, determined by the original division of the Greek text ; they also begin with the first verse of a section and finish with the last verse. They never begin the lesson in the middle, just as the Jews never start any lesson from the middle of a small Parasha, or the Samaritans in the middle of a Kissa. For the

Church the Books of the Bible stand on a different plane, and preference is given or no doubt was given to those chapters of the Prophets which lent themselves to a Christological interpretation. When the new dispensation dispensed practically with " the Law," it was obvious that no such prominence would be given to portions from the Law as is done by Jews and Samaritans.

It is curious how little is known of the beginnings of the ancient Christian liturgy. The recent researches of Glaue, *Die Vorlesung heiliger Schriften im Gottesdienste,* and the book of Harnack, *Uber den Privaten Gebrauch der Heiligen Schriften in d. Alten Kirche* (Leipzig, 1912), throw very little light on the reading of lessons from the Old Testament in the first two centuries of the Christian Church. But the investigation which I have carried out leaves no doubt as to the system and the practice followed in the primitive Church. The result from the lesson of the Church falls into line with the result obtained from the readings in the Synagogue and Kinsha. They all point in the same direction and prove mutually their antiquity. Direct dependence of one upon the other is utterly impossible, for though they agree in the main principle, they differ sufficiently in detail to obviate the possibility of any direct borrowing.

Another point is the size of the lesson of the Church. On an average it is about twenty-five to thirty verses ; herein again, no doubt, the Church follows the old example of the Jews where the smaller daily lesson certainly contained more than eight or nine verses. No question thus of a possible reading consisting of one or three verses alone even for a week-day, and still less for a Sabbath, Festival or other Holy Day. These lessons must have been of the size of the actual Parasha. As the matter is of still wider importance, I will mention here the lesson from the Old Testament read during the Lenten weeks (from Ash Wednesday to Easter) according to the Byzantine and the Syriac rites, limiting my-self to the lessons of the first ten chapters of Genesis; the former from the Triodion, the latter according to the list given in Maclean's *East Syrian Daily Offices*, page 284. In the Greek the lessons read are as follows:—

I. Mon., Gen. I. 1–13. Tues., 14–23. Wed., 24–Gen. II. 3. Thurs., II. 4–19.

II. Mon., III. 21 ff. Tues., IV. 8 ff. Wed., IV. 16. Thurs., V. 1–24.

III. Mon., VI. 9–22. Tues., VII. 5. Wed., VII. 6–9. Thurs., VII. 11–VIII. 3. Fri., VIII. 4–21*a*.

IV. Mon., VIII. 21*b*—IX. 7. Tues., IX. 8. Wed., IX. 18. Thurs., X. 1–9.

In the Syriac the reading from the first ten chapters of Genesis is :—

I. Mon., Gen. I. 1–20. Tues., I. 20–II. 8. Wed., II. 8 to end. Thurs., III. 1–20. Fri., III. 20 to end.

II. Sun., V. 18–32. Fri., V. 32 to end of VI.

III. Sun., VII. Fri., IX. 8 to end.

Of these two the Greek seems to be the older, and the other—the Syriac—a somewhat later division ; yet both follow the same principle of providing daily lessons from the Old Testament. They take as basis for their division what will be certainly a great surprise to students of the history of the Christian liturgy, a division of the text which coincides down to the minutest detail with the Samaritan division of the Hebrew text. It is noteworthy, for instance, that Genesis VIII. 21 should be broken up in the Greek lesson into two verses, and that one lesson should finish with 21*a* and the other begin with 21*b*, a division which coincides absolutely with the Samaritan division, and is not found even in the Septuagint.

It is not necessary to pursue this comparison much further. It is quite sufficient to prove (*a*) that the continuous reading of the text was the practice of the Church, (b) that the reading was extended over a good number of verses, although no one was called up, and the whole of the reading was left entirely to the priest, (c) that the ancient subdivision of the text into small Parashiyot was taken as the basis for the arrangement of the lessons, none venturing to break up these sections. If we then turn to the Palestine Syriac Lectionary of the Gospels, dating probably from the fourth or fifth century, the same tradition meets us for dividing the whole of the Gospels into large sections for the purpose of reading them as lessons during divine service, and finishing the reading in the course of one year. The tradition of the Church is thus uniform with that of the Kinsha and the Synagogue ; for the Christians certainly would not have invented an annual cycle or arranged the reading of the sacred Scriptures unless they followed a universally accepted tradition considered ancient, well established and holy. Nowhere is there to be found a trace of any other division of the Bible, and nowhere is there an attempt of establishing a cycle of lessons extending beyond one year.

The Karaites may be mentioned here, although they are of a very late origin ; but in view of their dislike to everything that appeared to them to be of Rabbinical origin, and their claim to be the representatives of the older, undiluted Biblical tradition, if they had found anywhere a practice which they thought to be of a recent origin, or an arrangement based merely upon Rabbinical interpretation, they would certainly have altered it, just to show their opposition and their independence. The yearly cycle as given by Bashyatchi in his *Aderet Eliyahu* (Odessa, f. 105a), is precisely the same as that of the Jews, nor does the author of this Karaite Code of Laws in any degree remotely point or allude to any other form of reading but the annual cycle. He says, moreover, it is based by them on the statement in the Book of Ezra (Neh. VIII. 18), " Also day by day, from the first day unto the last day, he read in the Book of the law of God," that is, as they explain it, from the day after Succoth to the same day a year hence. The *daily* lessons in the churches and the practice of the Anglican Church seem to rest also on this statement. The Karaites call their weekly lessons " Parasha," and they have no other name for them. They read the Parasha almost in the same manner as we do. In the Prayer Book it is mentioned that " on the Sabbath in which no Scroll is taken out the people read from the Humash, viz. the book; according to custom the Haham reads the first verse, the people continue and the Haham concludes." This reminds one very forcibly of the system prevailing among the Samaritans. But when they read out of the Scroll, they also divide the Portions into seven on the Sabbath, and the Kohen is the first to be called up to the reading.

The list of Haftarot given on f. 105*b* is not entirely different, as some have asserted, from that of the Jews. From Numbers to the end of Deuteronomy, with one or two exceptions, the Haftarot are precisely the same as those read by the Jews, and a notable fact is that the special Haftarot for the " three weeks of trouble " and the " seven weeks of comfort " are almost the same as the Jewish. Of the three between 17th of Tammuz and 9th of Ab two are identical. The difference, therefore, between Jews and Karaites amounts to very little; and is not much greater than that existing between the Sephardic, Ashkenazic, Yemenite, Italian, Persian, not to speak of other Rites. We find thus the same tradition even in the question of Haftarot, that only an annual cycle is known and practised. We see by their choice of chapters from the Prophets to be used as Haftarot that they believed the chapters read by the Jews as Haftarot rested on Rabbinical authority only; and therefore, whilst accepting the principle of the reading of the Haftarah, they often selected deliberately other chapters in lieu of those read by the Jews. Up to a certain date there was some latitude in the choice of the Haftarah, as the divergence between the various Jewish Rites shows.

But the Karaites never ventured to alter the reading of the Law ; they followed exactly the same principle and the same tradition as the Jews ; for it was to them an equally ancient and sacred tradition, although they claim for themselves an independent calculation of the calendar and different counting of the seven weeks which separate Pesach from Shebuoth. The latter falls with them always on a Sunday as with the Samaritans and the ancient Sadducees. But despite this difference, the division of the Bible is mainly the same, and they know only an annual cycle.

At a very late period, so late that its beginnings are not difficult to determine, a new word, Seder—or rather the plural, Sedarim—turns up, notably in Massoretic treatises, with a specific meaning. It is there employed to mark divisions of the Bible. I will not as yet discuss the interpretation placed upon this new division. For the time being we are considering this division of the Bible from a purely palæographical and archæological point of view. It has already been shown that the scroll of the Bible in accordance with the tradition preserved by the Jews, Samaritans, and Christians alike was written in a uniform manner and with definite divisions marked off, and that such divisions have never changed. On the contrary, they formed a rigid framework for any ulterior arrangement of the text of the Bible. So rigid was this division, that the Law would never allow the slightest deviation, and any change sufficed to make the Scroll unfit for religious service. The column was eliminated or so corrected as to reestablish the proper form of writing. It has been shown that the Parashiyot could not be divided ; and it was later on laid down as a rule that no man called up to the Law could break off the reading unless he either read to the end of that section (Parasha) or at least left three verses before the end to enable another person to be called up.

The great antiquity of this division is shown by the mode of writing the scrolls. A blank line originally divided one section from the other, and a larger space divided one of the five books from the other. The weekly portion falls in entirely with this arrangement, and no weekly lesson is known to begin in the middle of a section. Now this tradition is limited to the Pentateuch. No indications are found in the Mishna or Talmud of any such divisions of the other Books of the Bible, Prophets, Holy Writings, except for one or two rare instances where the words Parasha or Perek are used, to which reference will be made later on ; there is no question of Parashiyot as a regular institution or division. No rules are laid down for writing and dividing these Books of the Bible in a special, clearly prescribed manner, nor is there any direction as to what would make such a book fit or unfit for service when used for the reading of the Haftarah. The same holds good for the five scrolls, not excepting the Book of Esther. When the Talmud discusses at length, in the treatise Megillah, how the latter is to be written and read, no reference is made to any internal division or Parasha ; in fact, there existed none which has been authoritatively or universally recognised and followed as such, and there is nowhere greater independence than in the copies of these parts of the Bible.*

Even in the MSS. containing only the Haftarot, and therefore destined to be used in the Synagogue for religious service and to be read immediately after the Law, great obscurity prevails. There is no fixed tradition as to how these portions from the Prophets should be written and how they should be subdivided. No Haftarah nor any other portion of the Bible out-

---

* It is a pity that Prof. Kittle should have taken it wantonly upon himself to introduce irrelevant and misleading divisions in his edition of the Bible. He has no authority for it, and still less to decide which is to be a Petuḥa and which a Setuma (an open or a closed section) in Prophets and Holy Writings.

side the Pentateuch has ever been called Parasha.
If, however, the Sedarim represent and, as has been
assumed, stand in direct connection with the public
reading of the Law in the Synagogue, it is more than
surprising that no graphic trace of such a division
should be found in any MSS. of whatever age and place.
In those few MSS. in which the Sedarim are marked, this
is not done, let it be noted, in the Scroll but in the book
form; the letter ס (Seder) is written at the margin to
show where the Seder begins, just like any other Massoretic marginal note of late date and of no legal value.
There is no division inside the text; there is no blank
space left, there is no internal sign, nothing to show that
there is a break. Persons unacquainted with the Massoretic Sigla might be induced to believe that it is the sign
for Setuma, which by a mistake had got into the margin.
Even that ס is not found in any of the Biblical MSS.
before the twelfth century and rarely even later. But
what goes further to prove the recent and non-liturgical
origin of this division is that it has been extended
to the whole of the Bible. No one can maintain that
the Prophets and Holy Writings have ever been read
publicly in connection with the liturgy and in any consecutive order. That the whole of the Bible should
have been so divided is evidence that it has not been
done in obedience to any regulation or principle according to which they were to be used as lessons. There are
many books of the Holy Writings which have never been
used as such in their entirety, or in any large portions,
for any divine service; such as Ezra, Nehemiah, Daniel,
Chronicles, Proverbs, or even Job. The reading of
these books is mentioned in Mishna Yoma among
those which the sages read to the High Priest privately.
They were singled out for the reading to the High
Priest, no doubt, for that very reason that they were
otherwise never used in public worship. Of the
Prophets themselves, it is well known, only selected
chapters are read as Haftarot. It would be a remark-

able claim, after the whole of the Bible had been divided
into some 452 divisions for no liturgical purpose, to
say that the same division limited to the Pentateuch
rests upon a definite liturgical use to which the Pentateuch has been put. Either the division embraces the
whole and rests on a principle affecting the whole of the
Bible, or it does not. It cannot be claimed to be applied
in one way for one section (the Law), and to owe its origin
separately for that portion, whilst no explanation can
be given for the extension of that principle to the rest
of the Bible. If the Pentateuch had been divided into
150 weekly lessons for liturgical purposes, the division
of the rest of the books of the Bible could not have
been made for the same reason, as it cannot be applied
to the Prophets and Holy Writings. It is therefore
clear that Sedarim have nothing to do with Synagogue
lessons or Perikopes.

It cannot be denied that the other books of the
Bible must also have been divided into smaller sections ; but there is no fixed tradition for such division
nor any decisive authoritative rule as to the character
of the section, whether it be open or closed. It can
be shown, however, that the example of the Pentateuch
served as the model in general outline for the divisions of
the other parts of the Bible. The oldest division is that
of the Psalter, which has been broken up into five books,
like the Pentateuch. The Psalter was the hymn-book
in the Temple, as proved by the ancient testimony of
the Levites singing Psalms in the time of Ezra and
later (Rosh. Hash. 31a), an example followed by the
Synagogue and the Church. Curiously enough, the
Samaritans call their hymns " tehilot " (or, tehilelot),
probably the older name for our Book of Psalms—(so
Ben Asher)—" tehilim " being the later form and used
to differentiate between the Biblical book and other
liturgical hymns. To this day the Synagogue makes
large use of the Psalter. This division of the Psalter
into five books belongs to a very ancient period, long

before the Massora. Proof thereof is the doxology at the end of each of the last four books ; and in our daily morning service, after the doxology with which the Halleluyahs conclude, we also recite the doxologies of the preceding four books together, as if we had read the whole of the Psalter during that service.* The Psalter was subsequently divided into thirty sections, a certain number of Psalms being set aside for each day of the month ; a division with which we shall deal later. The five Megillot, or scrolls, no doubt owe their origin and arrangement to the same desire of following the example of the Law's division into five books. The five scrolls were used also in the liturgy. But besides this division of these books (Psalter and five Megillot) we must presume that all the books of the Bible were divided into smaller or larger sections, following the basis laid down for the division of the Pentateuch into Parashiyot, either when starting a new subject, or a new prophecy, or a new date.

It would be of real importance if the Sedarim could be shown to represent an ancient division. But the divisions found in ancient MSS. of the Bible are of a totally different character, agreeing in the main with the small sections or Parashiyot of the Pentateuch. The Septuagint is also subdivided into smaller portions, though those found in the Greek text do not tally with those found in some of the Hebrew manuscript Bibles. If we now continue our examination of the Sedarim we shall find that the tradition about the numbers is anything but reliable. According to one account there are 154, according to another 158, and according to a third 167 Sedarim. None of them can be explained on any possible calculation. Moreover, if we are to follow Ginsburg (*Introduction to the Bible*, pp. 33–4), there is a fourth tradition contained in a MS. with the Massora

---

* Of course each Psalm forms a small section for itself like the Parasha of the Law, and we find indeed some Psalms are quoted as Parasha or Perek in the Talmud, Ber. II, 1–2 ; Berach 9*b* and 13*b* ; Gittin 60*a* ; Rosh. Hash. 30*b*. (A small portion in Isaiah is also called Parasha : Meg. 24*a*.)

Parva which disagrees with the others. On examining these Sedarim a little more closely, we shall be struck by the incongruity of the size. Assuming for argument's sake that these Sedarim served some liturgical purpose and constituted the weekly lesson in the Synagogue, we find that some of them consist of seven, eight, or fifteen verses, whilst others run into chapters. Surely it is impossible to imagine that those who were responsible for such a division should not have tried to standardise these weekly lessons, and make them more or less of equal size. Are we to assume that those who used the Sedarim for their weekly lesson had gone entirely against the rules laid down for Jewish public worship, that they should establish for themselves new rules and regulations which flew in the face of all the tradition of the past; that they should have ignored the practice of the Temple and the practice of the Synagogue as described in the Mishna and the Talmud, that they should have ignored the ancient division of Parashiyot and started their weekly portions from the middle of these sections as, e.g., in Genesis xix. 1; xxvii. 28, etc., that they should deviate from the number of persons to be called up, the number of verses to be read on such occasions, all this for centuries, and, forsooth, in Palestine, without leaving a single trace in the practice and terminology of the Synagogue? Not only is there no mention anywhere in the whole literature of any weekly division by the name of Seder, but also the readings from the Prophets must have been entirely different and independent in size and selection of those that have formed the readings of the Prophets as Haftarot from remote antiquity. For the Sedarim in the Prophets are, almost without exception, of a much larger size than the Haftarot; a Seder often being equal to two or three chapters. Isaiah has only twenty-six, Ezekiel twenty-nine, the Minor Prophets twenty-one, and the whole of the Book of Psalms nineteen. If these Sedarim hold good also for Haftarot, what a profound difference between the obligatory weekly lesson of the Torah consisting of perhaps seven or eight verses, and the Haftarah from the Prophet of fifty or sixty verses!

In addition to this deficiency from a palæographical point of view of distinctive signs by which these Sedarim are marked off in the Scroll, there is also a complete absence of any direction or rule for the marking of such division. If one remembers the strictness. of the rules laid down for the open and closed sections, it is more than surprising that no care should have been taken, if this division into Sedarim were an old one, to lay down some rule or some legal guide for marking them in the Scroll. It is inconceivable that such a division could have obtained over a wider area over the whole of Palestine, and in ancient times covering the whole of the Talmudic period, without any legal formulation of the rules and principles underlying such division. How little they could be or have been connected with the history of the Scroll and the use to which it was put in the public service can be seen by the continued silence of all authorities, almost without exception. It is sufficient to quote Maimonides, especially as I shall have to refer to him in connection with the alleged three-year cycle. In his *Hilkhot Sefer Torah*, Sect. Ahabah, he devotes a long chapter (chapter VIII.) to a minute and detailed description of the open and closed sections of the Pentateuch. He enumerates each one and describes very carefully whether it should be open or closed, and he gives as his authority the famous model code of Ben Asher, originally kept in Jerusalem and then used by him in Egypt. But he never mentions even the word Seder, and does not seem to be aware of any other authoritative division of the Law but that into Parashiyot. No less interesting is the still more minute description of the Scroll by Meiri, who in 1305 wrote his *Kiryat Sefer*, containing a minute treatment of every letter, nay, of every jot and tittle,

in the sacred Scroll.   He calls every one of these smaller
sections by the ancient name of Parasha, but he knows
nothing of any other division of the Bible or of the
supposed Sedarim.   On the contrary, as far as I am
aware, he is the first to call our usual weekly Portion,
i.e. of the annual cycle, by the name of Seder.

I turn now from the palæographical to the philological
investigation of the word Seder and its use in Rabbinical
literature.   It will be found that in the whole of that
literature—Mishna, Talmud, Agadah—the word Seder has
only one definite meaning, that of order, the succession
of things, facts, deeds, performances, the complex of
actions that follow one another in a definite series.   It
has never been connected with any division or section
referring to the Bible.

There is not one single example which can be adduced, as far as I am aware, to show that it has ever
been taken as equivalent to Parasha, either in the
ancient meaning of the original smaller section, or in
the later development which made that word identical
with the weekly Portion (lesson, perikopes).   It is
necessary to settle this point as clearly as possible ; for
only thus many a misconception will disappear.   I will
take a few examples at random from the Mishna and
Talmud, and it will be seen that the word Seder has
never been used otherwise but as the designation of
order, or sequence.   What can we want more than the
expression " Seder of the Parashiyot," used in Megillah
III. 4 in connection with the discussion of the four
special portions for the four Sabbaths ? and it is furthermore stated (*ibid.*) that they (the Parashiyot) are read
Kesidran, i.e. in their proper " order."   We have the word
Seder Hayom (Mishna Yoma I. 3), meaning the whole
" order " of service for the Day of Atonement ; and
(*ibid.* v. 7) everything is described in proper " order "—
al haseder.   We have Seder Berakhot, " order " of the
blessings and benedictions, in Bera. 48*b*; the " order "
of the blessing after meals (*ibid.*).   We have Seder

Vidui, " order " of confession (*ibid.* 31*a*), Seder Tefilah, the " order " of Prayer (Rosh. Hash. 17*b*). Special stress must be laid on the following citation. When the Talmud wishes to describe the " order " of the books of the Bible (Baba Bathra 14*b*), it speaks of them as the Sidran Shel Nebiim, and Sidran Shel Kethubim, the " order " of the Books of the Prophets and the " order " of the Books of the Holy Writings. The Talmud does not refer here to any internal division called " Seder," but only to the sequence of the books. No less interesting is the reference to the " order " of the creation, which is called Sidrê Bereshit (Sabb. 53*b*, Kethub. 103*b*) ; whilst when these chapters are mentioned as " lessons " in the liturgy they are called Parashiyot, as shown above. We have, furthermore, the Seder of the Maamadot in Taanit III. 7, meaning the " order " of the successive Maamadot, but not referring to the Parashiyot read at the Maamadot. We have Seder Hakeriah, " order " of the reading of the Law, but nothing that would indicate that thereby was meant which special portion of the Law was to be read. It is simply used to describe the " order " in which the people are to be called up—Kohen first, Levite second, and Yisrael third, when the Scroll is taken out for the portion of the day, Sabbath, New Moon, Hanukah, etc. In Yoma 33*a* we find Abbaye arranges the Seder Hama'arakhah, or the " order " of the daily service in the Temple.

Turning to our Prayer Book we find, e.g. in the Mussaf Amidah, " *Temidin kesidran umussafim kehilkhatan,*" where seder and halakhah are used as synonyms ; and in the Ashkenazic form we have also Siddurē Nesakhēha, " order " of its drink-offerings, the form Siddur reminding one of the title " Order of Prayers," i.e. Prayer Book. So far has this word been identified with sequence and proper arrangement of the consecutive order of prayers, that the Prayer Book has got the name Siddur instead of Seder Hatefilah. Compare with this the Syriac name for the Prayer Book, Takhsa, which means "order." It would be easy to multiply examples which would prove one and the same fact, that the word Seder was never used in any other meaning but that of " order," and never applied through the whole of the ancient Talmudic literature either to any portion of the Bible or to any portion of the Law.

On the contrary, this title is employed for non-Biblical Rabbinical literature exclusively, while Parasha served to denote exclusively divisions of the Bible and notably of the Law. It is into Sedarim and not into Parashiyot that the Mishna is divided, and no one has ever used another term to designate the division of the Mishna. Speaking, for instance, of the Seder Moed everyone would at once know that the " order " of the Oral laws referring to the festivals is meant, whilst, for instance, no Parasha has ever been cited by the title Seder. One does not find in the whole literature, Seder Bereschith, Seder Noah, or a Seder Yithro, or any other. The fact that the word Sedarim had been applied exclusively, at any rate during the whole of the Talmudic period, to the compilations of the Oral Law ought at once to put us on our guard when we see the same name applied to the written Law. Moreover, when applied to the Mishna, the word Seder is the general title for a whole series of laws and ordinances which are subdivided into Masekhtot and Perakim. All these are new forms used exclusively in connection with the Oral Law and Rabbinical tradition. The word Seder does not as yet represent a small division, equivalent with the Parasha of the Bible. A long time must elapse and profound changes must take place before such a transfer could be possible ; and, as will be seen later, a change in the meaning attached to this word is due to a different school of thought and belongs to a period when with changed conditions a new significance was attached to older words.

Take now the word Perek, also seldom, if ever, used in connection with the Biblical books. It is applied part exclusively to Rabbinical literature and the same change in the use of the name has taken place many centuries later. Firstly, in the Mishna, the sub-division is called Perek (Perakim). Then we find Pirke Aboth, the "Chapters of the Fathers"; Pirke Hekhalot, "Chapters of the Heavenly Halls." We have Pirke de R. Eliezer, Perakim of R. Jehudah, and so on. They are never called "parasha"; and, on the other hand, none of the divisions of the Bible is ever known or quoted as Perek. Centuries elapsed; the Bible was divided by the Christians into chapters, and then the word Perek was used for this modern non-Jewish division of the Bible. It is found in the Massoretic closing notes of the various books of the printed Bible; but in the Massora we find layers in the terms used, some of extreme antiquity, and others of so recent an origin as these Perakim of the fifteenth or sixteenth century. A term found in Massoretic writings need not be considered as old unless it is proved by other evidence to be of ancient origin. The conclusion from the philological point of view is also obvious. Even if the Bible or Pentateuch would ever have been divided for liturgical purposes into smaller sections, if any proof would have been forthcoming that there was any practice but an annual cycle for the reading, and that there had been in general use another division for a cycle of three years or three and a half years, surely these divisions would have been marked by certain definite names clinging to them as has been shown to be the invariable rule with the weekly portion. No writer, with one single exception, to be noted later, down to comparatively modern times, has identified this division with any liturgical purpose, and has explained the Sedarim to have been introduced for such an aim. But a certain connection has been alleged to exist between the Sedarim and certain Midrashim. It is, therefore, of importance to establish in the first place the relation between the older Agadic compilations with these Sedarim, in order to

see whether such old works as the Mekhilta, Sifra,
Pesikta, etc., had any knowledge or took any cognisance
of these Sedarim. Those who have tried to identify the
Sedarim with the triennial cycle have never asked
themselves in what relation these stand, and have
rather hastily drawn conclusions from premises which
never warranted such conclusions, even if we should
agree that some of the later Midrashim start from
verses which mark the beginning of the so-called
Sedarim. Nothing even then would show that these
Sedarim served the liturgical purpose of an annual, or
still less a triennial, cycle, but would only show that the
Bible or the Pentateuch had been subdivided in an
additional manner. It will then be for us to find out
the reason, if we can, for such subdivision.

If we now examine the Sifra, the oldest of the halachic Midrashim, perhaps contemporary with the Mishna
or perhaps a little older, and in its structural arrangement no doubt going back to the tradition of R. Akiba,
we shall reach a more definite result. The agreement
between the Midrash and the smaller—not the weekly
—Parashiyot is so close as to leave no doubt that no
other division was recognised or known by the author.
The Sifra is divided into eighty sections, and Hoffman,
in his introduction to the Midrashim, shows that certain
portions had been deliberately left out of the Sifra.
The number of these omitted Parashiyot amounted
to fourteen or sixteen. These added to the eighty
would bring up the sum to ninety-six, the exact
number of Parashiyot, Petuhot, and Setumot, into
which Leviticus is divided. No room there for any
Seder, and no trace of any Seder. It is worth while
dwelling here, however briefly, on the terminology used
in the Sifra to designate divisions. It will show that
in addition to Parasha, also Perek is the most constant
term used ; the latter alternating as it were with the
former. In addition to these, other terms are sporadi-
cally used, showing that the terminology was still some-

what fluid, not yet rigidly fixed except in the case of the Parasha. The other terms found in the Sifra are Megillah, as Megillat Meṣora, (col. 134 ed., Venice), Megillat Emor (col. 184), and sometimes Dibbura, an archaic form for parasha (*vide* above), col. 85 and 211 ; once we find the word Sidra (col. 222) at the end of Behar. All these terms seemed to be used more or less promiscuously, and parasha itself sometimes designated a section, sometimes a lesson or perikope, and sometimes merely indicated the contents, such as Parasha Nega'im, Parasha Zabim, similar to Parashat Hamelekh in the Mishna.

An analysis of the Mekhilta may follow. As far as it has been preserved—and very likely it began with the present first chapter—it is divided into nine Masekhtot, and subdivided into smaller Parashiyot. No other term is apparently used. For the larger division the term Masekhet is used, which, as shown above, is applied to the sections of the Mishna, and which is never applied to any Biblical book. Masekhet means " textus "; hence our word text, a web, a thing woven together by the hand of the author. It will be evident that whilst the author of the Mekhilta keeps rigorously to the ancient division of Parashiyot and knows also the Perikope, he had no knowledge of any division of the Bible corresponding with Sedarim. If on one or two occasions the chapter of the Mekhilta begins with the passage where the Seder is now marked, it is a mere coincidence; for on those two occasions the weekly Perikopes begin in the same place (v*b*. and vii.). On the other hand, in three passages the author's division seems to run parallel with that found in the Samaritan Bible, starting from what is now a Samaritan Perikope (Nos. i., vi., vii.). On one occasion the Masekhet comes to an end with the Samaritan Perikope, as in ix*a*. In conformity with the halachic character of this Midrash, those chapters of Exodus which contain no Halacha are omitted in the Mekhilta, such as chapters xxiii. 20 to

XXXI. 11 ; XXXI. 18 to the end of XXXIV., XXXV. 4 to the end of the book, and very likely also chapters I. to XII., these being relegated to the Agadic Midrash. Moreover, it must be pointed out that some of the Masekhtot cover only small sections, such as those to Exodus XVII. 8–16, XXXI. 12–17, and XXV. 1–3. Of these the former contains the episode of Amalek connected especially with Purim, and the last two deal with injunctions concerning the strict observance of the Sabbath. But throughout there is no reference to the Sedarim, and not even a remote agreement with any division into Sedarim. It is obvious that at the time of the composition of the Mekhilta such division did not exist. Passing on from the Mekhilta to the Sifrē, we find here the weekly lessons are clearly marked, but these may be due perhaps to a late hand. On the other hand, it has the minute subdivisions of the text corresponding to a large extent with the division of the Bible into verses; each of these little divisions is called Piska, that is, a small school lesson, an agadic, or halachic interpretation—as the case may be—of one or a few verses together. Of no less consequence will be now an analysis of the Pesikta—the oldest collection of a purely agadic interpretation of the text both of the Law and of the Prophets, as far as they were read as lessons in the service. An examination of the Pesikta will serve also the purpose of bringing out the fact that to the author only one set of Haftarot and Parashiyot was known, and they were all enclosed within an annual cycle. He knew no two Parashiyot for any festival, or, for any one special day, two different Haftarot.

Another cycle (biennial or triennial) would obviously have produced a larger number of Haftarot, and each of these would have formed the subject for a separate homiletical interpretation. But the Pesikta knows only the one universally acknowledged set of lessons and Haftarot. But I will consider the Pesikta here solely

from the point of view of its relation to the Sedarim—
tracing whether there is any connection between them,
and whether the Sedarim lay at the basis, or were the
starting-point of the homilies—more especially because
the Pesikta is of a purely Palestinian origin, and it is
alleged that a triennial cycle was the rule in Palestine,
and that the Sedarim were the divisions of the Bible
in accordance with that cycle. The number of homilies
contained in the Pesikta—which, needless to add, is
also the oldest collection and goes back at least to the
fourth or fifth century—is thirty-two. Of these, thirteen
(XIII.–XXII. and XXIV.–XXVI.) take their text from the
Prophets, being Haftarot; and two (XXIX. and XXXI.)
have no text and will therefore be omitted. Of the
remaining seventeen not one starts from the same verse
as a Seder, unless it is at the same time the beginning
of a Perikope. On all other occasions the starting-
point is the old Parasha or section, and on some occasions,
the weekly Parasha; and what is of special significance,
we find also a remarkable parallel between the Pesikta
and the division into Perikope of the Samaritans. In one
of these instances the Pesikta agrees also with the Mekhilta (No. v.), but in the other two instances (Mekhilta
VI., XII.) the Pesikta is entirely independent and stands
by itself in this agreement. For each of these Pesiktot
we have Talmudic authority, some being already mentioned in the Mishna, others in the Talmud, the Babylonian as well as the Palestinian showing that the reading of these lessons as a fixed tradition goes back to
very ancient times, and was never questioned either in
Palestine or Babylon. From the foregoing examination
no doubt can be left that down to the fifth century at
least the Sedarim did not exist. Such a division of the
Bible in addition to, and superseding, as it were, that
into Parashiyot both as section and Perikope was not
known. It had no connection whatsoever with liturgy.
It was not allowed to be marked by any sign in the
writing of the text, nor did it influence the ancient

exegesis of the Law. Moreover, the legal authorities took no notice of it in laying down the rules for the writing or for the reading of the text. Still the existence of a division not only of the Pentateuch but also of the whole of the Bible into Sedarim cannot be gainsaid. It will be my endeavour to trace the late origin of these Sedarim, and to show the place which they occupy in the history of the text of the Bible and in that of its interpretation. It is for this reason that the examination of Agadic Midrashim in their relation to the Sedarim will be undertaken later.

In addition to the public reading of the Bible, and side by side with it, went the private reading or meditation. The preceding investigation has thus far led us to one result based on the archæological and palæographical facts preserved from ancient times and scattered throughout the whole literature. They all point unmistakably to the existence of only one system of public reading. The technical terms used leave no room for any other interpretation or for the existence of any other way of reading the Law in public, and prove that the system was to read the whole of the Pentateuch from the end of Succoth to the end of Succoth. It would be, however, a grave mistake to assume that the public reading of the Bible was the beginning and end of the use to which the Bible has been put. From a purely historical point of view it is clear that the public reading was only one aspect of the study of the Bible, and that before and concurrent with the public reading, the private reading and study must have been a universal practice. Whilst in Deuteronomy it is enjoined that the King should read the Bible (or such portions of it as were prescribed according to the tradition) once in every seven years to the assembled people, in the Bible the command of reading and meditating on the Law was repeated ever and anon. It is out of this private reading that the public reading grew; for it is not easy to assume that every Jew was sufficiently educated to

read the Bible for himself, and therefore the public
reading was instituted to assist in the fulfilment of
that duty, and to make the Book better known among
the masses. It would be almost superfluous to quote
here all the passages in the Bible where reference to
the reading and study of the Law is mentioned or
emphasised. From the first command to Joshua
(chap. I. 8) to the dying exhortation of David to Solomon (I Kings II. 3), almost to the last words of the
prophet Malachi and the most important public action
of Ezra (Neh. VIII. 8), all record the same fact, the reading
of the Bible in public and in private ; and the whole
of the later development rests and turns exclusively on
the study and application of the Law. From 1 Maccabees (I. 56 f.) we learn that many private persons
were possessed of books of the Law, which, by the order
of the King Antiochus, were rent and then burned by
fire. No doubt these were Bibles in the possession of
private persons who used them for their private reading.
I might in passing refer also to the " Sefer " of R. Meir,
a famous private model codex of the Law. So much
was " reading " identified with the reading of the Bible
that to the Pentateuch the very name " Mikra," i.e.
" the reading book," was given. The Bible was, in the
true sense, the textbook of the people. In this sense
our sages have interpreted the word that occurs in
Nehemiah, and they state that Ezra read . . . " bami-
kra " " in the Law " (Meg. 3a).

It is interesting to follow up the use of the word
Kara in the old Rabbinic literature, where we find it
almost exclusively used for Bible-reading. When,
however, the Mishna or the Oral Law is mentioned as
being read, another verb was substituted ; "tana" or
"shana."* In Mishna Yoma I. 6 the word Kara is used
to denote that the High Priest read the portion of the
Bible, and it is said that, in case he did not know how
to read, they taught him. Surely the High Priest

---

* Cf. Ket. 17a of one who read the Bible and studied the Mishna ;
dekarē vetanē.

could not have been an uneducated man : but though
the Hellenising priests may have had a very good
general Greek culture, they might not have been equally
well versed in the Hebrew reading of the Law. In
various parts of the Mishna (Meg. II. and III.) the very
same verb is used for the reading of the Megillah—the
Hebrew Scroll. The expression " keriat shema," the
private recitation morning and evening of the three
sections of the Bible known as Shemă (Deut. VI. 4–9,
XI. 13–24 ; Num. XV. 37–41), has become quite a
technical term, and occurs ever so many times in this
stereotyped form. It is unnecessary to multiply examples,
for the word is never used in any other meaning throughout the Mishna and Talmud except for reading the Law
in public as well as in private. To teach a man the
Bible was called " makrē," which does not mean simply
to teach him to read, but to teach him the Bible, as
is made clear by Ned. IV. 3. The meaning of the word
" mikra " was occasionally extended even to a small
portion of the Bible, not an entire volume, but a text
or portion of it (Sota IV. 2 ; Yeb. 11b), and in numerous passages the technical rule is laid down that no
" mikra " loses its original meaning whatever another
interpretation may put into it (Sanhed. 34a, 101a ;
Sota 14b, etc.). A Biblical scholar was called Kara,
that is, the " read one " (Kiddush 49b). Hence the
name of the Karaites, who call themselves Benē Mikra,
the children, or faithful followers, of the Mikra. A
man who calls himself Kara is a man who could read
(i.e. he knows) the Law, the Prophets, and the Holy
Writings. The development went even further, and a
verse of the Bible was then called Kera, a thing or piece
read. The original meaning of the reading had so
entirely been forgotten that this name was applied to
the verse. It is an alternate name for " katub," the
latter derived from the root " katab," to write. Hence it
often occurs in the Mishna and the Talmud. In the
ancient exegetical rules (in the Boraitha), R. Ishmael

uses this term exclusively to denote the verse. Kera as the " read " verse occurs in this meaning very often in the Talmudic literature (Berachot 2a; Sanhed. 45b, 71a; Moed. Kaṭ. 3b, etc.). This was the only name by which a verse of the Bible is described as such and quoted in the Mishna and in the Talmud. The application of the root Kara only and solely to the reading of the Law, is in itself a proof sufficient to show how universal the practice was. It is also of importance to notice here that Pasuk never means, or could mean, a verse in the Talmud. We shall presently deal with this expression, but for the time being it is sufficient to establish this practice of private reading and to show that it is very old, and that it had developed its own terminology differentiating its practice from any other reading or study. It was a devotional and didactic reading in the house, in the family, and in the school.

A statement in the Talmud makes it a law that a man is to finish his Parashiyot with the people, that is, he is to make his private reading concurrent with the public reading, not allowing the people to go ahead, but to keep pace with the public reading (Berachot 8a). We are also told that the teacher and the children may prepare their Parashiyot by lamplight (Tosefta Sabbath I. 12; Sabb. 13b), on which occasion the expression " Mesader Parashiyot " is used, which we must bear in mind. It shows that the pupils and teacher had to arrange their Parashiyot according to a definite order (Seder). We are told that R. Simeon ben Joḥai left no Parasha in the Torah which he had not studied (Sukka 25a). So important was the private reading of the Law that every man was expected to perform it every day, and to repeat the same blessing as when called up to read the Law in public. This practice has been retained to our very day. Small sections of the Law are read every morning, and the blessing is said in the earlier part of the daily service. A similar blessing is said on the Prophets when read as Haftarah.

The oldest examples of these blessings are found when the High Priest read the Law to the people on the Day of Atonement (*v.* above).   In order that the reading of the Holy Writings should not interfere with the reading of the Law and the Prophets and with the homiletical interpretation during the public worship, it was not allowed to read the Holy Writings during the Morning Service, or to meditate on them in the same manner. Yet in spite of this desire of keeping every part of the Bible in its proper place during the service, we find none the less that, whenever a man started reading the Holy Writings, he still was expected to say the blessing mentioned in Soferim XIII. 1.   This principle of private devotion and of continuous reading of the Law had become more and more a universal practice.   In the course of centuries it was extended from the Law proper to the Mishna and Talmud, and later to the mystical literature.   The original short ꞏ Maamadot, used only by the respective Mishmarot, became afterwards of general use, and the Maamadot already in the Siddur of Rav Amram* of the ninth or tenth century were extended over the seven days of the week, and additional pieces were added to them taken from the Rabbinical literature.

This was a natural development.   As already remarked, the principle which underlies the development of Jewish history, liturgy, Law, etc., is to preserve the old and to build upon it, enlarging and developing. Nothing that once had been the possession of the people was discarded, but if circumstances changed it was put to a different use.   The reading of the Bible had been, however, so engrained in the conscience and practice of the people, that it could only go on expanding and developing on the lines laid down by tradition and usage. Daily study and daily prayer went hand in hand, but study was considered superior.   A Beth ha-midrash enjoined greater respect and greater sanctity than

* *v.* Baer Abodat Israel Rödelheim, 1868, page 495 and note.

Beth ha-keneset—the school stood higher than the synagogue. "One may sell a synagogue to build a school, but one may not sell a school to build a synagogue." The mere study of the portions referring to sacrifices was equivalent to the bringing of them. Such is the Jewish Law. There is no need to dwell here on the deep attachment of the people to the practice which familiarised them with the contents of the Bible. In order to facilitate the understanding they did not shrink from adding the recital of the Targum—the lingua vulgare of the time. When that Targum or Aramaic translation became still more popular, and owing to the influence of Arabic domination was threatened with extinction, it also became somewhat of a holy language. This Targum developed later on into a more paraphrastic translation. The only points which I wish to note here are the slow expansion from translation into paraphrastic legend and homily, and the fact that each verse was read three times, twice in Hebrew and once in Aramaic. This recurrence of the figure three is very notable. It seems to play a very definite rôle in the history of the Bible in the synagogue. Not only is the Bible divided into three sections—the Law, the Prophets, and the Holy Writings—but the Bible is read by the Maamad three times daily. Each one reads at least three verses. The Bible is, moreover, read three times publicly during the week—on Saturday, Monday, and Thursday. Three persons are called up to the Law, representing the three divisions, Kohen, Levite, and Yisrael. Every verse must be read practically three times, twice in Hebrew and once in Targum. The Samaritans read their Parasha three times during the Sabbath—evening, morning, and midday (Ramsha, safra, and sehrem— this is their pronunciation of our sahoraim). One might mention here the repetition of Psalm cxlv. three times daily, not to speak of the thrice holy in the Kedushah.

The private reading was certainly not limited only

to the Law. It must have extended, in ancient times, over the whole of the Bible. It is quite true that in the public service, only the Law and the Prophets were allowed to be read; and nothing was allowed to intervene between these readings and the homiletic exposition which accompanied the reading: and with it, more or less, the service was brought to a close. It is for this reason that the Holy Writings were excluded; but we find that after Minḥa on the Sabbath it was allowed to read the Holy Writings. And, moreover, as mentioned above, a special blessing had to be said before the recital of these Writings. And this reading must have been half private, half public, more or less connected with the homiletical exposition in the afternoon, in which the Law, the Prophets, and the Holy Writings were equally represented. A Midrash has come down to us of uncertain date, though of late origin, called Agadat Bereshit, in which this three-fold reading has been preserved. The book contains eighty-four chapters composed of groups of three paragraphs each, in which the text for the first of the groups is taken for the homiletical exposition from the Law, for the second from the Prophets, and for the third from the Holy Writings, mostly Psalms. Here we have a proof for the further development of private reading and homiletical exposition in conjunction with the public reading. To this very day a remnant of the practice has been preserved, at any rate in the Sephardic rite. On Sabbath afternoon, at the conclusion of the Minḥa Service, three verses are read from the Parasha of the next week, although a large section had been read out of the scroll during the service. It is thus practically repeated. Then three verses are read from the Prophets, i.e. from the Haftarah of next week, and from the Holy Writings Psalm cxxxiv. is recited; or instead, three verses from the Megillot before the seasons of the year on which these are read in full. Other verses, among them two doxologies, are recited before and after the reading. In olden times the Targum to these verses was also recited, which was later replaced by the Spanish translation of the Targum, thus giving it fully the character of the study combined with the homiletical interpretation by the Meturgeman.

When an equal position was granted to the Oral Law in private study and reading, the Rabbis enjoined that a man should divide his time into three sections, and he should devote one third to the Torah (Bible), another to the Mishna, and a third to the Gemarah (Kiddushin, 30). In accordance with this principle, even in our prayers the first part of the service is made to contain portions from the Torah, Mishna, and Gemarah, by which means we are fulfilling this command of daily study, and at the conclusion of this section we say the proper Kaddish de-Rabbanan. The preeminence given to three is seen also in the " threefold blessing " of the priests, which may have been the starting-point. But the people obviously never rested content with the obligatory public reading of the Law three times only during the week, and the system of daily private readings was slowly evolved. It is best seen in the subdivision of the Psalter into thirty daily sections. Further systems of reading had accordingly been arranged extending over the year in which the Pentateuch was to be read. It was subdivided into daily lessons. Such a system of reading—extending over the whole year, and following the order of the Parashiyot or weekly lessons, and containing portions from the Law, the Prophets, the Holy Writings, Mishna, Talmud, Midrash, and Zohar—has been elaborated by Portaleone in his *Shilte Haggibborim*, Part III, f. 133*b*–170*a*, for every night of the year; and in the Ḥok Le Yisrael, by Ishak Barukh, each Parash is so arranged in daily readings that it is completed in the week in complete accordance with the statement of the Talmud. Each day contains lessons from the Law, the Prophets (Hebrew and Targum), the Holy

Writings, Mishna, Halakha, Zohar, and in later editions Mussar, providing thus a complete cycle of lessons for every day of the year.

The private reading was not confined to the house. Reading and study go hand in hand, for it was a reading with the object of imbibing the eternal truths of the Holy Writ. The Bible formed the basis of all education, and what was done at home was merely a reflex of what was done at school or the continuation of the education. The daily lesson was given at school, whilst the daily reading was afterwards continued at home, and it must have been the endeavour of the teacher, as it has been for so many centuries, to keep pace at school with the service in the synagogue, and to teach the boys always the Parasha of the week, so that they might be well prepared to follow the reading in the synagogue and to benefit by the homiletical interpretation which followed the public reading. The weekly portion must therefore have been divided into smaller sections for each day of the week, coinciding more or less with the private reading. It would be difficult to establish exactly these divisions for the reading and study. The arrangements of Barukh and Portaleone are of too late a date, and seem to be of too artificial a character to be a guide for that purpose. We may be able to find some traces later on for some such division of a purely homiletical didactic nature not liturgical; but it is first necessary to establish the fact that in addition to the division into Parashiyot, there was also another division which respected and preserved the older division into small sections, but divided the text according to its own needs and for its own purpose.

A name has come down to us for such a division which has often been misinterpreted. I mean the name Piska or Pasuk, the former the Aramaic, the latter the Hebrew term. This name changed in the course of time according to the new practice to which it had been put owing to the development of the Massora. A new meaning had been given to it at a much later period, just as was the case with Perek and even with Parasha ; and the word Pasuk was identified with " verse." It has been shown above that the real name for verse in the Talmudic period was Kera or Katub. At a later time the word Pasuk, when its real meaning had been forgotten together with the use to which it had been put in the older schools, became obsolete, and, as it meant division, it was taken over by the Massorites to denote the verse. It cannot originally have meant " verse," because the Bible was not yet divided into Massoretic verses, and it is the exact word corresponding with the Samaritan Ḳiṣṣa, division or section. There are many indications that the original meaning of the word was a section. It would explain what has hitherto remained somewhat of a riddle, and which had been taken as a proof for the very great antiquity of the Massoretic division of the text into verses. When we find in the Talmud (Hag. 15a), or even later, that Aher the scholar, or Neron the Emperor, or Haman are said to ˙have asked the boy coming home from the school to recite his Pasuk, hitherto translated verse, considering that the reply was seldom limited to one verse, and that the pupils were not expected to study in school only one verse during the day, the old interpretation cannot be correct ; but if it is understood that the boy was to quote something out of the Piska, of the *section* or daily lesson which he had studied, the difficulty is removed. And again, the Pissuk te'amim mentioned in the Talmud, which has been taken to mean the division according to accents, though such accents had not yet been invented, will now be fully explained : for it means a division of the text according to its contents, according to the Taam, in complete agreement with the definition of the word " taam "—contents—used throughout in the Talmudic literature. This corresponds with the principle of the division of the Bible described before, guided by the

" contents " of the text. We shall now better understand the meaning of Pesikta, to which reference has
already been made above ; and the reason why in
some of the ancient Halachic and Midrashic works the
section finished with the words Selik Piska. This agadic
interpretation refers not to one verse, but to the whole
section, of which only the first verse is quoted.

From the minute examination of the word Seder and
of the use of it from a palæographical and philological
point of view, as well as from the relation between a
supposed different division of the Law, called Sedarim,
and the ancient Midrashim as well as from the practice
and use of the synagogue, the house, and the school,
it is evident that a division such as is identified with
Sedarim did not exist up to a very late period. On the
other hand, it is perfectly clear that the practice of
private study and homiletic interpretation brought
about a subdivision of the text quite independent of
the liturgy and public reading. It is then, no doubt, and
that at a very late period, that probably the word
standing as a kind of abbreviation for Seder haparashiyot, the " order " of the Parashiyot, or Seder
Ha-limmud, the " order " of study, was used to denote
these divisions of the text into three weekly portions.
Such a division must have been originally identical
with the Piska, but as that word had already assumed
a different meaning, rather that of verse than section, the
other short expression—Seder—probably took its place.
This division for purely homiletical and didactic purposes is preserved more or less clearly in the Later
Midrashim, such as Yelamdenu, Tanhuma, and Rabbot.
It must be clearly understood that though there is a
close connection between these Midrashim and the subdivision or the larger subdivision of the weekly Parasha,
that does not prove that it stood in any connection
whatsoever with the public reading of the Law. It is
obvious that the homiletical interpretation could not
cover, in any one week, the whole of the weekly lesson.

No preacher could explain more than one small text, and no audience could be found to listen to an exposition going on for hours. There is no Parasha in these Midrashim which it would not take a long time to read, and much more time would be required to fully expound and explain by word of mouth all that is condensed in the written record. A division of the material was an obvious necessity, and the agadist or the interpreter—the preacher—started as a rule from one of the smaller Parashiyot (the closed or open section) with which the Sedarim in most cases coincide. On other and rare occasions he started with a verse which is now marked as a Seder. Even as late a compilation as the Agadat Bereshit shows still some independence of the division into Sedarim, for it just as often agrees with that division as it disagrees, and when it agrees in most cases " seder " and " parasha " are co-equal terms. The word seder or sedarim, therefore, denotes the agadic or didactic division of the Pentateuch. In fact, we find that the school is called Sidra, and the term in Leviticus Rabba, Resh Sidra, as head of the school, corresponding to the later Resh Metibta and Resh Kallah, fully bears out this interpretation. Looked upon from this point of view many of the difficulties which these Sedarim present, if taken as the weekly lesson, would instantly disappear. We shall then be able to understand better the peculiar discrepancy in the size of these Sedarim, to which reference has already been made. Why should certain Sedarim be limited to seven or eight verses and others be as long as two or three chapters ? Then why should some of these Sedarim begin in the middle of a Parasha ? It arises from the permission granted by the sages to the teacher to start his Piska, or Seder, wherever it suited him best, and as for the length, it will be observed that those chapters of the Bible which are either lessons for special Sabbaths, Festivals, or Holy Days, and therefore the subject of a special homiletical interpretation, e.g. the Pesikata, were no longer made the subject of the regular Sabbatical homiletical interpretation. The agadist could be satisfied to pass it over almost entirely, and the teacher could equally deal with it almost at one stretch, for these chapters were also the special readings in the service of the festive seasons. Other small chapters contain certain biographical details which became the centre and nucleus of a large cycle of legends. They stood by themselves, as it were, and a small section like that in Genesis xxII. would suffice for an agadist for more than one homily if necessary. It will be remembered that when discussing the Mekhilta, I drew attention to the difference in the size of the various Masekhtot, some of which were very small. The principle in both cases is exactly the same. The explanation given for the difference in the size of the Sedarim holds good also for that of the Mekhilta, with which it runs parallel. We shall therefore be able to understand better the number of the Sedarim for the whole of the Bible : for they must be taken as a whole together. Unfortunately the markings of the divisions in the Midrashim of the prophetical books and of the Holy Writings seem to have been obliterated. In our manuscripts and printed editions they are made to coincide with the divisions of the Bible, even with the latest. Just as there is no fixed tradition about Parashiyot in the Prophets and Hagiographa, so there is no tradition affecting the Midrashim based upon these texts. But we cannot fail to recognise in the figures preserved to us as to the number of the Sedarim the same division of the whole Bible for a threefold weekly study as is preserved in the Agadat Bereshit. The whole of the Bible is divided into 462 Sedarim, that is three times three readings a week, each consisting of three portions, Law, Prophets, and Hagiographa. In this calculation, of course, we have to reckon also the Leap Years, which have four weeks more, and for which provision had to be made, hence the fluctuation in the number assigned to the Pentateuch. It will be found thus that the real origin of the Sedarim must be sought in the school-room rather than in the synagogue. With this agrees also the late appearance in our literature of the word Sedarim with this meaning, which owes, no doubt, its origin to the Massoretic school that was anxious to find a word to designate this general division of the whole Bible. The word then appears for the first time, as far as I have been able to trace it, in the treatise Soferim (XVI. 10). The connection in which it appears is highly instructive.

The incident related in the Jer. Talmud of Rab. Joshua b. Levi (v. above) finding in a book of Agadah that the Law was divided into 175 Parashiyot, is here repeated, but enriched by the additional words, " and for this reason we have fixed them as Sedarim." It was in a book of Agadah (i.e. of homilies) that R. Levi found the Law divided into 175 sections, and to these sections at a late period the name Sedarim was given. The whole rests on a homiletical and agadic incident, and the explanatory gloss in Soferim comes, no doubt, from the School of the Massorites. Another reference to the Sedarim is alleged to have been found in the passage in the Sheeltot, chapter I., and is contained, let it be noted, also in a legend or agadah referring to the punishment of the wicked in Gehinnom during the week. It is said that the Sabbath rest of the wicked finishes at a certain period " when the Israelites completed their Sedarim " ; and this word has been taken to refer to the peculiar division of the Bible identified with that name. Anyone who had glanced at the passage in the Sheeltot would have found that nothing could be stranger than such an inter-pretation ; for the author continues to explain : " when the Israelites had reached the Sedarim of the going out of the Sabbath," meaning thereby the last verses of Psalm XC. and the whole of XCI., which precede the Kiddusha De Sidra, i.e. the Kiddusha in *Uba Le Sion*. But this legend does not stand alone. There are many parallels to it, one incomplete in Sanhed. 65b, another more complete in Tanḥuma Exodus Ki Tissa, paragraph 33, and a much more archaic and complete form in my Exempla of the Rabbis, No. xv., pp. 13 and 14, where the real translation of the passage reads: "when the Israelites finished the order (seder) of the service, including prayer, lessons, reading, and homilies." The reference to Job x. 22, taken from the Talmud Sotah 49a, is merely an allegorical interpretation, or a play upon words. The fact that this homiletical interpretation occurs already in the Talmud shows that there is not the slightest reference to any Bible lessons, and those who have based their argument on the Sheeltot have undoubtedly gone astray. It is not until we reach the En Hakoreh, a Massoretic grammatical treatise of the fifteenth or sixteenth century (South Arabian), that we find, and perhaps there alone, a clear identification of the title Sedarim with the division of the Bible in lessons arranged to suit a three-year cycle.*

A long space of time, however, had intervened between the Sheeltot and this other passage ; and before leaving the historical investigation of the Sedarim it is worth while pointing out further changes which have taken place in the use of this term. It must be mentioned that Ben Asher, the famous Massorite, the author of the model codex on which Maimonides relied, who is also the author of the oldest Massoretic treatise, *Dikduke Hate‘amim*, does not use the word Sedarim, as, in fact, no one did until the time of the " En Hakoreh " and Jacob ben Ḥayim (sixteenth century). Meanwhile, a certain confusion had arisen through the promiscuous use of the various terms for denoting divisions of the Bible; especially when each of the seven portions of the weekly lesson was also called Parasha. This word, then, had a threefold or fourfold meaning:

* I must add that I have searched in vain for the statement in the edition of Derembourg. I have not found the passage ; only Ginsburg gives it in his *Introduction to the Bible* (page 32).

the general division according to subject; the small division into open and closed sections; the larger division into weekly portions or lessons; and again, the small divisions of the weekly portion. The technical use in the legal compilations was reserved to the scholar, but for the popular use some arrangement had to be made, and whilst the Sephardim have kept the name Parasha for the weekly lesson, among other sections of the Jewish nation the name Seder or Sidra, practically an abbreviation of Seder Haparashiyot, became the common name for the weekly lesson. Parasha was then used for each of the seven sections of the Seder, and to this day the Sedra is the only name by which the weekly lesson is known among the Ashkenazic Jewry.

Before dealing with the supposed three-year cycle with which the Sedarim were alleged to have been identified or connected, it is advisable to recapitulate briefly the results which I have thus far obtained, for, if there is neither a palæographical trace of an ancient division of the Law into Sedarim, if there are no rules for the writing, if the name of Seder or Sedarim is on no occasion used in any other meaning but " order," especially " order of reading " and " order of study," if the ancient Midrashim were shown to be entirely independent of any such division agreeing with the Sedarim, if the division refers merely to the later practice of school reading and homiletical exposition, there is no room in the liturgy for such a division, and there has never been any connection between this division of a purely Massoretic and late origin with any public reading of the Law on Sabbaths and fixed seasons. Far from being an ancient division preceding that into weekly lessons, it was very late and of an ephemeral character. Nothing can therefore be based on this modern division to prove the existence of a three-year cycle, still less that it has ever been countenanced in Palestine over a large area, in great communities, and for a long period of time.

I turn now to the evidence which has been adduced to prove the existence of such a cycle. It will be found that there is only one reference in the whole of the Talmudic and Rabbinic literature to a supposed cycle of three years. In the Babylonian Talmud (Megilla 29a) a discussion is carried on as to the way in which the portion of Shekalim should be read at the beginning of the month of Adar. Rab. Tobi (Tobias) says the people of Maʻaraba (Bʼnei Maʻaraba) finish the Law in three years. It is doubtful whether Maʻaraba—as has hitherto been assumed—means always only Palestine and the whole of Palestine. The real meaning of the word is the " west," and it may just as well apply to any locality between Babylon and Jerusalem. It is well known that profound differences existed in many ways between almost every one of the large centres of Jews in these places, even between towns so close together as Sura, Pumpadita, and Nehardea. In Babylon itself various schools existed which differed on legal and, later on, on Massoretic questions, each one having its own teachings and traditions, even in matters Biblical. Equally profound are the differences between the various Massoretic schools in Galilee (Tiberius). The statement of Rab. Tobi is a mere *obiter dictum* of a man living at a great distance from Palestine. He himself may not have seen the practice at all, and he was telling it either from mere hearsay or in reference to one or another of those scattered Minhagim, which flourished so abundantly among the Jews of Palestine and Babylon. It was the very soil from which numerous Jewish sects sprang. They already existed there from olden times, and became more prominent later when the Karaite movement assumed such large proportions. We dare not, therefore, put into a single statement of this kind more than the author may have meant, as all the evidence adduced hitherto points to the contrary conclusion, and no other is found to support the former. Such an isolated statement is just as little proof for the general practice as, for example, the passage quoted by Muller (note 25 to Soferim x. 8), that according to the statement of "Rabbotenu Shebe-Ma'araba," "seven or eight persons are sufficient for Minyan at Barekhu and Kaddish," a practice of which nobody has ever heard and of which no other trace is found. What is further very interesting is that even for this alleged three years' cycle there is no uniformity. According to the Hilluf Minhagim—a very late compilation of uncertain date—in which the differences between Babylon and Palestine are set down, it is expressly stated that they used to read the Torah not in three years, but in three and a half years, and that they celebrated Simhat Torah on whatever Sabbath the finishing of the reading of the Law happened to occur. Moreover, it is stated that the custom of one village was not the custom of another village. This reminds one very strongly of the Mohammedan calendar, according to which the Ramadan is continually shifting through all the months of the year. The statement of a three and a half years' cycle runs counter directly to the statement in the Talmud, where Rab. Tobi speaks only of a three years' cycle, and let it be noted in addition that the mention of the three and a half years' reading dates probably from the ninth or tenth century, when almost every community was split up into warring sects, each with its own tradition and Minhag.

Thus far the three or three and a half years' cycle rests on doubtful references. The commentaries of Rab. Hananel and Rashi throw no further light on the passage in the Talmud. As commentators they merely endeavour to explain the meaning of the text without questioning its authenticity ; but the words of Rab. Hananel are very instructive. He says that "they divide the weekly Parasha into three sections," and he uses the word "posekin," that is, they make three Piska (or Pisikata) of each portion. He does not mention

Sedarim, and the actual division of the Sedarim certainly does not agree with such a division of the weekly lesson into three equal portions. The only one who refers to the practice more positively is Benjamin of Tudela, who says that in Cairo there existed two synagogues, one of the people of Palestine and one of the people of Babylon. The latter read the Law once during the year, and the other read it in three years, but on Shabuoth and Simḥat Torah the latter joined the former in the service in the synagogue. This is again a new version contrary to the Hilluf, and bearing out the peculiar vagaries of the Jewish communities at that time. Benjamin does not describe it as an eye-witness, he merely relates what he was told. I do not wish to imply that no such practice existed in a solitary synagogue. My contention is that it was only an isolated practice and certainly of a late date. It was not a generally recognised practice among the Jews of Palestine. This very statement of Benjamin proves it to have been a solitary instance, for Benjamin had just travelled throughout the length and breadth of Palestine. He describes the local customs very minutely and all the institutions he had visited. He is one of the oldest travellers who visited the Samaritans in Nablus, and gives us a vivid description of their synagogue and their life. If therefore it had really been a Palestinian custom he would have dealt at some length with it in his description of Palestine, or at least referred to it, and would not have mentioned it as a curiosity in one of the synagogues of Cairo. Cairo, it must be remembered, was the centre where many sects of Jews, Samaritans, Karaites, nondescripts lived together and often fought. No wonder if among them one synagogue existed with its own peculiar ways. But of how they divided and how they read the Bible no trace has been left.

Maimonides, who lived soon afterwards in Cairo, refers also to this custom rather contemptuously in Hilkut Tefilah, chapter XIII., paragraph 1, where he simply says—after stating that the annual cycle was the only established custom throughout Jewry—that there are some who read the Torah in three years, but this is not an accepted custom. He, of course, chronicled and tabulated whatever was found as a definite statement in the Talmud ; but though he records it, he none the less adds to it the qualifying statement that it was not a Minhag Pashut. He, moreover, may have heard of it as a local custom in Cairo ; he does not even refer to the place where it was done, and simply mentions it to condemn it. It is sufficient, then, to point to the way in which Abraham, the son of Maimonides, refers to the people who follow such a practice as ignorant, arrogant men who deliberately alter the Law.* We have reached now the last evidence, and the only one in which the Sedarim are mentioned in connection with this supposed three years' cycle—the reference in the En Hakorēh. This is a grammatical treatise preceding some of the manuscripts written in Yemen.

A careful examination of the work will reveal the fact that the author shared in the veneration of Maimonides with the Jews of Yemen. He simply copies the word from Maimonides, and he uses the same vague phraseology (" There are some who read the Bible once in three years ") without saying who these people were, without referring to Palestine as the home of this practice, without any hint as to how or where this practice obtained. He does not even mention Cairo, although the Jews in Yemen stood in close contact with the Jews of Cairo. Moreover, the Yemenite MSS., to which this treatise serves as an introduction, though they mark the Sedarim on the margin like so many other Massoretic signs, divide the text into perikopes in accordance with the annual cycle ; and no notice is taken of any other system of reading the Bible but the annual cycle through the rest of this Biblical treatise. It is clear that the author of the Ēn Hakorēh simply

* v. Büchler in J.Q.R., Vol. V, 1893, page 420.

refers to the Massoretic notice, which he interpreted in his own way, forgetting that the rest of the Bible is also divided by the Massorites into Sedarim without any reference whatsoever to any liturgical use. Now this is the sum total of the entire tradition in the whole of the Jewish literature for the existence of the so-called three years' or three and a half years' cycle. We can see now that it may have been a custom practised in sporadic synagogues and among Jewish sectarians who flourished down to the thirteenth or fourteenth century. The so-called Zadokite documents, published recently by Dr. Schechter, in addition to the testimonies of Seadyah in his Emunoth Ve-deoth and Shaharastani, give us an insight into Jewish sectarial life, of which those who believe that the development of Judaism has been running on smoothly like an undisturbed stream have scarcely been aware. To such a sect many vagaries may have commended themselves, but, basing our investigation upon the clear evidence of facts, there is not a single proof that a three years' cycle had ever been the practice in Palestine, or that it had been known in antiquity. That the Bible had ever been divided to serve such a purpose is nothing but pure imagination, and the study of the Sedarim themselves disproves the possibility that they represent such a division used for liturgical purposes. The whole tradition is unanimous that the Law had been read once a year, that the basis of the weekly perikope rests upon a very old division of the text which has been retained throughout the ages. It has been preserved in the Hebrew, Greek, and Samaritan Bible, and the annual cycle is the only one recognised by Jews, Samaritans, Karaites, and Christians alike. Any deviation from this ancient and time-hallowed institution would be an arbitrary enactment, for which no justification can be claimed in tradition and practice.

APPENDIX

THE SAMARITAN CALENDAR

I AM publishing here for the first time a complete Samaritan Calendar. From Scaliger in the sixteenth to de Sacy in the nineteenth century many attempts have been made to obtain a complete copy of the Samaritan Calendar, but all in vain. Various astronomical tables have found their way into the Crawford Collection ·now incorporated with the Rylands Library in Manchester, and a few more similar MSS. are to be found in my collection. But these do not give us a clue to the actual religious calendar.

The religious year was not the object of those investigations, nor do the astronomical tables contain the slightest hint as to the manner in which the Festivals are kept, or the liturgy arranged.

Codd. Harl. 5481, Harl. 5495 of the British Museum, is also of no help in either of these directions. It deals neither with the principle of the astronomical calculations of the Samaritans, nor with the religious divisions of the time. It contains mostly chronological indications with introduction taken from old liturgical hymns. Not one, in fact, as far as I am aware, has hitherto had access to such a Samaritan Calendar arranged for practical purposes and on the lines of the usual calendar.

At my request such a Calendar for the year 1329 of the Hegira (Mohammedan Era), which corresponds with August, 1910,–July, 1911, was prepared for me by the High Priest. In addition to this Manuscript, Cod. 1150, of my collection I have another Calendar (Cod. No. 858) arranged only for nine months, with somewhat more ample rubrics referring to the religious ceremonies. A third one (Cod. No. 857) is arranged for fifteen months, but is very brief; a mere pocket edition with the scantiest possible information. A number of other MSS., with astronomical tables such as Codd. 820, 1148, 1149, complete my collection of Samaritan calendars and astronomical tables.

The principle according to which the Calendar is calculated by the Samaritans is considered to be a "mystery" (just like the Jewish Sod Ha'ibbur) revealed by God to Adam, and then transmitted by Adam to Noah, the Patriarchs and Moses. It was then handed on to Pinehas the High Priest, son of Eleazar, who calculated it on the meridian of Sichem, and has thenceforward been preserved as a mystery by the successive High Priests unto this very day. The tradition is found in the closing chapter of the Samaritan Book of Joshua, edited by me, and in the oldest Chronicle, the Tolidoth ed. Neubauer.

No European scholars seem to have elucidated the Samaritan Calendar. Among my MSS. there is the Arabic work of Jakub ibn Ishak ibn Jakub ibn Abulfaraj (Cod. 1147), a writer of uncertain date (sixteenth to seventeenth century), who deals exhaustively with the Heshban Kushta, the *true* calculation as they call their calendar. In the first part he gives the traditional history of the Samaritan Calendar and in the second the theory and the practice of its calculation.

It is not here the place to follow these points further up. I mention them only to show to those who are interested in the history of the Samaritan Calendar and the comparative study of these systems that new and, to my mind, ample materials are now within easy reach.

One cannot speak of the Calendar of the Jews, Samaritans and other sects without being reminded of the extraordinary importance attached to these calculations. They are the corner stone, nay, the pivot round which all the heresies revolve. The fundamental differences between the sects turn mostly round the Calendar, and the history of the first centuries of the Christian Church knows equally fierce battles waged round the fixing of dates and settling of the Calendar. With these we have, however, now nothing to do here. The object of publishing this Calendar is principally to exemplify the division of the Law by the Samaritans into Weekly Lessons, and to show the exact manner in which the reading of the Bible had been adjusted by them to the seasons of the year, how the Festivals fare, and incidentally how the annual cycle works out on Samaritan ground. Other details of importance have been included. I therefore reproduce the Calendar practically in its entirety. I have only omitted the intermediate counting of the days of the weeks, which are of no importance whatever and can easily be supplied by any intelligent reader. The Sabbaths are indicated by *v*. With the exception of these figures *every other* item found in the Calendar has been reproduced. The MS. is of small size, but calligraphically though minutely written. The facsimile represents the exact size of the two pages 3 and 4. The Calendar is arranged according to the Mohammedan months, no doubt for practical purposes. Living among the Mohammedans their Calendar is for the Samaritans their Civil Calendar; they must regulate their daily life in accordance with it. The heading therefore contains the astronomical determination of the Mohammedan New Moon and the corresponding date of the Greek or Christian Calendar is given, and curiously enough in accordance with the Old, i.e. the Julian style. The Gregorian Calendar or New Style is added. The former is called Rumi, that is the Byzantine or Greek and also the Old Style, and the other is called the New or modern calculation (Ḥesban) or Style.

The Samaritan month is not mentioned by name but by the numeral, whilst the usual Hebrew names are used by the Samaritans to denote the months of the solar year. As I am dealing with these points elsewhere it is sufficient to have mentioned them for the understanding of the Calendar. I have transliterated the Calendar in its entirety from the Samaritan characters into the Hebrew, and I have reproduced, first, all the headings, then the dates being arranged in four columns. I have on each occasion given *all* the four figures: 1st, the day of the week (Sunday, Monday, etc.); 2nd, the Mohammedan date of the month, which day in the month it was; 3rd, the date according to the Old Style—the Julian; 4th, the date of the New Style—the Gregorian. The comparison between these dates is thus made easy.

In addition to these four columns there is in the MS. a large space devoted to entries affecting the religious life of the Samaritans. The lessons of the Sabbaths, the dates of the Festivals, the New Moons and other important items bearing on their religious conceptions and practices. All these entries have been faithfully reproduced. We can see here week by week how they divided the Law and also the occasions on which the weekly Perikope was omitted and other Lessons substituted.

I have also reproduced all the astronomical entries about the New Moon, when it happened, at which hour and what fraction of the hour and the day it happened. I shall not dwell on these, for they offer quite an unexpected problem. It will be seen, namely, that the proclamation of the New Moon is made at the time of the full moon. A curious passage in *Josephus, Antiqq.* III., x. 5, may thus appear in a new light.

The Calendar has been literally translated so as to make it accessible to a wider circle interested in the numerous problems connected with these calendars. The readings of the Sabbaths have been of course fully reproduced. They form the most important part, as it is for the sake of the Sabbatical Lessons that this Calendar is being published. In the translation the references to the chapters and verses of the Pentateuch have been added to each of these lessons. In order to show the exact relation between the Biblical Lessons of the Samaritans and those of the Jews, I have added to each of these. Bible Lessons the corresponding Lessons read by the Jews on each of the Sabbaths of that year.

Short notes added to the translation explain more fully some of the difficult points. In order to make the list of the Samaritan Bible Lessons more complete as found in actual life I have added also the list from the Calendar (Cod. 857) showing the permanency of the Institution and the manner in which these Lessons are read during the year. This Calendar starts with the eighth month and finishes with the ninth. It shows also slight discrepancies which are due to additional Sabbaths when the Parashiyot had to be subdivided. These I left untranslated as the references to the chapter and the verse of the Bible have been added, which make these divisions perfectly clear.

[P. 1] קבוץ חדש שעבאן והוא חדש החמישי בשעה 7 ד ועשרה
דקיקות מן יום הששי : המזדמן אל כג״ יום מן תמוז במחשב
קדמה : אשר ראשו יום החמישי והוא אחד ושלשים יום :

יומי השבוע : מספר ימי חדש שעבאן והו החמישי :
חדש הרומי במחשב קדמה : וזה במחשב ימה : מן חדש אב :

ו. א. כג. ה. זה ראש חדש החמישי והוא שעבאן :
(ש) בו פרשה מן פינחס בן אלעזר אל אחר ספר במדבר :
(ש) בו פרשה מן אלה הדברים אל ראו למדתי :

א. י. יד. א. ראש חדש אב בחשבן קדמה :
(ש) בו פרשה מן ראו למדתי אל כי יביאך : וזה הוא צמות הסכות :

א. יז. ח. כא. קראת חדש החמישי על א.ב. מן לילת א :
(ש) בו פרשה מן כי יביאך אל כי אתם עברים :

ה. כח. ים. א. ראש חדש אילול בחשבן ימה :
(ש) בו פרשה מן כי אתם : אל בנים אתם :

[P. 2] קבוץ חדש רמצון והוא חדש הששי בשעה עשתי עשר : וששה
וחמשים דקיקה מן יום השבת המזדמן אל כב : מן אב
במחשב קדמה : אשר ראשו יום חדה והוא אחד ושלשים :
ראש חדשי שנת ג. בשממטה :

א. א. כב. ד. זה ראש חדש הששי והוא רמצון :
(ש) בו פרשה מן בנים אתם : אל שופטים :

ד. יא. א. יד. ראש חדש אילול בחשבן קדמה :
(ש) בו פרשה מן שופטים אל כי יקח איש אשה :

ב. טז. ו. ים. קראת חדש הששי על ט.   נח. מן לילת השני :
(ש) בו פרשה מן כי יקח איש אשה אל היום הזה :

ז. כח. יח. א. בו פרשה מן היום הזה והיה כי יביאך : והוא ראש חדש
תשרי בחשבן ימה :

[P. 3] קבוץ חדש שואל והוא חדש השביעי בשעה השנית ושנים
וארבעים דקיקה מן יום השני המזדמן אל כ. מן אילול
במחשב קדמה : אשר ראשו יום הרביעי והוא שלשים יום ·

ב. א. כ. ג. ראש מועד חדש השביעי : והוא שואל :
(ש) בו לא יש פרשה : שבת עשרת יומי הסליחות :

ה. י. כט. יב. יום הכפור העצום : וענות הנפש :

ו. יב. א. יד. ראש חדש תשרי בחשבן קדמה :
(ש) בו פרשה מן והיה כי יביאך אל אחר התורה :

ב, טו, ד, יז, מועד חג הסכות : ראש שבעת הימים :

ה, יז, ו, יט, קראת חדש השביעי על ח, כח, מן יום ג, ה, :

(ש) שבת שבעת יומי חג הסכות לא יש בו פרשה :

א, כא, י, כג, ראש חדש תשרי בחשבן ימה :

ב, כב, יא, כד, יום השמיני עצרת :

(ש) בו פרשה מן בראשית אל ואדם ידע :

ג, ל, יט, א, ראש חדש מרחשבן בחשבן ימה :

―――――――――――

[P. 4] קבוץ חדש די אלקעדה והוא חדש השמיני בשעה הששית
ששה וחמשים דקיקה מן לילת הרביעי המזדמן אל כ, מן
תשרי במחשב קדמה : אשר ראשו יום הששי והוא אחד
ושלשים יום :

ה, א, כ, ב, ראש חדש אלקעדה והוא חדש השמיני :

(ש) בו פרשה מן ואדם ידע אל אל לבו :

(ש) בו פרשה מן אל לבו אל לך לך :

ב, יג, א, יד, ראש חדש מרחשבן בחשבן קדמה :

ה, טז, ד, יז, קראת חדש השמיני על ה, ד, מן יום ה, :

(ש) בו פרשה מן לך לך אל ויהי אברם :

(ש) בו פרשה מן ויהי אברם אל ויהוה פקד :

ה, ל, יח, א, ראש חדש כסלים בחשבן ימה :

―――――――――――

[P. 5] קבוץ חדש אלחגה והוא חדש התשיעי בשעה השנית וששה
ועשרים יום (!) מן לילת הששי : לגו תשע ועשר יום מן
חדש מרחשבן אשר ראשו יום השני והו שלשים יום :

ו, א, יט, ב, ראש חדש התשיעי והוא חדש אלחגה :

(ש) בו פרשה ויהוה פקד אל אברם (!) זקן :

(ש) בו פרשה מן ואברהם זקן אל ואלה תולדת יצחק :

ד, יג, א, יד, ראש חדש כסלים בחשבן קדמה :

ו, טו, ג, טז, קראת חדש העשירי על ד, מח, מן יום ו, :

(ש) בו פרשה מן אלה תולדת יצחק אל וישא יעקב רגליו :

(ש) בו פרשה מן וישא יעקב רגליו אל ותצא דינה :

(ש) בו פרשה מן ותצא דינה אל ויוסף הורד :

―――――――――――

[P. 6] קבוץ חדש מחרם והוא חדש העשירי שנת תשע ועשרים
ושלש מאות ואלף לממלכת ישמעאל : בשעה העשירית
וארבע דקיקות מן יום השבת : והוא חדש ט, : לגו תשע
עשר יום מן חדש כסלים בחהבן קדמה : אשר ראשו יום
הרביעי [הרביעי] והוא אחד ושלשים יום :

א. א. ים. א. ראש חדש מחרם וראש חדש טבת בחשבן ימה :

(ש) בו פרשה מן יוסף הורד אל ולוסף ילידו :

ז. יד. א. יד. (ש) בו פרשה מן ולוסף ילידו אל ויבא יוסף הביתה :

וראש חדש טבת לחשבן קדמה :

א. טו. ב. טו. קראת חדש העשירי על ה. ו. מן לילת א.

(ש) בו פרשה מן ויבא יוסף הביתה אל אל שדי נראה אלי :

(ש) בו פרשה מן אל שדי נראה אלי אל אחר ספר בראשית :

[P. 7] קבוץ חדש צפר והו אחד עשר בשעה השלישית וששה

וחמשים דקיקה מן יום השני לגו שבע עשר יום מן חדש

טיבת : אשר ראשו יום השבת והוא אחד ושלשים יום :

ב. א. ין. ל. ראש חדש אחד עשר והוא ראש המופתים : והוא חדש צפר :

ד. ג. ים. א. ראש חדש שבט בחשבן ימה :

(ש) בו פרשה מן ואלה שמות אל כי ידבר אליכם פרעה :

(ש) בו פרשה מן כי ידבר אל ואל אהרן זה שבת חקת המסבות :

ב. טו. לא.ינ. קראת חדש אחד עשר על ד. טו. מן יום ב. :

ג. טו. יד. א. ראש חדש שבט בחשבן קדמה :

(ש) בו פרשה מן ואל אהרן אל בחדש השלישי זה שבת צמות

הפסח :

(ש) בו פרשה מן בחדש השלישי אל ויקחו לי תרומה :

ג. ל. מו. כח. וחצי ורבע :

[P. 8] קבוץ חדש רביע הראש והוא שנים עשר בשעה החמישית

ושנים וארבעים דקיקה מן לילת הרביעי לגו ששה עשר

יום מן חדש שבט אשר ראשו יום השלישי והוא שמנה

ועשרים וחצי ורבע : חתמת חדשי שנת ג. בשמטה :

ד. א. מז. א. ראש חדש שנים עשר וראש חדש הדר בחשבן ימה :

(ש) בו פרשה מן ויקחו לי תרומה אל וזה הדבר :

(ש) בו פרשה מן וזה הדבר אל ויתן אל משה :

ג. יד. א. יד. ראש חדש הדר בחשבן קדמה :

ה. מו. ב. מו. קראת חדש שנים עשר על ה. לב. מן לילת ד.

(ש) בו פרשה מן ויתן למשה אל ויעש את הקרשים :

(ש) בו פרשה מן ויעש את הקרשים אל אחר ספר שמות :

[P. 9] קבוץ חדש רביע השני והוא חדש הראשון בשעה הששית

וששי וארבעים דקיקה מן יום החמישי והוא יום הששי :

לגו שמנה עשר יום מן חדש הדר אשר ראשו יום השלישי

והוא אחד ושלשים יום : בו מועד הפסח הברוך :

ז. א. יח. לא. ראש חדש הראשון והוא רביע השני :

ז. ב. יט. א. ראש חדש ניסן בחשבן ימה : בו פרשה מן ויקרא אל משה

אל צוי את בני ישראל :

(ש) בו פרשה מן צוי אל וישא אהרן :

ה. יד. לא. יג. יום טבח' :

ו. טו. א. יד. יום מועד הפסח הברוך : וראש חדש ניסן :

קראת חדש הראשון על מ. ד. מן יום ה, ו, :

(ש) זה שבת שבעת יומי חג המצות :

א. יז. ג. טז. ראש יומי אל עומר אצל השמרים :

ה. כא. ז. כ. יום מעד חג המצות :

(ש) השבת הראש מן שבע השבתות בו פרשה מן וישא אהרן

אל ואיש או אשה :

[P. 10] קבוץ חדש גמאד הראש : והוא חדש השני : בשעה השנית :

וששה וארבעים דקיקה מן לילת השבת לגו ששה עשר

יום מן חדש ניסן : אשר ראשו יום הששי : והוא שלשים יום :

ז. א. טז. כט. ראש חדש השני בו פרשה מן ואיש או אשה אל אחרי :

ב. ג. יח. א. ראש חדש איאר בחשבן ימה :

(ש) בו פרשה מן אחרי אל ובקצירכם :

(ש) בו פרשה מן ובקצירכם אל מועדי :

א. טז. א. יד. ראש חדש איאר בחשבן קדמה : וקראת חדש השני :

(ש) בו פרשה מן מועדי אל אם בחקותי תלכו :

(ש) בו פרשה מן אם בחקתי לאחר ויקרא :

[P. 11] קבוץ חדש גמאד השני : והוא חדש השלישי בשעה עשרי

עשר ושנים עשר דקיקה מן לילת חדה לגו חמשה עשר

יום מן חדש איאר אשר ראשו יום חדה והוא אחד

ושלשים יום :

א. א. טז. כח. ראש חדש השלישי והוא גמאד השני :

ב. ב. טז. כט. יום קהלה :

ד. ד. יח. לא. יום מעמד הר סיני :

ה. ה. יט. א. ראש חדש סיבן בחשבן ימה :

(ש) השבת השביעי חתמת שבע השבתות :

א. ח. כב. ד. מועד חג השבעות חתמת אלעמר מפרק חמשתי יומה :

(ש) בו פרשה מן במדבר סיני אל נשא את ראש :

ב. טז. ל. יב. קראת חדש השלישי על ג. ד. מן לילת ב. :

ד. יח. א. יד. ראש חדש סיבן בחשבן קדמה :

(ש) בו פרשה מן נשא את ראש אל דבר אל אהרן :

(ש) בו פרשה מן דבר אל אהרן אל שלח לך אנשים :

[P. 12] קבוץ חדש רגב והוא חדש הרביעי בשעה הששית וארבע
וחמשים דקוקה מן יום השני והוא יום השלישי : לגו
ארבע עשר יום מן חדש סיבן אשר ראשו יום הרביעי :
והוא שלשים יום :

ג. א. כז. ראש חדש הרביעי והוא רגב :

ז. ה. יח. א. ראש חדש תמוז בחשבן ימה : ובו פרשה מן דבר את
ראש (!) אל ויקח קרח :

ז. ט. כב. ה. קרח (!)

(ש) בו פרשה מן ויקח קרח אל וישלח משה מלאכים :

ז. ט. כט. יב. קראת חדש הרביעי אל ו. מ. מן יום ג. ד. :

ו. יח. א. יד. ראש חדש תמוז בחשבן קדמה :

(ש) בו פרשה מן וישלח משה אל פינחס בן אלעזר :

(ש) בו פרשה מן פינחס אל ויהי המלקח :

List of Parashiyot from Samaritan Calendar (Cod. 857).

As actually read.
The Calendar contains 14 months, i.e. from the 8th of the previous to the 9th of the next.

Genesis. P. 1. השמיני		
4,1	ירע אדם	2
8,21(b)	אל לבו	3
12,1	לך לך	4
17,1	ויהי אברם	5
21,1	ויהוה פקד	6

P. 2. התשעי		
24,1	ואברהם זקן	7
25,19	ואלה תולדת	8
29,1	וישא יעקב רגליו	9
34,1	ותצא דינה	10

P. 3. העשירי		
39,1	ויוסף הורד מצרימה	11
	ול(ו)יוסף ילידו	12a
43,26	ויבא יוסף הביתה	12b
48,3	ואל שדי	13

Exodus. P. 4. אחד עשר		
1,1	ואלה שמות	1
7,9	כי ידבר	2
12,1	ואל אהרן	3
	ויסע משה	4a

P. 5. שנים עשר		
19,1	בחדש השלישי	4b
25,2	ויקחו לי תרומה	5
29,4	וזה הדבר	6
31,18	ויתן למשה	7
36,20	ויעש את הקרשים	8

Leviticus. P. 6. הראשון		
1,1	ויקרא למשה	1
6,2	צוי את בני ישראל	2
9,22	וישא אהרן	3

P. 7. השני		
13,38	איש או אשה	4
16,1	אחרי	5
19,9	הפסח השני	6a
23,2	ובקצירכם	6b
מועדי :		

P. 8. השלישי		
26,3	אם בחקותי: אל עמלק:	8
	כל קהלה: כל מקרתה:	
	שבת הדברים:	
	חג הקציר:	

Numbers		
1,1	במדבר סיני	1
4,1	נשא את ראש	2

P. 9. הרביעי		
8,2	דבר אל אהרן	3
13,2	שלח לך	4
16,1	ויקח קרח	5
20,14	וישלח משה	6
26,11	פינחס בן אלעזר	7

P. 10. החמישי		
31,32	ויהי המלקח	8

Deuteron:		
1,1	אלה הדברים	1
4,5	ראו למדתי	2
7,1	כי יביאך	3

P. 11. הששי		
11,31	כי אתם	4
16,18	שופטים ושוטרים	5
22,13	כי יקח איש	6
26,16	היום הזה	7

P. 12. השביעי		
	[שבת עשרת יומי הסליות:] (!)	
30,1	והיה כי יבאו	8
	חג הסכות	
	שבת יומי חג הסכות	
Genesis	יום השמיני	
1,1	בראשית	1

P. 13. השמיני		
4,1	והאדם ידע	2
6,17	ואני הנני	3
8,21(b)	אל לבו	4
12,1	לך לך	5

P. 14. התשעי		
17,1	ויהי אברם	6
21,1	ויהוה פקד	7
24,1	ואברהם זקן	8
25,19	אלה תולדת יצחק	9

Cod. 1150

(Page 1)

Conjunction of the month Shaban, which is the Fifth Month 0 hour 10 minutes of the sixth day, which happens to be on the 23rd Tammuz according to the Old Style, whose first is on Thursday and which is of 30 days.

(The four columns are marked as follows.)

1. The day of the week. 2. The number of days of the month Shaban, which according to the Mohammedan Calendar is the seventh. 3. This column is the month of the Rumi [according to the Eastern Calendar (Old Style)] and the 4th is the modern calculation (New Style). This is here the month of Ab. [In the Jewish Calendar it was the month of Tammuz.]

Friday. 1. 23. 5. This is the beginning of the month which is Shaban, the 5th August, 1910.

Sabbath. On it the Parasha from Pinehas the son of Eleazar until the end of the book Bemidbar. (They read here evidently the whole of the rest of the Book of Numbers. Numb. 25, 11. to end. The Jews read on same Sabbath (August 6, Ab. 1) Massē. Numb. 33, 1. to end of the book.)

Sabbath. On it the Parasha from " Ele ha-debarim " (Deut. 1, 1.) until " behold I have taught you " (Deut. 4, 5.). (August 13th, Jewish Lesson, Deut. 1, 1–3., 22.).

Sabbath. The Parasha from " behold I have taught you " (Deut. 4, 5.) to " when he will bring thee " (Deut. 7, 1.). (August 20th, Jewish Lesson, Deut. 3, 22–7., 11.). This Sabbath is the Samot of Succoth. (*Note.*—Samot, a peculiar calendaristic term used by the Samaritans for a festive season, or rather a special Sabbath before the two festive seasons Succoth and Pesach, each time *six* weeks before the festival. They have special collections of prayers for these Samot (junction), but they do not seem to know the origin and true meaning. It is not here the place to discuss these Samot.)

Sunday. 17. 8. 21. Proclamation of the New Moon (i.e. Full Moon) of the Fifth Month for Sunday and Monday from the night of Sunday. [August 21st.]

Sabbath. Parasha from " When he will bring thee " (Deut. 7, 1.) till " for ye are passing " (Deut. 11, 31.). (August 27th, Jewish Lesson, Deut. 7, 12. to 11, 25.)

Thursday. 28. 19. 1. New Moon of Elul according to New Style. [September 1st.]

Sabbath. Parasha from "for ye are, etc." (Deut. 11, 31.) to "ye are sons" (Deut. 14, 1.). (September 3rd, Jewish Lesson, Deut. 11, 26–16, 17.)

(Page 2)

Conjunction of the month Ramadan, which is the Sixth Month on the 11th hour 56 minutes of Sabbath, which corresponds to the 22nd Ab according to Old Style, whose first is on the Sunday and is of 31 days.

The beginning of the third year of Shemiṭṭah.

Sunday. 1. 22. 4. New Moon of the Sixth Month. (Jewish Elul. The Jews have two days New Moon, Sunday and Monday; the Samaritans only Sunday.)

Sabbath. Parasha from "ye are sons" (14, 1.) to "judges and officers" (16, 18.). (September 10th, Jewish Lesson, Deut. 16, 18–21, 9.)

Wednesday. 11. 1. 14. First of the month of Elul Old Style.

Sabbath. Parasha from "judges and officers" (16, 18.) to "let a man take a wife" (22, 13.). (September 17th, Jewish Lesson, Deut. 21, 10–25, 19.)

Monday. 16. 6. 19. On it is the proclamation of the New Moon, 9 hours 58 minutes of the 2nd night.

Sabbath. Parasha from "let a man take a wife" (Deut. 22, 13.) to "this day" (Deut. 26, 16.). (September 22nd, Jewish Lesson, Deut. 26, 1–29, 9.)

Sabbath. 28. 18. 1. Parasha from "this day" (Deut. 26, 16.) until "when it will come upon thee" (Deut. 30, 1.).[a] (October 1st, Jewish Lesson, Deut. 29, 10–30, 20.)

[[a] *Note.*—This is evidently the Samaritan reading of Deut. 30, 1.]

And this is the first day of Tishri according to the New Style. [October 1st.]

(Page 3)

The conjunction of the month Shawwal, the Seventh Month 2 hours 42 minutes of Monday, corresponding to the 20th of Elul, Old Style, whose first is Wednesday and is of 30 days.

Monday. 1. 30. 3. The beginning of the First Festival of the Seventh Month. This is Shawwal. [October 3rd.] (The Samaritans were one day before the Jewish Rosh Hashanah, for Jewish Rosh Hashanah was on October 4th.)

Sabbath. No Parasha. It is the Sabbath of the ten days of Penitence. (October 8th, Jewish Lesson, Deut. 31, 1–31, 30.)

Wednesday. 10. 29. 12. The great awe inspiring Day of Atonement, the day of chastisement of the soul. [October 12th.]

Friday. 12. 1. 14. First day Tishri, O.S. [October 14th.]

Sabbath. The Parasha from "when it will come upon thee" (Deut. 30, 1.) to the end of the Law. (October 15th, Jewish Lesson, Deut. 32, 1–52.)

Monday. 15. 4. 17. The Festive Season of the Feast of Tabernacles. The beginning of the Seven Days. [October 17th.]

Wednesday. 17. 6. 19. The proclamation of the New Moon of the Seventh Month is 8 hours 29 minutes of the night of Tuesday to Wednesday. [October 19th.]

Sabbath. That of the Seven Days of Tabernacles. On it no Parasha. [October 22nd. The Jews also no Parasha.]

Sunday. 21. 10. 23. First day Tishri, N.S. [October 23rd.]

Monday. 22. 11. 24. The Eighth Day of 'Aṣeret. [October 24th.]

Sabbath. Parasha from "In the beginning" (Gen. 1, 1.) to "Adam knew" (Gen. 4, 1.). (October 29th, Jewish Lesson, Gen. 1, 1–6, 8.)

Tuesday. 30. 19. 1. First day Marheshban, N.S. [November 1st.]

(Page 4)

Conjunction of the month Dul Kaddar, the Eighth Month 6 hours 56 minutes of the night of Wednesday, corresponding to the 20th Tishri, O.S., whose first is Friday and is of 31 days.

Wednesday. 1. 20. 2. New Moon of Kada which is the Eighth Month. [November 2nd. This is the first of the two days New Moon of the Jewish Month Marḥeshvan.]

Sabbath. Parasha from "and Adam knew" (Gen. 4, 1.) until "unto his heart" (Gen. 8, 21b). (November 5th, Jewish Lesson, Gen. 6, 9–11, 22.)

Sabbath. Parasha from "unto his heart" (Gen. 8, 21b) to "now the Lord said . . . . get thee out" (12, 1.). (November 12th, Jewish Lesson, Gen. 12, 1–17, 27.)

Monday. 13. 1. 14. First day Marheshban, O.S. [November 14th.]

Thursday. 16. 4. 17. The proclamation of the New Moon of the Eighth Month 5 hours 4 minutes of Thursday. [October 17th.]

Sabbath. Parasha from "now the Lord said . . . get thee out" (Gen. 12, 1.) to "Abraham was" (17, 1.). (November 19th, Jewish Lesson, Gen. 18, 1–22, 24.)

Sabbath. Parasha from "and Abram was" (Gen. 17, 1.) to "and the Lord remembered" (21, 1.). (November 26th, Jewish Lesson, Gen. 23, 1. to 25, 18.)

Thursday. 30. 18. 1. First day Kislem, N.S. [December 1st.]

(Page 5)

Conjunction of the month Hijja, the Ninth Month 2 hours 26 minutes* of the night of Friday, corresponding to the 19th Marḥeshban, whose first is Monday and is of 30 days.

Friday. 1. 19. 2. The beginning of the Ninth Month. This is the month Al Hijja. [December 2nd.] (New Moon of the Jewish month Kislev.)

Sabbath. Parasha from "and the Lord remembered" (Gen. 21, 1.) until "and Abraham was old" (Gen. 24, 1.). (December 3rd, Jewish Lesson, Gen. 25, 19–28, 9.)

Sabbath. Parasha from "and Abraham was old" (Gen. 24, 1.) to "and these are the generations of Isaac" (Gen. 25, 19.). (December 10th, Jewish Lesson, Gen. 28, 10–32, 2.)

[*Note.*—It is to be noted the Parasha read to Jewish bridegroom on the Sabbath started from Gen. 24, 1.]

Wednesday. 13. 1. 14. The beginning of the month Kislem, O.S. [December 14th.]

Friday. 15. 3. 16. The proclamation of the Tenth (? Ninth) Month 4 hours 48 minutes of Friday. [December 16th.]

Sabbath. Parasha from "these are the generations of Isaac" (Gen. 25, 19.) to "and Jacob lifted up his feet" (29, 1.). (December 17th, Jewish Lesson, Gen. 32, 3–36, 43.)

Sabbath. Parasha from "and Jacob lifted up his feet" (Gen. 29, 1.) to "and Dinah went out" (34, 1.). (December 24th, Jewish Lesson, Gen. 37, 1–40, 23.)

Sabbath. Parasha from "and Dinah went out" (34, 1.) to "Joseph went down" (39, 1.). (December 31st, Jewish Lesson, 41, 1–44, 17.) [This is the first of the two days New Moon of the Jewish month Ṭebet.]

(Page 6)

Conjunction of the month Muharram, the Tenth Month, the year 1329 of the Mohammedan rule, 10 hours 4 minutes of the day of Sabbath, and that is month (written by mistake) corresponding to the 19th Kislem, O.S., whose first is Wednesday and has 31 days.

_____

* Written day instead of minutes in MS. by mistake.

Sunday. 1. 19. 1. Beginning of the month Muharram. Beginning of the month Ṭebet, N.S. [January 1st, 1911.]

Sabbath. Parasha from "and Joseph went down" (39, 1.) to "unto Joseph were born" (41, 50.). (January 7th, Jewish Lesson, Gen. 44, 18–47, 27.)

Sabbath. 14. 1. 14. Parasha from "unto Joseph were born" (41, 50.) until "and Joseph came into the house" (43, 26.). (January 14th, Jewish Lesson, Gen. 47, 28. to end of Gen.) The first of the month Tebet, O.S.

Sunday. 15. 2. 15. The proclamation of the Tenth Month 6 hours 6 minutes of the night of Sunday. [January 15th.]

Sabbath. Parasha from "and Joseph came into the house" (Gen. 43, 26.) until "The god Shaddai appeared unto me" (48, 3.). (January 21st, Jewish Lesson, Ex. 1, 1–6, 1.)

Sabbath. Parasha from "The god Shaddai appeared unto me" (48, 3.) unto the end of the Book of Genesis. (January 28th, Jewish Lesson, Ex. 6, 2–9, 35.)

(Page 7)

The conjunction of the month Saffar, that is the Eleventh Month 3 hours 56 minutes of the day of Monday, corresponding to the 17th day of Ṭebet, whose first is Sabbath and has 31 days.

Monday. 1. 17. 30. The Eleventh Month. This is the beginning of the miracles. This is the month Saffar. (This is the name of the month in which the portions of the Bible are read containing the miracles in Egypt.) [January 30th.] (Jewish month Shebat one day New Moon.)

Wednesday. 3. 19. 1. Beginning of the month Shebat, N.S. [February 1st.]

Sabbath. Parasha from "and these are the names" (Ex. 1, 1.) until "and when Pharaoh will speak unto you" (7, 8.). (February 4th, Jewish Lesson, Ex. 10, 1–13, 16.)

Sabbath. Parasha from "and when Pharaoh will speak unto you" (Ex. 7, 8.) until "and unto Aaron" (12, 1.). And this is the Sabbath of Mesabot. (February 11th, Jewish Lesson, Ex. 13, 17–17, 16.)

Monday. 15. 31. 13. The proclamation of the New Moon of the Eleventh Month 4 hours 46 minutes of Monday. [February 13th.]

Tuesday. 16. 1. 14. Beginning of the month Shebat, O.S. [February 14th.]

Sabbath. Parasha from " and unto Aaron " (Ex. 12, 1.) until " on the third month" (19, 1.). (February 18th, Jewish Lesson, Ex. 18, 1–20, 26.) This is the Sabbath of the Samot of Pesach.

Sabbath. Parasha from "on the third month" (Ex. 19, 1.) to "and they shall take unto me a heave offering" (25, 1.). (February 25th, Jewish Lesson, Ex. 21, 1–24, 18.)

Tuesday. 30. 15. 28. A half and a quarter. It means a half day and a quarter day to complete the solar year. [February 28th.] This is the first of the two days New Moon of Adar.

(Page 8)

The conjunction of the month Rabi I, which is the Twelfth Month, and is on the 5th hour 42 minutes of the night of Wednesday, which is the 16th of the month of Shebat, whose beginning is on Tuesday, which is of 28 days and a half and a quarter. The conclusion (!) of the third year of the Shemiṭṭah.

Wednesday. 1. 15. 1. Beginning of the Twelfth Month Hadar, N.S. [March 1st.] (This is the second day New Moon of the Jewish month Adar.)

Sabbath. Parasha from "and they shall take unto me a heave offering" (Ex. 25, 1.) until "this is the word" (29, 1.). (March 4th, Jewish Lesson, Ex. 25, 1–27, 19.)

Sabbath. Parasha from "this is the word" (Ex. 29, 1.) until "and he gave unto me" (31, 18.). (March 11th, Jewish Lesson, Ex. 27, 20–30, 10.)

Tuesday. 14. 1. 14. Beginning of the month of Hadar, O.S. [March 14th.]

Wednesday. 15. 2. 15. The proclamation of the Twelfth Month, 4 hours 32 minutes of the Wednesday. [March 15th.]

Sabbath. Parasha from "and he gave unto me" (Ex. 31, 18.) until "and he gave the boards" (36, 20.). (March 18th, Jewish Lesson, Ex. 30, 11–34, 35.)

Sabbath. Parasha from "and he gave the boards" (Ex. 36, 20.) to the end of the book Shemot. (March 25th, Jewish Lesson, Ex. 35, 1–38, 20.)

(Page 9)

The conjunction of Rabi II, which is the First Month on the 6th hour 46 minutes of Thursday and it is the 6th day, which is the 18th day of the month of Hadar, whose first is the

Tuesday and which is of 31 days. In this is the feast of the blessed Pesaḥ.*

Friday. 1. 18. 31. New Moon of the First Month, and it is Rabi II. [March 31st. This is the second day of New Moon of the Jewish Month Nissan.]

Sabbath. 2. 19. 1. Beginning of the month Nissan, N.S. Parasha from "and he called unto Moses" (Lev. 1, 1.) until "command the children of Israel" (6, 1.). (April 1st, Jewish Lesson, Lev. 1, 1–6, 7.)

Sabbath. Parasha from "command the children of Israel" (Lev. 6, 1.) until "and Aaron took" (9, 22.). (April 8th, Jewish Lesson, Lev. 6, 8–8, 35.)

Thursday. 14. 31. 13. The day of the slaughter (of the Paschal Lamb). [April 13th.]

Friday. 15. 1. 14. The day of the feast of the blessed Pesaḥ. First day Nissan, O.S., the proclamation of the First Month is 9 hours 4 minutes from Thursday to Friday. [April 14th.]

Sabbath. This is the Sabbath of the seven days of unleavened bread (Maṣṣot). [April 15th.]

Sunday. 17. 3. 16. The first day of the 'Omer. [April 16th.]

Thursday. 21. 17. 20. The feast day of the festival of Maṣṣot. [April 20th.]

Sabbath. The first Sabbath of the seven Sabbaths. Parasha from "and Aaron took" (Lev. 9, 22.) until "man or woman" (13, 38.). (April 22nd, Jewish Lesson, Lev. 9, 1–11, 47.)

(Page 10)

The conjunction of Djumada I, which is the Second Month 2 hours 46 minutes on the day of Sabbath, corresponding with the 16th of the month of Nissan, whose first was on a Friday and is of 30 days.

Sabbath. 1. 16. 29. Beginning of the Second Month. Parasha from "man or woman" (Lev. 13, 38.) until "after the death" (16, 1.). (April 29th, Jewish Lesson, Lev. 12, 1–15, 33.) [This is the second day New Moon of the Jewish Month Iyyar.]

Monday. 3. 18. 1. Beginning of the month Iyyar, N.S. [May 1st.]

Sabbath. Parasha from "after the death" (Lev. 16, 1) to

* Meaning the calculation is from 6 in the afternoon, evidently when according to the Jewish calculation the night of the 6th day had begun.

"and when ye reap the harvest" (19, 9.). (May 6th, Jewish Lesson, Lev. 16, 1–20, 27.)

Sabbath. Parasha from "and when ye reap the harvest" (Lev. 19, 9.) until "feasts" (23, 1.). (May 13th, Jewish Lesson, Lev. 21, 1–24, 27.)

Sunday. 16. 1. 14. Beginning of the month of Iyyar, O.S., and the proclamation of the Second Month 1 hour 24 minutes of the second day. [May 14th.]

Sabbath. Parasha from "feasts" (Lev. 23, 1.) to "if in my statutes" (26, 3.). (May 20th, Jewish Lesson, Lev. 25, 1–end of the book.)

Sabbath. Parasha from "if in my statutes" (Lev. 26, 3.) to the end of the book. (May 27th, Jewish Lesson, Numb. 1, 1–4, 20.)

(Page 11)

Conjunction of Djumada II, the Third Month 11 hours 12 minutes of the Sunday corresponding to the 15th of the month Iyyar, whose first was on Sunday and it is of 31 days.

Sunday. 1. 15. 28. Beginning of the Third Month, which is Djumada II. [May 28th. This is the first day New Moon of the Jewish month Sivan.]

Monday. 2. 16. 29. The day of the Gathering. [May 29th.]

Wednesday. 4. 18. 31. The day of the standing before Mt. Sinai. [May 31st.]

Thursday. 5. 19. 1. Beginning of the month of Siban N.S. [June 1st.]

Sabbath. The Seventh Sabbath, the conclusion of the seven Sabbaths. [June 3rd. Jewish Feast of Weeks, Friday and Saturday.]

Sunday. 8. 22. 4. The Feast of the Festival of the Weeks, the conclusion of the 'Omer at the going out of the 50 days. [June 4th.]

Sabbath. Parasha from "in the wilderness of Sinai" (Numb. 1, 1.) to "take the sum of the sons of Kehat" (Numb. 4, 1.). (June 10th, Jewish Lesson, Numb. 4, 21–7, 89.)

Monday. 16. 30. 12. The proclamation of the Third Month 3 hours 4 minutes of the night of Monday. [June 12th.]

Wednesday. 18. 1. 14. Beginning of the month Siban, O.S. [May 14th.]

Sabbath. Parasha from "take the sum of the sons of Kehat" (Numb. 4, 1.) until "speak unto Aaron" (6, 22.). (June 17th, Jewish Lesson, Numb. 8, 1–12, 16.)

Sabbath. Parasha from "speak unto Aaron " (Numb. 6, 22.) until " said " (13, 1.).   (June 24th, Jewish Lesson, Numb. 13, 1. to 15, 41.)

(Page 12)

The conjunction of the month Rajab, which is the Fourth Month 6 hours 54 minutes of Monday, which is (really) Tuesday, corresponding to the 14th day of the month Siban, whose first is Wednesday and has 30 days.

Tuesday. 1. 14. 27.   Beginning of the Fourth Month and it is Rajab. [June 27th. This is the second day New Moon of the Jewish month Tammuz.]

Sabbath. 5. 18. 1.   Beginning of Tammuz, N.S. Parasha from "speak unto the head " [this is here a mistake in MS., should be " said "] (Numb. 13, 1.) to " Korah took " (16, 1.).   (July 1st, Jewish Lesson, Numb. 16, 1–18, 32.)

Wednesday. 9. 22. 5.   Proclamation of the New Moon (rest missing, left incomplete, evidently started by mistake, *v.* below). [July 5th.]

Sabbath. Parasha from " Korah took " (Numb. 16, 1.) until " Moses sent messengers ". (20, 14.).   (July 8th, Jewish Lesson, Numb. 19, 1–25, 9.)

Wednesday. 16. 29. 12.   The proclamation of the Fourth Month 6 hours 26 minutes from Tuesday to Wednesday. [July 12th.]

Friday. 18. 1. 14.   Beginning of the month of Tammuz, O.S. [July 14th.]

Sabbath. Parasha from " Moses sent messengers " (Numb. 20, 14.) until " Pinehas " (25, 11.).   (July 15th, Jewish Lesson, Numb. 25, 10–29, 40.)

Sabbath. Parasha from " Pinehas " (Numb. 25, 11.) to " and the booty was " (31, 32.) [In some MSS. there is a Parasha marked also at 27, 1.]   (July 22nd, Jewish Lesson, Numb. 30, 1. to end of the book.)

JEWISH KNOWLEDGE OF THE SAMARITAN
ALPHABET IN THE MIDDLE AGES

THE Jews have never practically lost sight of the
Samaritans, unlike the Christians, who for at least
a thousand years had entirely forgotten their existence,
as no writer or pilgrim to the Holy Land speaks of
them with the solitary exception of Mandeville. It was
therefore a great surprise to the Western world when
at the beginning of the seventeenth century the darkness
began to be lifted, and through Scaliger, Huntingdon, and
Della Valle for the first time authentic news about the
Samaritans, their language, and their Bible began to
reach Europe.

The Jewish literature, however, knows no real inter-
ruption. Tradition flows on continuously from century
to century, and whenever the occasion arises new facts
are added to the old tradition. Jewish pilgrims like
Benjamin of Tudela and the famous poet Alḥarizi not
only visited the Samaritans in Nablus, but both gave
accurate and graphic descriptions of the people in Sichem,
of their peculiarities, their liturgy, and traditions. Benjamin
of Tudela, who flourished in the twelfth century (1160),
writes of them in a simple style befitting a traveller's tale.
Alḥarizi, who flourished at the beginning of the thirteenth
century (1216), who saw everything from the poet's
point of view, and who himself could indulge in bitter
sarcasm and irony, does not spare the Samaritans in one
of his Maḳamat. As I may point out on another occasion,
I believe that Alḥarizi had also made himself conversant
with some books of the Samaritan literature, among them
the Book of Joshua, for I believe that the whole setting

of his Maḳama with the story of the dove by which the besieged city is freed from the besiegers is nothing but an imitation from the episode of Shobakh of the Samaritan Joshua. It will be seen that Jews living in Palestine, as well as others who were travelling from the European continent, came often in contact with the Samaritans and tried to obtain from them some information about their literature, and more especially of their script.

There were two reasons which preserved the recollection of as well as the interest in that script. There were the comparatively abundant references to it in the older Talmudic literature and the Jewish coins. The Jews did not dispute the claim of the Samaritans that their alphabet was the genuinely "Hebrew" one, and more than once the opinion was expressed in the Talmud that it was in this "Hebrew" script that the Law was given on Mount Sinai (Sanhedrin 22a, Jer. Megillah, i, f. 71b, c), but that with the advent of Ezra a change had come and another script called Ashuri (probably Aramæan, not Assyrian as is generally thought) had been substituted for the older form of writing. No real reason has ever been assigned for this fundamental change. Probably in the eyes of the people it was quite sufficient to mark a separation between the two septs of the Jewish nation. Whilst they were engaged in mutual warfare no question was asked about such a change, as it required practically no other justification. But for all that, the older alphabet was not entirely forgotten, and it was used, as is well known, for the inscriptions on Jewish coins.

These coins date partly from the period before the destruction of the Temple (Simon, c. 135 B.C.), and some of them probably are as late as the beginning of the second century (Simon bar Kochba, 130 A.D.). No explanation has hitherto been found for this peculiar phenomenon. As the Jews had practically discarded their ancient Hebrew alphabet, why should they use it again in lieu of the one which they had adopted ? There was apparently no obvious cause why an antiquated alphabet should suddenly be used just for the coinage, which ought to bear the most popular script, and on which legends ought to be easily understood by the people for whom the coins were intended.

An explanation could be suggested for the non-use of the square character. It was regarded as a holy script, and was used practically exclusively for the sacred writings, and it might have appeared to the people to be a profanation to put the same script in which they wrote the name of God on the currency, which would pass from hand to hand, and easily pass from the hands of Jews to the hands of Gentiles. No such scruples virtually were attached to the other alphabet, just because it was now used among the Samaritans. Moreover, as the latter were almost as numerous in Palestine as the Jews, this Jewish coinage might have been intended also to be used by the Samaritans, for curiously enough no one has yet heard of a Samaritan coinage, nor is anywhere reference made to coins struck by the Samaritans with any direct mention of Sichem bearing Hebrew legends in their own script.

If, then, in addition to this consideration, it is accepted that the coins as struck by the Jews were issued by Simon the Maccabean in the last years of his reign (about 135 B.C.), just at the time when he had occupied part of Samaria and asserted his claim over that part of the country, it is not at all improbable that he used this script on coins intended for a common currency as a demonstration against the Samaritan claim that Sichem was the Holy Place. This might also explain why the obverse of many of the coins, notably those of the time of Simon the Maccabean, have a representation of the Temple with the legend "Jerusalem the Holy

One ". It was intended to show *urbi et orbi* that there was only one Sanctuary, one Holy Place, only Jerusalem. It was a symbol of victory over the Samaritans struck by the Hasmoneans, just as the Romans and Greeks struck similar coins as a sign of victory.

Now these streams of tradition, the one about the Hebrew origin of the "Kuthean", i.e. the Samaritan alphabet as found in the Talmud, and the other, the legends on the Jewish coins, have been the means of preserving the memory of the Samaritan script alive among the Jews. I have been able to gather some curious data about this knowledge of the Samaritan alphabet which might prove of interest.

They start from two heads. The one is found in commentaries on the passages in the Talmud, and the other is connected with investigations of the Jewish coins. The commentaries on the Talmud, however, are very brief. They do not discuss the script. They merely explain the tradition, and one of the commentators, viz. Rashi (*ob.* 1105), must, as we shall find, have even seen somewhere a Samaritan alphabet. He shows a close acquaintance with it. I will deal with this point later on, for it is only an allusion, though of no mean importance. Of far greater interest for the fact that the Jews were acquainted with the alphabet is that copies of this very alphabet have been preserved in ancient mediaeval writings.

In the first place I mention the MS. in the Bodleian Library (I cannot trace the number), a page of which I have been able fortunately to photograph. I give it here in facsimile (p. 617), with a transcript in Hebrew followed by an English translation.

The MS. dates from the twelfth or thirteenth century. The passage which I am reproducing here purports to be a direct copy of one of the numerous Responsa which emanated from the heads of the colleges and the leaders of the Jews in Babylon, who held authority over practically

העתקה מתשובות הגאונים ז"ל בפ' כהן גדול רבי אומ"
בכתב זה ניתנה תורה לישראל כיון שחטאו נהפך להם לדעץ
מהו לדעץ אנו למדונו לדעץ ויש ששונין לדחץ והוא הכתב
שהוא עכשיו לכותים ועד אן יוצאים כספים מטבעות בשקל
הקדש שעליהן כתב זה וזהו צורתו

Here is the copy of the alphabet in the MS.

ירוש" בפ"ק דמגלה תני רבי שמעון בן אלעזר אמ" משום ר"
אליעזר בן פרטא שאמ" משום ר" אליעזר המודעי כתב אשורי
נתנה התורה מאי טעמ" ווי העמודים שיהו ווים של תורה
דומים לעמודים א'ר לוי מן דמר בדעץ נתנה התורה עין מעשה
נסים מן דמר אשורי סמך מעשה נסים ר" ירמיה בשם ר" אלעזר
בר בא ור" סימון תרויהון אמרין תורת הראשונים לא היה
שלהם לא ה"א ולא מ"ם שלהם סמוך (סתום) הא סמך סתום. :

the whole of Jewry in their time.   The Geonim, as they are called, came to an end at the latest with the middle of the tenth century.   The copy, therefore, cannot be later, but it is evidently much older, and forms part of answers which these heads of the schools and colleges sent to queries about the elucidation of certain difficult passages in the Talmud.

Antiquarian passages were often those which required an explanation, for the Jews in Europe or in the West of Africa were not acquainted with all these details, with which the people in Babylon and in Palestine were often quite familiar.   One of these questions must have been the demand for an interpretation of the passage in the Talmud in which it was stated that the law had originally been given in the "Hebrew" script, but that it had been abandoned and another one substituted for it, the so-called square characters.   The translation runs as follows :—

" A copy from the Response of the Geonim, and this is what they say in the chapter Kohen Hagadol (Tr. San-hedrin, f. 22*a*).   Rabbi said the Torah was given to Israel in this script (Hebrew), and when they sinned it was turned into Da'aṣ.   What means Da'aṣ ?   We have been taught to know it under the form Da'aṣ.   Others explain it Dḥṣ, and this is the writing which is now that of the Samaritans.   And unto this very day there are silver coins current in the likeness of the Holy Shekel with this writing on them, and this is the copy of the letters. [Here follows the Hebrew alphabet with the corresponding letters of the Samaritan alphabet underneath.]   In Treatise Jer. Megillah, ch. i (f. 71*b*, *c*), we find R. Shimeon, son of Elazar, said in the name of Eliezer, son of Parta, who said it in the name of R. Eliezer the Mudite, the Law had been given in the Ashuri script.   Whence do we know it ?   'The hooks [vavē] of the pillar,' the vavē of the Law should be like unto pillars [i.e. the letter ׀ should look like a column—straight perpendicular line].

R. Levi said whoever said that the Law had been given in the Da'aṣ (Ra'aṣ) script, then the letter ע was miraculously written; whoever said it was Ashuri, then ס was miraculously written. R. Jeremiah in the name of R. Elazar Baraba and R. Simon both said in the Torah of the Ancients neither their ה (הא) nor their מ (מם) were closed,[1] but ס alone was closed."

The explanation of the last sentence is that these letters forming a complete circle could not have been kept in the Tablets of the Law unless by miracle, for they were cut out of the stone, and there was nothing to keep the central portion attached to it.

The commentators of the Talmud have merely discussed the meaning of that mysterious word Da'aṣ, Ra'aṣ, or Dḥṣ without coming to any satisfactory conclusion. If the correct reading be Da'aṣ one might almost feel inclined to see in it the terminus technicus for the wedge-like Assyrian–Babylonian writing, for which hitherto no Hebrew name has yet been discovered. But this is merely a conjecture, and it might lead me far astray were I to follow up the question as to whether the Jews were intimately acquainted with the Cuneiform script, and if so, why no name of this kind of writing has been preserved.

The variation mentioned in the first part of this Responsum is quite in conformity with the phonetics of the Samaritans, who make no difference between the gutturals and often substitute ע for ה, and ה for ע, and, as we shall see, also pronounce ע, ה, ח, א, almost without any distinction, in fact so much so that the signs of these letters are used promiscuously to designate often one and the same sound.

If we now examine more closely the shape of this Samaritan alphabet we shall find that in the main there is a close agreement between this script and that used by the Samaritans, yet there are some differences which are

[1] In MS. the reading is סמוך ; in the Talmud the reading is סתום.

not due to the inventive genius of the scribe, but probably
rest on much older tradition. It will be noticed that not
a few of the letters terminate with small ringlets instead
of with straight lines: ת, פ, נ, ו, ה, ז, ג, א. Others are
somewhat changed and difficult to recognize, like פ, ז, ו,
ה, ט, נ. But, for all that, it cannot be gainsaid that the
copyist reproduces here a genuine Samaritan alphabet, in
which the square character is beginning to change and
approximate more or less to the cursive script. These
ringlets seem to be of a very archaic origin, and show that
this alphabet had been used also for quite a different
purpose than the mere writing of Samaritan books.
Rashi, in his commentary to the above passage in the
Talmud (Tr. Sanhedrin 21b, s.v. לבנאה), says this was
the alphabet of the Samaritans and was also used in
amulets and charms and Mezuzot. The ancient alphabet
evidently had become the mystical alphabet, and the
letters were used in such charms down to recent times,
sometimes being distorted out of recognition and
distinguished by the fact that the corners are rounded off
in small ringlets. No doubt the Samaritan alphabet
had become a mystical alphabet to those who did not
understand it or to those to whom it appealed as being
the very alphabet in which, according to the tradition
recognized by the Jews as correct, God Himself had given
the Law in this script. It was therefore the script best
fitted for all mystical purposes, as it was endowed with
a significance and value lacking in every other script.
Rashi, then, must have seen such an alphabet similar to
the one in the facsimile here reproduced. This would
prove the accuracy of the copyist in the manner in which
he reproduced the old Samaritan alphabet.

Maimonides describes and denounces this practice
(M. T. Hil. Tefillin, v, 4). The correctness of this view,
that ancient alphabets became in time mystical alphabets
and that this has happened with the Samaritan, is borne

out by the list of such alphabets found in a MS. in the
possession of Mr. David S. Sassoon. The MS. is of
Oriental origin. It is written in the year 1465–8 (1776–9
Seleucid), and is part of a compilation called Sha'ar
Harazim (not the book with a similar title ascribed to
Todros ha Levi, but one of a much later date). It consists
of 465 chapters, being mystical prayers or sympathetic
prescriptions, love philters, amulets, charms, etc. The
book is mostly composed in Hebrew.

There are some chapters written in Arabic. They
contain mysteries (Sodot) ascribed, curiously enough, to
the Fayyumi, by which name the Gaon Seadyah of the
ninth century is usually known.

I am reproducing here the Samaritan alphabet from the
MS. kindly placed at my disposal by Mr. Sassoon—

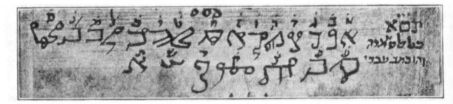

It is paragraph 461, and is called in the margin
כט אלסאמרה and underneath והו כתב עברי, i.e. " the
Samaritan alphabet, which is the Hebrew writing". The
form approximates very much more closely the actual
Samaritan, but not a few agree very closely with the one
reproduced before. We have here also the Hebrew
equivalent letters written above the corresponding
Samaritan signs; and we find that they also have those
peculiar ringlets to which attention has been drawn and
which show that this alphabet served magical purposes
at a later time.

We turn now to the other stream of information, which
has kept alive the remembrance of the Samaritan alphabet,
although it was not put to any mystical use—the legends

of the shekel, to which reference is made also in the Response of the Geonim. This identification of the Hebrew script of the shekel with the Samaritan script brought the Jews in close contact with the Samaritans in Palestine and helped to keep alive the knowledge of the script among the Jews.

Azaryaḥ de Rossi, one of the most prominent Jewish antiquarians of the time of the Renaissance, devoted a special chapter to an investigation of the Jewish coinage, and notably to the legend of the Shekel. He has gathered in that chapter of his famous book *Meor Enayim*, printed by him in Mantua, 1574, much curious information, of which I am giving here only those parts which affect us directly in the question before us, for he discusses in addition to the legend many other problems connected with the shekel, which are now beside the mark. We learn from him among others that many Jewish travellers from Italy in going to Palestine did not shun contact with the Kuthiim or Samaritans. On the contrary, they entered into friendly relations with them and obtained from them much information. Furthermore, these travellers made ample notes of that information, and brought or sent it home in notebooks in which they had set down the knowledge which they had gathered. Some of these collections had come into the hands of de Rossi, and he gives us extracts therefrom which prove of great value, the loss of which must be deemed also a loss to the world at large. It is from such collectanea that de Rossi is able to reprint a complete Samaritan alphabet, which I am reproducing here from the first edition, f. 171a. On f. 171b we have a very rude representation of a shekel. Before discussing the form of the letters of this alphabet I had better sum up here the information contained in the *Meor Enayim*.

In chapters 56–8, ff. 171a–8b, we find there in the first place from these short references by de Rossi, that the tradition had been continued uninterruptedly down to the sixteenth century.

"On the letters of the alphabet of the other side of the river Eber Hanaha and on the Holy Shekel. Towards the end of our work we are now discussing also some types of letters not of our script, but of that script which our sages called Tr. Megillah I, San. ch. 2; they called it 'Hebrew Script', namely, that of the other side of the river, which they also called the script ליבנאה, the interpretation of which is (as given above in the name of Rashi) like the script on amulets and mezuzot, and is still used by the Kuthiim (Samaritans). Also Maimonides, in the Commentary of the Mishna Yadayim, chap. iv, writes about it that that is the script used by the people called Al Samira, viz. the Samaritans. And according to what I have seen in a Ḳonṭras (compilation) sent by a reliable man from the Holy Land to Rabbi Petaḥyah Ida of Spoleto, who also taught him the Arabic language, and his son the Rabbi David Mosheh shewed me (those notes) here in Ferara, and also according to what afterwards was told to me by the wise man Samuel Marli in Mantua from the Itinerary of the Holy Land of Rabbi Moses Bassolah; and all the novelties which he had seen during that journey, in the very autograph of the above-mentioned man, and also what has been shown unto me there in Mantua by Reuben of Perugia, the script which had been given to him by one of the Christian scholars in Bologna as found in a very ancient book upon which they place great reliance. The following is, then, the form of the Samaritan alphabet, and this is the language of the above-mentioned Rabbi Moses Bassolah :—

The letters of the Kuthiim which are found on the coins follow here. It consists of three rows of two lines each, and under the Hebrew is the corresponding Samaritan letter. Many are double, e.g. twice א, twice ה, twice ט, twice ו, etc.

Then follows—

"At the end of his commentary to the Pentateuch, Nachmonides (1263) writes as follows: 'The Lord has blessed me that I reached Akko, and I found there among some of the local old men silver coins with inscriptions (engravings). On one side like a blossoming almond rod, on the other side the likeness of a flask, and on both sides round it was a very clear inscription, and they showed the writing to the Kuthiim (the Samaritans), and they read it at once, for that is the Hebrew writing which has been preserved by the Samaritans as it is mentioned in treatise Sanhedrin. And they read (the legend) on the one side "Shekel of Shekelim" and on the other side "Jerusalem the Holy One". And they say that the emblem on the one side denotes the blossoming rod of Aaron, and that on the other side the flask of Manna. We weighed it in the scales, and its weight was 10 silver, i.e. half an ounce, as Rashi mentions. And I have seen also similar coins of half weight, and they weigh half a shekel, which was the shekel of the sacrifices' (thus far Nachmonides).

"But I (the writer—de Rossi) also, thank God, have seen one of these Shekelim, and I also have seen a coin in the hand of the widow of Isaac Hagiz, the Sephardi, who was one of the inhabitants of Ferara, but who had gone to Jerusalem and died there and was buried in the

Vale of Jehosaphat, about a mile from Zion. And this woman being overburdened with children, she returned to her eldest son, Rabbi Yomtob, who was managing his father's business in Ferara. Round that coin I found written in the above-mentioned letters Shekel of Israel. In the middle a flask and the letters שׁר above, which according to my opinion are the initial letters of 'Shekel of David', and on the other side 'Jerusalem the Holy One', and in the middle a rod with three blossoms, according to the accompanying two illustrations.

"I (de Rossi) believe that Nachmonides made a mistake when he wrote 'Shekel of Shekelim' instead of 'Shekel of Israel'.

"I (de Rossi) think we can read also ירושלים הקדושה or ירושלימה קדושה, i.e. by reading ה to the previous word for as it is found in Jer. Talmud, Megillah, ch. i, the Jerusalemitans used to write ירלשלימה ירושלים, which was also a Samaritan practice.

"We pass on to another quotation from the Responsa of Moses al Ashkar (end of fifteenth century)—' Know that I have found a large number of coins of shekel and half-shekel, and on some of them is written year so and so of the comfort of Zion; year so and so of King so and so; and on one I have found the image of a palm (*lulab*) and citron (*etrog*) tied on to it, and a Jew who was an expert in that writing said to me that on one side was written in Greek letters and Greek arms, and on the other side was Hebrew writing; evidently, then, this coin must have been struck when the Jews were under the Greeks,' etc. The letters which Abraham de Balmas brings in the first chapter of his *Makneh Abraham* are clearly not the letters of the coins." Thus far the abstract from de Rossi.

We learn thus that Maimonides of the twelfth century was fully conversant with the Samaritan alphabet, and he knew that the Hebrew script mentioned was that of the Samaritans of his time. No doubt he must have met

some of the Samaritans in Egypt, as at his time a large
colony flourished in Egypt, and Samaritan fragments
have been found among the papers rescued from the
Genizah in Cairo.

Still more interesting in de Rossi is the mention of
Nachmonides, who after he had emigrated from Spain
and finished his commentary in Jerusalem met Samaritans
in Akko who were able to read to him fluently the ancient
Hebrew script of the Jewish coins. Various people had
been in close connexion with the Samaritans, as not only
was the alphabet preserved in one of these notebooks,
but we find there a reference to the Samaritan use of the
word חסד for "curse".

If we turn now to the alphabet reproduced in facsimile
from de Rossi we shall find that this alphabet agrees much
more closely with the script used by the Samaritans than
the one reproduced from the MS. of the thirteenth century.
The former must have been taken from the writings current
among the Samaritans. There are no ringlets, no twisted
forms, and the Samaritan letters correspond entirely with
the Hebrew printed above them. But we find here a good
number of letters represented by two signs. A comparison
with the Samaritan script will solve the difficulty. We
have here, in fact, both the uncial form of the Samaritan
corresponding with the square form of the Hebrew, and
we have the cursive form of the letters called by the
Samaritans half-letters. It is not here the place to discuss
which of the two is the older one, but it is certainly an
interesting fact to find that not later than the beginning
of the sixteenth century the Samaritans used the cursive
writings alongside with the other.

With the beginning of the seventeenth century the
Samaritan alphabet became the property of the Western
world.

Massoretisches im Samaritanischen.

I. Samaritanische Bibelaccente.

as gesamte Gebiet der Semitischen Philologie, welches für den Meister und Nestor keine Geheimnisse hat, wird unzweifelhaft von berufener Seite vollauf vertreten sein, um Prof. NÖLDEKE den Dank zu zollen, der ihm so reichlich gebührt. Ich beschränke mich auf einen ganz kleinen Winkel dieses so umfangreichen Gebietes und will einen kleinen Beitrag dazu liefern, da auch dieser von NÖLDEKE vor Jahren beleuchtet wurde (Göttingen 1862). Die Mitteilungen, die ich mache, beruhen zunächst auf unmittelbarer Erfahrung, die ich persönlich aus dem Munde einer anerkannten Autorität gesammelt habe, und die daher den Wert der Tatsache gegenüber der rein spekulativen Hypothese besitzt. Im Oktober 1902 kam nach London von Nablus ISHAK BEN AMRAM ha-Cohen ha-gadol und brachte mehrere samaritanische Handschriften. Eine derselben wurde vom Britischen Museum erworben, und die größere Zahl der anderen kam in meinen Besitz. Während seines Aufenthaltes verkehrte ISHAK täglich in meinem Hause und von ihm habe ich mich über viele Einzelheiten unterrichten lassen, die bisher trotz aller Vorgänger doch ziemlich dunkel geblieben waren. In erster Reihe las er die hebräisch-samaritanische Bibel mit mir, und ich ließ ihn in meinen Phonographen hineinsprechen, sowohl um die Aussprache des Hebräischen und des Targum zu fixieren sowie auch um die Art des Vortrages der Bibel in der Synagoge und die Art der Recitative

der anderen liturgischen Stücke während des Gottesdienstes, besonders aber des Priestersegens, des Gesanges Mose's im Exodus
und des Liedes im Deuteronomium kennen zu lernen. PETERMANN
hat zwar schon in ausgezeichneter Weise die Aussprache des
Hebräischen in Nablus erlernt und sein Resultat in den *Abhand-
lungen für die Kunde des Morgenlandes* (V, 1876) veröffentlicht.
Mein Gewährsmann ist nun der Sohn desselben Hohenpriesters,
AMRAM, der seiner Zeit PETERMANN als Lehrer im Samaritanischen
zu der Transkription des Hebräischen nach samaritanischer Aussprache
verhalf. Wir sprachen Hebräisch miteinander und verständigten uns
ganz vortrefflich, besonders da meine sefardische Aussprache der
seinigen nahe kam, denn ISHAK ist ein wohlbewanderter Mann. Daß
er jetzt die Stelle als Hohepriester nicht einnimmt, kommt daher, daß
er zu jung war als sein Vater starb, um diese Würde antreten zu
können, und so wurde sie seinem Oheim SHALMA übertragen. Unter
den von ISHAK erworbenen Hss. befindet sich auch eine von ihm selbst
verfaßte Zusammenstellung der Unterschiede zwischen dem hebräischen
Texte der Bibel und dem samaritanisch-hebräischen. Dieser letztere
ist überschrieben קשוט „Wahrheit"! Er versuchte sogar mich von
der Echtheit und Wahrheit der sam.-heb. Rezension zu überzeugen.
Ich hatte es jedenfalls mit einem Manne zu tun, welcher die Bibel
und den Gottesdienst genau kennt und als Vorbeter in der Synagoge
fungiert, also am besten im Stande war, mich über Vieles zu be-
lehren. Er brachte nun drei Bibelhandschriften mit, von welchen
eine vom Museum erworben wurde. Diese ist unzweifelhaft eine der
schönsten hebr.-sam. Hss. in Europa und vielleicht in der Welt. Eine
Beschreibung dieser wundervollen Hs. hat der Bibliothekar am Museum
Rev. G. MARGOLIOUTH in der *Jewish Quarterly Review* XV, 1903
pp. 632—639 geliefert. Die zweite Hs. ist ein kleines Ms. in 12°,
Pergament, welches ich weiterhin noch genauer beschreiben werde,
und die dritte eine Rolle, die eine genaue Abschrift der uralten Rolle
sein will, welche im Allerheiligsten in der Synagoge in Nablus be-
wahrt wird. Es ist aber bestimmt keine Abschrift jener ältesten Rolle
— denn diese wird kaum angerührt —, sondern von einer der anderen
drei Rollen, die nach Angabe dieses Priesters sich dort befinden.
   Bei dieser Gelegenheit möchte ich bemerken, daß ISHAK mir auch eine
Photographie mitbrachte, die ebenfalls von jener alten Rolle gemacht
sein soll. Als ich sie aber unter dem Vergrößerungsglase genauer

untersuchte und ihm meine Zweifel an ihrer Echtheit ausdrückte, lachte er und sagte, die Samaritaner würden ja nie daran denken, die alte heilige Rolle einem photographischen Apparate auszusetzen; aber Besucher, besonders „'Arelim" kämen häufig nach Nablus und wünschten eine Kopie von der alten Rolle zu bekommen, so habe man eine andere photographiert, und diese sei das Original für diese Kopie, und, fügte er hinzu, „nicht jeder, der nach Nablus kommt, bringt ein Vergrößerungsglas mit und untersucht die Photographie." Da Schlüsse aus der Schrift dieser Photographie gezogen worden sind, so ist die Feststellung dieser Tatsache nicht ohne Belang.

Die Hs. im Britischen Mus. ist nun eine der wenigen ganz vollkommenen Hss., die sich in Europa befinden. Es fehlt kein einziges Blatt, und die Hs. ist, soweit ich konstatieren kann, die einzige in einer öffentlichen Bibliothek sich befindende mit einem Kolophon am Schlusse des Pentateuch. Von den anderen Hss. im Mus. sowohl als auch in der Sammlung CRAWFORD, jetzt JOHN RYLANDS in Manchester, wo die älteste Hs. ist (vom Jahre 1211), hat keine ein solches Kolophon. Nur der Codex Barberini in Rom soll nach der Angabe bei HEIDENHEIM, *Bibl. Sam.* I p. XXXIV auch ein Kolophon haben. Wie mir Herr COWLEY, der Bibliothekar der Bodleiana in Oxford mitteilt, sind auch die dortigen sam. Bibelhss. entweder am Ende defekt, oder wenn sie überhaupt ein Kolophon haben, so beschränkt es sich auf die Angabe der „Kessen".

Die wahre Bedeutung dieses Kolophons ergab sich mir aber erst, nachdem ich es genau mit ISHAK durchgelesen und er mir die einzelnen Zeichen erklärt hatte. Das Dunkel, das über diesen Zeichen schwebt, hat Mr. MARGOLIOUTH veranlaßt, zu schreiben (*ibid.* p. 634—4): "Below the above summary of sections is the following mnemonic rubric regarding the lections of the Pentateuch" und weiter: "An account of the Samaritan order for reading the Law was given by Mr. COWLEY in the *Jewish Quarterly Review* for October 1894; but no mnemonic rubric is given there, nor can I gather a detailed explanation of the rubric from the account contained in the article just mentioned". Er betrachtet also diese Angabe als eine mnemonische Rubrik für die Reihenfolge der Lektionen in der Synagoge. Hinter jedem Worte steht aber je ein bestimmtes Zeichen, und dies hat er übersehen; das davor stehende Wort bezieht sich nun aber ausschließlich darauf. Es sind die Namen der betreffenden Zeichen! Vor die Hs. in's

Museum gelangte, las ich das Kolophon mit dem Priester und gebe
nun zunächst den Text wieder, wie er im Original steht und auf dem
auf S. 535 No. I beigegebenen Facsimile erscheint. Ich lasse hierauf
die Transkription folgen, genau nach der Aussprache des Priesters,
und werde dann die Erklärungen soweit wie möglich in seinen eigenen
Worten wiedergeben. Bei dieser Gelegenheit drucke ich das ganze ab
in der Aussprache ISHAK's und zugleich die im Texte enthaltenen
Angaben über Schreiber und Datum der Hs.

*Ani h̆ébed 'áni al raṣṣón Ádonái Abrahám bin Ia'úb bin Tábiyah
bin Sáádah bin Abraham admibáni Fígmah katábti zét hatoráh ha'edo-
šah al šémi téhyi barakátah áli ŭél malamédi-ŭél chál 'áli Yišrael
ámen: évšénat erbaím ŭešába almamlachót báni Yišmael vui millu é
orán odi et Ádonái ŭašaél oto yesa'édni al mechtafót kámoah ámen
ámen ba'mal ben 'Amrám.*

Von allen andren Fragen abgesehen — wird doch nun die Aussprache
dieses Kolophons von autoritativer Seite festgestellt und manches
Zweifelhafte aufgeklärt — weise ich nur auf die Lesung des Wortes וסעה
hin, welches sich nun nach der Angabe des Priesters als eine Abkürzung
herausstellt und somit die Hypothesen beseitigt, die an dieses Wort
geknüpft wurden. Es ist auch bemerkenswert, daß man schon im
XIV. Jhrh., als die Hs. geschrieben wurde, sich solcher Abkürzungen
bedient hat.

Das andere Kolophon lautet nach der Aussprache von ISHAK:

*Turá temumá barúch noténa kilúl kél 'ésse araóta téša maót uši-
ším ušiša b̆ámăsfar: Sedaréi ma'arata áfsa' ₊, énged ", annáu •, er-
kénu |, šeyála ⁖, báu ⁖, zĕífa ⸱, atmaú ⸲, zíf =⁚, túru |:; madda' mak-
šeb ufem emyáteb elkál 'ad menún.*

Soweit dieser Text, den I. noch als *ashara erkuním* bezeichnet,
d. h. die zehn Modalitäten, in welchen der Bibeltext öffentlich vor-
getragen wird. Seine detaillierte Erklärung ist nun wie folgt:

afsa' sei Schluß des Verses, Abschluß und Ende; *énged* sei eine Art
schleppende langgezogene Art zu lesen, halb fragend wie Gen. 29, 4, 5
(er zitierte diesen Vers als Beispiel: *ŭayaómer . . . ái . . . me'iran*);
anna'u = langsames Lesen; ib. v. 12. 13, und als Erklärung des Wortes
und Begriffes zitierte er וינח אלה; *erkenu* = langgedehntes Lesen ארך;
šiyála = Frage; *báu* = *darásh* wie יבקש ה'; *zĕi'a* = Ausrufen צעק; *atmaú:* =

Wunder und Überraschung: wie in מה עשה; *zif* = Ärger und Entrüstung
wie חרה אפי; *túru* = Lehren und Gebote wie in יורו משפטיך.

„Wissen, Aufhorchen oder Aufpassen und Aussprache (wörtlich:
Mund) gehören zu jedem Einzelnen von diesen". Alle diese Beispiele
sind so von ihm zitiert. Er hat demnach das Wort „Makšeb" so
aufgefaßt, als ob es mit Qaf und nicht mit Kaf geschrieben wäre, und
hat es auch nicht guttural gelesen. Als ich ihn darauf aufmerksam machte, meinte er: es sei alles eins; dies sei die richtige Bedeutung, und diese letzten drei Worte bezeichneten die für alle „Sedarei"
geltenden Bedingungen, denn ohne genaues Verständnis und Aufpassen, wie diese gesprochen würden, und ohne die genaue Wiedergabe seien sie wertlos. Es seien eben nur 10 „Erkunim" bekannt
und nicht mehr.

Da ich mich mit dieser kurzen Erklärung nicht zufrieden gab,
drang ich in den Priester, mir die Bedeutung dieser Zeichen durch
biblische Stellen, wo sie angewendet würden, genauer zu bestimmen.
Ich gebe nun die Zitate genau nach seiner Aussprache und füge den
hebr. Text jedesmal bei:

Enged: Ŭayai ʿol aṣhófar alak uázak méod (Exod. 19, 19). ויהי
קול השופר הלך¹ וחזק מאד.

*Ánnáu: bi adáni laish débarim anáki gem mitámol gem mišélšom
gem míaz dabérak alabádak ki kábed fa ukábed líshon ánaki*
(Exod. 4, 10). „Hier wird die Stimme gesenkt beim Lesen der unter-
strichenen Worte". בי אדני לא איש דברים אנכי גם מתמול גם משלשם גם
מאז דברך אל עבדך כי כבד פה וכבד לשון אנכי.

Zếʿa: la yehye lak elóem aʿérem alfáni! latéši: oder vor den
Worten: *šéšat yémim teesa maasek.* לא יהיה לך אלהים אחרים על פני
לא תשא. ששת ימים תעשה מעשיך² (Exod. 20, 3 u. cf. v. 9).

*Siyála: ŭelkelótema míyal fáni aadáma: šúb miʿarón abáak ŭen-
nám al errá lamák zékor labrahám elésak elyaʿób* (Exod. 32, 12—13).
ולכלותם מעל פני האדמה שוב מחרון אפיך והנחם על הרעה לעמך זכור לאברהם
ליצחק וליעקב³.

Erkénu: éšar áta šékeb alía lák etténena ŭelzérak ŭáyae zérak

---

¹ Mas. Text: הולך
² Er hat nach d. Gedächtnisse zitiert: M. T. תעבוד ועשית כל מלאכתך
³ Im Mass. T.: ולישראל

káfar áres (Gen. 28, 13—14). ‏אשר אתה שוכב עליה לך אתננה ולזרעך‏
‏והיה זרעך כעפר הארץ.‏

    *Báu: sélaḥ na lûn aám azé kagádal ésdak kaéšar našáta lám
azé memúsrem uád ána* (Num. 14, 19). ‏סלח נא לעון העם הזה כגדל‏
‏חסדך כאשר נשאת לעם הזה ממצרים ועד הנה.‏

    Atmaú: Der ganze Passus Exod. 33, 12 seq. und 34, 5—7. *uyárad
Ad. baánan uyettésab ímmo šámma uaye‘rá éfšam Ad. uyabár Ad.
alfáno ŭeye‘rá Ad. Ad. el réum ŭánun árek ébèm uráb ésed ŭámet násar
ésed lálafim náša ûn uféša uetá una‘á lu yena‘é. fó‘ed ûn ábot al bánim
ŭál bánebánim.* ‏וירד יי בענן ויתיצב עמו שם ויקרא בשם יי ויעבר יי על פניו‏
‏ויקרא יי יי אל רחום וחנון ארך אפים ורב חסד ואמת נצר חסד לאלפים נשא‏
‏עון ופשע וחטאה ונקה לא ינקה. פוקד עון אבות על בנים ועל בני בנים.‏

    Turú: kullu Mišaftim: (d. h. Kapitel 21—23 von Exod., die der
jüd. Abteilung Mišpatim entsprechen, besonders aber Kap. 21
und 22).

    Zíf: ŭayaár abó: yédak téye bó baráišoná leamíto. ‏ויחר אפו:‏
‏ידך תהיה בו בראשונה להמיתו:‏

    Identisch mit diesem Kolophon und in anderer Beziehung noch
viel ausführlicher ist das Kolophon in meinem Cod. Or. 800. Ein
Facsimile dieses zweiten Kolophons veröffentliche ich auch hier (S. 536
No. III). Es enthält außer den obigen Zeichen noch manche Angaben,
die ich bisher nur hier gefunden habe. Die Hs., auf Pergament geschrieben, stammt aus dem Jahre 915 Heg., wie sich aus der Note des
Kopisten ergibt, der nach samaritanischer Art zwischen den Zeilen
von Fol. 181 b (Deuteron. I 1) und Fol. 188 a, die hemistichisch geteilt
sind, in den Zwischenraum die das Datum ergebenden Buchstaben
geschrieben hat. Die Hs. ist in Ägypten geschrieben. Soviel ich
weiß, ist es die einzige Hs., deren ägyptische Provenienz außer Zweifel
steht. Sie ist mit großer Sorgfalt geschrieben und, wie ich glaube
nachweisen zu können, nach einem uralten Muster. Sie hat nun
mannigfache Schicksale erlebt. Von Ägypten kam sie nach Gaza
in Palästina, wo sie, zusammen mit noch zwei anderen Pentateuch-
Codices, von einem gewissen ṬABYAH' BEN ISHAK ha-Cohen gekauft
wurde, als er gerade in Gaza war, um sich dort eine Frau zu holen
und die sam. Gemeinde im Aussterben traf. Er brachte diese Hss.
nach „Eschkem" im Jahre 1180 Muham. Ob unser Codex schon da-
mals defekt war oder erst später die ersten und die letzten fünf

Blätter eingebüßt hat, läßt sich aus seiner Angabe fol. 181 nicht bestimmen. Als die Hs. nachher im Jahre 1285 Muham. in den Besitz
des AMRAM BEN SHALMA kam, fand dieser sie schon in diesem defekten
Zustande, und er hat das Fehlende mit großer Sorgfalt nachgetragen.
Es ist derselbe Hohepriester, den ich schon oben als einen Freund von
PETERMANN erwähnt habe und für welchen er das Exemplar korrigiert
hatte, welches PETERMANN nachher herausgeben sollte. Sein Sohn
ISHAĶ hat nun mir diese Hs. verkauft. In dem Kolophon heißt es, daß bei
der Erbteilung die Hs. ihm als Erbteil zugefallen sei. AMRAM BEN
SHALMA hat nun am Schlusse des Pentateuch ein ausführliches Kolophon
angebracht. Es ist das vollständigste, das bisher bekannt ist, und
enthält die vollständigsten massoretischen Angaben, die sich bisher
meines Wissens in irgend einer samaritanischen Hs. erhalten haben.
Auf die einzelnen Angaben, die von nicht geringer Bedeutung sind,
gehe ich momentan nicht ein, da ich mich ausschließlich mit den
Zeichen beschäftige, die nicht nur AMRAM hier im Texte angibt,
sondern auch ISHAĶ noch erläuternd am Rande wiederholt und die
im Texte fehlenden Zeichen nachträgt, die ganz genau mit den im
Cod. Brit. Museum übereinstimmen. Daß er diese von einer der
alten Hss. in der *Kenschä* in Eschkem abgeschrieben hat, kann keinem
Zweifel unterliegen. Aus dieser erläuternden Randglosse ersieht man,
daß es eben nur 10 *Sedarei Ma'ratah* gibt und daß die Reihe hier
mit *atmáu* schließt. Cod. Barberini enthält nun eine dritte Liste derselben Zeichen, die aber von HEIDENHEIM (l. c.) unrichtig abgedruckt
worden ist.

Wie alt sind sie? Wessen Ursprunges? und in welchem Zusammenhange stehen sie mit den verschiedenen Systemen der semitischen Schriftvölker des Altertums? Ebenso schwierige Fragen wie
alle, die sich auf die Geschichte des Textes der hebräischen Bibel
und den Anfang der Massora bei Juden und Syrern beziehen.

In erster Linie muß untersucht werden, ob wir es hier mit
einem willkürlichen Syteme zu tun haben, welches, wie es im
Syrischen bei Išo der Fall war, nur das Werk eines Mannes war
und sich dann nur einer sehr beschränkten Anwendung erfreute,
oder ob es ein allgemein anerkanntes System war, welches von Allen
gleichmäßig benutzt wurde? Erstreckt sich ferner die Anwendung
dieser Zeichen auch auf die Pentateuchrolle, oder ist sie auf die Buchform des Pentateuch beschränkt und schließt somit an die Praxis

der Juden an? Bekanntlich gibt es keine vollständige alte sam. Pentateuchrolle in Europa, und die wenigen Fragmente, die sich davon in den Bibliotheken von Petersburg und London befinden, sind entweder verhältnismäßig jung oder nicht genügend beschrieben, um uns darauf eine entschiedene Antwort zu geben. Das einzige sehr alte Fragment in meinem Besitze, von welchem ich ein Facsimilie veröffentlicht habe (*Illuminated Hebrew Bibles*, London 1901), welches ich dem XII. oder XIII. Jahrhundert zuschreibe, enthält nun bloß zwei dieser Zeichen und zwar die ersten in der Liste: *Afsa'* und *Enged* d. h. Schluß und in vielen Fällen Mitte des Verses.

Außer diesen Zeichen, natürlich mit Ausnahme des worttrennenden Punktes, findet sich keine Spur in der alten Rolle, und ebensowenig in der modernen Abschrift, die ich von ISHAK erworben habe. Er hat sich darin jedenfalls mehr gewissenhaft gezeigt als man bei einem modernen orientalischen Kopisten erwarten könnte, dem die alten Zeichen vielleicht unwesentlich erscheinen würden. Jedenfalls findet sich keine deutliche Spur von irgend einem der anderen acht Zeichen. Am Schlusse der einzelnen „Kessen" und in derselben Reihe sind natürlich auch in der Rolle drei oder mehr Punkte zu finden aber nicht in dem leeren Raume zwischen den „Kessen" wie in den Hss. in Buchform. Es hat sich also in der Rolle bei den Samaritanern wie bei den Juden doch eine altertümlichere Form der Schreibung erhalten. Nicht so genau haben es die Samaritaner mit dem Buche genommen, welches nicht für liturgische Zwecke bestimmt ist und somit mit größerer Freiheit behandelt werden kann, wiederum genau wie die Juden es mit ihren Bibeln getan haben. Von diesen Hss. ist die in der Ryland's Library wohl eine der ältesten. Ihr folgen chronologisch die anderen drei, von welchen Facsimiles in den *Publications of the Palaeographical Society* veröffentlicht wurden. An diese schließen sich der neue Codex des Br. Museums und zahlreiche sehr alte Fragmente in meinem Besitze, und außerdem mein oben erwähnter Codex Nr. 800. Wenn man nun all diese alten Hss. untereinander vergleicht, ergibt sich das interessante Resultat, daß, je älter ein Codex ist, desto zahlreicher diese Zeichen angewendet sind, und je jünger ein solcher ist, desto mehr der Gebrauch derselben verschwindet. Man hat wohl im Laufe der Zeit immer mehr das wirkliche Verständnis für diese Zeichen verloren, und da der Gottesdienst sich immer mehr auf Nablus beschränkte,

da die alten Gemeinden in Damaskus, Ägypten und Gaza allmählich
verschwanden, so hat der politische und soziale Niedergang der Gemeinde auch einen entsprechenden Niedergang des Wissens und des
Interesses für solche genauen diakritischen Interpunktionszeichen her-
beigeführt. Bei den Juden hat sich die Zahl solcher Zeichen im
Laufe der Jahrhunderte vermehrt, und verschiedene Systeme, die wohl
ursprünglich unabhängig von einander entstanden waren, sind später
zusammengeflossen und haben so unser kompliziertes System hervor-
gebracht. Die Syrer dagegen haben immermehr die Anwendung
ihrer mit der Zeit sehr komplizierten Systeme ihrer Interpunktion auf-
gegeben, und im höheren Maße dann die literarisch viel ärmeren
Samaritaner. So finden sich alle Zeichen im Cod. Cambridge von
1219 (Plate 38 der *Palaeogr. Society*), Codex Barberini anno 1227 (ibid.
Pl. 89) hat schon eine geringere Anzahl und weicht ein wenig in der
Form ab, ob zwar die Grundformen dieselben bleiben. Cotton Claud.
Brit. Mus. von 1362—63 hat auch schon wieder einige weniger und
weicht auch einigermaßen von den früheren Formen ab, aber auch
hier nur in der Art der Anwendung der Grundlinien, während das
Prinzip dasselbe bleibt. In meinem Cod. ist der Gebrauch dieser
Zeichen schon ganz eingeschrumpft und hat sich nur sporadisch erhalten. Auch weichen die Hss. unter einander sehr ab, in der Kon-
sequenz mit welcher sie diese Zeichen dem Texte beifügen. Es
scheint mehr von der Laune oder dem Wissen des betreffenden Ab-
schreibers abzuhängen, ob und wie häufig er von denselben Gebrauch
macht. Eine feste Norm läßt sich nicht konstatieren, und wenn in
einem Codex ein solches Zeichen sich findet, so ist das noch keine
Gewähr dafür, daß es sich auch an derselben Stelle in einem anderen
Cod. finden wird. Eine von bestimmten Gesetzen geregelte Norm
hat sich nicht herausgebildet, und dadurch ist eine gewisse Willkür
in die Handhabung und Setzung dieser Zeichen eingetreten. Über
den Charakter derselben läßt aber die Setzung, wo sie sich nachweisen läßt, kaum einen Zweifel aufkommen: Bei einer Frage finden
wir häufig ᵂ ad ᷱ; Ausrufung ⁊ zif ⹀: Exod. 22, 10—19. Das Facsimile No. II (S. 535) eines alten Fragmentes Gen. 24, 20—33 in meinem
Besitze enthält Beispiele von solchen Zeichen. Was also das Alter
derselben betrifft, so ergibt sich als notwendige Schlußfolgerung,
daß dieses System, da wir, je höher wir hinaufgehen, einen desto
ausgiebigeren und verständigeren Gebrauch desselben finden, jeden-

falls um Jahrhunderte älter sein muß, als die älteste Hs., in welcher sich diese Zeichen nachweisen lassen. Da wir sie vollkommen ausgebildet schon im Codex Cambridge aus dem Anfange des XIII. Jahrhunderts finden, so dürfte es nicht als übertrieben betrachtet werden, wenn wir das IX. Jahrhundert als den Termin ansetzen, wo sich diese samaritanische Bibel-Punktation herausgebildet hat oder in ein System zusammengefaßt wurde. Wie weit hinauf sich die Anfänge ansetzen lassen, hängt nun von dem Verhältnisse ab zwischen diesem und ähnlichen Punktationssystemen bei den anderen Völkern, besonders aber bei Juden und Syrern.

Sollte aber trotz ISHAK noch ein Zweifel über den wahren Charakter dieser Zeichen obwalten, so würden die Namen derselben ihn beseitigen. Ungleich den meisten syrischen und hebräischen Namen der Accente sind die samaritanischen vollkommen durchsichtig und lassen sich aus der Sprache leicht erklären, wie es auch ISHAK in seiner Weise getan hat. Sie sind eben nur rein syntaktische Interpunktionszeichen, die nur auf einen ganzen Satz als solchen sich beziehen. Sie haben gar keine musikalische Bedeutung, es sei denn daß sie bestimmte Modulationen der Sprache bewirken, die sich bei Frage, Zorn, Wunder, Ruhe und Behaglichkeit von selber ergibt. Es handelt sich also nur um Kolon und Semikolon, um Ausrufungs- und Fragezeichen etc. Wenn auch nicht konsequent durchgeführt, da diese Zeichen nicht regelmäßig benutzt werden, jedenfalls nicht in den Codices die sich erhalten haben, so unterscheiden sie sich doch klar genug von den anderen beiden Systemen der Syrer und Juden, in erster Reihe durch größere Einfachheit und auch durch die geringere Anzahl der Zeichen, die zur Anwendung kommen. Diesen beiden Systemen gegenüber nehmen die samaritanischen Zeichen eine gewisse Selbständigkeit und auch größere Primitivität ein. Aber es läßt sich kaum bezweifeln, daß wir in diesem Systeme nur einen Ausfluß ähnlicher Tendenzen haben, die sich zu einer bestimmten Zeit um den Text der Bibel drehen und zu dessen besserem Verständnisse beitragen sollten, zunächst wohl nur, um die syntaktische Konstruktion für den Leser festzustellen. Ein Versuch, durch äußere Zeichen die Bibel zu kommentieren! Keiner von den dreien, die zunächst in Betracht kommen: Juden, Syrer und Samaritaner, hat sein System ganz unabhängig erfunden, wenn auch jeder einzelne nachher in seiner Weise die ursprünglichen Elemente zu einem Systeme weiter ausgebildet hat. Die verschiedenen Stufen, welche das Syrische System durchgemacht hat, zeigen die von PHILLIPS, MARTIN, DIETTRICH etc. veröffentlichten Texte der Jacobiten und Nestorianer. Die hebräischen Accente sind schwierig zu verfolgen. Altes handschriftliches Material von abweichenden Traditionen ist sehr spärlich. Fragmente in Berlin, Oxford und Cambridge und Hss. in meinem Besitze werden vielleicht etwas mehr Licht in dieses Dunkel bringen. Aber aus dem wenigen Bekannten läßt sich schon eine allmähliche innere Entwickelung nachweisen, wie zuletzt KAHLE gezeigt hat (*ZDMG*, 1901, LV p. 167 ff.). Im Samaritanischen sind wir am schlechtesten daran, denn auch für diese primitiven zehn Zeichen sind wir bisher nur auf zwei oder drei Hss. angewiesen, von welchen bis jetzt nur eine einzige bekannt war, während die andern beiden hier von mir zum ersten Male behandelt sind.

In welchem Verhältnisse steht nun dieses samaritanische System zu den andern in der Form, der Zahl und in den Namen der Zeichen?

In der Geschichte der massoretischen Zeichen im allgemeinen lassen sich drei Stadien der Entwickelung nachweisen. Das erste, wo alle Bezeichnungen nur durch Punkte gemacht wurden, das zweite wo eine Linie, in den meisten Fällen eine senkrechte Linie, sich hinzugesellte, und erst in dritter Reihe der Kreis oder Doppelkreis als schlängelnde Linie. Alle drei sind in den jüd. Accenten vertreten, und obzwar jetzt zu einem organischen Ganzen verbunden, lassen sich doch diese drei Stadien nachweisen: zuerst in den punktierten Buchstaben im Pentateuch, dann in den Vokalen und zuletzt in den Accenten; überdies lassen sich die drei Stadien auch in verschiedenen Systemen nachweisen. Im Syrischen dagegen begegnen wir nur dem Punkte, der sich zu einem Doppelpunkte entwickelt, aber dabei stehen bleibt. Das Samaritanische hält nun eine Mittelstellung ein, indem es sowohl Punkte als auch Striche verwendet; zu dem Kreise oder Halb- und Doppelkreise ist es noch nicht fortgeschritten. Merkwürdig ist nun, daß, obwohl der einzelne Punkt als Worttrenner gewiß von sehr alter Zeit her gebraucht wurde — Beweise dafür phönizische und hebräische Inschriften —, die Reihe der massoretischen Zeichen mit dem Doppelpunkte begann, und nicht mit dem fetten Punkte des *Anna'u*. Hierin stimmt der Samaritaner genauer mit den Juden überein als mit den Syrern, und wie bei den Juden schließt jeder Vers mit dem vertikalen Doppelpunkte. Neben-

bei sei bemerkt, daß in sehr alten hebr. Hss. die vertikalen Doppelpunkte am Schlusse des Verses etwas höher über die Linie zu stehen
kommen als die Buchstaben, so daß der zweite niedere Punkt in
einer Reihe mit den Buchstaben steht, der obere aber über denselben
fast wie ein Ḥolem. Wenden wir uns nun zu den Strichen, so finden
wir bei den Samaritanern: Einzelstrich, *Erkenu* /, Strichpunkt: *Zei'a* ⌐,
und Strich und zwei Punkte : *Turu* /:. Zwei Striche und zwei Punkte
Z'if =:. Daraus entwickelt sich der spitze Winkel, indem zwei Striche
wie *Erkenu* / und *Zei'a* ⌐ verbunden werden, wovon einer schräg
ist: so erhalten wir *Baú* ⌐ mit einem Punkte darüber, *Sheyala* mit
zweien darüber ⌐ und schließlich zwei vertikale Punkte damit verbunden in *Atmaú* ⌐:.

Wenden wir uns nun zu den hebräischen Accenten, so
sind wir durch die Fragmente in Cambridge und Oxford glück-
licher Weise in der Lage, von unerwarteter Seite eine direkte Parallele
in den allgemeinen Grundzügen zu diesen Systemen zu finden. Die
dort vorhandenen Accente bestehen zunächst aus dem einfachen und
dem Doppelpunkte, von welchem einer horizontal und der andere vertikal
ist, dann aus Strichen und Winkel (s. KAHLE, l. c. p. 179—180 und
187). Was ihre innere Bedeutung gewesen sein mag, syntaktisch
oder musikalisch, muß noch unerörtert bleiben, und für verfrüht, ja
geradezu verfehlt betrachte ich es, diese Accente mit dem komplizierten Systeme, das in unseren Bibeln jetzt als massoretisches vor-
liegt, direkt zu vergleichen und dadurch den Wert derselben bestimmen zu wollen. Es ist meiner Meinung nach nicht angebracht
zu behaupten, daß ein Punkt oben genau diesen oder jenen Accent
vertritt, weil wir ihn nachher so in dem anderen Systeme finden. Es
muß nur eines festgehalten werden, nämlich daß zur Zeit und in
der Schule, wo jenes System allein gehandhabt wurde, andere Prinzipien galten für die Setzung bestimmter Zeichen. Wie viel davon
in unser massoretisches System übergegangen ist, muß erst noch
untersucht werden. Aber a priori betrachte ich beide unabhängig
von einander in den Prinzipien, welche in der Setzung bestimmter Zeichen
an bestimmten Teilen des Verses den Schreibern vorschwebten. Hier
haben wir jedenfalls Punkt, Strich und spitze Winkel mit der einzigen
Ausnahme eines Zeichens, welches wie ein etwas offener Kreis aus-
sieht und mir verdächtig vorkommt. Dieselben Grundelemente sind
auch in dem besser bekannten Systeme vorhanden, nur sind sie dort

anders gehandhabt worden. Wir haben nun in dem massoretischen System in unseren Bibeln, welches von Vielen als das Tiberianische bezeichnet wird, ebenfalls Punkte in: Rebia, Zaqef und Segol; Striche in: Maarich, Tarḥa, und obere: Pašta, Gereš, und doppelte Linien: Geršin oder Trein Ḥutrin und Maarichin, die auch als "Trein Ḥutrin" bezeichnet werden; Punkt und Strich: Tebir; zwei Punkte und Strich: Zaqef gadol. Verbindung von zwei Linien zu einem Spitz-Winkel: Šofar holech, oder Munaḥ, Mahpach oder Yethib, und Atnaḥ welches letzteres nur ein auf seinem Schenkel stehender Spitzwinkel ist und so auch in den alten Hss. erscheint, wo alle anderen Linien nur gerade sind, aber je nachdem nach rechts oder links schräg gezogen sind, nicht halbrund wie in modernen Drucken, Maarich, Tarḥa und Tebir, Pašta, Gereš etc. erscheinen. Aus alten Hss. ersieht man auch, daß Darga ursprünglich nur ein Doppelshofar ist, dessen Teile in entgegengesetzter Richtung auf einander gesetzt sind ⌐ = ⌐, und Šalšelet mehrere solcher Šofar mit einander gebunden, so daß eine aus spitzen Winkeln bestehende Kette entsteht. Von den runden und geschlängelten Accenten wie Talša, Qarnei Parah, Zinnor oder Zarqa sehe ich ab, Pazer dagegen gehört mit in diese Liste, weil auch dieses Zeichen in alten Hss. rechts nur eine vertikale kleine Linie hatte, die die horizontale in der Mitte schneidet so: ⊢, also weder Winkel noch Halbkreis ist wie in modernen Drucken. Ich habe hier טעמים und משרתים zusammen erwähnt, obwohl sie nicht alle derselben Zeit angehören, und viele darunter, besonders die משרתים, späteren Ursprunges sind. Die Untersuchungen von KAHLE machen es wahrscheinlich, daß auf Grund alter Traditionen die Zahl der Hauptaccente „Ṭa‘amim" zum Unterschiede von „Neginoth" sich auf zehn beschränken läßt. Wir kommen somit auf dieselbe Zahl, die sich im Samaritanischen erhalten hat. Die Übereinstimmung ist mindestens auffallend und kann kaum auf einem Zufall beruhen. Und wenn man aus dem Labyrinthe und dem Wuste der syrischen Tradition die Hauptaccente ausschält, so wird sich die Zahl der wichtigsten und ursprünglichsten auch auf zehn reduzieren lassen, die eben mit den grammatischen Forderungen am besten übereinstimmen und einen besseren Einblick in die Urgeschichte der biblischen Accente gestatten, als wir sie bisher gehabt haben. Trotz der samaritanischen Accente ist es aber kein leichtes, die zehn ursprünglichen im Hebr. festzustellen. In solchen Fragen muß man sich einerseits vor äußerlicher Ähnlich-

keit hüten und andererseits auch nicht absolute Identität erwarten.
Begriffe können leicht von einem Volke zum andern wandern, aber
in der Aufnahme und Anwendung derselben muß man jedem eine
gewisse Originalität lassen. Die tiefgreifenden Unterschiede zeigen, daß
keines der Systeme von dem anderen direkt entlehnt hat. Es genügt ja,
wenn wir annehmen, daß ungefähr im fünften Jahrhundert sich allmählich in Palästina und Syrien die Praxis eingebürgert hat, den
Text der Bibel durch einige wenige Zeichen zu interpretieren oder
besser zu „interpungieren". Wenn dann in den verschiedenen Systemen,
die auf dieser ursprünglichen Grundlage sich aufgebaut haben, eine
Ähnlichkeit in Zeichen und sogar in Namen sich nachweisen läßt, so
sind wir deshalb doch noch nicht berechtigt, eines direkt vom anderen
abzuleiten. Dazu gehört eine absolute Identität sowohl in Form als
auch in Namen, besonders aber auch in Bedeutung oder Anwendung
derselben. Ich muß mit um so größerem Nachdrucke gegen voreilige
Schlüsse warnen, die aus solchen scheinbaren Analogien gezogen
werden können, als gerade in letzter Zeit die Neigung dazu immer
stärker wird. Ich denke dabei nicht nur an PRÄTORIUS' und KAHLE's
sonst sehr anregende und wertvolle Untersuchungen, sondern auch
an den letzten Beitrag von CONSOLO, der in den *Verhandlungen des
Hamburg. Orient.-Kongresses* p. 214 ff. eine Liste der hebräischen Accente
und der musikalischen Noten der Griechen und Lateiner veröffent-
lichte, die in Form und musikalischer Bedeutung mehr oder minder den
hebräischen entsprechen sollen. CONSOLO ist einer der besten Kenner
der hebräischen Liturgie und traditionellen Cantillation und zugleich
ein hervorragender Tonkünstler, so daß man seine Behauptungen
nicht so leicht von sich weisen kann. Er leidet aber unter der
fehlerhaften Anschauung, daß alle biblischen Accente ursprünglich
eine musikalische Notation darstellen, und kommt daher zu einigermaßen falschen Schlüssen. Wir müssen von dem Standpunkte aus-
gehen, daß die ältesten Accente nichts mit der Musik als solcher
zu tun hatten, aber daß umgekehrt ihnen später eine musikalische
Bedeutung zugeschrieben wurde, als verschiedene Systeme zu einem
zusammenflossen und man mit dem Reichtum von Zeichen nichts
anzufangen wußte, wenn man sie nur als Interpunktionszeichen
auf den Vers als Ganzes bezogen hätte. Man kam daher auf den
Gedanken, besonders den später hinzugefügten Accenten die musikalische Bedeutung beizulegen, die sie nun in der Liturgie besitzen

Die Cantillation ist gewiß älter als die Zeichen, wie aus verschiedenen Stellen im Talmud und Midrasch hervorgeht. Aus eigener Erfahrung kann ich behaupten, daß es zumeist nur die kreisförmigen und oberhalb des Wortes stehenden Accente sind, welche wenigstens bei den Sefardim einen ausgesprochenen musikalischen Charakter haben. Sie sind auch nicht als reine Wortaccente aufzufassen, da sie ebenso häufig auf der tonlosen Silbe des Wortes zu stehen kommen wie diejenigen Zeichen, welche jetzt auf der betonten stehen, besonders Talša, Zarqa, und Segol. Ebenso verhält es sich ja mit „Pašta" und Qadma, welches sich nicht am Worttone hält. Daß die ältesten Formen nicht ursprünglich über die Buchstaben gesetzt wurden, ersieht man aus dem Syrischen und dem System der Fragmente, sowie im Pesiq und Sof Pasuq, welches durch Silluq eigentlich überflüssig gemacht, aber doch beibehalten wurde. Die Tendenz der massoretischen Entwickelung ist Anhäufung des gesamten Materiales. Nichts wird verworfen oder aufgehoben, was sich überhaupt erhalten läßt. Die Massora ist eben nicht eklektisch. Dadurch aber ist geringer Verlaß auf diese sich häufig widersprechende Tradition. Wie unsicher die Tradition der ältesten Accente ist, hat jüngst KAHLE nachgewiesen, l. c. Schon im zehnten Jahrhundert hatte man keine klare Anschauung mehr über das Wesen und den Ursprung derselben, und die Namen wechseln in jeder Liste, die uns überliefert worden ist. Noch heute existiert ein Unterschied in den Namen und auch in der Cantillation, bei den Aschkenazim und Sefardim. Die Letzteren kennen überhaupt nicht das Wort Munaḥ: es heißt Šofar holech. Anstatt Mehupach nennen sie das Zeichen Mahapach, „Maarich" steht für „Mercha" und „Tarha" für „Tifḥa"; auch in Bezug auf Talša, Karne Parah etc. unterscneiden sie sich von einander. Sie nennen jedes Metheg: Ga῾ya. Die Tradition der Accente ist sehr schwankend. In einer Hs. in meinem Besitze Cod. 86, welche die Hagiographen enthält, findet sich eine sehr lange Liste von Accenten, die die persisch-babylonische Tradition darstellt. Der Codex ist außerordentlich interessant, dadurch daß er häufig einer ganz anderen massoretischen Tradition der Hagiographen folgt, und obzwar erst gegen 1490 in Khashan von einem Gelehrten für einen Gelehrten geschrieben (wie das Kolophon zeigt), ist der Text häufig anders vokalisiert und die Accente weichen in den meisten Fällen in ihrer Anwendung von den bekannten massoretischen

ab, wenn auch die Zeichen nicht ganz verschieden sind. Dem
Schreiber hat gewiß ein alter „Muster"-Codex als Vorlage gedient.
Wenn nun ein Vergleich zwischen diesen verschiedenen Systemen
unter einander und dann mit den syrischen und samaritanischen gezogen werden soll, so muß man zeitweilig von der landläufigen Anschauung absehen und mit Hilfe des neuen Materials an die Lösung
der Frage herantreten. Wir müssen uns eine größere Freiheit gestatten und mit einer allgemeinen prinzipiellen Übereinstimmung zufrieden sein. Ein erster Anstoß von Außen ist nicht ausgeschlossen,
nur ist der Beweis dafür kein zwingender. Es handelt sich ferner
darum, das Maß zu bestimmen und die Grenzen zu ziehen. Daß das
Beispiel der griechischen Interpunktion im allgemeinen in späterer
Zeit einen Einfluß ausgeübt haben mag, läßt sich a priori ebenso
wenig verneinen als bejahen, ist aber, soweit es das Hebr. betrifft, nicht
anzunehmen. Noch viel weniger kann eine direkte Entlehnung für
biblische Accente in Betracht kommen. Eine parallele Entwickelung
kann wohl stattgefunden haben, aber da es sich um bibl. Texte
handelt, so wird die Priorität dem Griechischen nicht zugesprochen
werden können. Aus dem Gesagten geht hervor, daß die Anfänge der Accentuation im Hebräischen wohl nichts andres gewesen
sind, als reine Interpunktionszeichen, ebenso wie bei Sam. und Syr.
In der Wahl der Zeichen ist jedes System dann seinen eigenen Weg
gegangen, aber in dem Prinzip, von dem diese drei ausgegangen
sind, zeigt sich doch eine so innige Gleichartigkeit, daß sie nicht ganz
unabhängig von einander entstanden sein können. Wenn nun auch
die sam. Zeichen sich eng an die ältesten hebr. der Fragmente
anschließen, so ist doch die Verbindung zwischen den syrischen und
samaritanischen Namen bis zu einem gewissen Grade enger als mit
denen der Juden. Daß das betreffende Zeichen nicht in allen Systemen
denselben Namen trägt, ist nach dem bisher Gesagten nicht zu ver-
wundern. Namen und Zeichen brauchen sich nicht zu decken. Es
genügt darauf hinzuweisen, daß in der ältesten Liste der syrischen
Accente (PHILLIPS, *Appendix* I) Namen für die Lesezeichen vorkommen, die den sam. genau entsprechen und zwar Pasuqa Schluß =
sam. *Afsa'*, Garura oder *Naguda* = sam. *'Nged* Continuatio, Meshae-
lana = sam. *Sheyala* Frage; Metdamrana = sam. *Atmaú* Wunder;
Menihana = sam. *Annaú* Ruhe; Mesalvana = sam. *Baú* Bitte; Paquda
= sam. *Zei'a* Befehl; und Mehavyana möchte ich mit *Erkenu* Hin-

weis vergleichen. Ob Qaruya = *Zif* oder *Ze'ia* zu nehmen ist oder
= *Turú*, lasse ich dahingestellt.

Nicht so leicht ist es, Parallelen mit den Namen der hebräischen
Accente zu finden, da die ursprünglichen Namen und die Bedeutung derselben schon längst verschollen sind und nur hie und da leise Spuren
davon sich erhalten haben. Die ganze Grundlage, auf welcher sich das
Accentsystem ursprünglich aufgebaut hat, hat sich im Hebräischen
verschoben. Der Vers als solcher wird jetzt in seine einzelnen Bestand-
teile aufgelöst und jedem einzelnen Wort wird eine separate Behand-
lung zu Teil; Wort- und Satzton ist mit musikalischen Noten verquickt.
Alle Verse werden nun nach einer Schablone behandelt, und es wird
keine Rücksicht auf den idealen Inhalt genommen. Die Länge oder
Kürze der Verse bestimmt die Anzahl und Ordnung der Accente, die
angewendet werden. Aber je höher wir hinauf gehen und je älter
die Fragmente sind, die an's Licht kommen, desto geringer ist die
Anzahl der Zeichen. In diesen Fragmenten und in den Traditionen
der verschiedenen massoretischen Schulen hat sich hin und wieder
eine Spur von der ursprünglichen Einfachheit der Gliederung und ge-
ringen Zahl der Zeichen erhalten. Leider sind uns die Namen nicht
übermittelt worden. Die jetzt bekannten Namen der Accente sind
zumeist modern, das ersieht man aus der Tatsache, daß sie nur von
der Form derselben herrühren. Die späteren Massoreten, die auch
neue Zeichen hinzufügten, hatten die ursprüngliche Bedeutung der
alten Zeichen vergessen und so benannten sie diese nach der Form,
in welcher sie sie vorfanden, es sei denn, daß der eine oder der andere
Name so fest eingewurzelt und durchsichtig war, z. B. wie Atnaḥ
und Silluq, daß daran nicht zu ändern war. Ich bin mir noch lange
nicht sicher, daß die Namen nicht im Laufe der Zeit von einem
Zeichen zum andern übertragen worden sind. Unter den Accenten
haben sich nun Namen erhalten, die unabhängig von der Form sind
und mehr der syntaktischen Bedeutung entsprechen. Dahin gehören
Namen wie Pesiq und Atnaḥ „Mitte", „Ruhe" und „Ende", Schluß des
Verses, die an die sam. *Afsa'* und *Anaú* erinnern. In der alten Liste,
die Ibn Balaam zugeschrieben wird, finden wir „Nagdah", welches
sam. *Nged* entspricht; Maarich und Tarhha deuten gleichfalls auf die Art
des Lesens hin und schließen sich als solche an *Erkennu* an, Tebir bricht
das Lesen ab, und Pazer zieht es in die Länge, Geriš treibt es an. Da
die meisten dieser Zeichen in fast jedem Verse zusammen vorkommen, so

haben sie nicht mehr die Kraft einzelner Interpunktionszeichen, die sich auf den ganzen Vers erstrecken. Wenn ich sie aber aus der Anzahl der Accente heraushebe und hier behandle, so ist es um zu zeigen, daß in der Liste der Namen sich doch noch manches archaische Material erhalten hat, das unabhängig ist von der Form, und daß sie ursprünglich wohl andere und weitere Bedeutung gehabt haben und allein oder in Verbindung mit einem oder zwei anderen den ganzen Vers beherrscht haben. Genau wie im Samaritanischen und Syrischen. Und wenn man die alten Texte genauer untersucht, so wird man gerade diese Zeichen unter den ältesten finden, die für die biblische Accentuation gebraucht wurden.

Aus diesen Vergleichen ziehe ich nun noch einen weiteren Schluß: auf die Zeit, für welche wir den Anfang dieses samaritanischen Systems ansetzen dürfen. Das Samaritanische steht, wie wir gesehen haben, dem Syrischen am nächsten in Bezug auf die Namen der Zeichen. Wenn es sich bewahrheiten sollte, daß diese Namen erst dann in das Syrische aufgenommen waren, nachdem im VI. Jahrhunderte die Werke von Aristoteles übersetzt waren, so hätten wir einen Terminus a quo für die Entstehung der Namen. Die Zeichen können etwas älter sein und auch die Zahl derselben könnte Anfangs sich auch nur auf fünf reduzieren lassen, und könnten sie somit mit den ursprünglichen vier oder fünf Abteilungen des Syrischen übereinstimmen. Die Namen wären dann hinzugefügt worden, zuerst im Syrischen durch die Nachfolger von Yusaf von Ahvas, oder von ihm selber; und wären dann von den Syrern zu den Samaritanern gelangt, die sich gewiß gesträubt hätten, etwas von den Juden, mit welchen sie in Jahrhunderte langer Fehde lebten, anzunehmen. Der tiefergehende Unterschied zwischen sam. und hebr. Namen der Accente schließt aber die Möglichkeit derselben Quelle für die letzteren aus.

Jedenfalls glaube ich, daß für die Frage nach dem Ursprunge der hebr. Accente durch den Vergleich mit den samaritanischen und syrischen auf Grund des von mir hier zum ersten Male im Zusammenhange behandelten neuen Materiales eine von der bisher versuchten verschiedene Lösung möglich ist. Zunächst muß eine innere Scheidung der Accente, die durch Form und Namen bedingt und durch die Parallele mit den anderen Systemen gekräftigt wird, vorgenommen und auf diese Weise die Schichtung klar gelegt und ein besserer Einblick in die innere Entwicklung gewonnen werden.

Welche Bedeutung diese sam. Zeichen nach dieser Richtung
hin auch haben mögen, so ist ihr Wert für den sam. Text noch ungleich größer und verdiente daher eingehend behandelt zu werden.

2. Zahl der Kessen, Worte im Texte des sam. Pentateuch.

Ich beschränke mich in diesen weiteren Angaben auf das in
meinem Cod. Or. 800 enthaltene Kolophon, dessen Facsimile hier erscheint (No. III), das der Hohepriester AMRAM von einem alten Codex
abgeschrieben haben muß, um definitiv die Zahl dieser eigentümlichen
Abteilungen des Pentateuch nach sam. Tradition festzustellen. Aus
den von mir verglichenen Codices des Brit. Museums habe ich das
Resultat gewonnen, daß die best authentifizierte Zahl sich auf 966
beläuft. Mit dieser stimmt die Zahl derselben, wenn wir die einzelnen
Posten zusammenzählen, wie sie sich am Ende jedes der fünf
Bücher finden und zwar: Gen. (fol. 59b) 250, Exod. (fol. 107b) 200,
Levit. (fol. 137b) 135, Numeri (fol. 181a) 220 und schließlich Deuter.
161 „esse" wie ISHAK das Wort las. Mit dieser Gesamtsumme
stimmt auch die Angabe des neuen Cod. des Brit. Museums Or. 6461.
Die Londoner Polyglotte gibt nicht die Summe des ganzen Pentat.,
und in fast keinem anderen Cod. des Brit. Mus. ist die Gesamtsumme
gegeben, mit Ausnahme von Cott. Claud. Am Schlusse der einzelnen
Bücher findet man aber die Angaben der „Kesse" der betreffenden
Bücher. Wenn man diese zusammenzählt, so ergibt sich als Gesamtsumme für die Polyglotte 964 Kesse. Nun enthält mein Ms. eine
zweite Angabe, der zufolge die Summe sich auf 960 „Kesse" beläuft,
und darin stimmt diese Hs. mit Cott. Claud. Brit. Mus. überein. Der
Abschreiber AMRAM hat einfach eine sehr alte Kopie abgeschrieben, der er
diese Notiz entnommen hat, und hat sich nicht die Mühe genommen, die
einzelnen Posten, wie sie sich in der Hs. finden, zusammenzuzählen. Er
traute gewiß seinem Originale und rechnete nicht noch einmal nach.
In welchem Zusammenhange diese Kesse mit den Abteilungen der
hebr. Bibel stehen, wird man nur dann positiv feststellen können,
wenn die Pentateuchrollen beider Recensionen mit einander genauer
verglichen sein werden. Ich habe den Versuch gemacht mit dem
Fragmente der uralten Rolle in meinem Besitze und bin zu dem
überraschendem Resultate gelangt, daß die meisten der sam. „Kesse"
genau dort beginnen, wo sich im Hebräischen eine Petuḥa (seltener

eine Setumah) findet, und in vielen Fällen auch mit dem alten „Seder" übereinstimmen. Die Zahl aller Petuḥot und Setumot in der Bibel beläuft sich aber nur auf 669, ein Drittel weniger als die Kesse der sam. Version des Pentat., welche also in kleinere Stücke geteilt worden ist. Wenn man nun die alten syrischen Hss. der Bibel und die griechischen Hss. vergleicht, so stößt man auch da auf ähnliche Abteilungen, die bisher aber weder berücksichtigt noch viel weniger untersucht worden sind. Man hat nur auf „Stichen" geachtet und diese Abteilungen der Texte ganz ignoriert, trotzdem sie gewiß auf alter Grundlage basieren und unzweifelhaft in innigem Zusammenhange mit diesen bisher nicht genügend erklärten Abteilungen des hebräischen Textes stehen. Ich muß mir aber die detaillierte Untersuchung auf eine andere Gelegenheit aufsparen und ebenso die Wiedergabe von ISHAK's Bericht darüber. Es genügt hier eine alte „massoretische" Tradition nachgewiesen zu haben, die sich auf alle alten Versionen und Rezensionen des Pentat. erstreckt und bisher, soweit ich sehe, ganz unbeachtet geblieben ist.

Unmittelbar nach der Angabe der Zahl der „Kesse" findet sich, und nur in dieser Hs., eine Angabe der Zahl der Worte des Pentateuch. Sie beläuft sich beim Samaritaner auf 86,362, gegenüber den 81,404 der hebr. Rezension nach GINSBURG's Ausgabe der Bibel. Ein Plus auf Rechnung des Sam. von 4,958 Worten. Daß der sam. Text mehr Worte enthält als der hebr., ist sattsam bekannt. Hier haben wir zum ersten Mal eine genaue Angabe der numerischen Differenz. Sie ist nicht ohne Bedeutung, wenn auf Grund des inzwischen sehr gewachsenen Materials eine neue Ausgabe der samaritanischen Rezension unternommen und das Verhältnis zwischen Samaritaner und Hebräer auf's Neue festgestellt werden sollte. Aus meiner Untersuchung (*Illuminated Bibles*, London 1901 p. 33 sqq.) hat sich mir jedenfalls das Resultat ergeben, daß je älter eine sam. Hs. ist — und besonders wenn sie eine Rolle ist, also für den liturgischen Gebrauch und infolge dessen mit größerer Sorgfalt geschrieben ist — um so geringer die Unterschiede sind sowohl im Zusetzen als Auslassen von ganzen Worten oder einzelnen Buchstaben (scriptio plena und defectiva). In dieser „massoretischen" Notiz haben wir nun zum ersten Mal eine genaue Angabe, von welcher aus man die verschiedenen Hss. prüfen kann. Ob diese Notiz verläßlich ist, kann sich eben nur nach einer eingehenden Prüfung zeigen.

Leider ist es die einzige, die sich in den in Europa befindlichen Hss. erhalten hat. AMRAM würde sie aber nicht hinzugeschrieben haben, wenn er sie nicht in seiner Vorlage gefunden hätte. Ich bin bemüht herauszufinden, welche Hs. in Nablus ihm als Vorlage gedient hat. Bei den in der kleinen Gemeinde obwaltenden Verhältnissen ist es aber momentan fast unmöglich, von der Ferne eine befriedigende Antwort zu erhalten. Man muß die Sache an Ort und Stelle verfolgen und dort die wenigen Hss. persönlich einsehen, wenn man überhaupt Zutritt zu denselben erhalten kann.

In noch erhöhtem Maße wäre es wünschenswert, eine weitere handschriftliche Bestätigung zu finden für die nächste Notiz, die ich als die wichtigste unter allen bisher gefundenen betrachte.

Unmittelbar vor den zehn Zeichen steht nämlich folgendes: „Abgeschrieben (oder: überliefert) von unseren Vätern den reinen, auf ihnen das Wohlwollen (Gottes)!, genau wie sie es kopiert (oder „überliefert") haben, nach den siebzig Ältesten." Auf meine Frage an ISHAK, wer denn diese siebzig Ältesten seien, antwortete er mir: *aze'enim bamadbar*, die siebzig von Moses gewählten Ältesten. Auf meine weitere Frage: „wie verhielt sich das nun zu ihrer Behauptung, daß ihr ältester Codex, auf welchen sie sich immer berufen, von „(Abishua) Pinehas ha-Cohen" geschrieben sei?" wurde er stutzig und konnte mir keine Antwort geben. Die Frage über diesen Pinehas ben Elazar hacohen kann ich hier nicht erörtern. Ich glaube aber, daß es sich um einen gewissen Pinehas handelt, der in alter aber historischer Zeit in Damaskus einen Codex abgeschrieben hatte, denselben wie ich glaube, den sie noch heute in Nablus besitzen und anachronistisch auf den biblischen Pinehas beziehen. Der Wunsch einen Codex zu haben, der älter als irgend einer der jüdischen Tradition ist, spielt dabei auch mit. Aber darauf kann ich momentan nicht eingehen. Es würde sich aber, wenn sich meine Konjektur bestätigen sollte, dadurch das Alter ihres ältesten Codex feststellen lassen und auch die Basis zeigen, auf welcher ihre etwas verworrene Tradition beruht. Das ließe dann den Raum frei für diese Notiz hier, deren weittragende Bedeutung nicht zu unterschätzen ist; denn sie ist unzweifelhaft ein direkter Hinweis auf die Septuaginta In der gesamten nachbiblischen Literatur kennt man nur diese 70, die Verfasser der griechischen Version. Die samaritanische Tradition weist also hier direkt auf die griechische Version hin als die bessere, der sie in ihrer Rezension, im Widerspruche zu der hebräischen der Juden, gefolgt ist. Daß ein inniger Zusammenhang zwischen diesen Rezensionen existiert, braucht ja kaum bemerkt zu werden. Von dem Momente, wo die samaritanische Version in Europa bekannt wurde, ist diese Ähnlichkeit und Verwandtschaft zwischen Sam. und LXX aufgefallen und Gegenstand eingehender Vergleiche und Untersuchungen geworden. Aber eine direkte Bestätigung von Seiten der samaritanischen Tradition hatte niemand erwartet. Ich glaube, daß dieses Kolophon der erste Hinweis auf die LXX in einem Cod. des sam. Pentateuch ist. Alles was bisher über das Verhältnis zwischen diesen beiden gemutmaßt wurde, muß der Tatsache weichen, daß zu einer bestimmten Zeit der Zusammenhang und die Abhängigkeit der beiden Versionen von einander in der sam. Tradition sich noch erhalten hatte. AMRAM, der Hohepriester, der dieses Kolophon abgeschrieben hat, hat es nicht erfunden, und bei seiner sonst bezeugten Gewissenhaftigkeit ist nicht daran zu zweifeln, daß er alles, was sich jetzt am Schlusse dieser Hs. findet, von einem alten Codex abgeschrieben hat.

Interessant ist das Wort, das hier für „Abschreiben" oder „Tradieren" gebraucht wird: עתק *ateq*, im Pent. nur Gen. 12, 8 und 26, 22, Targ. S.: אסתלק und עקר übersetzt. Bekanntlich haben die Juden später das Wort besonders nach Prov. 25, 1 als „Abschreiben" und späterhin sogar als „Übersetzen" gebraucht. Die Karäer haben es als „Überlieferung" = מסר genommen und so in ihrer Literatur gebraucht. Wo haben die Samaritaner es in diesen Bedeutungen hergenommen? Ich habe beide Möglichkeiten zugegeben und daher sowohl „Abschreiben" als „Überliefern" übersetzt. ISHAK sagte: „*katebu*". Es ist nicht ohne Bedeutung, das Wort so bei den Samaritanern zu finden wie bei den Juden in talmudischer und den Karäern in nachtalmudischer Zeit. Der Sprachschatz der Samaritaner ist seinem hebräischen Gehalte nach bisher nicht genügend untersucht worden. Es bleiben noch viele sam. Probleme zu lösen. Mögen diese kleinen Beiträge hier als ein Scherflein zu dem Versuche der Lösung betrachtet werden!

I

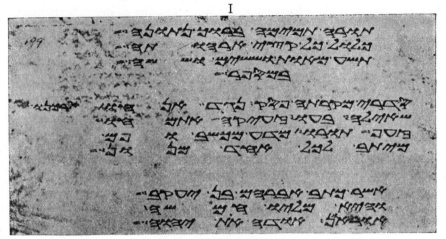

Cod. Brit. Museum.

II

Cod. Gaster 805 C (Gen. 24, 20—33).

Facsimile III umstehend.

III

Cod. Gaster 800 fol. 217ᵃ.

M e r x (Adalbert): Der Messias oder Ta'eb der Samaritaner. 5
Nach bisher unbekannten Quellen. Mit einem Gedächtnis-
wort von Karl Marti. Gießen 1910. (Beihefte zur Zeitschrift für die alttestamentl. Wissenschaft, XVII.)

Die älteste Korrespondenz mit den Samaritanern wird durch
Thomas Marshall im 17. Jahrhundert zu einem jähen Abschlusse 10
gebracht, weil er die Nachrichten über den samaritanischen Messias,
die durch Huntington u. a. nach Europa gebracht wurden, zu
Missionszwecken benutzt und den Samaritanern Christentum predigt.
Trotzdem hat das Interesse an dieser Frage nicht abgenommen und
ist immer wieder zur Sprache gekommen in dem ferneren Briefwechsel, 15
der sich weiter entsponnen und sogar in dem letzten von Kautzsch
veröffentlichten Briefe einen Nachhall gefunden hat. Der Name
des vermeintlichen samaritanischen Messias, sowie dessen theologische
Bedeutung ist bisher verschiedentlich gedeutet worden. Eine große
Literatur darüber verzeichnet schon Gesenius und einen reichhaltigen 20
Nachtrag Montgomery, p. 246 ff. Aber bis auf die letzten Jahr-
zehnte beruhte die ganze Spekulation auf der Ausdeutung der verschiedenen Briefe, die vom Ende des 16. Jahrhunderts an nach
Europa gekommen waren, und auf einigen Andeutungen in den
spärlichen liturgischen Hymnen, die bis dahin veröffentlicht wurden. 25
Erst seit den letzten Jahrzehnten des 19. Jahrhunderts fließen
die Nachrichten etwas reichlicher, und diese haben ihren zeitweiligen
Abschluß in dem vorliegenden Werke von Merx gefunden. Es war
aber dem Verfasser nicht beschieden, das Buch zu veröffentlichen.
Bei dem Imprimatur, welches er dem letzten Bogen beigefügt hatte, 30
überraschte ihn der Tod. Professor Marti hat sich nun der liebe-
vollen Aufgabe unterzogen, die letzte Gabe des großen Forschers
den Gelehrten darzubieten, nicht bloß als Andenken an den Verstorbenen, sondern weil auch er die richtige Ansicht teilt: daß
„der Samaritanismus als Faktor in der Geschichte der religiösen 35
Bewegungen, zur Zeit als das Christentum seine Lehren formte,
eingestellt werden muß".
Das Buch enthält nun eigentlich 5 Texte, denn Nr. I (Vor-
bemerkungen) bietet einen Teil eines samaritanischen Liedes, zu
dem Nr. II (Ein liturgisches Lied über den Ta'eb oder Messias) 40
gehört. Beide sind nämlich Teile e i n e s u n d d e s s e l b e n liturgischen Hymnus des Abischa für den Versöhnungstag (15. Jahr-

hundert); Nr. III (Die biblischen Beweise) arabisch, anonym; Nr. IV
(Die Widerlegung der Hibat ibn Naǧm, „die einem gewissen
Schaich Ibrahim aus der Familie Qajas gehört") und Nr. V (Ein
Midrasch über Sintflut und Auftreten des Messias - Ta'eb). Die
5 letzte Seite wird durch einen „Kalender mit Vergleichung der
samaritanischen und Hiǧradatierung" ausgefüllt. Alle diese Texte
sind von einer deutschen Übersetzung begleitet und dogmengeschicht-
lich nach allen Seiten hin erläutert. Eine Beurteilung des von
Merx Geleisteten zerfällt nun ganz natürlich in 2 Teile: 1. in den
10 philologischen und literarhistorischen auf der einen, und 2. den
dogmengeschichtlichen auf der anderen Seite, und die Untersuchung
demgemäß in 1. über die Geschichte und Beschaffenheit der Texte,
die uns hier „nach bisher unbekannten Quellen" geboten werden,
und 2. über die Frage nach der Bedeutung des Ta'eb-Messias vom
15 samaritanischen Gesichtspunkte, denn dieser allein muß der aus-
schlaggebende sein. Die Tragik der so viel besprochenen und so
wenig gekannten Samaritaner scheint sich auch auf ihre Literatur
zu erstrecken. Es wird viel davon gesprochen, aber die wenigsten
scheinen sie zu kennen, ja nicht einmal das, was bisher in Europa
20 geleistet worden ist. Wir haben hierfür einen schlagenden Beweis.
Bei der großen Verehrung, die ich für den verstorbenen Prof. Merx
hege, ist es mir äußerst peinlich, darauf eingehen zu müssen. Ich
bin fest überzeugt, daß Prof. Merx in gutem Treu und Glauben
gehandelt hat. Um so merkwürdiger und sonderbarer sind nun
25 folgende Tatsachen: Auf dem Orientalistenkongresse 1889 legte
Prof. Merx der gelehrten Versammlung ein liturgisches Lied über
den Ta'eb vor, bestehend aus 48 Doppelversen, die er in der Gothaer
Hs. Nr. 963 entdeckt hatte; im Jahre 1893 erschienen die Akten
und im Jahre 1894 druckt Prof. Hilgenfeld denselben Text noch
30 einmal ab und führt das Thema weiter aus. Daraufhin schreibt
D. Cowley im „Expositor" 1895, p. 161: „It seems strange that when
a learned Professor is cataloguing MSS. the most extensive collection
of the texts already printed should escape his notice. It is almost
incredible that a *second* learned Professor, after an interval of
35 nearly five years, should still ignore the literature of the subject.
But Samaritan studies have unfortunately suffered a good deal from
this kind of treatment"; denn lange bevor Merx seinen Text entdeckt hatte, hatte Heidenheim in der samaritanischen Liturgie, die
1887 erschienen war, pp. 85—99 den ganzen Hymnus abgedruckt,
40 von dem der von Merx entdeckte Text nur ein Fragment war.
Aber Cowley selbst wußte auch nicht, daß Heidenheim viele Jahre
vorher in seiner Vierteljahrschrift, Bd. V, Zürich 1873, pp. 169—182
unter dem Titel: „Die Christologie der Samaritaner" den wichtigsten Teil dieses Hymnus und zwar die Buchstaben ה, ו (nur einige
45 Zeilen), ז, und einen Teil von ח [denn die vielzeiligen Strophen
sind alphabetisch angeordnet], den samaritanischen Text mit gegen-
überstehender deutscher Übersetzung, Anmerkungen und Erläute-

rungen veröffentlicht hatte. Hilgenfeld's Aufmerksamkeit wurde
von Heidenheim darauf gelenkt, und er erkannte dann im folgenden Jahrgange (1895) die Priorität Heidenheim's an. Alles das
scheint Herrn Prof. Merx entgangen zu sein. Daraufhin veröffent-
lichte Heidenheim diesen Tatbestand in seinem „Commentar Mar- 5
qah's" (Bibliotheca Samaritana, Bd. III, p. XXX—XXXI, Anmerk.).
Trotz alledem wurde derselbe ganze Hymnus noch einmal von
Prof. Merx entdeckt (!), in einem von ihm erst später erworbenen
handschriftlichen Gebetbuche der Samaritaner für den Versöhnungstag. Auszüge hieraus erscheinen nun hier unter Nr. 1 und decken 10
sich — wie natürlich — mit den Edd. Heidenheim. Eine sonderbare Verkettung von Tatsachen, und es ist verwunderlich, daß der
Herausgeber dieser Tatsachen nicht mit einem Worte gedenkt! So
wenig ist man mit der samaritanischen Literatur vertraut. Aber
diese Frage hat noch eine andere, für den Text selbst bedeutsame 15
Seite; denn so sehr unzuverlässig die Herausgabe der Texte, die
Heidenheim besorgt hat, ist, — in manchen Fällen hat er das Un-
glaublichste geleistet, wie ich anderswo zeigen werde, — so hat er
doch, wie schon Cowley bemerkt hat, gerade d i e s e Texte mit der
größten Sorgfalt herausgegeben und eine Kollation damit oder mit 20
dem Original im Brit. Mus. hätte an manchen Stellen zu anderen
Resultaten geführt, als sie uns jetzt vorliegen. Auch ich besitze
noch einen Text davon Cod. 849 fol. 12^b—19^b, und hätte ich vorher davon gewußt, so hätte ich diese Hs. zugleich mit anderen, auf
die ich noch zu sprechen komme, dem verstorbenen Herausgeber 25
zur Verfügung gestellt. Bei diesen äußerst dunklen und schwierigen
Problemen kommt es sehr viel auf minutiöse Detailfragen an, besonders da es, wie Merx selbst anmerkt, kein leichtes ist, sich in
den Gedankengang der Samaritaner hineinzuleben, „daß die Übersetzungen unter vielen Vorbehalten gemacht sind, weil das Samari- 30
tanische sprachlich nicht leicht zu überwinden ist, wenn man nicht
arabische Übersetzungen hat. Es liegen hier überall Fußangeln,
durch die man leicht zu Falle kommt, und welche große Vorsicht
und Umsicht des Bearbeiters erfordern!"
Ich selbst habe mich der Mühe unterzogen, diese Texte mit 35
den Hss. zu kollationieren. Schon dadurch ergibt sich an sehr
vielen Stellen ein anderer Sinn als der von Merx ermittelte. Es
ist unmöglich, hier auf alle Einzelheiten einzugehen: es hieße denn,
die Texte noch einmal ganz abdrucken und ganz anders übersetzen.
Ich muß mich mit einigen Beispielen begnügen, die von ent- 40
scheidender Bedeutung sind. Ich führe auf: p. 7, Z. 2: מקדשי lies
מבקשי; p. 8, Z. 1: שה לו lies לושי. Die darauf folgende Übersetzung von Merx muß auch eingehend geändert werden. Ich beschränke mich auf die folgenden Sätze, die bei Merx so lauten:
„Der Garten Eden ist auf meinem heiligen Berge gepflanzt, der 45
Gottesstätte Garizim, auf welcher rings um ihn auf vier Stand-
plätzen (Säulen?) Heiligtümer gesammelt sind. Und ich will sie

dir erklären, da deren Kenntnis in meinem Kopfe ist. Eins nenne
ich Aburtha (Durchgang), in dem die Priester walten (רשא?), und
eins Altar (Abraham's, dem befohlen wurde, ein Schaf zu nehmen),
eines Ackerstück, wo mein Haupt erhoben wird, und die Mitte ist
5 der ewige Hügel, der Platz der Heiligtümer".

Man muß sich in die Dogmatik, in die religiösen Vorstellungen
und in den liturgischen Gedankengang der Samaritaner eingelesen
haben, um diesen Text richtig zu verstehen. Nach samaritanischer
Anschauung lag das Paradies auf dem Berge Garizim, und dort
10 haben sich die wichtigsten Ereignisse der biblischen Geschichte ab-
gespielt. Vier dieser sind es, die Abischa hervorheben will. Es
muß also lauten: . . . . „auf welchem (Garizim) diejenigen, die
(Gott) gesucht haben, sich dort, gleich vier Grundpfeilern, rings
um ihn versammelt haben. . . . . Eines ist: K i r y a t h
15 'Aburtha, wo die Hohenpriester sind" (d. h. der Platz, der Kirjath
'Aburtha heißt, nicht weit von Schechem, wo nach samaritanischer
Tradition die Hohenpriester von Eleasar an begraben sind. Die
Gräber werden bis heute noch gezeigt). Der Name 'Aburtha, Ma-
burtha oder Mamortha kommt schon auf römischen Münzen vor,
20 die in Sebastia (Neapolis) z. Z. der römischen Herrschaft geschlagen
wurden (v. Juynboll, pp. 294—96). Das samaritanische Wort
ארשי bedeutet: Häupter (eine Metathesis von ראשי). „Und eines
ist: der Altar Abraham's, der zur Sara sagte: Knete (das Mehl für
das Brot zum Empfange der drei Engel", s. Genesis 18, 6 לושי).
25   „Und eines ist: ‚das Feldstück‘, wo mein Haupt erhoben wurde"
(das Feldstück, welches Jakob s. Z. bei Schechem sich angekauft
hatte und wo die Gebeine Joseph's, des Hauptes des Stammes der
Ephraimiten, begraben wurde, s. Genesis 33, 19 und Jos. 24, 32).
„Und die Mitte: ‚der ewige Hügel‘, der Platz der Heiligtümer".
30   Im nächsten Texte, im 6. Liede ist p. 9 ein ganzer Vers des
Originales ausgelassen. Den letzten Halbvers, Zeile 4 von oben:
בקצת שמעתי נבי אקים להם etc. übersetzt Merx: „Ich habe es teilweise gehört. Einen Propheten werde ich ihm erwecken" etc. etc.
Merx hat das Wort בקצת mißverstanden; es ist aber nichts anderes
35 als der samaritanische Ausdruck für Kapitel oder Paragraph (פרק
im Hebr.) und soll heißen: „In dem Kapitel, (welches mit dem Worte)
שמעתי (anfängt)"; denn die Paragraphen oder Kapitel werden ge-
wöhnlich nach dem ersten Worte benannt   Der letzte Halbvers
wird übersetzt: „Es wird auf dir jeder Fleck sitzen etc". Das
40 Samaritanische dafür lautet: ישרי עליך כל מומה וגו'. Merx hat
nicht erkannt, wie es auch Anderen ergangen ist, daß כל מומה
oder כל מאום „alles" und nicht „nichts" bedeutet. Und die Stelle
heißt also: „Und alles wird dir recht sein".
     Im nächsten Texte p. 10, Z. 2 פתרתי ומה wird von Merx
45 übersetzt: „was ich erläutert habe". Im Samaritanischen bedeutet
aber . . . ומה „und n i c h t" d. h. habe ich erläutert auch nur einen
Teil . . . Zeile 9 anstatt האמן בתרו lies: יאמן באתרו und anstatt

wie Merx zu übersetzen: „wird jeder Einzelne nach ihm glauben",
muß übersetzt werden: „und jeder Einzelne wird an seinem Orte
fest sein" (d. h. die Menschen werden z. Z. des Ta'eb in Ruhe und
Sicherheit wohnen). Überhaupt müßte die Übersetzung des zweiten
Teils eine ganz andere sein! P. 12, Z. 36 statt קמם: lies נקמך 5
„erlöse sie von deiner Rache", und die 2. Hälfte des Verses:
וזכור ברית אקרי heißt nicht: „und erinnere dich des ursprünglichen
Bundes", sondern entspricht dem hebr.: וזכור ברית אבות, „und
erinnere dich des Bundes mit den Vorfahren". Zeile 39 anstatt:
„und rede kein Wort gegen den Abtrünnigen etc." muß übersetzt 10
werden: „rede kein Wort für die Abtrünnigen etc." (denn Moses
tritt nach samaritanischer Auffassung als Fürsprecher „für" das
Volk und nicht also Ankläger „gegen" auf). Und so steht auch
im Handschrifttexte Zeile 67 anstatt Merx: יתבלל משה חיבים die
Variante: יתפלל משה בעד החיבים. Zwischen Zeile 74—75 ist 15
eine ganze Zeile ausgelassen. Ebenso fehlt die zweite Zeile im
Texte p. 16. Hier will ich mich bloß auf ein oder zwei Bemerkungen beschränken. Zeile 3 חתמת etc. heißt nicht: „Siegel
von Fünfungen von Tagen", sondern „der Schluß der 50 Tage,
die als 'Omertage vom Passahfeste bis zum Schabuothfeste gezählt 20
werden, das sind also die (kanon.) 50 Tage. Zeile 4 בתורה הקור
wird von Merx übersetzt: „in der Thora sind sie vereinigt". Der
Strich über dem ה bedeutet aber, daß dieser Buchstabe wie ב gelesen
werden muß. Das Wort ist also הקבו zu lesen und geht auf den
Ausdruck der Bibel zurück: נקבו בשמות (Num. 1, 17) d. h. „wird in 25
der Thora durch drei Namen bezeichnet", wie sie auch in den drei
folgenden Zeilen genannt werden: 1. חג הקציר, 2. וחג שבעות und
3. ויום הבכורים. Merx verzichtet darauf, den Text, den er p. 17
abdruckt, überhaupt zu übersetzen. Ich will nur einige Varianten
mitteilen, und zwar: Zeile 13 anstatt מורעד lies הכבד, Zeile 14 30
anstatt מן lies מנה. Diese Halbzeile 17 נגד פסק מקרא ist von
großem Interesse und ich würde mich nicht wundern, wenn sie
Andern, die mit der Geschichte der samaritanischen Akzente nicht
vertraut sind, unüberwindliche Schwierigkeiten geboten hätte. Es
bedeutet nämlich: daß „sie die Thora lesen gemeinsam, die ganze 35
Nacht bis am Morgen, nach den Modulationen der Akzente: מקרא
פסק נגד" (s. Gaster in Nöldeke's Festschrift, p. 513 ff.). Wir
haben hier nebenbei auch den wertvollen Nachweis, daß noch im
14. Jahrhundert die Namen der samaritanischen Akzente und das
Lesen der Thora nach diesen Akzenten als feststehende Tatsache galt. 40
Zeile 18 anstatt אל lies עד == עד („bis"). Ich gehe nun zu Text II
über, der wie schon oben bemerkt, bisher mindestens dreimal abgedruckt und mehrere Male übersetzt und kommentiert worden ist.
Ich will nur ein oder zwei merkwürdige Fehler, die schon von
Anderen verbessert wurden, aber hier nichtsdestoweniger stehen ge- 45
blieben sind, anführen. Zeile 27: ויבלל לשן העברים: ויתגלו לשן
עבראיתו von Merx übersetzt: „Und er (der Ta'eb) wird die Sprache

der Juden (Ibrim) verwirren, und die Sprache seines (echten) Hebräertums wird geoffenbaret werden", was natürlich Unsinn ist. Die Juden werden nachher speziell Zeile 41 als והיהודים bezeichnet. Die Hss. haben aber richtig הערבים und die Übersetzung ist: „Und
5 er wird die Sprache der Araber (ערבים) verwirren". Und das ist der einzige korrekte Sinn der Stelle; denn die Samaritaner nennen ihre Sprache die richtige, die also z. Z. des Ta'eb zur alleinigen Herrschaft gelangen wird. Die gezwungene Erklärung p. 41 fällt somit weg. Zeile 31 steht הדבב welches auch richtig als „Feind"
10 übersetzt ist; in den Hss. dagegen הדבר, was natürlich „Leiter" oder „Führer" bedeutet und einen besseren Sinn gibt. Zeile 36 druckt er דא זכרו; es muß aber wie in den Hss. דאזכרו (als ein Wort) gelesen werden; „die (Stämme), die in der Thora erwähnt werden". In der Übersetzung dieses Textes hat Merx leider sehr häufig den
15 wahren Sinn mißverstanden. Ich will mich auf zwei Beispiele beschränken. Zeile 6—7 sind von ihm folgendermaßen übersetzt: „Und dies Gedicht ist richtig, und dein Leben besteht in dem, was du hörst. Von wem sie zu mir gekommen sind und bis (wann) nach mir er kommen wird, das wird mein Wort dir (?) verkünden
20 in dem Preise des Ta'eb und seiner Herrschaft"; . . . Es muß aber folgendermaßen übersetzt werden: „Und dies Gedicht ist richtig, und bei deinem Leben, du hast nie gehört desgleichen weder von denjenigen, die vor mir gekommen sind, noch (wirst du hören) von jenen, die nach mir kommen werden. Meine Worte werden dir
25 verkünden den Bericht des Ta'eb und seiner Herrschaft". Zeile 46: Dazu gibt Merx p. 31, Note 3 auch die Variante der anderen Hs. und übersetzt: „siehe auf, es schaut mein Auge" . . . Es muß aber heißen: „O! daß mein Auge ihn gesehen hätte, diesen Ta'eb und seine Majestät" . . . Dadurch, daß Merx häufig den Text miß
30 verstanden hat, ist es selbstverständlich, daß viele der Schlüsse, die er zieht, unhaltbar sind. Ich komme späterhin noch auf diese theologischen Ausführungen zurück. Ich kann jedoch diesen Text nicht verlassen, ohne auf einen chronologischen Mißgriff aufmerksam zu machen. Merx hat offenbar Abischa, den Enkel, mit Abischa, dem
35 Großvater verwechselt. Letzterer, der der Verfasser der liturgischen Hymnen war, war nie Hohepriester (s. mein Artikel im Journ. of the Royal As. Soc. 1908). Und er starb 778 Hedschra = 1376, während sein Enkel 880 Hedschra = 1475 starb. Es ist also Merx ein Irrtum von 100 Jahren unterlaufen!
40 Die zwei folgenden Texte sind arabisch, davon enthält der erste die biblischen Beweise und ist von Merx aus einer einzigen Hs. aus dem Jahre 1891 abgedruckt worden. Es ist sehr sonderbar, daß der Name des Verfassers und der Titel dieser Abhandlung in der Merx vorliegenden Kopie fehlen. Ich selbst besitze zwei
45 Hss. dieses Textes (Cod. Gaster 866 vom Jahre 1281 Hedschra = 1864, fol. 2—7 und Cod. 879 vom Jahre 1320 Hedschra = 1902, fol. 18 b—22 a). In beiden lautet der Titel folgendermaßen:

المقاله الشافيه فى ثبوت الدوله الثانيه تاليف حكهين غزال الدويك

also, eine Abhandlung über die zweite Weltperiode oder zweite Weltherrschaft von Ghazzāl al Doweik (Doek), der merkwürdigerweise, soweit ich ersehen kann, kein besonderes Gedicht darüber verfaßt hat. Ich habe nämlich in meinem Bande der Liturgien, 5 der die Gebete für den Versöhnungstag enthält, vergebens danach gesucht. Nun aber finden sich sonst alle auf den Ta'eb beziehenden Gedichte in diesem Bande. Da dieser arabische Text sich inhaltlich mit einem Gedichte deckt, welches Abraham al-Ḳabasi verfaßt hat, so kann man getrost voraussetzen, daß Ghazzāl al Doweik älter 10 sein muß als Ḳabasi; denn man darf wohl voraussetzen, daß, nachdem diese biblischen Beweise zusammengefaßt und ausführlich erörtert wurden, sie erst nachher in ein Gebet poetisch verarbeitet wurden. Abraham al-Ḳabasi verfaßte sein Sīr al-Ḳalb (s. mein Cod. 882) 938 Hedschra = 1531. Also muß der Verfasser des 15 arabischen Textes jedenfalls vor 1531 gelebt haben. Er würde sogar noch viel älter sein (10. Jahrhundert), wenn er mit Ṭabyah b. Dartah identisch wäre! Ich maße mir nicht an bei meinen beschränkten arabischen Kenntnissen ein Urteil darüber abzugeben, in welcher Weise der arabische Text herausgegeben worden ist. In 20 einigen Stichproben, die ich gemacht habe, sind kaum irgendwelche wesentliche Unterschiede zu finden. P. 63, Note 2 bestätigt mein Codex die zweite Konjektur von Merx. Ibid. p. 63 fehlt in meinem Codex: اللهم امين. Der oben erwähnte al-Ḳabasi ist nun der Verfasser von Text IV, p. 68 ff., den Merx Qajas nennt, ein Fehler, 25 der sich wohl durch das arabische Schriftzeichen leicht erklären läßt, aber doch unverzeihlich ist, denn der Verfasser war ein Mann, der eine große Stellung unter den Samaritanern eingenommen hat, denn er war ein angesehener samaritanischer Priester in Damaskus, der mehrere Male Reisen zu den Samaritanern in Sichem und anderen 30 Städten unternommen hat, und die Samaritaner wissen von ihm ganz wunderbare Dinge zu erzählen.

Der letzte Text ist der hebräische Text, den Merx Midrasch nennt, der aber eine allegorische Umdeutung und Anpassung der Geschichte der Sintflut ist. Von dieser besitze ich auch zwei Hss., 35 eine, Cod. 879, fol. 16 b—18 a und eine andere, die mir der jetzige Hohepriester abgeschrieben, Cod. 876, p 1—10. In der letzteren Hs. ist der Titel hebräisch und lautet folgendermaßen:
בשם יהוה. אמר אדונן הרב פינחס: רצון יהוה וסליחתו עליו; אמן.
Im anderen Cod. heißt es: 40

هذا الكلام نقلته من خط سيدى الوالد الامام عمران . . . . وذاكر
انه ناقله من خط سيدنا الريس فنحس المصنف . . .

Also eine Abschrift, die Imran (Amram) von dem Originale des Pinehas, des „מצניף" gemacht hatte. Auf meine Anfrage, wer

der Verfasser sei, antwortete der Hohepriester, er hätte vor mehr
als sechshundert Jahren gelebt, und das würde uns wieder in das
14. Jahrhundert hinauf führen, und der Verfasser wäre dann nicht
der Zeitgenosse des Ḳabasi, sondern der „Hohepriester" Pinehas, der
5 Vater des Abischa, der 1363 starb. Es muß in diesem Zusammenhange hervorgehoben werden, daß der Ḳaṭef (Blumenlese d. h. bib-
lischer Verse) für den Versöhnungstag regelmäßig mit dem Verse
Genes. 8, 4: „Und die Arche ruhte" beginnt. Ein gedanklicher
Zusammenhang wurde also von uralter Zeit ohne Zweifel zwischen
10 der „Wasserflut" der Vergangenheit und der „Sündenflut", die der
Ankunft des Ta'eb vorhergehen soll, angenommen und daher die Erklärung in Genes. allegorisch gedeutet. Justinus Martyr führt übrigens
diesen Gedanken ausführlich im christlichen Sinne aus, was Merx
entgangen ist bei der Erklärung dieses Textes. Eine Vergleichung
15 mit den anderen Hss. ergibt auch hier viele Varianten, von denen
nur einige hier bemerkt werden sollen, da sie zur Erklärung des
Textes beitragen dürften. Um die Vergleichung zu erleichtern,
habe ich die Zeilen von M.'s Text gezählt. Zeile 2 nach ברוך יהוה
add. אשר. Zeile 6 ופורגה lies ופורגג welches bedeutet: „der da hilft"
20 (nicht „interzediert" wie Merx konjiziert). Zeile 13 ועשתם lies
ועשית. Zeile 21 streiche יום. Zeile 26 anstatt עם lies את.
Zeile 29 streiche יהוה. Zeile 34 lies להחיות anstatt לחיות.
Zeile 37 streiche על השהב und 38 anstatt משה lies השהב. Zeile 43
statt אתך, welches Merx Schwierigkeiten verurscht hatte, lies אתם.
25 Zeile 46 streiche פנותה. Zeile 48 streiche von ההרים ... bis הארץ
und lies dafür האמת על פני כל הארץ. Zeile 49 anstatt הטובים
lies הטורים, wie Merx Note 1 conjiziert. Zeile 51 anstatt הרשעים
lies הישרים wodurch der Text einen ganz anderen Sinn bekommt.
Zeile 53 streiche וישראל und ואת (zweimal). Zeile 57 anstatt
30 את השהב lies אך השהב „und so blieb nur der Schaheb" ...
Zeile 58 fehlen folgende Worte hinter ותשע: וארבע שנה מאות,
wodurch die Rechnung richtig wird. Merx hat schon bemerkt,
daß hier eine Zahl ausgefallen sein muß. Zeile 61 statt רימהר
lies והחמס und die Worte von וירצבו ... bis וארץ sind zu streichen.
35 Zeile 62 statt השכהנה lies השכנה. Zeile 66 statt רגלה lies
רגלם und streiche שבעת. Zeile 67 streiche פנותה. Zeile 68 statt
על פי lies לפני und Zeile 70 statt הארץ מינן lies ארץ כנען.
Die darauf folgende Zahlensymbolik und Gematria, die, wie
Merx selbst anerkennt ursprünglich samaritanisch sein muß und
40 nicht von den Juden entlehnt, da die Zahlendeutungen auf den
samaritanisch-hebräischen Text beruhen, sind bei Merx arabisch, in
meinen Hss. dagegen hebräisch, d. h. in der ursprünglicheren Form.
Das Arabische ist eine Übersetzung daraus. Auch ist der Text
etwas ausführlicher und man ersieht daraus den Grund, warum die
45 Zahlenspielerei hier angeschlossen ist. Es soll nämlich durch diese
Berechnung des Zahlenwertes bestimmter Verse bewiesen werden,
daß für alle Daten und Zeitangaben der Beweis immer in der Bibel

selbst zu finden sei. Und so soll auch hier bewiesen werden, daß
die Sintflut der Fanuta 2941 Jahre dauern wird. Und ebenso sollen
noch andere Daten aus dem Bibelvers bewiesen werden. Anstatt
مسميح haben die Hss. יְשׁוּעַ und außerdem noch folgende Verse
Deut. 31, 18: הַסְתֵּר אַסְתִּיר פָּנַי מֵהֶם בַּיּוֹם הַהוּא עַל כָּל הָרָעָה אֲשֶׁר 5
עָשׂוּ und Deut. 31, 29: כִּי הַשְׁחֵת תַּשְׁחִיתוּן וְסַרְתֶּם מִן הַדֶּרֶךְ, welche
ihrem Zahlenwerte nach als 2943 (resp. 2942) berechnet werden.
Soweit die philologische Seite und die Geschichte der Texte.

In bezug auf den theologischen Inhalt werde ich mich ganz
kurz fassen. Ich glaube dadurch dem Verfasser größere Gerechtig- 10
keit widerfahren zu lassen, wenn ich das hier in diesen Texten
Gebotene als eine Phase des Glaubens an den Ta'eb bezeichne, wie
sie sich im Schrifttume des 13. und 14. Jahrh. wiederspiegelt.
Aus dem historischen Zusammenhange herausgerissen und in die
Vergangenheit hinaufgerückt, bietet sie keine verläßliche Darstellung 15
der samaritanischen Anschauungen über den Ta'eb. Die verschiedenen
Verfasser und Dichter setzen eine solche Anschauung voraus. Wenn
sie vom Ta'eb schreiben, dann wissen sie, daß ihre Zeitgenossen
nicht erst aus ihren Schriften und Hymnen die Lehre über den
Ta'eb gewinnen werden. Sie setzen voraus, daß der Begriff des 20
Ta'eb, wie er von alter Zeit überliefert war, den Samaritanern ge-
läufig war, daß sie ihre Anspielungen verstehen und in ihren Ge-
dichten bloß eine poetische Verherrlichung des Ta'eb sehen werden,
ohne erst daraus zu lernen, was der Ta'eb sei. Nicht aus diesen
Schriften ist deshalb die Lehre vom Ta'eb zu ziehen, und die 25
dunklen Andeutungen sind nicht in der Weise aprioristisch zu
deuten, wie es alle bisher getan haben, Gesenius, Merx, Hilgenfeld,
Cowley etc. etc., die nur mit späterem Material operiert haben.
Man muß viel weiter hinaufgehen, und hätte Merx die Schriften
des Marḳa, der vielleicht ein Jahrtausend älter ist, eingesehen, so 30
wäre er bestimmt zu ganz anderen und positiveren Resultaten gelangt. Wie unzuverlässig auch die Ausgabe von Heidenheim sein
mag (Commentar Marqah's des Samar., Weimar 1896), so hätte Merx
doch mindestens daraus erfahren, daß eine vollständige Hs. von
Marḳa sich in der Kgl. Bibliothek zu Berlin befindet, die er hätte 35
einsehen können und müssen. (Es sind außerdem mehrere Disser-
tationen über Teile derselben Hs. erschienen.) Es finden sich nun
bei Marḳa viele Stellen, wo er über den Ta'eb ziemlich ausführlich
spricht, so Heidenheim pp. 22, 46 und 94—95 und sonst, aus
welchen man erschließen könnte, daß der darin erwähnte Ta'eb 40
Josua oder Joseph als König gleichgestellt wird — was noch das
Wahrscheinlichste ist, und nicht, wie Heidenheim glaubt, ein Joseph
redivivus ist. Die Grundzüge sind wohl dieselben, wie sie sich
bei Abischa finden, welche die Kontinuität einer alten Tradition
durch die Jahrhunderte beweisen und darauf spielt er an, aber 45
in der Tätigkeit und in der Identität der Person scheint eine Ver-

schiebung der Begriffe stattgefunden zu haben. Fest steht jedenfalls
für alle Samaritaner nur, daß der Ta'eb, wie ihn schon Gesenius u. a.
gedeutet hatten, derjenige sein wird, der die Herrschaft zurück-
bringen wird, nicht ein redivivus, ein Verstorbener sein wird, der
5 zurückkehrt, sondern einer, der die Gnadenzeit, die Wiederherstellung des Tempels und die Darbringung der Opfer auf dem Berge
Garizim bewerkstelligen wird. Nun scheinen sich zwei Gesichtspunkte in der Idee des Ta'eb gekreuzt zu haben: die Königswürde
und die Hohepriesterwürde. In einigen Texten kommt daher die eine
10 Ansicht zum Vorschein, während in anderen die zweite erkennbar
ist, und dadurch ist die Konfusion in der korrekten Auffassung
des samaritanischen Ta'eb entstanden. Es ist hier nicht der Platz,
diese Frage erschöpfend zu behandeln. Ich muß mich daher auf
einige Punkte beschränken. In dem arabischen Briefe vom Jahre
15 1684 an die vermeintlichen Brüder in England sagen die Samaritaner u. a., daß der Ta'eb sterben und begraben werden wird bei
Joseph und daß es geschrieben steht in dem Buche Josua. Juynboll, p. 52 hat schon darauf aufmerksam gemacht, daß davon nichts
in dem Texte steht, den er herausgegeben hat. Eine etwas ver-
20 schiedene Rezension des arabischen Textes has sich jedoch bei den
Samaritanern erhalten, die aus dem 15.—16. Jahrh. stammen soll,
und von der ich eine wörtliche Abschrift in samaritanischen Buchstaben besitze (Cod. Gaster 890). Dieser Text geht nur bis zur
Geschichte Alexander's (inkl.). Alles Übrige von Kap. XLVII ed.
25 Juynboll fehlt in dieser Handschrift. P. 35 findet sich nun folgendes
kurze Kapitel:

פצל.

תלאת אזכיא מקאבל תלאתה מלוך: תלאתה אזכיא קבלי הרגריזים
ותלאתה מלוך שמאלי לגבל גריזים אלאזכיא אבראהים ואסחאק ויעקב
30 ואלמלוך יוסף ויושע ואלתאיב אלדי יקום פי אלדולה אלתאניה ויקבר
מיתהם. עליהם אלסלאם אגמעין:

d. h. „3 Fromme entsprechen 3 Königen, 3 Fromme im Süden vom
Berge Garizim und 3 Könige im Norden vom Berge Garizim. Die
3 Frommen sind: Abraham, Isaak und Jacob, und die 3 Könige
35 sind: Joseph, Josua und der Ta'eb, welcher erstehen wird z. Z. der
2. (Welt-) Herrschaft und wird dann bei ihnen begraben werden.
Friede über sie alle!" Dieser Text mußte den Schreibern in Nablus
im 17. Jahrh. vorgelegen haben, denn darauf beziehen sie sich. In
dieser Gleichstellung als König ist die Erklärung zu suchen für
40 die Identifizierung mit Josua, die schon sehr alt sein muß. Nicht
bloß erwähnt ihrer Eulogios, sondern wir finden auch einen ähnlichen Gedankengang bei 'Abdallāh b. Sabā, dem Begründer der
Schi'a, der wie Schahrastāni erzählt, daß er, „als er noch Jude
war, von Josua bin Nun, dem Erben des Moses, Ähnliches auszu-
45 sagen pflegte, wie (später) von Ali", d. h. unzweifelhaft eine Wieder-

kehr (v. J. Friedlaender, Zeitschr. f. Assyr., Bd. XXIII, p. 303, 320 und XXIV (1910), p. 4 ff.). Aus Marḳa scheint hervorzugehen, daß er mit Joseph in Verbindung gebracht wird, aber unzweifelhaft in derselben Weise, daß seine Weltherrschaft ebenso groß sein wird wie die des Joseph. Über seine Abstammung erfahren wir 5 jedoch nichts.

Die andere Tradition, die den Ta'eb wiederum mit Moses in Verbindung bringt und sogar identifizieren will, ist teilweise angedeutet in den Liedern etc., welche ihn Opferdienste bringen lassen, die doch nur ein Priester (Levite) darbringen konnte und 10 von denen ein Israelit (Ephraimite) ausgeschlossen war. Das wird wohl der Sinn der Weissagung des Hohenpriesters Aḳbun sein, die er sterbend seinem Sohne Nathanael machte (s. Merx, p. 34). Dafür gibt es nun eine viel ältere Stütze in der von mir entdeckten samaritanischen Apokalypse Moses, in samaritanischer 15 Sprache, mit deren Herausgabe ich beschäftigt bin. Diese Assumptio schließt mit einer Prophetie Mosis über die Zukunft. Zwar dunkel ist der Rede Sinn, aber genügend klar, um daraus die Anschauungen der Samaritaner über die zukünftige Wiederherstellung der irdischen und göttlichen Macht auf Erden kennen zu lernen. 20

Trotz der von mir beanstandeten Punkte kann man doch nicht umhin, dem verstorbenen Professor Merx dankbar zu sein, daß er jedenfalls diese Texte gesammelt und herausgegeben und in der Weise beleuchtet hat, wie seine umfassende Gelehrsamkeit nicht anders erwarten ließ. Ich möchte noch einmal ausdrücklich betonen, 25 daß mir nichts ferner liegt, als einen Zweifel an der Ehrlichkeit und Gewissenhaftigkeit des Verstorbenen zu äußern. Es ist nur ein Beweis dafür, den gerade einer der hervorragendsten Vertreter der samaritanischen Wissenschaft erbringt, daß es sehr schwierig ist, das zerstreute samaritanische Material zu übersehen und daß 30 man an die Herausgabe samaritanischer Texte nicht gehen darf auf Grund einer einzigen zufällig in die Hände geratenen Hs., ohne vorher genaue Umschau zu halten und sich zu erkundigen, ob nicht noch andere Hss. zu haben sind. Wenn ein Mann wie Merx, der schon manches Samaritanisches geleistet hatte, so sehr irren konnte, 35 wie wenig berufen sind Andere, die noch nichts geleistet haben, über samaritanische Sprache und Literatur ein Urteil abzugeben.